ANTHONY BURGESS

by the same author

REWARDS AND FAIRIES by Rudyard Kipling
An Edition
STAGE PEOPLE
A Harlequinade
THE MEMOIRS AND CONFESSIONS OF A JUSTIFIED SINNER
by James Hogg
An Introduction
THE LIFE AND DEATH OF PETER SELLERS
An Elegy
THE REAL LIFE OF LAURENCE OLIVIER
A Romance
THE MAN WHO WAS PRIVATE WIDDLE
Charles Hawtrey: 1914–1988
A Dirge

Anthony Burgess

ROGER LEWIS

ff
faber and faber

First published in 2002
by Faber and Faber Limited
3 Queen Square London WC1N 3AU

Typeset by Faber and Faber Ltd
Printed in England by Clays Ltd, St Ives plc

A CIP record for this book
is available from the British Library

ISBN 0-571-20492-9

2 4 6 8 10 9 7 5 3 1

To Anna

'I need so little, a bottle of ink,
and a spot of sunshine on the floor –
oh, and you. But the last isn't a small
thing at all.'

Vladimir to Véra Nabokov

'The biography stands, fat and worthy-burgherish on the shelf, boastful and sedate: a shilling life will give you all the facts, a ten pound one all the hypotheses as well. But think of everything that got away, that fled with the last deathbed exhalation of the biographee. What chance would the craftiest biographer stand against the subject who saw him coming and decided to amuse himself?'

Julian Barnes, *Flaubert's Parrot*

'Has it occurred to you . . . that maybe your final form of this ought to be a narrative of your writing it, the people you've talked to, rather than a novel-like story of me? I see the situation as a fascinating way to get into what a man's life is really like. And of course, at the end of it, neither of them, subject nor writer, *knows* . . . I think there's no biography so interesting as the one in which the biographer is present. I think it's a wonderful story, the whole thing: trying to get me, the people who won't speak, the people who do speak, the different versions, the meetings, the sources – and out of this comes the story.'

Orson Welles

'*Q.* – On what occasions do you lie?
A. – When I write, when I speak, when I sleep.'

Anthony Burgess

Contents

List of Illustrations

Page xiii: Cartoon of Anthony Burgess by Adrian George, published in *The Times Saturday Review*, 3 November 1990, to illustrate 'A beginner's guide to burgessing' by Fiona MacCarthy. (Courtesy of Adrian George)

Page 311: 'Les Amis Muets', a strip cartoon by Martin Rowson, published in the *Sunday Correspondent*, 28 October 1990. (Author Collection)

Plate section

Lynne Jones and John Wilson on their wedding day, Bournemouth, 22 January 1942. Photographer unknown. Used to illustrate 'Burgess the betrayer' by Richard Heller in the *Mail on Sunday*, 11 April 1993. (Author Collection)

'It has been a sin to be prolific only since the Bloomsbury Group made it a point of good manners to produce, as it were, costively.' Burgess in Etchingham, 1968. (Timepix / Rex Features)

'Anyway, I'm actually a composer.' Burgess in Chiswick, 1968. (Timepix / Rex Features)

'That stick makes you look venerable. You look *venerable*, Anthony.' Graham Greene. (Timepix / Rex Features)

Paolo-Andrea (*aet.* seven), born to Liliana Macellari and Roy Lionel Halliday on 9 August 1964. Photographer unknown. Captioned 'Andrea is a very expressive child. He is very free. He is very confident in himself,' the picture appeared in the *National Elementary Principal*, Volume L, Number 6, May 1971. (Author collection)

Liliana – known as Liana – the daughter of Contessa Maria Lucrezia Pasi della Pergola, arriving at Burgess's Memorial Service, 16 June 1994.

Photograph by Ian Jones, which accompanied the report 'Tribute to talent's full bloom' in the *Daily Telegraph*, 17 June 1994. (Courtesy Ian Jones)

Homage to Quert Yuiop – 'I get angry at the stupidity of critics who wilfully refuse to see what my books are really about. I'm aware of malevolence, especially in England.' (Timepix / Rex Features)

Caesar Burgess – a bust sculpted in Bracciano by Milton Hebald, who gave this photograph to Roger Lewis. (Courtesy of Milton Hebald)

The Art of Caricature: David Levine (*New York Review of Books* originally, and also used by the *Observer* to illustrate Martin Amis's review of *Little Wilson and Big God* on 22 February 1987. It is also incorporated in the jacket design of the Hutchinson edition of *Homage to Qwert Yuiop*); Martin Rowson (*Sunday Telegraph* magazine, accompanying Geoffrey Wansell's 'Man of the Week' column on 8 September 1985); and William Rushton (whose drawing appeared on the contents page of the *Independent* magazine on 28 September 1989. Entitled 'Anthony Burgess in transit', it illustrated the short story 'The Endless Voyager', taken from the collection *The Devil's Mode*.) (Courtesy of the artists or their estates)

The iconic artwork by Philip Castle for the poster of Stanley Kubrick's *A Clockwork Orange*. An exhibition, 'Philip Castle: *A Clockwork Orange* Poster Design', opened at the Sho [*sic*] Gallery, 73 Curtain Road, London on 20 April 2000. (Courtesy of the Ronald Grant Archive)

Dust jacket for the first edition of *A Clockwork Orange* (Heinemann, 1962). Illustration for Lot 291 in the sale of Valuable Printed Books and Manuscripts, Sotheby's, London, 13 December 2001. (Courtesy of Sotheby's)

Two stills with Malcolm McDowell as Alex in Kubrick's film of *A Clockwork Orange*. (Courtesy of the Ronald Grant Archive)

The Grand Old Man of Letters: John Wilson, otherwise known as Anthony Burgess, 25 February 1917 – 22 November 1993. Photograph by Jane Bown. (Courtesy of Jane Bown / Camera Press)

Chronology and Select Bibliography

1917 Born John Burgess Wilson, 25 February, at 91 Carisbrook Street, Harpurhey, north-east Manchester, to a Catholic Lancashire family. Son of Joseph Wilson, book-keeper and pianist, and dancer and singer Elizabeth Burgess Wilson. 'My mother had no living relatives. Family disappeared. Didn't know her at all. An unusual woman, judging from the photographs, a very beautiful blonde . . .'

1918 15 November: his only sister, Muriel, aged eight, dies of influenza and broncho-pneumonia in an epidemic. His mother, aged thirty, dies four days later of influenza and acute pneumonia.
His father and he lodge with his Protestant aunt – his mother's sister – Ann Bromley and her two daughters, Elsie and Betty, at Delauneys Road, Higher Crumpsall.

1921 Commences formal education (briefly) at a local Protestant school, where he is known as Jack Wilson.

1922 Father remarries Maggie Dwyer (neé Byrne) the landlady of the local pub, the Golden Eagle, Lodge Street, Miles Platting. 'I was politely (or not so) told to get out of what had become a West Indian preserve,' Burgess commented sixty years later. His step-mother has two daughters, Agnes and Madge.

1923 Attends St Edmund's RC Elementary School, Upper Monsall Street. 'I was still weak and unmuscular through having no proper mother,' he said.

1924 Moves to a tobacconist's shop, 21 Princess Road, Moss Side.
Attends Bishop Bilsborrow Memorial Elementary School, Princess Road.
Moves to live in an off-licence at 261 Moss Lane East.
Agnes marries Jack Tollitt and they live over the tobacconist's shop.

Madge marries Clifford Kemp. Attends the Church of the Holy Name, Oxford Road, 'a stronghold of British Jesuitry, [which] would soon have to be deconsecrated for lack of a sufficient congregation. Islam was growing, Irish Catholicism disappearing.'

1927 Stepsister, Agnes, gives birth to Dan at 261 Moss Lane East, which was to be 'turned into a shebeen before it was demolished'.

1928 Contracts scarlet fever and stays at Monsall Isolation Hospital, Monsall Road, north-east Manchester. Holiday in Torquay and Torbay – an essay on Torbay published in the children's corner of the *Daily Express*. Illustrations published in the *Manchester Guardian* and *Daily Express*.

Attends Xaverian College secondary school, Victoria Park, Rusholme (since 'turned into a Muslim ghetto'), on a scholarship.

1936 Sits for Customs and Excise examination. Comes 1,579th.

1937 October: starts at Victoria University of Manchester (formerly Owen's College) on an English Literature degree course.

1938 18 April: his father dies in Fallowfield, a district of Manchester, of pleurisy and influenza, aged fifty-five.

1939 Short story, 'Grief', is awarded five guineas as the best piece of undergraduate writing, judged by Harold Nicolson.

Meets Llewela (Lynne) Isherwood (as he called her – though the middle name appears on no official document) Jones, an Anglo-Welsh Protestant and fellow student, aged eighteen, daughter of the Headmaster of Bedwellty Grammar School. They get engaged. Tours Belgium, France, Holland and Luxembourg with Lynne and her friend Margaret Williams as Nazi anti-Semitism grows – Burgess's 'Celto-Lancastrian' nose is considered Jewish.

1940 Writes dissertation (now lost) on Christopher Marlowe's *Doctor Faustus*.

Graduates with a IIi BA Hons in English Literature from Manchester University.

October: his stepmother dies from a heart attack. Gives private tuition in English and mathematics to a pupil who had been ill with cardiac rheumatism and had missed going to school. Is paid twenty-five pounds. 'I was ending my civilian life well off.'

17 October: joins the Royal Army Medical Corps at Eskbank, near Edinburgh.

1941 Posted to the 189 Field Ambulance of the B Company at Cheviot Hall, near Morpeth, Northumberland. Over-extends his leave to stay with Lynne in Manchester and the military police come after him for desertion. His copy of *Finnegans Wake* is 'generally thought to be a code book'.

Moves to the Entertainment Section of the 54th Division and becomes musical director of Army dance band, the Jaypees, based at Moreton-in-the-Marsh, Gloucestershire.

1942 22 January: marries Llewela (Lynne) Jones in Bournemouth registry office, as sergeant.

Undergoes training to transfer to Army Educational Corps. Posted to Emergency Medical Section of a lunatic asylum at Winwick, near Warrington, where he undertakes speech therapy with patients.

1943 New Year's Day: posted to Infantry Training Centre, Peninsular Barracks, Warrington. Lynne works in London at the Board of Trade.

November: posted to Gibraltar as a training college lecturer in Speech and Drama. In London, Lynne, pregnant, is allegedly mugged and attacked by GI deserters; she miscarries.

1946 Promoted to sergeant major. Discharged, returns from Gibraltar to London to live with Lynne on Baron's Court Road. Teaches sergeant-instructors at the Mid-West School of Education, Brinsford Lodge, near Wolverhampton, under the aegis of Birmingham University.

1948 Appointed Lecturer in Speech and Drama by Ministry of Education at an Emergency Teacher Training College, Bamber Bridge, near Preston, Lancashire.

1950 Appointed English teacher at Banbury Grammar School, Oxfordshire, and lives in the village of Adderbury. Volume of poems sent to Faber and Faber is rejected by T. S. Eliot. The verses will later turn up as 'Some uncollected early poems by F. X. Enderby', an Appendix to *Enderby Outside*.

Writes for the *Banbury Guardian*.

1953 Writes *A Vision of Battlements*, which is rejected by Heinemann as a first novel.

1954 Having been interviewed for the post in London in the New Year, in August he and Lynne travel east, where Burgess is to be an Education Officer for the Colonial Service, Malay College, Kuala Kangsar.

1955 Transfers to Teachers' Training College, Kota Bharu, Kelantan. Works on an anthology of English literature in a Malay translation.

Lynne's mother dies from cancer of the throat; they do not return to Britain.

1956 Publishes *Time for a Tiger* (London, Heinemann) under the pseudonym Anthony Burgess.

1957 Returns to Europe with Lynne on 4 August, spending five days in Istanbul (at the Alp Oteli, Beyoglu), arriving in England on 11 August. Holiday in Rome and London, where he meets Graham Greene. Revisits Banbury in October. Until their departure for Brunei, the Wilsons are based with Lynne's family in Aylestone, Leicester, where her sister, Hazel, and widowed father are now living.

1958 Education Officer for Colonial Service as English Language Specialist, Sultan Omar Ali Saifuddin College, Brunei, Borneo. Publishes *The Enemy in the Blanket* (London, Heinemann) as Anthony Burgess, over which he is served with a libel writ.
English Literature: A Survey for Students (London, Longmans Green) is published under the name John Burgess Wilson.

1959 Collapses in the classroom in Brunei and invalided home. Tests for a possible brain tumour are conducted by Dr Roger Bannister at the Neurological Institute in Bloomsbury, London.
Publishes last novel in trilogy, *Beds in the East* (London, Heinemann), as Anthony Burgess. Lives briefly in Hove and Brighton before the purchase of 'Applegarth', Etchingham, East Sussex.

1960 *The Doctor Is Sick* (London, Heinemann; New York, Norton).
The Right to an Answer (London, Heinemann; New York, Norton, 1961).

1961 Publishes *Devil of a State* (London, Heinemann; New York, Norton, 1962) – a novel about Brunei, which is relocated in Africa for reasons of libel.
One Hand Clapping published under the pseudonym Joseph Kell (London, Peter Davies).
The Worm and the Ring (London, Heinemann). As a result of a libel action by Gwen Bustin, secretary of Banbury Grammar School and Mayor of Banbury, the novel is withdrawn – reappearing as a revised edition in 1970.
July: catastrophic yet profitable trip with Lynne to Leningrad – for the Russian sounds he hears will inspire the dialect of *A Clockwork Orange*. His talk about Lynne's hospitalisation,

'A Rash in Russia', is broadcast twice on the radio, in mid-September and late October.

1962 Extensive broadcasting on the BBC – especially talks for *Woman's Hour*.
May: publication of *A Clockwork Orange* (London, Heinemann; New York, Norton, 1963).
Writes *St Peter's Summer*, which becomes *Honey for the Bears*.
Autumn: publication of *The Wanting Seed*.
The New Aristocrats by Michel de Saint-Pierre (London, Gollancz) – translated with 'Llewela Burgess' from the French, *Les Nouveaux aristocrates*.
The Olive Trees of Justice by Jean Pelegri (London, Sidgwick and Jackson), translated with 'Lynn [*sic*] Wilson' from the French, *Les Oliviers de la Justice*.

1963 Death of Lynne's father.
Holiday in Gibraltar and Tangier, where Burgess meets William Burroughs. It's another *Carry On*-style expedition, with Burgess fed a sleeping potion by a doctor who deems him 'unstable and violent when drunk'.
Having completed the writing of *Nothing Like the Sun*, his contribution to the forthcoming Shakespearean quatercentenary, in the autumn Burgess and Lynne fly from Gatwick to Jersey, Seville, Marrakesh and Tenerife, where 'Lynne came out in violent red spots' and Burgess has a psychic vision about Kennedy's assassination – which duly takes place.
December: meets Liliana [Liana] Macellari, an Italian researcher in applied linguistics at Cambridge, who is separated from her black Bostonian husband, Ben Johnson, a lawyer.
Inside Mr Enderby (London, Heinemann) published as Joseph Kell and reviewed by Burgess himself in the *Yorkshire Post*.
Honey for the Bears (London, Heinemann; New York, Norton, 1964).
The Novel To-day (London, Longmans Green and Company, for the British Council and the National Book League).

1964 Early spring: finalises purchase of 24 Glebe Street, Chiswick. Stays in Etchingham from 15 July for six weeks to write about Joyce for Faber and is 'as Joyce-impregnated as I'll ever be', he tells Huw Wheldon, the BBC (Television) Head of Documentary and Music Programmes.

9 August: Paolo-Andrea is born to Liliana Macellari at Bethnal Green Hospital, London. Roy Lionel Halliday is named as the father on the birth certificate.
First entry as Anthony Burgess, novelist, in *Who's Who*.
The Eve of Saint Venus (London, Sidgwick and Jackson; New York, Norton, 1967), illustrated by Edward Pegram.
One volume edition of *A Malayan Trilogy* (London, Heinemann).
Nothing Like the Sun: A Story of Shakespeare's Love-Life (London, Heinemann; New York, Norton).
Short story, 'An American Organ', *Mad River Review*, Vol. 1 (winter 1964–5).
Language Made Plain (London, English Universities Press; New York, Crowell, 1965), published under the name John Burgess Wilson.

1965 15–30 January (though in his autobiography he says it was 'in February'): flies to Dublin with Christopher Burstall to make a sixty-minute film about Joyce for the BBC series *Monitor*, produced by Huw Wheldon. Burgess is paid one hundred and seventy-five guineas, for the provision of a forty-five minute script, his appearance in film sequences, and the dubbing of his own commentary. He received a further fifty guineas for consultations, 'recces' and viewing sessions, 'as required'.
Appears on BBC2's *Take It or Leave It* and other programmes.
Returns to Chiswick; Lynne begins to deteriorate and vomits blood – a portal haemorrhage – and goes into hospital for a transfusion. They visit Abergavenny in South Wales.
Appointed drama critic for the *Spectator*, concert and opera critic for *Queen*, and contributes a regular 'London Letter', beginning in late summer, to the *Hudson Review*.
The Long Day Wanes: A Malayan Trilogy (New York, Norton).
The Man Who Robbed Poor Boxes by Jean Servin (London; Gollancz), translated from the French *Deo Gratias*.
Here Comes Everybody: An Introduction to James Joyce for the Ordinary Reader (London, Faber and Faber).
A Vision of Battlements (London, Sidgwick and Jackson), illustrated by Edward Pegram.

1966 Spring: goes to America (without Lynne) for conference on literary translation at Long Island University, New York. Back in London, a Harley Street specialist confirms that the sclerotic calf pain is

due to failing arteries, caused by high cholesterol levels.
Translates Berlioz's opera *L'Enfance du Christ* (*The Childhood of Christ*) into English for BBC2.
Tremor of Intent: An Eschatological Spy Novel (London, Heinemann; New York, Norton).
'Five Revolutionary Sonnets: From the Novels *Inside Mr Enderby* and *Enderby Outside*', *Transatlantic Review*, no. 21 (summer).
'The Sword', *Transatlantic Review*, no. 23 (winter 1966–7).
Introduction to *Augustus Carp, Esq. By Himself: Being the Autobiography of a Really Good Man*, by Henry Howarth Bashford (London, Heinemann).
Edits and introduces *The Coaching Days of England 1750–1850* (London, Elek; New York, Time-Life).

1967 Introduction to *The Moonstone* by Wilkie Collins (London, Pan Books).
Gives a talk at Amherst College, Boston. Travels through Massachusetts and stays with his Norton editor, Eric P. Swenson, near Hartford, Connecticut. Speaks at a literary festival at Vanderbilt University, Nashville, in Tennessee, and meets Richard Ellmann. Visits East and West Berlin to write an article for *Sunday Telegraph*, staying for a weekend at Kempinski Hotel on the Kurfürstendamm. 'This meant philosophising superficially and coming to the brash unequivocal conclusions appropriate to popular journalism.' Burgess would be without peer in this.
Edits, with Francis Haskell, *The Age of the Grand Tour: 1720–1820* (London, Elek; New York, Crown).
Edits *A Journal of the Plague Year* by Daniel Defoe (Harmondsworth, Penguin).
'From *It's the Miller's Daughter*: A Novel in Progress', *Transatlantic Review*, no. 24 (spring).
Contributes to *The God I Want*, edited by James Mitchell (London, Constable).
The Novel Now: A Student's Guide to Contemporary Literature (London, Faber); retitled for America as *The Novel Now: A Guide to Contemporary Fiction* (New York, Norton).

1968 Travels to Los Angeles at the invitation of Warner Brothers–Seven Arts to discuss a script for a film inspired by his novel *Nothing Like the Sun*, to be called *The Bawdy Bard*; stays in the Manhattan Hotel opposite Grauman's Chinese Theater.

February: leaves Etchingham for Lynne's last London season of parties – e.g. a *Time-Life* reception at Bruton Street.
On 25 February, following a massive portal haemorrhage, Lynne is admitted to the general hospital in Ealing. She dies at 5.30 a.m. on 20 March of cardiac and liver failure in Central Middlesex Hospital, Park Royal, Ealing. She is cremated at Mortlake. The only mourners, in addition to Burgess, are Lynne's sister Hazel and some acquaintances from Amherst College and their wives, who happen to be in town.
Burgess returns to Los Angeles a week later to discuss the Shakespeare film with William Conrad, who wants to produce.
In London, meets Liliana Macellari again and discovers she has a son; having house-hunted on Malta during August, on 9 September they marry in a registry office in Hounslow. She is thirteen years his junior and the daughter of Contessa Maria Lucrezia Pasi della Pergola and the late Gilberto Macellari, an actor.
Travelling through France, Italy and Sicily in the Bedford Dormobile, they arrive at their villa in Lija, at the centre of the island of Malta, in October.
Leaving Liana and Paolo Andrea behind, Burgess returns to London in November, for a discussion about the Enderby film, *A Blast from the Smallest Room*, and then proceeds to Los Angeles to work on the Shakespeare film script. Spends Christmas on the cruise ship *Uganda*, between Malta, Naples, Ajaccio, Tunis, Barcelona and Mallorca. Gives lecture on censorship to Maltese Jesuits.
Publications this year include: *Enderby Outside* (London, Heinemann).
Enderby, comprising *Inside Mr Enderby* and *Enderby Outside* (New York, Norton).
A joint edition of *A Clockwork Orange* and *Honey for the Bears* (New York, Modern Library).
Introduction to *Last Exit to Brooklyn* by Hubert Selby, Jr (London, Calder and Boyars).
Introduction to *Titus Groan* by Mervyn Peake (London, Eyre and Spottiswoode). 'It remains essentially a work of the closed imagination, in which a world parallel to our own is presented in almost paranoiac denseness of detail.'
Urgent Copy: Literary Studies (London, Jonathan Cape; New York, Norton).

'The Muse: A sort of SF Story', *Hudson Review*, no. 21 (spring).
'Somebody's Got to Pay the Rent', *Partisan Review*, no. 35 (winter).

1969 Lectures throughout the American Pacific north-west and on 'Elizabethan Pronunciation' at the Stratford Summer Festival (Ontario); visits Montreal; lectures to a class in Harvard for 'an easily earned thousand dollars'.
Summer in Deyá, Mallorca, with Andrea and Liana, where he teaches a course on European studies to students from Dowling College, New York.
In the autumn he conducts a lecture tour of the American west coast, starting in Vancouver and finishing in Los Angeles. Henry Miller comes to hear him on *Finnegans Wake*, 'but he did not stay to the end'. Elected Fellow, Royal Society of Literature; Writer-in-Residence, State University of North Carolina at Chapel Hill.
Edits *A Shorter 'Finnegans Wake'* by James Joyce (London, Faber).
'A Benignant Growth', *Transatlantic Review*, no. 32 (summer).
Poem, 'Imagination Is Your True Apollo', *New York Times* (12 July).
'Genesis and Headache', in *Afterwords: Novelists on Their Novels*, edited by Thomas McCormack (New York, Harper).
'Gibraltar', in *Integrated Writing*, edited by R. C. K. Ginn (Beverly Hills, Glenco Press).
'Words', in *Essays by Linguists and Men of Letters 1858–1964*, Volume 2 of *The English Language*, edited by Whitney French Bolton and David Crystal (Cambridge University Press).
Introduction to *Autobiography* by G. K. Chesterton (London, Hutchinson).

1970 Early spring: departs from Malta with Liana for Rome, Bombay, Singapore, Perth, Melbourne and Sydney, Australia, and various towns in New Zealand ('There was a fair amount of resentment down there'); opens the Adelaide Arts Festival; stops off at Nandi, Honolulu, Fiji, Hawaii, San Francisco, and London, where he meets Stanley Kubrick.
June: delivers lecture on 'Obscenity' for the Malta Library Association in the Science Lecture Theatre of the University of Malta. 'The audience was fascinated: some were confused; a few were openly hostile: never had obscenity been analysed in public before!' stated the MLA Publications Board.

They move to Piazza Padella, Bracciano, Italy – pays for house 'by smuggling dollar royalty cheques into the [Italian] peninsula and paying them into the bank account of an expatriate American sculptor living near Rome'.
Shakespeare (London, Jonathan Cape; New York, Knopf).
Introduction to *All about H. Hatterr* by Govindas Vishnaodas Desani (New York, Farrar, Straus and Giroux).
'What is Pornography?', in *Perspectives on Pornography*, edited by Douglas A. Hughes (New York, St Martin's).
Introduction to Mozart's *Don Giovanni* and *Idomeneo* (London, Cassell).
Autumn: Visiting Fellow, teaching Creative Writing, at Princeton University. Commutes once a week to teach Creative Writing also to postgraduates at Columbia University; Andrea attends John Witherspoon School, 'where he was not happy'. Visits Atlanta to address English teachers on the English language. Gives talk on Charles Dickens at Yorke University, Toronto.

1971 Spring: publication of *MF* (London, Cape; New York, Knopf).
At the end of the academic year ('The Burgess family was not wanted in Princeton') he sails back to Naples on the *Leonardo da Vinci*. Drives to Trieste for International Joyce Congress; visits Pola – where Joyce taught – in Yugoslavia (Croatia): 'The [Neapolitan] guard at the frontier did not sing but he shouted, and he had to be punched.'
Returns to Minneapolis in the summer to work on his incidental music for *Cyrano*. His translation, *Cyrano de Bergerac* by Edmond Rostand, is published in September (New York, Knopf). Plans are afoot to turn this into a Broadway musical.
Acquires lease on 16A Piazza Santa Cecilia, Rome. He and Liana are continually robbed. 'The response of the Questura was a scolding for being a victim.'
In the autumn, to London to see a preview of *A Clockwork Orange*, the film based on his novel, produced and directed by Stanley Kubrick, starring Malcolm McDowell. The reception staff at Claridge's think Liana is the Italian-speaking nanny. Hopes to work with Kubrick on a film about Napoleon.
Writes his magisterial entry on 'The Novel' for the *Encyclopaedia Britannica*.

1972 January: flies to Minneapolis, for work on songs for *Cyrano*, and to New York, to publicise Kubrick's *A Clockwork Orange*. Warner Brothers put him up at the Algonquin. Malcolm McDowell, he discovers, has been billeted at the more luxurious Pierre.

Accepts two New York Critics' Awards on Kubrick's behalf at Sardi's. Kisses Mary Ure at the reception. She dies soon afterwards. Returns to Rome via London, where he faces bitter criticism in the press and on radio (particularly from Jimmy Savile) about the violence of Kubrick's film.

March–April: translates and adapts *Oedipus the King* by Sophocles for the Tyrone Guthrie Theater, Minneapolis. (Text, published by the University of Minnesota Press in association with the Tyrone Guthrie Theater, contains Burgess's correspondence with the director, Michael Langham, and the composer, Stanley Silverman).

Provides the English language voice-over passages for the Dustin Hoffman film *Alfredo Alfredo*. Is paid in bundles of 'non-taxable cash'.

Begins work for Vincenzo Labella and Lew Grade on *Moses the Lawgiver*. Is paid in-kind by acquiring adjoining property in Bracciano to extend his original house.

In the summer, goes to the Cannes Film Festival for more publicity on Kubrick's behalf. Meets Groucho Marx. *L'Orange Mécanique* shown in France 'to highly intellectual plaudits'.

Publication of *Stanley Kubrick's A Clockwork Orange* (Ballantine Books, New York): still photographs and transcribed dialogue from the film. 'The meeting with Anthony Burgess I remember best was in Brown's Hotel, where we met for a drink,' recalls Sir Frank Kermode. 'He arrived in a fury and threw on the table a large paperback with the title *Stanley Kubrick's A Clockwork Orange*. He said that Kubrick bought the book for a pittance and thereafter allowed Burgess absolutely no rights in it.'

From September, works as Distinguished Professor of English at City College, New York; teaches Joyce's *Ulysses*, Shakespeare, and Creative Writing. They stay in 'famous feminist and man-hater' Adrienne Rich's flat on Riverside Drive, Manhattan, but Burgess is secretive about his exact address. Andrea attends Dalton School on Park Avenue. 'His schooling lacked continuity. This was all my fault.'

11 November: gives a lecture as part of the tribute to Joseph C. Wilson, deceased, honorary chairman of the board of trustees of Rochester University.
Introduction to *The John Collier Reader* by John Collier (New York, Knopf).
When not in New York, tours to Florida, Louisiana, Colorado and Maine to give lectures. 'My major problem was a lack of money.'
Oedipus the King opens in Minneapolis. The musical *Cyrano* is cast, with Christopher Plummer in the lead.

1973 New Year: commutes between New York and Minneapolis to work on the lyrics for *Cyrano*; has difficulties with the immigration officials crossing to Canada for the try-out in Toronto; further try-outs held at the Colonial Theater, Boston; *Cyrano*, 'based upon Anthony Burgess's adaptation of *Cyrano de Bergerac*', opens on 25 March at the Palace Theater on Broadway. 'Plummer Triumphs in Musical "Cyrano"' hails the *New York Times*. It soon closes. 'Cyrano out of Breath' laments the *New York Times*, on 20 May.
9 May: files suit in the High Court, London, against Warner Brothers, Si Litvinoff and Max Raab, executive producers of the film *A Clockwork Orange*, alleging conspiracy to defraud him of the motion picture rights to his novel.
June: receives medal from National Arts Club as winner of their Sixth Annual Award in Literature.
Returns to Italy aboard the *Michaelangelo*, late July. Building works at Piazza Padella, Bracciano, now complete. Resumes operations on *Moses* project in the Santa Cecilia flat and also begins to draft *Napoleon Symphony*.
'The Case for Diversity', in *New Movements in the Study and Teaching of English*, edited by Nicholas Bagnell (London, Temple Smith).
'Is America Falling Apart?, in *The Norton Reader: An Anthology of Expository Prose*, edited by Arthur M. Eastman (New York, Norton).
Joysprick: An Introduction to the Language of James Joyce (London, Deutsch).
Obscenity and the Arts (Valletta, Malta Library Association), a limited edition of his lecture (see June 1970), which was 'slowly but carefully turned into type-script from the magnetic tapes, and the editing was done by the author himself'.

1974 April: The villa in Lija is confiscated by the Maltese government – Burgess had never obtained the necessary (temporary or permanent) resident's permit, nor had he paid any taxes. 'The Maltese claim I've abandoned the property and have ordered me to surrender possession and the keys. This is a totally vindictive act – a naked confrontation between the state and the individual' (*New York Times*, 11 April).

Sets off to tour the Alps and visits Ansedonia, Montalbuccio and Siena in the Bedford Dormobile whilst writing the script of *Jesus of Nazareth*, for which he has prepared by perusing 'the New Testament in Greek'. The first draft is 'considered ludicrous by Franco Zeffirelli. I expected this.'

May: Zeffirelli has received Burgess's draft and indeed calls it a 'Gospel potpourri' which 'ultimately destroyed the charismatic, mystical nature that for me sustained the character of Christ'.

English Literature: A Survey for Students (London, Longmans), a new edition of the book first published in 1958 under the name John Burgess Wilson. Actually revised in Bracciano in 1971. Now dedicated 'To Liana'.

The Clockwork Testament: Or Enderby's End (London, Hart-Davis, MacGibbon; New York, Knopf, 1975).

Napoleon Symphony (London, Jonathan Cape).

Poem, 'O Lord, O Ford, God Help Us, Also You', *New York Times Magazine* (29 December).

'The Novel', entry in the *Encyclopaedia Britannica*, finally published (University of Chicago Press).

Begins composing a symphony for the orchestra of the University of Iowa. First movement completed by Christmas, the remainder by the following April.

1975 January: travels from Rome with Vincenzo Labella to discuss *Jesus of Nazareth* with the ABC network in New York, followed by a lecture tour: Florida; Wisconsin; Sacramento to Vancouver.

Commissioned by Cubby Broccoli and Guy Hamilton to write the script for *The Spy Who Loved Me*. 'I knew from the start it would not work.'

Collapses at a Quaker College in the Mid-West and again in Pittsburgh.

Returns to Europe and is a jury member for Cannes Film Festival.

Writes *Beard's Roman Women* on the road in the Dormobile.

Summer in Montalbuccio and in Monte Carlo, where the Burgesses search for an apartment.
Teaches the modern novel for half a semester at the University of Iowa. Gives piano accompaniment to Fritz Lang's *Metropolis* at Iowa University film festival.
22 October: performance of his Symphony No. 3 in C by the University of Iowa Symphony Orchestra, conducted by James Dixon.
At Bracciano, writes libretto for a musical based on Trotsky's visit to New York in 1917; the score to be composed by Stanley Silverman (unproduced). One of Burgess's lyrics later performed on BBC radio.
Script on life of Freud for Canadian television (unproduced).
Introduction to *The White Company* by Arthur Conan Doyle (London, Murray).
Script of a disaster movie, *Puma*, for Richard Zanuck and David Brown of Universal Studios (unproduced). This will be recycled, along with the Trotsky and Freud projects, as *The End of the World News*.
Broadcast of television mini-series *Moses the Lawgiver* directed by Gianfranco De Bosio, produced by Vincenzo Labella, starring Burt Lancaster, Anthony Quayle, Ingrid Thulin and Irene Papas. ITC Entertainment Corp.
In his spare time Burgess translates the obscene poems of Giuseppe Gioacchino Belli.

1976 'On Christ's Nativity: Five Sonnets', *Times Literary Supplement* (23 January).
The Burgesses move to 44 rue Grimaldi, in the Condamine district of Monaco.
Liana 'almost distractedly' buys a house in Callian, the Var, Provence, France.
Writer in residence for six weeks in the spring, University of New York, Buffalo.
Delivers speech on Shakespeare's possible contribution to the King James Bible at a bicentennial festival in Washington. Recites Anglo-Saxon with Jorge Luis Borges at the Argentine Embassy.
To Culver City to discuss *Puma* with Zanuck and Brown, who want John Frankenheimer to direct. Stays at the Beverly Wilshire. 'This was not a good hotel.'
Returns to Monaco and adapts a screenplay from Mary Stewart's

The Crystal Cave. Carlo Ponti is interested in *The Wanting Seed* as a vehicle for Sophia Loren. 'But financiers were scared of cannibalism as the solution to the world's feeding problem.'
Fruitless visit to New York to discuss further film projects on 'Vinegar Joe' Stilwell and Aristotle Onassis.
Film, *Gli Occhi di New York* (*The Eyes of New York*) (Milan, Mondadori).
Beard's Roman Women (New York, McGraw-Hill; London, Hutchinson, 1977). Photographs by David Robinson.
A Long Trip to Teatime (New York, Stonehill).
Long poem, *Moses: A Narrative* (London, Dempsey and Squires).
New York (Amsterdam, Time-Life) Photographs by Dan Budnik *et al*.

1977 January: Andrea (now calling himself Andrew) attempts to commit suicide. Liana breaks her leg in two places; operated upon at Hôpital Princesse Grace, Monaco.
They move to Callian. Visits Keats's grave and lodgings and makes documentary on Rome for the Canadian television series *The World's Great Cities*, produced by John McGreevy.
Abba Abba (London, Faber).
Broadcast of television mini-series, *Jesus of Nazareth*, directed by Franco Zeffirelli; script by Anthony Burgess, Suso Cecchi d'Amico and Franco Zeffirelli, starring Robert Powell.
L'Homme de Nazareth, translated by Georges Belmont and Hortense Chabrier. (The novel *Man of Nazareth* does not appear in English for another two years.)
Jesus of Nazareth, adaptation of the screenplay, by William Barclay, photographs by Paul Ronald (London, Collins).
Foreword to *Anthony Burgess: A Bibliography: Works By and About Him Complete with Selected Annotations*, by Paul W. Boytinck (Norwood Editions).

1978 *1985* (London, Hutchinson; Boston, Little, Brown).
Ernest Hemingway and His World (London, Thames and Hudson; New York, Scribners).
Introduction to *Maugham's Malaysian Stories* by Somerset Maugham (London, Heinemann).

1979 Spring: presented with Critic of the Year prize ('a plastic plaque and a cheque for two hundred pounds') by Margaret Thatcher at the Savoy Hotel, London.

Much journalism for British, American and Italian press. Personally deposits the fees in Switzerland 'in a bank I will not name'.

Goes to Salt Lake City, Utah, Key West, Florida, and Kansas City to film *Grace under Pressure*, a documentary film (London Weekend Television) about Ernest Hemingway, directed by Tony Cash.

Man of Nazareth (New York, McGraw-Hill).

The Land Where the Ice-cream Grows (London, Benn).

Scrissero in Inglese (*They Wrote in English*), two volumes (Milan, Tramontana).

Works at *Earthly Powers*, which he'd been drafting since 1972 and which has had the various working titles of *Eagles in My Life*, *The Creators* and *The Prince of the Powers of the Air*. Gabriele Pantucci, of Artellus Ltd, Burgess's representatives in London, brokers a deal with Simon and Schuster in New York.

1980 Interviews Graham Greene in Antibes for the *Observer*.

Spring: delivers T. S. Eliot Memorial Lectures at the University of Kent, Canterbury, on the relationship between music and literature.

Flies to Kuala Lumpur and visits Ipoh, in Perak, and Kuala Kangsar for *Writers and Places*, a BBC television series, directed by David Wallace.

Debates and speaks at Edinburgh Festival; visits Andrew in Inverness. Writes overture for Scottish National Orchestra. 'My mother's roots were up there somewhere.'

Autumn: delivers the four John Crowe Ransom Memorial Lectures (more on the relationship between literature and music), Kenyon College, Ohio.

Revisits Manchester for a television programme made by Granada. Is filmed looking at Xaverian College and Moss Lane East: 'the shops over which I had lived as a boy were no more'.

Winter: trip to America with Liana to publicise *Earthly Powers*, which is a Book of the Month Club choice. Stays at the Plaza. Celebratory dinner to launch the novel at the Four Seasons ('the rack of lamb was too tough to eat'). Publicity tours to Chicago, Boston and Washington. Returns to London on Concorde. 'It was three hours late in taking off.'

Earthly Powers (London, Hutchinson) is nominated for Booker Prize.

Refuses to attend the gala banquet, claiming he doesn't have a dinner jacket. Prize goes to William Golding for *Rites of Passage*. 'It's bloody awful. It's so bad you have to think there's a reason in it.'
Preface to *Modern Irish Short Stories*, edited by Ben Forkner (New York, Viking Press).
Foreword to *Anthony Burgess: A Bibliography* by Jeutonne Brewer (New Jersey, Scarecrow Press).
Introduction to *Private Pictures*, photographs by Daniel Angeli and Jean-Paul Dousset (London, Jonathan Cape; Mondadori, Verona).

1981 January: broadcast of the television documentary 'A Kind of Failure', about a revisit to Malaya, for *Writers and Places* series.
They move to their house on rue des Muets, Callian, to escape noise of the Monaco Grand Prix.
A Malayan Trilogy, translated by Liana, appears in Italy as *Malesia!* and wins the Premio Scanno.
Special languages created for *Quest for Fire*, a film produced by Michael Gruskoff, directed by Jean-Jacques Annaud, based upon the novel *La Guerre de Feu* (1911) by J. H. Rosny-Aîné, screenplay by Gerard Brach.
Travels to Paris, Oslo, Stockholm, Vienna and through Germany to publicise the various translations of *Earthly Powers*. Georges Belmont and Hortense Chabrier win the Charles Baudelaire prize for the year's best translation, and Burgess wins *le meilleur livre étranger de l'année* prize for *La Puissance des Ténèbres*.
'Anthony Burgess's Rome', the script of his documentary, appears in *Cities*, adapted from the television series conceived by John McGreevy (London, Angus and Robertson; Canada, Lester and Orpan Dennys).

1982 2 February: broadcast of the operetta *Blooms of Dublin* on Radio Telefis Eireann and BBC Radio Three, produced by John Tydeman and Michael Hefferman. Music and lyrics originally written between 3 and 22 August 1971 whilst commuting from Italy to Minneapolis for *Cyrano de Bergerac*.
Introduction to the *Aerodrome* by Rex Warner (Oxford University Press).
12 May: Honorary Doctorate awarded by University of Manchester.

The Cavalier of the Rose, adapted from the opera *Der Rosenkavalier* by Richard Strauss and Hugo van Hofmannsthal (New York, Metropolitan Opera Classics Library; London, Michael Joseph, 1983).
The End of the World News (London, Hutchinson).
On Going to Bed (London, Deutsch).
This Man and Music (London, Hutchinson).

1983 Afterword to *The Heritage of British Literature* (New York, Thames and Hudson).
First performance 21 July: yet another revised translation of *Cyrano de Bergerac* by Edmond Rostand is produced by the Royal Shakespeare Company at the Barbican Theatre, London, directed by Terry Hands and starring Derek Jacobi.

1984 'A Personal View', in the catalogue of *The Thyssen-Bornemisza Collection of Modern Masters*, Royal Academy of Arts.
26 March: *Enderby's Dark Lady* (London, Hutchinson).
Ninety-Nine Novels: The Best in English since 1939 (London, Allison and Busby).

1985 20 January: presents 'The Rage of D. H. Lawrence', a *South Bank Show*, broadcast on the ITV network.
April: broadcast on NBC of twelve-hour mini-series, *A.D. – Anno Domini*, directed by Stuart Cooper, produced by Vincenzo Labella, for Telepictures Corp., starring Ava Gardner, James Mason, Anthony Andrews and Fernando Rey.
7 May: Burgess and Liana travel to Oxford by rail to meet Richard Ellmann and Roger Lewis.
13 May: *The Kingdom of the Wicked* (London, Hutchinson).
9 September: *Flame into Being: The Life and Work of D. H. Lawrence* (London, Heinemann).
23 October: First night of Weber's *Oberon*: 'A New Version by Anthony Burgess', Theatre Royal Glasgow, produced by Graham Vick, conducted by Sir Alexander Gibson. Burgess attends a performance at the Apollo Theatre, Oxford, on 10 December, with Roger Lewis.
7 November: libretto for *Oberon Old and New* is published (play by James Robinson Planché, music by Carl Maria von Weber; London, Hutchinson).
30 December: broadcast of *L'Enfance du Christ*, a television interpretation of the oratorio by Hector Berlioz, ITV network.

Publication of *Cyrano de Bergerac by Edmond Rostand Translated and Adapted for the Modern Stage* – to give it its full title (London, Hutchinson).
Moves for several months each year to Lugano, Switzerland. 'The chalet was purchased by Liana . . . and I tried to efface myself totally and present her to the Swiss as a *sole fem* [*sic*] not well-off whom a man occasionally visits.'

1986 1 March: *Homage to Qwert Yuiop: Selected Journalism 1978–1985* (London, Hutchinson) and as *But do Blondes Prefer Gentlemen? Homage to Qwert Yuiop and Other Writings* (New York, McGraw-Hill).
April: *A.D. – Anno Domini* broadcast on BBC television.
10 July: Honorary Doctorate awarded by University of Birmingham.
28 August: *The Pianoplayers* (London, Hutchinson).
27 November: first night at London Coliseum of *Carmen* (adaptation of libretto and translation) for English National Opera. Produced by David Poutney and conducted by Mark Elder.
Carmen: An Opera in Four Acts, 'Libretto by H. Meilhac and L. Halévy, based on the story by Prosper Mérimée, translated into English' (London, Hutchinson).
Blooms of Dublin, 'A Musical Play Based on James Joyce's *Ulysses*' (London, Hutchinson).
Introduction to *The Colonel's Daughter* by Richard Aldington (London, Hogarth Press).

1987 25 February: *Little Wilson and Big God: Being the First Part of the Confessions of Anthony Burgess* (London, Heinemann). Awarded the J. R. Ackerley Prize for 1988.
A Clockwork Orange, 'a play with music based on the novella of the same name' (London, Hutchinson).

1988 Introduction to *Venice: An Illustrated Anthology*, compiled by Michael Marquesee (London, Conran Octopus).

1989 2 March: *Any Old Iron* (London, Hutchinson).
The Devil's Mode, short stories (London, Hutchinson).

1990 *You've Had Your Time: Being the Second Part of the Confessions of Anthony Burgess* (London, Heinemann).
6 February: first night of play *A Clockwork Orange – 2004*, at the Barbican, produced by the Royal Shakespeare Company, directed by Ron Daniels and starring Phil Daniels as Alex, music by The Edge and U2.

1991 *Mozart and the Wolf Gang* (London, Hutchinson).
The Long Day Wanes: A Malayan Trilogy, paperback reprint (London, Penguin).
5 July: Honorary Doctorate awarded by University of St Andrews.

1992 8 October: having undergone a bronchoscopy and treatment at Memorial Sloane-Kettering Cancer Center, 1275 York Avenue, New York, Burgess is told that his lung condition is inoperable.
9 October: speaks on 'Translation' at Cheltenham Festival of Literature.
Eulogy delivered at the memorial service for Benny Hill.
A Mouthful of Air: Language and Languages, Especially English (London, Hutchinson).
'Sonata no.1 for great bass recorder and piano' (Hedon, Da Capo Musica).
Nothing Like the Sun. A Story of Shakespeare's Love Life, paperback reprint (London, Vintage).

1993 24–29 May: *Chatsky*, adapted from Griboyedov's *Woe from Wit*, and directed by Jonathan Kent, previews at the Malvern Festival Theatre before moving to the Almeida, London.
22 November: dies of lung cancer in the Hospital of St John and St Elizabeth, St John's Wood, London, aged seventy-six.
A Dead Man in Deptford (London, Hutchinson).
'Concertinos, Cor Anglais Orchestra' (Harlington, Saga Music Publications).

1994 25 February: in Lower College Hall at the University of St Andrews, a dinner in Burgess's honour had been planned on what would have been his seventy-seventh birthday. Though he'd died, the invitations had already been printed and sent out – so the celebrations went ahead anyway. In the unavoidable absence of the Guest of Honour, selections from *A Dead Man in Deptford* were read out by Dr Michael Herbert, the modern literature specialist in the School of English.
16 June: 'A Memorial Celebration for the Life and Work of Anthony Burgess', in St Paul's Church, Covent Garden, London.
Future Imperfect, omnibus edition of *The Wanting Seed* and *1985* (London, Vintage).
'Study for Cor Anglais or Oboe' (Harlington, Saga).
'Master Coate's Pieces for Piano' (Harlington, Saga).
'In Time of Plague' (Harlington, Saga).

1995 *Byrne: A Novel* [actually a poem] (London, Hutchinson).
One Man's Chorus: The Uncollected Writings, selected with an introduction by Ben Forkner (New York, Carroll and Graf).
The Complete Enderby (London, Penguin).

1996 *Childhood and Youth* (London, Penguin). Extracts from *Little Wilson and Big God* (1987).
'A Little Concerto for Oboe and Piano' (Harlington, Seresta Music).

The above has been compiled from the various Burgess bibliographies, Boytinck's, Brewer's, plus the ancillary checklists and addenda by Beverly R. David, in *Twentieth Century Literature* (July 1973), Carlton Holte, in *Twentieth Century Literature* (January 1974), and Samuel Coale, in *Modern Fiction Studies* (Autumn 1981). I have also cross-checked various dates with actual first editions, contemporary newspaper articles and reviews, the interviews Burgess himself gave, unpublished letters and manuscripts, and other related books by homunculi like Lew Grade and Franco Zeffirelli. In Burgess's own memoirs, *Little Wilson and Big God* and *You've Had Your Time*, the chronology is often faulty. He gets the Christopher Plummer *Cyrano* musical wrong by a full year – and the sequence of events goes haywire after that. He seems to imply that work on the *Jesus of Nazareth* script was done in the summer of 1973; yet Zeffirelli in *Jesus: A Spiritual Diary* says that Burgess delivered his draft in May 1974, having worked on it only during the previous sixteen days. Also, throughout the summer of 1973, Burgess was still busy on *Moses the Lawgiver*, going into the dubbing booth and re-recording Burt Lancaster and Anthony Quayle's dialogue so that they sounded, well – so that they sounded more like Burgess: 'I feel, ha ha, very much a civilian here, Joshua, me boy.' In addition to which, *Napoleon Symphony* ('an attempt to unify a mass of historical material in the comparatively brief space of about 150,000 words') had to be written at some point. From his own accounts, I don't know if Liana broke her leg once, twice, or whether she was as accident prone as Norman Wisdom. Similarly, he implies that Paolo-Andrea's suicide attempt was in 1977 – except that in a profile in *The Face* (1984) he says that the sad drama happened when the boy was nineteen, i.e. in 1983. Yet, as we'll see, it always suited his purpose to be inexact.

It was a hectic life – there's an amazing amount of racing around, especially in later years, when he must virtually have lived at airports waiting for the aerial bus rides. I've been unable to pin-point dates for trips to San

Juan, in Puerto Rico, when he lectured on Communications to a conference of American magazine proprietors, or quite when he was at the university in Nantes, talking about Hopkins and Eliot, and where he formed a relationship with Professor Ben Forkner that has given rise to The Anthony Burgess Center, The Anthony Burgess Newsletter and The Anthony Burgess Society (a.k.a. Les Amis D'Anthony Burgess), which operate from the Faculté des Lettres, Langues et Sciences Humaines at the Université d'Angers. The spirit of all this reminds me totally of The Goon Show Preservation Society, which collects and catalogues old recordings and fugitive bits of silliness much as the scholar-squirrels gather in Brittany to wonder at the reality of Burgess's electric organ, donated by his widow.

I have barely mentioned above his vast contribution to BBC radio programmes during the early sixties; nor have I attempted to straighten out his various lecture schedules and tours. He was also an enthusiastic delegate at conferences. Thomas F. Staley, the Director of the Harry Ransom Humanities Research Center at the University of Texas at Austin, met Burgess at a Modern Languages Association (MLA) conclave in Denver and at a Joyce convention in Monaco. They were also (Mr Staley tells me) 'on a program together' in London. What's all that about? Ulick O'Connor informs me that on 16 and 17 June 1991, Burgess attended the Joyce Summer School in Dublin and was paid two thousand pounds to deliver a lecture – the same Joyce lecture he'd been peddling for thirty years.*

* Here's Our Man strutting his stuff in Holland, as described to me in a letter of 2 February 1999, from Eric de Kuyper of Nijmegen:

> At the end of the eighties, I was deputy director at the Netherlands Filmmuseum (equivalent of the BFI), where we wanted to attract a larger audience for our silent movie programmes. Therefore, I was very much interested in Burgess's *The Pianoplayers* and I decided to try to invite him for a lecture in Amsterdam.
>
> After several calls between his agent and his wife the date and the price were set (in our eyes a large amount, I think two thousand pounds) and the programme decided. I think it was on the suggestion of his agent that we decided to have in the first part of the programme one of Mr Burgess's compositions: a song after d'Annunzio for tenor. In the second part we had the lecture of Mr Burgess about music and literature, and finally the evening was concluded by the rediscovered and restored Fritz Lang silent film, *Hara Kiri* [1919]. I remember that after the show Mr Burgess congratulated the piano-player, and sat down at the piano to demonstrate how his father would have played at the time for the silents. It was very funny and it was visible that he was enjoying it very much playing the fool for part of the audience leaving the theatre.
>
> All in all it was a successful evening and I think Burgess appreciated a lot the performance of his music. After it we went for a drink at his hotel; he insisted for a 'good hotel', with a preference for the Hotel Américain (which I think was not a good choice). In the taxi he was talking a lot, nicely arguing with his wife: the subject as I remember was language and linguistics – of course.

A full list of his musical compositions is another job again. He had a dozen careers all at once – novelist, journalist, composer, pundit, television and radio personality, would-be Broadway and Hollywood operator, translator, after-dinner speaker, showman, academic lecturer, teacher; he was all over the place, like Ulysses blown on and off course by the fickle gods.

A biography, however, should be much more than the arrangement of dates and the filling in of days. Behind the times to be made public, from private diaries and letters, there exists, for the critic to face, the murky world of the imagination, the ambiguous world of inspiration. How can we fashion a portrait of an artist? How can we gain access to, and assess, a stranger's life and his personality? To solve such problems, this book will have three main objectives, each of them interwoven and kept going in each section. (1) I attempt to uncover the principles and preoccupations of all the fiction, critical studies, articles, reviews, music and interviews; (2) I place Burgess in the wider context of European literature and cultural history, by glancing at the subjects he impinges upon and descends out of; and (3) to find out how the citizen who died as Anthony Burgess formed himself out of John Wilson (born on 25 February 1917), a Lancashire Catholic of mixed Irish and Scottish breeding, I have conversed with those who'd chanced to meet and work with him – from schoolmasters and editors to movie moguls, actors, academics and army colleagues. What is the relationship between the man and the writer the man became? The book traces and accounts for the transmogrification. As Chesterton said, 'A great genius may appear in almost any disguise; even in the disguise of a successful novelist.'

Prologue

Mr P. Larkin, CH

A service of thanksgiving for the life of Mr Philip Larkin, CH, was held in Westminster Abbey yesterday. The Right Rev Edward Knapp-Fisher, Sub-Dean, officiated, assisted by the Rev Alan Luff, Precentor and Sacrist, and Canon Trevor Beeson. The Rev F. C. Copleston, the Rev Willie Booth, Prebendary G. Irvine, the Rev D. J. Atkinson and Canon T. G. Grigg, were robed and in the sacrarium.

Mr Ted Hughes, Poet Laureate, read the lesson, and the prayers were led by the Precentor and Sacrist. Miss Jill Balcon read from the preface to "All What Jazz" and "Love Songs in Age", "Church Going" and "An Arundel Tomb" by Philip Larkin. The *Jazz* group played "Blue Horizon" by Sidney Bechet and "Davenport Blues" by Bix Beiderbecke. The Sub-Dean pronounced the blessing. Among those present were:

Mrs C E Hewett (sister), Mr and Mrs R Parry, Mrs M Price, Mr and Mrs V Thorpe, Mr E Larkin, Mr G Larkin, Lord Stewart of Fulham CH, Lord Dainton of Hallam Moor, Lady Kilmarnock, Lord Wilberforce (Chancellor, University of Hull) and Lady Wilberforce, Mr Norman St John Stevas, MP, Lady Violet Powell, the Hon W G Runciman, the Hon M Summerskill, Sir Bernard and Lady de Bunsen, Lady Bullard, Sir Mervyn Brown, Sir Patrick Neill, QC, and Lady Neill, Sir William and Lady Rees-Mogg.

Miss M Jones, Mr Kingsley Amis, Mr and Mrs A Burgess, Mr R Faber, Professor W Taylor (Vice-Chancellor, University of Hull), Mr P J Kavanagh, Mr and Mrs P Levi, Mr Harold Pinter, Mr Anthony Powell, Mr J Treglown (Editor, "Times Literary Supplement"), Miss C Tomlin, Mr A N Wilson, Mr M Wheeler-Booth, Mr and Mrs B J C Wintour, Rear Admiral A J Whetstone, the Very Rev Alan Webster and Mrs Webster, Dr M A Baird, Mr P Bailey, Mr M Couchman, Dr J M Bellamy, Councillor H Dalton (Chairman, Humberside City Council) and Mrs Dalton.

Mr J B Vent (Old Coventrians' Association), Mr P Taylor (chairman and treasurer, The Poetry Workshop and Society of Civil Service Authors) and Mrs Taylor, Mr B Morrison (The Poetry Book Society and "The Observer"), Mr G B Richardson (Oxford University Press), Mr M Le Fanu (general secretary, Society of Authors), Miss Pamela Lewis (Nottingham Poetry Society), Mr B Fothergill (Council of the Royal Society of Literature), Miss Barbara Hill (Poetry Society), Miss M Walmsley ("Encounter"), Miss J Elkins (honorary secretary, Blackheath Poetry Society), Miss L Edward (Tennyson Society), Mrs M Smith (honorary secretary, The National Council for Educational Standards), Mr Keith Jeffrey (FVS Foundation, Hamburg), Mr A J Loveday (secretary, Standing Conference of National and University Libraries), Mr A Wilson (president, Library Association) with Mr G Cunningham (chief executive), Mr P Castle (Castle Park Hook, Architects).

Professor R L Brett, Mr A J Bell-Wilson, Dr H Annis, Professor J H Appleton, Squadron Leader G M Bailey, the Rev J Clerkin, Professor R G R Bacon, Dr A Flick, Mr R Hamlin, Professor N Page, the Rev T Russ and Canon Anthony S B Rowe.

Mr Anthony Burgess

A memorial celebration for the life and work of Mr Anthony Burgess was held yesterday at St Paul's, Covent Garden. Canon Bill Hall, Senior Chaplain of the Actors' Church Union, officiated. Excerpts from the works of Anthony Burgess were read by Mr Michael Ratcliffe (*Homage to Qwert Yuiop*), Mr John Tydeman (*Mozart and the Wolf Gang*), Mr Antony Sher (*Inside Mr Enderby*) and Mr John Walsh (*A Dead Man in Deptford*).

During the service recordings of the author reading from his works *Little Wilson and Big God* and *Nothing Like the Sun* were played. Mr Auberon Waugh and Mr William Boyd gave addresses.

The Sixteenth of June, recorded music from *Blooms of Dublin*, words and music by Anthony Burgess, was played. The Barbican Virtuosi played *Adagio* from Mr Burgess's String Quartet. *In Time of Plague* by Thomas Nashe, an unaccompanied choral work by Mr Burgess, was performed by I Fagiolini. Among others present were:

Mrs Burgess (widow), Mr Andrew Burgess (son), Mr Ned Sherrin, Dr and Mrs S G Owen, Mrs E Raeburn, Mr and Mrs M C Battestin, Mrs William Boyd, Mr Anthony Thwaite and Mrs Ann Thwaite, Professor and Mrs Jack Allanson, Mrs Katherine West, Mr James Duckworth, Mr and Mrs Alan Williams, Mr David Day, Mr John Hughes.

Mr Christopher Hawtree, Mr Blake Morrison, Mr and Mrs Andrew Sinclair, Mr Peter Lewis, Mr William Cooper, Ms Penny Perrick, Mr and Mrs A J Parker, Mr David Lodge, Mr J Wilshire, Mr Kevin Jackson, Professor Hermione Lee, Mr Richard Cohen, Mr Paul Levy, Mr Charles Pick, Miss Lesley Gardner, Mr Colin Thubron, Mr Roger Lewis, Mr Stephen Musgrave, Mr Richard Roberts, Mrs Mic Cheetham.

Miss Gail Rebuck (Random House), Mr Simon King, Mrs Sue Freestone, Mr Tony Whittome and Mrs Elizabeth Sich (Hutchinson), Miss Angela Martin and Miss Helen Fraser (William Heinemann), Mrs Martha Smart (Poetry Book Society), Mrs Fanny Blake, Mr Peter Carson and Mr Peter Mayer (Penguin Books), Mr Brian Perman (Book Trust), Ms Tamer Karet (Medallion), Ms Nicky Gerard (*The Observer*), Mr John Coldstream and Miss S Herbert (*The Daily Telegraph*), Mrs Aridea Fezzi Price (*La Voce*), Mr George Bull (Royal Society of Literature), Miss Kate Pool (Society of Authors).

Mr Alastair Niven (Arts Council of England), Mr Richard Wortley (BBC Radio Drama), Mr Mark Bowles (Saga Music Publishing), Dr Nicholas Godlee (University College Hospital), the Rev Mark Oakley (St John's Hospice, St John's Wood), Mrs Lyn Williams (Globe Education, Shakespeare's Globe), Mr Michael Rubinstein, Mr John Rubinstein and Mr Bernard Nyman (Rubinstein Callingham) and Mr Ian Lewis (Medici Galleries).

'I said to Joyce in a bar in Paris in 1924: "Well, you gave George Russell an eternal and unbreakable alibi for that afternoon. But I know and he knows that he was not in the National Library."' *Earthly Powers*

Philip Larkin's memorial service was reported in *The Times* on 15 February 1986, Burgess's on 17 June 1994. (Misspellings of proper nouns in original.)

7 May 1985

Burgess appeared, slowly but firmly, up the steps from the tunnel under the tracks at Oxford railway station, like he was coming out of a hell-mouth in a Faust play. The 5.17 from Paddington was delayed, and Professor Richard Ellmann and I had been hanging about on the platform for half an hour, feeling expectant. 'Just think of all the famous people who've come up those stairs,' mused Dick, an American who'd been enticed from his native land to hold the Goldsmiths' Chair of English Literature.* His predecessor was Lord David Cecil. One of his successors is Hermione Lee. Though he spent most of the academic year hanging about his condominium at Emory University, Atlanta, where he received a lucrative stipend from Coca-Cola, now and again he did come to Oxford for appearance's sake. He had been working on a biography of Oscar Wilde since 1959. With its sensitivity to people's

* Ellmann was my supervisor (though he didn't do much supervising) for a doctoral dissertation on Ezra Pound, of which I wrote not one word. We became friends and used to dine lavishly at the Randolph, sending the bill to *Punch*, at Tudor Street, EC4, materially helping to close that magazine. We were both aware of a Bloom/Dedalus dynamic in our relationship. I was immensely cocky and callow, Ellmann wholly lacked the Oxford way of people being interested in each other only for their own advantage. He didn't seem interested in people at all and was wrapped up in his (dead) subjects' lives. 'Wilde moved house today,' he once told me, by way of indicating his progress in the MS. When he died in May 1987, Burgess wrote in the *Observer*, 'I first met Dick Ellmann in Nashville, Tennessee, in 1966 . . . He wrote nothing that was dull, inelegant, or lacking in profound humanity . . . At Oxford he brought American commonsense and a European sensitivity to his teaching' – which makes him sound ripe for the Henry James treatment. Burgess concluded his tribute by claiming, 'It gives me a small consolation to know that I received one of his last letters, kind and witty as always, saying that he had gained some pleasure from my most recent book.' Burgess's *Any Old Iron* (1989) is dedicated 'In Memory of Richard Ellmann/1918–1987'.

feelings and sorrows, I personally prefer it to his magisterial book on Joyce.*

'Wilde and Lord Alfred Douglas,' I ventured. 'Sir Harold Macmillan . . .'

'I was thinking of Zuleika Dobson,' said Ellmann, wistfully.

At that moment my friend John Wain pushed a laden trolley past us. Wain was a minor novelist and former Professor of Poetry, an Honorary Fellow of St John's and of Brasenose, where he could be found most lunchtimes quaffing (the only word) from his personalised silver tankard. He'd recently been anointed CBE. As Philip Larkin once said, 'Isn't England a marvellous, free, open country? Take a chap like old John Wain, now. No advantages of birth or position or wealth or energy or charm or looks or talent – nothing, and look where he is now . . .' Where he was at that exact moment was trying to get his luggage wagon (which naturally had a wonky wheel) through the pressing crowd. Wain was flustered and irritable, which I'd always taken as his normal state. He used to come round to my rooms at Magdalen with his girlfriend, Brenda, and they'd spend the evening arguing, quite nastily, too. Towards the end of his life he went blind and cut a Homeric, Miltonic, Borgesian figure in the Senior Common Rooms. I fancy he even moved about with the aid of a tall wooden staff.

We told him that we were waiting for Anthony Burgess, and he did a pantomime of horrified recoiling and flinching, as if at an invisible serpent. 'Oh God! Oh Christ! Oh no! I'll leave you to it then. I'm off – to Bangor and Stoke-on-Trent.'†

* *Oscar Wilde* was published by Hamish Hamilton (posthumously) in 1987. Ten years later it formed the basis of a dreadful film, *Wilde*, starring Stephen Fry – whose very-pleased-with-himself demeanour was a million miles away from Ellmann's portrait of a doomed and ironic (and iconic) Dubliner who, despite the self-destructive infatuation with Bosie, was a family man of intense loyalty. The role needed the sensibility of an Alan Bates. Jude Law as Lord Alfred Douglas was about right. Burgess claimed that he'd once had an acrimonious correspondence with the real Lord Alfred Douglas about the merits of Gerard Manley Hopkins: 'I was able to submit a letter explaining sprung rhythm to the pederastic fool.'

† Having since looked up Burgess's comments on Wain's work I regret he had to hurry away to his train – I could have witnessed a punch-up. In his British Council pamphlet *The Novel To-Day* (1963), Burgess, adopting his best housemaster style, wrote, 'John Wain first impressed, in *Hurry On Down* (1953), with subject rather than form . . . We now see that, though he still has good fictional material, he lacks a great deal of the equipment of a man like [Kingsley] Amis.' The summings-up are decidedly beta-double minus: 'weary rather than bright'; 'he does not prune sufficiently, so that what should be sharp is often long-winded'; and finally (magnanimously), 'Yet there is always evidence of a fine mind behind the sloppiness.' Come *The Novel Now* (revised edition 1971), the buttons are off the foils: 'atrocious construction'; 'indifferent style'; 'a pawky but undistinguished prose'; 'remarkably careless'; and (devastatingly) 'he ought to consider giving up extended fiction'.

Ellmann aside, nobody at Oxford took my Burgess interests seriously. Had he been the historical Anthony Burgess who wrote sermons and doctrinal treatises, the chaplain to the parliamentary garrison in Coventry and a member of the Westminster Assembly, who *fl.* 1652, I'd have had little difficulty from Oxford's pear-shaped drones. My Burgess had the handicap of being (and the bad taste to be) still alive.

Wain once told me, a little maliciously, that he'd been a delegate at a conference in the American Midwest. Burgess was there – or rather he wasn't there. He stayed in his motel room typing a James Bond script for Cubby Broccoli. (This much is true – Burgess wrote a screenplay for *The Spy Who Loved Me.**) I was meant to take this as a revelation of vulgarity. Burgess was to be deplored, dismissed.

He finally arrived at 5.40, accompanied by his wife, Liliana, known as Liana, who was dumpy, vivacious and Italian – a character. The dedicatrice of many of his later books, including *Earthly Powers*, she was like a Captain of Artillery attending a Head of State. Burgess was straight-backed and formal. He was wearing one of his greenish-reddish yellow tweed jackets which, owing to his Daltonianism or monochromatism, he believed to be a muted brownish grey. (It's the one question polymathic Burgess couldn't have answered: What colour's an orange?)

'Is it still term? Are you having exams? In Manchester we'd be finished on May the twentieth,' he said with a booming voice. He was like an old-fashioned teacher or dignitary, a man heavy with responsibilities, coming into a classroom or canteen on a tour of inspection, concerned that he's not regarded as a joke. I was glad that Wain had vanished.

We all went to find Ellmann's rusty, seldom-washed car, to drive the short distance to New College. Burgess sat in front of me, lofty and still and with a parade-ground bearing. Ellmann smiled and chuckled self-consciously. The way he had of lowering his head and coyly glancing up at you – or at the road – from under his brow, Princess of Wales fashion, was a slumpedness, a slackening of his neck muscles, which we didn't know then was a symptom of motor neurone disease.

Liana and myself, smiling politely, were flung upon each other's laps as Ellmann took us through the city, turning corners by mounting the kerb,

* 'I was engaged on a lecture tour of the USA at that time,' Burgess wrote in the *Sunday Telegraph* (14 June 1987), 'and in one Holiday Inn bedroom or another, I hammered out a story which involved a gross Orson Welles villain in a wheelchair whose ambition was no longer to serve either Russia or Mammon but to humiliate the world . . . My script, as I foresaw, was rejected, but my oil tanker (a camouflaged floating palace for the chief villain) was retained.'

grazing bollards and scattering cyclists. (Why is it that the clever men of Oxford, who know all there is to be know'd, also have to drive like Mr Toad? Burgess himself had never driven a motor vehicle.) She informed me that she was reading *The End of the World News*, with a view to translating it into Italian. 'It is so good – issa brilliant! I'm taking notes.' At one time she'd made a living as a translator, with Thomas Pynchon's *V* and *The Crying of Lot 49* to her credit. What I most noticed at the time was the extreme tutti-fruittiness of her accent, though as Kingsley Amis remarked, after he'd met her, in fairness a strong Italian accent is not to be unexpected in an Italian. What I think now, however, is how odd it was to praise in such lavish terms her husband's work with her husband present. In England we'd be much more laconic – indeed, we almost deliberately glory in our modesty and, in public at least, friends, husbands and wives are more likely to mock one's shortcomings. This is how Burgess's first wife, Lynne, dead of cirrhosis in 1968, operated. 'Mr Burgess disappoints!' she'd say. I wonder to this day if he comprehended the layers of raillery and affection in her attitude to him. She was from South Wales.

What must have appealed to Burgess about Liana was that she seemed to refuse to have any understanding of English subtleties and customs, of our leg-pulling and wit. She was ignorant of our elaborate codes of irony and put-down; she had no patience with our reticence and indirection. He was drawn to her as he was to living in exile – foreignness got him going. 'Writers need light to write,' he once said, 'and I have been granted more light by the Mediterranean sun than by the perpetually overcast skies of England.' Living in Malta, Monte Carlo, Rome, on the lake at Bracciano, and in Provence, he could thus dazzle us with epic subjects like Napoleon, Jesus, Attila the Hun, Mozart or Cyrano de Bergerac. Those left at home, the Amises, Murdochs, Drabbles and Byatts, subsisting in an England that has 'been too cosy, too easy to live in', have avoided the shocks of the life overseas and hence have had to 'make literature out of suburban adultery'. Or so he maintained – in fact Burgess's complaints about 'the narrow insularity of British life' and the philosophy of art he adumbrated from this reveal more about his own mind – with its sham splendour – and restlessness than it does about the writers and the community he abandoned.

I said to Liana, wasn't *The End of the World News* based on aborted plays and film scripts – the disaster movie section, the musical about Trotsky, the operetta on Freud? This instigated an instant tirade about the iniquities of Hollywood moguls and impresarios. 'Lew Grade – a veelenous, veelenous man!'

Burgess, who'd been murmuring to Ellmann about Joyce, broke off to say, 'But this is Lawrence's centenary! I've done a book, very rapidly, for Heinemann, who've woken up to the fact it's Lawrence's centenary!' I'd already read *Flame into Being*, his account of the life and work of D. H. Lawrence, in proof. It was to be published on 9 September. As with many of Burgess's biographical opuscules (Hemingway, Keats, Orwell, Shakespeare, and Joyce of course), the actual subject is Burgess himself, and the mood can be a bit swaggering and self-congratulatory, too. The first chapter at least came clean, unimproveably so: 'Lawrence and Myself When Young'. Burgess explained how he and his literary playmate were both from working-class families and northern industrial cities (Manchester and Nottingham); both were, as infants, branded as *mardarse*,

Eh, th'rt a mard-arsed kid,
'E'll gie thee socks . . .

– meaning that they were sensitive, bookish and mollycoddled; both went to provincial universities (Burgess was never to stop saying that Oxford and Cambridge persons snubbed him, which shows how much my advocacy registered), and 'William Shakespeare was another Midlander who did not go to Oxford'; both married foreign aristocrats (Frieda von Richthoven and Liliana Macellari, daughter of La Contessa Maria Lucrezia Pasi Piani della Pergola); both elected to live abroad (Lawrence just about everywhere, searching, amongst other goals, for a climate hospitable to his damaged lungs; Burgess in Malaya and Brunei, the Côte d'Azur, Switzerland – the labyrinth of his adventures implying this attempt 'to get out of the narrow cage which inhibits the English novel, to avoid writing about failed love affairs in Hampstead'); both believed themselves persecuted by a British boorishness and scorn for imaginative pursuits – Lawrence had trouble with the censor long before Lady Chatterley dropped her drawers. Burgess was sued for libel by a school secretary who recognised herself in *The Worm and the Ring*; there was a prudish fuss over *A Clockwork Orange*; the critics, he complained, would vex him and mock his fluency to his dying day: 'I always felt there is a kind of resentment in England, as though I was resented for being able to write without too much difficulty.' All in all, 'literature is essentially subversive, and Lawrence is a witness (or martyr, which means the same thing) for that truth'.

Subversive, perhaps, because it upends preconceptions; it makes it new, to use Ezra Pound's phrase; it locates bliss in the commonplace, to use

Thomas Mann's phrase. Subversive, perhaps, because it *doesn't* promote moral good – which is the lesson for all the arts in *A Clockwork Orange.* Alex loves Beethoven; after listening to the music he goes out on the rampage. Lawrence was a witness to sexuality; his subject, the mythical and ritualistic; his world, the dangerous forests of the mind ('the divine unconscious'). Burgess interprets him as a theological Freud, a psychoanalytic Blake: 'Lawrence's entire output adds up to a unity to be read rather as one reads the Bible . . . Like all Britain's prophets, he preached to a wilderness.'

It's impossible not to form the impression that Burgess, whose primary link with Lawrence is that they were both egotists, needed to feel embattled – and, as with Coriolanus, everybody had to hear about it. There was a great deal of self-seeking manipulation in his behaviour, in the advertising of his hurt quality. There was something precarious about him – but he wanted to be like that. We'd now arrived at New College and, the afternoon light having faded, we wandered around the silent darkness of the grassy quadrangles. 'Very charming, very charming,' Burgess muttered as some girls went past. 'Nymphets, undergraduettes. English girls are so well-fed nowadays.' If this was to presage a lunge, or a quick shape-change into a bat so he could bite them on the neck, nothing happened. But Burgess's gaunt, wan features and red-rimmed eyes were certainly vampiral. I'd expected him to be tanned – otherwise what is the point of living in the Mediterranean? – but he looked waxy and pallid, long deprived of the sun. And how are we going to describe his hair? The yellowish-white powdery strands were coiled on his scalp like Bram Stoker's Dracula's peruke, not maintained since Prince Vlad the Impaler fought off the Turks in the Carpathian mountains in 1462. What does it say about a man that he could go around like that, as Burgess did? Though he was a king of the comb-over (did the clumps and fronds emanate from his ear-hole?), no professional barber can be blamed for this.* I thought to myself, he has no idea how strange he is. What did he think he looked like? He evidently operated on his own head with a pair of garden shears. Was he indifferent to his appearance? That one can be ruled out. The actorish mannerisms, the voice, the wielding of the cigarillo, the silk handkerchief, the whole Burgess plumage, imply a high level of personal vanity. Yet, if he genuinely believed he was concealing his baldness, he must have

* This biographer drew the line at traipsing around the Mediterranean to see if any coiffeur had a black and white 8" x 10" of Anthony Burgess in the window and to ask if it was good for business.

been tremendously wrapped up in himself to suspend belief that wilfully. He also had a strange idea of his audiences' (or spectators') credulity – except he could never imagine the thoughts and reactions of others – just as there's no sympathetic or spiritual contact with his readers. It was clear, from a few moments in his company, that he was unlikely to ask your opinion about anything. He was not interested in what you'd do or think or say.

In the short run, however, the nicotine-stained fuzzy bush at the summit of his frame served to distract from the ugliness of the rest of his face, which raised a vague reminiscence of a snapper turtle or tapir. He also appeared to have unnaturally long lower teeth, the colour of maize, and no upper set to speak of, the top of his mouth or lip having become elongated to conceal his gums, like a baboon. Ellmann was showing us the William of Wykeham statue – Wykeham being the bishop who'd obtained a papal bull for the endowment of Winchester school in 1378 and who issued a charter for the foundation of 'Seinte Marie College of Wynchestre in Oxenforde', i.e. New College, in 1379. As Burgess, on the *Parkinson* show in 1980, had complained that, until the Catholic Emancipation Act, Lancashire families such as his were forbidden from attending universities and public schools ('If we had talent or temperament we used to go into the entertainment business'), a monument to the original Wykehamist was unlikely to make him brimful with euphoria. 'Very gothic,' was all he said. 'A very vivacious virgin,' said Liana, of William's companion, St Mary. 'Was this Judas College?' asked Burgess, the second Max Beerbohm reference of my day.

We went to see what Burgess called 'the dark ravine' of New College Lane and then to the cloisters. Liana told me that the architecture reminded her of the monastery or city where Shakespeare meets Cervantes in a fanciful episode in one of her man's (many) unrealised film scripts: Valladolid, situated a hundred and fifty miles north of Madrid. It has a university and a granite cathedral. In the fifteenth and sixteenth centuries it was the capital of Spain, and Shakespeare and his acting troupe are there with the delegates attending the Hispano-British peace colloquies. According to Burgess, Shakespeare and Cervantes fall out over who was first to create the Don Quixote/Hamlet, Sancho Panza/Falstaff universal archetypes.* Burgess, explaining to me that Shakespeare will have stayed

* The sequence survives as 'A Meeting in Valladolid', collected in the short-story collection *The Devil's Mode* (1989). Sounding like Burgess himself castigating the Hampstead School, Cervantes rails at Shakespeare: '"I say this of you English – that you have not suffered. You

at Oxford on his way between London and Stratford – 'It's where he watered his horses' – perked up as he examined the memorial plaques dedicated to John Galsworthy (1867–1933) and Hugh Gaitskell (1906–63). 'I never knew he died so young,' he said delightedly of the latter. 'Didn't they give Galsworthy the Nobel?' I asked – a mistake. 'Yes indeed, 1932. I remember it well. The following year a Russian won it for the first time. Ivan Bunin, he translated Byron. It's all political. I was up for the Nobel Prize a few years ago, but I was beaten by somebody else. . .' William Golding, I had the sense not to say. 'My books were being solemnly read by the committee in Stockholm.'

He went on ahead to join Ellmann. As the century's two great Joyce enthusiasts strolled together in learned comradeship, what did they talk about? Pension plans, investments, tax-avoidance schemes, offshore bank accounts, bonds, gilts, blue-chip stock and securities. I was reminded of Burgess's Shakespeare, wasting time in Spain, wishing he was back in Warwickshire 'collecting debts . . . and negotiating for the purchase of arable land'.

'I claim my old-age pension now,' he said to me in triumph, 'though there was some difficulty with the computer in Newcastle-upon-Tyne' – where the offices of the then Department of Health and Social Security (Records Branch) were situated. And I'm sure there indeed was some head-scratching and microchip popping – as John Wilson, the man behind the mask of Anthony Burgess, would not have paid any United Kingdom income tax and National Insurance contribution since 1954.

'I have to keep writing in order to live and pay the bills,' he began – and certainly the upkeep and maintenance charges on the white marble palazzo in Malta, the house in Bracciano (actually two knocked together – the building work all paid for by the labour on *Moses the Lawgiver*, which starred Burt Lancaster), the mill house in Callian, the villa in Lugano, Switzerland, the two apartments in rue Grimaldi, Monaco, plus various properties in London, Paris, and Rome, must add up. But that's not what he meant. He meant he was as poor as a church mouse.

---

do not know what torment is. You will never create a literature out of your devilish complacency. You need hell, which you have abandoned, and you need the climate of hell – harsh winds, fire, drought." "We have done our best," Will meekly said.'

In addition to Shakespeare and Cervantes, *The Devil's Mode* is full of strange meetings: Hamlet and Dr Faustus; Debussy and Shaw; and Shaw is in the audience at a Sherlock Holmes violin recital; Browning, Debussy and Mallarmé in Dublin with Gerard Manley Hopkins; Hopkins and a word-child who'll grow up to be James Joyce. For Burgess it is a literary universe, where all his heroes and influences are kith and kin.

'My books are taxed in the place of publication, except for England, which has a treaty. Though if I give a lecture here, that's paid net of tax.' To indicate that he was a man who had to count the pennies, he grew worried about the waste of electricity – all those curtainless windows with lights glaring. I explained they were communal staircases. He thought it improvidence.

We made our way back to the car, and thence to Ellmann's house at 39 St Giles. Why do academics choose to live in such squalor? Only in films do professors sit on Queen Anne furniture, sip vintage port from crystal goblets and fondle calf-bound first editions. At Ellmann's place the chairs were broken, the sink clogged with tea leaves and his daughters' draining knickers, Christmas cards from the year before last were still up, and the windows were so unwashed and opaque, they put me in mind of that line in Eliot about the yellow fog rubbing its back and muzzle on the panes. The building was clad in a rickety trellis and a pair of sooty, unpruned lime trees overhung the street, like claws.

The room we were shown into, off the entrance passage, was not romantically gloomy – lamplit or gaslit; it was dark because the boss was going easy on the forty-watt Mazda bulbs. There was a bed in there, too. On the wall, a signed Cocteau print. Perhaps it was Mary Ellmann's boudoir in the normal run of events. Ellmann's wife had suffered from strokes and cancer for years; it was always sad to see her shuffle about, snapping at Ellmann, who'd be hovering over her, half embarrassed, half solicitous. Nobody ever expected that he'd be the one to die first. Present during the ensuing scene, she made no contribution.

Burgess, remembering that this was Oxford, started complaining about *The Oxford Companion to English Literature*, as edited by Margaret Drabble and recently published. 'She would have liked to leave me out. The first thing I did was look up myself, Dick, A. S. Byatt and Frank Kermode.'* Liana added that Kermode had written the best review of *MF*. She forebore to add that, as 'The Algonquin Oedipus', it was printed in the *Listener* on 1 June 1971.

'Claude Lévi-Strauss's *The Scope of Anthropology* stirred me a great deal,' Burgess vouchsafed. 'Riddles, incest, the functioning of the mind.

* Kermode is not there; Ellmann, we are told, was 'educated at Yale University and Trinity College, Dublin', which was exactly so; and of Antonia Byatt we are informed 'Her sister is the novelist Margaret Drabble.' Burgess is described as a writer who 'displays a flair for pastiche, satiric social comment, and verbal invention'. In the revised edition of 1995, Burgess's dates are given as '1917–1994', generously giving him an additional year of life.

I've fallen out with my French translator though, unfortunately. He was a leader in the Hitler Youth. He'd changed his name to that of a red wine. Tell me, Dick, which white wine did Joyce drink?'

'People come to blows over that,' was the evasive reply. Ellmann, meantime, was making a meal of fetching gin and tonics. A tray had to be taken back and forth to some far-off pantry. No bottles were left conveniently to hand. A plastic tub of what might have been called guacamole made a brief appearance. Ellmann may have held seven honorary doctorates and written masterpieces of twentieth-century biography, but as a host he needed to stay and see the teacher after class.

'There is a post-structuralist discussion of *Goldfinger* out in France,' said Burgess, reverting to his theme. 'Structuralism should be about the unconscious – about the shapes and forms that we find ourselves imposing on the world, to make sense of it.'

'Like Catholicism, Marxism or psychoanalysis, it's the search for certainties,' I piped up. 'Wasn't your *Tremor of Intent* your James Bond homage?' I didn't want to insult him by saying pastiche or rip-off. Given the sink-it-at-the-box-office subtitle of 'An Eschatological Spy Novel', instead of action set-pieces and hair's-breadth escapes, what we got were sermons on faith and patriotism and parallels made between a secret agent's debriefing and the confessional. At the end, the spy gives up being a spy and goes to Dublin to be a priest. Less Ian Fleming, then, than Graham Greene. There's one detail I always enjoyed: the spy's top fly button conceals a microphone.

'In Copenhagen they call that book *Martyrernes Blod*,' said its author.* 'There was a martyr in my own family. He was executed for publicly refusing to acknowledge Elizabeth I as head of the church.' This bit of ancestral history is included in the novel. In quite a few of his books, crucifixions, torture and being burnt at the stake are described with relish.†

* In Rio de Janeiro it's *A Ultima Missão*, in Buenos Aires, *Trémula Intención*, in Paris, *Un Agent qui vous veut du bien*, and in Stockholm, *Skuggen ar ett Svek*.

† '. . . the body of Edward Roper tasted the fire. He screamed high and loud as his garments blazed, then his skin, then his flesh. Then through the smoke and flames his disfigured head, the hair an aureole, was seen to loll. . .' The passage in *Tremor of Intent*, covering two pages, purports to come from Hearne's *British Martyrs*, which is of course Burgess's version of John Foxe's *Book of Martyrs*, more correctly entitled *Acts and Monuments of These Latter and Perilous Days, Touching Matters of the Church*, first published in 1563. Actually, this is all about Roman Catholic persecution and Protestant martyrdom during Queen Mary's reign – and that's the twist in Burgess's plot ('You bloody benighted idiot, Roper. Curse your stupidity, you stupid idiot . . . you haven't even the sense to look up the facts . . . all wrong, totally bloody wrong').

The funny thing was, Burgess still smarted about these injustices done to his relatives in the sixteenth century as if it was yesterday. 'We died for the faith. We stood up for what we believed in,' he added.

'That was a long time ago, though, wasn't it?' I said placatingly. It was certainly a long time to bear a grudge, but then for thirty years Burgess had been complaining at every opportunity that Geoffrey Grigson had given him a bad review. We were saved from a new outbreak of a sectarian religious war by the entry into the room of a beef-faced white-haired party called Gordon N. Ray, the editor of Thackeray's letters and papers (in four volumes), the author of several critical studies of Thackeray, and of a book which examined the relationship between Thackeray's fiction and personal history. He had clearly never heard of Anthony Burgess and asked him where he was from – an innocent enough opener.

'Manchester,' answered Burgess – true in the sense that Sir Isaiah Berlin originally came from Riga and the Ellmann great-grandparents emigrated to Highland Park, Michigan, from Bucharest, but this couldn't have been what Ray meant. Except to make a television programme about it for Belgian television, to accept an honorary degree, and to call in on his book-signing tours, Burgess hadn't set foot in Lancashire since the war. 'It used to be a great city. Cottonopolis. Music – we had the Hallé. A great newspaper – the *Manchester Guardian*. Now it's a run-down dirty place full of West Indian shebeens. I went to the university there, not to Oxford. Liverpool, Leeds and Owen's College, Manchester, formed the Victorian University of the English North. By my day it was the Victoria University of Manchester. I read for a very linguistic, phonological degree. We looked to the North – a lot of Germanic, Scandinavian pride. We had to go to Iceland to do part of the course. It's probably softer options now.'

'Anthony spends most of the time in Monaco,' I threw in. This was also

---

The mentality of martyrdom and guilt is explored in *The Worm and the Ring* ('His recusant family had lost land, been barred from the universities, that he, Christopher Howarth, might have the right to apostatise'), where the hanging, drawing and quartering of a traitor is described; and an execution of alleged Catholic traitors is very fully described in *Nothing like the Sun* ('The hangman's hands reeked. Then he went with his hatchet for the body as he would mince it fine'). The opening chapter of *Man of Nazareth* is a DIY lesson on crucifixions ('The manner of executing a criminal in those days, as I have seen too often with my own eyes, was somewhat in the manner I shall now describe'); and *The Kingdom of the Wicked* entirely concerns the colourful martyrdoms of Christ's followers. Despite what he told Michael Parkinson – 'I became associated with violence chiefly because of the film made by Stanley Kubrick. In consequence they have turned me into some kind of expert on violence which I really know nothing about' – violent death and persecution are prevalent in Burgess's work well beyond the pages of *A Clockwork Orange*.

the first time I'd called him by name – by any name, for there was a variety to choose from, in addition to Mr or Dr Burgess. Liana called him Antonio, as if he was a waiter about to come round with the giant peppermill. Ellmann called him John. Everybody who'd known him prior to 1968 when, like Byron in the Beerbohm cartoon, he kicked the dust of England from his shoes, called him John. I would have liked to have had the courage to do so – the Anthony Burgess business was an act, after all. But I was to know him as Anthony. (Only Zeffirelli called him Tony and Lew Grade, to his eternal credit, called him Tone-Boy.) But – Antonio, John, Anthony: he never once smiled bemusedly or twinkled at the absurdity of being called lots of names simultaneously. You'd think that, by a complicit gleam in his eyes, he'd signal that he was making a conscious show of his indifference. It contributed to the aura of everything around him seeming unreal.

'Monaco was like Ruritania, before Grace died. An outpost of Hollywood, too, with these yachts arriving. Onassis wanted Marilyn Monroe for Rainier, who is a playboy. When Grace married Rainier, Americans thought she was going off to become the madam of a high-class gambling saloon. She was a cultured, intelligent, well-read woman, Grace. She even read my books. I've set up the Princess Grace Library in her honour. A collection of Irish books, especially music – sheet-music of popular songs, which Joyce knew, didn't he, Dick?'

Ellmann, having only heard the words *library* and *sheet,* as he'd been off-stage getting Gordon Ray his drink, said, 'There was recently a Joyce Conference organised by a Professor Kidd, of Virginia. He is concerned about the pagination of the first edition of *Ulysses*. He thinks the page numbering is of significance. On page sixty-nine there has to be a mention of oral sex. I think this is fringe loony stuff.'

Of all the preposterous projects Burgess got up to – and it's a wide field, from playing Scrabble in Malay, to wanting to translate *Finnegans Wake* into Italian,* to the stone-age dialect workshops he conducted with Desmond Morris for *Quest for Fire*, to the New Grove-style catalogue he

* The idea for this one came to him on board a transatlantic liner in 1971. Having taken against his fellow travellers (the Italians ate too greedily and everybody else was sunbathing – 'mindless solar worship'), he shut himself in a cabin with Liana and a copy of his own *A Shorter Finnegans Wake* ('This is one of the most entertaining books ever written,' according to 'A. B., London, 1965') and set about devising *pHorbiCEtta*, 'forbicetta' being the Italian for earwig – thus Humphrey Chimpden Earwicker, Joyce's hero, and the initials HCE that stand for Here Comes Everybody and Haveth Childers Everywhere. I wonder how far they got with it?

compiled for himself in *This Man and Music* (which included incidental music for *Moses* deemed 'unacceptable to Sir Lew Grade'), to the way he could remember his army serial number, 7388026, only by 'converting it into a tune on the Chinese principle of notation' – it's hard to beat his involvement with the Princess Grace Irish Library, 9 Avenue Marie de Lorraine, Monaco. I thought he meant he was the curator, but the curator was Dr Georges Sandulesco, a Swede born in Romania of a Greek mother, and who had studied Joyce at Leeds and Essex. (I can't rule out the possibility that he was a Burgess creation.) Having proclaimed that there were two thousand songs embedded in the text of *Finnegans Wake*, Burgess had a piano wheeled into the library so he could sit at it and play them all. He said this was for the entertainment of tourists and visitors.

'Princess Grace was more gracious and royal than any of the British Royal Family, except for Princess Di. But then she was a trained actress.'

Liana, who'd been constantly staring and wondering, said, 'See Napoli and Di.'

'Do you have any family, Mr Burgess?' asked Gordon Ray.

'I have a son, Paolo Andrea, who has become a Caledonian. We have to call him Andrew. He destroys all my writings which refer to my Irish roots. He wants to find our Scottish roots and connections. *The Encyclopaedia Britannica* mentioned that one of my grandmothers was Irish, a Finnegan from Tipperary. My set now has an odd volume missing. This is a real, Oedipal experience. An attempt to strike the father dead, and to have no family ties – to be independent. He is trained in cuisine. He and I cook, Liana shops. He was once a cook at Durrants, off Baker Street, where we stay.'*

'There's a community spirit at the hotel,' said Liana. 'It's like Bologna.'

Durrants, situated behind the Wallace Collection and just off the Marylebone High Street, is a quaint Georgian (1790) building popular with publishers, who often billet visiting authors there. I've seen Muriel Spark, Paul Auster and Jan Morris in the lobby. Within, it is a long, narrow premises with brass and mahogany appointments, like Captain Nemo's *Nautilus*. It has an intimate wood-panelled bar with blunderbusses and muskets in glass cases. The seats are of a rich red leather. On the wall is a large oil of a nude woman with a particularly hairy snatch. I call it *The 'Baccy Pouch*, and it looks like they found it decorating the set

*Though not always. On one occasion a publisher or the BBC inadvertently (?) booked him into not quite so nice a place round the corner – and in his paranoid way he made much of this. Did it signify that his stock had fallen?

in a Western. I myself have been staying at either Durrants or the Basil Street Hotel since I returned to live in England in 1995. The barman told me Burgess preferred to drink bottles of Tiger beer in the pub next door.

Burgess seemed indignant that Andrea – or Andrew – had only been required, when in the hotel kitchen, to chop cucumbers. He felt that was an insult – as if without ado one could take over and be Antonio Carluccio. In his novels there is much on rich food – for example, the duel of overeating, the battle of the bellies, in *Tremor of Intent* (a version of the baccarat game between Bond and Le Chiffre in *Casino Royale*); or the Edwardian plenitude of a menu card Toomey recollects in *Earthly Powers*:

Saumon Fumé de Hollande
Velouté de Homard au Paprika
Tourte de Ris-de-Veau Brillat-Savarin
Selle d'Agneau de Lait Polignac
Pomme Dauphin Petits Pois Fine-Fleur
Sorbet au Clicquot
Poularde Soufflée Impériale
Salade Aida
Crêpes Flambées au Grand Marnier
Coffret de Friandises
Corbeille de Fruits Café Liqueurs

He didn't only lavish attention on high-quality eateries. There are many mentions of Lancashire hotpot in his biographical writings; of Sandwich Spread, Marmite, Golden Syrup. *One Hand Clapping* is virtually a catalogue of food in the fifties: chops and onions and sliced potatoes in layers; gammon and a fried egg; tinned steak and kidney pudding; pie and cake and jam. But there is equally as much, in his work, on weak stomachs. Fancy cooking is an indulgence – he doesn't really approve of it. It shouldn't be more than a basic refuelling. His characters are always vomiting. They have broken teeth and can't chew. His attitude to sex is similar – it's bestial, and filled him with shame.

For now we were making do with Ellmann's dip and a Ritz cracker. 'We have been to Inverness with Andrew,' said Liana. 'He was injured in a car crash in January, on Friday the thirteenth.'

'I warned him not to go out. Sometimes it is right to be superstitious,' said Burgess.

'Are you working on something at the moment?' asked Gordon Ray, his career in the Thackeray archives still not having taught him that this is the query authors hate most, as it implies they are dabblers who only take up their pen now and again, on a whim; and Burgess, of all people, was nothing if not industrious.

'I'm writing a novel called *The Sovereignty of the Sword*, about the rediscovery of Excalibur. It's about the Celts.' This became *Any Old Iron*, another of his inflated epics which encompassed the sinking of the *Titanic*, the Great War, the Russian Revolution, the Spanish Civil War, the Second World War, and the victims of Yalta, and thereby avoided any reverberations of failed love affairs in Hampstead. It reached number five in the bestseller list.

If Andrew – or Andrea – was prohibiting Irishry, Burgess was doing the next best thing and looking at the Welsh. *Any Old Iron* sees Welsh Nationalists steal the shards of Excalibur from the Hermitage in Leningrad, in the hope that its magic powers will aid their cause. Reminiscent of the Nazis wanting to make evil use of the Ark of the Covenant in an Indiana Jones picture, or even of Tolkien and his talismanic rings, at least to my mind, to its author's the influences on the book were Tennysonian and Wagnerian. He turned to me and said, 'My first wife was from Blackwood, near Bedwellty in Monmouthshire. Her father was headmaster of the school there. I used to visit, and picked up bits of Welsh. I wrote a song, 'These Things Shall Be', as a celebration for Bedwellty Grammar School. In the new book I want to revisit the Welsh language.'

I took this as an opportunity to say I knew the area well – indeed that I was (in the Isaiah Berlin and Riga sense) from just down the road; and that of those who passed the Eleven-Plus at my primary school in Bedwas, one year they went to Bassaleg, near Newport, while the next year's successes went to Bedwellty.* If I'd hoped for or imagined we were about to share some South Wales reminiscence I was wrong. I could have told him that I'd met former colleagues of his late father-in-law. I can appreciate

* By the time it was my turn the Socialist Revolution had done away with grammar schools, and I was self-educated at Bassaleg Comprehensive – though architecturally still the twin of Bedwellty and both were ruled by the same education authority. School mastering is a major Burgess theme. Other beaks who became authors include William Golding, Gwyn Thomas and Robert Bolt. *Q:* Does this limit them? 'I love teaching,' Burgess said in 1972. 'Once a teacher, you can't do anything about it, you're always one.' The effect on his novels is that they turn into parades of erudition. The tone can be hectoring – almost like that of a man who has never been to university. The trouble with teachers is that they are always convinced that they know more and that they know better; they also expect obedience. Freed from the constraints of a classroom and a fixed syllabus, they go in for big themes, post-apocalyptic visions and scripts for David Lean, of all film directors the most lofty.

now that a biographee doesn't want a biographer trampling over his precious past, at least not in his presence (as if what were we? Each other's non-identical twin?); and nor would he want to be caught out. You'd not easily pick up bits of Welsh in the Rhymney Valley, as it is an English-speaking region. You may, though, hear Italian – in all the Feccis, Berni and Sevini cafés. (The actor Victor Spinetti is from there or thereabouts.) Burgess strangely never mentioned those. Overall, however, he was ill at ease referring to Lynne with Liana sitting there. What second wife wants to know that the first wife can still run through your husband's mind, nearly twenty years on? Lynne, though, with her injured soul, is in book after book, creating drama. Morose and exuberant, scornful and uproarious, the violent extremes of Burgess's heroines kept his Welsh dragon very much alive.* In *Beard's Roman Women*, as Leonora, she actually comes back from the dead (like Coward's blithe spirit Elvira) to haunt her widowed husband, her voice being heard on the phone singing Christmas carols from beyond the grave. 'This is your wife speaking, do you hear, that was lost and is now found again, and the name is Leonora Beard, née Pritchard.'

He'd pretty much ignored Lynne's heavy drinking and general self-destructiveness when she was alive; he'd felt helpless. It was a sad affair. Yet she was back within reach in his novels, a tormenting, tragic muse. It was as if he had to commemorate or remember her not so much privately as secretly – in fiction. *Any Old Iron*, published four years after our meeting, does indeed revisit the Blackwood–Risca–Monmouthshire region; and when Ludmilla signs a cheque she simply inscribes 'L. Jones', as Lynne would have done. When Ernest Jones, Freud's disciple and biographer, travels to Vienna, in *The End of the World News* (published three years prior to Burgess's appearance in Oxford), it is Jones's Welshness which Burgess is at pains to describe, a theme that meant aspects of Lynne were churning inside the novelist. These were his ways of having her to hand whilst writing about something else; his way of resurrecting her and surreptitiously keeping her close. Here is an interesting question about Burgess: did his work deteriorate as Lynne faded

* Lynne is both Laurel and Lavinia in *A Vision of Battlements*; Fenella Crabbe in *The Long Day Wanes* (*The Malayan Trilogy*); Sheila in *The Doctor Is Sick*; Veronica in *The Worm and the Ring*; Lydia in *Devil of a State*; Beatrice-Joanna in *The Wanting Seed*; Belinda in *Honey for the Bears*; Vesta Bainbridge in the Enderby books; Aderyn, the Bird Queen, in *MF* ('the mistress of magic owls who ask difficult riddles under pain of death'); and the list goes on from there.

directly from it, as her sorrowful mystery receded? (But she was inextinguishable.)

'It was a long marriage,' he said to me, 'nearly thirty years.' His descriptions of Liana, by contrast (she's Paula Lucrezia Belli in *Beard's Roman Women*: 'You talk of loving me. It is just my body you want'; there's inevitably similarly lubricious material on her in volume two of his memoirs, *You've Had Your Time*), are sentimental and superficial. You felt he was having to watch what he said, and the passages are false and unreal – indistinguishable from his eulogies of Sophia Loren.

He abruptly asked Ellmann about progress on the Wilde opus. 'I'm inserting extra chapters, incorporating notes from box files. There are a few hundred books I need to go through,' responded the professor, who'd be fiddling and fussing to this day, had he not learned that he faced the most morbid of deadlines. The corrected proofs were found by his bed when he died.

'I've put him in *The Kingdom of the Wicked* as Selvaticus,' said Burgess. 'He is banished from Rome by Claudius for sodomy. His follower is Petronius.' The novel was to be published on 13 May, six days hence.

History, the nightmare Stephen Dedalus tried to wake up from, was currently Burgess's habitat; he was having to be content to slumber in its embrace, and Catullus's phrase *una nox dormienda* (the one long final night of death – the big sleep) runs through *The Kingdom of the Wicked* as a refrain. History was *currently* Burgess's inspiration, in addition, because he'd talk of himself, in Mediterranean and Alpine exile, as being cut loose from the current of modern British life. The reality of his homeland was dead to him. Exile is a post-mortem state; when making – like Leonora on the phone – ghostly visitations to publicise a book he used to say he felt foolish 'trying to work out how much the types of coins are worth . . . It's the currency you see, the daily currency of life. . .' A chronological elsewhere was the only territory he could lay claim to. He was an exile both in time and space.

Already, by the eighties, when I first read them, Burgess's early novels had a distinct period flavour. Enderby, the menopausal picaro, capers through a country of Beatles and Beat poets, of nylon chic and Union Jacks, of Morris Minors, Jags and lately demobbed war veterans. When he was resurrected in 1984 (*Enderby's Dark Lady*), Enderby (a town, incidentally, near Leicester) was to be located, if the book's vernacular was any clue, somewhere in the Indiana of the seventies: a place of sun-goggled hipsters, flared breeches and long caroline locks. Uneasy about the dated modernity, Burgess shifted the bulk of the novel into a remote past (Enderby living the life of Shakespeare) and a remote future (Enderby the author of a sci-fi nonsense about time-travel).

The Sovereignty of the Sword was to have been set in pre-war Wales and, I was to learn, sixties Leningrad, which he had visited with Lynne.* There were reports that Burgess was also in the midst of a big book about Manchester set in the thirties. That so prodigal a man could be tapping out two epics simultaneously there was no doubt (he bought a pioneering word-processor to hurry production); and the two projects merged to become *Any Old Iron*. But the interesting point is that again he was recollecting and fabricating history – as of course Joyce did by looking at a June day a decade after it had elapsed.

But historical romance, which is what Burgess confects, does not, as Joyce's epic does, penetrate into the minds of its characters to listen to their thoughts. Historical romance is costume drama in prose, a novelistic wax museum. In the V&A clothes section, and at Madame Tussaud's, the curators labour to get details right. So too Burgess. *The Kingdom of the Wicked* is a product of research. An appendix testily informs us of beetle-browed hours spent with the Graeco-Latin edition of the New Testament, with *Die Romfahrt des Apostels Paulus und die Seefahrtskunde in römischen Kaiseralter* by H. Balmer . . . and so on. The backdoor of the Monaco atelier saw more book-laden carts than George Eliot's house when she drudged at *Romola*.

Fearful, with justification, that the Doctor of Divinity affectations and fustiness would impede the sale of the novel to the multitude, Burgess pretends to peddle the text through a diseased shipping clerk called Sadoc: 'The opinions, interpretations, errors . . . of the supposed author . . . are not always mine.' Sadoc benignly muddles things. We are to credit that this chronicle is hidden behind more layers of reticence than Henry James, more occult paper-puzzles than Borges ('the Argentine Burgess'). Sadoc writes in demotic Greek which Burgess has pretended to translate. Secondly, speech is reported in dialects and languages we don't actually hear – for example, 'You seem to have difficulty with our Aramaic. Would you prefer that I spoke in Latin?' – and yet we read only Burgess's eccentric Victorian English. The headmasterly author's note alone informs that Tacitus, Suetonius, Josephus and the Acts of the Apostles were consulted 'in the original tongues'. Burgess wants us to applaud his learning

* Their adventures became *Honey for the Bears*.

(*'Plaudite! Plaudite!'* shouts his Nero) whilst also appreciating a ripping yarn. The contrary tugs between highbrow and lowbrow feature in all his books. Toomey, in *Earthly Powers*, writes bestsellers but can't quite manage art; Enderby dreams of art but a succession of brides drags him into the marketplace; Robert Loo, in *The Long Day Wanes*, is a composer of genius but dissipates his talent by writing pastiches and movie scores.

Burgess's two heroes miraculously survived the extremes of intellectual gravity and the personal angle. Shakespeare made money and wrote masterpieces (*Nothing Like the Sun*); Joyce wrote masterpieces, worked hard, survived on charity (*Here Comes Everybody* and *Joysprick*). The duopoly had recently become a triumvirate: D. H. Lawrence was Burgess's latest wish-fulfilling self-image, with his *Flame into Being* centennial celebration. Yet Lawrence, like many of the Modernists, is as remote in terms of the calendar as the Victorian age. 1885 was the year of the *Mikado*.

When Ellmann was off on one of his time-ticking-away trips for extra (flat) tonic water, Burgess told me brightly that he'd read the Joyce biography countless times. He knew passages by heart. He knew Joyce's own works by heart. But how different were these men, the author and the professor. Yes, they both worshipped Shem the Penman (as Joyce called himself); they were, by temperament, both parsimonious and cagey. But where Ellmann spent his career perfecting two books (*James Joyce* was extensively revised for Joyce's hundredth birthday in 1982), Burgess produced at least two books each year. Ellmann was a thoroughgoing scholar; Burgess's scholarship, as in *The Kingdom of the Wicked* Appendix or the prefatory note to the novella *The Eve of Saint Venus* – worth quoting in full:

> This is based on a tale told by Burton (*Anatomy of Melancholy:* Pt. 3, Sec. 2, Mem. I, Subs. I) which he got from Florilegus, ad annum 1058, 'An honest historian of our nation, because he telleth it so confidently, as a thing in those days talked of all over Europe . . .'

– all this appears to me a mockery of scholarship. Though I do not question the intensity of Burgess's work (he was driven; he never relaxed), much of the fanatic pedantry has the quality of stage scenery. It's an entertainment. The idea that he was in possession of complete knowledge was a mad illusion. And where Ellmann could see the human relations within Joyce's world of words or behind Wilde's paradoxes and epigrams, for Burgess literature was language; its components sparkled like a grain of salt and he loved to toss his arcane vocabulary at us: diastematophobia, brontophobia, diopters, presbyopia, epigones, manducatory, piacular, disembogued, tissage. (This isn't language as shared communication – it's to use words to keep yourself aloof and isolated. It's an avoidance of intimacy with the reader.) He admired overt craft. The fiction he singled out in *Ninety-Nine Novels*, in 1984, was the heavily symbolic, highly stylistic works of say, Rex Warner or Malcolm Lowry. There's nothing ambivalent, uncertain or instinctive in Burgess's work; like a Victorian painting, his groupings, shapings, tints and textures are all framed and typified and laborious. There's little by way of human association or real human conduct. He saw not characters but particles. He was never natural.

When Ellmann returned, Burgess asked for directions to the lavatory. 'In America they call the jakes the offices. Which way's your office, Dick?' He marched off, and Liana and I talked of the Shakespeare film that never was, variously to have been called *Will!* or *The Bawdy Bard*.* 'I found his script, all damp, in Bracciano. The story was going to begin in Oxford, with Shakespeare encountering Giordano Bruno and John Florio.' So the city had another use beyond being the stopping-off point between Stratford and The Globe? I was reminded of the F. E. Smith anecdote – of how he'd regularly call in to use those marble and Royal Doulton tile pissoirs in Whitehall Place. When the porters eventually explained to him that this was the National Liberal Club, and was he a member?, he gasped in mock incredulity, 'You mean there's a Gentleman's Club in this building as well?' Bruno was an Italian philosopher, eventually burned by the Inquisition, who believed that the human soul strove to achieve mystical union with the infinite universe. Born in Nola, he was called the Nolan by Joyce, as if he were Irish; and Burgess, if he knew his Ellmann as well as he claimed, will have known that one of Bruno's quotations became Joyce's–Stephen Dedalus's rubric: 'No man can be a lover of the true or the good unless he abhors the multitude; and the artist, though he may employ the crowd, is very careful to isolate himself.' This is certainly how Burgess – and Burgess's Shakespeare – kept himself apart, keeping himself under constant pressure, aggressive, alone, in the forest of his thoughts.

Indeed, aside from the discomposed central figure in each of his novels, an Enderby say or, in the Malayan things, Victor Crabbe, Alex in

* When, in 1998, the Gwyneth Paltrow vehicle *Shakespeare in Love* came out, for which Tom Stoppard, amongst many others, won an Oscar, I was reminded of Burgess's project. (His Hollywood experiences were recycled in *Enderby's Dark Lady*.) John Madden's film is about Will-as-Amadeus; and it is also about how the cinematographer has lit La Paltrow's cheekbones and celebrated her blondness. (Her tawny beauty contrasts with the London mud and murk.)

A Clockwork Orange, or the likes of Howarth, Hillier, Foxe, Denham and Howard Shirley in the early fiction, and Christ, Moses and Napoleon later on, there is a loathing for the human race, the drooling mobs with broken teeth; the snarling, grunting disciples, soldiers, colleagues, hoodlums, pupils and patients – who'll betray you, as Alex feels himself to be in the play adaptation (1987) of the Kubrick film: 'Traitors and liars,' he screams at his gang. 'Is the whole world full of nothing but liars and treacherous brutal vecks that call themselves droogs?' Other people obviously only existed to try Burgess's characters' (and, by safe inference, Burgess's) patience. (Such was the chronic, lingering state of his misanthropy, was the anger actually directed at something inside him?) Though here he was in a room with five other people in Oxford, it was hard to conceive of Burgess as in company, as being part of a group – instead, like an actor, he talked to a crowd, full of affectations and games to impress us.

Heralded by gushing and flushing, he came back saying, 'How good to have a life of Ben Jonson in there. My old tutor in Manchester, L. C. Knights, published a book on Jonson.* I met him years later – in 1976 – at a conference in Washington. He wasn't at all pleased to see me. Rather cold. I think he resented it that I was a writer.' And he launched into a recitation from *The Poetaster*:

> Time was once, when wit drown'd wealth; but now,
> Your only barbarism is t'have wit, and want.
> No matter now in virtue who excels,
> He that hath coin, hath all perfection else.

'I'm very fond of *The Poetaster*, though I've never seen it acted,' he continued. 'Shakespeare is Ovid.'†

'Liana was telling me of the Shakespeare film.'

'Yes – meant to be a film, with Peter Ustinov as Ben Jonson; Maggie Smith; David Hemmings. We moved to Malta on account of the film, which never happened. Joseph L. Mankiewicz was to have been in charge.'

It was probably because Burgess had wanted the bardic biopic to demonstrate the historical origins of the American spoken language that

* *Drama and Society in the Age of Jonson* (1934).

† There is a trenchant account of *The Poetaster or His Arraignment* in Burgess's biography, *Shakespeare* (1970): 'Shakespeare loved Ovid . . . but it is doubtful if Ben would give him the satisfaction of being Ovid on stage. He recognised also that, little as he approved [of] his undisciplined art, he could not shove Will in with the rest of the poetasters. He was too big for easy lampooning . . . In spite of everything, they were friends.'

the project was dropped. He'd perplexed and bored the Hollywood executives by explaining to them that, 'Whatever the dialect, the whole back area of the mouth is cut off from vocalising' – as if who needs a lecture on phonetics? This is where John Florio, an Italian refugee who'd studied at Oxford, came in useful. His Italian–English dictionary of 1611, *Queen Anne's New World of Words*, had allowed linguists to deduce how words would have been pronounced in the seventeenth century. That is to say, how Shakespeare himself sounded. Hence the scene between the lexicographer and the playwright, in a setting not unlike New College cloisters. Florio reappears, by the way, in Burgess's novella about Keats, *Abba Abba*. The poet is given the Italian's dictionary as light reading on his deathbed. 'Master Kates, Shakespeare would call me. I have had the revelation this morning of hearing Shakespeare's voice' – much as Burgess fancied he'd heard Lynne's voice, and Beard, Leonora's.

Before he went into exile, Burgess earned six hundred pounds a year. Then he hit the jackpot, with the American Book of the Month Club and the sale of the film and dramatic rights of *Nothing Like the Sun*, and he made eighty thousand pounds, which after taxation would have left him with five thousand pounds: 'so I had to flee to some dull paradise like Malta'. (As he'd sanctimoniously put it in the autumn of 1968, placing himself in the third person, 'Art comes before country, and he saw in this windfall a chance to write the books he felt were in him.')

I said that it was whilst on honeymoon, on the island of Gozo in 1982, that I'd first bought and read his novels: *The Eve of Saint Venus* – reprinted in 1981 'as a loyal tribute to the Prince of Wales and his bride' (Hamlyn paperbacks, £1.10) – and a paperback of the operatic *Earthly Powers* (£1.95). Because Burgess had no sense of humour, I didn't add, in the manner of Arthur Lowe's Captain Mainwaring, who'd learned to play the bagpipes on his honeymoon, that there wasn't much else to do – though in a way that was the case. An island twenty-six square miles in size and lying four miles north-west of Malta, Gozo, together with Comino, formed a British Crown Colony. Anna and I grew fed up of looking at Roman cart-ruts and other ancient remains. Instead I wallowed in Burgess's fecundity and catholicity. It was a turning point. I read everything of his I could lay my hands on. I adored his spectacle and noise, his flamboyance, the surface pleasures of his prose. And there, piled high upon the roll-top desk, they soon were: *Homage to Qwert Yuiop*, a selection of twinkling journalistic squibs; *The Pianoplayers*, a whore's remembrance of post-Great War Lancashire; *Blooms of Dublin*, the conversion of *Ulysses* into lyrics of a Broadway musical (lyrics already aired, actually, in *Earthly Powers*). From the shelves of charity shops, antiquarian booksellers, mail-order catalogues, flea-markets, jumble sales, hospital libraries, county lending libraries weeding out their stock, and the back-rooms of general stores in provincial towns and the windows of specialist places on the Charing Cross Road, I gradually amassed his five dozen or so titles. When he died on 22 November 1993, at the age of seventy-six, what seemed worse than no more Anthony Burgess was the prospect of no more Anthony Burgess operas, novels, essays, reviews, lectures, opinions. He was torrential – and it was as if Niagara had stopped flowing; he was irresistible. If, as he said of Mozart, 'ultimately artists must be judged not merely by excellence but by bulk and variety', then on his own estimation he was now sitting amongst the gods. Open a newspaper in New York, Paris, London or Rome – there he always was, loudly having his say on the pressing issues of the moment (e.g. the fall of the House of Windsor or the difficulty of obtaining decent sausages in Monaco). Go into Waterstone's or Barnes and Noble, and there would be the gleaming display of his latest fiction, on Christ's Apostles, Christopher Marlowe, or the search for the sword Excalibur. Because he'd raise whirlwinds, he was beloved of talk-show hosts ('I'm ashamed of sad, drab, vulgar Britain,' he'd inform a television audience of millions); and he'd go on the radio to promote his writing and take our breath away by saying categorically: 'Actually I am a composer.'

Composer, scribbler, polemicist – the greatest man, as he'd be the first to tell you, never to win the Nobel Prize for literature (or for literature, science, medicine and the promotion of peace rolled into one) – Burgess was, in fact, a non-stop performer. Physically, he resembled an old-fashioned actor like Freddie Jones (the pomaded grey hair, the ostentatious puffing upon a panatella, the silk handkerchief billowing from the jacket pocket); and his voice, a baritonal boom, was made to reach the back of the gallery – or the classroom. For Burgess was a magnificent teacher. He loved to tell us things. His novels, like *Abba Abba*, are crammed with digressions on linguistics and phonetics. He loved arcane languages (when he ran out of new ones to learn he invented his own – as in *A Clockwork Orange*); he was greedy for knowledge and eager to impart it, if we paid attention. He was tetchy, iconoclastic, indulgent and, like a teacher standing before the blackboard, dinning his ideas into us, he was anxious to keep our attention by throwing in grand words – palinogue, autophagous, endogamy – to send us scurrying for a dictionary. He was a frightful show-off and his strong (bad-tempered and obstinate) personality infused every sentence he wrote.

This was the party who, at Ellmann's place in Oxford, was not letting me down. (There's consummate artistry in the way he presented himself.) Yet what, as a young man, I thought of as his sophistication and worldliness was really vulgarity, a desire to be striking; he aimed for grandeur but instead what he was getting was grandiosity, a different thing. He was fizzy, unstoppable, though none of his characters is living and laughing. *Earthly Powers*, when I first read it, was broad and bizarre; it seemed to take in everything – an encyclopaedia. I myself was wholly taken in, swept up by it, along by it. What a concept – Toomey the writer who has met famous people, who has worked all over the shop, from Malaya to Hollywood, and who makes an odyssey through the twentieth century's dark heart. It was a manic book – more than very slightly half-mad in its scope. It was even frightening. But my suspicion now is that it was a pastiche of a great novel, rather than being a great novel. Burgess wants us to be aware of his effort. His voice is always heard – that single psyche present. This book, like many of his others, has flamed into being by the force of his will. Everything is deliberate. For all his apparent polymathic range, I think he worked narrowly: the good and evil debates and Catholic agonising; the Stanley Unwin* verbiage; the manufactured and artificial action scenes; the way he looks at emotions from the outside. And so on.

> The sounding cataract
> Haunted me like a passion; the tall rock,
> The mountain, and the deep and gloomy wood,
> Their colours and their forms, were then to me
> An appetite . . . That time is past,
> And all its aching joys are now no more,
> And all its dizzy raptures.

Burgess as he seemed to me then; as he seems to me now: it's a double story. How I was then; how I am now, aware of lost opportunities, lost

* Stanley Unwin (1911–2002) was a self-proclaimed 'Professor of Unwinese', a nonsense language which sounded like segments of *Finnegans Wake*: 'Goldyloppers trittly-how in the early mordy, and she falloped down the steps. . .' Goodness knows how, but he had a full-time career in light entertainment on the basis of his gobbledegook, and he appeared in *Carry On Regardless* (1961). 'Kenneth Williams,' he said, 'like so many other comic pros, understood the conscious stream concealed in my dialogue and it was always inspiring to work with him.'

time. It is a fact that books and authors suffer alteration over the years; we question our former attraction and are amazed by it. Where once I was attuned to his egotistical sublimity and vividness, this appears, after a lapse of time, straightforward calling-attention-to-itself behaviour (on his part) and a need to hide intellectual insecurity behind over-literariness (on mine). His sense of separateness, initially heroic, has come to appear pathetic: what's so big about being unfit for ordinary life and too proud to deal with problems in the material world? Burgess knew about almost everything, indeed, except the world he was living in. Susan Boyd, the publicity director at Heinemann when *Little Wilson and Big God* was published, called him long distance to wish him a Merry Christmas. 'Eh?' he said – and then over his shoulder he shouted, 'Liana! You'll never guess! It's Christmas!' He'd failed to notice the season. 'Is there a subject on which you are not an expert?' he was once asked on a radio show – and an honest and comprehensive answer would have had to include unguarded feelings, domestic familiarities, normal, simple emotions, an instinct for beauty, sympathy and understanding. He's the least intimate and spontaneous of writers. There's little insight into the variety or inner lives of others – or of himself.

My need to know about Burgess twenty years ago: what lack or absence in me was being compensated for? I was youthful, full of ambition and ideals; he was a constellation, larger than life-size, a writer's writer, crammed with allusions. He was, as Carlyle said of Danton, 'a gigantic mass of ostentation', and the piratical swagger was alluring and I had an abiding affinity with it. The facets which you are taken in by when you are young – the languages, the apparent wide knowledge – genuine academics and professionals, people in the know, see it as so nonsensical, it's beneath them to contradict Burgess's bluster. His success came from impressing people who didn't quite know better; he was left alone by those who did. He fell into that gap, and made a fortune for himself. It worries me that henceforward he is going to have a spurious reputation (for the wrong reasons), pumped up by second-rate scholar-squirrels from unheard-of institutions who'd condone doctoral dissertations on 'Taming the Rock: Myth, Model and Metaphor in the Novels of Anthony Burgess', 'Utopias, Subtopias, Dystopias in the Novels of Anthony Burgess', or 'The Uses of the Grotesque and Other Modes of Distortion: Philosophy and Implication in the Novels of Anthony Burgess' – titles which are well beyond any excuse of esoteric curiosity and which strike me as to be of such imaginative laxity as to sound abject piss.* Twenty years on from my days as a student prince, if I'm allegedly repudiating the lion of my late adolescence, it's no doubt because deep down I continue to feel close to him. As Dickens said of Mount Vesuvius, 'There is something, in the fire and the roar, that generates an irresistible desire to get nearer to it.' His dedication and intelligence can't be denied and though he has zoomed and plunged in my affections and esteem, and though I am realising that I'm no longer the person who first loved his work, I can still respond to a man who refused to live contentedly and calmly. He was fantastical and theatrical – and my changed perspectives mean that I want to look beyond the colour and dash. I want to know about the complicated emotions behind the words, words, words. I want to examine his callousness and underlying fears; his psychological interior; his chillness. It's fascinating, his sense of being lost and on the outside of things; his ways of failing to engage with people ('It's *Christmas*?'). He was withdrawn – and withdrew himself all the way to the South of France, and points round about, where he liked to portray himself as forgotten and suffering. Re-reading his books, new meanings emerge. The remorseless detachment was always apparent, as was the sense of savagery underneath – but now I detect panic and anguish on the other side of that anger; so much of his life was about grief and loss and his despairing love for Lynne, and for a mother whom he never knew: the Beautiful Belle Burgess who died in the influenza pandemic after the end of the First World War. Add to this the (faulty – obviously) diagnosis in 1959 that he had a brain tumour and a year to live – and we can see the meaning of his work: mortality.

Where, originally, I may have found him exalting – proof that, if you knew how to use it, language could make magic: control the seas and move the planets, like Prospero – now his work seems dank, rain-swept, nocturnal, sooty. Manchester is in his nodular, irksome prose rhythms. You'd think there'd be a division in Burgess between the Lancashire lad and the dweller in the Mediterranean sunshine, but he managed to make both equally unhealthy. It's crapulous, hung-over work, its author

* I speak with feeling – and I speak with authority, having had occasion, in the past, to survey many a learned journal article on Burgess, e.g. in *Papers on Language and Literature*, *Modern Fiction Studies* (vol. 27, no. 3, autumn 1981, was an Anthony Burgess Special Issue), *English Language Notes* and *American Notes and Queries*. The academic approach to him is enshrined in books by Aggeler (a professor at the College of Humanities, University of Utah), Coale (a professor at Wheaton College, Massachusetts) and Morris (who 'teaches the modern British novel' at the City College of the City of New York University, where Burgess himself was a Distinguished Professor of English in 1972).

reproachful, weary, and oversensitive to light and noise. Asked what the side-effects of being an author might be, he listed haemorrhoids, excessive smoking, dipsomania, impotence, an over-reliance on caffeine and dexedrine, dyspepsia and chronic anxiety – and he was in the right of it there.

He was incredulous that I'd bought his books on Gozo, a place where I was happy.

'How can they be on sale there now? I'm banned on Malta – it's a terrible place. They censor everything. Swimwear advertisements were scissored out of imported copies of English newspapers. Proof copies of my own novels were confiscated by a couple of ancient near-illiterates at the post office in Valletta. The government confiscated even our house in the end.' He seemed put out that his books were no longer prohibited – though he never did revise his anti-Maltese set-piece speech in the light of the new information, a tiny yet telling example of how he was insufficiently absorbed by what other people told him.

Alert to the awkwardness, Gordon Ray said that a biography of Thackeray had been written by a lady who lived on Gozo. I asked Burgess if *The Worm and the Ring*, the Banbury novel, was based in some way on *The Rose and the Ring*,* and instead of answering he started reciting –

> Here begins the pantomime,
> Royal folks at breakfast time.
> Awful consequence of crime!
> Ah, I fear, King Valoroso
> That your conduct is but so-so.

'I loved *The Rose and the Ring*. Who reads it now? I had it read to me as a child. I like the way Thackeray gets his rogues to recount their exploits as if they were thoroughly moral and lawful people – Barry Lyndon and Jonathan Wild, not wicked at all. And in *The Rose and the Ring*, when Prince Bulbo holds the magic rose he stops being the fat buffoon he really is and is transformed into the Prince of Crim Tartary. What's that poem about Werther? Can you quote some of it?' And as he beat Gordon Ray to a recital of the whole of 'The Sorrows of Werther', I realised that, Holmes-like, I had been thrown a clue. Burgess, like the Crim Tartary illusion, was essentially a fake. I mean, he's a fictional

* In *English Literature: A Survey for Students*, originally written in 1957, when Burgess (as John Wilson) was working as a teacher in the Federal Training College at Kota Bharu, he calls the book 'one of the best-loved of all Victorian fantasies'.

character. He's a fabulous animal. He doesn't exist. Being Burgess was – forgive the alliteration – a bogus business, and I can't believe that he himself was really being taken in. The bombast and charlatanry of his memoirs, *Little Wilson and Big God* and *You've Had Your Time*, do suggest, however, that these books are paradoxically true to how he'd become, detached from society, a stranger upon the earth. He's so implausible, and that's what I rather enjoy about him now, the outlandish interplay between Burgess and John Wilson; the upright private man and his opportunistic, shady side. How did Wilson readjust his balance and get to be Burgess? It's an atomic split, a split personality: the factual and the fictitious; the real thing and falsehoods. The courteous man of letters, the wide-ranging and generous reviewer, the diligent writer of novels, the stirring pundit, the lecture-platform professional and conference delegate – and then the angry, essentially insane person he'd have us believe he turns into in pubs, at passport controls, when sighting a policeman, if encountering anyone in uniform or authority. He's reckless, loud, quick with his fists and wields a swordstick: 'Fuck off! I've got cancer!' was his war cry. He flouts the law, is flung into gaol, is on the run. He's transgressive – obsessed with criminality and wildness. His papers are never in order. He's an impossible traveller, quarrelling with hoteliers, cooks and porters. To listen to him, he only ever came across misery and discomfiture and provocation. The food is bad, the beds lousy, everybody is insolent. In interviews and autobiographical works he was expansive and explosive; he called attention to a troubadour–bohemian image of himself. On television his face and body are twisted, wracked. The pursed mouth, the twitching muscles in his cheeks – the tormented artist. This was the public character, the folderol merchant. Inside Burgess, however, like the grub in the apple, lurked Wilson, who exemplified the virtues of industry, application, and moral seriousness, and who hankered for decorum and respectability. He worked harder than anybody – and what Chesterton said of the Jekyll and Hyde story we can apply to Wilson and Burgess's: remember, only one man was born and one man died.

Thackeray had many aliases – James Yellowplush, Michael Angelo Titmarsh (*The Rose and the Ring* was published in 1855 under the name of M. A. Titmarsh) and George Savage Fitzboodle; and Barry Lyndon metamorphosed into Redmond Barry, Barry of Barryogue, Captain Barry and Redmond de Balibari. In Burgess's world it is his alter ego F. X. Enderby whose life is a sequence of onomastic disguises. Hogg Enderby, Piggy Hogg, and so on – and how relevant is it that James Hogg, of *The*

Confessions of a Justified Sinner, had an editor called John Wilson (1785–1854) who, when Professor of Moral Philosophy at Edinburgh University, a post he held for thirty years, published no original material and had his lectures ghost-written by a friend in Birmingham? Under the pseudonym Christopher North, Wilson contributed satires and short stories to *Blackwood's Magazine*. When he was in Malaya, Wilson called himself Yahya bin Haji Latiff. *One Hand Clapping* was published under the name of Joseph Kell, as was *Inside Mr Enderby*. John Burgess Wilson was the author of *English Literature: A Survey of Students*, translated as *Igirisu Bungakushi* by the Japanese. In writing to the BBC, he'd sign off his letters –

John
J. B. Wilson (Anth. Burg.)

or

John
Anthony Burgess etc.

or

This is *Anthony Burgess / John Wilson* writing

or

{ *John Burgess Wilson*
Anthony Burgess }

Here's a man, therefore, obsessively passing through multiple roles, costumes and designations* – who changed his name, his habitat and his wives – so what remained continuous about his identity? He was like Cyrano de Bergerac,† who resembled Prince Bulbo and sounded like the euphonious Crim Tartary, writing letters and love poems and passing

* Philip Larkin to Anthony Thwaite (13 August 1966): 'The whole of English Lit. at the moment is being written by Anthony Burgess. He reviews all new books except those by himself, and these latter include such *jeux d'esprit* as 'A Shorter Finnegans Wake' and so on . . . He must be a kind of Batman of contemporary letters . . . I suspect a Mediterranean background.' Kingsley Amis to Philip Larkin (5 December 1980): 'Anthony Burgess's gusto and exuberance springs from his brilliant bum . . .'

† One day a doctoral student will examine and trace the genesis and dilemmas of Burgess's work on Rostand, whose play he kept going back to, from his earliest translations, used for a production in Minneapolis; his lyrics and book, which ended up briefly on Broadway; the endless rewrites and backstage dramas whilst on the road; the songs and orchestral interludes he composed and which were scrapped; the revisions for the Royal

them off under another person's name. Cyrano is captivating and seductive – yet in secret. His real self remained unknown. As I left the St Giles house, the one-man chorus was declaiming:

Werther had a love for Charlotte
Such as words could never utter;
Would you know how first he met her?
She was cutting bread and butter.

Charlotte, having seen his body
Borne before her on a shutter,
Like a well-conducted person
Went on cutting bread and butter.

Shakespeare Company – *Cyrano de Bergerac* was finally a success with Derek Jacobi in 1983, directed by Terry Hands (Burgess's translation was used again by Antony Sher in a touring production in 1997, directed by Gregory Doran). We need a variorum edition of the many texts, for there were twelve versions of a hundred-page libretto in 1973 alone, stretching from the drafts published in the *Malahat Review* (January 1971) to the synoptic edition ('Translated and Adapted for the Modern Stage') published by Hutchison in 1985. In 1990, Burgess provided the English-language subtitles for the Gerard Depardieu film, directed by Jean-Paul Rappeneau. The screenplay was by Jean-Claude Carrière. *Cyrano de Bergerac* was nominated for five Academy Awards.

I

Jack Be Nimble 1917–37

I don't like to meet my heroes – I prefer to be free to imagine them. Ellmann never met Joyce, but he did encounter Wyndham Lewis in Notting Hill, blind and querulous: 'I'm blind – *and I don't like it*!' the old Vorticist had growled; and he'd once glimpsed Ezra Pound across a canal in Venice, and Pound had raised his arm in greeting, like a wave from Odysseus. During the war, when he was enlisted as a Yeoman Third Class (a low-grade sergeant) in the American Navy, Ellmann's knee was briefly perched upon by Marlene Dietrich. The closest he got to Wilde was to befriend Wilde's grandson, Merlin Holland – though I believe there was a bit of a to-do over Ellmann's conclusion that Oscar had died from an attack of meningitis which was the legacy of tertiary syphilis. And indeed – what descendant would want that residue swimming about the gene pool? (Ellmann was being over-speculative. The certified cause of Wilde's death was an intracranial complication of suppurative otitis media.)

Another reason for avoiding Burgess was that I knew the drill, I knew the lore. The way he chain-smoked Schimmelpennincks, put six tea-bags in his morning cuppa, praised Kingsley Amis for transliterating *corm beef*, *tim peaches* and *vogka*, spoke Anglo-Saxon with Jorge Luis Borges,* preferred living in a Bedford Dormobile, greeted people by asking, 'Do I owe you money?' and parted from them by saying, 'I take it you're paying for

* My favourite account of this apocrypha is in *Henry Root's World of Knowledge*, by William Donaldson (1982): 'Though both these great polyglots could speak each other's language better than a native, they found it more agreeable [when they met] to converse in ancient Norse.' Actually, what they did, at a conference on Shakespeare in Washington in 1976, was jointly to recite the Old English 'Caedmon's Hymn', which Burgess will have known from studying Henry Sweet's *Anglo-Saxon Reader* at Manchester University. In *You've Had Your Time* he misquotes it (though admits 'I may have got the dialect wrong'), a fact which speaks for itself.

this lunch?'[*] Several times a season (and each new moon brought in another book to publicise), the distinguished novelist would come to England, like a monster rising from the deep, to appear on television with Michael Parkinson ('For a Lancashire man to live in Monaco is the height of poshness,' gushed the son of Barnsley), Clive James (*Q*: 'What makes a great writer?' *A*: 'Death!'), Terry Wogan ('I don't know who Terry Wogan is'[†]), Bernard Levin (who exclaimed, 'Look how you use language, man!'), Jeremy Isaacs ('Do I show off? Does Shakespeare show off? He was a tremendous player with words') or Sue Lawley ('All men dream of fat women, never thin women,' he told her dogmatically); he'd broadcast on radio with Anthony Clare (a charmer who normally could almost read the thoughts of people); he'd hold an audience with Melvyn Bragg ('I spent quite a bit of time with Anthony Burgess over the years'[‡]); and for the purposes of a magazine or newspaper profile he'd talk to Martin Amis, Jonathan Meades, Alice Thomas Ellis, Jonathan Coe or Lorna Sage, and they'd be overawed in the presence of the master. He was the star-turn at the Edinburgh Festival, the Cheltenham Festival of Literature, and at the Way With Words Literature Festival at Dartington he delivered the inaug-

[*] On the principle that it takes one tightwad to nail another, Burgess fell out with Graham Greene over the matter of a bill. 'He is very parsimonious. I took him to lunch – he never offered to pay. I don't enjoy his books any more and he doesn't like me or my work.' Burgess had met Greene in Antibes to write a profile for the *Observer*, 'God and Literature and So Forth', which appeared on 14 March 1980. (It is reprinted in *Homage to Qwert Yuiop* as 'Monsieur Greene of Antibes'.) They clearly didn't get along – Greene, the senior by thirteen years, relishing signs of infirmity, mock-courteously refers to Burgess's 'venerability' (because Burgess sports a walking stick); Burgess, in his turn, imputes second-rateness with comments like, 'With all except one of your novels filmed, and several short stories, you're exemplary as the filmable novelist.' On a technical point, as Burgess only picked up the tab at La Marguerite ('it was the parodic *haute cuisine* at its most vulgar – the thick floury sauces that Escoffier condemned') as part of a newspaper commission, all his expenses would have been automatically reimbursed.

[†] This despite appearing on *Wogan* six or seven times. The remark appeared in *Fiction Magazine*, vol. 3, no. 2 (summer 1984). Over the years the joke became a straightforward insult. 'And who are these people who are thought so important on television?' he asked John Walsh, in the *Standard*, on 19 May 1988. 'This Wogan person, a man with a little Irish charm but nothing else . . . These people are simply not interesting.'

[‡] Though Burgess turned down the invitation to be a subject of *The South Bank Show* itself, because the fee was too small, he presented a special edition of it called 'The Rage of D. H. Lawrence', transmitted on 20 January 1985. 'Lawrence is the patron saint of writers not having an Oxford or Cambridge education and who are despised by those who have,' he pontificated. The programme was chiefly memorable for an inadvertent comic moment when Burgess was compelled to do a piece to camera from the top of a hedgerow or next to an electric fence because the adjacent field was owned by the family on whom Lawrence based the Critches in *Women in Love*, and (according to Burgess) 'they still resent the portraiture and will not let me trespass on their land'.

ural Terence Kilmartin Memorial Lecture (1992). He collected honorary degrees from Manchester, St Andrews and Birmingham. At the University of Kent he gave the T. S. Eliot Memorial Lectures ('I had always had grave doubts about Eliot's taste and, indeed, intelligence'). Occasionally, traffic went in the opposite direction, Russell Davies reeling around Venice with him, or Nigel Williams making a visit to Bracciano, or Robert Robinson and Duncan Fallowell smoking him out in Monte Carlo. No matter what their nipping and eager air, however, Burgess's interrogators and acolytes, across a thirty-year period, each got the same performance – his conversation was a monologue, delivered in his exhibitionistic Victorian actor-manager voice. So predictable was the entertainment, one of those singalong prompt-boards may as well have dropped from the flies so that we could all join in, as at a pantomime. He always led off with how neglected he was; how he received insufficient recognition. 'I don't think England likes its writers . . . It's a philistine country. The only country in the world where a man of letters is actively looked down on; where it is a matter of pride that the Royal Family love only horses . . . Still, the stupidity of the English as a whole has and will be, I suppose, their salvation . . . The lack of appreciation in my own country grieves me deeply . . . I think it's because I'm a Catholic from the north-west, as simple as that. They just don't like us in the south . . . I've had a long swathe of time in which people have been snide and uncomprehending – and this should not happen . . . One does feel a little bitter. A little aggrieved . . . If they can give Jimmy Savile a knighthood, well, the honours system is so dishonoured that one wouldn't want it . . . I'm subject to terrible bouts of anger, being over here. It's the programmes on the television, the things you read in the papers . . . We came here on the tube, and you see signs saying, "Give up your seat for an elderly person." I suppose I'm an elderly person, but they don't . . . Writers are feared and despised . . .'

When Burgess started wailing in this key it was certainly useless to try and contradict him or think you could prevent him. A note of unemphatic irritation crept into his delivery when Anthony Clare probed him about loneliness; and when Bernard Levin said, 'You are an extraordinarily cerebral man. But where's the heart?', Burgess took this as an opportunity to say how scholars at a conference turned their backs on him – 'final confirmation that I'm not an intellectual'. But this was not what Levin had meant, and when it was explained to Burgess that a scholar is not the same thing as an intellectual, Burgess retorted that if we were to look up his big words in a dictionary his vocabulary had probably been used wrongly.

Eyes screwed up, smoking hard, it was a dare – he wants to get off this point. 'Graham Greene only writes two hundred words a day, anyway,' he stated, as if one's daily word-count was now (or had been all along) the topic. 'You have great control over your literary technique – and over your feelings,' Levin summed up, leaving it there.

Accused of over-production, or praised for being prolific, Burgess gave the same stock answer: 'I write a thousand words a day. At that rate you'll write *War and Peace* in a year . . . or very near the entire output of E. M. Forster.' This would be the cue for him to insist that it's a class thing, being reviled for getting on with the job and for making money at it: 'To discover virtue in costiveness was a mark of Bloomsbury gentility. Ladies and gentlemen should be above the exigencies of the tradesman's life.'* But the opposite of constipation or refined anal retentiveness isn't the healthy evacuation; it's diarrhoea (there's toilet imagery = creativity symbolism aplenty in the Enderby books), and yet Burgess gave every appearance of truly believing that quantity, dolled up as a continuous firework display, with whizzing Catherine wheels and foaming light-fountains, could in itself be a sign of quality; instead of its being, which is surely nearer the case, a substitute for quality. 'No, I don't pause between books,' he admitted in 1990. 'In fact I'm usually writing more than one at a time.' His work, like Attila's sacking, raping and pillaging, monotonously catalogued in the novella 'Hun' (contained in *The Devil's Mode*), became a pointless activity. It's not fecundity, in his later books, but conspicuous waste; or like Attila's battles, a meaningless feat of endurance.

His motivation? Everybody who met Burgess would hear about his nervous collapse in North Borneo in 1959, where he was employed as an English instructor at the Sultan Omar Ali Saifuddin College in Bandar Seri Begawan, Brunei. 'One day in the classroom I decided that I'd had enough . . . I just lay down on the floor. I was picked up and shoved into the local hospital. Various elementary tests were given and then I was sent home to England. Eventually my wife was told there was evidence of a cerebral tumour, but it was inoperable. She told me that they gave me a year to live.' A benign interpretation is that Lynne was being mischievous. But the legend is that, unemployed, Burgess sat at his typewriter and polished off *The Doctor Is Sick*, *Inside Mr Enderby*, *The Wanting Seed*, *The Worm and the Ring* and *One Hand Clapping*, one after the other, during the pseudo-

* 'Mozart was both craftsman and breadwinner,' Burgess told Lorna Sage in 1992. 'Like nearly all musicians, he wrote on commission. It's only in literature that Bloomsbury rules take over – this Bloomsbury business of not writing very much.'

terminal twelvemonth. Actually, *The Worm and the Ring* had existed in draft form at least as early as 1954, when Burgess (as Wilson) was still at Banbury Grammar School; colleagues on the staff had read it. But there's no gainsaying Burgess's optimism, hoping to leave his prospective widow well-provided for with royalty payments. And the mighty engine he'd set going inside him wasn't to cease functioning until his death, nearly thirty-five years later. As a matter of fact, such was the stockpile, or such was the period it took for his dynamos to run down, reviews he'd written continued to appear in newspapers posthumously, the novel in verse, *Byrne*, was published two years after he'd died, and the essay collection *One Man's Chorus* emerged in 1998, five years after he'd died. It's as if, in some ghostly fashion, he's continuing to bring us airs from heaven or blasts from hell.

At the centre of his work there was a fretting about time and its ebbing; a worry about night falling and the infernal fires approaching. Burgess is precise about measuring time in his fiction (Burgessian boldness and insubordination is offset by a sharp Wilsonian rage at disorder and irresponsibility), and when Spindrift has his wristwatch stolen from a hospital locker in *The Doctor Is Sick*, he is propelled into a life of crime and chaos. Alex's life of crime, in *A Clockwork Orange*, is a history of mechanised thuggery. He is converted from being automatically bad into being automatically good. Nando and Paolo Tasca, the volatile Italians in *Devil of a State*, fight over a stolen pocket watch and enact the Oedipal crime of parricide: as the son measures himself towards manhood, the father measures his own decline. *The Long Day Wanes*, also known as *A Malayan Trilogy*, monitors the crepuscular end of the British Empire, its characters watching their power fail like parodic Wagnerian gods. At one point we see 'the Western sky put on a Bayreuth montage of Valhalla'. At another point we hear that 'the white man's day is coming to an end. Götterdämmerung.' The coming to an end of the world itself is charted in *The End of the World News*: day by day our planet moves nearer its fatal collision with a rogue star.

Burgess's vision was apocalyptic – he was convinced (his) time was running out. What he enjoyed about living in Lugano, towards the end of his life, in a new chalet where the heating system hummed like a ship's engine and the nuclear bunker in the basement was used to store back-copies of *Corriere della Serra* (many containing articles by himself), was that the looming mountains 'impose their sempiternity upon my ephemerality'. Something would last, at least. 'Swiss clocks keep good time and the Alps look scrubbed . . . There are worse places.' After the famous death sentence was passed and he'd decided to compose novels, and the energy and industriousness never slacked, and he continued to sustain himself through work ('The only way I can live with myself, I find, is to justify my being here at all, and the way of justification is the way of work. I feel guilty when I am not writing, and so I write'), and it was as if he'd turned himself, like his Swiss hot-water boiler, into a machine ('I'm not proud of my work by any means. But I am proud of my persistence – of pushing on at it'), no wonder he could gather his journalism as *Homage to Qwert Yuiop*, for he did seem espoused to his typewriter keyboard. His characters, too, in his fictions, are less bundles of thoughts and impressions than cybernauts with components prone to error. Keats dies messily in *Abba Abba* (and the real Keats once wrote to Reynolds, 'until we are sick, we understand not'); Shakespeare dies syphilitically in *Nothing Like the Sun*; Freud dies cancerously in *The End of the World News*; and Herod, in Burgess's adaptation of Berlioz's *L'Enfance du Christ*, is afflicted with migraine – his cure: mass infanticide:

> Sleep, still my aching brain;
> Sleep, ease my anguished spirit.
> Unfold your wings
> And bear me from this prisonhouse of pain.

People don't have thoughts; they have bodies which decay, appetites which need fulfilling – and everything stems from this. Burgess's humans are humanoids, spouting theories about Free Will and Predestination, Freudian psychoanalysis, Hopkins' poems, or the correct recipe for Lancashire Hot Pot. They give lectures. And in *The Wanting Seed* and *1985*, for instance, history itself – the characters' environment – is robotic. There is no progress, only repetition. The future depicted is an exaggeration of the egregious elements from the present – as the sci-fi glam-rock landscape in *A Clockwork Orange* was an exaggeration of the Mods and Rockers trend of the early sixties.

Burgess's tendency to exaggerate could be regarded as preachy, slip-shod and over-boisterous. (Geoffrey Grigson said that the personality behind the prose must surely be 'coarse and unattractive'.*) It is, nevertheless, what gives

* Burgess never forgave Grigson (1905–85) for this remark, made within a review of *Urgent Copy*, itself a gathering of book reviews, published by Jonathan Cape in 1968. Grigson's piece, 'Insatiable Liking', appeared in the *Listener* on 7 November 1968. He collected it in his own book of essays, *The Contrary View: Glimpses of Fudge and Gold* (New

a great deal of his work a broad, slapstick edge – and it is what prevents him, at his best, from being portentous and stuffy. Farce is a mechanical form: characters whizz from one catastrophe to the next, and Burgess's novels, with their busy plots and people built from the outside in, are farcical picaresques. His characters are automata who do his bidding. (He would never have claimed, as Kingsley Amis did, that novel-writing involves 'some non-conscious level'.) Their pratfalls and collisions are engineered malfunctions – Enderby whirls about London, Rome and Tangiers; Paul, in *Honey for the Bears*, capers around Leningrad; Edwin, in *The Doctor Is Sick*, travels in the criminal underworld; Hillier, in the Ian Fleming pastiche, *Tremor of Intent*, has fast-paced adventures in Istanbul; Ron Beard is chased by whip-cracking lulus in *Beard's Roman Women*; Toomey is made to jostle with famous writers in *Earthly Powers* (originally called *The Creators*); and there are the wandering disciples and apostles in *Man of Nazareth* and *The Kingdom of the Wicked*; the wandering tribe in *Moses: A Narrative Poem* . . . Burgess himself, in his memoirs, makes his own life, too, seem like a Boulting Brothers film.

—

Jersey, 1974). Grigson also reviewed *The Doctor Is Sick* (in the *Spectator*, 25 November 1960). The paradox is that Grigson, a poet and literary journalist, the author of *A Skull in Salop* (1963) and *Montaigne's Tree* (1984), is to be remembered now chiefly as a footnote in the Burgess story (or also as the husband of Jane Grigson, the cookery writer, and as the father of Sophie Grigson, another cookery writer). As late as 1992 – i.e. *twenty-four years later* – Burgess was complaining, 'I still smart from a review excreted by the late Geoffrey Grigson. In noticing a volume of essays I had published, he said: "Who could possibly like so coarse and unattractive a character?" This, I think, was unjust and impertinent . . .' In *Little Wilson and Big God*, Grigson's alleged enmity (Burgess interestingly couldn't discriminate between his Burgessian literary persona and any independent personality beyond his own work) is crankily ascribed to the Protestant/Catholic South/North divide: '[Grigson], son of an Anglican country vicar, was acknowledging an alien culture gruffly subsisting outside the covenant of the Protestant establishment. The coarseness is in the Wilson family, and it is bound to be unattractive to Southerners.' I doubt whether this motivated Grigson at all; nor would he have been conscious of such prejudice. He simply thought Burgess pretentious and inflated – he attacked Edith Sitwell on the same grounds. Burgess's revenge, nevertheless, was to mention Grigson at every available opportunity with elaborate sarcastic courtesy. 'I'll never forget,' he said in a rare moment of candour in 1983, 'and I'll always get those people if I can.' Grigson would most often be mentioned in obscure American publications (*The Hudson Review*, *The American Scholar*), and the reference must have been baffling to Burgess's readers – unless they assumed that a Grigson was a folkloristic noun synonymous with Aunt Sally or April Fool, i.e. a laughing stock. I'm particularly fond of the Author's Note tucked away at the back of *Moses: A Narrative*, a book seen by few people as the publishers, Dempsey & Squires, in London, and Stonehill, in New York, both vanished. After mentioning the 'coarse and unattractive' sobriquet, as made by 'Geoffrey Grigson, the . . . reviewer and poet', and writing about himself in the third person, he continued: 'This is an extreme expression of a pretty widely held attitude which makes Mr Burgess's thumb shake with rage as it counts the banknotes which he periodically takes from under the mattress of one or other of his many houses.'

What with his saturation in Joyce (on whom he wrote two book-length critical studies), it might be anticipated that Odysseus, the supertramp, is the progenitor of Burgess's meandering, lost picaros. In fact, the origins are in Oedipus. Odysseus's destiny was to return home (as Leopold Bloom does); Burgess's characters, like the Theban king, end up without home or homeland – as Burgess himself drifted from house to house, complaining of exile, buying and discarding property. In 1972, he actually wrote *Oedipus the King*, a loose and 'neurotically distorted baroque' adaptation of Sophocles' play, for the Guthrie Theater, Minneapolis. And if you look at his novels, they are full of mythical motifs: rootlessness, attitudes to kinship and power, riddles.

In *Beds in the East*, Victor Crabbe is bitten on the foot by a scorpion. He is bandaged and limps: 'I am now Club Foot the Tyrant . . . But I didn't kill my father and I didn't marry my mother.' What, in that case, is his Oedipal crime? If Crabbe is a representative of colonial usurpers, his transgression has been against history: the British stole the history of Malaya from its rightful owners; they usurped the throne. In Malaya, the British had no roots. They interposed between the Malays and the Malayan past: they appeared, as from nowhere, to govern, as Oedipus did in Thebes. Crabbe may seem more like the Sphinx, another creature which arrived unheralded bringing its curses. So may the British seem sphinx-like (or *sphingyne* in Burgess's coinage); the novel deplores their Westminster legislature and gadgets like refrigerators. So too may Oedipus. He, at a moment of despair in Burgess's Minneapolis translation, believes himself to be a duplicate of the Sphinx.

Oedipus discovers that he has been living a lie: present information completely alters the complexion of the past. Thus Crabbe – who discovers that his first wife, whom he remembers as a golden goddess, had had a lover. The golden goddess, retrospectively, becomes a cheat. Looking back in anger and seeing the truth, Crabbe is maddened. Like Oedipus, he was not given a choice to choose wrongly: his life itself was cursed with misfortune. Trying to scour memories of his first wife by escaping East, Crabbe only busied himself, unknowingly, towards having to confront the reality of those memories. There is a dreadful – clockwork – symmetry about his fate.

Crabbe is a man to whom things happen. He does not initiate business himself. He does not change (except for growing older and more ill) throughout the trilogy. He is the fixed point in the spinning world; and he is the fixed character in the spinning world of Burgess's output.

From Crabbe to Toomey to Christopher Marlowe, in *A Dead Man in Deptford*, we have essentially the same personage: outcasts more sinned against than sinning; persons of action rather than thought. From Crabbe, Burgess's persecuted descend. Oedipus, under different names, appears in book after book. (In *Honey for the Bears* there is even a 'Doctor Tiresias' on hand to explicate; and when Paul, the confused hero, remarks on a soapy aroma, there is a leap to 'something from his past . . . it was his mother washing herself down in the scullery in Bradcaster, himself about ten with an Oedipus limp still'.)

Another of Burgess's conceits, along with his arias that he was neglected, wilfully misunderstood and sneered at by the critics, and that he was once death-marked and had yet survived, was that the Oedipus complex meant nothing to him. 'Freud laid so much emphasis on the relationship of a child with the mother, setting up the Oedipus complex, the war with the father, and so on. I don't think this could have happened in my own life,' he told Anthony Clare, 'because I never had a mother substitute and my relations with my father were rather lukewarm.' But the absence of something – love, compassion, comfort, warmth, security – can be felt more keenly than its presence, which can (and maybe should – it's what mothers are for) be taken for granted. It is revealing that when he saw a preview tape of Berlioz's oratorio *L'Enfance du Christ*,* which he had translated and dramatised for Thames Television, he wept. He kept asking his literary agent, who had accompanied him, and who had two young boys, 'What is it like being a mother? What does it feel like to be a mother?' He was most taken with the mezzo-soprano who'd played the Madonna, Fiona Kimm, a singer from the English National Opera. Yet when he met her, he was slightly disappointed – she wasn't quite a reincarnation of the BVM after all, and one has to think of Keats's Lamia or Larkin's Jill, fantasy women whose physical reality doesn't measure up to the daydream, who are diminished. Later, putting the record on the turntable at his flat in Chiltern Court, he'd stop the disc and replay the scene where the Holy Family flee to Egypt to escape Herod. 'Open your door/To a mother and child./We have trudged from Judea,/Seeking a refuge here.' Despite what he'd say, being parentless and rootless was affecting him in a deeper, sadder way than he'd care publicly to acknowledge. He was like a man who'd trained himself not to need affection – and in book after

* Broadcast on ITV on 30 December 1985. The original stereo soundtrack was released on vinyl, CD and cassette by ASV Records. Burgess's text was supplied in the slipcase.

book, Burgess tries to exalt his heroes as independent, as self-created; and as he said of himself in 1968: 'I was brought up by an Irish stepmother and had very little love, very little affection, not that I wanted this very much, and I went purely to the local schools in Manchester. I had no intellectual companionship, no intellectual stimulants at all. Everything I did, I did on my own. I read on my own. I taught myself music on my own. I owe nothing . . . If I had achieved anything, I owe nothing at all to family, nothing at all to environment . . . I was just totally alone and I learned to live without family, without affection.' He was a virgin birth, unspotted by neither nature nor nurture. Describing an abandoned child who'd never known a mother's love (not only Oedipus – but also Moses in his basket bobbing amongst the bullrushes): this was a way of dramatising himself, of informing us he was special; and his novels and plays are filled with changelings and foundlings – or with lonely men (Enderby, Cyrano), men isolated by their genius (Shakespeare, Marlowe, Freud), or men jeered at and betrayed (Jesus, Toomey, Carlo Campanati – who becomes Pope Gregory XVII). Why did Burgess imagine his childhood in this way? Like an actor, he was aware of the impression he was making; that he was being different. His simplifications and freakishness became part of his strivings to be epic; and his assumption of a new identity – Wilson into Burgess – was part of this myth or fairy story. His complexity and fascination, for me, dwell in the strategems he adopted to help invent for himself, in the pages of his books, an autobiography; an alternative life (and an invisible one: in February 1986, Anthony Burgess was listed by *The Times* as being present at Philip Larkin's memorial service. Wherever he was that day, he was not in Westminster Abbey.*) By having a suite of aliases, he had the freedom of an actor who swaps costumes and parts. *One Hand Clapping* and *Inside Mr Enderby* were written by 'Joseph Kell', and 'Anthony Burgess' was not only the pseudonym of John Wilson – pseudonyms, we are told in *MF*, hold privy secrets. Why, the epigraph to that novel quotes the First Folio stage direction of *Much Ado About Nothing*, which marks the entry of 'Jacke Wilson', who played Balthazar and sang to the ladies to sigh no more. When Miles

* By a neat coincidence, almost too good to be true, though I myself was listed in *The Times* as having been present at Burgess's own memorial service, held on Thursday 16 June 1994 at St Paul's Church, Covent Garden, I, too, was actually elsewhere. As Toomey says to George Russell, who'd been in bed with him on the real Thursday 16 June 1904, when Joyce, in *Ulysses*, says he was at the National Library in Dublin talking about Shakespeare with Stephen Dedalus, I'd been furnished with 'an eternal and unbreakable alibi for that afternoon'. I wish I could confess I'd been tumbling with shepherdesses in the bracken.

Faber – M. F. – wakes from a nightmare, his watch has stopped at 19.17, the year of the birth of John Wilson. *The End of the World News* presupposed that Burgess had died; the text was purportedly edited by John B. Wilson, B.A. (Manc.). And in *Abba Abba*, Keats and his acquaintance, the Italian poet Guiseppe Giacchino Belli, unravel a family tree that connects Romantic Italy with the Wilsons in Manchester. Keats acquires Florio's dictionary and figures out how Shakespeare spoke: 'He spoke like an Irishman.' Belli's sonnets, translated by one J. J. Wilson from Manchester ('He worked and lived in Manhattan until his death in 1959'), are described as 'a kind of proto-*Ulysses* . . . With awe and something of fear, John felt as if he were being instructed by the dead in person, souls of poets dead and gone.' For John, read John Keats; and John Wilson.

Borges, he often claimed, is 'another form of Burgess'; and in 1980 he said to Graham Greene: 'I see you have a volume of Borges here, the man who kindly calls himself the Argentine Burgess.' Borges it was who said, in *On Writing*, that 'to be a writer is, in a sense, to be living a kind of double life'; and what with Burgess/Borges, Burgess/Wilson and Burgess/his own heroes, my biographee is the father of all his characters and all his characters are the father of him – and of his readers. When asked by the *Paris Review* to describe the perfect reader of his work, Burgess gave a personal snapshot: 'I think every author wants to *make* his audience. But it's in his own image, and his primary audience is the mirror.' Burgess was alone with himself, enclosed in his own writings and in the writers – Lawrence, Joyce, etc. – to whom he felt a certain closeness. His fictional heroes duplicated his fads and worries and sense of alienation. Enderby, especially, in four novels, shadows all of his creator's ventures with caricatured equivalents – from living in Hove, to working on film scripts, to collaborating on a Shakespeare musical, to being a Visiting Professor in New York.

F. X. Enderby is Burgess's self-administered palliative treatment – the so-called cerebral tumour, for instance, became, in *Enderby Outside*, complete madness. Enderby loses his memory and is forced to pass himself off as somebody else. He decides to call himself Piggy Hogg, and as James Hogg's *Confessions of a Justified Sinner* is a tale about the relationship between two brothers, it is the vagaries of the fraternal bond which link Enderby and Burgess – and Burgess and Wilson? Brotherhood is important in many texts: the ties between individuals and within groups (the expats in Malaya, the staff-room in *The Worm and the Ring*, Alex's droogs, the disciples in the Jesus books, Moses and Aaron and their tribes). Burgess was interested in the splitting of the personality, in communities of rivals; like selves, comparable individuals – as in a family. ('Friendless I can never be,' wrote Dickens in *Master Humphrey's Clock*, 'for all mankind are my kindred, and I am on ill terms with no one member of my great family. But for years I have led a lonely, solitary life; – what wound I sought to heal, what sorrow to forget, originally, matters not now.')

To make Anthony Burgess out of John Wilson – to perfectly extract a famous writer and walking–talking encyclopaedia – what did he have to learn? What was lost? What in any event was he trying to accomplish through these self-renewals? He has said (in *Napoleon Symphony*) that a writer is a conqueror. He has also claimed that a writer wants to create a papery universe to rival the physical universe created by God. In *Ulysses* we hear that after God, Shakespeare has created most. Do we approach, here, a motive behind Burgess's manic productivity? A duel? It's as if, in the tensions and releases of his work, he was trying to strike a divine spark, achieve a divine vision. But of one thing I'm certain, as I note his bitterness and calculate his angry needs: Burgess cannot be happy.*

When I was watching *Moses the Lawgiver* ('The Epic Story of a Man, a Hero and a Nation'), and wondering whether, because the majority of the actors were Italian and didn't understand English, this was why there was no mass rebellion when the cast was asked to mouth (the sounds would be dubbed in later) an approximation of lines like, 'Your divine majesty has touched upon an interesting, indeed compelling, theological point'; it occurred to me suddenly that Burt Lancaster, debating,

* Reviewing a book called *Beethoven and the Voice of God* by Wilfrid Mellers (*Observer*, 13 February 1983), Burgess stated that 'His title . . . is clearly blasphemous.' His own attempt to (his word) fecundate the world with his billions of words and (his words again) wax exceedingly mighty was similarly unregenerate – or greedy. It was as if he wanted to outperform the Almighty. Over the Christmas holidays in 1966, for example, he wrote fifteen thousand words on the Grand Tour, an essay on precognition, a study of 'The American Jew as Voice of the Nation', a 'little piece' on Mark Twain and *Finnegans Wake*, a short story 'about talking blood', reviews of Malcolm Lowry, the Pre-Raphaelites, and Milton, plus 'other things I've forgotten'. I can't help agreeing with my friend Duncan Fallowell, however, who also finds Burgess's harping on about the virtues of productivity *annoying*; the writer's job is 'to produce a masterpiece, not churn out *stuff* . . . You "fecundate" the world far more effectively with one amazing book than with fifty mediocre ones. What Burgess is really doing in all this has nothing to do with literature . . . He is indulging his machismo.' A counterfeit machismo, as it happens, because he was sexually impotent. He once wrote a couplet about it:

Mr Anthony Impotent Burgess
Pretends he's controlling his urges.

deliberating, propounding, fatigued and ill-looking, was exactly like Burgess himself. Can this have been deliberate?* Lancaster began his career by playing grinning acrobatic crimson pirates and matured (unlike Kirk Douglas – who remained all teeth and dimples) into a large-frame crackpot patriarch. There's always a hint of madness and detachment to him – J. J. Hunsecker, the all-powerful newspaper columnist in *Sweet Smell of Success*; Happer, the cosmos-gazing tycoon in *Local Hero* – and he was drawn to the role of Moses because (he said), 'Burgess is a wonderful man, a great novelist. He saw God as a very tough customer with whom Moses was always in conflict. That appealed to me immediately – me fighting God!' As God's voice, groaning and growling in the mountains or emerging from the burning bush, is also Lancaster's voice (in the same way that Olivier played not only Hamlet but dubbed the Ghost's part, too), an interesting point is made about the actor's grand scale. Throughout the six-hour film, Lancaster either looks like a bear, thick-set and emerging from hibernation, or else, hacked and carved, he resembles the rocks amongst which he sits. He's not, therefore, physically like Burgess; he's like Burgess in giving the impression that his real thoughts are elsewhere, e.g. (in Lancaster's case) up on Cinecittà's reconstruction of Mount Sinai, amidst the dry ice, or attending to Ennio Morricone's heavenly choirs in the desert. 'God works through the dust and the smoke and that pillar of sand,' he intones meaningfully. He's imposing – and evasive. He's continuously agonised by the feeling that he is being watched; that he is being on trial. As the Egyptians suffer rivers of blood, boils and running sores, and plagues of frogs, locusts and wretched dialogue ('We are trying to avert these inexplicable nuisances from the innocent people'), Moses is stubborn, intractable. With the Pharoah, demanding freedom for the slaves, he's like Burgess giving one of his lectures on good and evil – and, as with Burgess, his idea of freedom is decidedly illiberal and wanting.

* *The Clockwork Testament* (1974) is dedicated:

To Burt Lancaster
('. . . *deserves to live, deserves to live*.')

The line is from the Moses story, where Miriam, Moses' sister, consigns the bulrush cradle to the waters:

> 'Live,' whispered Miriam, 'live.' A current took the
> Cage, cradle, ark and swirled it shoreward,
> Into the reeds . . .

In the television production, Miriam was played by Ingrid Thulin, the Swedish actress best known for her work with Ingmar Bergman.

Reaching the Promised Land requires a ruinous self-denying obedience; the laws Moses gives out are full of restrictions and prohibitions. He's above or lacking in ordinary warmth, and he believes himself to have a monopoly on intensity and insight. In Schoenberg's opera, Moses is stumbling and uncertain, depressed and authoritarian. Charlton Heston, in the De Mille film, glowers in a long white curly beard and looks like a steel engraving in a Victorian edition of the Old Testament. (Fact: as a boy, Burgess used to masturbate over the etchings of servant girls and semi-draped tribes-persons in the family Bible.) Burgess's Moses, to which Lancaster was attuned, is an egocentric agent, imperious and wrathful, and everything he does or says is slightly off-register.*

This is the effect Burgess himself has on me when he is doctrinaire. His familiar bag of tricks would range from the anthropological ('The Welsh can't take drink, you know'), to the boastful ('Rousseau was very candid about his sex life. So am I'), to the surprising and off-putting ('Garlic is the nicest smell in the world – very very erotic in a woman'), to the reac-

* The Moses/God/Lancaster/Burgess relationships, with their mirrorings and schizoid splits, would have been further developed in a script Lancaster wanted Burgess to write for him on 'the life of Schroeder, the schizophrene who had interested Freud'. I have a feeling that the commission was meant to have been about Daniel Paul Schreber, whom Freud never met, but whose dreams he analysed from a transcribed memoir. Schreber, a German magistrate, had spent ten years in lunatic asylums. He wrote a long account of his nightmares and delusions – of how he conversed with God, trees and birds. As Hans Eysenck explains, in *Decline and Fall of the Freudian Empire* (London, 1985, p. 58): 'Freud concentrated on two particular illusions which he thought to be fundamental; Schreber's belief that he was being changed from man to woman, and his complaint of having suffered homosexual assaults . . .' From all this stuff Freud deduced that repressed homosexuality was the cause of paranoid illnesses, the unattainable love objects being (in Schreber's case), his father, his doctor and God. 'Freud argued that the origins of the condition lay in a childhood Oedipal conflict in which Schreber, due to fear of castration, had become fixated on the notion of sexual submission to his father. This unconscious drive was kept from the adult Schreber by a series of psychoanalytic defence mechanisms. These involved converting it into its opposite – hatred . . .' Can intelligent people ever have been taken in by such balls? Eysenck adds that, 'Critics have pointed out that Schreber's sexual deviation was transsexuality, rather than homosexuality, and his mental illness was schizophrenia, not paranoia,' but it is still balls. But what a role for Lancaster, perfect for his gallery of dignified misfits, from *Birdman of Alcatraz* to *The Swimmer*, from Don Fabrizio, Prince of Salina, in *The Leopard*, to Lou, the bookies' runner, in *Atlantic City*. In 1974, Lancaster and Gianfranco De Bosio (who directed *Moses the Lawgiver*), wanting to discuss the project with Burgess, flew to meet him in Iowa City, where he had a temporary teaching job in the local university. Talks didn't proceed far, however, as Burgess was excitedly involved with the Music Department's forthcoming première performance of his Symphony No. 3 in C, which Lancaster and his associate were compelled to sit through, poor buggers. Though Lew Grade was prepared to finance the film, no more was heard about 'my promise of a script on Schroeder'. (Did Lancaster receive the dedication of *The Clockwork Testament* in the wild hope that he'd play the 'schizophrene' poet Enderby instead?)

tionary ('I don't feel at home in England anymore, can't understand the coinage – decimalization was a great error'), to the pathetic ('I always feel as though I'm going to be poor again'), to the reproachful ('Graham Greene put carrots into a Lancashire hotpot'), to the ribald ('Holofernes was the name for the penis, you know'), to the testy ('Don't ask me if I was disappointed that I didn't get the Booker Prize, the Booker Prize is nothing, it's one of those silly little British games'), to the uncomprehending ('I was puzzled by the London poster stating that *Milk Delivers Bottle* and I do not quite understand the new meaning given to *wanker*'), to the paranoid ('The English don't like people to know too much – polymath is a term of abuse'), to the very paranoid ('I feared that possibly the State was all too ready to take over our brains and was turning us into good little citizens without the power of choice'); and whilst, on the basis of such over-rehearsed scraps and greasy relics, it was always possible to be irritated by Burgess's habit of self-praise and affectation, I'd no more want to bawl at him to come off it (as Kingsley Amis did) than I'd have preferred Olivier to jettison the false noses and the wigs. The didacticism and false jocularity were all too easily parodied by Craig Brown, in *Private Eye** ('Breakfast, literally speaking the fasting of one's breaks or, from the early Nordic "Brrr – eat fast", as the Vikings would say when the weather was chilly . . .'); the sound of him was imitated by John Sessions, in a radio play by William Boyd called *Hommage to AB*† ('Wedged as we are between two eternities of idleness, there is no excuse for being idle now. Who said that? . . . Me! Me! I did! Me, Anthony Burgess'); and the vengeful, snarling, uncouth, sneering Burgess was the one who went to dinner at Paul Theroux's house in Chapter Five, 'The Writer and His Reader', in *My Other Life*.‡ It is in this book (subtitled 'A Novel') that Theroux

* 'Etartnecnoc: Anthony Burgess's Diary' was published on 2 March 1990. It is collected in the author's anthology, *Craig Brown's Greatest Hits* (1993).

† I have also heard Sessions do Burgess at a party of Craig Brown's; and he did the Burgess voice-overs for the BBC2 documentary, *The Burgess Variations*, broadcast on 26 December 1999.

‡Talking about Oedipal father/son schisms, how tiresome it must be for Paul Theroux, author of forty or so books, to have been so quickly eclipsed by his son Louis (First Class Honours in Modern History, Magdalen College, Oxford, 1991), whose fame is derived from a sixty-minute *faux naif* television interview with Jimmy Savile? Burgess, of course, despised Savile, for debasing the Honours List, for his 'promotion of musical garbage', and for announcing on the radio that *A Clockwork Orange* could incite people to violence. This 'made me boil and wish to inflict Grievous Bodily Harm on Savile,' fumed Burgess – rather justifying Savile's point. Paul Theroux's account of the apocryphal night with The Mighty Anthony (which 'took place on November 14th 1981. Or perhaps it didn't') first appeared as 'A. Burgess, Slightly Foxed' under the departmental heading FACT AND FICTION in *The*

describes an evening he also spent with the Queen. The style is that of a memoir – the tone is exactly that of Theroux's journalism and travel pieces, where we assume that the first-person narrator and diary format pertains to Theroux himself – and he's been cagey about whether the events described actually took place or not. With regards to *The Great Railway Bazaar* or *The Happy Isles of Oceania*, I think we can believe that he undertook those excursions; though would the texts in themselves be less sincere and authentic if it was revealed that, all along, Theroux had never been further than the end of his street at Medford, Mass., where he was born? The truest poetry is that most feigning – and in *My Other Life*, as in *My Secret History*, the Paul Theroux who walks around in the stories, whom people talk to and respond to, is meant to be a different entity from the Paul Theroux on the book's jacket and spine. Did he derive this stuff from Burgess – or from Borges, who supplied *My Other*

New Yorker, on 7 August 1995. There are substantial alterations between the magazine version and the hard-cover version, published the following year. His wife Anne changes into Alison, for instance. William Empson's attempt to seduce a student with the line 'I want to kiss your pretty little thing with my mouth' becomes the less decorous 'I want to put your pretty little thing in my mouth' – and Burgess's non-surprise at the anecdote is ascribed to bisexuality: 'at various times during his first marriage he and his then wife had experimented with a *ménage à trois*. "I've tried just about everything Burgess wrote"' – which is perplexing, and perplexing punctuation. Doesn't Theroux mean, '"I've tried just about everything," Burgess wrote'? Or is it he, Theroux, who has tried everything Burgess wrote [about]? Quite a few paragraphs are added, augmenting the idea that Theroux is a Burgess disciple – provincials who didn't fit in and who were drawn to far-off lands, Burgess to Malaya, Theroux to Nyasaland and Uganda. He meets his man in Singapore. 'I want to become a novelist,' he says. 'I know your work,' Burgess replies. 'You are already a novelist.' There's a lot more of this brothers-of-the-pen bonding. 'He wrote an introduction to the French translation of a novel of mine, *Les Conspirateurs*, and, as a joke, signed himself Antoine Bourgeois.' But there's a hint of a growing distance, too: Theroux isn't quite the green-horn. 'I loved his work' in *The New Yorker*, becomes 'I valued his work' in the *My Other Life* version, and, at table, Burgess is even more snarly and disputatious towards poor Lettfish, the collector of his first editions and manuscripts (hence it is a pun on *foxed* as in damp-stained paper as well as being a word for tricked or deceived). One plausible-sounding moment, however, failed to make the transition from *The New Yorker* to the book. Burgess wants to know if any lawyer has ever become an author: 'John Mortimer is a barrister,' Lettfish says. 'Are you suggesting that he is a writer? Because if you are, I would find that insulting,' growls Burgess.

He was indeed dead jealous of Mortimer's urbanity and popularity. The erudition and crapulousness of Enderby and Rumpole of the Bailey may be similar, yet Burgess never had a success to compare with Mortimer's adaptation of *Brideshead Revisited* or his script for *A Voyage Round My Father*. It particularly rankled with Burgess that it was Mortimer who dramatised the six-part ATV series *Will Shakespeare* (starring Tim Curry and Ian McShane) in 1978. He claimed that he'd undertaken the *Jesus of Nazareth* project for Zeffirelli because otherwise 'they'll hand it over to that lawyer fellow, John Mortimer, and you might get a disaster' (the *Sunday Tribune*, 20 May 1985).

Life with an epigraph: 'I do not know which of us has written this page'?*

Having himself lived in Singapore and explored Malaysia, and having written extensively about hot exotic places, Theroux, in a way, has come closest to re-traversing Burgess's landscapes and he participated in a television documentary, 'Burgess at Seventy', broadcast as an edition of the (now defunct) *Saturday Review,* on 21 February 1987. 'Burgess is full of gusto and his books are for sale all over South America,' we were told. 'He is truly international.' This is the Burgess who gets into Theroux's tale, an endless traveller, jet-lagged, crapulous, collapsing over dustbins in the street, knowledgeable about foreign foods and customs, jaundiced, immensely ungracious, and knotted and crackling with anxiety. Whether or not the disastrous dinner party, of prawn curry and coconut milk, occurred in reality (did Theroux ever meet V. S. Naipaul? Has he ever bought a train ticket by himself?) is irrelevant. It is a wholly convincing and plausible portrait of Burgess the small-minded and resentful public performer – who 'ground out his cigar butt and lit another one and blew smoke assertively, squinting behind it, as though planning an attack'. Theroux's Burgess is focused, yet distracted; and whilst evidence of the self-melodramatising author, whom Theroux captures so well, is easy to find ('I never found opium-smoking addictive'; 'I have the teaching urge. I was giving my wife a long lecture in bed this morning on the musical elements in Joyce's *Ulysses*' – unless that was the Burgess household's private code for copulation; or 'I began publishing late – thirty-eight, the age Joseph Conrad was when he first started, but then [death's-head deprecating smile] he had to learn English first'), how did he see himself? What did he know himself to be like?

When Burgess looked back at his younger self, or incarnation, he saw a boy genius. In *Little Wilson and Big God*, he says that he learned to read by scanning the captions on the screen in silent movies. His father played the piano in cinemas. He taught himself music and once claimed that, 'I could read Cyrillic, having studied the original score of Stravinsky's *Le Sacre du Printemps*.' He learned Greek and read Cervantes in not merely Spanish but Catalan. He wrote out the menu for his school canteen in Latin ('with coffee as *kupha*, a Modern Greek borrowing from the Turkish'). And so on; and then he wondered why he wasn't popular: 'I was either distractedly persecuted or ignored,' he once said of his childhood. 'I was one

* To quote from the Author's Note: 'These characters do not exist outside this intentionally tall story . . . There are some names you know – Anthony Burgess . . . Queen Elizabeth II . . . but they too are alter egos, other hes and other shes. As for the other I, the Paul Theroux who looks like me – he is just a fellow wearing a mask . . . The man is fiction, but the mask is real.' I can quite quickly lose patience with this kind of titting about.

despised . . . Ragged boys in gangs would pounce on the well-dressed, like myself, and grab ostentatious fountain pens.' Was it his swottiness which kept him apart? Or his ingrained temperament? Day in, day out, he walked home alone. He certainly did himself no favours by the ungracious way he received prizes – his attitude was, who dares presume to judge *me*? When, as an infant phenomenon, ditties of his or drawings were printed in boys' comics, he says he was 'angry' at coming top. His reaction was to be the same when, stationed in Gibraltar at the end of the war (aged twenty-eight), he won the Governor's Poetry Prize of a guinea and had then 'trounced the mean quality of the verse . . . and gained enemies'; and it was the same once more in 1979 (aged sixty-two), when he was dubbed Critic of the Year and given 'a plastic plaque' by Mrs Thatcher, whom he proceeded to denigrate as being in possession of 'a mediocre mind'. Another – lofty, contemptuous – ploy of his was to fail an examination on purpose, to advertise his disdain for the whole process. As a student at Manchester University he failed a French course because 'It has never been my preferred foreign language'; and when he wins a prize for a short story (adjudicated by Harold Nicolson), he is scornful as he didn't want to be a successful writer but a great composer. Up in London to sit the tests for the Licentiate of the Royal Academy of Music and the Associateship of the Royal College of Music (Composition), he contrived to fall out with the inquisitor, Herbert Howells.*

* Herbert Howells (1892–1983), a pupil of Sir Charles Stanford and Sir Hubert Parry, taught theory and composition at the Royal College of Music for over half a century. He went in for large-scale choral works, such as *Hymnus Paradisi* (1938). He accumulated lots of honorary doctorates and fellowships, a CBE and a CH. A survivor from an era of Elgaresque oratorios – all those solemn settings of Gerontius, Job, Saul and Caractacus – Howells lived long enough theoretically to have heard Burgess's Joycean operetta, *Blooms of Dublin*, which musicologists (e.g. Hans Keller) and Joycean specialists (e.g. Denis Donoghue, the Professor of English and American Literature at University College, Dublin, since 1965) laughed to scorn when it was broadcast on Radio Telefis Eireann and Radio 3 on the evening of 2 February 1982, Joyce's hundreth birthday. 'Burgess's pathetic pastiche,' wrote Keller, 'evinced a centrifugal incompetence which pervaded its entire orbit, so that continuous listening became impossible for any naturally musical ear, professional or naive . . . Senseless tonal and rhythmic antics . . . take the place of even the most elementary invention . . .' Way to go, Hans! Burgess was mightily indignant. 'I began my artistic career as a composer, am academically trained in the craft, and wrote a score which may not be impugned . . .' he seethed. In retaliation he immediately wrote *Homage to Hans Keller* for four tubas, a sort of lavatorial blast. When asked if this piece had any connection with the Hans Keller who'd panned him in the *Listener*, he said no, it's another Hans Keller, like Gielgud who said (to Edward Knoblock), 'There goes the biggest bore in London, second only to Edward Knoblock – I mean the *other* Edward Knoblock.' Keller, who had emigrated to London from Vienna in 1938, at the age of nineteen, co-founded the magazine *Music Survey*, served on the BBC staff from 1959, and was considered an expert in the field of analytical criticism and modern composers. Three years after Burgess's gaseous tribute, he died.

'I failed the practical tests less through incompetence than through truculence' – how stupid or infantile is that? He sat the civil service examinations for HM Customs and Excise and came 1,579th.

Whether people were being nice to him or horrible, he had difficulty with authority, officialdom or being sized up – with other people being (as he saw it) presumptuous. He could never cope with criticism, and the second volume of his memoirs, *You've Had Your Time*, embarrassingly goes on and on about the bad reviews he'd received. (He never mentions the intelligent, perceptive appraisals he'd also occasioned over the years.*) Burgess's first words to Robert Robinson, who had travelled to Monte Carlo, in 1976, to interview him for *The Book Programme*, were, 'I have been a critic myself, Bob, as indeed you have – you were one of the people twelve years ago whom I had it in for. You reviewed a novel of mine about Shakespeare . . . Yes, and you said that learning dripped from every sentence like sweat from the end of a nose.'

* From, amongst others, Peter Ackroyd ('For one thing, the words have never failed him,' *The Times*, 26 February 1987); Martin Amis ('his evident, and superabundant, natural gifts', *Observer*, 22 February 1987, and collected, along with three other glowing pieces on Burgess, in *The War Against Cliché: Essays and Reviews* 1971–2000 [London, 2001]); Malcolm Bradbury ('Anthony Burgess is a writer of prodigious range and exhilarating versatility,' *No, Not Bloomsbury* [London, 1987]); John Carey ('a giant', *Sunday Times*, 22 February 1987); David Caute ('Burgess has written a novel epic in its sweep, subtle in its portraiture, graceful in its unforbidding exploration of ideas, and brutally funny' – of *Earthly Powers*, in the *New Statesman*, 24 October 1980); Shirley Chew ('. . . he has given fragments enough of his individual vision to convince us of its intensity and importance, and of the continuing vitality of his work', *Encounter*, vol. XXXVIII, no. 6, June 1972); Jonathan Coe ('one of the most interesting minds of our time', *Sunday Correspondent*, 28 October 1990); Carol M. Dix ('his great body of writing [is] such a gift to contemporary English literature', *Writers and their Work: Anthony Burgess* [Harlow, 1971]); D. J. Enright (*Nothing Like the Sun* 'is a clever, tightly constructed book . . . full of the author's old verbal ingenuity, with something of Shakespeare's to boot . . .' *Man Is an Onion* [London, 1971]; '*Earthly Powers* carries greater intellectual substance, more force and grim humour, more knowledge, than ten average novels put together,' *A Mania for Sentences* [London, 1983]); David Lodge ('wonderfully entertaining', *TLS*, 27 February 1987); Fiona MacCarthy ('a near-miss genius', *The Times*, 3 November 1990); Julian Mitchell ('His invention and imagination are both enormous, and they almost always work happily together,' *The London Magazine*, February 1964); Jonathan Raban ('He is surely the most intelligent English novelist alive – the only man writing in distinctively British English who can match, say, Günter Grass or Saul Bellow in sheer mental energy and agility,' *Encounter*, November 1974); Christopher Ricks ('No doubt he has been embarrassed by the gratifying words of reviewers; to deserve them all, he would have to be a much better novelist than Dickens,' *New Statesman*, 5 April 1963); Lorna Sage ('full of imagination and curiosity', *Observer*, 12 November 1989); John Sutherland ('In so far as a reader's absolution counts he has mine, and my admiration as well,' *TLS*, 26 October 1990); and Mary Warnock ('he [has] the power to turn memory of the ephemeral past into present, and perennial, truth', *Sunday Telegraph*, 22 February 1987).

Robinson, to his credit, salvages what is promising to be an ugly moment by joking, 'Really? I was rather good in those days.' Clive James, similarly hoping for a cosy chat with the magus, was also disconcerted to be told that his less than wholly laudatory ruling over *1985*, the Orwell spoof, had still to be forgotten and forgiven and called for condign punishment. Burgess allowed James to squirm a little before launching into his set-piece about how 'to write costively is a post-Edwardian affectation. My own production is in the tradition of Wells and Dickens.'*

You don't have to be a Viennese witch-doctor to conclude that Burgess was a little deranged, nor to suspect that his deep terror and isolation grew out of his childhood. Man and boy, he believed himself to be oppressed, and he believed himself to be different. He was animated by a dark pride and rage – and his recollections of his youth, in *Little Wilson*

* James's article, 'Look Forward in Mild Irritation', appears in *From the Land of Shadows* (London, 1982) and was originally published in the *New York Review of Books* in 1978. 'Burgess,' he writes, 'would probably like *1985* to be thought of as a teeming grab-bag of ideas. In fact it is a scrap heap.' It is a wonder that the novelist (who always claimed he liked a brawl), when he walked on to the set of *The Late Clive James*, on 11 May 1985, didn't punch his host in the face.

Clive James remains an interesting case – or head-case. He can never decide whether to emulate John Bayley and Christopher Ricks, and compose wide-ranging critical commentaries, or whether to be a professional nincompoop on television, introducing Japanese game shows or presenting himself in travel documentaries as a sort of Australian innocent abroad, like Barry McKenzie. His programmes have self-non-effacing titles like *Clive James on Television*, *The Late Clive James*, *Saturday Night Clive*, *The Talk Show with Clive James*, *Clive James: Fame in the Twentieth Century*, *The Clive James Show*, *Clive James and the Calendar Girls*, *Clive James Meets Roman Polanski* and *Clive James Finally Meets Frank Sinatra*. He's clearly hungry for fame – but he was far better writing about television than appearing on it, where his exertions to prove himself an entertainer wore thin. Actually, the person whom he most resembles is Burgess – look, for example, at the fancy foreign-language epigraphs garlanding the books, the intellectual boastfulness, and all the over-done effects of autodidacticism. On page eighty-five of *Reliable Essays: The Best of Clive James* (London, 2001) there is a perfect Burgessian sentence. Describing how a particular grammatical error may have come about, James says: 'This habit has something to do, I suspect, with a confusion between the English past participle and the Latin ablative absolute.' It is that *I suspect* which makes him a prat. This is blatant showing off – and (like Burgess) James is riven by his two attitudes or voices, Coco the Clown and the po-faced contributor to the *London Review of Books*; the low-brow and the high-brow. (Only S. J. Perelman, to my knowledge, combined a light and deep tone or prose style without strain.)

In the *Guardian*, on the day before he made his appearance on James's television show, Burgess said of his protégé: 'He's a very good journalist, but the novel he wrote [*Brilliant Creatures* (London, 1983)] was disastrous, I thought. A bit of a chip on his shoulder about being Australian. He's getting bald and he's getting fat.'

and Big God, or fictionalised in *The Pianoplayers* and elsewhere,[*] read like the equivalent of angry chords bashed on a keyboard. Other children, whom he was compelled to meet at St Edmund's Roman Catholic Elementary School, on Monsall Road, where he was cast as a whey-faced Picasso blue-period pierrot in a play, and at the Bishop Bilsborrow Memorial Elementary School, next to the tram depot on Moss Side, barely register as human. Meagre, stunted and stooping, they could be Squeers' pupils, fed on a diet of brimstone and treacle. And this was how Burgess looked back at Wilson – when talking about earlier parts of his life, the struggles of his life, he always put it in terms of literature; so for his childhood he's Oliver Twist, Pip or David Copperfield, or Dickens himself, at the blacking factory. 'I was in an ugly world,' he says in his memoirs, 'with ramshackle houses and foul alleys.' Manchester, situated on the Irwell, in the south-east of Lancashire, thirty miles east of Liverpool, was the centre of the English cotton-manufacturing district, with many other textile and related industries, and it had many fine buildings, including a gothic Town Hall and Assize Court House, and the John Rylands Library. The city grew enormously during the Industrial Revolution, and its economic and political struggles at the beginning of the nineteenth century were severe, and included the Peterloo Massacre – when, in 1819, a group of workers gathering in St Peter's Field to discuss and demand parliamentary reform were fired upon by the army, by order of the magistrates. Thirteen died, six hundred were wounded. Burgess only referred to the event in passing – 'The Central Library and the Town Hall Annexe, which I am old enough to remember being built, preside over what used to be St Peter's Fields, where the Peterloo Massacre took place . . . They are as elegant as anything in England'[†] – for, as regards indignation, his mind was fixed further back, on the Elizabethan martyr called, like himself, John Wilson, who'd been executed for refusing to acknowledge the Queen as defender of the faith. Burgess's Manchester is a phantasmagoria of colliery brass bands and choirs, orchestras and opera houses, Catholic recusants sneaking off to secret meetings and toasting

[*] E.g. worked in to articles on Chaplin and Benny Hill, where Burgess would ally himself with stars who 'learned their trade through the hard grind of popular stage entertainment' (*One Man's Chorus*, p. 355). Even though it was his father who'd played the piano in theatres and music halls, Burgess had an affinity with anyone famous who'd served an indigent apprenticeship.

[†] As an indication of how, to Burgess, Manchester was an imagined rather than a real place – its events mythical rather than historical – the effects of the Peterloo Massacre are cordoned off within parentheses: '. . . (it is still bitterly remembered) . . .'

Bonnie Prince Charlie, the Young Pretender; he recalled 'hard-headed magnates and cotton-brokers gorging red meat in chophouses'; the streets are bustling with mad or simple servant-girls, ragged men playing tin whistles; and I can just about smell the coal, fog, beer, urine, hair oil, pipe smoke, wet mackintoshes, sulphur and soot. I can see the brightly coloured comic papers he read, *The Funny Wonder*, *Chips*, *Gem*, *The Magnet*, *The Boys' Magazine*; the bustle of the department stores; the streets, pubs and silent-movie cinemas; the sauce bottles, advertisements and jingles: it was a Dickens world of hot muffins and pikelets, or (as he remembered) mutton stews and nutmeggy custards.

Despite the plenitude and energy, the Christmas parties, the sing-alongs:

We'll be merry
Drinking whisky, wine and sherry,
All be merry
On Coronation Day . . .

– despite all the laughter and animation, however, Burgess felt Wilson to be malnourished and barefoot, shut away in attics like Smike. Though surrounded by people and by kindly acts, such as being taken to concerts given by the Hallé, he nevertheless preferred to feel isolated, 'run down and weak', 'a mere household animal', more constitutionally frail than Paul Dombey, with rheumatic fevers and scarlet fevers (necessitating a stay in the Monsall Isolation Hospital, Northampton Road – where 'I learned hate' because, believing he was about to die, he mismanaged the bedpan and was rebuked by a nurse), with frequent fainting fits and nightmares. He faints when he sees a map of the night sky – he's appalled by the endlessness of the heavens. He gets the willies when he opens an atlas – all that space; all those demarcations and wiggly lines. He enters a public library – he panics. The laws of gravity seem so improbable, occasionally he sees the impossibility of walking and movement and stumbles to a bench. He is colour-blind and greens, oranges, violets and blues merge muddily. Though as myopic as Mr Magoo, he refuses to wear spectacles and, in later life, entered a bank in Stratford-upon-Avon and ordered a drink. The first time he masturbated, he got giddy and passed out. He is prone to migraine headaches, vomiting, and pains in his bowels. The prevalent sickliness, I think, the image he gives of a child driven in on itself, a back-street urchin able to accept neither praise nor blame, is consistent with his grown-up personality. He felt himself to be a rejected creature. He was filled with fear and mistrust – and this made him angry, violent, envious and cruel. He was always the victim – and always innocent. The physical, nutritional or economic deprivations he imputed to his earliest days are, in fact, metaphors of his emotional neediness. The dilapidated buildings, the tumble-down pubs, the garrets with gurgling water pipes, the dirt and decay, dust and rust: the Fagin's den atmosphere, the old curiosity shop spookiness, is a portrait of the future artist as a psychological cripple, cut off from other children – as, in years to come, he'd cut himself off from people generally. When his uncle, Jack Tollitt, took him to see Manchester City play (the only time Burgess attended a sporting fixture in his life), all that's recalled is the uncouthness of the crowd – a mob out of *Barnaby Rudge*, no doubt complete with pitchforks and flaming torches. Watching his family at the table, breakfasting on Bass and a pork pie, dining on grilled sweetbreads, they strike him as common and coarse. He's contented (or feels safe) only on his own, up in the loft, surrounded by his father's discarded books, listening to classical music on his crystal set.

A biographer is duty-bound to insist that one's subject's childhood was traumatic [Greek, *traumatos*, for wound]. The parents were feckless, or overprotective, neglectful, or clinging. There has to be a dysfunctional background of alcoholism, wife-beating, disloyalty, political extremism and sexual perversity. For how else to account for the abnormality of being a famous actor, soldier, painter, poet, novelist, or what-have-you? If it was a childhood of agreeable picnics and games on the lawn, they'd be as boring as the rest of us. There must be hurts and strangeness to exorcise – and luckily Burgess's primal injury is first rate. He made no secret of it. Here's how William Boyd distilled the story in *Hommage to A.B.*:

> . . . one night in 1919 when I was two years old my father came home on leave from the army to find both my mother and sister dead. Spanish influenza.* I lay chuckling in my cot while my mother and sister lay dead on a bed in the same room . . . There was no doubt that God existed. Only a supreme being could contrive a world-wide influenza pandemic after four years of unprecedented suffering

* Thomas Pynchon, in his story 'Entropy' (collected in *Slow Learner*, London, 1985) uses the *grippe espagnole* to signify a generalised post-Great War malaise: 'And that tango. Any tango, but more than any perhaps the sad sick dance in Stravinsky's *L'Histoire du Soldat*. He thought back: what had tango music been for them after the war, what meanings had he missed in all the stately coupled automatons in the *café-dansants*, or in the metronomes which had ticked behind the eyes of his own partners? Not even the clean constant winds of Switzerland could cure the *grippe espagnole*: Stravinsky had had it, they all had had it.'

and devastation. He removed half my family and provided me, instead and in due course, with a stepmother . . .*

Dickens, who loved a death-bed scene, such as little Nell's last moments, which are filled with heavenly harps and angelic choirs, couldn't have contrived a better tableau. Between September and November 1918, the influenza virus killed between twenty and forty million people, certainly more than in the circumjacent First World War. Spanish flu reached every continent and country. The first case was reported on 4 March 1918, in Kansas; by April it had spread across the States and had reached Europe – taken by the soldiers crossing the Atlantic for the last big push in the mud of Flanders. There was a serious outbreak at Brest, a port used by the American troops. Once the sick army left its crowded troop transport for crowded hospitals, in crowded cities, the disease flourished. The virus infected the inner lining of the respiratory tract, damaging the alveoli – the tiny air-filled sacs in the lungs – filling them with fluid, making it impossible to breathe; without sufficient oxygen, or oxygenated blood, the skin became discoloured (cyanosis): patients went black. For some macabre reason, it killed the young and healthy rather than the old and infirm. That Little Wilson's mother had been a lusty singer and dancer in the music halls completes the pictorial effect. Burgess's private misery is turned into an engraving – ivory and black, like one of Cruikshank's illustrations, black and grey and cross-hatched, dense with rain and poverty. The alleys and tenements filled with yellow fog; the actors, clowns and acrobats; the cracked mirrors and glass lamp-shades; the slippers, plumed hats and crumpled clothes . . . Elizabeth Burgess was billed on the posters ('pleonastically' as her son would point out) as 'The Beautiful Belle

* Boyd takes his wording from *Little Wilson and Big God* (p. 18). The account also turns up in *This Man and Music*: 'I was born in Manchester in early 1917 while my father was serving in the Pay Corps. When I was eighteen months old he came home on leave one day from his barracks in Preston to find my mother and six-year-old sister dead from Spanish influenza and myself chuckling away in my cot' (p. 11). It was a regular starting point in interviews. 'My father came home and found my mother and sister dead in the same room and myself on the bed alive,' he told Samuel Coale in *Modern Fiction Studies* (autumn 1981). 'I was only about four months old, less than a year.' The post-bellum flu epidemic carries off an actor friend of Toomey's in *Earthly Powers*: 'It must be hard for my younger readers to take in the fact that a man could die of influenza. We of that age had electricity, gas, automobiles, rotary printing presses, the novels of P. G. Wodehouse, canned goods, Gold Flake cigarettes, mass destruction, aeroplanes, but we did not have antibiotics.'

Burgess'. Allegedly she was in the chorus at the Ardwick Empire and 'she also understudied for Josie Collins, the dark brooding star of *The Maid of the Mountains* and reputedly a bit of a bitch'.* Born in 1887, José Collins, to spell her name correctly, was an actress, vocalist and dancer who'd begun her career as a child performer with Harry Lauder, touring with him in musical comedies and pantomimes. She played roles like Madame von Gruenberg in *Vera Violetta*, Zuricka in *The Rose of Ispahan*, the Countess Rosalinde Cliquot in *The Merry Countess*, and Camille Joyeuse in *The Happy Day*. It was at Christmas 1916 that she had played Teresa, the girl taken hostage by a band of brigands and who falls in love with their chief, in *The Maid of the Mountains* at the Prince's Theatre, Manchester, which ran for three years. In Manchester she also played Dolores in *The Southern Maid* (1917) and Peg Woffington in *Our Peg* (opening on 24 December 1919 – but by then her understudy was dead).

The 'once famous Ardwick Hippodrome' [*sic*] appears in *Byrne*, the novel-in-verse published posthumously:

> It was all conjurors and dancing dogs,
> And veteran sawers of a girl in half,
> Arthritic troupes that clumped about in clogs,
> Comedians who never raised a laugh
> Except in sentimental monologues . . .

José Collins' career, which Belle Burgess shadowed; those effusive operettas filled with trilling gauze-clad sopranos; the garishness of the make-up and the decrepitude of the old vaudevillians; the improbable plots: there is an air of strangeness about this brightly lit non-naturalistic world, which I find intensely melancholy. I think it's to do with the simplicity of the ideals and dreams – love conquering all; handsome princes and princesses sweeping you off to join the aristocracy; betrayals and treacheries coming right; reconciliations – and how this all contrasts with the forlornness and shoddiness backstage; and how these shows and all

* No doubt. She was married three times: (1) Leslie Chatfield; (2) Lord Robert Innes-Ker; (3) Captain G. B. Kirkland, R.A.M.C. *The Maid of the Mountains* was composed by Harry Graham and Harold Fraser-Simson (book by Frederick Lonsdale):

> If faithful to my trust I stay,
> No fate can fill me with dismay.
> Love holds the key to set me free,
> And love will find a way.

the men and women who were in them and who watched them are gone. The Burgess story is particularly full of vanished lives. I have the original death certificates before me.

The reality is slightly (but significantly) different from the recapitulations half a century on. For a start it was the sister, Muriel Burgess Wilson, who died first, aged eight years, on 15 November 1918 (not 'early 1919'), at the family home (and Little Wilson's birthplace), 91 Carisbrook Street, Harpurhey, in the sub-district of Blackley, Manchester. The cause of death is given as (1) Influenza, (2) Broncho-Pneumonia, (3) Cardiac Failure, and was certified by J. Kerr Bell, L.R.C.P. There was no post-mortem examination. The registrar, Mr Whittaker, was informed the same day, at the Prestwich Register Office, by Joseph Wilson, Lance Corporal, Army Pay Corps, Preston, and a cashier at the wholesale meat market, who'd be in attendance at the death. So much for the tale of the feckless father wandering in from his barracks, or looking in as an afterthought, or coming back from the pub. Elizabeth Wilson, aged thirty, died at the same address four days later, on 19 November, of (1) Influenza, (2) Acute Pneumonia, (3) Cardiac Failure, and again Dr Kerr Bell certified that life was extinct – and again Joseph Wilson was present at the death. Mr Whittaker didn't register the death until 21 November. Did a weekend closure supervene? There was no autopsy.

Burgess's telling of the tale was always suspiciously neat and schematic – like in *Earthly Powers*, where a miracle turns out to have evil consequences and good becomes bad; or *A Clockwork Orange*, where free will and predestination intertwine and subvert the notion of moral choice; or *MF*, where male and female and black and white switch positions. His story about his mother and sister had become crystallised, static – delivered like an actor who has mastered the technique of wringing sympathy from us. It doesn't seem real at all. That his father had been there throughout; that his mother watched her daughter die in agony: behind Burgess's story is a considerable domestic tragedy. Yet he could never confront or discuss or extrapolate passions like these. As a novelist his distinction is that he avoids complex feelings and shades of meaning; personal interactions – he steers clear. Not that, with this scene in Carisbrook Street, he has made anything up exactly – it's more that the actuality is much more poignant and heartbreaking. He doesn't misconstrue it, but the real story is stronger; the mystery of human relationships is deeper and sadder. He doesn't want to deal with any of that. Why? Because it'll un-man him? Overwhelm him? The millions of words he wrote – the books, articles, the long interviews he gave: they were a bulwark against the horror inside him. He wrote to keep back his thoughts, and not (particularly) to articulate them. Hence he's disconnected, choked off. He spent his life circling off and avoiding what was on his mind. In this lay the expertise – the masterful poise. All that trapped emotion – like Oedipus, the fear of what he blinded himself to was vast. Like Oedipus, it was to do with who he is.

The loss of his mother, when he was nineteen months old, meant, he claimed, that, 'I was always frightened of giving myself, frightened of declaring love and frightened of friendship. I had no infantile cushion to which I could refer when I entered into an emotional relationship. I think the situation now,' he confessed to Anthony Clare in 1988, seventy years on, 'is that I have no friends.' Talking about the flu episode and its aftermath to Jeremy Isaacs, however, twelve months later, what might have seemed accidental now appeared more of a design, a reductive, austere philosophy: 'I've never expected too much from life – from other people.' He had no role in life save to shut himself away from it, he seems to be saying. He once vouchsafed that 'the emotional coldness' established in childhood 'has marred my work'; and if we add to his burden of guilt and misfortune the death of Lynne, in 1968, he became not a heartless writer or a loveless writer: sometimes he could be an insane or sociopathic writer. I'm thinking of the way he recollected an episode during the war. He has been made up to sergeant and posted to Winwick, near Warrington – to a lunatic asylum. Many of the inmates are syphilitic, which gives Burgess the notion that illness can generate genius – thus his theory of Shakespeare, in *Nothing Like the Sun*. One of the doctors asks if he'd like to watch a post-mortem examination, so Burgess notes that the body is 'a mess of meat, a few jugs of blood and a tangle of entrails'. On another occasion, to while away the time, Burgess watches a laboratory technician dispose of aborted foetuses and dead babies by cutting them up with a pair of scissors. What's shocking is that Burgess doesn't even register a horrified fascination. He often lacks taste, but the complete lack of feeling here, as he breezes past these details, which strike neither pity nor terror in his marrow, suggests the dispassionateness of a madman or of a benumbed child. You always get the impression of a man writing, not a person feeling – or (when Lynne dies) a husband suffering. He's similar in his reaction to his father, in connection with the deaths of Elizabeth and Muriel – he never gives any mind to Joseph's grief, because he doesn't wish to be noticed experiencing grief himself.

He gets it into his head that there was resentment (his word – his favourite word*) that he had survived.

In his childhood he looks on death – and dead children received pitiless treatment in his work. Whilst Howarth, in *The Worm and the Ring*, is mooning over Hilda, his young colleague, his son Peter climbs on the school roof, falls, and is impaled on the railings. 'The children held themselves off from the body . . . They saw with horror and fascination what was proper for films and thrillers . . . They held back as if it would bite them.'† The incident – including the impersonal tone – is transferred to the novel from the Manchester past. Eddie Mitchell,‡ aged nine, climbed up a drainpipe to the roof of the Temperance Billiard Hall, to retrieve a ball, and plunged on to a spiked fence. 'He crawled home, lay down on the family sofa, and said: "Nobody knows what I've been through." Then he died.' The bleak stoicism is blackly funny – it's a northern comic's joke.

* Despite the affinity with Joyce, both personal and stylistic; despite Joyce wanting to be a saint, his life one long martyrdom – and Burgess subtitles *Little Wilson* a volume of confessions, the temptations of St Anthony; despite all this, Burgess never once makes Wilson seem Joycean; nor are Burgess's novels Joycean in their impression. This is because Joyce was motivated by a sense of love and irony; Burgess is motivated by a sense of hate and sardonic mockery.

Little Wilson and Big God is spiked with ferocity; it bristles with indignation and persecution. Wilson's father had 'mingled resentment and factitious gratitude' that the boy survived when the mother died; 'I sometimes resent my father'; 'I . . . was perpetually angry' as a child; 'I was either distractedly persecuted or ignored' at school; 'I was one despised'; 'I . . . was angry at gaining first prize'; of Handel and Bach: 'I rather despised these diatonic harmonies'; 'I felt weary, lonely'; in hospital: 'I learned hate'; 'I was reared emotionally cold'; 'I detested equally the canon and his gormless curate'; Catholicism makes him 'despise small patriotisms'; A. J. P. Taylor 'earned my enmity'; of Burgess being more famous than L. C. Knights, Wilson's former tutor: 'I think he resented this'; of the French: 'I resent their exquisiteness'; of soldiers: 'they learn their hate from their own side'; of his superior officers: 'They earned resentment'; 'I was also resentful . . . resent . . . resentment . . .'; 'I resented my wife, as all men going East have to . . . I resented my wife . . .' And so it goes.

Burgess looks back in anger; he's like Alex in *A Clockwork Orange* on the rampage. Anger, detestation, resentment, humiliation: they are Burgess's representations of earthly powers – energy perversely creative.

† Improbably (though this *is* a novel), we later learn that he has pulled through – but no information percolates to the reader as to the effects of the accident on those involved. 'He's going to be all right. They thought he'd die, you know . . . It's Howarth we have to feel sorry for. Poor Howarth,' is hardly adequate. Burgess himself evidently quite forgot these lines, for when recounting the plot in *Little Wilson and Big God* he says categorically that after his fall the boy 'dies in agony'.

‡ Three hundred pages later, in *Little Wilson and Big God*, Eddie Mitchell has become Alec Mitchell. Why the confusion or slip? Alec was the name of the husband of the woman upon whom the fictional Hilda was based. Eddie was John Wilson's father-in-law.

More nauseating and macabre is the response of Eddie's sister, Lily. She invites Little Wilson round when the family is out, strips off and lies down pretending to be a corpse. Wilson is meant to tickle the body back to life – which sounds like that bit in *The Old Curiosity Shop*, where children are found playing in a churchyard and one wee moppet lies upon a fresh grave, half hidden in the bed of leaves. He explains to Nell that it is not a grave – 'it was a garden – his brother's. It was greener, he said, than all the other gardens, and the birds loved it better because he [used] to feed them. When he had done speaking, he looked at her with a smile, and kneeling down and nestling for a moment with his cheek against the turf, bounded merrily away.'

Is Burgess's impassive style preferable to this forced sentiment and sickliness, which is like the worst kind of Victorian genre painting? But I think Dickens's and Burgess's intentions are the same – whether by prettifying infant mortality or by being insouciant, it's an event or experience they are at pains to put at a distance and control reactions towards. (They are to be well-protected by their style.) For the massacre of the infants scene in Zeffirelli's *Jesus of Nazareth*, little bundles are tossed from windows and the Roman soldiery rush into houses with daggers glinting. Peter Ustinov, immense as Herod in scarlet and brocade gold robes, rages in his palace, throws a wine cup to the mosaic floor, and looks as if he is about to burst into a villain's aria from Puccini. The same scene in *Man of Nazareth*, the novel from which the television production was drawn, is less operatic and camp – but in its own way much more wordy and artificial: '"And now," Herod calmly said, "You can kill all the new-born. Do you hear me? Kill them all – all the boy-children. No, the girls as well, it will take too long to sort out the sexes. Be on the safe side . . . All those up to a year old. Two years for that matter. The safe side . . . Go on, you – take your men and let your men take their swords. Make sure they're sharp. To Bethlehem. Hack. Lunge. Chop. Kill."' A sergeant says to a colleague, 'Easier, lad, with these soft small bodies . . . Nothing to it. They're just soft squashy things.' You'll find the affectlessness, too, in *The Kingdom of the Wicked*, when the Christian children ('some hundred of them') are dressed in lambs' fleeces and flung to the lions in the arena games. The audience murmurs its disapproval – not about the gratuitous cruelty, but because they are bored. (The equivalent episode in *A.D. – Anno Domini*, the Vincenzo Labella twelve-hour mini-series, sees Alun Armstrong, as a sort of harassed theatrical dresser backstage, trying to encourage the doomed youths into their costumes – it is grimly, determinedly, unfunny.)

Childhood, the message seems to be, is there to be dispensed with ('Children are uncreative. They can only imitate,' he said dogmatically and implacably); and it fits the pattern almost too perfectly to know that when Burgess, stationed in Gibraltar during the war, hears from Lynne, who has had to remain in London working for the Ministry of War Transport, it is to be told that she's been attacked during the blackout by unknown assailants, kicked and punched, and that she has suffered a spontaneous abortion. (This is not to assume that Burgess was the father.) You'll find the attack in *A Clockwork Orange*, where it is viewed from the perspective of the thugs: 'The writer veck and his zheena were not really there, bloody and torn and making noises. But they'd live' – and it is interesting to note that Burgess shows no interest in or sympathy for the victim herself, nor for her husband. And my point is, when we know the reverberations of dead babies in his life – his sister; a mother's tears; the assault on Lynne and her despairs – then a sequence like the one in *Moses the Lawgiver*, where children are rounded up, thrown into cages and drowned in the Nile whilst the Egyptian troops sing this shanty:

> Here's the way we earn our pay:
> We've been ordered off to slay
> Little Jews so long as they
> Have balls between their legs . . .

– such moments, so cold-blooded in his writing,* reach down to his terrors and desires, and to the irreparable deaths, in his history. As a child, it was as if he did not really belong in that state, but somewhere, or as something, else. 'When I went to school,' he reminisced, 'I was already able to read. At the Manchester elementary school I attended, most of the children could not read, so I was dragooned into the job of a kind of class monitor. This put me a little apart, [made me] rather different from the rest.' Like Oliver amongst Fagin's gang, he was distinct – and this is the isolated consciousness of his books; he lived and concealed himself inside his work, which was a repository of his personality, a storehouse for whoever existed behind the Wilson, Burgess, Kell aliases; and as a child, too,

* In the television version, the infanticidal soldiers are off on a spree and the sequence is shot without much style or terror. *Moses: A Narrative*, however, makes it plain that the Egyptians want to cull the tribes of Israel because they consider them vermin. ('This zest for breeding – it is the mark of/An animal race.') There's a particularly nasty image of rats gnawing at the babies' corpses floating in the Nile – fortunately that one was not transferred to the screen, either.

there'd been no shortage of names. He's John Burgess Wilson on his birth certificate, coming into the world (and Harpurhey) on 25 February 1917; his mother was labelled as 'Elizabeth Wilson formerly Burgess'. The birth was registered on 13 March, by his father. He was known, however, as Jack Wilson, or Little Jackie, or Johnny Eagle, or once he got to university, J. B. Wilson. Left, after his mother's funeral, to fend with relatives, you feel that he can't grow up quickly enough – and there's never any youthful spirit in Burgess's work. His imagination didn't retain the wonder of a child – neither the intensity, nor the innocence. Primal forces – predatory, liberated, fearless urges – only gripped him with language, as he immersed himself in the flutings, hisses and buzzes of speech, in the prattle or babble of linguistics. The general state of things is a middle-aged moroseness and crotchetiness – his essence, formed by humiliation, rejection and castigation, which hardened him (and gave him an air of self-congratulation, too).

Proust's belief that art or books come from 'the deep self, which is only to be found by disregarding other people and the self that knows other people' is a particular puzzle with Burgess, because whilst he did disregard other people and was not sociable, a deep private self was also what he avoided, when writing. Instead, what burns through, what had been collected and retained in his memory, was a sense that he had been surrounded by menace. After his mother's death he was looked after by his mother's sister, Ann Bromley, a war widow, who had two daughters, Elsie and Betty. Aunt Annie bought him a wind-up gramophone, which he broke. Of his cousins, Elsie died single and Betty's husband died on their wedding night. He was made to sleep in a cold room in the house on Delauneys Road, Higher Crumpsall, and the picture on the wall, of a minatory gypsy woman mouthing the word 'Beware!', made him hysterical. He imagined that the picture would open at night like a casement, and that serpents and goblins would tumble towards his cot. His father, meantime, had a Bob Cratchit existence during the day, keeping the account books at Swift's Beef Market and scoring neat lines with ink and an ebony ruler. At night he drank and played the piano at a pub on Lodge Street, in the district of Miles Platting, called the Golden Eagle, a large premises of ale bars and singing rooms, polished brass pumps and sawdust. 'You don't see pubs like this anymore,' said Burgess in 1981. 'I don't know whether the pub is still there. I know that the eagle itself, the huge golden eagle outside, was bought by the Anglican church for use in front of a pulpit. I don't think you'll see those pubs anymore . . . Open at six in the morning, open until midnight. Meals were served, free lunches, a colossal lot of drink . . .'*

In 1922, the year of *Ulysses* and *The Waste Land*, as Burgess would not have needed reminding, Joseph Wilson married the landlady, Margaret Dwyer, née Byrne; fat, illiterate, always belching and picking her teeth, it's hard to tell her apart from Mrs Gamp or the Widow Corney. She quells drunks with a truncheon and knuckle dusters. She complains continuously about obscure headaches and gastric spasms. She pokes her earhole with hairclips. Her bunions play up. She's a cartoon virago who drops her aitches and, in her rooms, 'there were no books even as part of the décor. Books were timewasters or worse. When, in my teens, I came home with a 1683 chapbook bought for twopence, she shrieked at it and put it on the fire with the tongs: she had heard of the Great Plague and here was a paper bubonic rodent.' Her chief crime seems to have been that she was lower-

* This aspect of Burgess's life and the long-gone world of the Golden Eagle is the subject of *The Pianoplayers*, written *c.* 1979 and published in 1986. Purportedly the memoir of Ellen Henshaw, these are clearly the recollections of Little Wilson. The hero, the pianoplayer Billy Henshaw, Ellen's papa, is a portrait of Burgess's real father, Joseph Wilson – a rather romanticised portrait, but the indigence, sparky wit and gentle showmanship seem accurate enough. Billy Henshaw makes his living ('If you could call it a living') providing accompaniment for the last days of silent movies whilst the Vitaphone looms. His wife and son having died in an influenza epidemic (as of course Burgess's mother and sister did), he brings up his surviving daughter on his own, or with the casual help of the floozies who pass through his life, or bed. There is little money; there is petty thievery; jobs and homes change weekly. Ellen and Billy traipse from tenement to shanty, consuming bully beef, strong tea and malt vinegar. 'It was not the best place in the world for a kid to be brought up.'

The infant Ellen sits in the stalls of verminous picture-palaces every night. 'I know the films from, say 1924, to the time of *The Singing Fool* as well as anybody in the world.' Billy, meanwhile, brilliantly vamps away, his versatility unappreciated by the whelk-sucking mob: 'my dad never complained . . . a man of resource, as he called himself'.

Ellen, too, is resourceful. Edging into adolescence, she begins to attract the leers of wheezy old men. One such asks her to skivvy for him, but 'it wasn't the cleaning up he was interested in as you can guess'. If she is groped, at least she is paid off for her pains – or pleasures, for Ellen, receiving expectations of fifteen bob a week from hiring out her body, has a premonition of the future which will consist of the oldest profession in the world.

Whilst it wouldn't be difficult to rig up an argument saying that prostitution is an allegory of Burgess's career – Burgess the old tart who never turned down a commission ('I refuse no reasonable offer of work,' he said in 1978, 'and very few unreasonable ones'); and whilst a psychologist might advance the theory that Ellen and Billy are a projection of what Muriel's life could have been like had she survived to live with Joe, had Little Wilson, baby Jackie, been the one to die – the energy and interest of *The Pianoplayers* reside in the nostalgia for olden days and being brought up hard. 'I miss all those things now, I can tell you, and there's no real way of calling them back.' The end-of-the-pier shows, glorious in their tattiness; the spicy food; the big brassy pubs, with singing-rooms and snugs; the cobbled alleys; the sooty streets with trams; the flashing of frilly knickerbockers and the downing of bottled Bass; days when you could guzzle chocs and smoke fifty Woodbines, 'and nobody said it was bad for you'.

middle class – the way Liana is always proudly billed as the *contessa* on his dustjackets shows how ashamed Burgess was of his own origins. Burgess's revenge is to become absurdly swotty – he must have been very trying, a perfect pain in fact, especially as his stepmother it was who bought him a bookcase for his Everymans, collected plays of Bernard Shaw and H. G. Wells novels. As when he commented that 'I sometimes resent my father's failure' to tell him stories about his mother, to fill him in about The Beautiful Belle Burgess, mistaking the silent grief for purposeful indifference or unkindness,* so too he refused to see that Maggie Dwyer and her family – a large clan of greengrocers, poulterers, publicans and plumbers – did offer him love and affection, had he wanted to accept it. There's almost a Jewishness to them (another big contingent in Manchester), in the way that no value is put on openness and emotional honesty (it'll expose you); they are close – closed – yet also there's a lot of boasting and showing off, an ostentation that certainly Burgess shared. The name-changing, the tall tales and reinventions – these characterise people fleeing religious persecution or political repression, and Burgess used to give every indication that the Catholic Emancipation Relief Act of 1829, which enabled Roman Catholics to sit in Parliament and be eligible for all public offices (save Lord Chancellor), had only happened the week before last.† But his hurt

* Burgess knew that his parents had met at the Ardwick Empire, where his father was deputising in the pit band for the regular pianist 'who was down with alcoholic gastritis', according to *This Man and Music*. He also believed that his father had gone to Glasgow, in his capacity as a book-keeper, and had returned with Elizabeth Burgess as his bride. It would be convenient to find a link between the soubrette, Little Wilson's mother, José Collins and Sir Harry Lauder, as the latter pair were at the Theatre Royal, Glasgow, in *Aladdin*, and José Collins played Little Bluebell to illustrate Lauder's song 'I Love a Lassie'. But there is no evidence for this. Nor have I found any Wilson–Burgess marriage certificate in Scotland or England.

As for Elizabeth Burgess's ancestry and birth, working backwards from her death certificate there are two possibilities: that she was born on 20 January 1888, at 32 Heaton Street, Ardwick, near the theatre, in the district of Chorlton, Manchester, the daughter of John Burgess, a velvet embosser (presumably something in the textile trade), and Emma Burgess, formerly Acton; or else she was born on 15 July 1888, at 29 Walton Street, St George, Manchester, the daughter of David Burgess, a general labourer, and Harriet Burgess, formerly Wilson – coincidentally. Poignantly, both births were registered by the mothers, who both signed the document with an X ('The mark of Emma Burgess,' 'The mark of Harriet Burgess'). To go from illiteracy like that to Burgess's own stupefying hyper-literacy – *delabialisation*, *supersessive*, *intervallar*, *anapaestic* – is somehow searing.

† Penal laws against Catholics were repealed towards the end of the eighteenth century. They could purchase freehold land and intermarry with Protestants, teach and practise law, from 1792. I wish somebody had stood up to Burgess, when he whinged about persecution, and challenged him about the St Bartholomew massacre of Protestants in France in 1572, the war with Spain in the later sixteenth century, and the 1605 Gunpowder Plot.

pride won't allow him a happy existence. He is convinced he is unwanted, and slinks off to his attic, 'an annexe for junk and a stepson'. It wasn't as lonely as all that, however, under the eaves. Phyllis Cornthwaite and Glynis from Wales, the live-in maids, who also slept in the loft, introduced him to sex – unless that's another of his tall tales. We'll never ascertain the truth at this distance. Glynis also set fire to the laundry rack. Perhaps she and Burgess had been applying too much friction to his crystal set.

He's taken on holiday to Blackpool – on the beach he reads Ibsen and Schopenhauer and Kant's *Critique of Pure Reason* 'in a bad translation'; he is taken to London, and they stay at the Strand Palace Hotel, and whilst Maggie fusses with her dentures, her stepson sketches musical settings for the songs in *Sweeney Agonistes* ('I recorded these in Milan in 1981'); they go to Scarborough and Charles Laughton is on duty as a waiter in the hotel restaurant – which must be news to Simon Callow, Laughton's biographer, who'd placed his subject in the West End by the late twenties. In Wales, they wave to David Lloyd George on a steamer off Anglesey. This was not, then, a neglectful, poverty-stricken time and, the tenancy of the Golden Eagle relinquished by 1924, the Wilsons founded and developed a tobacconist and off-licence business, with properties at 21 Princess Road (telephone Moss Side 1274), 261 Moss Lane East, 47 Princess Road and 2 Leabrook Road, Fallowfield* – a district where, according to Burgess, 'Every father . . . shagged his daughters on the corner of the kitchen table at Saturday throwing-out time. Incest that was called.' No doubt he was being fanciful. Agnes, one of Maggie's grown-up daughters, married Jack Tollitt, from Chorlton-on-Medlock. They had two children, Sheila and Dan. Madge, Burgess's other stepsister, married Clifford Kemp, of Collyhurst, and they had a son called David. (Burgess never forgave Clifford Kemp for calling Shakespeare 'a flat-footed highbrow'.) Dwyers, Tollitts, Kemps and Wilsons lived and worked amongst the thin reek of Gold Flake, Players and Woodbines. They did well out of the thirties because even in an economic slump drinking and boozing still went on – the wholesale tobacco store and the retail beer, wine and spirits shop trade flourished. Though Burgess wouldn't want to admit it, this paid for his education. It was his means of subsistence. It paid for violin lessons at Mr Bradshaw's School of Music on Moss Lane East, as a child, Xaverian College, in Rusholme Park, as a teenager, and Manchester University, later on. He went up (or took the tram across town) in October 1937. His father died on 18 April the

* Joseph Wilson, however, died at 5 Leighbrook Road, Withington – Burgess has slightly misremembered the address.

following year, aged fifty-five. (1) Cardiac Failure, (2) Pleurisy, (3) Influenza, certified by F. S. Catto, M.B. Joseph Wilson was intestate and left nothing except his bowling woods, a pair of binoculars and a fountain pen. In his memoirs, Burgess again adopts the flat comic voice that fails to be funny. The room fills up with Dwyers, Kemps, Tollitts and Wilsons and the devout death-bed scene, with everybody kneeling and praying, is undercut when his father mutters, 'What does bloody God think he's bloody playing at?', shits himself, and drops off the twig. Looking upon 'the husk with its collapsed sphincters',* Burgess composes a poem: '. . . when I saw his end was near/My brain was freer/And scrawled a cancellation then/of all the accidents of birth.' It is a moment of liberation – and of intense loneliness. Burgess was to be a man related to no one except himself. He'd appraise himself, watch himself go by – and all he wanted from the world was total surrender. (On another occasion he said his father's last words were: 'Bugger the priest. Give me a pint of draught Bass.'†) Maggie moved back to 47 Princess Road, to be with the Tollitts. Jack Tollitt kept the shops open all hours and 'I grew frightened of him,' Burgess claimed – as if he's having to confront Mr Murdstone. Little Wilson is now 'the orphaned wraith on the periphery', and has to share a room with young Dan (b. 1927), who grew up to become a travel agent. Burgess's father appears in dreams and, as a revenant at a Hallé Concert of Beethoven's 'Eroica', waves to his son and vanishes. The first words he'd spoken to baby Johnny had been 'He may be a new Napoleon.'

* Death-bed realities, described with the objectivity of a hospice nurse, occur in *The Right to an Answer*. 'And your father is now in his coffin, you say, and the coffin is next door in the next room? Ah, well, that is a chapter closed. And tonight you resume your old bed, which, by fortunate chance, has now clean sheets on it, and your father's bed is not for use, it bearing on its mattress marks of the dead and the incontinence of the dead.' In his review of *The Oxford Book of Death*, edited by D. J. Enright (in the *TLS*, 6 May 1983), Burgess returned to the fascinating topic of the physical reality of the hour of death, when subject becomes object: '. . . the real trouble about dying . . . is fighting for breath and losing, and leaving behind a body which discharges its excrements with abandon and makes death disgusting rather than ennobling'. Further on in the article, he repeats himself: 'We expect to feel guilty, because we, the children, are being made room for, but we do not expect to feel disgusted. The desperate asthma, the rattle, the rictus are so mechanical and depersonalizing, and the collapse of the excretory system, with its aftermath of a ruined mattress waiting days for the garbage cart, is a sub-Rabelaisian joke in very bad taste.'

† Burgess's death-bed verses are also Enderby's for his father, in *Enderby Outside*. We are told that they come from a privately printed volume called *Independence Day*:

> So when I knew his end was near
> My mind was freer
> And snapped its thumb and finger then
> At the irrelevance of birth . . .

Lancashire Catholicism is a subject in itself,* yet it is not too facile to state that the religion took people in one of two directions: it could be liberal-minded and embrace the music hall, the acting profession and entertainment – a social hinterland of boarding-houses, drinking and stage names; or else it could be doctrinaire and puritanical. Burgess himself would embody both extremes, being conservative and radical, priggish and insubordinate. (He never got the hang of young people and would bridle and bristle at long hair and pop music like a beef-faced retired colonel in Angmering-on-Sea.) The Wilsons, however, represented indulgence, in his view. Burgess's paternal grandfather, another Jack Wilson, kept a pub in north-east Manchester full of piglets and songbirds called the Derby Inn. His wife, Mary Ann Finnegan, from Tipperary originally, presided over a witch's kitchen that produced cannibalistic-sounding rice puddings with thick brown skins and black puddings bursting with blood. Newspapers were a source of wonder to the couple. Were the necrology columns reportage or a premonition? Were the events recorded as having happened in the wide world, involving Prussians and Russians, fact or fiction? Burgess once had an idea to publish a novel in the format of a newspaper – a dying man would see the unfolded *Times* on his bed and he'd 'deliriously trace all his past life as though it were the contents, news items, editorials, crossword puzzle, everything'. (Was he pre-empted in that kind of palaver by B. S. Johnson?) It's an interesting way of constructing a biography, too – and how amazed these barely literate, humble people would have been to see the coverage given to their grandson at his death. 'Anthony Burgess, the polymath, dies at 76,' said the *Daily Telegraph* on the front page, on 26 November 1993. 'Burgess was blessed with a quick and restless mind, coupled with an immense capacity for work.' *The Times* gave his death front-page attention, a huge obituary and a leader: 'Literature has lost a great moralist.' Burgess may have hated Maggie Dwyer for her ignorance and uncouthness, for exposing him to philistinism and misery, but he was proud of George Patrick Dwyer, who ended as the Catholic Archbishop of Birmingham.† 'I don't quite know how George and I were related,' he said

* Interested readers should consult Steven Fielding's *Class and Ethnicity: Irish Catholics in England 1880–1939* (1993), in which the author draws on Manchester/Salford for his examples; *Irish Migrants in Modern Britain 1750–1922* by Donald M. MacRaild (1999); *The Irish in Britain 1815–1939* by S. Gilley and R. Swift (1989); *The Irish Community in Britain* by C. Lloyd (1995); and 'The Irish in Nineteenth Century Britain: Problems of Integration' by M. O. Tuathaigh, in *Transactions of the Royal Historical Society* (1981).

† I am grateful to the Birmingham Archdiocesan Archives, Cathedral House, St Chad's, for the following information:

in 1989. 'My Irish stepmother was his aunt, which made him a kind of step-cousin.' George chain-smoked, using a special holder found in Rome, which kept nicotine stains off the fingers that would celebrate the Eucharist. It snowed in his presbytery of meat and drink. 'Here I shall leave my bones,' he said at the celebratory dinner after his Birmingham enthronement, 'if anyone can find them.' He was a Pickwickian figure, whom Burgess remembers helping to choose the Christmas turkey for family parties. He enjoyed the poetry of Baudelaire, knew his Hopkins, and during the fuss about *A Clockwork Orange*, 'he was quick to defend it as a moral study that was not scared of looking evil in the eye'. Fat, gourmandising, full of himself, he may be glimpsed as Carlo, the ebullient, corpulent prelate in *Earthly Powers* who is revealed, in the final reel, to be an orphan of unknown parentage – precisely Burgess's own fantasy; as Carlo snarls to Toomey:

> No friends. No brothers, no sisters, no father, no mother. Like Oedipus, you remember . . . If God can accept loneliness, so can his servant. I don't want any of you . . . I don't want you. You're a hindrance . . . I elect loneliness . . .

If George Dwyer, 'spouting in a Lancashire accent', was a physical expression of Catholicism in the tradition of Rabelais, then the Tollitts were narrower, more buttoned-up. It was the Tollitts who were exemplars of industry and spiritual discipline, the Princess Road house congested with pictures of the Pope and hagiographs of the Sacred Heart, the Mater Dolorosa, St Anthony and John the Baptist. Jack Tollitt, 'a fierce and pedantic Catholic', put his stepbrother-in-law to the task of delivering cartons

The Most Reverend George Patrick Dwyer, D.D., Ph.D., B.A., Archbishop of Birmingham, was born on September 25th 1908, in Manchester. He went to school at St Bede's College in Manchester and prepared for the priesthood at the Venerable English College in Rome, being ordained on November 1st 1932. He stayed on in Rome to complete his Doctorate in Theology at the Gregorian University. On his return to England he went up to Cambridge University and took an honours degree in Modern Languages. From 1937 to 1947 he was on the teaching staff of his old school, St Bede's. When Father (later Cardinal) Heenan re-founded the Catholic Missionary Society in 1947, he asked his old friend of student days to join him and for the next ten years Father Dwyer visited every part of the country preaching, giving talks, leading retreats, writing for the press and editing the Society's magazine, the *Catholic Gazette*. On the appointment of Father Heenan as Bishop of Leeds in 1951, Father Dwyer became Superior of the Society. In 1957 Father Dwyer succeeded Bishop Heenan in the See of Leeds, being consecrated on September 24th 1957. He was translated to the Archdiocese of Birmingham on October 7th 1965. Since the Second Vatican Council, each Nation has its own Commissions for putting into effect the Conciliar Decrees. Archbishop Dwyer was a member of the National Theological Commission and until his retirement, on September 1st 1981, was Chairman of the National Liturgical Commission. He died on September 17th 1987.

of Swan Vestas to the retail outlets – an odd job you can tell Burgess thinks is beneath him; but what really rankles is the way he has been quite usurped. A stepchild, he has no status in the menage. Jack, who drives a polished Austin Saloon, and who during the war became, like boorish Mr Hodges the grocer in *Dad's Army*, an Air Raid Precautions Warden, 'a pedant about blackouts', edges Burgess out, as Mr Raj edges Denham out of his own home in *The Right to an Answer*. Seemingly deferential and civil, actually Mr Raj is formidable and decidedly creepy. The novel was written after Burgess's return from the East, when he felt a stranger now in England; but the idea that he was an outsider reached much further back, to the time when the fact that he was alive at all was a source of jealousy and mistrust. Mr Raj believes Negroes to be an inferior species – and Burgess was convinced his stepfamily considered him a lesser breed, too.

The result of being raised by a family not quite his own – who were a little more than kin and less than kind – who took him in (as he maintained) on sufferance, was that he didn't think he was born to be the same as other people. At Xaverian College, a gloomy place covered with wet ivy, where lots of foreign (Jewish) pupils were taught by madmen (i.e. Jesuits who couldn't desist from dishing out canings and beatings), he was the teachers' pet ('I wish I had three hundred John Wilsons,' wrote Brother Martin in a report), who read *Don Quixote* four times, wrote a verse play about Luther, learned Hopkins by heart, composed a three-hundred-page symphony ('the Luftwaffe, in the name of Beethoven, was probably right to destroy it in 1941'), and revised for the Higher School Certificate, to get to university as a scholarship. Step-cousin George, then a priest teaching French at St Bede's College, Manchester, persuaded Maggie, 'who did not believe in higher education', to allow Burgess to study for his matriculation. ('George put her right.') He'd have liked to have read for a music degree, which required preliminary qualifications in Latin – a subject which the great linguist always flunked, despite a facility for translating the lyrics from Fred Astaire musicals into Ciceronian prose.* He believed that one of his perfect papers must have been mislaid; when, at Manchester, he fails Latin again, it was because the professor had sponsored the production of a Euripides play Burgess had criticised in a student magazine. So he studies English – and he was never to stop moving words around. His history is literary history.

* You can't help but admire the panache of the special acknowledgement to 'the Graeco-Latin edition of the New Testament published in Graz and furnished with an apparatus-criticus by Augustinus Merk, S. J.', which is to be found at the end of *The Kingdom of the Wicked*. Thurber couldn't have topped it.

11

Sex and Violence 1938–46

What if you are *not* shaped by your early years? That's what Burgess was determined to set out to prove ('I had no real upbringing'*); he was self-generated, a triumph of the will, his identity a matter of illusion and conviction. In his memoirs and other autobiographical pieces – fragments of the Burgess myth are scattered throughout his fiction and non-fiction† – he seems outside his own story, an onlooker. He stares at things from a distance – from the high windows of his attics or from the corner where he sits, making no secret of the fact that (a) his stepfamily was unfit to be responsible for him, and (b) from the first, Manchester, with its meat markets and leather trades, breweries and cabbage-sellers, was to be treated as a home no longer. He made himself dispossessed, and peculiar. But the exterior world would always leave him scared and wondering. He didn't like Malta because of its 'philistinism – a fruit of British occupation'; there was also 'far too much philistinism' in Australia, he reported, after opening and spending a 'Writers' Week' in Adelaide. He had hopes for Rome ('the air smells of the anarchic full-life'), yet before long it gets to be 'very wearying', too noisy, the press of the traffic is ruinous to the nervous

* *New York Times Magazine*, 3 November 1968.

† Re. fiction, Enderby has stepmother trouble, writes awful poems, and works on the Shakespeare musical, to no avail, as Burgess did; Toomey lives in Burgess's Malta house and writes the Joyce operetta; *A Vision of Battlements* is Burgess in Gibraltar; *The Worm and the Ring* is Burgess in Banbury Grammar School; *The Long Day Wanes* is Burgess in Malaya; *Devil of a State* is Burgess in Brunei; *The Doctor Is Sick* is Burgess sick; *Honey for the Bears* is Burgess and Lynne in Leningrad; *Beard's Roman Women* is Burgess bereaved; and so on. Re. non-fiction, the Joyce and Shakespeare, Hemingway and Lawrence books are Burgess-on-Burgess books; and even his reviews were sprinkled with Burgessian boasts: *Tunes of Glory* is 'one of the ten best films ever made, said Alfred Hitchcock to me in the lift one day at Claridge's' (*Observer*, 6 October 1985); or 'I possess Josephine Baker's old Gaveau upright piano, long neglected and beyond repair' (*Observer*, 28 January 1990).

system, the Tiber is polluted, and the air unbreathable – it is a dying city, and also one 'dim on literary excitement'. He goes to New York, to teach at City College – and that's wrong. He despises the food and he hates the students, feeling 'oppressed' by their jeans and espadrilles. The longer he spends abroad, the more he becomes a caricature of provincial Englishness – pretending not to understand slang, disliking the greeting *Hi!* ('too casual'), an 'aged outsider'; and if he thought he was resembling Evelyn Waugh, as an ironic moralist and sophisticated satirist of modern times, the effect is more of Alf Garnett, as played by Warren Mitchell: 'a sort of broken Coriolanus, a reviled or mocked misfit', according to Burgess, who didn't appear to grasp that *Till Death Us Do Part* was a comedy.* Going on about the layabout young, with their long hair and leather jackets, complaining about the cult of drugs ('that promotes an instant Xanadu'), photographers, Beatles-type groups, 'grinning TV pop-show personalities', models like Twiggy, mini-skirts, the replacement of half-crowns, florins and shillings, bobs and tanners by decimal coinage, being called *love* 'by the half-literates of the theatre', loathing the 'ghetto language' of blacks, who should be taught to speak good English, and the Italianness of Italians ('Play "Rule Britannia"!' he yelled at the military band in the Piazza Santa Cecilia), Burgess is (like Alf Garnett) a bigot and a buffoon and at the other end of the scale from endearing. The taste for indulging in mean and selfish ranting predetermines that if, for example, Burgess is aboard ship, the only way he can avoid his fellow passengers, 'a somewhat philistine gang' of (he believes) Mafia chieftains and New York Jews, is to slope off grumpily to the First Class lounge bar and compose a sonata for a harmonica. Callian, in Provence, at least had a parking space for the Bedford Dormobile, and Lugano, in Switzerland, was so boring there was nothing to do except write, for 'nobody comes to stay with us' – hardly a surprise. As for Monte Carlo, 'I don't go out,' he said in 1989. 'I don't have any friends here. I used to be a friend of Princess Grace, but she's dead now.' As ever, he was encircled by the ill-bred and by parvenus: 'Yes, Michael York is around the corner. Ringo Starr is somewhere, and that Swedish tennis fellow, Borg, runs a shop . . . But they're a philistine lot mostly.'

* Burgess was trying to describe Johnny Speight's *Till Death Us Do Part* to the readers of *The Hudson Review* (spring 1967). Not only does he not divulge that it is a comedy show (which became *All in the Family* when reconceived in the States, with Carroll O'Connor as the pig-headed Archie Bunker), he omitted to mention Alf's racism – he wants to ship out the immigrants – his snobbery and his swearing. (He's coarse and unattractive, as Geoffrey Grigson might say.) My other examples of Burgess's liverishness in this paragraph also all come from American journals – principally *The American Scholar*, 1967–73.

All people ever do is accord him disrespect. 'Nobody has ever heard of me,' he mutters in exasperation. Being against the young and the old, he's also not keen on academics or fellow authors, such as the representative Margaret Drabble, 'content to plough a traditional and parochial furrow'; yet nor is he, despite his exiles, truly international, like Beckett and Borges. He is uncomfortable with the English establishment; and abroad he falls out with the natives. He never learned to relax. He hates staying put, though if he travels he is plunged into a maelstrom of lost documents, missed connections, and fractious and exasperating officials out to get him. He hates his body, which plays tricks on him with gum boils, dyspepsia and bronchitis, which he treats with an anal pessary. I think he hated being a human being – and was only to be happy inside his head. 'Books are heavenly,' wrote Marlowe. 'Lines, circles, letters, and characters: Ay, these are those that Faustus most desires' – Burgess too. When Enderby is told that literature is about the emotions, he retorts, 'Oh very much no. Oh very very very much no and no again. Poetry is made out of words.' Of course it isn't – poetry and art are manufactured from what Macbeth calls 'the current strong, obscure and deep,/The central stream of what we feel indeed' – which is what language is called upon to represent; but this is an interesting indication of how Burgess saw his job, and why his work often sounds like a translation – not quite alive. The voice of the novels, the tone of the journalism: it is much the same – slabs of prose, like a stone-by-stone copy of an ancient edifice, a monument to the author's own knowledgeableness and exaggerated behaviour. His work is fake-old (*Nothing Like the Sun*), fake-grand (*Earthly Powers*), like a Victorian Gothick castle or railway station. It is an industrial process, too; he's an industrialised writer, clocking in and drinking three pints of strong tea, working all day, cooking in the evening. 'One day,' said William Morris, 'we shall win back art to our daily labour'; and, initially at least, Burgess liked Rome because 'art is part of daily life. One makes one's statues or poems or books as one bakes bread or mends shoes.' He didn't mind the noisy square where he lived, either, because it was the noise of beavering: 'I rather liked the noise; it was the noise of men at work, men making fake antique furniture or genuine bedsteads. I thought that I was part of the activity and that my work was somehow as useful as theirs.' Eventually, he listened to money singing, and the chink of coins being counted in Monte Carlo was to prove a more beguiling music to his ears.

Like bricks, which you can learn to lay, games you can learn to win, or confidence tricks one can learn to pull off, words one can learn to use.

One of the benefits of the neologisms in *A Clockwork Orange*, he claimed, was that by the end of it the reader 'would be brainwashed into learning minimal Russian';* and when challenged about his rococo lexicon – *desquamated*, *logomachy*, *stichomythia* – he was unrepentant. His far-fetched language was part of his concept of improving yourself: 'If my books are not read, it's because their vocabulary is too big, and people don't like using dictionaries when they are reading novels. I don't give a damn.' To which the only possible reasonable response is *pig's arse*. He couldn't sincerely have believed he was educating us with those big words of his. ('Incidentally,' mused Jeffrey Bernard, 'I have been wondering why Anthony Burgess will insist on using the word "micturate". I conclude that he is an English language swank. Whether it is correct or not is neither here nor there. What's wrong with "piss"?') Though words were his occupation, his compulsion, the pointless unintelligibility is there to block us off. And though his pedagogical mannerisms were profuse – look at the number of textbooks he wrote, beginning with *The Young Fiddler's Tunebook* (unpublished) in 1947 – there's a distinct limit to his approachability. Despite his exuberant nature and the actorish showing-off in front of the Sixth Form effects, he deploys language and literature to preserve his loneliness and arrogance. Through books and music – and his books are musical: patterned, shaped, carefully worked out, having taken the measure of their themes and counter-themes exactly – he tried to outsoar the forces of environment and family life and connect himself, instead, to a family tree of famous authors: Shakespeare, Hopkins, Joyce, Lawrence, and so on. He wants us to define him by what he has read – which appeared to be everything. (He read himself into insanity – as Nabokov said of Don Quixote.) Literature embodies 'all the memories of the world', to use Alain Resnais' phrase about the Bibliothèque Nationale in Paris; and Burgess was spellbound by questions of lineage and identity, by links and allusions – Enderby has his associations with James Hogg; in *Nothing Like the Sun*, Shakespeare's impregnated Dark Lady returns to the Far East and, as the narrator ('a character called Mr Burgess . . .

* *Minimal* is the word. Robert O. Evans, from the University of Kentucky, in 'Nadsat: The Argot and its Implications in Anthony Burgess's *A Clockwork Orange*' (*Journal of Modern Literature*, vol. 1, 1971), says that though the roots of Burgess's borrowings are 'mostly Slavic', the bulk of the Russian is introduced in the first fifteen pages, and then repeated and repeated (*droogs*, *rassodocks*, *vesches*, *horrorshow*, *veck*, *devotchkas*, *viddy*, etc.) until the words become familiar. Evans estimates there are only about fifty Russian derivations, which constitutes but three per cent of the text. The rest is rhyming slang, puns or pure verbiage.

progressively drunker and drunker on Chinese rice spirit') explains, 'He sent his blood out there. I am of his blood . . .'; *MF* is about incest as the mad dream of the dispossessed: no family one minute, deep enmeshment in one's family the next; *Abba Abba*, the very title referring both to the rhyme scheme of a sonnet and to the Hebrew for father (and one of Christ's last words on the cross), rigs up a genealogy to join Keats and Belli's friend Giovanni Gulielmi, i.e. an eighteenth-century John Wilson, to singers, barmaids and meat-market clerks in Manchester; the private struggles of Carlo, in *Earthly Powers*, are to do with his heredity; the religious trilogy, *Moses: A Narrative*, *Man of Nazareth* and *The Kingdom of the Wicked*, which deals with the Acts of the Apostles, particularly Saul's transformation into Paul, concerns foundlings, changelings and 'God's new pretty tricks in the way of making children without fleshly coupling . . . You will be talking next of spiritual parenthood'; the tales that constitute *The End of the World News* celebrate the 'transcendence of our dungy origins': psychologically, with Freud, ideologically, with Trotsky, and physically, with the invention of the space rocket; and *Byrne*, the long poem composed on his death-bed and published two years after he'd cooled, is named for Burgess's stepmother's ne'er-do-well brother, Jim Byrne, who made a single fleeting appearance in Manchester to announce, in September 1939, that there'll be no war, and quotes Joyce (without acknowledgement) to the effect that 'paternity was but a legal fiction' and argues that 'True fatherhood's a thing you cannot prove.'*

Whilst Burgess was a disciple of Joyce – all this rebuttal of actual home and family is the obnoxious Stephen Dedalus wanting to create a fanciful world of his own outside Ireland – Burgess himself was not a Modernist. He's curiously old-fashioned (the dominie with his grammar and spelling tests) and the morals and meanings of his work are always apparent, which they aren't in *Ulysses*, despite the technical trickeries. He is steeped in Joyce, he defers to Joyce, articles and whole books on Joyce poured forth, but he wasn't like Joyce, try as he might – e.g. by making Enderby a cousin of Leopold Bloom, disclosed composing poetry on the lavatory, or by deriving his Shakespeare theories from Stephen's discussions with the egg-heads in the National Library, where they prove 'by algebra that Hamlet's grandson is Shakespeare's grandfather and that he himself is the

* In *Ulysses*, the riddle is expressed thus: 'Well: if the father who has not a son be not a father can the son who has not a father be a son?' Burgess quotes the passage in *Here Comes Everybody* (p. 131) and glosses it as meaning an 'image of that special paternity of the imagination . . . defined in terms of what it is not'.

ghost of his own father', or by using Virgil in *A Vision of Battlements* like Joyce used Homer as a structure for his day out in Dublin.* And yet why isn't he the Joycean? Because Burgess isn't interested in what other people are like. His own consciousness and will power are all there is. Enderby, straining at stool in Seville, drafts a verse which is pertinent here:

> Time and the town go round like a river,
> But Darwin thinks in a line that's straight.
> A sort of selection goes on for ever,
> But no new species originate.

Ends are fused with their beginnings (the subtitle of *The Clockwork Testament* is *Enderby's End*), the circle is closed, and nothing much that's new is going to happen – as how could it with this species of only one member? Going round and round, shooting off into space – the meaning is the same: Burgess is the one who's fit to survive – yet at the cost of being derivative and monotonous. The dilemmas of Robert Loo, in *Beds in the East*, are played again, in *Earthly Powers*, when Domenico Campanati half-deliberately fails as a serious classical musician to earn a fortune knocking off film scores; Catholic apostasy and guilt beset every Burgess hero, without exception; *Nothing Like the Sun* is retold as the text for the picture book *Shakespeare* (reprinted in 1996 without the illustrations); *Oedipus the King* and *Blooms of Dublin* are inside *Earthly Powers*; *The Pianoplayers* and *This Man and Music* contain the Manchester scenes of *Little Wilson and Big God*; *Language Made Plain*, hastily partly altered, was passed off as a big new study of language, *A Mouthful of*

* *Ulysses* has 'meant more to me, as a writer and as a private person, than I can well hope to express', he wrote in the *Observer Magazine* (20 May 1979). 'To call it my favourite novel is, I see, shamefully inept. It is the work I have to measure myself hopelessly against each time I sit down to write fiction.' Three years later, on 31 January 1982, he told the same newspaper: 'I have to approach [Joyce] not merely as a reader or as a fellow writer working, to some extent, in his shadow, but as one who, while still a boy, recognized a temperamental kinship.' Which is to be taken to mean a gravitation towards the Joyce who was educated by Jesuits at Clongowes Wood College in Kildare and Belvedere College in Dublin (= Burgess at Bishop Bilsborrow Memorial Elementary School and Xaverian College); whose mother succumbed to a terminal illness; who had a feckless father (though Joseph Wilson held down his book-keeping job without complaint); who was suffused with religious guilt; who was a musician; whose modes of attack were 'silence, exile, and cunning'; who wandered Europe, ending up in Switzerland (where he died in 1941); and whose work is full of polyglot puns. 'Like James Joyce,' said Burgess grandly (*Observer*, 5 May 1985), 'I heard the call of art.' I don't think we'd have found Joyce, however, churning out why-oh-why pious pieces for the *Daily Mail* on football hooliganism or appearing live on a late-night LBC phone-in radio show to take a call from Sonia of Hendon. But the Nora Barnacle = Molly Bloom = Lynne = Liana formula is about right.

Air[*]. (Chapter headings in the former, 'Piercing the Iron Curtain', for instance, or 'The Breaking of Babel', become in the latter 'The Russians Are Coming' and 'Can Babel Be Unbuilt?') 'Good work,' I recall hearing him say more than once, referring to the left-overs from a script that he'd cobbled into one of his religious novels, 'should not be wasted' – and nobody could quibble at the cunning way he recycled his own bitter juice. 'Produce! Produce!' thundered Carlyle, invoking the Gospel of St John. 'Were it but the pitifullest infinitesimal fraction of the product, produce it in God's name . . . Whatsoever thy hand findeth to do, do it with thy whole might. Work while it is called today; for the Night cometh wherein no man can work . . .'

Industrialisation, for Burgess, however, was not merely a way of celebrating God; it was a way of challenging him. In *Here Comes Everybody*, he explains that: 'The fundamental purpose of any work of art is to impose order on the chaos of life as it comes to us; in imparting a vision of order the artist is doing what the religious teacher also does . . . But the religious teacher's revelation is less a creation than a discovery, whereas the artist feels that – God rather than God's servant – he is the author of order.' Order, however, will depend upon the kinds of dream their author has; what is at stake is the quality of his mind. Thus, in Burgess, first, the nervous prevarication between high and low art – and his jealousy of Graham Greene ('We do not expect, as with Giuseppe Verdi, a new direction in Mr Greene's old age; we expect, and we get, a concise summation of the characteristic virtues'), Umberto Eco ('Read this book and you will never again have to wonder how an Italian monastery functioned in the Fourteenth Century') and John le Carré ('Admirers of John the Square will find here what they have learnt to expect and to admire'), who achieved the bestsellerdom and an audience which Burgess craved and was denied. What really mattered to him, therefore, wasn't merely the battle between popularism and the recondite, but status. There again, as William Morris pointed out, badness, whether aesthetic or moral, may be caused by the lazy pleasures afforded by careless wealth. The jukebox in the Malayan jungle and Robert Loo's abandonment of his promise, the films made from Enderby and Hopkins' poetry, the lending-library fiction

[*] Burgess's disquisitions of language had their first outing under the name of John Burgess Wilson in 1964. Essays published in *Encounter* – 'Powers That Be' (January 1965), 'The Great Vowel Shift and All That' (May 1966), 'Making de White Boss Frown' (July 1966), 'English as in America' (February 1967), 'Partridge in a Word Tree' (July 1969) and 'Language as Movement' (January 1970) – were incorporated in a revised edition of *Language Made Plain*, published in 1975.

of Toomey: these would tie in with Morris's argument that 'Nothing should be made of man's labour which is not worth making; or which must be made by labour degrading to the makers.' Remember Burgess in his motel rooms typing a James Bond script or in the back of his Bedford Dormobile hammering out another draft of the *Jesus of Nazareth* screenplay for Lew Grade, whom he denounced (whilst pocketing the shillings) as 'very ignorant, incredible the depth of it, but gets things done'? Secondly, Burgess's idea of order, and his mental make-up, is signified by his fancy for the discipline and formality of grammar and linguistics. Language, in Burgess, creates the content. His information about his ancestors is divulged in terms of how they spoke and sounded, and by the Lancashire hotpot they ate: speaking and swallowing. And of course he can't mention Manchester speech without having a go at the 'centralizing linguistic culture' of London and the south, which ironed out regional dialects – yet where did his own sonic boom come from? Elocution lessons? 'We provincials have suffered in forcing ourselves to conform,' he announced in 1987, writing from 44 rue Grimaldi, Monaco. One of Burgess's biggest inadvertent jokes was to call a book *Language Made Plain*, because he makes it complicated, in my view. When he talks about substituting 'an alveolar nasal for a velar one' or of 'palatizing his unvoiced alveolar fricatives', I haven't a clue what he means – except that he is showing off and being boring. He can't have friends or cronies at school – they have to be persons 'true to the etymology *khronios*'; even as a hungry baby he was like the vociferously verbose Leonard Sachs, compère of *The Good Old Days*, the music-hall show broadcast from the City Varieties, Leeds. Instead of crying for more milk, it's a question of 'the lactal ducts never refilling fast enough'. With Lynne dead in her hospital bed at the Central Middlesex, all he can think about is that the origin of the word *acites*, one of her symptoms (a distension of the abdomen), is the Greek *askos*, a wineskin, and that one of her last acts had been to rebuke a Singapore nurse in fluent Mandarin Chinese, 'astonishing me with a sleeping knowledge of the language I never knew she had'.

Clamour and confusion are concealed by language, and for Burgess living details become a literary process. He reminds me, therefore, less of any modern (or Modernist) artist, where the many-sidedness of existence is acknowledged and presented in a multitude of experimental ways, than of a late Victorian or Edwardian man of letters – his equivalent in painting being William Powell Frith, whose vast, thronging canvases of Ramsgate Sands, Derby Day or railway-station platforms and booking halls prompted Wilde to enquire innocently whether it was really all done by hand? Such, too, are Burgess's modes of exaggeration – the bejewelled vocabulary, the polishings of his prose – the effect, though picturesque, is that the books are assembled by clockwork. His love of words is robotic.

Who the goddess of love is we well know (in Greek, *aphrodiastikos* means 'lecherous', *aphrodiazein*, 'to copulate'). The god of language was Hermes (or 'the rogue god Mercury' as Burgess calls him), often represented in Classical statuary as a priapus. In many parts of Greece (Peloponnese, Argos, Megalopolis, Kyllene), he and Aphrodite were worshipped together. They certainly commingle in Burgess, who even talks of taking his dictionaries, like mistresses, to bed. *Homage to Qwert Yuiop* contains several dozen fervid pieces on dictionaries and sundry encyclopaedia: a veritable seraglio. Burgess always kept on his desk the *OED*, the *American Heritage Dictionary*, a 1926 Webster, plus works on slang, etymology, quotation, euphemism, anecdotes and Yiddish, the effect of which touched his every sentence. *A Malayan Trilogy* is full of South-East Asian tongues. *The Doctor Is Sick* is about a phonetics expert and the language of the criminal underworld. *Abba Abba* makes John Keats a pioneering philologist. *Honey for the Bears* plays games with Cyrillic script, as Paul Hussey becomes Pavel Ivanovitch Gussey. (The flyleaf of Burgess's copy of Waldemar Schapiro's *Russian Gem Dictionary* [1959] is inscribed 'Ivan Vilson' in perfect Cyrillic.) And the neologisms in *A Clockwork Orange* derive from the cockney dialect upon a Russian base. *Baboochka* is 'old woman', *droog* is 'friend', *pretty polly* is 'money'. To write the novelisation and script for Zeffirelli's *Jesus of Nazareth*, Burgess went back to Greek and Hebrew editions of the Gospel, discovering a Bible rife with puns. The famous phrase about humped beasts and needles' eyes is a confusion of *kamilon* (rope) with *kamelon* (camel). On the cross, Jesus did not call out *Eli, eli, lama Sabacthani*, but *Elie, elie* . . . 'This is the vocative of *helios* in its demotic unaspirated form. He was calling on the sun.' In Amos, Chapter 8, verse ii, Burgess glosses 'a basket of summer fruit becomes a portent of Israel's end' by informing us that in the original 'basket' is *qais* and 'the end' is *qes*. A play on words, in other words. *Harlot* to Chaucer meant 'maid-servant', *knave* once meant 'young man' (the German *knabe*), *apricot* comes from Arabic *al-precoq* which comes from Latin's *praecox*, or early fruit. Such snaps, crackles and pops of information were put to use in *Quest for Fire*, a film about Stone Age man, directed by Jean-Jacques Annaud, in 1981. It was based on the novel *La Guerre du Feu*, written by J. H. Rosny-Aîné in 1909 and first published in 1911.* Burgess devised a prehistoric creole, or a new language patched out of existing ones (*crioulo* is Portuguese for 'a slave born in the master's household'), by ransacking his grammars. To make a word, he says, 'begin with a lip sound, continue with a back vowel, end with another lip sound'. In the film, *dondr-dondr* (a Chinese duplication from the Greek for tree) means 'a forest'; a stag is *tirdondr* (German for deer, *Tir*, with the antlered branches). Juggling, somehow, Japanese and Russian, *muuv* emerges as the word for 'breast'.

Could he conceivably have been taking the piss? Who did Burgess think he was being? James Murray? Murray, 'a godfearing teetotal non-smoking philoprogenitive bizarrely polymath dominie', was the editor of the *Oxford English Dictionary* – a great project which, by scientifically classifying the exfoliations of language, the evolution and pedigree of words, is related to Victorian biology and the work of Charles Darwin. Murray learned new lingos by translating the Bible (for instance, a Chinese Book of Genesis); and he was intrigued by dialects, those remnants of ancient tongues (Anglo-Saxon, Gaelic, Cornish, Welsh) which in his day were still spoken in remote regions, surviving like Romantic ruins. And the second wordsmith Burgess wrote articles on is George Borrow, a lackadaisical genius, in contrast to Murray, who was so formal he wore his doctoral cap even at family meals. Yet for all his sloppy manner (he was a supertramp happier living with gypsies than with gentry), Borrow knew hundreds of languages, attending the Great Exhibition of 1851 to be seen 'yapping away in Armenian and Turkish and Manchu'. Burgess himself, having spoken Anglo-Saxon with Borges and read *Don Quixote* in Catalan, by 1989 was ready to learn Japanese ('it takes me a week to learn one phrase. That can't be right'). He wanted to be able to startle the Sons of Nippon, whom he kept running across in London or New York hotels, with the inscrutable information that *ringo wa ume yori yasui desu*: apples are cheaper than plums. He was also brushing up his Hebrew and encouraging Liana to learn Arabic. 'Soon,' he announced, 'we'll be able to read the

* J. H. Rosny-Aîné, the pseudonym of Joseph Henri Boëx, was born in Belgium on 17 February 1856 and died on 15 February 1940. He seems rather a Burgessy figure, publishing one hundred and seven novels under his own steam and a further forty in collaboration with his brother, Séraphin Justin Francois Boëx, who died in 1948. Titles include *L'Immolation* (1887), *L'Impérieuse Bonté* (1905), *L'Appel au Bonheur* (1919) and *La Vie Amoureuse de Balzac* (1930).

Quest for Fire ('The future began 80,000 years ago'), with locations in Europe, Iceland, America, Canada and Kenya, took four years to shoot. The costumes – animal pelts daubed with mud – amazingly won an Academy Award.

Koran in the original to see if Salman Rushdie is mentioned by name. On the whole, though, I suspect the Koran'll be a bore in any language.'*

Murray (1837–1915) and bohemian Borrow (1803–81) are clues to an understanding of Burgess. Despite his fluency in Joyce's life and work, his knowledge of Pound, Eliot and Lawrence, his omniscience about contemporary fiction (*The Novel Now* was thrice revised), he is not himself, ultimately, a modern writer. As a displaced craftsman from the nineteenth century, he is the very *last* Edwardian man of letters. His essay collections express enthusiasm for H. G. Wells – who is the 'patron saint of all who scribble fast for a living, of all guttersnipes and counterjumpers who make the literary grade', especially those born on 25 February 1917 at 91 Carisbrook Road, Harpurhey, Manchester.† Wells's *The Outline of History* was given to Burgess as a boy and he grew up absorbing Mr Polly's philosophy that 'Human history becomes more and more a race between education and catastrophe.' The mad logic of G. K. Chesterton (whom he heard on the radio in 1936 saying, 'They talk about things being as dull as ditchwater. For my part, I always think of ditchwater as teeming with quiet fun,' and whose *Autobiography* Burgess once introduced‡), his convivial religiosity, was also much admired – though not by

* Burgess hated Rushdie, though not for the usual reasons. He believed that *The Satanic Verses* was deliberately inflammatory. 'I think he may have been encouraged to write a scandalous book by his publishers . . . Let's put it this way – I don't think his publishers were displeased' – i.e. by the sales figures. But that could be overlooked. What really rankled was that, when Burgess appeared with Rushdie on a television show, they were made-up and ready to go, 'then he insisted on having a haircut. A free one. I didn't like that.' If only Burgess had thought of that scam first! (Though it would have been a brave beautician who'd rethink that rug.)

† '"Sesquippledan," he would say. "Sesquippledan verboojuice."' *The History of Mr Polly* (1909) – a half-misquotation of Horace's *sesquipedalia verba*: 'his words a foot and a half long'.

‡ 'The works of Gilbert Keith Chesterton have never lacked praise, but the praise has never lacked qualification,' wrote Burgess in the Introduction to *Autobiography*, in 1969. Chesterton's verbal fluency made him seem wayward and frivolous when being most devout. To a troubled Catholic like Burgess, the unorthodox orthodoxy was beguiling. Instead of wrestling with your immortal soul and being convulsed by guilt and a sense of worthlessness and sin, like Burgess was (or Greene), Chesterton advocated a life of beer and high spirits: 'Drink because you are happy, but never because you are miserable . . . Never drink because you need it, for this is rational drinking, and the way to death and hell. But drink because you do not need it, for this is irrational drinking, and the ancient health of the world' ('Omar and the Sacred Vine', in *Heretics*, 1905). How would that have gone down with Burgess, whose wife died of cirrhosis? His only criticism was that the Chestertonian rude-health-and-happiness business was countermanded by a century that saw the Spanish Civil War and Nazi gas chambers, and that perhaps GKC's sheer innocence was 'a kind of madness' (*Homage to Qwert Yuiop*, p. 324). Chesterton was ignorant of the nature of evil. Nevertheless, in *The Worm and the Ring*, Howarth is an outrage to

many now except Burgess. 'The trouble with Chesterton,' he said presciently, 'is that he is not Kafka' – though maybe Lewis Carroll or Sir William Schwenk Gilbert are? Burgess admired Carroll's business acumen (he 'worked his publishers hard'), the riddles and games he played with his name ('He Latinised Lutwidge to Ludovicus or Lewis and Charles to Carolus or Carroll'), and for being a 'double person' who was also a 'single writer', like Twain and Clemens, or for that matter Wilson and his derivations. Alice's looking-glass world, the mazes and paper puzzles, and the grand eccentrics shimmering in Wonderland, is Victorian respectability running riot. Realism has become surrealism. Its topsy-turviness is that of a lunatic asylum, filled with catatonics, obsessives, and psychopaths with delusions of grandeur or omniscience. G and S?* I was surprised, watching Mike Leigh's *Topsy-Turvy*, to find that Anthony Burgess is listed at the end amongst the acknowledgements. Why should this be so? Sullivan has a walk-on part in the Sherlock Holmes pastiche 'Murder to Music', in *The Devil's Mode* (he's glimpsed drinking champagne at the Savoy Theatre), and Burgess reviewed Arthur Jacobs' biography *Arthur Sullivan: A Victorian Musician* favourably. Did Leigh clip that out? 'Anyone who has ever produced an orchestral score will appreciate what Sullivan's labour was like,' wrote Burgess, 'the long nights with twenty-odd-stave paper, dotting in his notes with exquisite neatness and the speed of shorthand, his fingers stained with incessant cigarette smoking, always – like Mozart – fighting to meet a deadline': this is an image exactly duplicated in Allan Corduner's performance. Gilbert's librettos Burgess praised for being 'subversive and sexually perverse'; he was 'the most accomplished lyricist who ever lived' – and if we think about the plots of *Pinafore* (1878), *Pirates* (1879), *Mikado* (1885) and *Gondoliers* (1889) for a moment, we'll realise they are about bastardy, parental abandonment, foundlings, arranged marriages, children gone astray, lost siblings – all Burgess's changeling reveries. Sir Joseph Porter's tribe of cousins, aunts and sisters – this 'crowd of blushing beauties' whom he 'reckons up by dozens' – is like an incest-ridden harem; and when Buttercup confesses that 'I practised baby farming', it was her mistake that sent Ralph off to be an Able

his prudish wife because he disavows 'the sort of Catholicism that Veronica wanted to see in him: it was swearing and boisterous and made no reference to chastity'.

Burgess's party trick was to recite Chesterton's long poem 'The Rolling English Road' in its entirety.

* Burgess reviewed the television productions of *The Yeoman of the Guard* and *Iolanthe* in the *Listener*, on 17 September and 15 October 1964, respectively.

Seaman and Corcoran to grow up to be a Captain. 'How could I do it? I mixed those children up!' It's a joke, really, about nature and nurture ('That you are their Captain is an accident of birth'), a satire on the foolishness of conventional morality, class and social snobbishness. Gilbert was also attentive (like Carroll – like Joyce) to language's overlaps and puns. Frederic's destiny and plight in *Pirates* is founded upon Ruth's mishearing pilot as pirate: 'The words were so much alike!' The pirates themselves, meantime, are all boohoo-ing orphans.

For Burgess, the late Victorian/Edwardian era was Elgar's First Symphony, the loss of the *Titanic*, the death of an agricultural society, the growth of the suburbs, the fear of war, Freud's *Interpretation of Dreams*, a devotion to tradition, a humanist wisdom, and a sense of 'spiritual dispossession' and a feeling that culture was 'threatened'. He saluted the flamboyance of Cunninghame Graham ('a surplus of interests and images – these mar him as a writer'); and he made two attempts to film a life of Edward Lear,* whose predilection for limericks and nonsense verse is somehow suggested in his highly coloured, hallucinogenic watercolours of animals and plants and foreign landscapes done for the Zoological Society of London and the British Museum. Shaw, Burgess simply described as 'a man of my time'. Clearly the Edwardianism goes deep – plunging Burgess into the discoveries of Freud†. Kipling is 'a poet of doubt and division, with hysteria not far from the surface'. Elgar (whose death in the spring of 1934 Burgess remembered seeing in the paper), Kipling's musical analogue, is similarly a variation of enigmas and packed with neuroses. We need, argued Burgess, to delve into artists' lives to sort out the 'neurotic

* One was to have been with Michael Powell as the director/producer. Powell told me that he and Burgess spent their script conferences talking about *Lavengro* and *The Bible in Spain*, by George Borrow. The other version was to have been a vehicle for Peter Ustinov, Burgess's Herod and (had it been made) Ben Jonson in *Will!* 'I know nothing of Ben Jonson,' Sir Peter told me. 'I read the Lear script (very good), without realizing it was by A.B.'

† I think I am glad we did not get to see (or hear) Burgess's long-promised Freud opera (there is a Freud scenario in *The End of the World News*), to have been called *From Soma to Psyche*. Act I: Freud argues with the medical establishment, trying to get them to accept that madness is not physical but of the psyche. Act II: Freud explains to a patient that he's suffering from the Oedipus Complex – that he loves his mother. Act III: a flashback to Oedipus himself, putting his eyes out – 'the upward displacement of the testicles'. Act IV: Freud is attacked by a man whose ill wife has been told that her problems are concealed in her sexual desires. Act V: Freud is having trouble with his fractious disciples when he is struck down by cancer of the jaw . . . Which is I believe how far Burgess got. He had an idea for the cancerous tumour to become a character in its own right, sung by a counter-tenor: 'You, Doctor Freud, have insisted on the separating of the soul from the body. Now here I am, the body. What are you going to do about it . . .?'

hates and neurotic sentimentalities' which intrude into poetry and music. (Billy Henshaw, in *The Pianoplayers*, like Burgess's father, claimed to have been present at the première of Elgar's First Symphony, played by Hallé in 1908.) The late nineteenth century, apparently so self-assured, is actually nervous – even narcotic. Sherlock Holmes (about whom Burgess wrote that short story, 'Murder to Music'), the embodiment of calculating self-awareness, is a cocaine addict. All of this, the boredom, the horror and the glory of Burgess's century's beginning, is the subject of Burgess's favourite English novel (*Ulysses* is Irish), Ford Madox Ford's *Parade's End*, 'a superb summation of Edwardian values'.

Imagine Burgess tapping about the promenade and to the casino in Monte Carlo a century ago, and his manic productivity would not be out of place (Wells has been mentioned; what of Trollope, or Gosse, or further back, Walter Scott?); rue Grimaldi, where the word-processor now lies dormant, even still is a thoroughfare of iron ornament and stucco grapes. And all those other houses: Burgess was a man of property, Soames Forsyte redux. He believed in 'energetic individualism' (his phrase when reviewing *One Hundred Nineteenth-Century Lives*), enterprise, self-discipline, fast travel, wealth, and a mechanistic approach to its creation. Grandiose effects, as in the soaring melodies played by the heavy brass in an Elgar symphony, have to be produced under conditions of great control. Apparently, Frith found genuine acrobats, for example, too jumpy and fidgety. He could only work from models who'd been trained to keep still. He employed people to scout for the right physiognomies. 'What is it to be this time?' Jacob Bell asked him. 'Fair or dark, long nose or short nose, Roman or aquiline, tall figure or small? Give your orders.' He worked incessantly. For the race meeting picture, *Derby Day*, models dressed as jockeys took turns to pose on a wooden horse. Friends would speak to him of the way he'd be 'dropping in here and there little gem-like bits into the beautiful mosaic you have so skilfully put together' – and Frith's brush-strokes are like Burgess's words, diverting us towards an apprecia-tion of the sheer toil that has gone into the manufacture. Such a consider-ation deflects the critic from his job: the quality of the work under scrutiny. As early as 1964, Julian Mitchell was worrying in the *London Magazine* whether 'the sheer volume' of Burgess's work 'has scared off the critics', and nearly forty years on it still does so; but Burgess made the deluge part of his aesthetic. In *The Novel Now* he explained that each book a writer publishes represents a fragment or splinter of what's inside him – and the whole of what is inside his head will be signified, in the end, by 'at least a shelf', i.e. you measure artistry by the yard. The problem here is that early, immature experiments will have to be permitted the same space as the sophisticated visions of one's maturity. The sum of the parts will not be greater than the totality – and nor is it, with Burgess. Though his work demonstrates great versatility, the versatility is always the same. To read one's way through all of Burgess's work (and how many have done that – except me?) is to make a startling discovery. It's all the same. (He was sesquipedalian.) Incidents in the Malaya novels, of the fifties, theological debate, conceptions of fidelity, the behaviour of the expatriate community, the attitudes of warring tribes and factions, the quicksilver operations of language, the tentacles of fate, introduce us to themes duplicated in *Earthly Powers*, and this suggests that Burgess achieves the singular feat of using a variety of locations, a thesaurus of words, a host of historical periods both fore and aft of the present, in order to show that the distinguishing quality of his mind is that it had always been made up.

For this reason it was impossible to teach him anything. He once went to a poetry reading given by Cecil Day Lewis at Manchester Grammar School – the enemy camp, in Burgess's view, because the pupils are Protestants. Day Lewis happens to mention that he didn't think he'd ever composed a sonnet. Oh, yes, you have, shouts out Burgess, and 'I began to deliver from memory: "Nearing again the legendary isle/Where sirens sang and mariners were skinned . . .",' which he says was the Xaverian pupil making 'a social or class gesture', but which seems to me straightforwardly and off-puttingly cocksure. Similarly, when he gets to Manchester University, the practical criticism sessions, where the names of the authors of the passages to be studied are concealed, hold no mystery for him – 'I could not help recognizing some of the texts,' he says. Old English, which he'd quote with Borges, got off to a head start because 'I had been studying a little Anglo-Saxon on my own.'*

He always liked to be one up – and his guard was always up. They had him on *Call My Bluff* once, the programme being recorded at 4.30 p.m. on 28 January 1968 at Studio 6, Television Centre. The fee was fifty pounds. He was a disaster. He quite failed to enter into the spirit of the show and pretend he didn't already know the big words – his attitude was to be flabbergasted that people weren't handling and using obscurities like *acroamatical*, *apocope* and *apotropaic* in ordinary everyday conversation. On Boxing Day 1983, I saw him on an edition of *The Book Quiz* – which was a version of his Manchester practical criticism class. The panel had to

* See Appendix A, p. 397.

spot who wrote what, and it was impossible to tell what Burgess actually knew or was pretending to know as he huffed and puffed and growled behind his curtain of smoke. Salinger 'catches the rhythms of adolescent speech'; Hemingway's 'journalistic style is presented as art. His writing in the *Kansas City Star* is the same writing as later'; Gertrude Stein had a 'muscular, simplistic style'; Norman Mailer 'is a parodist of his own reading of the New Testament and the Penguin Homer'; C. P. Snow 'had a knowledge of the world of science and Whitehall ministries, a world which novelists often don't know about'*; of Ezra Pound, 'I did not know he could be so amusing'; and W. H. Auden 'made his poems out of dictionaries' – as Burgess himself created *A Long Trip to Teatime* out of a section of an encyclopaedia and described a hotel lobby in *MF* using words and definitions picked at random from a page in W. J. Wilkinson's Malay–English dictionary.†

What all this means, the childhood buried in books, the teenage swotting, the undergraduate cramming, was that Burgess felt he had to value literature (and music) above everything else. Nobody, you feel, had anything to offer him – and in the books that he himself wrote he doesn't flirt with the reader; it's not a soothing or collusive prose. His tone is for the parade ground or class delivery. His dependency on the Tollitts and the Dwyers, his stepfamily, had made him both vulnerable and restive; a displaced person – as later he'd volunteer to be a displaced person by moving abroad. So he made a new or alternative existence for himself with words, giving the impression that his published work was still only a partial transcription of that extraordinary, prolix world going on inside his head. 'There's not a lot of time left,' he lamented in 1989, 'and a great deal left to be said.' The books emerged as from an endless ticker-tape. Each morning, when he began to pound at Qwert Yuiop, it was as if, he claimed, he was reading off a telex, like Shakespeare in the sci-fi short story, 'The Muse', collected in *Enderby's Dark Lady*, who receives a visit from a spaceman. The time-traveller has come to Elizabethan London from an alternative universe in the distant future (or something) and hands the playwright, a mediocre credulous fellow living in a lane off Bishopsgate, a sheaf of dramas, which Will then spends the rest of his career copying out in his own hand. 'When poets had talked of the Muse

* *Nothing Like the Sun* is dedicated to 'Pamela and Charles Snow'.

† Or so he told *Writer's Digest* in August 1975, where he said the hotel description was built up from p. 167. In *This Man and Music*, however, it is now p. 113 that he utilized and the 'Malay (or Indonesian) – English' dictionary was compiled by R. J. Wilkinson.

had they perhaps meant visitants like this . . .? Humming a new song . . . he went on, not blotting a line' – and starts to forge *The Merchant of Venice*, though not before rejecting and throwing into his rubbish bin a bit of pseudo-Shakespeare, or genuine Burgess:

> Consider gentlemen as in the sea
> All earthly life finds like and parallel
> So in far distant skies our lives be aped
> Each hath a twin each action hath a twin
> And twins have twins galore and infinite
> And e'en these stars be twinn'd . . .

The idea that one's real progenitors are the past artistic masters with whom one has an affinity derives from *The Picture of Dorian Gray*,* where Wilde spells out how 'one had ancestors in literature, as well as in one's own race, nearer perhaps in type and temperament, many of them, and certainly with an influence of which one was more absolutely conscious'; and Burgess's like and parallel, living in his brain and in his passions, were (he hoped) Joyce and Shakespeare. But, though he had a skill for wordplay, he lacked any sense of human differentiation or any sympathy for human oddity. He's in a continuous state of irritation. Thus, with his facility for etymology and verbal showmanship, he came to wrap himself up in a paper universe – he was a paper man – his words deployed as confetti, bonbons, artillery. Burgess is the least intimate of authors – and one of the worst in literature at love or sex scenes. Actually, affection or the erotic don't concern him. He prefers illnesses, machines, assertions of power and intellect. A psychologist would explain him in a jiffy.

I have before me a stack of scientific papers on what is called Attachment Theory, or Reactive Attachment Disorder, which is all about

* Wilde, evidently, is the source for the theme in *Ulysses* about searching for an alternative, more suitable parentage than the one bestowed by nature. 'It seemed to him,' says Wilde of Dorian, who has been dwelling on the great heroes of literature and painting, 'that in some mysterious way their lives had been his own.' Thus, Odysseus and Hamlet in Joyce, and Joyce, Shakespeare and the Edwardians in Burgess. Joyce bought an Italian translation of *The Picture of Dorian Gray* on 16 August 1906, in Rome. He regarded Wilde as being, like himself, a Dubliner who was 'the miserable man who sings of joy' . . . 'a betrayed artist and exile' (Ellmann). Joyce's involvement with a performance of *The Importance of Being Earnest* in Zurich, and the acrimony which ensued, is the subject of Stoppard's *Travesties* (1975 – Ellmann's *James Joyce* appears in the Acknowledgements section of the Faber text). Burgess tried to copy this technique – of putting a famous figure getting up to farcical deeds in an unexpected place – in the (unrealised) off-Broadway musical about Trotsky's visit to New York in 1917. You'll find it in *The End of the World News*.

the effects on a child of emotional deprivation caused by its separation from (or the death of) a parent – or caregiver, in the disgusting jargon of the hour.* In terms of biological importance, there is an 'internally driven motivation' (i.e. instinct) for a baby to imprint or form an attachment, which precedes the drives to mate and feed. It is necessary for fundamental survival and a sense of identity. This provides the infant with security. If the bond is shattered, if there is a sense of disconnectedness, there will be problems with self-esteem and self-confidence throughout the rest of life. 'The infant's primary needs are touch, eye contact, movement, smiles, and nourishment,' say the shrinks. 'Through this interaction, the child learns that the world is a safe place and trust develops. Attachment is reciprocal, the baby and caregiver create this deep, nurturing connection together. It is imperative for optimal brain development and emotional health, and its effects are felt physiologically, emotionally, cognitively and socially.' If a baby loses its primary caregiver, it learns at a pre-verbal stage that the world is to be mistrusted, and this lesson 'has taken place at a biochemical level in the brain'. As Dr Keith Reber explains in *Progress: Family Systems Research and Therapy* (vol. V, 1996): 'Reactive Attachment Disorder is an inability to form normal relationships with others and an impairment in development, usually caused by pathological parental care,' which in this day and age may include domestic violence, substance abuse, and the Lord He Knoweth What Else, not simply a pre-Raphaelite vision of one's mother floating away with the Fellow in the Bright Nightgown. A sufferer from Reactive Attachment Disorder may be identified if they show signs of a few (or more) of the following symptoms:

1. Superficially charming to get what he wants.
2. Lacks genuine affection with primary caregivers.
3. Controlling, bossy, manipulative, defiant, argumentative, demanding, impulsive.
4. Preoccupation with fire, death, blood, or gore.

* The information in this section derives from *What Is Attachment Disorder?* (Evergreen Consultants in Human Behavior, Colorado, 2000); *Attachment Theory: A Brief Overview of Attachment, the Behaviours of Those Insecurely Attached and an Introduction to the Counselling Approach Known as Educational Therapy* by Michelle Vaughan (Worcester Educational Psychology Service); 'Fostering the Child with Attachment Difficulties' (a memorandum from Claire Burgess, Primary Care and Support Project, Worcester, to Health Authority colleagues, 24 September 2001); 'Children at Risk for Reactive Attachment Disorder: Assessment, Diagnosis and Treatment' by Keith Reber; *Progress: Family Systems Research and Therapy*, vol. V, 1996, pp. 83–98 (Phillips Graduate Institute, California).

5. Aggression towards others or self.
6. Destructive, accident-prone.
7. Rages or has long temper-tantrums, especially in response to adult authority.
8. Poor eye contact, except when lying.
9. Blames others for his problems.
10. Lacks self-control.
11. Lacks cause-and-effect thinking.
12. Lies, steals, shows no remorse, no conscience, defiant.
13. Has difficulty maintaining friendships.
14. Persistent nonsense questions and incessant chatter.
15. Grandiose sense of self which lacks trust in others to care for him.

I don't know about the experiments and clinical trials, or the grids of statistics they drew up in the field, but it seems to me that the students of the mind needed to look no further when compiling this list than to go through Burgess's memoirs and novels. It's all here. The strong feelings of loss caused by his mother's death when he was nineteen months old created the deeply troubled child who became an anxious adult. (His insides were all wrong.) And if it is the purpose of a biography to see how a personality can come into existence, then Burgess is now generating out of Wilson, making his feebleness into force, the bother and burden of living diverted into the meanings and memories, the evocations and suggestions, of his art. Playing off his actual, biological ancestry with the pedigree he found in literature, he was still intent on suffering, however. He'd made himself tiresome at home – he was supercilious at university. He thinks that his musical knowledge made for 'a kind of social ostracism', and his roll-call of the lecturers, H. B. Charlton, L. C. Knights, J. D. Jump, is an identification of the enemy. 'I, twenty years old and too knowledgeable, was marked.' They probably considered him a pretentious prick. A. J. P. Taylor, in Manchester before going to Magdalen, in 1938, wrote on one of Wilson's history essays, 'Bright ideas insufficient to conceal lack of knowledge,' which is the judgement most of us would pass after glancing through *Abba Abba*, where he tries to be a Keats expert (the details are lifted from Robert Gittings), *A Mouthful of Air*, where his opinions on contemporary spoken English evidently ossified in the early sixties, and *Mozart and the Wolf Gang*, where he affects omniscience about late eighteenth-century composers, and has celestial discussions amongst the shades of Berlioz, Rossini, Schoenberg, Gershwin and the rest of them – and the remarkable thing is, they all sound like Burgess ('I resent that', 'There seems to be a lot of resentment going on this heavenly day', 'talking of resentment', 'you must all admit to resenting Elgar'*). Against these, his huge article on the novel in the *Britannica* is magisterial, and his biblical books, despite their vulgarity, are at least as good as Henryk Sienkiewicz's *Quo Vadis?*, a novelist who won the Nobel in 1905. (Burgess's response, years later, was to say that Taylor was 'too young to respect' – he'd have been thirty-one.)

When Burgess recalled Wilson's classmates, Reginald Bate, Douglas Rankine Mason, Denis Crowther Gaunt, it is as if he's taking the names off a register or out of a yearbook. (How well did he know them?) Other students only impinge on his life to make him feel plaintive and haughty. He writes for and edits the university magazine, *The Serpent*. Back copies of this, along with a tobacco jar that bears the university coat of arms (a snake writhing under a rising sun – the motto Virgil's *arduus ad solem*), decorate Dr Shawcross's bungalow in Kuala Kangsar, in *Earthly Powers*. Some of the poems Wilson contributed to the paper appear (as Nero's – on Hannibal) in *The Kingdom of the Wicked*: 'Proud with his pachyderms piling the perilous passes'; other bits of doggerel were stored away for Enderby. The enmities between the rival student poets, the factions and sects in Manchester turn up in many of Burgess's works; he was always scenting the air for treachery. Jesus, Moses, Napoleon, Freud, all his huge heroes, suffer from fools. Enderby is endlessly beleaguered by philistines. Wilson, as an undergraduate, was always trying to correct people; and in wanting to put his superior knowledge to good use he can't see why he is

* Burgess derived the format of a heavenly symposium – conversations amongst the notable deceased – from Brigid Brophy's *The Adventures of God in His Search for the Black Girl*, which he praised in the *New York Times Book Review* section on 25 August 1974.

Brophy's book contains one particular idea of genius – that Jorge Luis Borges was really Ambrose Bierce, who in 1899 discovered a longevity plant in the Andes.

I can't help thinking, however, that *Mozart and the Wolf Gang*, though short and late (148 pp; 1991), is none the less Burgess's most megalomaniacal production. Getting everyone in history to meet everyone else, all these tyrants and geniuses competing and arguing: when Robert Lowell used to start post-prandial speculations along those lines, according to Jonathan Miller, a manic attack and breakdown was not far off. There's an element of madness in the lordly dissolution of time and space so that (as here) Wagner and Beethoven, suspiciously weighing each other up, appear alongside Gluck and Prokofiev, who are doing the same. The author further disintegrates himself into 'Anthony' and 'Burgess' components to carry on a schizophrenic debate about the purpose and meaning of music, which concludes with his shibboleths that 'without craft there can be no art' and 'the gulf between the serious and the merely diverting is now firmly fixed'.

always 'sneered' (his word) at. He claims that his (rejected) review of *Finnegans Wake* would have been as perceptive and pioneering as Edmund Wilson's, in the *New Republic.* He is sacked from being a pub pianist because 'I showed off by playing the Jupiter movement from the full-score of Holst's *The Planets.*' He says that he was in any event wasting his time, as his accompaniments were far more competent than the efforts of the amateur singers. He goes away and composes an operetta about Copernicus, who'd argued that the Earth rotated about the Sun and that the Earth was not the centre of the Universe.

Wilson himself stuck to his own eccentric orbit. You'd have thought that he'd whizz away with a brilliant degree. He later stated that 'My own English department stressed the Teutonic ancestry of the language and seemed to offer the humanistic study of literature as a bait for catching potential scholars of Old Norse' – no problem there, you'd imagine, for the man who was at his happiest when immersed in a sacred world of words. Yet he failed to take a First. He says that the Chief Examiner's chair had collapsed under him, which put him in a bad mood during the Wilson *viva voce.* We know that he'd frequently done badly in Latin and French; but Burgess wrote many times about the Honours thesis on Christopher Marlowe, having been drawn to Shakespeare's contemporary for his Catholic guilt and conflicts – the Faustian desire for both damnation and salvation. *A Dead Man in Deptford* came out of this. In 1981, Burgess remembered:

> I was the more impelled to want to write my thesis on Marlowe, because it was 1939–1940, and the bombs were dropping. You know, the Nazis were overhead. One was writing one's thesis with the bombs going over. Indeed, we did our examinations with a raid in a huge glass-roofed gymnasium, looking at the bombs going over. So literature, then, wasn't a pretty game. You were tied up with the matter of life and death. So I felt that Marlowe, certainly *Doctor Faustus*, had something to say to us then. You know the moment was coming when whatever you felt reality was like, the bomb would drop and there it was. I wrote with some fervour on Marlowe. I felt that this was not purely an academic subject.

The strange thing is, however, when I searched through the departmental files in Manchester, it was impossible to confirm that his final-year dissertation was on Marlowe, since no entry was made either in the marks ledger or on his record card (which stated that he was 'good at English and Music') as to his topic. Undergraduate dissertations were kept only for five years, then destroyed. So perhaps he had one of his mutinies and didn't hand it in? Or (as he claimed) the Luftwaffe came for it? In which case mercy would have been shown and he'd have been awarded the equivalent of an aegrotat grade. Whatever, he received a IIi, or Upper Second – a disappointment.* It hadn't helped that he'd always referred to Professor H. B. Charlton, whose much-reprinted *Shakespearian Comedy* came out in 1938, as Professor H. B. Charlatan. Charlton may have lectured and published on the plays, but his student claimed descent from them, John Wilson (1515–1674) being a composer and lutenist, who set Shakespeare's songs; and Jacke Wilson, as we know from *MF*, was the singer named in a First Folio stage direction for *Much Ado About Nothing*, coming in to sing 'Sigh no more ladies' in Act II, scene iii. If that's not charlatanry, I don't know what is.

John B. Wilson BA (English IIi, 1940), as he appears in the faculty's List of Graduates, may have had biological antecedents and a stepfamily about whom he was not prone to be possessive; and Anthony Burgess B.A., D.Litt., F.R.S.L., as *Who's Who* billed him, was a 'gigantic brain' (as Dickens called Mr Pickwick), stuffed with odds and ends of literature; but with literature, Burgess once said, 'you're dealing with sex and violence. These remain the basic themes, they're the basic themes of Shakespeare whether you like it or not' – and yet I wonder how much he knew about either? His war service was conspicuous for the distance he was kept from any bullets or bombs. The only time his life was in danger was when he was nearly shot by his own men. He'd ticked off his platoon for not caring that Count Basie had cribbed from the slow movement of Tchaikovsky's Fifth in some jazz piece – this was a bit of pedantry 'I should not have known'; or at least not have crowed about in his shitty way. And with sex I can't help wondering – did he ever kiss a girl? His lack of an affectionate nature is so evident. I don't mean particularly his super-

* Amends were made on Wednesday 12 May 1982 (Founder's Day), when Professor D. S. R. Welland concluded his Address:

> [. . .] *Earthly Powers* has, in two years, sold more than 140,000 copies in the United Kingdom alone and its French translation has been awarded the French prize for the best foreign book. If recalling him today to the scenes of his early life widens that audience and reinvigorates still further his great talent, Manchester will be usefully strengthening the bonds that were formed in the vicinity of this University sixty-five years ago.
>
> Mr Chancellor, Your Grace, I present to you in his own University and in the hall in which he may well have sat his Finals, Anthony Burgess for the degree of Doctor of Letters, *honoris causa* [. . .]

ciliousness towards his stepfamily, who offended him by being riff-raff (the only one he approved of was George Dwyer, because he was an Archbishop – and with regards to Liana's being the Contessa Pasi, a fact significant enough to be mentioned on his jacket blurbs, you never heard the Amises reminding us that Hilly was the Countess of Kilmarnock); or his obnoxiousness to his peer group and superiors; or his moaning generally, like Trevor Howard playing a crusty and bloodshot old boy seeing out his last days on the terrace of the Royal Bombay Yacht Club in a comedy film. I mean that he is the least flirtatious or serenading of writers. There's no attempt to win us over. He's brash, loud, and his sentences are always dressed up. He tells us about his characters; he doesn't draw us into them. There's no sensuality. He always describes sex with distaste – it's loathsome to him, an embarrassing need or requirement, like going to the lavatory. Copulation is a mechanistic business – unpleasurable; and he never acknowledges simple randiness because he could never let go like that. Once there has been an 'engorgement with blood of the genitalia,' he wrote in 1988, 'we are possessed and we are no longer ourselves'. He described H. G. Wells's womanising as 'glandular restlessness' – and to Burgess sex was always a bestial business of anatomical drives, bodily emissions and muscular itches. Nevertheless, it was something to boast about. The press release for *Any Old Iron*, published when he was seventy-two, contained the reassuring information that 'his erotic life does not seem yet to be at its end', and it will have ended, as it began, inside his head.

Too wholly wrapped up in linguistics, Burgess quite failed to notice the sexual intensity of his beloved Hopkins' poetry – the colliding, intermingling words; the ecstasy. The figure of Christ as a chevalier, the hawks, the storms and the seasons: it is electrically, sexually charged. And Shakespeare's sex life, in *Nothing Like the Sun*, is about his life as a stretcher-case, as the spirochaetes course through him, making him delirious. Lust and filthy fornication roam the realm, and here's one of the bard's wet dreams:

> . . . that vision of the golden trull, the black nipples,
> the flash of breast-muscle, even the fierce small fists upraised,
> haunted his sleep and oft, in the dawn, lashed his seed
> to cold and queasy pumping out.

Sweaty and chilly simultaneously, sex is feverish, swinish. The nuns and priests responsible for Burgess's early education hadn't helped, as they gloated about punishment and eternal damnation for the sins of the flesh. As a seven-year-old, Wilson had had an unrequited crush on a classmate, Joan Price, and he never forgot the hot flush of humiliation at being rebuffed – 'falling in love is dangerous', or merely a madness, indeed, and as well deserving of the Jesuitical canes and straps as if you'd spouted rank heresy. That girl who lay down pretending to be dead near her brother's coffin and who wanted Wilson to tickle her back to life – it is actually *more* revealing of his attitude to sex as death if that recollection was an invention.

There were the Welsh maids in the attic; there's a fourteen-year-old girl, Edith, with whom he rolls on the floor ('Boys cannot make love. Nature is so eager to shoot young seed that she forgets what it is for'); and he is picked up by a woman librarian and taken back to her house in Ardwick, where 'tumescence renewed itself'. They are 'Protestant, of course', these hussies; and what *is* this persistent fantasy that he is a great leg-over man? He makes orgasms as alluring as vomiting, and he could torment himself as never before once at university. 'I sat in the classroom with genuine women,' he said in 1985, recalling the seminars on Old Norse and Anglo-Saxon. 'The men . . . sat on the opposite side of the room from the women . . . I once tried to sit among the women students for a lecture on John Keats, but that was regarded as provocative . . . We only met women students transformed into bare-shouldered lipsticked sirens at formal dances . . . I even married a fellow-student, though she was in the history not the English department. For a student of Old Norse to marry another student of Old Norse would have seemed incestuous.'* He repeated the point in his autobiography: 'There was something incestuous in mooning after someone of our own year and our own school.' Girls whom he shunned in case they were his psychic siblings were Trixie Brayshaw, Marjorie Bottomley, Pat Wilson and Rosalie Williams, who half a century later played Mrs Hudson in Granada's *Sherlock Holmes* series. He had a similar reasoning for not approving of his stepsisters' marriages: 'There was a whiff of incest in this too easy consolidation of the faith and blood' – i.e. of Catholic families intermixing. He'll always raise this matter if he can – it's a fear of contamination. Yet he desired it, too. *MF* is a hymn to incest and in *Earthly Powers* Toomey and Hortense, the brother and sister, are brought together like Giovanni and Annabella, the wanton siblings in *'Tis Pity She's a Whore*:

* Old Norse specialists have, in fact, conjoined without deleterious effects – congratulations to Professors Peter and Ursula Dronke, of the Faculty of Modern and Medieval Languages, Cambridge.

The love of thee, my sister, and the view
of thy immortal beauty hath untuned
All harmony both of my rest and life.

– or, as Burgess rewrites the scene:

> 'Lie down with me,' I said, 'just for a little while . . . Lie down, with my arms around you.'
>
> 'What is this?' She was amused but spoke acutely. 'Are you trying to make yourself normal? Through a different kind of abnormality? . . .'
>
> 'Quotha,' I said, 'since the context could be taken as Jacobean . . . that incest play by John Ford. Jacobean . . .'*

Incest, ethically and socially repugnant, is the ultimate transgression; yet for Burgess, who never knew his mother or sister, it is the ultimate bond of reconciliation, too – what if they weren't dead but still out there wandering in the world, anonymous, waiting for him? 'I must confess,' he said in 1985, 'that I have never enjoyed even the most innocent relations with either an Englishwoman or an Irishwoman' – just in case he broke the taboo. Instead (he bragged) he has had carnal knowledge of Chinese, Malay, Buginese, Tamil, Singhalese, Bengali, Japanese and Algonquin women – all prostitutes, all impossible to trace. (Or perhaps it was the same prostitute – there's a lot of racial overlap in the Federated Malay States.) We'll have to take his word for it, that his 'seed has been set to work to help generate new life' all over the shop. What does he think he is? A pollinating flowering plant?

There are many mentions of homosexuality in his work, and of impotence. *The Wanting Seed*, *Honey for the Bears*, *Earthly Powers*, of course; enough for Anthony Powell to confide in his journal (Wednesday 15 June 1988) that 'when I first heard of him (we have never met) [Burgess] was vaguely spoken of as bisexual, never as a thoroughgoing queer'. Queerishness was imputed by Christopher Ricks, too, in his inscrutable article 'The Epicene', in the *New Statesman* (5 April 1963), when he decoded Belinda and Paul Hussey's newly discovered bisexuality, in *Honey for the Bears*, as meaning that the novelist is now personally advocating 'a rather pleasant virtuosity'; Paul Theroux also alludes to

* In 1960, Burgess said he 'wasted a month' trying to adapt 'John Ford's *'Tis Pity She's a Whore*, a grim story of brother and sister incest' as a novel, to be called *Sealed with a Loving Kiss*. He said the result was 'improbable', but the shreds and tatters of his project survive in these later works.

the charge (without adverse comment) in his dinner-party short story. It was one of Burgess's chestnuts that the Ricks article came in handy when he needed to fend off the attentions of a predatory female doctor in Tunbridge Wells, whom he'd consulted about his sclerotic leg. ('Professor Ricks, I said, had not taken it far enough.') What signals were being misread by others other than the Kentish quack? For homosexuality (and impotence) in Burgess's work refers to infertility, creative deadness – literature feeding off itself, books being made out of books. Everything, as he said on the *Book Quiz*, explaining the self-referential style of Salinger, 'turned in on itself' – and, his eyes gleaming, he used his hands to mime hugging something to your own bosom. What was his was his. ('Nearness in birth or blood doth but persuade a nearer nearness in affection', as Ford's Giovanni says.)

The verbosity, too, was suspicious. 'Wordiness is effeminacy and unforgivable,' as Kipling had told Edmund Gosse, sternly. I think his personal manner, also, was capable of being misconstrued: the long hair, the genteel prickliness, the splayed hands and the way he waved his Schimmelpenninck cigar around, the orotund voice – the vanity. He was affected. He had the touched-up suavity of one of those middle-ranking Royal Shakespeare Company character actors, bitter that they'll never be offered better roles than Egeus, Leonato, Holofernes or Sir Oliver Martext. And then there was Lynne, voluble and aggressive – less like a female than a female impersonator, complete with wig. 'Jane and I had a posh party,' Kingsley Amis told me. 'We'd hired a butler, caterer, the works. The Burgesses arrived, they said, in a chauffeur-driven limousine, which would pick them up to take them home again. It was a fucking mini-cab driver! "Would you like to come in for a drink?" I said, having been expecting the Admirable Crichton in a grey uniform and peaked cap. "No thank you, mate," said this cockney. "Oh, all right. Make it a small brandy, if I may." You should have seen Lynne in action. A gin martini every time the tray went round.'*

A headstrong shrew happiest getting paralytic in the pubs of Fitzrovia,

* I talked to Amis about Burgess on 23 September 1986 ('I can tell you some stories about Burgess . . .' – and he did). Lynne at a public gathering, making an exhibition of herself, appears at the end of Chapter Fifteen of *Difficulties with Girls* (1988), where she is lightly disguised as Vera. Jenny is Jenny Standish, the novel's heroine:

> An outburst of swearing in a female voice started up a few feet away. One or two of the words might have been unfamiliar to Jenny but she knew most of them. The one doing the swearing was the four-eyed little Vera, and the one being sworn at was a tubby man who was quite old, old enough for that not to happen to him, at any rate.

or so Burgess would imply, she is the most important person in his story. Wilson was brought up by women – stepsisters, a stepmother, his mother's sister, Ann Bromley, and his cousins, Elsie and Betty – none of whom, he claimed, could conceal the reluctant way they tolerated his existence. There was no lovingness. He was lonely and sad. This is why he found Lynne so necessary. She treated him like a child, nagging him, scolding him, humiliating him in company and in full view – and with impunity. But at least she was paying him maximum attention. Barely in control, as the booze got to her later on, she was none the less never to be accused of not being natural and sincere. Her raw emotion contrasted with his art and craft. She was first seen in the Chorus of Women of Canterbury, in a student production of *Murder in the Cathedral*, wailing about martyrdom and blood. For their first date, he took her to see *The Lady Vanishes* (just released – 1938) at the Gaumont, and like his mother and sister, Lynne would vanish from Burgess's life eventually, washed away on a tide of Tanqueray bottles. But that wouldn't be for thirty years – yet even so, what a haunted film. What Burgess would have observed, on that original trip to the pictures, was that Michael Redgrave's Gilbert Redman was, like himself, an amateur music scholar and a high-minded bumbler; and Lynne, like Margaret Lockwood's Iris Henderson, was forthright, proud-minded, unsettled, and a bit of a slapper, too. Foreign journeys, crowded trains, soldiers and secret police, menacing doctors, folk songs, puzzles about identity (does Miss Froy exist or not? Did Burgess? Did Joseph Kell?): the atmospherics of a world on the brink of war and catastrophe, the Hitchcock themes, would be the paranoid Burgess themes also, in all his novels, from *A Vision of Battlements* to *A Dead Man in Deptford*. Fugitives, espionage, the persecution of the innocent, wrongful arrests – these are particularly on view in the Marlowe novel. Jack (the narrator) cannot even be sure of his hero's name. 'What are you – Merlin or Marlin or Morley?' 'I am Marlowe or Morley or Marley . . . Merlin is a magical name. Some call me by it.'

As Eva Marie Saint yanked Cary Grant up to her top bunk, and as Kim Novak enticed James Stewart up the belltower, so Lynne took the

---

'I can't drop you in Fulham on my way to Muswell Hill,' he kept saying, mostly a bit at a time, 'because they're in opposite directions.'

'You' was the word Vera came back to most often, though she used a great many other ones in between, and she finished each paragraph by shouting, '. . . you.'

After a time the tubby man moved off towards the street door with Vera following him and still shouting until her voice was lost in the general hubbub.

initiative and marched John (as he always was to her) back to her room in Ashburne Hall of Residence. Burgess felt he had been led there by a sign in *Finnegans Wake*, where there is a character called 'J. B. W. Ashburner'. When people start believing that messages have been left for them in literature it is normally time for the men in white coats to bring on their butterfly nets.* Blake is a frequent source for crank mail – and in one of Burgess's poems printed in *The Serpent* (and later given to Enderby) there is a dedication 'To Tirzah'. Tirzah, he later explained, 'was a character in Blake's prophetic books who stood for the physically maternal. I do not propose checking on this'† – and in this verse of his there is a metaphor of the vagina or birth-canal as 'the gate/where the army went through', which suggests that Burgess quite believed copulation always to be a matter of siege and battering rams, invasion and conflict, and so it was with Lynne. Soon his 'tool of biology' is getting a regular work-out, his 'painful erections' are ministered to, and the 'glandular secretions of the young' are of such volume he's compelled to complain about the mounting cost of condoms, pessaries

* Joyce's book 'knew of the burning glands I took to Ashburne Hall', Burgess maintained. This would make slightly more sense if the reference was accurate. The name in *Finnegans Wake* is not J. B. W. Ashburner but 'Mr G. B. W. Ashburner' (p. 369). Ashburnham is the illicit lover in Ford's *The Good Soldier*.

† Lazy sod. Tirzah was not a character in Blake's prophetic books – it was a town in northern Israel captured by Joshua. The battles are recounted in stirring and typical fashion in the Old Testament. See I Kings 14–16 and II Kings 15: 14, 16. In the Song of Solomon (6: 4) we find: 'Thou art beautiful, O my love, as Tirzah, comely as Jerusalem, terrible as an army with banners.'

Here's Blake's actual poem (1794), which Burgess was cribbing:

TO TIRZAH

Whate'er is Born of Mortal Birth
Must be consumed with the Earth
To rise from Generation free:
Then what have I to do with thee?

The Sexes sprung from Shame & Pride,
Blow'd in the morn; in evening died;
But Mercy chang'd Death into Sleep;
The Sexes rose to work & weep.

Thou, Mother of my Mortal part,
With cruelty didst mould my Heart,
And with false self-deceiving tears
Didst bind my Nostrils, Eyes, & Ears:

Didst close my Tongue in senseless clay,
And me to Mortal Life betray.
The Death of Jesus set me free:
Then what have I to do with thee?

and other pharmaceutical and hygienic requisites. As Gore Vidal said to the Midlands fictionalist Jonathan Coe, do we really want to know all this about Anthony's cock? (His arguments with army doctors about whether or not he should be circumcised frequently pop up in his writings. 'I stuck to my prepuce,' Burgess assures us).*

Lynne, according to Burgess, had, like Constantinople, long since been occupied and was promiscuous to the point of nymphomania. He tried to be sanguine about this, defiant almost, but when talking about her on the radio twenty years after her death he was still in a state of despair: 'With regard to my first marriage, my wife [was] almost philosophically unfaithful. She . . . established the general principle that to sleep with anybody was in order . . . She would sleep with anyone.' In his memoirs he says she behaved 'in the manner of Molly Bloom'; and earlier, in *Little Wilson and Big God*, he says of his own mother that 'it would be easier to recreate her in fiction, relating her to Molly Bloom . . . than to wrestle with a virtually non-existent reality'. Which makes me wonder what he believed Joyce's character to be like? To me she's Penelope, the patient wife of Odysseus, waiting for her husband to return. She may be having a fling (with Blazes Boylan), but she can see her suitor for what he is; and she's lonely, grieving for her lost child, Rudi, and grieving for her lost youth, lost time, in Gibraltar, as a daughter of the regiment. She's domestic, romantic, well-disposed. She runs the household efficiently (she can quote the going price of oysters, potatoes and new handkerchiefs); she's pleased with how she can look (and badly wants to save up for a peach-blossom dressing jacket 'like the one long ago in Walpoles only 8/6 or 18/6'); and she has an ear for poetry, and for the sensuousness of poetic things: a big juicy pear, a white rose, pepper trees, white poplars, fresh vegetables in the market covered with dew, and the fig trees in the Alameda gardens. Burgess seems to know none of this. His Molly is a vamp, a damned witch, full of mischiefs manifold and sorceries terrible, 'coming to Dublin speaking and thinking like any low Dublin fishwife', as he told the *Paris Review*, in 1972, re-emphasising the point he'd once made in *Here Comes Everybody*: 'Molly is eternal earth, rolling round unsleeping on her creaking bed. Dirt is of her essence.'

* There's ample on circumcision rites in *The Kingdom of the Wicked*: 'And why had God decreed that the snipping of the foreskin . . . should be the condition of entry into the army of the chosen? Because the foreskin capped the tree of generation, human procreation being the moon that reflected divine creation's solar light.' In the *Moses* film, Gianfranco De Bosio felt it was necessary to show us Irene Papas lunging at a naked baby boy with a knife and then dropping this worm-like flap of skin on the cooking fire.

Lynne didn't listen to his musical compositions, was bored by his enthusiasm for Joyce and Hopkins, and for three decades was a foul contending rebel and graceless traitor to her loving lord. So what did he see in her? Irrational, irresponsible, subject to fits of rage – was she not an exaggerated version of what he believed he was used to? And what, beneath his anger and defensiveness, he believed he deserved? He wanted to be in the grip of powerful, manipulative women, overflowing women, who'd be quick to react, who'd be crazy and obsessive. He wanted to feel helpless – and Lynne was a way of inflicting punishment on himself. She was his destroyer – yet also his angel. Without her there was too much high seriousness; too much of the life of the mind. She pushed him into life. For all that they were two raging fires meeting together, she was his chance of love. The equivocal dispositions do battle in his books, where blatant vulgarians, nagging and shrill, contrast with white goddesses or kindly dark ladies. It's a breach that is in his own nature, too: the grammarian and linguist, the self-disciplinarian and musician trained in counterpoint, on the one hand, and the ranting sword-stick wielding Quixote in his Dormobile, on the other, driving to Yugoslavia to re-enter Italy disguised as a tourist purely and simply in order to benefit from a visitor's concession of petrol coupons.

The pomegranate had two halves, as it were: the super-sensitive aesthete and then the concatenation of ugliness and excesses; cleanliness and order and what John Cheever (quoted by Burgess in the *Observer* on 3 February 1985) called 'the ancient human lusts and expectations that pick up men and women and dash them screaming on the rocks of their own desires'. Thus, Burgess's life, and Burgess's books, with the almost slapstick veering between confidence and collapse, sneering and snarling, struggles and sacrifice. The ghostly muse, a divine source of inspiration, makes sporadic visitations in Enderby's sphere, for instance; as does her opposite number, the monstrous stepmother. When Burgess's father remarried the proprietress of the Golden Eagle, Maggie Dwyer's fate was to become all the cartoon harridans who afflict Burgess's protagonists. Stepmothers are usurpers ('My stepmother would take time off from the beer pumps to clout me. I would cry and be called, as D. H. Lawrence had been called, mardarse') – and yet what happens, with Enderby anyway, is that *all* the women he is entangled with change into this Sycorax. Vesta Bainbridge regresses from a beauty into a beast ('You've been doing your damndest to turn into my stepmother'); Miranda Boland becomes 'thin and evil'; and when Enderby, after being a fugitive in Tangiers, eventually finds himself the manager of a café, he calls the sea-front establishment La Belle Mer, a pun on the French for stepmother. An anonymous lady appears in the bar and demands to read Enderby's poetry. She deciphers it Oedipally. For all he knows, she tells him, his stepmother might be his real mother. The thought that his true mother and his false mother are connected is too terrible to contemplate. Yet the transference does occur, in a way, in Burgess's Shakespeare fantasia, *Nothing Like the Sun*. Will's Muse begins as a golden goddess, takes on sexual connotations, then she takes on connotations of sexual illness. She's like Lynne, dealing with her John's 'burning glands'.

It was curtains for Maggie Dwyer or Margaret Wilson (prop. of M. Wilson's), as she was more properly known, one morning in October 1940, soon after her stepson had roused her with a cup of tea – a valet's duty he discharged with revulsion because he could never stop hearing the way she sucked the drink up thirstily into her dentureless head. Burgess is back in the kitchen, there's a thump from upstairs, and the old girl has fallen out of bed with a heart attack. 'I was more an outsider than I had ever been,' he wails. In a move that Freud himself would have had to mull over, he pinches his stepmother's identity card, and he and Lynne utilise it to book a hotel room under the guise of Mr and Mrs Wilson – which is what they would indeed rightfully become. The engagement ring was purchased with the prize money from Harold Nicolson – Burgess's closest association with Bloomsbury. (He believed that the prose of Virginia Woolf, Vita Sackville-West's friend, would have been much improved if she'd been 'seduced in a Manchester back-alley'.)

'What's left for me but marriage?' asked Margaret Lockwood's young sophisticate rhetorically, in *The Lady Vanishes*. Lynne could have given the line a similar ironic spin. She could always slip off her wedding and engagement rings if she felt like going on the prowl. Her debasement of the sacrament of marriage and of what the ring symbolised lurks behind the title of the novel *The Worm and the Ring*, where Veronica, hysterically chaste, is Lynne in reverse. Burgess alludes to Wagner's ring – the power that is given to those who wear it – and also to the grub in Blake's rose, gnawing away at happiness and innocence. When she was attacked during the blackout, the thugs broke her finger trying to wrench the ring off – unsuccessfully. It's an unsparing detail when she died that the funeral director had to snap her metacarpus finally to free the band of gold. But marriage? And marriage to Burgess? The way he was convinced he was being hurt and exploited made her strength and protection necessary –

and people like being necessary. Lynne was also equally as insecure herself – why else did the grog grip her so early on, the pints of cider and gin chasers? Being Welsh had a lot to do with it – or Welsh in so far as Monmouthshire is concerned, which is not the Wales of the Welsh language, leeks and love spoons, but a place (in those days) of coal mining and poverty. Then (as now) it was always raining or promising to rain.

Lynne was born on 24 November 1920 at 11 Nursery Terrace, Sirhowy, Tredegar, to Florence Jones (née Jones) and Edward Jones, schoolmaster. It is important to grasp how high up the social tree teachers were back then, and Lynne – registered as Llewela* – would have been brought up in a family treated as gentry, with books in the home, stained glass in the hall, a bottle of sherry on the sideboard, the tennis rackets, in their wooden presses, hung up in the garage, an account at both Howells and Morgans (Cardiff's department stores), church rather than chapel, a place on the bench, and an involvement in local administration. Lynne's father had studied chemistry to M.Sc. level at Manchester and served in the Royal Army Medical Corps during the Great War as an officer attached to Field Marshal Allenby. He saw action with the Egyptian expeditionary force in 1917, attacking the Turks, driving northward beyond Jaffa, and capturing Jerusalem, Damascus and Aleppo, where the armistice was signed. Ted Jones Science, as he was inevitably known in the valleys, invented a sort of mobile incinerator, which was widely used by his army on the march. Lynne had 'a strong fixation on her father', Burgess was to say sternly, liking to suggest a form of unacknowledged incest between them. What he was actually seeing, for the first time, was a parent and child who got on. There was an elder sister, Hazel, who was her mother's favourite. I do worry, though, about the extent and merit of Burgess's psychological discernment.†

The Worm and the Ring is about the construction of a new grammar school, generally believed to be based on Burgess's experiences at Banbury. The school is a modern Valhalla, its staff configurated variously after the Wagnerian gods (Woolton is Wotan, Lodge is Loge, Fria is Fry,

* Though not as Llewela Isherwood Jones, as Burgess always claimed. On her father's side there was meant to be a connection with the Bradshaws of Marple Hall in Cheshire and, 'through that, with Lady Charlotte Isherwood. Of Christopher Isherwood, who appears as Bradshaw in *Mr Norris Changes Trains*, neither the Jones father nor daughter had heard.' This, like the crowing about Contessa Liliana Pasi Piani della Pergola, is one of his little snobberies.

† And whilst I'm ticking him off, it may be noted that his father-in-law was never called, as he is in the autobiography, 'Eddie', but 'Teddy' or 'Ted'.

and so on). In that beyond the squabbling deities and the bickering dwarves (i.e. the pupils: Albert Rich is Alberich, wouldn't you know) there's this gleaming building project going on, the novel may also refer to Bedwellty. Mr Edward Jones M.Sc. came from Newbridge County Secondary School to be the head of Bedwellty in 1934 – but first they had to find a site and put the place up. A contract was finally awarded to Rees Edwards, Builders, of Tredegar, in 1935, following the issue of application for tenders. The architect was Colin Jones of Newport. The site was to be a bog at the southern end of Aberbargoed. Lynne's father helped to calculate the allowances that needed to be made for the shifting of the foundations. In December 1936, he told the Governors that 'the laying of the grounds was now progressing well', from which we can deduce that there'd been concerns that the edifice was sinking, like Atlantis. What was to be known as the Bedwellty County Secondary School, under the jurisdiction of the Monmouthshire Education Committee, officially opened on Thursday 9 September 1937, its catchment area extending to Maesycwmmer, Bedwas and Machen – and thus to my own overlap with an edge of Burgess's world. The Chairman of the Governors was reported in the local paper as saying, 'What would they not now be able to accomplish in commodious and up-to-date premises which they would soon be occupying?' – exactly the brave-new-world rhetoric of Gardner in *The Worm and the Ring*. The cost of the new school was £40,000. Lynne's father wrote in the log book, of his first day in office: 'It was a very wet day. It rained incessantly . . . The school was crowded to capacity.'

Amongst the throng was Lynne, who became the Head Girl. Her father being the founder and first Chairman of the County Amateur Athletics Association, she played tennis and hockey and swam for Wales. There were flourishing Library, Debating and Dramatic Societies, captained by Lynne. One of Ted Jones Science's innovations was the introduction of a Students' Representative Council, consisting of a pupil (or 'scatophagous hawk' in Burgess's phrase) from each form, and an HMI report commended its 'usefulness in the training of self-government and giving real responsibilities in certain departments of school life, under the supervision of the Headmaster'. Lynne was the convenor. During the war, when the Air Training Corps was formed, in February 1941, the school set up its own squadron, with the Headmaster as Officer Commanding. If it hadn't been for the fact that Lynne was in Manchester by then, writing her thesis on 'French Policy in Morocco 1912–1914', as part of her course in Economics, Politics and Modern History (she graduated with a IIi in 1942

– 'Lynne had achieved a degree no better than my own,' Burgess remarked tartly), she'd no doubt have been promoted on the spot to Group Captain.

Lynne, in her own realm, was quite the vivacious lady, taunting Burgess with news of all the local lads with whom she'd frolicked, like Carmen playing with Don José. One of the beaux, Rhys Evans (though given Burgess's faulty memory it might have been Rees Edwards the builder), had knocked upon her gate and devirginated her in Cefn Fforest and fully expected matrimony to ensue. He and young Wilson eyed each other warily. 'It was clearly time for me to get out of Blackwood,' said Burgess, looking back as if at the Wild West. In the Introduction to his adaptation of the Bizet, published in 1986, Burgess said that the opera *Carmen* was about 'the destructive animality of a certain kind of woman', and you know who is on his mind. 'A female is in general gall and wormwood, but she has two good moments,' wrote Mérimée, 'when she is in bed and when she is dying.' Our thoughts on Lynne are coloured by our knowledge of the news of her death. What had been carefree and confident in her youth became stupid and vulgar later on, when she began to scold and raise up such a storm that mortal ears might hardly endure the din; her zest for strangeness and risk became all exposed nerves and excitability. Burgess's sure and concentrated manner wasn't going to help. I think the real horror of her disorder and death lay in the attempts she made to reach him, how she realised that this was impossible, and how she succeeded only in destroying herself. But nor did it help leaving Wales. She'd been at her happiest and most fulfilled at Bedwellty County Secondary School – which as a result of the Education Act (1944) became Bedwellty Grammar School in 1945. Her father retired in August 1949. Burgess remembered with contempt that 'she was convinced that she had learnt more from her history master Britten than distinguished professors like L. B. Namier could ever teach'. Good shot, Burgess. The history beak was actually Mr J. C. Britton, who retired in 1945. Sir Lewis Namier, chairman of the department in Manchester from 1931 to 1952, was indeed eminent – but he was also (according to Isaiah Berlin) 'vain, proud, contemptuous, intolerant, quick to give and take offence [and] an appalling bore'. You can use many of those epithets for Lynne – and for Burgess too, once he'd found his stride. But Namier's cosmopolitanism was going to be very dismissive of a vision which began and ended with the Rhymney Valley, where Lynne had led a life of pleasure, power, freedom and glory. At the risk of imparting an anthropological generalisation of Burgessian distinction ('We don't have an intellectual class'; 'Romans despise the Pope'; 'London is an alien city with an alien monarch'), Welsh people are nervous wrecks the other side of Chepstow Bridge. There's a great sense of inferiority – for what has the tribe achieved? There's nothing much going for them: the homoerotica of rugby football, male voice choirs, pit-head baths; the kind of actor who overdoes machismo (Richard Burton, Stanley Baker) or pop-eyed eccentricity (Hugh Griffith, Anthony Hopkins); poets and novelists too fond of their own wish to glitter (Dylan Thomas, Gwyn Thomas); the sing-song bloody accent. Monmouthshire, particularly, is a wearying place, as it can't decide how Welsh it is, yet it's not England, either. Like Lake Wobegone, it is lost or trapped in the fold in the map. The people are tiresomely chirpy and nosy, talking indefatigably but not listening to what's being said. There's a facile atmosphere – as if everyone is in on some never specified joke. The effect can be demoralising, and this was Lynne's inheritance. She couldn't transplant herself easily, hence the drink and the need to create effects and make scenes.

Lynne's uprooting and departure proved ruinous; Burgess's arrival in Wales is what taught him to be a teacher. (It definitely didn't teach him a writer's observational skills – his dismal, comical Welsh folk, indeed-to-goodness-ing and look-you isn't it-jabbering, are less than trite, a *joke*. Which begs the question, how tenable are his Malays?) The impression his future father-in-law made on him cannot be underestimated. Here was John Wilson, the callow hanger-on from an extended stepfamily of small-scale shopkeepers; the Joneses were bourgeois pillars of the community. Young Wilson didn't quite know who he was or what he wanted to do, beyond having vague ideas about being a composer (hence the propitiatory hymn, 'These Things Shall Be', he wrote for Bedwellty in 1947, the school's tenth anniversary). In Ted Jones he saw what could be a career path – and Burgess's pedagogic vocation would bring dignity and fulfilment, as well as frustration. He was a teacher in the army, in Malaya and in Borneo, as well as at Banbury. When he came back from the East with the phantom tumour and said he sat down and wrote nothing but novels, actually he was trying (and failing) to get back on the staff at Banbury. Once he was established as an author he was frequently visible on the lecture podium and he enjoyed collecting temporary professorships and fellowships. Increasingly the bossy and mannered Victorian headmaster, he traipsed across America delivering talks, though this would be another opportunity for moaning. In 1973, he went to the University of Rochester to give a presentation at the Eastman School of Music and 'played a few bars of Elgar on the piano'. He was paid a thousand dollars. After the agency had lopped off its thirty per cent and hotel and travel expenses were deducted, was the fistful of dollars left over worth the effort? Nevertheless, onwards he went, to Louisiana, then to Troy, New York state, where the airport was snowbound. He had to get to Grand Rapids, Michigan, the next venue, by bus, 'four hours of slip, grind, and squelch'. Why did he do it? He put so much energy into these impracticable excursions. Indeed, he was always in transit, going from one house to another ('I find that I have certain signposts of exile stuck all around the Mediterranean . . . All this sounds like wealth, but it is really improvidence'), or one book to another ('There is a deliberate attempt not to do the same thing twice. I think that would be cheating'), or one book-signing session to another* ('I get recognised more in New York than here. G. K. Chesterton the English used to recognise, because he was fat and wore a cloak and a pince-nez. Shaw was recognised. But Graham Greene? Nobody would know who he is'), an endless voyager; and what this advertised was a man who lacked roots, for whom there was no place where loves and loyalties don't change and remain steady and were absolutely his. The best he could hope for was to play the role of the outgoing man of letters, making public appearances on chat shows and the publicity circuit, at literary dinners and in classrooms, and all the time that he is talking to you he is keeping his distance.

Always restive and looking like he was ready to flee, he was saved from aimlessness by the call to arms. Since taking his degree he'd been humping fag cartons for the Tollitts and tutoring (for 35/- a week) a boy who'd missed out on his schooling through long bouts of rheumatic fever. After the death of his stepmother he'd moved out of the flat above the shop, at 47 Princess Road, where Warden Tollitt had decreed a nine o'clock curfew, and had rented a room on Ducie Avenue. His new landlady, a crone called Mrs Hacey, allowed Lynne to stay, and put a special pan of chips on to feed the fornicators. ('Take it while you can get it, like my old man used

* Not only in Britain and America, but across the Continent. 'Winterreise', in *One Man's Chorus*, is an account of a journey through Germany to promote *Earthly Powers*, or *Der Fürst de Phantome*. Because Hans von Richter had conducted the Hallé's Wagner concerts, and because, at Manchester University 'my subject was Germanic philology', he left the country 'with an emotion I had not expected: homesickness'. Going to Spain on a similar errand (his pockets crammed with pesetas – royalties handed over in cash), he feels Spanish. He makes comparisons between the Catalan language and the Lancashire dialect and (in *Byrne*) says that there is a Spanish element in the Irish – and thus in the Manchester–Irish – owing to sailors shipwrecked from the Armada in 1588 coming ashore and, resigning themselves 'to pigshit, peat and mud', deciding to 'tickle these mad Irish with our blood'.

to say,' she'd cackled.) On the recommendation of Mr A. J. Laramy, her old science teacher, who'd already taken up a post with the Ministry of Supply, Lynne, once she'd obtained her degree, was to fill in as an assistant principal at the Board of Trade, where she was involved with the distribution of clothing coupons. She was transferred to London and to the Ministry of War Transport, in Berkeley Square. Eventually she was to be set the task of victualling the small craft of Operation Overlord, but what she most enjoyed was being taken by lots of different men to lots of different pubs and clubs, where she'd open the pipes with three pints of beer. Burgess, meantime, had pitched headlong into the plot of *Carry On Sergeant*. He spent six weeks as a raw recruit at Eskbank, Scotland, passing out as a Nursing Orderly Class 3 in the Royal Army Medical Corps. Like a Graham Greene character wallowing in squalor and malaria, Burgess seemed rather to relish the deprivations and the humiliations, the chronic constipation and the filth. He hated the bloody-minded warrant officers and NCOs, and they hated him right back. When an instructor referred to the velum as the uvulva by mistake, 'I was able to put him right.' He says he was 'resented' for being able to play the piano and for composing tunes for the bugle. He hates the marching and the drilling – 'responding like clockwork to orders' – and really he's enjoying himself having such a lot to hate, happy not having to wash or to change his clothes, having plenty of ready-made enemies; no women about. 'I was marked,' he said, with satisfaction – as he had been at school and at university. He is posted to a Field Ambulance Station at Morpeth, Northumberland, and is told, 'You are not wanted here, you know. We are a band of brothers. You are intruders.' This, like his own vials of wrath poured upon a Company Quartermaster Sergeant ('Allow me to deliver a solemn valedictory anathema, sir . . .'), is inconceivable as actual speech;* and his scrapes, such as throwing a bucket of dirty water over the NAAFI manager, or knocking off a corporal's cap, or scrubbing and polishing a corridor so well people slip and break hips ('the casualty reports were heavy'), belong to those of comical conscripts like Charles Hawtrey's Private Golightly, and they are a bit fatuous even then. What Burgess is trying to tell us is that Forces life was farcical; what actually comes across is that he was scheming, bossy, conceited and humourless.

Having shown an interest in the bagpipes, he was transferred to the Entertainments Section of the 54th Division (Home Forces) and joined a

* 'May your remaining testicle shrivel and your useless prick drop off at the root. May you wake crapulous . . .' etc. It is lifted from Jonson's *The Poetaster*.

band called the Jaypees, stationed at Moreton-in-the-Marsh. The concert party played for detachments of gunners and sappers in Gloucestershire village halls. Burgess was not popular amongst his fellow musicians – Bill Elliott, Harry Walkling, Ted Norman, Bill Brian, Ted Wright, Dick Nutting and Bob Morgan – because he told them off if they missed a cue and he insisted on prolonging his own solo passages with riffs derived from Debussy. None the less, he was well enough satisfied with his arrangements and compositions to include them in his ersatz-Grove or Biographia Musicalis catalogue forty years on:

> 1939: *Blackout Blues* – a group of cabaret songs in English . . .
>
> 1941: *An Afternoon on the Phone* – arrangement for six-piece dance orchestra of Debussy's *L'Apres-midi d'un Faune* . . .
>
> 1943: *Reveille Stomp* – for large dance orchestra.
> *Purple and Gold* – march for military band . . .

There were also settings of poems and songs by Sassoon, Wilfred Owen, Eliot and Hopkins. He fancied his chances as being Kurt Weill, John Philip Sousa, Richard Rodgers, Franz Schubert and Sir Edward Elgar rolled into one. But he didn't even reach the level of Bruce Montgomery (who published improbable thrillers as Edmund Crispin), the Oxford composer who began so promisingly and declined very fast, abandoning opera and oratorio projects to write the score for *Doctor in the House* and *Carry On Constable*.* Burgess's full orchestral scores and incidental music for *Will!*, the Shakespeare film, *Cyrano de Bergerac*, Lew Grade's *Moses the Lawgiver*, and so on, were met with by embarrassed coughs. Lord Grade did humour him once, however, by commissioning a song for Barbra Streisand. It was finally decided 'that she had better not' sing it, otherwise her career would suffer such a setback, she'd be in Brooklyn again hoofing for throw-money and babysitting for Jay Landesman.

Burgess felt that his intellectual capacities were not being quite utilised plonking out waltzes for gormless soldiers. He was 'resentful' that he was never invited to become an officer, and many of his war years involved cleaning latrines and disposing of kitchen swill. (Clearly not everybody went to crack the Enigma code at Bletchley.) From Moreton-in-the-Marsh he went to Eye, near Diss in Norfolk, Wakefield, in Yorkshire, Winwick, near Warrington, and to Chester, where he took a woodwork course.

* In 1964, Montgomery wanted to make an opera out of Burgess's *The Eve of Saint Venus*, but the composer was 'losing hope and energy'.

His report stated that he 'seemed nervous of his tools'. This is the madness of *The Wanting Seed.* Tristram Foxe, enlisted, shuttles around England, yet everywhere seems the same. Hang on a minute! Everywhere is the same! The soldiers have been trapped inside a gigantic film studio. 'Loud amplifiers. Magnesium flashes. Electronic war, a gramophony war.' War, it transpires, has been artificially created by the government to thin the pullulating population and turn the country into 'a clean house full of happy people. But every house, of course, has to have a drainage system. We're that,' explains a civil servant – who could be from Lynne's own ministry. The corpses are recycled as food for the starving millions. Burgess was always to say that there is nothing inherently wrong with cannibalism, and that he himself had eaten roasted baby in New Guinea. In *Earthly Powers*, it is argued that the Holy Eucharist is basically a cannibalistic ritual – bread and wine transubstantiated into the body and the blood – and in a Foreword to a reprint of *The Wanting Seed*, in 1982, Burgess looked forward to the day when we will 'find cans of meat in our markets called Mench or Munch, human flesh seasoned with sodium nitrate'. He was annoyed when his idea was stolen by Harry Harrison for the novel *Make Room! Make Room!*, which became the film *Soylent Green*, with Charlton Heston and Edward G. Robinson. I wonder what the reaction of Bulwer Lytton's shade was, as *The Wanting Seed* is derived from *The Coming Race* (1871), in which the people of the future are nourished by a mysterious extract called Vril. The problems of overcrowding, the battle of the sexes, the nature of evolution – all Burgess's themes come from Bulwer Lytton.*

* 'Bulwer Lytton (1803–73) is now scarcely read, though his *Last Days of Pompeii* has been filmed, and his *Rienzi* inspired an opera of Richard Wagner. *The Coming Race* anticipates modern "science fiction", with its race of underground supermen living on a nourishing substance called Vril,' we may read in *English Literature: A Survey for Students.* (I'm not even going to *mention* the schoolboyish connections between coming, sperm, seed, and other sticky equivocations.) Edward Bulwer Lytton, variously Edward Bulwer, Edward Lytton Bulwer, or Lord Lytton, was a Burgessian prototype. A prolific and opportunistic author, who moved into any form or style (science fiction, social commentary, historical reconstruction), if that's where a readership might be, his collected works fill thirty-eight chunky volumes. His novels (like Burgess's) are full of archaeological research and fictionalised kings, popes and emperors. 'Everything he wrote,' said Edmund Gosse, 'sold as though it were bread displayed to a hungry crowd.' In addition to the fiction, he published eleven volumes of poetry, two essay collections, translations, and a history of Athens. He was a friend of Dickens and later became a Member of Parliament and Secretary for the Colonies. 'That he is not much remembered in his own right would have surprised his contemporaries,' we are told in *The Cambridge Guide to Literature in English,* 'for during the mid-19th century he was widely regarded as England's leading man of letters.'

Cannibalism, the consumption of one's own species, is the very extremity of incest, the mating with one's own family, so Burgess's interest in it is consistent. The Second World War too, was, for him, less the putting to rout of the King's enemies than a vindication of his personally held belief that the biggest threat to Britain was the British – a culture that was turned in on or against itself. As he told *The Face*, in 1984, pontificating in the bar at the Savoy, 'we detested our officers so much, far worse than we did the Germans. There had to be that Socialist landslide in 1945 when Attlee got in. That paved the way for the Angry Young Men from the provinces, it paved the way for the breakdown of the system, but of course the system still exists – it always will, it's incredibly powerful.' Little Wilson's provincial paranoia was always humming and thrumming away. The war entrenched his prejudices, and was curiously congenial to him. It provided bombshells. He was shocked into an awareness of, if not other individuals, then of the death of something or other: 'The vision of Hell in *Doctor Faustus* seemed not too irrelevant. "I'll burn my books – ah, Mephistophilis."' Burgess was to remain a war writer. His pride and independence made him, by temperament, prickly and quarrelsome.* As I have mentioned, the word which chimes through his memoirs, for example, is *resentment*. His father resented him; his stepmother resented him. He is resented by Protestants, by the nuns who taught him, by religious people generally. When he joins up, the Forces seem disorganised ('I felt anger at their unprofessionalism') and his discovery is that soldiers 'learn hate from their own side'.

* Anger is Burgess's trademark, like the roar of the MGM lion. The emotion is big in his work: Enderby's flourishing of a swordstick with passion; the tatterdemalion bruisers in *A Clockwork Orange* and the mobsters in *The Doctor Is Sick*; the fights and spats in *Tremor of Intent* (a parody of the parodic Ian Fleming) and *Honey for the Bears* (West vs. East in Leningrad); the potency of potentates and scabrous aliens in *Devil of a State* and *The Right to an Answer*; the grotesquerie of Bonaparte in *Napoleon Symphony* and Carlo the burly pontiff in *Earthly Powers*. Indeed, anger is Burgess's representation of an earthly power, an energy signalling a divine afflatus. Moses foments the Promised Land and liberation from Egyptian tyranny through anger. Freud, in *The End of the World News*, through pain and anger inculcates the theory of psychoanalysis – an inner Promised Land of the afforested mind. Aptly, Burgess's Freud is conveyed as a thankless, sinned against Moses; Burgess's Moses, the primordial Jewish patriarch, is conveyed as a proleptic Viennese physician, lamenting mothers and taboos on incest.

Anger links Burgess with Hemingway, whose titanism he celebrated in a Thames and Hudson picture book, *Ernest Hemingway and His World*; with Norman Mailer, a contemporary whom he warily reviewed in the public press; and, further back, with the intemperateness of Wyndham Lewis and the genial rage of Ezra Pound – who both founded a magazine to enshrine invective, called *BLAST*. Burgess's autobiography, *Little Wilson and Big God*, is another blast of lively temper – raging, raging against the dying of the light, casting a harsh light on a dark horse.

Burgess (as with his taste in women) evidently thrived on opposition; he was forever putting himself in embattled positions. (Though he received thousands of laudatory reviews for his work later on, it was only carping and criticism which he took to his bosom. He liked to feel aggrieved, hard done by.) His wartime novel, *A Vision of Battlements*, set in Gibraltar, depicts an anti-establishment pro-anarchic masochistic mood; *The Wanting Seed* sets Tristram Foxe (who possesses Burgess's own military number)* to roam a futuristic England that has branded him a criminal. He is one of the 'wretched wanderers' press-ganged into an exterminatory World War I-style combat, complete with trenches and mouth-organ music. His sin, in an overpopulated world, is to be surrounded by an 'aura of fertility'. He thinks himself the only normal man on the planet – a one-man race apart – and such a view, of course, is paranoid. But then look at Burgess's intense individuality. He seems to have found it difficult to get on with people who knew less than he did. His huge self-involved, self-tormenting intelligence, until he found an outlet for it as a creative writer at the beginning of the sixties, was a curse. 'I was perpetually angry,' he said of his youth. 'I felt weary, lonely.' He failed tests on purpose by telling the school or army invigilators 'about the irrelevance of analysis to the aesthetic experience and I denied the validity of the task set'. He was intractable; impossible. (You can see where the aggression in *A Clockwork Orange* comes from.) He couldn't keep or find a permanent job. Yet this is the man who, in 1942, applied for a transfer to the Army Educational Corps, to teach his fellow conscripts in the ways of enlightenment. He was summoned to the Army Educational Corps depot at Wakefield and, using pamphlets issued by the Army Bureau of Current Affairs, got himself trained in the rudiments of the British Way and Purpose Scheme and promoted to sergeant. The theory was that soldiers should be encouraged to discuss the reasons for the war, its conduct, and the nature of the enemy; 'to think rationally, to examine prejudice in the glare of reason'. According to Burgess, 'the men did not understand and they were bored'. Telling them about 'a postwar life of greater cultural and political awareness', informing them about the constitution and the empire, was senseless, was nothing. As he'd veered off the syllabus to bore the men with the International Phonetic Alphabet, his classes, lectures and discussion groups were considered 'not educational' by his superiors – who were agog that on one occasion he invited along a Nazi prisoner-of-war

* 7388026 is also the secret code to open an electronic gate in the disaster-movie sections of *The End of the World News*.

to give a talk on the 'essential cultural brotherhood of the Germans and Anglo-Saxons', as if the prose extracts in Sweet's *Anglo-Saxon Reader* could smooth over the aberrations of the Reich and Hitler's desire for world domination and the eradication of the Jews. Well, at least the Nazis in Buenos Aires would be able to chant Caedmon with Borges, if they ran out of conversation. ('I felt, as often before, that I was marked.')

He hates the officers; he hates the toothless excused-boots illiterates whom he has to teach. He hates the American soldiers who (he claims) 'sneered at a rationed and beleaguered people'. He hates girls and housewives because all they want is to be 'shagged by the Yanks'. He hates the army fodder, yet when the Tollitts push the boat out to welcome Lynne, that's not right either – 'the lavishness of food and drink was obscene'. The apocalyptic vision of *The Wanting Seed* thus isn't a satirical exaggeration; it is how Burgess felt. People are born and must die as soon as possible. It's like an insane doctrinaire Catholic conspiracy, an interfusion of sex and violence, love and death. War, Tristram Foxe decides, is 'a massive sexual act, culminating in a detumescence which was not mere metaphorical dying. War, finally, the controller, the trimmer and exciser, the justifier of fertility.' He's like a ranting Thomas Malthus, who in an *Essay on the Principle of Population* (1798; 1803) argued that the progress of the human race was held in check by the limited supply of the means of subsistence, and that if the human race increased more rapidly than its food supply, a conscious and deliberate limitation of the birth rate (or an acceleration of the death rate – through warfare) had to be effected. As he was working in a lunatic asylum at Winwick, and after a spell at the Infantry Centre and Peninsular Barracks, Warrington (where he stole pass-forms by signing himself J. Joyce and E. Pound), was based at another hospital at Walton, Liverpool, which specialised in venereal diseases, it must have been hardly a straightforward task to distinguish Burgess from the actual inmates.

With all these meanderings and postings, he and Lynne's time together was fitful. Her department of the Board of Trade having been billeted in Bournemouth, they were married there in the Register Office on 22 January 1942. He was twenty-four, she was twenty-one, and they both gave their address as 17 Frances Road, Bournemouth, in the District of Bournemouth, in the County Borough of Bournemouth. It was in another south-coast town, Hove, that they'd roost after the calamitous return from the Far East – it was where all the books were produced in the pseudo-terminal year. Enderby lives here or hereabouts, too, in an out-of-season seaside resort – in generic 'sharp marine' weather, amongst 'the gull-clawed air', where the tide may be observed 'crawling creamily in'. The honeymoon lasted for an afternoon, then the criss-crossing of the country continued, the riots and tussles Burgess precipitated wherever he went picked up again, and Lynne, off now to London, mingled with accountants from Price Waterhouse, the whole of the Scotland Yard Special Branch and Parliamentary Under-Secretaries from the Board of Trade and the Ministry of War Transport. She took a flat at 122 Baron's Court Road, which is where Toomey lives in the days of his indigence. ('It was gasring cookery. A kind of ragoût. A tin of bully beef with onions and carrots . . . The ragoût had a faint odour of metal . . . It's not nice having to sleep in the odour of bully. And onions.') Her gallivantings at the Wheatsheaf, the Black Horse, the Bricklayers Arms, the Marquess of Granby, the Highlander and the Duke of York; the society of poetasters and hack journalists who subsisted on the sale of review copies; the alcoholics, black marketeering gangs and glass smashing: this was to be faithfully reported or duplicated in *The Doctor Is Sick* (dedicated 'to Lynne'), where Sheila Spindrift neglects her husband and carouses in wicked afternoon drinking dens with criminals and bent coppers. How accurate is this Fitzrovian/Soho scenario, for Burgess puts himself and his wife in the midst of high and rheumy bohemians like Julian Maclaren-Ross, who wore a rancid raincoat (which burst into flames when Aleister Crowley put a curse on it) and published short stories; Gilbert Wood, who had a phobia about rats and painted the pictures used to furnish rooms in film sets; Nina Hamnett, a Pembrokeshire-born artist who'd worked in Montparnasse as a model; and Dylan Thomas, cadging cash and writing scripts for the Ministry of Information? It's a wonder Burgess and Lynne didn't pose for a portrait by Augustus John, another toper at the Wheatsheaf Tavern (double rum and brandy), which was kept by a Jewish family called Kleinfeld, not Klein, as Burgess recalled. Everyone alive back then claims to have met Dylan Thomas and stood him a drink at least twice. Burgess goes one better and alleges that Lynne slept with Cwmdonkin Drive's Rimbaud, whose favourite tipple was orange squash. ('He was not very good at sex,' Burgess confided to the *Western Mail*, in 1987. 'He just wanted somebody to cuddle up to.') It all sounds like a regurgitation of Maclaren-Ross's own *Memoirs of the Forties* to me,* with bits of Dan Farson's accounts of the French and the Colony Room, of Francis Bacon and John Deakin and their gilded gutter lives,

* Burgess called Julian Maclaren-Ross, whose stories appeared in *Lilliput* and *Penguin New Writing*, and who appears as the brilliant but unstable sponger X. Trapnel in Powell's *A Dance to the Music of Time*, 'a symbol of wartime Bohemia'. He claimed to have admired

thrown in. Burgess knew that the Duke of York was situated off Jekyll and Hyde Alley (so called, said Maclaren-Ross, 'because it was the sort of place through which Mr Hyde flourishing his stick rushes low-angle on the screen'), but he forgot to tell us its actual name was Newman Passage, and was the sinister byway used by Michael Powell for a murder scene in *Peeping Tom*. He also unaccountably forgot to tell us that Nina Hamnett and Maclaren-Ross were so shaken by the film *The Lost Weekend*, they had to be administered a stiff rum before being strong enough to hail a taxi back to the Wheatsheaf. (Nina, who had affairs with Roger Fry and Anthony Powell, died in 1956 as a result of a fall from the window of her flat in Westbourne Terrace on to the railings below. She was another Welsh person stranded outside Wales.)

The bibulousness, the smoke-laden saloon bars, the mobsters and government officials, the tarts and society beauties, burglars and art dealers; the film extras, scenery painters, chorus girls and poetasters: it's like the last five minutes of the Roman Empire, or Bulwer Lytton's *The Last Days of Pompeii*, with its moral lesson that the eruption of Vesuvius was well-deserved.† Speaking in the sinking city of Venice towards the end of his life, Burgess said, 'What you remember about the past is the truth. The falsifications are a tribute to the power of one's own memory.' Did he quite mean this? It's not dissimilar (as dissimulation) to Toomey's remark about novelists making enthusiastic but hazardous eyewitnesses – asked by the Archbishop to verify a miracle of Carlo's, he says, 'We lie for a living. This . . . makes us good believers, credulous anyway.' Also, old men forget.

Burgess's musical scores – but it transpired that what he was praising was the neatness of the dots, dashes and squiggles, inked in by hand, which he said resembled a Persian manuscript. Maclaren-Ross had worked as a vacuum-cleaner salesman for a firm called Sucko in Bognor Regis. His experiences informed the novel *Of Love and Hunger* (1947), where the salesman is seduced by randy housewives, one of whom gives the hero 'a kiss like a mouthful of rice pudding. Her teeth didn't get in the way and she knew what to do with her tongue.'

All of Maclaren-Ross's works are long out of print: *The Stuff to Give the Troops* (1944), *Better than a Kick in the Pants* (1945), *Bitten by a Tarantula* (1945), *The Nine Men of Soho* (1946), *The Funny Bone* (1956), *The Weeping and the Laughter* (1953), *Until the Day She Dies* (1960), *The Doomsday Book* (1961), *My Name Is Love* (1964) and *Memoirs of the Forties* (1965). Books discussed in the Fitzrovian pubs, but never actually written, had titles like *Threnody on a Gramophone*, *The Sea Coast of Bohemia*, *Khaki and Cockayne* and a second volume of autobiography, *Lost Atlantis*.

† The volcanic climax in Pompeii was borrowed for *The Kingdom of the Wicked*: 'The floor trembled again; brimstone fumes sailed in . . . Smoke, fire and lava. Lungs filled, choked. A black pall began to be pulled over the day's serenity . . . The lights out, time's ruination, our mother our killer, an uncaring deity, so everything ends, a figure of the finality and nothing done.' *Götterdämmerung*, you might say.

In *Earthly Powers*, though the homosexual hero jostles with Fordie, Ez, Tom Eliot and Willie Yeats, he doesn't know that the lesbianic novelist Radclyffe Hall was called John by her friends and there is a scene set at Green Park underground station ten years before it was built. Do we have here laziness and ignorance on Toomey's part? On Burgess's?* It might, therefore, have been more to the point for him to have said that the

* He'd never allow himself to be corrected, claiming that the errors in *Earthly Powers* (as, for example, catalogued by David Holloway in the *Telegraph*) were intentional – to see if we were on our toes, presumably, though his huffing and puffing if caught out being sloppy was like Captain Mainwaring when he says with false jocularity, 'Well done, men, I was wondering who'd be the first to point this out!' As Burgess cried to a student reporter from *Isis*, 'the errors were deliberate . . . [Toomey's] going to get things wrong. I like understanding from those who read my books, I don't get much from the people in England.' Well, Amis's *The Old Devils* is set in Swansea and Glamorganshire not Newport and Monmouthshire, despite what Burgess stated when reviewing it; and if it comes to that, it's Robert Donat not Richard, as he would have it in *Little Wilson and Big God*. He was also offended, however, by the stupidity of his readers if an error had crept in and nobody did complain: 'A few weeks back I published a review in the *Observer* and there was a gross error – not my fault – when the name Marx was confused with Mach [Ernest Mach – Austrian physicist and philosopher who measured the speed of sound]. The sentence became such obvious nonsense that I expected a massive response. But no-one noticed. Not a peep. It's disturbing.'

That comment comes from an unused portion of interview material sent to me by Richard Rayner. (A truncated question-and-answer session, co-scripted by Jonathan Meades, 'In Conversation with Anthony Burgess', appeared in *The Fiction Magazine*, in the summer of 1984.) Emboldened, perhaps, by Burgess's comments, Rayner used his space when reviewing *You've Had Your Time*, to list the errors he'd found: it should be Alan Ladd *Jr.* at the head of Twentieth-Century Fox, not Alan Ladd; Sam Goldwyn and Jack Warner are transposed; Mods and Rockers were not engaged in pitched battles as early as 1960; and so on.

You can tell that polyglottal Burgess took huge delight in being able to state that he could vet all the translations of his works that kept appearing ('I would say that the German translation of *Earthly Powers* is better than the original'); and it was pure bliss to announce that: 'It's an author's duty to watch the translation . . . There were some fabulous blunders in the Italian translation of *Jake's Thing*. Kingsley should have watched that.'

Why, however, couldn't those close to him have physically restrained him from publishing articles like 'The Anachronist Strikes Back' (*TLS*, 2 August 1985), his volcanic eruption over Peter Howell's (actually docile) review of *The Kingdom of the Wicked* (*TLS*, 31 May 1985)? The worst Howell could find to say is that the novel's narrator is able to quote Juvenal years before he was born and wrote, yet Burgess foams at the mouth about the critics 'having a stab at me again'. You know he is going to mention the precedent of Shakespeare and the clocks striking in ancient Rome, Brutus and Cassius wearing hats, and Caesar getting knifed in the doublet . . . and so he does.

The most embarrassing (or most splendid) example of Burgess's blowing his top and making a *complete fucking fool* of himself was his reaction to English National Opera's production of his *Carmen* libretto ('this leaden balloon', Paul Griffiths, *The Times*, 29 November 1986; 'one of the ghastliest examples I've seen' . . . 'total unfocussed chaos', Nicholas Kenyon, *Observer*, 30 November 1986). He wrote a piece in the *Observer*, on 28 December 1986, fulminating against the philistines and claiming (ineffably) that '*I guessed beforehand* that both the director and the singers would howl about unsingability, unactability and over-literariness. This sort of thing always happens.' (Italics added.)

powerful falsifications and fabrications of memory are a tribute to the mind's capacity to fictionalise and to make its own connections and truths. It selects, edits, anthologises; it imposes its own symmetries and coherence; and it deceives and conceals. Can George Orwell really have seen Burgess smoking Victory cigarettes at the Mandrake Club, Meard Street, and then gone directly back home to put a soldier puffing on Victory cigarettes in the manuscript of *Nineteen Eighty-Four*?* Does it matter what is imagined and what is authentic?

Behind autobiography (the art of discovering what a person stands for) and its mirror image, biography (the science of why people behave as they do); behind all the bluster of existence, expressed as anecdote, reminiscence, apocrypha, reportage; behind the exposing and withholding, there should lie the quality of myth. Burgess's story has this dim air of unreality, with Lynne as his idea of a licentious Molly and Burgess himself as the long-suffering Bloom. Lynne was exaggerative, crude, impulsive, sociable. She's eager to be entertained and adored late nights, gaiety and movement. Burgess, by contrast, is calculating, deliberate, stony, and with a deep distrust of the world. Look further, however, and there's a depressing side to the Fitzrovian partying, 'the hazy days and unremembered nights', as Beryl Bainbridge put it, referring to the life of Jeffrey Bernard, who perpetuated the noncomformist tradition; and Lynne didn't have the skills of Francis Bacon (placenta-pink pictures) or Jeffrey Bernard himself ('In all the years I have never once been bored by Jeffrey Bernard,' Graham Greene exclaimed†) to transcend this environment. An affected carelessness and getting drunk were all she was ever to aspire to – she tried to recreate its spirit wherever she went, in Banbury, Malaya, Chiswick. It was her dead end. Burgess, equally a part of the nonconformist tradition, was intent more on creating his own personal myth as a man who is exceptional, isolated; and he projects into his works his special feelings and anxieties by making his lack of engagement into a peevish and contemptuous, hard and shiny, personal style. When he indulges in bouts of

* Orwell's looking at London in the forties, and projecting it as the futuristic eighties, is discussed further in *1985*, in which book Burgess also alleges that Orwell put a curse on the Mandrake Club and a pub called the George – for if ever you had a drink there with Dylan Thomas, Louis MacNeice or Roy Campbell, 'on your next visit [you] learned they were dead'.

† Jeffrey Bernard was most put out when Burgess snubbed him in Old Compton Street, in the summer of 1987. 'I called out to him, but he pressed on.' Two years previously, Burgess had spent an afternoon in the Colony Room telling Bernard the meaning of life. The trouble was, Bernard forgot what he said.

manliness or suggests a pride in squalor and roistering, or when he brings on fat-bellied garlic-smelling characters and avoids elegance and delicacy, it's an act – like Richard Burton (who was to have played Enderby in a film), informing us of his hard-living off-screen antics because he's fretful that we'll judge him (as he's only an actor) as a man who is inadequate and soft. 'By those who look close to the ground,' said Dr Johnson, 'dirt will be seen.' This is Burgess in Gibraltar, a compound of arrogance and deliberate wrong-headedness.

He received notice of his posting overseas in November 1943. He left from the Transit Depot at Marylebone on a slow train for Avonmouth and a ship that zig-zagged out into the middle of the Atlantic before returning to the Bay of Biscay. He was not to see Lynne again, save for a brief leave two years later, until his demobilisation in May 1946. As with his mother and sister, here's another relationship predicated on an absence. Burgess's separation from others (in a specific and general sense), and his view of himself as wanting to be a notable victim, is getting to be the pattern. Also – his uppishness. Molly Bloom came from Gibraltar, and Burgess has a few emendations to make ('Joyce had got Molly all wrong') regarding the imprecision of the Spanish dialect in *Ulysses*, the unlikelihood of Molly's father being a major, and the impossibility of a mixed marriage between an Irish soldier and a gypsy-ish girl from the Rock. As he explained to the *Paris Review* ('It's a matter of great literary import'):

> There's a social thing. In a very small garrison town like Gibraltar with this man, Major Tweedy, whose previous wife is Spanish, his half-Spanish daughter would speak either Spanish as a first language (and not with the usual grammar) or English as a first language – but certainly both languages, in the first instance in an Andalusian way, and in the second instance in a totally class-conscious, pseudo-patrician way . . . [It] is an image of Nora Barnacle and not of Molly at all.

This, from the Burgess whose Bedwellty denizens talk like a bad amateur production of *Under Milk Wood* done by Pakistanis (in Pakistan) and whose Celtic characters in *Any Old Iron* are Taffies the same way that I'm a Dutchman. The man had no ear for speech as it is spoken colloquially by real people. Recalling Burgess's involvement with *Jesus of Nazareth*, Zeffirelli said that the main problem facing himself and his co-writers, Suso Cecchi d'Amico and Emilio Gennarini, was to dismantle the script for each scene with the actors 'in order to find speakable words'. Left to Burgess, the Disciples and Apostles would have sounded how Victorian

Bible illustrations look: formal, stiff, ponderous, and with lots of bearded men being angry and gloomy. Anger and gloom, however, are at the core of Burgess's personality. If he didn't quite register how people actually talked to each other, it was because his mind was too busy correcting their mistakes and lapses. In his fashion, he was as rare-fied and sensitive an aesthete as Wilde's fops, who maintain that egotism is delightful because the world will never weary of watching a troubled soul 'in its progress from darkness to darkness'; and in Gibraltar, Burgess sank himself in a lonely funk, which was to be the chief characteristic of the protagonists in his novels, who find unrest and catastrophe everywhere they go.

Gibraltar was taken from Spain by the British in 1704, and it has remained of strategic importance as the entry to the Mediterranean. Sporadic attempts were made over the years to recover the lost peninsula, so the garrison was kept in a permanent state of readiness. By the late nineteenth century there were approximately twenty thousand residents, two-thirds of whom were belonging to the occupying force. Cannons signalled the opening and closing of the frontier gates – servants and Spaniards had to hurry back to La Linea, a place noted for its brothels and seedy bars. Smuggling and black marketeering were rife. On the Rock there were art galleries, a ruined castle (converted into a prison) and, in the Alameda Gardens (where Molly Bloom flirted with the officers), concerts were held. There were spectacular views of Spain and, across the Straits, of the Atlas Mountains and Morocco. Thackeray, in 1844, described the Rock as 'always beautiful, especially at evening, when the people are sauntering along the walks, and the moon is shining on the waters of the bay and the hills and twinkling white houses on the opposite shore. Then the place becomes quite romantic; it is too dark to see the dust on the dry leaves.' A hundred years later, Burgess found it a shit-hole. Far from its being a model colony where one sat shaded by palm trees to read or to take tea, it is crammed with bored soldiers drinking themselves silly, disease, bed bugs, and the scrofulous Barbary apes, flourishing by order of Churchill.

He'd been sent to the Rock as an instructor in German, and was also ordered to teach Spanish, French and Russian. From the start he's truculent – belligerent. He claims that he starts fights, gets into brawls with dockers, is flung into prison for mocking Franco, is thrown out of bars – all on an implausibly regular basis. What might be taken as a journal of the Gibraltar years is the novel *A Vision of Battlements*, where the Army Educational Corps becomes the Army Vocational and Cultural Corps, and where Molly's rebuke to Bloom, 'Rocks! Tells us in plain words!' becomes, right there on page one, a big blonde Wren's, 'Aw, come on, tell us in plain words.' Burgess (or Wilson) is Richard Ennis, or *Sinner* backwards. 'A first novel as autobiographical as it's possible to find,' Burgess confessed to Bernard Levin; so here we go with the Burgessian crosspatch in a foreign location, sleeping with young native girls in the afternoon, guilty about a neglected wife, and having problems with his superiors. Human beings are no more than an assemblage of weak stomachs, rotting teeth, and bodily functions; they are devoid of any distinctive life – they certainly don't have heart. The only layers characters possess are anatomical, physiological. People are all nerve fibres and tissues. It was his first novel, and I read it last. Just the other day as a matter of fact – and is it his best? The book is not rushed; it is not over-hasty. The paradox of late-period Burgess, or even the Burgess who became a feature on the literary scene in the sixties, is that though he's prolific, industrious, indefatigable, it was all to become a laborious routine; as an artist he was lazy, incurious. (Much of his work isn't art – it's pop journalism.) There was a lethargy of thought. I don't feel that about *A Vision of Battlements* – its weariness is that of the forties malaise; as with the Malaya novels, there's an exhausted end-of-empire atmosphere, which Burgess has captured, and which perhaps is only fully visible now; and he'd had to be there, sensitive to it, alert. *A Vision of Battlements* is an alert book. The war has been won (or the end is in sight); and Burgess feels a personal sense of defeat, of wilt – literally so: Ennis fails to satisfy Lavinia, not much is to be done with her, and she vanishes from the story, like Lynne left in London. There is no sense of victory, only of impotence. Yet how could critics so misunderstand this novel, saying it is comic? ('The brilliant and hilarious war novel by the author of *Nothing Like the Sun* and *A Clockwork Orange*,' runs the blurb for the Ballantine paperback edition, in November 1966. 'A dazzlingly funny novel of love, war and the army . . .') Admittedly, Burgess himself was taken aback by the judgement, too. Roland Gant, of Heinemann, 'kindly called me into his London office and gave me a glass of Empire sherry and said: "You know, we like your novel, it's funny." I was surprised because I had always seen myself as a creature of gloom and sobriety.' Exactly so – *A Vision of Battlements* is despairing.* Of course there are faults: the symbolism and allusion, stolen from Joyce; caricature

* America produced *The Naked and the Dead*, Britain *A Vision of Battlements*. The pusillanimity of our Second World War literature (perhaps of our literature generally compared with American machismo – machismo plus operatic self-pity, from Ahab to Willy Loman, it

in place of characterisation; the plot – too much happens. But a lot of his books are here already – the violence of *A Clockwork Orange*; the disdained artist figure (Enderby); the Mediterranean location (Gibraltar is like the Malta of *MF*); the affinity with abroad (and suffering in the heat); the alien scenes and smells; the light and the stink; all the God business; and Lynne hovering over it – his work is haunted by her. The character of Concepcion, had she lived, might have grown up to become Liana – oh, these dark girls – *dark ladies* – who slink through the books! (It's as if he is going to be on the look-out for things in life which he'd prophesied in his stories.)

None of Ennis's battles, however, with God, girls, a wife, a mistress, irritate quite as much as his difficulties with his oafish superiors. From his stepfamily to the Faculty at Manchester, Lynne's suitors to army officers – or, in Burgess's novels, from the headmaster and his deputy in *The Worm and the Ring* to the colonial officers in the Malaya books, from Alex's gaolers and the psychologists in *A Clockwork Orange* to critics and readers in the memoir *You've Had Your Time* – Burgess had problems with obedience, with respecting manners and codes. (He was alone in a world of enemies.) He resisted the hierarchical world – unless he's on top – and in *A Vision of Battlements* Ennis's enemy, Major Muir, is based on Burgess's adversary, Major Meldrum. Of Muir it is observed: 'He spoke often ungrammatically, with a home-made accent in which Cockney diph-

---

ought to be added) was a taunt of Mailer's: 'Has not the time come for the British writer to face the disagreeable notion that, compared to us in America, he has been slack, has fought his battles with too little, and surrendered too often to those peculiar betrayals which are worked in the name of good taste, caution, and the public trust?' (cited in *The Time of Our Time*, 1998). Burgess, in many respects, would go along with this, his own works intending to be tidal waves of rhetoric, as opposed to the piddling rivulets of Amis, Murdoch, Drabble, Angus Wilson, and so on, the cast of his British Council pamphlet *The Novel To-Day* (1963) and his 'Student's Guide to Contemporary Fiction', *The Novel Now* (1967; revised 1971). As he said in 1985, 'One of the reasons I left England was that I didn't want to be associated with the British school of literature and its small-minded themes – Hampstead Heath adultery etc. . . .' [etcetera and ellipsis in original]. The paradox with Burgess, however, is that for all the vastness of (say) *Earthly Powers* – taking on a history of the twentieth century; hundreds of pages of tiny print – its scale is small. Nobody changes; nobody alters when they learn things. Toomey, as Mailer would say, is *slack* – as all Burgess's sufferers are. Even his titans (Napoleon, Jesus, Freud, Moses) are mulish. And the linguistic skills, which are meant to open him out, seem to me antiquarian. He polishes his vocabulary like a Victorian minerologist putting specimens in a glass cabinet. Burgess once met Mailer in New York. 'Burgess, your last book was shit,' said Mailer with finality. Burgess also encountered John Steinbeck. 'Fuck off,' said Steinbeck, when Burgess had asked him, at a Heinemann party, how he intended spending the Nobel Prize cheque. (The incident also occurs in *Inside Mr Enderby*.)

thongs stuck out stiffly, like bristles. His ignorance was a wonder. But he had power, pull, in high places'; and in *Little Wilson and Big God*, Meldrum enters (to pantomimic boos and hisses) as a detestable slave-driving boss who 'seemed to me to have little justice in his inventory. Nor any compassion.' He knows nothing about Eliot or Dante, Hölderlin or Kafka, is a bureaucratic tyrant, compiling endless pedestrian progress reports and 'dull forecasts of quantitative glory', and he surrounds himself with warrant-officers who ensure his orders are executed. One such was Mr Crump, whom Burgess considered an obsequious bully. It was Crump who met the new draft on Christmas Eve 1943. 'We all knew we were not going to get on with Crump,' he recalled, and Crump and Meldrum – splendid Dickensian names – 'earned resentment'. What's certainly pathetic, however, are Burgess's mean little gestures of defiance, forgetting to salute or smoking without permission. He believes that his insubordination and the scrapes he gets into around the town portray him as a man of action. This isn't gleeful, delighting mischief, though; it is sour, hysterical behaviour. What are we to make of his attempted rape of a young Gibraltarian? 'I grabbed a girl and hungrily kissed her' – and he's 'resentful' of her screams. Burgess is insolent, insulting, concealing the phrase 'Meldrum is a fucking fool' as an acrostic in a film review; and if his problems with authority are predictable, so is his pretentiousness. 'I composed one Sunday, in the intervals of reading Hemingway's *Fiesta* in German, a setting of a song by Lorca,' he informs us. If Max Beerbohm, Evelyn Waugh or even Craig Brown had written that sentence it would be a masterpiece of satire, a complicit mix of the languid and the preposterous. Burgess expects to be taken literally – there are no undercurrents or overtones. When he doesn't get on with people or feels he is being mocked for his cleverness, he doesn't seem to know how condescending he is, what a target he makes himself into; and Lynne, at least, knew how to deal with him: with affectionate derision and irony. Sergeant Richard Ennis could enter into the spirit of that; he hasn't given up on people yet or acquiesced in failure and defeat. Maybe Sergeant John B. Wilson was like that, too. But the Burgess who looked back at his youth after nearly half a century lacked any perspective of humour. What we have instead is an 'air of injured sanctity' – to use John le Carré's phrase about the impression created by his convicted confidence trickster of a father. His music written on the Rock, a Sonata for piano, a Retreat for flute and drums, a Prelude and Fugue for organ, a Nocturne, and an Overture for a large orchestra (entitled 'Gibraltar'), plus a Sinfonietta ('abandoned') and a Mass in G for chorus and orchestra ('abandoned') are faithfully listed in his 'Biographia Musicalis', in *This Man and Music.* I am absolutely certain that none of this is offered up as a joke. And when Meldrum and Crump turn up in Burgess's novels (as 'the more detestable of my minor characters'), again it isn't comedy; it is revenge. Here they come, for example, in the opening chapter of *Inside Mr Enderby*:

> 'Crump,' called the major-general in an etoilated martinet's voice. 'Crump. Crump.' He was not reminiscing about the First World War; he wanted the barman to replenish his rum-glass. Crump came from behind the bar . . . with a false smile both imbecilic and ingratiating . . . 'Yes, General,' he said. 'Similar, sir? Very good, sir.'

It's a Mrs Meldrum who is Enderby's landlady ('The less he saw of her the better') and she evicts him; and it is a Meldrum who, as Principal of the South London (Channel) Unitary School (Boys), is Tristram Foxe's supervisor in *The Wanting Seed*: 'You realise that it's not up to me who fills these vacancies. It's up to the board. All I can do is recommend.' He is full of such mealy-mouthed platitudes and malice: 'Things are very tricky these days. In confidence, fella, you watch your step . . . One false step . . . and you'd be out. Yah, out.' Crump and Meldrum, the one doing the dirty work of the other, or dancing attendance upon the other, represent officiousness, of a kind that is bound to clash with a free spirit. In *A Clockwork Orange*, there is a man writing a treatise about moral philosophy, which is also called *A Clockwork Orange*, and Alex reads a sentence or two before tearing the typescript into big snowflakes: 'The attempt to impose upon man, a creature of growth and capable of sweetness . . . laws and conditions appropriate to a mechanized creation, against this I raise my sword-pen.' To Burgess, his commanding officers in Gibraltar and the interchangeable Blimps and autocrats in his fiction, which culminate in Paul Maxwell Bartlett, Co-ordinating Principal, Combined Space Research Projects of Columbia, Princeton, MIT and the University of Pennsylvania, and a Special Attachment to the US Navy with the temporary rank of Rear-Admiral, in *The End of the World News*, a man who is going to decide who has a useful enough trade to be worthy of a place aboard the spaceship, or Ark, which will fly away from Earth and avoid the apocalypse when the planet collides with an asteroid – all that these men want, Burgess believes, is mastery. Meldrum, in particular, knew no pity. He refused Burgess compassionate leave when Lynne was attacked; nor would he allow Sergeant Stevens leave when his baby daughter was killed in an air-raid. 'The dead could not be made undead, said Meldrum with infuriating reasonableness.' This gets directly into *A Vision of Battlements* – Sergeant Bayley's son is killed: 'He died. Young John. My son . . . My only son . . . And I never saw him . . . And Muir wouldn't let me go home.' Interestingly, it is Ennis who comes out with the callous and fatuous comment: 'But, you know, it isn't as though you'd ever seen him. I mean, it's easier for you than for her', i.e. than for the mother; and isn't this the way Burgess froze his own emotions when it came to subjects like loss and grief?

In *1985*, he summed up his attitude to the forties by saying, 'the British class system found its most grotesque expression in the British Army . . . There was, to say the least, a general antipathy on the part of the troops towards their officers, a great gulf of manners, speech, social values, a chasm between those who had to lead and those who did not want to be led.' This was certainly his own position – yet his own position was also, in a way, the opposite. If women turn into his stepmother, Burgess could turn into Meldrum. During his three-week leave in 1945 he finds he doesn't like being home; he doesn't like Welsh children or Welsh pubs, when he visits Blackwood with Lynne; he doesn't like the 'new world of frankness and insolence' – though it is precisely his own frankness and insolence, when confronting Crump and Meldrum, that he had been at such pains for us to admire, was it not? Ennis leaves Gibraltar to find 'A new world, I believe. Wide boys, drones, a cult of young hooliganism. State art. Free ill-health for all . . . The *Daily Mirror*'s increasing circulation . . . Reality will seem very unreal over there.' Ennis becomes Howard Shirley, in *One Hand Clapping*, who is so nauseated by the post-war liberties that he plans a dramatic suicide; or he's Denham, in *The Right to an Answer*, or Lydgate, in *Devil of a State*, who find England so fully intolerable that they vanish abroad on business – coming back, of course, periodically, to give us a good wigging. The strong feelings of impatience are Burgess's own; and we've seen how John Wilson was Richard Ennis, a Burgess self-image *aet.* thirty. But what did other people think? Burgess originally departed for Gibraltar in a draft of five – with Harry Stevens, a Welsh sociologist, Ben Thomas, a Welsh mathematician, 'a morose Lancashire woodwork expert called Albert Parker', and Jimmy Wilkinson, a teacher of French. A year after *Little Wilson and Big God* was published, Burgess himself sent me the following letter – without comment, without prejudice:

Dear John,

I often listened to the BBC2 book programme, which occasionally puts on a panel of speakers to discuss new publications. They had a programme on James Joyce, whom I know was a favourite of yours; and indeed you took part. However, first things first. It was only when they were reviewing your autobiography that I realised that Anthony Burgess, the author of *The Little Wilson and Big God*, was none other than John Wilson with whom I worked in Gibraltar for two years. What prompted me to write to you was the impression I got that your remarks about Captain Meldrum – later Major Meldrum, the Command Education Officer – were less than just. Indeed, they were bordering on the scurrilous. I felt that this was very unfair indeed because Meldrum, if he is living at all, will be a very old man and in any case his family will still be around and you were very hard indeed on him. I have a feeling that, in a Freudian kind of way, you were blaming him for the mishap you had, also for Harry Stevens'* unfortunate and very sad loss of his baby. No matter what Meldrum would have done or said, it would have been wrong in your eyes, for the simple reason that he was unable to send you home on leave, and I think you were assuming that he had powers he did not possess.

As it is now over forty years since we were together in Gibraltar, no wonder you got names wrong: for example I am Norman Parker not 'Albert', Frank Allen was the W.O.1., not Frank Barton, and W.O.1. Crump, as I remember, was Norman Crump. I do not really see why you should get uptight over people like Crump – he was a loner, suffering from 'Rockitis', anxious to get away. Frankly, we just simply left him alone. He didn't want to be one of us and I didn't particularly want to be a friend of his and it didn't worry me to the extent you made out in your autobiography.

Your memory is faulty over the names and I suggest you were at fault in other respects also. What I thought I'd do was to set down my memories of my time in the Army Education Corps, bearing in mind, and I must emphasise this, that I am speaking from a time-span of over forty years [. . .]

Like you, when I joined the Army Education Corps, I was sent to one of the rotten jobs. From your autobiography, you seemed to finish up in a psychiatric hospital. I was sent to a glasshouse, staffed by

* Burgess spells the name 'Stephens'.

thugs transferred from the various infantry regiments, who were given three stripes and told to get on with it.

I well remember my first lecture to the soldiers under sentence. I was told to talk to them about 'why you are in the war'. What a daft idea! I entered this vast room in a cotton-mill in Heywood, Lancashire, and inside the room, placed about six feet from the wall, was a vast cage. The men were housed in this cage with their bunks three tiers high. To listen to me they had to sit on the few chairs available or on the floor in the middle of the room. I was taken aback by this experience and instead of trying to tell these people 'why you are in the army', I simply gave them (a) an outline of the stage of the war at that point and (b) a sketch of some of the developments that were going on in preparing for the post-war period. Foolishly, I invited questions at the end of this talk and one man stood up and said: 'It's all very well for you to talk about how the war is going, and what is going to happen after the war, what about us here in this bloody cage? Here we are,' he said, 'and at night time we have got these buckets into which we have to piss and shit – what kind of existence is that for so-called human beings?' Well, I had no answer to that and I was very glad when the session finished. Like you, I had the experience of teaching some of these men basic English. Many were illiterate. They had to parade each day and I well remember when they dragged a man out from solitary confinement. He had obviously been beaten up, his face was all swollen and he had to be assisted to his feet. I was quite sick over this, so much so that later I went to see the Commanding Officer, who I was quite sure didn't know, or care, about what was going on. I asked him 'was it really necessary to have this man beaten up in this kind of way?' Shortly afterwards I found that I was on embarkation leave.

It would be early December that I had to report, as you did, to the transit camp in West London prior to going overseas. It would be about December 12th and we had to arrive by 23.00 hours. When I arrived there were three others there. One was called Wilkinson, who was a linguist; one was Harry Stevens, who was the economics man; Ben Thomas, a W.O.2 – he was a maths man; and myself, a qualified teacher specialising in handicrafts with also technical qualifications in the Construction field. Later, indeed shortly before lights out, you arrived and I distinctly remember asking you about your background. It seemed to be English and if I recall, your M.A. was taken by a research project on Shakespeare. Wilkinson said, 'I knew it, it's a bloody circus'; and sure enough we were really a mixed bag. You were quite drunk. You started to tell us about your evening which was spent in a pub in Soho which was very crowded. You mentioned names like Dylan Thomas and other names I did not know. You were sitting next to your wife, I believe she was called Lynne, and on the other side of her was a man who was trying to make up to her and began to fondle her. What you were upset about was that your wife seemed not to object to this and eventually you had to go. You became quite maudlin over this and I believe you were also weeping. I felt so sorry for you because I had left my wife, who was pregnant with our first child, and we were all feeling pretty low.

The next morning we were taken to the boat train which went very slowly to Avonmouth. We arrived there in the dark and I recall going into this dimly lit ship. It was one of the Highland class converted banana boats. It was called the *Highland Monarch*. We sailed up the Irish Sea and eventually to the Firth of Clyde, where we joined a huge convoy which set off about December 14th and sailed out across the Atlantic. It was very rough. I was very sick, and for several days I was in my bunk which began to look like a coffin. It had deep wooden sides. I became so weak that I couldn't stand and eventually I had to be carried up to the ship's hospital, where I was placed in a cot, on gimbals, and fed with beef tea. We arrived in Gibraltar on Christmas Eve 1943. It was dark and I was astonished to see the Rock was quite well lit up. For some reason or other I assumed that everywhere had a blackout, but it looked quite dramatic from the boat.

We were met by W.O.1. Crump and, as you say in your autobiography, we had to split up. Two of you went to the Moorish Castle and three of us to the Engineers' Barracks, at Europa point. We only slept there one or two nights because we were attached to the Garrison Mess which was in the middle of the town, in Engineers' Lane. We simply dumped our kit on the bunks and then were taken to the Garrison Mess where I well remember hearing dance music as we approached. I thought, 'Good, there's a dance on' – but on getting inside I found that there was a three-piece band playing in the corner and the men were simply lying around – some under the tables, some under the seats, most of them were quite drunk, and it seemed so odd to me that there wasn't a single woman in sight. I viewed with astonishment some of the things that went on. Most of the Warrant Officers and sergeants were regulars and each of them seemed to have a speciality turn. One man, who although quite drunk, stood in one corner singing 'In My Sentry Box' and at the end of every verse he had to discard a piece of clothing. He eventually finished up stark naked, but he was still singing 'In My Sentry Box', and no one was taking a blind bit of notice of him. Another man gave a turn playing a mouth organ through his nose – which seemed disgusting to me but the others seemed to enjoy it. A third one gave a recitation about a visit to the zoo. So the night went by, people giving their little turns, and I was getting more and more miserable. Eventually we were able to get back to our bunks at Europa Point.

The following morning I walked right up to the top of the Rock on my own. It was a beautiful day. I looked north to see the snow capped Sierras in Spain and I looked south-east to see the Blue Atlas mountains in Africa. It was a magnificent sight, but I felt very homesick and very lonely.

A couple of days later* we had a staff meeting with Captain Meldrum and Crump, and there we met the sixth member of our team, a chap called Jack Curling. He was a schoolmaster with a science degree. He had an enormous chip on his shoulder and he couldn't get on with Crump at all. I think he was very glad to see us. At the staff meeting, Meldrum told us he was going to call together all the Unit Education Officers and he expected each of us to give a brief talk about our background and what we could do. He pointed out that there was a problem in Gibraltar of boredom and low morale and he referred to 'Rockitis' – the first time I had heard this word, which is really self-explanatory. It is a kind of disease which Crump had in a big way. You refer to this meeting with the Unit Education Officers in your autobiography – I do not recall any people walking out from your talk. Certainly some of them walked out but they simply wanted to use the Gents. They'd been sitting still for quite a long time, listening to myself, Harry Stevens, and other people. Your talk was quite amusing. Harry Stevens was very professional, as you would expect from an ex-W.E.A. lecturer. I don't remember or recall what Ben said, but I was to make a feature of attacking this problem of 'Rockitis' by, first, linking the men's studies and interests with home and, secondly, by having courses which would assist them in civilian life. Like us all,

* Burgess says that the meeting was on Christmas morning itself and that, 'There were no seasonal greetings. We were merely told what we had to do.'

I worked very hard on the Rock. I had selected a man from each unit, brought them down into the town to give a talk on instruction techniques, kitted out each unit with a workshop for handicrafts, and I also started teaching technical subjects in the Gibraltar Evening Institute – telecommunications, structural engineering, building and construction . . . The technical subjects were quite successful. With language subjects, on the other hand, they would enrol in their hundreds for Spanish and after a few weeks you'd finish with about twenty. I think a lot of soldiers thought that they would attain a language merely by attending a class.

I got to know my colleagues reasonably well. Harry Stevens clearly was an expert lecturer and he seemed to walk the length and breadth of the Rock giving his talks on the British Way and Purpose, and so on. Thankfully I hadn't to do that because I was busy on the technical side. He was very unfortunate indeed when he lost his child and we were all very sad over it. All of us hoped that he could get away on compassionate leave, but unfortunately transport was very difficult at the time and I don't believe that Meldrum had the authority to put him on a ship or the Sunderland flying boat. I am pretty certain he put the case forward to the Garrison Commander, but he was unsuccessful. I do not recall your problem, John, of your wife having a miscarriage, but then as I said before – it is forty years ago.

I well remember Ben Thomas. He was older than us. Most of us were in our mid-twenties, but Ben I would think was in his mid-thirties – half a generation older. He was something of a father figure. He was supposed to be a very good mathematician, but as far as I remember the only evidence we had of this was that Ben kept telling us so.

Then there was the other chap, Wilkinson, the linguist – ginger haired who, when we first met him on the boat, told us a number of stories and then laughed like a drain. He was still telling the same stories months afterwards, but this time he was the only one laughing. He still carried on telling the same old stories. I found him a terrific bore. He was also, I think, involved in the debriefing of the Free French and Free Dutch who came through the border from time to time. Perhaps you don't remember, but every so often a convoy of lorries would disappear during the night into Spain (presumably with petrol and other goods) and come back before dawn with a load of escaping prisoners of war, Free French and Free Dutch, and Wilkinson was involved in some of the debriefing that went on. I recall that he was rather indiscreet in that he told us about it as well. You say in your book he went off the Rock in disgrace.* I don't remember this at all. He was still there when the release scheme came out [. . .]

Then there was Crump himself, who was very taciturn and I recall that he went to O.C.T.U. after a few months. Much later, perhaps twelve months later, this other W.O.1 arrived called Frank Allen, not Frank Barton as you state in your book. You describe his appearance quite well.† Ben took an immediate dislike to him. Whether through jealousy or not I do not know. In fairness to Frank Allen, he did at least assist Meldrum with the administrative work. I do not recall Ben ever doing anything on the admin. side. Indeed I don't know what he did to warrant W.O.1 status. Incidentally, Ben made quite a lot of money on the side teaching English at school certificate level to the Gibraltarians.

Now I come to Meldrum himself. In my view he was a good administrator. He seemed to have few ideas, but any ideas that came along he would process them and do everything possible to make them come about. I have reason to be grateful to Meldrum for assisting me in the work I did. I had the greatest co-operation from him in terms of sheer administration. Personally I hated admin. so it was quite useful to be able to tell him what was required and he set it in motion. He arranged for potential instructors from each unit to come down and have about a week's course with me. Also, when I required lecturers with various qualifications for the technical subjects, he seemed to have access to records and he put me in touch with suitable people. So from a professional point of view, I could not fault Meldrum. Everything was put into buff coloured files. He had a whole pile of these and whatever the topic, he had a file for it.

Frankly that kind of work bores me stiff, so I have always been grateful for other people who have been able to do it. On a personal level he was pleasant enough. I do not know what you expect from these people. He was a regular soldier, a Captain, and he deployed us to the best of his ability. I think you were grossly unfair in your comments about him, in that when poor old Harry had his bereavement I am quite sure he tried to get Harry off the Rock on compassionate leave, but he was only a Captain and he would not have that degree of authority. Another fact in your book which is wrong – Meldrum was

* Burgess alleges that Meldrum more or less had Wilkinson killed by sending him out to fight in Burma – to a 'death among the snakes and leeches'.

† 'A moustached and double-chinned bluffer.'

awarded the M.B.E. and not the O.B.E., which you say was 'other buggers' efforts'. This rather hackneyed story is the result of a conflict between your imagination and the truth. Where you have a conflict between truth and a good story I rather think truth becomes a casualty. You must have known it was the M.B.E. and not the O.B.E.

We were all invited to a party in the Officers' Mess which I think was in the Governor's house. By this time of course Captain Taylor had arrived on the Rock and you seemed to take an immediate dislike to him.* I had little to do with him. I thought he was a bit smarmy. Perhaps that's unfair, as he and I had no professional contact at all. At this party you had rather more to drink than was wise and I remember seeing you sitting down in the corner with Taylor and you proceeded to tell him how much you disliked him! It doesn't exactly make you friends with people and Taylor had to sit there with that silly grin on his face while you said: 'You know, Taylor, I never did like you ever since you came on the Rock.'

I seem to be left with a description of yourself and myself. We were very contrasting types, remarkably so. You were a lapsed Catholic, I was a Nonconformist, not terribly religious after having had a few shocks. You had been raised in Manchester, I had been raised in a country village at the end of the Rossendale valley. You had gone to a Catholic school, had been taught by Jesuits, a Catholic Grammar School and Manchester University. I had gone to the village school, served an apprenticeship in my Father's business, and then proceeded to Technical School at Bury and the Royal Technical College at Salford, where I attended courses for over ten years (three nights a week and every Saturday morning). So we couldn't have a greater contrast between you and me. I do not mention this in any envious kind of way. I just mention it because there was a tremendous difference between us in terms of knowledge and judgement. My heroes were people like Professor Lethaby, T. H. Huxley, Rousseau, particularly with his education of Emile, L. P. Jacks, and I read a great deal of Bernard Russell.† I was also very keen indeed prior to the war on politics, particularly pacifism and the Peace Pledge Union. So I volun-

* Captain Taylor is 'a willowy sapper', 'an intellectual Methodist', and a 'bloody fool', whose crime, in Burgess's view, was to call people by their Christian names.

† W. R. Lethaby (1857–1931) was an author, architect, and Principal of the London County Council Central School of Arts and Crafts; he was made professor of design, Royal College of Art, in 1900. His publications included *Westminster Abbey and the King's*

teered for the services with my eyes wide open. From time to time, I would start a conversation with you, perhaps I would mention something about Robert Louis Stevenson, with his interests in construction;* or perhaps Herbert Read,† and what he had to say about design, but then the conversation would be switched to your topics and your heroes, and from being a conversation it became simply a monologue. I was always amazed at the breadth of your knowledge particularly in the field of philosophy and phonetics. One of your heroes obviously was James Joyce, and I seem to remember that you put on a short course on the history of philosophy or something along those lines. Anyway, I came to the conclusion that your knowledge was encyclopaedic – a mile wide and half an inch thick, but to be fair we were young and we had not yet had enough experience of life to make use of our knowledge or to be able to make sound judgements.

Your main interest was in the field of music and I remember you composed a symphony. I went along to listen to its première, which was held in the Engineers' Hall. It was played by a scratch orchestra made up of the soldiers, sailors and airmen on the Rock. Coming from a Lancashire village, I was raised on choral music. Even in our own village we had an orchestra, but I think the limit of their repertoire was 'In a Monastery Garden'. However, I went along to this première

---

Craftsmen. T. H. Huxley (1825–95), doctor and scientist, published many books and papers on geology, comparative anatomy, physiology and zoology. He was Professor at the Royal College of Surgeons, President of the Royal Society, and Privy Councillor. Jean-Jacques Rousseau (1712–78) was the political philosopher and educationalist. *The Social Contract* (1762) gave the French Revolutionaries their slogan *Liberty, Equality, Fraternity*. His views on education were expressed in the novel *Emile*: the natural goodness of human beings versus the corrupting influence of institutions; if society treats you as ugly, you become ugly. His *Confessions* influenced the breast-beating of Burgess's memoirs. ('I was trying, in my humble way, to emulate the candour of those authors [i.e. Rousseau and St Augustine] while in no manner laying claim to a comparable literary distinction.') Lawrence Pearsall Jacks (1860–1955) was a theologian, who was educated and later preached at Liverpool and Manchester, and whose publications included *The Education of the Whole Man*. Bertrand Russell (1872–1970) attempted to apply the rules of mathematics and logic, as expounded in *Principia Mathematica*, to the more traditional philosophic problems of morality, meaning and truth. His pacifism led to imprisonment during World War I. Russell was the Distinguished Professor at the City College of New York, a Chair which Burgess was to occupy in 1972.

* The author of *The Strange Case of Dr Jekyll and Mr Hyde* won a silver medal whilst at Edinburgh for a paper on lighthouse building, 1871.

† Herbert Read (1893–1968) was a critic and poet who, after posts at the Victoria and Albert Museum and Edinburgh University, founded the Institute of Contemporary Arts in 1947. His publications included *Art and Industry* (1934), *Art and Society* (1937) and *Education Through Art* (1943). Knighted, 1953.

performance of your symphony. Really, John, I could not understand it, it simply seemed to me a cacophony of discords, but it didn't seem to bother you, although I felt so sorry for you when the reception was very mixed, very low-key in fact. But good luck to you, and obviously you enjoyed doing it, and I was in no position whatever to criticise because, frankly, I did not know enough about music to know whether it was good, bad or indifferent, it just sounded cacophonous [. . .]

You say in your book that you opposed having to teach the returning Gibraltarian children.* I cannot recall any opposition from anybody else – indeed, we were glad to help. It seemed to me that if there was no objection to private coaching for money, then it was downright immoral to object to teaching the children who could not afford to pay privately. Nor do I like your snide comments about plumbers.† You do not have to be very perceptive to realize that soldiers waiting for demobilization and worried about getting a job are more likely to be interested in plumbing, wood-work, metal-work and other technical subjects, rather than Goethe, Wittgenstein, or even James Joyce.

I realised quite quickly that the future of education was technical education, so I completed my Associateship of the Royal Technical College (now of course Salford University) and shortly afterwards joined the staff of the first Technical Teachers' Training College at Bolton. I moved up the ladder – Lecturer, Head of Department, Vice-Principal to Principal [. . .] On the personal level I have three sons and one daughter and my wife who bore them died of cancer when she was forty-six. She was a very fine woman and I was desolate. I remarried in 1964 – another outstanding but different kind of woman. She raised my children and it has been a very happy marriage.

Well, John, I don't really know why I'm writing such a long letter to you, other than from a sense of injustice to Meldrum [. . .]

Yours,
Norman Parker

* 'I cancelled the class and told Major Meldrum why. I was not here, I said, to provide colonial education: that was the job of colonial officials not military instructors.' His grouse was fiscal: civilian functionaries did not pay income tax as Gibraltar was a free port. British soldiers, however, received tax demands like anybody else. It was for the tax advantages that Burgess went to Malaya – and Malta – and Monte Carlo – and Lugano.

† 'Education had to be vocational as well as inspirational. The men must be taught trades. Plumbers and commercial artists had to be given three hasty stripes and inducted into the corps . . . The more humane subjects became a sideshow.'

As a postscript to all this: at an orang-utan rehabilitation centre deep in the jungles of Sarawak, Borneo, in 1999, I met a retired high-up from the Army Educational Corps, who told me that Norman Crump and Bill Meldrum (who never married) were to end their days together in an Officers' Benevolent Home near Chalfont St Giles (think Eric Sykes and Terry-Thomas in *Monte Carlo or Bust*) and that whenever the name came up, or if they saw that scaly domed head looming out at them from behind the cigar smoke on *Wogan*, or if they heard his episcopal voice on the radio, or glanced at one of his articles in the newspaper, for the rest of their days one or other of them would say: 'Don't talk to me about Anthony Burgess!' and they'd each go purple in the face.

III

Happy Days 1947–54

He was known, by the Regimental Sergeant-Major, as Schoolie or School Sarnt, and by his comrades (puzzlingly) as Tug – as in jerk? Or as in 'a small powerful boat for towing larger boats and ships' (*OED*), which might be a metaphor for the guiding, steering function of a teacher? For all Burgess's hatred of petty rules and regulations (and his determination to flout them), he began to enjoy his last few months in Gibraltar. He organises gramophone concerts, writes for the local papers, leads Meldrum a dance, and his 'expertise and experience' make him in demand for his British Way and Purpose lectures – which, as he rightly said, were of their nature rather schizoid. On the one hand there had to be a celebration of our history and our heritage (i.e. what we were fighting to protect); the Empire and painting the map pink. Yet on the other hand (and this is what we were fighting to bring about), the troops were encouraged to devise a future free from totalitarian menace and built around a Welfare State – but wouldn't that mean the undermining of a ruling class, of kings and crowns? People were expected to be both reactionaries and rebels – and Burgess certainly was, claiming (in 1984) that, 'I was always so conservative that my conservatism looked like communism.' He was formally bidden farewell from the services at the Demobilisation Centre at Aldershot in May 1946, having voyaged back to England on a rat-infested ship where the rats went into the stew consumed at meals. He joined up again, in a civilian capacity, almost immediately.

The education scheme for an army serving in wartime conditions had been grouped around three subject areas: the Humanities (History, Geography, Economics and International Affairs); what were called the Utilities, or the vocational subjects and trades; and Arts and Crafts. Burgess had whined that his areas of interest were being undermined by the emphasis on training and technology, but the fact of the matter is that the Army was quite aware of the wide range of talents and knowledge at its disposal now that so many men had been called up, and the number of potential students far exceeded the country's official school population. Hence, Burgess had no real difficulty getting employment as a sergeant-instructor (or as an instructor of potential sergeants in the AEC) at the Mid-West District School of Education, Brinsford Lodge, near Wolverhampton – a town, he said, populated by hump-backed dwarves, refugees from Wales originally, who were engaged in iron smelting. The courses were run by the Workers' Educational Association and appointments (and pay – allotted by the Treasury) came under the administration of Birmingham University Extra-Mural Department.* The University's Military Education Committee was itself answerable to the Regional Committee of the Central Advisory Council for Adult Education† in His Majesty's Forces, and their Command Officers, in the words of *The Story of Army Education*, by Archie White, were not meant 'to advise, but to

* Though Burgess's association with the University of Birmingham was only an administrative convenience, it was enough of a link for the institution to want to award him an Honorary Doctorate, which was conferred at a ceremony on 12 July 1986. As the Public Orator explained, 'He taught Education Corps instructors in what he refers to as "a kind of concentration camp run by the Ministry of Supply near Wolverhampton"; . . . he was attached to this University's Extramural Department . . . Anthony Burgess is the most adventurous and energetic writer of his generation; he is erudite; he is invariably instructive. I trust that his classes in that concentration camp near Wolverhampton realised how privileged they were.'

† CAC, for short. Not all of Burgess's obstructionism was going to bring this institution down, his smoking without permission, letting his hair grow, not washing his khaki drill, his back-answering. In addition to Birmingham there were twenty-two other Regional Committees based at the extra-mural departments of universities, from Exeter to Aberdeen. Before financial support was approved by the Treasury, initial funding and initiative were provided by the YMCA and the Pilgrim Trust. A Director of Education was appointed by the War Office, and Brigadier C. G. Maude, Inspector of the AEC, was in charge of recalling those members of the Corps who'd be able to make themselves available to meet the demand for teachers – Burgess was part of this recruitment. A council of fifty members, drawn from the Regional Committees, met annually in London; an Executive met monthly. As the official publication, *Education in the Home Forces*, explained, 'CAC possessed useful powers of access to Ministers, Under-Secretaries and Army Councillors' – and was quite the corridor of power, as tramped by C. P. Snow who (writes Burgess in *The Novel To-Day*), in the *Strangers and Brothers* sequence, explores the moral and psychological dynamics of how individuals become members of groups and how groups formulate decisions: 'reasonable men will arrive at a reasonable decision, one that, if it pleases no single individual or group, will do the least harm'. In *A Clockwork Orange*, the conflict between different kinds of justice becomes not (as in Snow) a Senior Common Room or Whitehall Smoking Room debate, but a clinical sci-fi nastiness. Snow believed that right and gentility would prevail, Burgess did not.

make provision for lecturers, tutors, and teachers, and to co-ordinate that provision'. Burgess's superior was a Lieutenant-Colonel Scriven, whom he seldom saw; what he had seen he didn't like.

Meant to be giving classes on International Affairs, European History, Musical Appreciation, Drama and Politics, Burgess believed himself to be 'faintly despised', and so sulked. The Army personnel had the temerity to call him by his Christian name. He can't win respect, he believes, moreover, because he's not in uniform. The usual riots and punch-ups take place whenever he pops his nose round his door. 'There was a great deal of rage about,' he says – mainly emanating from himself, let's be fair. It is snowing heavily – the big freeze of 1947. He can't face the idea of sex with any of the auxiliary women troops staying at Brinsford Lodge because 'there had always seemed to be a hint of incest' in the prospect of a relationship with a colleague – as there had been with his female classmates at Manchester. (*That* old excuse again.) Where was Lynne? Getting fat on pints of beer in the pubs of Fitzrovia and clubs of Dean Street, neglecting to do the washing-up or dusting at her flat in Baron's Court, and rather enjoying being fought over by two brothers from Tredegar, whom she knew from the past (and to whom Burgess said she was distantly related), Eddie and Herbert Williams. Herbert had been a Deputy District Education Officer in Shrewsbury and was presently Chief Instructor at the AEC Depot in Blackheath, holding the rank of major. Eddie was a manager of a bank in Calcutta, who was home on leave. Both men (apparently) wanted to marry Lynne and the three of them lived together in a rented mock-Tudor house in Henley. When Burgess turns up, Lynne pretends he's her brother ('You bad boy. Why didn't you telephone that you were coming?').

Surely this is the plot of a musical comedy? It is an episode full of mix-ups and misunderstandings – and strange loyalties or observance. It was Herbert, after all, who'd been looking after Lynne whilst Burgess was in Gibraltar all those years. They'd met at a poetry recital given by Louis MacNeice, had gone together to see Olivier's *Henry V* (which was released in 1944), and matters had escalated from there. If Burgess expected his rival to be dashing and martial he was in for a shock – Herbert was fat, bald and short, with an array of nervous winks and blinks, like he had the ague. Nonetheless, he it was who introduced Burgess to Scriven and got him out of the post-demob doldrums. As for Eddie, he was 'small and plump but masterful', recalled Burgess, and he blandished Lynne with promises of P&O staterooms to India and a palace in West Bengal run by servants. So what we have here is: Act One – Lynne as a Barbara Stanwyck or Shirley MacLaine figure, a runaway bride, flouncing around and being actressy with the pair of brothers (let's make them twins – so both can be impersonated by Claude Rains) scurrying eagerly around her. Burgess appears, the cuckold, like Ford in *The Merry Wives of Windsor*:

> My wife hath sent to him, the hour is fixed, the match is made. Would any man have thought this? – See the hell of having a false woman! My bed shall be abused, my coffers ransacked, my reputation gnawn at; . . . Fie, fie, fie! Cuckold! Cuckold! Cuckold!

– Verdi could set this to music; except we are not in Windsor but nearby Henley-on-Thames, where Eddie's bank has leased a pad, staffed by black marketeers and an amusing pair of servants called Gwen and George Tagg (played by Una O'Connor and Eric Blore). The regatta is on. Burgess (being played by Edward Everett Horton) sees John Betjeman* on the towpath gathering material for a poem (another of his glimpses of the great – like Lloyd George in Anglesey or Charles Laughton in Scarborough):

> When shall I see the Thames again?
> The prow-promoted gems again,
> As beefy A T S
> Without their hats
> Come shooting through the bridge?
> And 'cheerioh' and 'cheeri-bye'
> Across the waste of waters die,
> And low the mists of evening lie
> And lightly skims the midge.

Betjeman can lead a lavish Hollywood chorus sequence, with nymphs on horseback and bicycles, the subalterns and their freckled girlfriends, the young men in their blazers and boaters, the proud parents and ladies with parasols, and everybody is laughing and waltzing in the sunlight – and through this singing and dancing throng, which makes Cecil Beaton's Ascot scene in *My Fair Lady* look drab by comparison, Burgess wanders

* Betjeman appears in *Earthly Powers* as Dawson Wignall, the Poet Laureate. Toomey (and by safe inference Burgess) doesn't care for the poetry – 'insular, ingrown, formally traditional, products of a stunted mind . . . his droolings over girl's bicycles and gym tunics and black woollen stockings were chilled by whimsical ingenuities of diction.'

grimly, singing to himself (in counterpoint) about his helplessness. Act Two – Lynne and Eddie go to Eastbourne. Burgess creeps after them and spends a humiliating week following them into pubs. Eddie vanishes when he receives a telegram requesting his urgent recall to Calcutta because his deputy at the bank has unexpectedly died. (Is the wire counterfeit? Did Burgess fabricate its despatch?) Lynne and Burgess celebrate their reunion back at the Baron's Court Road flat by shaving each other's pubes – somewhere along the line they have caught crab lice (*phthirus pubis*). Lynne having 'dealt briskly with my engorgement', as Burgess says (and that must have made her day), we have a fast fade out.

It's in *The Doctor Is Sick* where Lynne's gavotte with The Boys from Tredegar is to be found – as Sheila Spindrift's coming and going with Leo and Harry Stone. Leo's baldness, the put-upon Edwin observes, 'was more advanced than that of his twin. His accent had a patrician overlay, as if he had sometime been a superior salesman.' And Burgess's search for Lynne in Eastbourne is duplicated when Edwin looks for Sheila at the Farnworth Hotel. 'He had not thought it possible that there should be so many Farnworth Hotels . . . Still, that would be something more to do, finding the place. Now he had many hours to fill in.' The mystery really is why has Burgess been so ineffectual? In the Army, or in fact in any other sphere or group or place you care to name, if there's a snigger about Lorca or a detrimental remark about Honegger (the French composer whose *Pacific 231* was a musical representation of a steam locomotive), then he is quick to hit out with his fists. But he does nothing to defend Lynne or to assert his rights as a husband. He is not even testy. He says of Herbert, 'I liked the man' – for (unlike Lynne) he can talk about Latin poetry and he has a nice tenor voice. Eddie he doesn't care for quite as much because his degree was in mathematics – but he at least received it from Jesus College, Oxford, which outranks any qualification from Manchester. I think what was happening here was that Burgess wilted before their masculinity. It was in character for him to be in conflict with the world – he had a talent for loneliness, and accepted it. He's always fretting about guilt – but guilt implies transgression, and what did he do wrong? What he means is shame – a sense of sexual failure (a failure of manliness); and at least Lynne was being loved and protected. Secondly, Burgess from the earliest age, had inured himself to the forces of environment and family life. Lorca's verse and Honegger's music did mean more to him than real people; and in a strange way Lynne's adulteries didn't mean anything to him, in comparison, which is why we get no sense of hurt – only of a bizarre enjoyment of the sexual envy.* There was part of him that didn't object to humiliation – that sought it, indeed. He was enough of a Catholic to relish being a tormented soul. The two obvious questions – How did Burgess see these rivals off? Why did Lynne elect to remain with Burgess? – are, in effect, connected. Eddie, back in Calcutta, married a judge's daughter, and Herbert returned to his officer's quarters in Blackheath, never to be heard from again. They leave without ado (if the telegram from the bank was sent by an accomplice, then the deputy manager's death was at least still a consistent fabrication); and my own suspicion is that once Burgess turned up, Lynne's swains were glad to be rid of her. Who, in actuality, would want to align themselves with her ruinous boozing? Once you'd seen her project a stream of vomit, like the trumpet of the Archangel Gabriel, six feet across a room, you'd seen everything. It's so sad, the decline from a sheltered and provincial childhood to a non-life as an afternoon-club drunk and good-time girl. She returned to her husband because there really was nobody else – and Burgess's Catholicism wouldn't countenance divorce in any event. 'Lynne accepted,' he said, 'that it was less trouble to be a more or less faithful wife to me than to be a shuttlecock between the Williams brothers.' There is a sort of submissiveness in both Lynne's and Burgess's attitudes to each other, as if they are the left-overs and nobody else will have them.

As a result of that attack in the blackout, Lynne suffered from a condition called dysmenorrhoea – excessive muscular spasms of the uterus, which caused cramps, hormonal changes, which meant mood swings, and vaginal bleeding of such degree that she'd rinse and swill out her own bedsheets at hotels. It ruled out, anyway, sexual intercourse – and Burgess was able to fool himself into believing that, after all, perhaps she'd been chaste. Let us allow him to think that if he wants to. Her waylaying by the footpads, however, had a longer-term effect than any prohibition on complete carnal knowledge; and her physical ailment did slowly heal with the ingestion of a synthetic oestrogen called Stilboestrol, a drug, by the way, carrying the risk of vaginal cancer, and which may (they'd not have known this then) have exacerbated the nausea, fluid retention and breast enlargement everybody ascribed to her drinking and the side-effects of cirrhosis. The deeper consequences, though, were not anatomical, but psychological. If the actual attack on Lynne is described in *A Clockwork*

* It is this episode to which Paul Theroux alludes in 'The Writer and His Reader' (*My Other Life*, p. 200): 'during his first marriage he and his then wife experimented with a *ménage à trois*'.

Orange, the aftershock of the attack is described by J. W. Denham, in *The Right to an Answer.* His mistress, Michiko, had been assaulted by teenagers and near-raped, and the mental injury 'meant that she didn't want me, nor did I want to touch her, though I felt anger, compassion and pity and other cognate emotions . . . And then, of course, I came home one day to find . . . Michiko not there anymore.' Instead of bringing them together, the violence meted out to Lynne drove them apart. Coping with a trauma can do this: the psychic scar tissue makes it not possible to submerge your life in someone else's. They shared the same (single) bed on their visits to each other at Baron's Court Road or Brinsford Lodge, but they found each other unaccommodating. They made each other's lives hard. Lynne's heartiness and Welsh coarseness were gradually dulled and deadened; Burgess's pride and self-righteousness became a personal style.

It was not quite a misalliance, though, for nothing about either of them was easy or natural. Her sorry belief in a romantic fairytale was the legacy of a Monmouthshire upbringing. After the loving childhood (it seemed such a shame to leave it), she couldn't cope with adulthood – with its disappointments, curtailments, longings and dissolvings. Hence, the drinking trough, the recourse of those who fear a clear consciousness, who are disinclined to see things in their true colours. Burgess, meantime, would ruthlessly present his marriage (in interviews; in his memoirs) in such a way that Lynne's affairs and carousings was behaviour which had nothing to do with him – he's so detached, it's not even something that's impossible to endure. But the real atmosphere was more dense than this. He'd drive her towards bouts of bad behaviour so he could then believe she was rejecting him; he had a need for the raucous and the pattern of his life is an avoidance of continuous harmony. He couldn't settle. 'There's an anger, an emotion looking for an object,' he said in 1992. Everything set him off, from a visit to London ('I hate to see people wearing three hundred pound trainers. People are not elegant anymore, they're not speaking properly, becoming inarticulate'), to a trip to Rome ('I'm disgusted with its corruption, thieves, sour people and sour wine'), which is why, I think, wartime had a liberating effect on him. The larger, grander, historical events were a magnification of his personal inadequacies and anguish – and the war became a means for exhilaration, bravado, abandon; it let him off having to be peaceable.* Many of his books refer to it, or have

* A trait he shares with my other characters. The breakdowns and tantrums of Peter Sellers and Spike Milligan and their experience of the war inspired *The Goon Show*, which is crammed with gunfire and explosions, corrupt officers and dopey privates. It is a comic

their origins in it, or derive their energy from it: sci-fi battles and destructiveness; raping and pillaging; executions; the historical fiction – which is the twentieth century in costume. Burgess liked to give the impression he was a violent man – he boasted to Kathleen Winfield, his Senior Mistress at Banbury Grammar School, that on a return visit to the town, in 1957, he'd offered to fight sundry 'Teds, layabouts and Yanks . . . in the urinal of some pub or other' – and certainly he had a kind of mechanical or brute force. There was an indestructible stamina for work, as he pressed words from himself, seeing the human character or personality as a mechanism he could quell or dominate. (He'd flatten people out, literally and figuratively.) The rhymes of *Byrne*, for example, thud and thump along, like a steam engine. It is an industrial process. His personal manner was hectoring and didactic, and he required noise, change, chaos, detritus across his desk, car smashes and brawls. This is why he flinched from non-threatening women, easy-going women. If those autobiographical ciphers, his characters, are anything to go by (Ennis, Enderby, Crabbe, Denham, Hillier, Beard, not to mention Shakespeare and company), he needed to be fooled, cheated, cuckolded, fleeced, and entrapped by women. The oddest instance of this is the male-rape episode in *Beard's Roman Women*, where a dead wife keeps coming back from beyond the grave to thwart the widower's chances of securing a new wife. A quartet of naked Furies shimmers into the flat, pinion Beard, and taunt him for his 'detumescent state'. Cracking a whip, one of the witches says, 'We're in control, and we have what we want!' (Male rape happens to Enderby, too, in *The Clockwork Testament*: 'Everything off. I want to see you in your horrific potbellied hairy filthy nakedness' – it's clearly a regular porno fantasy of the author's.)

Who Leonora Beard and Paula Lucrezia Belli are it is easy to guess; and who else but Burgess would describe a marriage as an 'incestuous . . . semiotic complex', because the man and the woman are turned in on each other and ignore the wider world? Yet between Lynne and Liana there's another female in this novel, *Beard's Roman Women*, whom he calls Miriam, his lost love. Beard had met her originally after the war: 'You used to be Sergeant Bloomfield. I remembered so much, summer of forty-six and so on. You. That Western Command course I came to give

---

re-enactment of the war. Laurence Olivier's heroic war-leader qualities led obviously to *Henry V*, which was made as a propaganda film with government assistance. In reality, Olivier wasn't quite so adroit a soldier: in the Fleet Air Arm he caused such damage, it was as if his function was to make the enemy feel overconfident.

the lectures on. How to run a Forces radio station and all that nonsense.' He meets her, years later, at the airport – a place, Beard says, which has the significance of the crossroads in *Oedipus* ('if you waited, you never knew. A mad secret chance'). She's lost her lustre a little, naturally, in the intervening years, has filled out a bit, but 'the eyes never changed'; she's still feisty, and is happy to reminisce about their affair, decades ago, when they'd rolled around naked. She also taunts Beard with the news that the 'body you remembered as rather a nice body' is now riddled with cancer. A journalist and war correspondent, she's off to cover the shoot-outs and bombings in the Middle East and hopes she'll be felled by a stray bullet. She intends outwitting the death her illness has got planned, and has already prepared the headline for her obituary: 'Daughter of Israel falls, but not of cancer of the rectum.' Later, when he is discussing his own health with a Dr Bloomfield (Beard has started to suffer from convulsive facial twitchings – Major Herbert Williams's complaint), we learn that Miriam's wish came true. 'She got splattered two hours before the cease-fire. A marvellous girl.' Her death was therefore the perfect exercise of human choice – like Concetta Campanati, in *Earthly Powers*, another old bird wasting away from cancer who decides to get herself shot instead. In her case, she tries to assassinate Heinrich Himmler, misses, and is killed by an SS guard. (One has to wonder how much Lynne's drinking herself to death and Burgess's smoking himself to death were likewise extreme libertarian positions?)

In the ice-bound winter of 1947, at Brinsford Lodge (not a requisitioned mansion but an abandoned Ministry of Supply Nissen hut), there may be found what appears to be the origin of Beard's romance. Burgess says that he fell headlong in love with an ATS sergeant who was attached to the school. She was a Jew from London and 'her cell, or mine, became a nut of sexual riot'. It was his revenge on what he imagined Lynne was doing back in London, Henley and Eastbourne. In his memoirs, Burgess emphasises 'the odours of heat', the way he'd gone 'erotically mad' with his Jewish girl. 'I should have married this girl,' he sighs. But who was she? Given that Burgess can remember the name of Lynne's history teacher from Bedwellty or the name of a public house landlady in Shrewsbury, the date of haircuts, or what he was doing the day *before* Kennedy was whacked (reading *El Cid* in Tenerife, 'to help my Spanish'), his coyness in not revealing her identity is jarring. In *Beard's Roman Women*, Miriam, the one-time Sergeant Bloomfield, is now known as Mrs Moishe (Moses) Gillon. 'A bit incestuous,' jokes Beard – as Miriam was of course Moses' sister. In the archives of the BBC, more specifically in the files of *Woman's Hour* for 1962, I found a note Burgess had sent to the producer, Jean Burns,* recommending, as potential contributors to the programme, literary friends of his ('That's just in case you should want them sometime') called Diana and Meir Gillon, of 30 Ravenscroft Park, Barnet, Hertfordshire. *The Wanting Seed* is dedicated to 'The Unsleeping Gillons', a reference to their own novel (they wrote, like Il'f and Petrov, jointly), *The Unsleep*, a dystopian satire about what would happen to the human race if slumbering was abolished and we failed to tell the difference between dreams and reality. So have I, cross-referencing Miss Marple fashion, uncovered the webs and fibres of Burgess's grand passion? When he says he'd been 'set upon by Dionysus', the god of wildness and ecstasy, was he alluding to Diana the huntress, goddess of the moon? (Women are always associated with moon imagery in the Enderby novels – their fickle affections wax and wane, they are thin and narrow-minded or rounded and gross, they obey only the cycles of tides and lunar months: they are lunatics.) What is more likely is that here we have evidence of Burgess's tendency (as in *The Unsleep* – which is briefly mentioned in *The Novel Now*) to mingle falsehood and the truth. He had a fantastical streak, and this is what comes out in those reflections of his memoirs. It'll happen again in Banbury – where he talked of committing adultery 'spectacularly if discreetly with a fellow member of staff': once more the party is unnamed, and I tracked her down, and it's all lies. According to Professor Raanan Evelyn Zvi Gillon, who holds the Chair of Medical Ethics at Imperial College, London, and who is Diana and Meir's son (Lynne and Burgess attended his twenty-first birthday party in 1962), it was his parents who helped John Wilson, fresh from Malaya and knowing nobody, to get established in literary London, suggesting him for reviewing jobs, generally supporting him and being appreciative of his work. The Gillons introduced him to the PEN International Club,† a society founded in 1921 by

* Burgess had a busy sideline as a broadcaster on the Third Programme throughout the sixties. ('I suppose, to avoid ultimate confusions, I'd better say here that "Anthony Burgess" is only my pseudonym, and that my real name is as below [John Wilson]. Please call me by whichever name you like,' he informed Miss Burns, on 31 May 1960.) His note about the Gillons is dated 26 February 1962, the day after his forty-fifth birthday. It was also his biographer's birthday, by the way. I was chuckling in my bassinet ('. . . a changeling, a goblin baby dumped in . . . a pram', as is said of Carlo, in *Earthly Powers*).

† Despite the philosophy of the Society, Burgess wasn't much of a one for brotherly love. He never had any time or respect for the concept of black or ethnic studies. In 1971, he complained that 'At various universities, I've seen black men who are treated very indulgently, over-indulgently. They are allowed to do what they want, take what they want,

C. A. Dawson Scott and John Galsworthy to defend freedom of expression and promote understanding between the poets, playwrights, editors, essayists and novelists of every nation. This is the kind of generosity and warmth Burgess later signally failed to acknowledge, as he tried to confect this image of a self-created Don Juan.*

A make-believe relationship has the advantage over a real one in that you can direct its course; and it's masturbatory; and if Lynne had her dysmenorrhoea, Burgess had his spermatorrhoea, which began to afflict him the night his father died. Is the word his own coinage (e.g. like *numismatorrhea*, in *The Doctor Is Sick*, to indicate the discharge of pennies from a pay-phone)? It means, anyway, wet dreams. According to my handy *Visual Dictionary of Sex*, edited by Dr Eric J. Trimmer (1978), this is a condition related to premature ejaculation and involves feelings of inadequacy, failure and anxiety. 'Wet dreams are simply a method of some release of sexual tension . . . [They] occur during sleep without an individual being able to remember any kind of dream, sexual or otherwise. [Or they can] occur as part of a sexual dream . . . a dream [which] is odd, bizarre, or sexually disturbing.' Whatever is afoot inside the skull at night, which is sending signals to the genitalia, the point is no other person is present – indeed, it's more solitary even than masturbation, because no conscious act is involved in the gush, spurt or dribble. Sex has

drop what they want. I met one young man in Philadelphia, a young black, who wanted to learn music. But he wouldn't learn music from whites because it was "tainted" music. Well, this is bloody ridiculous . . .'

Burgess just didn't get it, did he? This is the man who threw the Catholic Emancipation (Relief) Act of 1829 in your face every two minutes and who lost no opportunity to tell you about the oppression of *his* people, the Lancashire Catholics. There's another unpleasant section to be found in *You've Had Your Time*. Burgess's dreadful Symphony in C is being rehearsed at Iowa City and Jim Dixon (so that's what happened to Lucky Jim?), the conductor and Head of the Music Department, has an argument with what you know Burgess is longing to call an *uppity nigger*: 'There was trouble with the timpanist, who was black. Like many blacks, he insisted that he had a natural sense of rhythm, but this Jim Dixon had denied. "You ain't got no rhythm, baby," he had said. Jim Dixon had none of the fashionable squeamishness about race,' nor any concept of what is insulting and ignorant and what constitutes good manners, either. Anyway – 1973, March, New York, Burgess attends a PEN symposium on 'Authorship and Commitment', and uses his address to vilify the 'ghetto language' of black people, which he believes is merely a sign of their all-inclusive deprivation; they should be taught (and compelled to learn, speak and write) good classical English. This didn't go down well. 'There is a growing assumption, in New York at least,' he says sniffily, 'that reason is an outmoded device of conviction.' This because an *uppity nigger* had coolly articulated, 'Do you honestly think you are going to get away with that remark?'

* Burgess joined PEN International in 1962 and ceased paying his dues and resigned in 1965.

been drained of all emotion and feeling. The body, asleep, has a mind of its own – hence Burgess's fascination with *Finnegans Wake*, a book about a man dreaming, composed in dream language. 'To represent a dream convincingly, one needs a plastic language, a language in which two objects or persons can subsist in one and the same word,' as he explained in *Here Comes Everybody*, the Joyce book with the spermatic pun in the title. According to Burgess, in Earwicker's dream, insect means incest, wives merge with daughters, and the whole thing is about guilt and sin, resurrection and redemption. For a writer and personality like Burgess, who is so hard-headed and high-minded, dreams represent freedom – 'shadowiness, confusion, the melting of one personage into another, of youth into age, friends into enemy: these are of the essence of the dream', and of Burgess's own imaginative procedures, it can be said. Thus, good reviews of his work are remembered as hostile, friendly acts are wiped from the memory bank, disagreements are inflated into full-scale personal attacks, not being praised unreservedly and all the time means a conspiracy by Oxford-educated critics to neglect or denigrate him, girls he knew become mistresses he shagged half to death and women who were nice to him were the wives who got away, running from the presence of the sun, following darkness like a dream. Burgess always felt himself to be exceptional and as Earwicker absorbs or embodies Joyce's heroes, from Adam to Humpty Dumpty, so Burgess – the pseudonym – absorbed John Wilson's, from Moses and Jesus to Shakespeare and Freud; and of course Burgess did his utmost to subsume Joyce himself. The 'malinchily malchick' ('my little boy') Russian idiom of *A Clockwork Orange* is in *Finnegans Wake*, as is the phrase 'timidly twomeys', which gives Toomey in *Earthly Powers* his name, and is a reference to the merging of opposites and not knowing which twin is which; and the Russian heritage of Anna Livia Plurabelle inspired the Russianness of Ludmilla Jones, the Lynne character in *Any Old Iron*, who even resides at Lynne's old girlhood address, 2 Sunnybank Road, in Blackwood. Fancy knows no limits, as they say, and what Burgess appreciated most in Joyce was how, by having Humphrey Chimpden Earwicker as the ultimate father-figure, who has a wife and begets sons and daughters, the theme of repetition and return can be exploited and 'the dead and resurrected gods' get to be transmitted from generation to generation, 'to live on . . . in the flesh and spirit of others', as Shakespeare, in *Nothing Like the Sun*, lives on in the East, through the Dark Lady's progeny, or as the hero of *Byrne*, 'spending seed' and 'fertilising' the world indiscriminately, is Burgess's own ultimate founding father, with children everywhere, of every colour, culture and creed.*

The spermatorrhoea, as I said, commenced after Joseph Wilson handed in his dinner pail; and from what I can understand of his drift, the spunky stream has to do with lineage: 'the voiding of my father as donor of the seed that had become myself', as Burgess puts it, suggesting that when it came to orgasms he was like a salmon strewing milt; could sex ever be more impersonal? Toomey (the twin) similarly suffers. He awakes from a nightmare 'grotesquely engorged and pumping out seed'. The next night he finds 'seed pumping out' six times! A consultation is made with Dr Einaudi of Milan (the name of Burgess's own Italian publisher, incidentally; elsewhere in the novel there is a gynaecologist called Dr Belmont, after his French translator, and a Dr Pantucci, named for his literary agent: what is this association between genito-urinary specialists and the world of letters?). Toomey is told he is 'suffering from spermatorrhea, an ailment pretty rare in Italy', precipitated by guilt, depression and loneliness. The problem recedes if, when he is making the beast-with-two-backs with his pick-ups, visions of his mother flash before his eyes. Thus cured, he goes off to a concert at the Salle Gareau where Domenico's symphony is to be performed. From the description ('jazz riffs on wa-wa trumpets and glissading trombones'), it sounds like one of Burgess's musical compositions – and the muted reception of the modernistic clonking and squealing is reminiscent of that report about the orchestral suite in Gibraltar.

So – what do we have here? Premature or unprompted ejaculations; self-disgust; mythical overtones (primeval fathers, earth mothers); sleep and dreams; Joycean allusions; shame; fantasy; ghost women and wish-fulfilment women; fertility versus sterility; fecundity versus the moribund: what a lot was going on inside Burgess's head. What it can be (like a sauce) reduced to, I think, is the relationship between sexual energy and creative energy ('Blot no line: let it come, pumping out,' Shakespeare advises himself in *Nothing Like the Sun* when working on *The Comedy of Errors*); and where Picasso, in paint and (virtually) in reality, wanted to pulverise his mistresses, taking possession of them body and soul, and where Degas thought of the canvas as a partner he'd besplatter in an artistic adventure, for Burgess there was 'a very strong masturbatory urge: the urgent need to spend seed in order to get on with the job of writing'. No wonder his favourite dauber was Dali, whose most famous picture is *The*

* The text of *Byrne* itself is protean, having been translated into Czech, Latvian and Polish as well as the usual languages.

Great Masturbator, a lurid photograph, as it were, of a state of mind, a dream portrait, which the old surrealist's biographer, Ian Gibson, decodes as representing 'the painter's fear of sexual contact and of impotence, while the closed eyes [are] oblivious to external reality. [He] is only concerned with the erotic fantasies being played out in the theatre of his mind.'*

I'd say that here is an intriguing description of Burgess, too. Like Dali, he was over-ripe and self-intoxicated, a draughtsman rather than a creature of depth and flexibility. Natural life is threatened – the work is filled with phantoms and puppets. His prose, like Dali's placing of pigment, was a thing of sheen and glimmer. His past, again like Dali's, had to be mythologised. For, let's face it, his lower-middle-class upbringing was not exactly *Angela's Ashes*, yet he told Martin Amis that the Lancastrian childhood was 'poverty-stricken'; and it was certainly not an excuse for his arias of self-pity and bile. I think he enjoyed feeling betrayed and put-out, a martyr to something or other, and Lynne (like Gala) was his goad and scourge – and the likes of his London Jewess, or Diana Gillon, a mannequin in his mental stage-set, an 'auriferous goddess', to use a phrase from *Homage to Qwert Yuiop*, meaning bearer of gold. Whilst still at Brinsford Lodge he had to chair a quiz for members of the Auxiliary Territorial Service, constituting teams from the blondes and the brunettes. They were short of blondes, so a brunette had to join the blonde team. 'Am I as dumb as that?' she asked crossly. Burgess tried to mollify her by explaining that it was tall fair Celts who'd conquered and superseded the diminutive, swarthy Silurians, whom one could see round and about in the industrial Midlands. 'Blondes belong to the privileged races, such as the Germans.' Was this a clever remark to be making in the forties? He then backtracked and claimed that blondeness can signify goodness and cleanness and that 'the great dark women of literature, like Cleopatra and Anna Karenina, are goddesses of defeat'. He stuck to this curious view, for Lynne, on the pretext that her hair was thinning, was later to wear a

* Ian Gibson, *The Shameful Life of Salvador Dali* (London, 1997), p. 206. In his essay on the Thyssen-Bornemisza Collection of Modern Masters (Royal Academy of Arts, 1984), Burgess described Dali's *Dream Caused by the Flight of a Bee around a Pomegranate a Second before Awakening*, praising its 'beauty, skill, theatricality, inspired vulgarity, [and] eye-opening mythopoeia. This is the Dali of 1944, when, we are told, the technique was becoming too slick and the ideas banal. The Baron [Thyssen] clearly likes the work, and I cannot blame him.' Burgess's admiration for Dali as his favourite painter was also included in his responses to 'The *Correspondent* Questionnaire', compiled by Rosanna Greenstreet, in the *Sunday Correspondent*, 10 December 1989. (The trait he most deplored in himself was 'excessive modesty'.)

blonde wig. And it was his curious views ('Nobody likes the French. Even the French don't like the French'; 'Any of us can sit down and write a novel in which Jesus Christ is the son of a whore and all Christ's disciples homosexuals') which got him a reputation for eccentricity. After the blonde bombshell insults and misunderstandings, Lieutenant-Colonel Scriven transferred him briefly to a camp belonging to the Army Ordnance Corps at Nesscliffe, situated between Shrewsbury and Oswestry. He didn't like to mention this much, because it goes against the grain of how shabbily he was treated, but he had honorary officer's rank and dined in the officers' mess – and it was from this billet that he applied for and landed the post of Lecturer in Speech and Drama at Bamber Bridge Emergency Training College, in the Ribble Valley of southern Lancashire, near Preston.

It was the nearest he came to moving back home, or at least to his birthplace. Did he revisit the Wilsons much? The impression he gave was that they belonged to a galaxy far, far away. In 1962, he was still making an effort. He told Jean Burns, of *Woman's Hour*, that as he was going to have to make the journey to Leeds, to attend a *Yorkshire Post* literary lunch, 'I'd better go and see my relatives in Manchester and save on the train fare'; and in 1968 he told a reporter from the *New York Times Magazine* that 'I have an uncle of ninety who is still a Communist, though a Catholic (and a master plumber, incidentally),' which implies that this Uncle Jack, his father's brother, was at least fleetingly in his thoughts. Matters start to get a bit weird after that. 'Jack,' he said in 1987, 'died recently in his nineties' – so time must stand still in Burgess's world if nobody ages significantly in twenty years. Stranger still, they have a Lazarus-like ability to pop back. At a Waterstone's literary dinner in 1989, he told everybody, 'My Uncle Jack is still alive at ninety-six – a plumber.' And yet asked, later the same year, if anyone now ever called *him* Jack, he replied that Jack Wilson did come back occasionally. 'In 1988,' he said, he'd been in Manchester to sign books and 'an ancient man came along and said, "I'm your nephew." Another ancient man said, "I married your niece." Various people I did not recognise.' Another time he told the story, in 1989, the two old men have merged together to form a single, ghostly entity: 'A very very very old man said, "I'm your nephew married to your niece." I got extremely frightened by that.'* So much for Daniel Tollitt. This is an instance

* We are in a surrealistic realm now – or perhaps a short story by Jorge Luis Borges. In December 1993, I received a letter from a Mr John Anthony Wilson, who told me he possessed an inscribed copy of *You've Had Your Time*, given to him at a public signing session in Oxford. 'I pointed out to [Burgess] that I had been born into a large Catholic family in

of how disconnected he became – and it is a process we can detect as well underway at Bamber Bridge. One of the ways he kept apart from people was by treating them as yokels or as an amusing tribe: the Welsh, the Malays, the Romans, the Americans, each received the pseudo-anthropological treatment. As in his short story 'The Muse', he travels across time to come and listen to their quaint uses and abuses of language. The Lancastrians at Bamber Bridge (remember this is 1948) speak like characters in *Sir Gawain* or *Beowulf*. 'I became professionally interested in dialectology,' says our Professor Higgins,* and he roves the hills and dales with a little notebook, identifying and transcribing the 'Danish sounds in local speech' and utilising the International Phonetic Script, which makes words look like Tolkien's Elvish. Tolkien, in his capacity as Rawlinson and Bosworth Professor of Anglo-Saxon at Pembroke College, Oxford, maintained that it was all downhill after the Norman Conquest – all that Frenchification despoiling the Old English – and Burgess had a similar racist philosophy, except he went back further still, wanting to purify us of the influences of the Angles, from the Danish peninsular, who invaded in the fifth century, and of the Germanic peoples, who migrated to our shores at a similar period. Do only the Druids get his vote, fantastically dressed in wild flowers as they were? Interviewed in Wales about the Welshness of *Any Old Iron*, he claimed that, 'In principle I'm in favour of Welsh nationalism – and of the Celts recovering England, too. Excalibur could be a rallying point to drive the bloody Anglo-Saxons out. They are the invaders. But it'll never happen.' No, I think they have become pretty well assimilated since the Bronze Age. He believed himself to be completely Celtic, which was to account for his 'imagination, wit, fancy, the spirit of paradox, inspired illogicality, and the rest of the Celtic gifts', best exemplified in Oscar Wilde, Brendan Behan and Dylan Thomas – men who were all sacrificed to 'the Anglo-Saxon gods of dullness'. And sure enough, 'I have

---

Harpurhey, north Manchester, and that my name was John Wilson . . . I gave a copy of *Little Wilson and Big God* to my ninety-year-old uncle, who now thinks he is the "Jack Wilson" referred to therein.' So, in 1993, a month after Burgess's own death, Uncle Jack is still capable of metamorphosis and resurrection?

* Shaw's character, Burgess noticed, was based on Frederick J. Furnivall, founder of the Early English Text Society, who is described by Elisabeth Murray, in *Caught in the Web of Words: James Murray and the Oxford English Dictionary* (which Burgess writes about in *Homage to Qwert Yuiop*), as a man who 'never understood, or attempted to understand, the quality of tact. It was a species of dishonesty. What he held to be true was to be enounced in the face of all opposition, with unfaltering directness and clarity; what he held to be false was to be denounced with Athanasian intensity and resolution.' Burgess quotes this with approval.

sometimes romantically seen myself as one of the potential Celtic literary victims . . . I do not like the Establishment and it does not like me . . . I will beat the Anglo-Saxons yet.' Surely he knew that the Celtic revival was a fantasy of the late eighteenth century, involving invented costumes, folk art and fake rituals – the forgeries of Ossian, the castles of William Burges, the archaisms of Thomas Chatterton, and Welshmen dressing up in bedsheets like the Ku Klux Klan? (If we were to substitute Aryan for Celtic and consider his views on racial superiority and Anglo-Saxon 'deviousness' in the light of other eugenicists of modern history, Burgess would be considerably more than just a bloody fool.)

His home country was a phonetic museum, and he was like Kipling's Puck, picking up not flints and minerals but words and phrases. 'Art witshert?' or 'Art wit-shet?' meant 'Art thou wet-shod?', thus 'Are your shoes wet?' Lynne was asked this when she ran from a cloudburst into a pub. 'Oo's getten showder-wartsh' conveyed the information that 'She's got a pain in her shoulder.' Burgess once heard it said of his grandmother that 'oo's getten 'eed-warch'. The imprecation 'I'll play Amloth with thee, lad!' meant that it was not Shakespeare or Thomas Kyd's mad Dane whose wrath would be released, but Saxo Grammaticus's, who'd written (in Latin) an account of the original Norse folktale of Amleth, the prince who feigns idiocy as a ruse. At Bamber Bridge (known as the Brigg), Burgess produced an amateur dramatic rendition of a complete First Folio *Hamlet*, presented in two halves on consecutive nights. Words were things to him, objects, jewels. They are what he gets emotional and meaningful about. Big words, odd words, fallen-into-disuse words. They were his companions. Lynne? She was with him now, living in the tiny study-bedroom which had been allotted to the married couple at the end of a student dormitory. The college itself was simply a former American Army training camp which the Ministry of Education had hastily taken over. Ex-servicemen were being encouraged to go into the teaching profession, and Burgess helped to give them their basic thirteen-week course in educational theory and practice. He taught a course in the history of European drama and gave classes on the art of speech. For *Hamlet*, which brought both these specialisations together, Lynne helped with the wardrobe. When they did *Murder in the Cathedral*, for which Burgess wrote incidental music, she was in the chorus, as at Manchester. Much of their time was spent in the British Legion, listening to the locals tell jokes in the manner of Stanley Holloway (Olivier's gravedigger in his *Hamlet* film, and Billy Wilder's, too, in *The Private Life of Sherlock Holmes*, where the Baker Street wizard is a disaffected

Hamlet): a man, having missed the last bus home, is offered the other half of a double bed where his friend's kid brother is already lying. In the morning, asked if he has slept well, he says, 'Yes, except your kid's arse isn't half cold.' 'Aye, well,' comes the reply, 'he's been dead three days.' Grim humour – cuddling up to a corpse: it's the buffoonery of Elsinore. For a short while, at least, Burgess enjoyed being here, sharing meals with the mature students, pounding the piano in the pubs – except that pub piano-players are 'usually despised' for being more competent than the amateur wailers and warblers they are accompanying, a frequent complaint. Soon, though, the charm of an enclosed society wears thin. The 'incestuously ingrown social habits' of the rustics start to disgust him. There's no privacy. Scandal and gossip are what people are thriving on, not culture. Families gawp at their television sets and eat chips. Women go shopping with curlers still in their hair. Merry England, with its self-sufficient communities, is vulgar and common. His wife, of course, wasn't much comfort. She believed she had to drink continually to replace the blood that was being leaked away. The 'perpetual menstruation [necessitated] a corresponding intake of fluid. She was not able to have any children or even to have intercourse for a long time,' Burgess told *Playboy* in 1974. 'The gynaecological complex begot its own psychological aura. Things never got really right again. And so she just resigned herself to the idea of wanting to die and drank steadily. I couldn't stop her. Finally she got what she wanted.'

Could he have stopped her? Could he have done more to *try* and stop her? The detached, clinical tone he took in interviews and his own memoirs surely wasn't how he was when they were alone? When she suffered her first massive portal haemorrhage and was rushed to hospital in Ealing for a blood transfusion and a splenectomy, in early March 1968, Burgess was asked by the surgeons, 'How well do you know your wife?' They couldn't believe that even the most negligent of husbands would fail to notice chronic alcoholism. He looked at them blankly. How can one explain that it's possible simply to be tormented by life? Or that he himself was a man difficult to reach? Things were not happy at home, therefore (and his domestic routines were fully audible to his class of trainees at the other end of the shed); and nor was he fulfilled at work. 'I taught a kind of minimal language, minimal German and that sort of stuff, you know,' he said in 1971. 'I taught educational courses to regular soldiers who had to take exams to get promotions. I taught current affairs a great deal . . . What I did twice a week with most classes was to read to them as well as I could, dramatically differentiating the roles in the dialogue . . . Odd words and concepts would come up, and one could write these concepts on the board and discuss them and then go back to reading . . . [Yet] you are handicapped by being up against a lack of quickness, a lack of a quick ear and the quick brain. There is no good in pretending.' The problem was, any old Tommy-this and Tommy-that and Tommy-go-away was being shoved through the course for a Cert. Ed., to supply teachers expeditiously for the rising birth rate. (There were not a few of these old duffers still clogging the classrooms of industrial South Wales council schools when I came along at the end of the Age of Aquarius.) And besides which, the job at the Brigg was not permanent. Having responded to dozens of advertisements in the *Times Educational Supplement*, Burgess finally secured a position at Banbury Grammar School, to begin in the autumn of 1950.* Talking in 1968, he makes it sound as if he was mortified from the outset – an affronted Nicholas Nickleby:

> I was teaching in a grammar school – that is, a state secondary school for brighter children, selected by examination at the age of eleven. I was a senior English master in a grammar school. In Banbury. 'Ride a cock horse to Banbury Cross', and so on. It was a school of great reputation, a very good school in fact, and I enjoyed the work. But my salary as a grammar school master was less than five hundred pounds a year. My salary as a master with a good degree, working five days a week, doing games supervision, running the dramatic society, was far less than that of the average market gardener. One didn't mind about that. One could put up with five Woodbines a day and a couple of halves of draught cider, which I think was threepence a half. But the horror was that one's own students, one's own pupils in the sixth form, had read books one had not read oneself because their parents were rich enough to be able to afford to buy them. The humiliation, as it were the cultural humiliation, was so extreme that one had to do something about it. The only thing to do was to get out and make a new start . . .

– in Malaya, where his salary was a vastly improved one thousand nine hundred pounds a year, out of which he easily afforded a cook, amah and driver; and he'd pay no income tax. Thence, Malta, Monte Carlo; you know the drill.

It is the jealousy and peevishness which is so uncompelling; the

* 'You're nearly forty,' Howarth's wife Veronica says in *The Worm and the Ring*. 'You're just a grammar school teacher with no prospects. You're not even getting interviews.' We can hear Lynne giving that rebuke.

clamminess of his cupidity.* Let's look further, or seek another perspective. I have before me a dozen buff-coloured copies of *The Banburian*, the magazine of Banbury Grammar School, half a century old. Is there anything more like a burial mound than an ancient school magazine? More dusty and creepy and plangent? All that youth and hope and ambition – and the pupils are going to be septuagenarians now, or dead. 'Our congratulations to Isabel Cadd and Dorothy Noon, who have been advanced to prefectorial rank'; 'Welcome home to Janet Tattersall, whom many Old Banburians will remember as Janet Middleton.' I love the names, the Hickmotts, Blinkhorns, Trumps and Gallimores, the Lickorishes, Wimbushes, Shipps, Pratts and Bustins: this is a Shakespearean roll-call, like Bullcalf, Mouldy, Shadow and Wart, Falstaff's recruits, or Oatcake and Seacoal, from Dogberry's platoon. It is, in fact, a completely Shakespearean landscape, with swallows circling and owls blinking against the light. Banbury, pop. fourteen thousand (in the fifties), is a market town in Oxfordshire, famous for its livestock market and pastries with spicy currant fillings. It was as snug as Sir John's Windsor, as self-contained as Olivia's Illyria, with aldermen and box hedges, assembly rooms and goose fairs. It is situated only twenty miles south-east of Stratford-upon-Avon, and is on the old stagecoach route to London. Bardolph calls Slender 'You Banbury cheese!' (in *The Merry Wives of Windsor*), and Burgess's evocation of Stratford-upon-Avon is his memory of Banbury† – rendered

* This rant, delivered to an interviewer in America, is almost word for word Howarth's speech to his wife when he sees a car salesman paying for a round of drinks with 'a dirty wad' – '"You see?" said Howarth, grinning malevolently . . . "And I just have enough for one half of cider. And tomorrow's bus fares." He began to swear rhythmically and roundly, with much showing of his lower teeth.'

There's plenty on the clink and chink of money in *The Worm and the Ring*, yet whereas, in Wagner's opera, the hoarding of gold is a corrupting activity, in Burgess it is the corrupt or the philistines who are already in possession of riches – and *he* wants those riches, believing wealth to be more his due. He complained yet again to Geoffrey Aggeler, who interviewed him for a critical study in 1972: 'Tradesmen were spending fortunes in pubs, standing everyone rounds of whisky and gin whilst teachers and musicians had to drink draught cider at twopence half penny the glass.' *Tradesmen*? Wasn't he himself the stepson of the corner shop? The snobbery and indignation was to be Burgess's consistent attitude, nicely brought out in Michael Mewshaw's article, 'Do I Owe You Something', in *Granta* (issue no. 75, autumn 2001): whenever he runs into the Great Man, at receptions or book launches, 'as if in a recorded announcement, Anthony [always] asked, "Do I owe you something? A letter? A recommendation? Money?"' It was a successful (and shitty) way of ensuring he'd never be pledged for those things.

† The real Stratford-upon-Avon he hated, 'a most ghastly place. Have you been there, Liana?' he asked in the presence of an interviewer from the *Malahat Review*, in 1971. 'Better not go, awful place. The theatre's good, except the audiences are lousy, so obviously sort of Women's Institute.'

poetically in *Nothing Like the Sun* ('Air blue and sweet over the greenery where the hares darted . . . the butchers sharpening their knives . . . Sweet hopeful air . . . with a wild south-westerly whisper of afternoon rain . . .'); and he's no less lyrical in the biography, *Shakespeare*, where he describes a borough which 'sat in a fine wooded valley and was surrounded by crops and cattle'. The school prizes were distributed one year by the District Commissioner of Tanganyika, and the next year, 'In the absence of Lady Grasett, who was indisposed, Sir Edward Grasett presented the prizes'; there is the announcement of the death of King George; there's a trip on the last passenger steam train service between Banbury and Kingham (*n.b.*, the overgrown platforms and sidings are still visible from the Cotswold Line and look like Roman remains); an excursion by Midland Red Motor Bus is made to Stratford-upon-Avon to see Peggy Ashcroft and Anthony Quayle (Burgess's future Aaron); the Dedication of the War Memorial is conducted by the Bishop of Dorchester; there are the harvest camps at Evesham in flawless weather to gather the plums; the examination passes; the rugger games and hockey matches lost and won; the display of nests and birds' eggs on Open Day; the announcement of the early death by cancer of a physics master; the weddings and reunion dinners: all that hope and effort and struggle, which has sped away from us. And Burgess is here – as John Wilson – in the midst of it, and he had no idea we'd one day be watching. There he is supplying the incidental music for *A Midsummer Night's Dream* ('The School Orchestra played an overture and entr'acte composed by Mr. Wilson'), or he's taking part in a Staff Brains Trust (with Miss Winfield, Mr Batts and Mr Draper) to debate such topics as progress and the degeneration of the male, or (on 28 January 1953) he's addressing the VIth Form Forum ('at very short notice') on Modern Drama, with illustrations from Shaw, Eliot and Auden ('the American accent was much appreciated!'), or he's writing a review of the Banbury Grammar School Choral Society's performance of Handel's *Samson* in St Mary's Church ('Perhaps the true heroine of the evening was Miss Muriel Pawley, who brought to her organ accompaniments [a] profound realisation of the limitations and strength of her instrument'), or telling us (under the pen-name Adolphus Trout*) about their rendition of

* Adolphus Trout is Burgess's nudge towards Augustus Carp – he was a fan of *Augustus Carp, Esq., by Himself: Being the Autobiography of a Really Good Man* (1924), which he'd first come across in 1940, and he set himself the task of discovering the identity of the anonymous author. (The subtitle of his own memoirs, *Being the First Part of the Confessions of Anthony Burgess*, alludes to Carp's construction.) In 1965, he asked readers

Mendelssohn's *Elijah* ('of Miss Marita Quelch's performance what will remain in our memory is the exquisite quality of her top notes' – a spoof notice? The date is Thursday 1 April 1954), and at the Christmas Bazaar, away from the bric-a-brac stalls and tables of babies' bibs, dolls, sweet-filled snowmen, bottles, pickles and preserves, he lodged himself in the Medical Room as Professor Sosostris, the palmist ('people emerged from the Medical Room, their eyes glazed with horror . . . Many of those who crossed his palm with silver are now of the opinion that ignorance is bliss' – in the course of the afternoon he foretold sixty-three marriages, seven legacies, fifteen sea voyages, a hundred and twenty births and one sudden death*).

A pupil who appears frequently in the magazine is Valerie Tryon, whose father was the Languages Master. She obtained her L.R.A.M. at the age of sixteen and won an Open Scholarship to the Royal Academy of Music in 1951, obtaining nearly one hundred per cent in the practical examination. By the following year she had been awarded the Silver Medal Albanesi Prize and was giving a recital in Leicester, and in 1953 she won the Harold Samuel Bach Prize, the Cuthbert Whitemore Prize and the Principal's Prize. Whatever happened to her? She gave a recital in Banbury Town Hall, in aid of the 'Wireless for the Bedridden' Fund, and Burgess composed a sonata specially for her to play.† Another name cropping up is

of the *TLS* if they knew of the book (which has always been a cult comedy and had never caught on like *Diary of a Nobody*, which it resembles), and from the replies he discovered that the author was Sir Henry Howarth Bashford, M.D., F.R.C.P., Chief Medical Officer to the Post Office, Medical Adviser to the Treasury, and Honorary Physician to King George VI. Apart from this book and contributing specialist pieces to *The Lancet*, he wrote *Vagabonds in Perigord* and *Wiltshire Harvest*, and died in 1961. Burgess wrote an Introduction to *Augustus Carp* for a reprint by the Boydell Press in 1985. Two years later, exactly the same piece became the Postscript for a reprint by Penguin. The Edward Gorey-ish illustration of the Rev. Simeon Whey in the original edition is the spitting image of the young Burgess. (The actual artist was Marjorie Blood who, as Mother Catherine, was a member of the Order of the Sacred Heart at Roehampton Convent.)

* He retained an interest in the occult. *Earthly Powers* may be seen as the working out of curses and conundrums. Malaya was full of black magic. There are wizards and witches in *Tremor of Intent* and *MF*. His notion of Shakespeare's Dark Lady (and of the uses and abuses of the Muses in the Enderby novels) involves the supernatural. He once put a spell on a boat in the harbour at Monaco, using a Greek and Roman formula taught to him by Peter Green, professor of classics at Iowa. It sank.

† She emigrated to Canada soon afterwards. I located her in Ontario, whence she told me: 'I played his sonata from the manuscript for him. Unfortunately, in all the moving I've done, the sonata has got lost. I regret this of course. The piece as I remember it was a short one-movement work, around ten or fifteen minutes, with dissonances, but in a rather romantic vein.'

Sonia Hunt, who is in the First XI Hockey team, sang three soprano solos in *The Messiah* at the church in Middleton Cheney, on 7 March 1951 ('There could be very few adverse criticisms,' said the report in the magazine – written by Burgess), and was Mistress Ford in *The Merry Wives of Windsor* ('It was enough to turn one green with envy of Falstaff when she focussed her magnetic allure on him'). Burgess even took the trouble to notice her absence: 'Miss Sonia Hunt, owing to indisposition, was unable to sing', wrote 'J. B. W.' of Handel's *Samson*. She still lives near Banbury and has been long married to Martin Blinkhorn, who owns the town's camera, hi-fi and electrical goods shop. They met at the Old Banburians Dramatic Society when John Wilson was directing its shows. 'John Wilson was a hero to me,' she told me. 'He liked to talk to the Sixth Form as if we were adults. I was in his class. I was in the plays he produced, in school and in Adderbury. I was in the Upper VIth, and he wanted me to write the libretto for his opera! I mean, what a thing to ask! We were all impressed when he said he was a composer – for he knew all about literature, too. A great teacher – an inspiring teacher. I couldn't believe it when I read his autobiography, and he says how lustful he was. The other girls in my class – it's what we used to discuss together, how completely *asexual* he was. We were seventeen. We were aware of things – and yet John Wilson behaved so well. Never so much as the vaguest pass. He didn't seem interested. Strange.'

Was there a huge amount of foaming, frothing, seething sexual frustration being kept under strict (Jesuitical) self-control? Suggesting that they collaborate on making an opera together perhaps was Burgess's idea of a seduction technique. He pottered with *The Eve of Saint Venus* for years, from 1952 until its publication as a novella in 1964. It's the tale of a man who puts a ring on a statue of Venus, and she comes to life.* It is constructed like a drawing-room-and-French-windows comedy, exactly the kind of play mounted by amateur dramatic societies, with off-stage thun-

* This is the only known instance of Burgess (the man who knew too much) not knowing that other, related adaptations of his source existed. He's so wrapped up in a version of the tale told by Robert Burton in *The Anatomy of Melancholy* (1621), it escapes his notice that Ogden Nash and S. J. Perelman had collaborated with Kurt Weill on a Broadway show, *One Touch of Venus* – exactly the same story – in 1943. (Weill had wanted Marlene Dietrich for the role of the goddess and settled for Mary Martin.) A film version, with additional material by Harry Kurnitz, was released in 1949, a scant three years before Burgess began work. It starred Ava Gardner (Burgess's Agrippina, Nero's mother, in *A.D.*) who, in her later years, as a permanently sozzled old vamp, could have played Lynne in a biopic to perfection. Nash and Perelman's source was *The Tinted Venus* by F. Anstey (the pseudonym of Thomas Anstey Guthrie), written in 1885.

der and lightning effects, a droll low-class maid to carry tea trays in and out, and a sentimental ending ('I never felt less tired in my life, but I'll come back to bed') that provides a neat curtain line. The characters are Sir Benjamin Drayton, Mr Crowther-Mason, Spatchcock, Ambrose, Julia and Diana. There are on/off betrothals, tiffs and makings-up, night-before-the-wedding nerves and Ernie Wise dialogue ('Goodnight, Mummy. Thank you for everything, especially for being my mother,' says Diana. 'I've fulfilled my biological function and I always felt it would be nice for someone to thank me for it,' answers Lady Drayton). Though derivative – here's some Christopher Fry, over there's some of Eliot's verse-plays, here's some William Douglas-Home – the intrusion of theology is Burgessian ('Oh,' says the vicar, 'sin is my hobby. Not, of course, the commission of sin, ha ha, but the study of it'); and, intriguingly, the inner meanings of the work, its tremulousness and guilt-racked longings, speak directly to his own concerns. As a vision of marriage as an indissoluble state, a trap once the choice has been made, it can be seen to be haunted by Lynne. 'I've missed the boat, haven't I, I've failed,' says one of the characters. 'Oh, why does nothing happen? I'm doing my best, aren't I, O God? . . . I feel as if I'm winding up a watch with a broken spring . . . There's something missing.' As Sonia Blinkhorn (née Hunt) told me, they all thought Lynne was a witch – a pagan goddess. 'She'd give you a baleful look – she was horrible to children. She wasn't at all like you'd have imagined John Wilson's wife. You'd picture him with a lovely, intelligent woman, sweet-natured . . . I'm sure she was intelligent, but she was this mad creature, who drank all the time. She almost never came to school functions. He didn't seem to have a wife where a wife was expected, accompanying him to plays, concerts, or speech days.' Thus, in *The Eve of Saint Venus*, to do battle with the virago summoned from hell ('The gods are still alive, aspects of the . . . moving, widening, unifying pattern') there has to be her opposite, a dream of a fair woman, the character of Diana – a Diana Gillon or Sonia Hunt, as in Diana the goddess of the hunt: 'waif-like, wet', 'a pretty flushed girl, angry, full of words' clad in a 'Chinese dressing gown that was all dragons'.

Howarth, in *The Worm and the Ring*, dwells upon how it wasn't fair, 'the whole system was wrong in allowing them to flaunt their country-girl breasts, proud of the way they tautened the regulation white school blouses . . . It was sex all day long, damn it, whichever way you looked at it.' It could all so easily happen, he fears, 'an encouraging hand on the shoulder, a smack on her buttock as she goes down the corridor, a kiss in the dark at a school party.' These are the saucy ruminations which went directly into his autobiography ('A mixed school is a dangerous place for susceptible male teachers'); and were he a teacher now, in our super-cautious age, he'd be had up on a charge of perversion – especially as his enthusiasm for young girls (in Gibraltar he appraised the frisky natives and in Warrington he was jealous of the American GIs who were mobbed by fourteen-year-old minxes) is actually an extension of his incest fantasy. In *Finnegans Wake*, you can discover whatever you fancy looking for; hence for Burgess it is an epic about incest and guilt, HCE's 'twitch of longing for his daughter, especially as his wife is old and has lost her looks', he tells us in *Here Comes Everybody*. 'This guilt is never far to seek in a man who, himself ageing, has an ageing wife and a nubile daughter,' he generalises. If he'd had a daughter, would he have pounced upon her? An impossible speculation – who can say? But he was madly possessive – and possessed a mad logic, that children were purely and simply one body with their parents. 'An incestuous longing for his daughter is a pathetic attempt,' he further said of Earwicker, 'to remain loyal to his wife while indulging the last spurt of desire for a body comely and sweet as cinnamon.'* Mistress of the cottage at 4 Water Lane, Adderbury, which had been purchased with a loan from Lynne's father, who'd retired in 1949, and which Burgess (pissily) named Little Gidding, Lynne definitely fits the bill as the wife who's no longer an oil painting. ('He put out a hand to Veronica,' it is said of Howarth, 'pitying her for her lost beauty [and] her frustration.') And if I'm glad he didn't have real daughters, the Banbury schoolchildren were his daughter surrogates, or filial harem, which he kept safely locked inside his head, as a masturbation scenario. When he described the habits of Dylan Thomas, for instance, in 1974, he was really referring to himself: 'His sexual activities normally took place in the bathroom; he was a great masturbator. [Writers] often go into the bathroom to masturbate. Thomas did this all the time. Quite a number of artists masturbate, then they write.' Or then they teach – or produce plays. Sonia Hunt was in *The Chiltern Hundreds*, which was performed on 12, 13 and 14 July 1951 (she 'looked, as always, well', remarked the reviewer in *The Banburian*); it was not a success. 'A mere flaccid mass of stock situations, lifeless characterisations and limp dialogue,' wrote somebody signing themselves 'I. V.' in the school mag. Old 'I. V.' could have been prophesying Burgess's later novels. 'There were few chances for

* *Cinnamon* is a word Burgess used in association with Shakespeare, that is to say Stratford-upon-Avon and the Midlands, that is to say, Banbury.

the producer. Lights had to be switched woodenly off and on, and the proscenium arch a prison made . . . The producer informs me that Clara, the duck, provided a Sunday dinner for him. The sensation of eating a character, he tells me, though satisfying in one way, was gruesome in another. It was as though Hamlet was awaiting burial in one's own back garden.' After incest, therefore, cannibalism. Sonia Hunt's future husband, Martin Blinkhorn, was the Earl of Lister.

For the October Drama Week, held in the Town Hall, Burgess inflicted Eliot's *Sweeney Agonistes* on the borough. The review (again by 'I. V.') is a masterpiece of tact:

> This [work] was chosen for its historical significance (the first 'modern' poetic play) as well as for aesthetic merits which, if unperceived by many of the audience, began to appear startlingly to many of the cast. Martin Blinkhorn played Sweeney, the man dimly aware of being in hell, but unable to do much about it . . . A harpy-like gin-drinking Chorus scared itself with the nightmare finale. John Wilson produced.

His next effort was the Old Pupils' production of Aldous Huxley's *The Giaconda Smile*, performed on 6, 7 and 8 December. Again, the house was sparse. Kathleen Winfield saw it and tried to be enthusiastic about 'Mr John Wilson's able direction' and the cast, at least, was audible, the décor was 'very pleasing' and the scene shifting was done 'quickly and efficiently'. Martin Blinkhorn had the task of playing Henry Hutton, the worldly intellectual humanised through suffering – and you can see Burgess's hand here, choosing material about saving souls and his Catholic hang-ups. 'It is regrettable that such a good performance received so little support,' it was later reported, but the play was 'a severe test' – which was rectified by the more purely entertaining presentation of Christopher Fry's *A Phoenix Too Frequent* as part of the school's Diamond Jubilee celebrations in 1953. The scenery was again 'delightful', the lighting effects 'effective', the stage management 'unobtrusive', and in the programme the bold statement or command 'You will like the play' was signed 'John B. Wilson'. Again, Kathleen Winfield is our eyewitness:

> John B. Wilson is to be commended for a finished production, though a more obvious sarcophagus would have added to the illusion that the scene was a tomb, and the position the two women had to take up when lying asleep forced them to adopt somewhat inelegant postures.

One of the women, Dynamene, was played by Moyna Morris. As

Moyna Patricia Boyle she'd been a pupil at the school, and had married in 1946. She'd joined the school staff with a temporary appointment in March 1950, a term prior to Burgess. Her husband, Alec, had passed out top of his pilot's course at Wellesbourne, Warwickshire, and his wings and the Mountford Trophy, for being the best Pilot Officer on the course, were presented to him by John Profumo MP. He was posted as a Technical Officer to the Royal Aircraft Establishment at Farnborough, where his wife intended joining him in July 1953. By September of the following year he'd successfully accomplished a long list of tests for the Staff Qualifying Exam at Cranwell and he was eventually to become Air Marshal of the RAF, Sir Alec Morris KBE, CB – and Moyna, Lady Morris, was another of Burgess's muses, one with whom he'd 'conducted an adulterous affair [as a] way of avoiding mischief', i.e. with the nymphets. Again, as with his other dangerous liaisons, intimacy didn't get further than the inside of his head.

'He was an extraordinary man, even then,' Lady Morris told me a few years ago, looking back to the early fifties, 'erratic in his teaching, production of plays, and lifestyle. I played Juno in *Juno and the Paycock*, which he produced,* and I figured as Hilda Connor in the withdrawn Heinemann book, *The Worm and the Ring*, but didn't feel it was a matter for legal action – as Gwen Bustin, the school secretary did!' As Veronica will no longer permit sexual intercourse,† Howarth's lusts and desires fix upon this 'fit, well-off, well-dressed' young maths teacher, whose husband is a major in the Engineers:

> It was a queer and disturbing life, being surrounded daily by young flesh, watching the shy slow blossoming of childish breasts, the rounded flanks growing yet rounder . . . But was it safer, to court Hilda Connor? . . . He saw her sturdy legs in hockey dress. 'Come on, girls!' Yet he had smelt Schiaparelli's *Shocking* on her . . . and had admired the slim blood-tipped fingers that gripped a vicious marking pencil.

* In his review of Garry O'Connor's *Sean O'Casey: A Life* (in the *Independent* on 17 March 1988), Burgess stated that O'Casey, who had experimented with a variety of names (Jack Casey, Sean O'Cathasaigh, Johnny Casside), was unplayable. 'I once directed *Juno and the Paycock* for an Oxfordshire dramatic society; the actors had great difficulty with the brogue . . .'

† She shares Lynne's obscure wound – or stigmatum: 'I've told you before, Howarth,' says Dr Leary, 'a woman's internal economy is a very strange and subtle thing. We still don't know much about it, you know . . .' And again: 'A woman's system is a queer thing. Delicately balanced. Mind and body are intermixed, more so than in a man. The thing cleared up a bit when [she] was happy [and] had some sense of security.'

You can just see him tolling his own bell as he writes this – with one hand. Her husband away at his military base, Hilda resides with her mother in the village of Rodforth. Moyna Morris, too, with a husband stationed elsewhere as a Flight Lieutenant, kept house with her mother – at Chipping Warden, a village north of Banbury. 'He made very little effort to disguise Banbury,' she told me. 'It is *thinly* disguised. The streets, tea shops, the pubs, the people. I remember when he was writing *The Eve of Saint Venus*, as a play not a novel. He was a struggling writer, very disorganised. He was amazed that I knew how much money I had left in my bank account. I told him, you keep a running balance on your counterfoils in your chequebook. He was impressed, incredulous, stared at me. He was not a man who smiled, except wryly, and then very occasionally. There was a sense of deep unhappiness somewhere – he'd tell me things about Manchester, but you never knew what to believe – that his mother was in the music hall and she'd died and left him crying in his cot. He always told me these marvellous stories – the cot, with his dead mother and sister. I didn't believe any of it.'

Did she mind being Hilda Connor? 'I thought it foolish to press for legal action, and identify yourself in the book. Gwen Bustin wanted me to join her in the action. I knew Gwen well – my daughter was her goddaughter. There are many incidents in the book between Hilda and Howarth that are me and John, but it's all very embroidered. He didn't paw women about – but in all his books he loves to put in this stuff about being the great stud. It's cerebral. We didn't have a physical relationship. We never went to bed – the most he did was put his arm around me once, for a split second. He did bombard me with letters and poems – he'd pin them on the school noticeboard for all to see. I was very young when I knew him – and to be honest I couldn't cope with this onslaught. Alec knew all about it. He said I should laugh about it, and I suppose he was an exciting person. Alec liked him. He was a good companion. Entertaining – the way he'd handle language. But his womanising! Who believes it? It was such the reverse of that, I'm sure he was impotent.'

So John Wilson fooled nobody; it was Anthony Burgess who'd do that.*

* Reviewers were always happy to take him at his word, e.g. 'A Don Giovanni burning with resentment,' in the *Spectator*, on 28 February 1987, which was a piece by myself as a matter of fact. But I was on to something when I wrote: 'Burgess writes up Wilson's past in the lineaments of libertine Frank Harris' – for Harris (1856–1931), who published a four-volume autobiography entitled *My Life and Loves*, was a notorious braggart and liar. His plays and books, *The Man Shakespeare* (1909), *Shakespeare and His Love* (1910) and *The Women of Shakespeare* (1911), influenced *Nothing Like the Sun*. He was played by Jack

In *The Worm and the Ring*, Howarth persuades Hilda to go to the cinema in Charlbury, works upon her at school, by sitting next to her during assembly or in the canteen (where he declares his love), and the relationship reaches its climax when the pair of them escort a party of children on an educational visit to Paris. 'We can never be really together,' sighs Howarth, staring into his Pernod. 'We could be together now, in bed, if you really cared enough about it,' retorts Hilda, 'instead of moaning in this insipid Catholic romantic way of yours. We could be together tonight.' They bang away whilst the church bells ring out for Easter Sunday. 'We were both mad,' they agree later. There was indeed a trip from Banbury Grammar School to Paris, which took place between 28 March and 5 April 1953. The group stayed at the Craigmore Hotel in London and caught the channel boat *Lisieux* at Newhaven. The crossing was rough and there was much puking. They disembarked at Dieppe and took the train to the Gare St Lazare, where a coach met them for Issy. There then followed a round of sightseeing and expeditions to cafés and bars, exactly as in the novel. At the Hotel de Ville, kites were given to parties of English schoolchildren to fly on Coronation Day. Moyna Morris was the supervising member of staff – accompanied by her husband, who was on leave. 'It actually did happen, the Paris trip,' Lady Morris told me. 'It was my husband in charge of the boys, not John. He substituted himself.'*

And what an illuminating, wish-fulfilling substitution. In the novel, the erotic entanglement suggests that Hilda and Howarth have a compulsion to hurt each other and their absent spouses. But Burgess doesn't have the

Lemmon in the film *Cowboy* (1958). Wilde, about whom he wrote a book, told Harris, 'You are a man of dominant personality . . . You require response, or you annihilate.' Shaw called him a 'pugnacious Captain Kidd'. His editor, Lyle Blair, called him 'undoubtedly a charlatan, unscrupulous [and] flamboyant'.

To interviewers who tried to broach the subject of his libertinism, Burgess would either be: (a) evasive: 'I feel happier in Italy where you can have a major row with your wife in public and it's regarded as acceptable grand opera. I don't like the terrible upper middle-class reticence you used to get in Somerset Maugham's drawing-room comedies.' Or (b) he'd trot out the mad incest theory: 'I've always felt that Englishwomen had to be approached in a brotherly manner rather than in an erotic manner. I've always preferred women of the Mediterranean.'

* 'I wrote a very good account of Paris before I ever went there,' he boasted in 1971. 'Better than the real thing . . . Paris was a town I always tried to avoid. But I've been more and more in it recently and find that the account of Paris I wrote (although it smells of maps and tourist guides) is not unlike the reality. This is also true with Joyce's Gibraltar in *Ulysses*; one has no need to visit the country to write about the country.' This will rather depend on whether what you want to achieve is topographical accuracy, which any fool with a Baedeker can confect, or some kind of psychological landscape – which is altogether harder to counterfeit. Burgess felt safer with externals.

skills or psychological penetration to make anything of this. (Burgess could write, with *Flame into Being*, a lively study of Lawrence, whose novels are filled with the tribulations of schoolmasters, but he's a million miles away from Lawrence's understanding of sensation and the power of human relationships.) All the clever allusions and underpinnings to Wagner and Joyce in the world can't disguise the fact that *The Worm and the Ring* is very minor. Nothing is emotionally charged. (The emotions that gave rise to it aren't in it.) You ought to want to believe that Hilda is holding herself back; that then Howarth can't satisfy her, which would link up with his problems with Veronica and the excuses of her obscure gynaecological complaint. Jealousy and sexual obsession and how this is intimately painful – these were his subjects, but he avoids them. A passionate fling – and how there is no future in it. For in real life he was agonised by seeing Alec and Moyna Morris together. It was like Diana and Meir Gillon, or even Lynne and Herbert Williams,* when they were together and he was in Gibraltar. He looked at couples from the outside, from which vantage point a relationship could look serene, and it filled him with longing. Even in his own marriage he was left out. Lynne's passive hopelessness made him feel entirely alone. This was to make him, paradoxically, closer to the character based on Gwen Bustin, over which he was sued, and the book withdrawn and pulped, than to Howarth, the successful adulterer. (Though the ending is an accurate forecast: Howarth, with wife and son, emigrates to Italy.) Frumpy old Alice has a sad crush on the ineffectual Headmaster, Mr Woolton. She also has ideas above her station. These are the words complained of in the libel writ, as evidence of Burgess's malice and his intention to whip up ridicule and contempt:

> Alice is only a secretary . . . She belongs to the town, as her family has for generations, and . . . this town loves scandal better than anything.
>
> . . .
>
> [Alice had] given forty years of her life to [the school]: nobody else had been as loyal as that. And yet, as the yellowing records showed, she hadn't been exactly a prize pupil. She hadn't even played any games.
>
> . . .

* The novel's villain, Dr Gardner, who plagiarises Howarth's thesis on Baudalaire – i.e. appropriates or steals what's not his – has the first name Herbert. Of his expensive tastes in gin or fountain pens it is said sneeringly, 'Only the best for Gardner.'

> Was there no escape from this incubus [frets Woolton]? . . . His rough rejection of her desire to insinuate herself further into his life . . . would engender spite and a will to wound.
>
> . . .
>
> 'Oh, she's a bit deranged,' said Frederica Woolton. 'She's the sort of woman who should have got married ages ago. It's too late now, I'd say.'
>
> . . .
>
> She's just pitiable, that's all.
>
> . . .
>
> She seemed to be suppressing an old maid's excitement.
>
> . . .
>
> She came along with a pain in her chest [says Dr Leary]. When I asked her to take her blouse off, she looked at me with a mixture of, well, excitement and outrage . . . She seemed to be the sort of woman who might scream that I was trying to rape her . . . She seems definitely unbalanced, the sort who might shout out dirty words under an anaesthetic.

Though Burgess made the pathetic excuse* that it was a complete coincidence if his school secretary bore any resemblance to the actual school secretary, everybody in Banbury at once saw the accuracy of the portrait – and Gwen Bustin rather proved that she was indeed a hysterical dried-up old duenna by reacting in the way she did, i.e. by hiring Colin Duncan QC to express her outrage in open court that she'd been portrayed in a book as a hysterical dried-up old duenna. One can only feel sorry for her. Banbury Grammar School was her whole existence. She's all over the pages of *The Banburian*, editing the News of Old Pupils section, appealing for donations for the War Memorial panels, collecting the money for the Stratford-upon-Avon theatre trips, organising Reunion Dinners, keeping things going. In 1954, she became Mayoress of Banbury, and the

* In his entry on the Novel in the *Britannica*, Burgess despairs on behalf of the poor novelist who, whilst 'depicting purely imaginary characters and situations', blunders innocently into a libellous minefield. This is hypocritical. He knew full well when he was putting people he'd taken umbrage against into a book, e.g. Crump and Meldrum. He'd do it again in *The Long Day Wanes*, eliciting another libel writ from a former acquaintance. Wise to his operations, Heinemann made him rewrite *Devil of a State* to conceal its Brunei background and relocate it in Zanzibar. Strangely, there is a mention of the deployment of the law of libel in *The Worm and the Ring* itself, as if he was deliberately provoking ructions: 'You've published these lies,' Dr Gardner tells the girl whose diary has been read out. 'You're guilty of a libel . . . A libel is the publication of lies intended to harm a person.'

school 'wished her success and happiness in her round of duties' – and though it is easy to scoff at this provincial self-importance (at the displays of dancing, in aid of the Mission for Seamen and the British Sailors' Society, 'arranged by Miss Bustin in her capacity of Mayoress of Banbury,' etc.), as a satirical target, the old darling was too soft. Burgess *was* being malicious. Why? Dr Leary was a real Banbury doctor – and the Mayoress's doctor. The whole thing's a taunt – and a masochistic one. It's Burgess himself who is suffering from frustration and hysteria and who might 'one of these days . . . be really dangerous. Sex does queer things to people . . . It rends them like a departing devil' – and the exorcism scenes in *The Eve of Saint Venus* and *Earthly Powers* are ceremonies to purge the body of its demonic lusts, its devices and desires. Money and sex, and the shortage of both, are what exercise his mind, from first to last. He should've sat for Francis Bacon.

Self-loathing and bitterness, however, cannot fill the whole of a life, even when the roster of resentments is as pathological and comprehensive as Burgess's. If as a lover he was a lunatic (and the Victorians may have been right all along: it does sap your sanity), as a teacher and a colleague he was a success. I went to Stretton-on-Fosse to meet Thomas Atkinson, who was the History Master, and he's in the novel as Mr Keyte, where fun is made of his big ears, pillar-box aperture grin and enthusiasm for rugby, which Mr Atkinson actually did coach. Expecting, therefore, a punch-drunk Halloween pumpkin, I was relieved to encounter a spry and elegant nonagenarian, hailing from the days when schoolmasters were several cuts above the washed-out ignoramuses and timid social workers who today are entrusted with the nation's young fine minds. If this was a film, Thomas Atkinson would be played by Michael Hordern.

'He was a good man to have on the staff, John. Second-in-command in the English Department under Kenneth Carrdus, who was educated at Brasenose and had a rich wife. He used to love these big words. He'd stand there and they'd flow from his mouth – *philoprogenitive* was one I remember. He was a splendid chap. Everyone was fond of him – but I don't recognise the gruff and cantankerous Anthony Burgess who appears on the television. It must be a joke. I arrived at the school in 1947. There was a background of politics at the place, gossip about this or that faction, hearsay, and John picked up on all that and worked it into his novel. My university was Manchester – like John – and the staff at the school was full of ex-army people, all of us glad to be out of uniform. John was in Educational and Vocational training – EVT – we all were. Anything to keep the troops quiet. We used to have a drink with him and Lynne in Adderbury, at the Bell. They lived in this small terraced decrepit cottage. She was quarrelsome. Drank a lot. When we heard that she'd been ambushed in Malaya, everybody thought, well, it's a wonder she wasn't ambushed in Banbury. She was not a lady, if you know what I mean? I remember he was so sad on his birthday once when she'd forgotten – so he brought cheese and a half bottle of Beaujolais into the staffroom. God knows where he got that from – this was Banbury soon after the war. He said theatrically, "No one's remembered m'birthday!" But that was an act – all his grandiose ways are an act. He was a sensitive man, John. There was this school excursion to Windsor – the Diamond Jubilee Commemoration Trip. Every single person in the school went. Military planning for it. A special train hired. A boy was singled out by Mr Rose, the Headmaster, a boy picked from the throng and held up as an example of unforgivable slovenliness and how he was letting the school down – all that sort of thing, how this was exactly what you mustn't be like, and so on. John said to me, "I could've wept when that boy was humiliated." And he went up to the boy and said, "Look, I'm sorry this has happened." Gwen Bustin was Mr Rose's secretary – of course there were rumours about their relationship. There always are. He wrote *The Worm and the Ring* whilst he was at Banbury, though it wasn't published for years. And he wrote a play, *The Gods Have Hot Backs*, which became *The Eve of Saint Venus*. He was a great one for titles. Have you read *Earthly Powers*? Contains every sexual perversion. It makes me angry to see him on television or in the paper, roaring away as Anthony Burgess, coarsening himself, travestying himself and degrading and begrudging Manchester, denigrating his past and the man he was. Why couldn't he have cultivated a quiet confidence? He never mentions that he was John Wilson, a teacher at Banbury. He suffered from a lack of money – was at the bottom of the salary ladder, and he felt very strongly about this, though we were all in the same boat. I got the impression he always knew he'd be famous, that he wasn't going to stay. We saw him when he came back from Malaya – we had a meal at the White Lion. He was going in for being a flamboyant bohemian and it was an embarrassing spectacle, awkward. They were very drunk – Lynne was drinking whisky. He'd published a few novels by then and he told me pompously, "Fame comes *very* slowly." Who did he think he was, all of a sudden? That's not how I want to remember him. The John I knew was a kind man and a good colleague. He used to bring his dog to school. He loved that dog. How to find a home for his dog when he left for Malaya was a great worry. I read once that when he revisited England from Monte Carlo he stayed at Claridge's or the Ritz, or somewhere like that. My wife and I sent him a postcard, "It's a long way from the Bell at Adderbury to the Ritz!" We never heard from him. We were in Crete with Alec and Moyna, and there was this spare chair at the café table. "Do you know who I wish was sitting there, who I'd love to talk to again?" And Moyna said, "I know, I was thinking the same – John." We all sent a postcard, saying he'd been simultaneously in our thoughts, but he's never replied. He's cut the cable on his past. Won't get in touch with old friends. We'd love to have seen him then, in Crete. Quite eerie, the way he crossed our minds. I think the only reference he made to Banbury was to say that he felt he'd been "drowning in honey", whatever that meant. "Time, gentlemen, please" was his catchphrase. He'd say it at the end of a lesson when the bell went. "Time, gentlemen, please." At the end of a staff meeting. Always.'

It is what Charles Ryder says about his enchanted summer with Sebastian Flyte at Brideshead and then in Venice: the time passed 'quickly and sweetly – perhaps too sweetly; I was drowning in honey, stingless'. Was the Banbury episode simply such indulgent floundering? He called Adderbury and the Cotswold villages 'drearily picturesque'; and for that matter he never ceased calling Manchester a great ugly slum, whereas I personally treasure its conglomeration of charcoal-toned civic buildings, the Victorian High Gothic turrets and rotundas, like a municipal Gormenghast. He wanted to be the free and reckless hero – like Joyce's Shakespeare, in what he called 'the most delicious' passage in his favourite book: 'Christfox in leather trews, hiding, a runaway in blighted treeforks from hue and cry. Knowing no vixen, walking lonely in the chase. Women he won to him, tender people, . . . ladies of justices, bully tapsters' wives. Fox and geese.' Joyce's image is of a cunning little farmyard-raiding Hamlet, beholden to no one, a fugitive and a martyr. This is how Burgess wanted to see himself, rushing through, scattering feathers, an enigmatic stranger, swashing his buckle. He couldn't have any affectionate words to say about Banbury (or anywhere he lived and was made welcome), because nostalgia implies a tie or emotional bond. He was determined only to look back in anger. It wasn't a clean anger, a righteous anger. There's a shrillness and crudity to it. Burgess possessed a shifty, narrow-eyed defiance; he believed himself to be intractable and was permanently insulted or injured; and it is this bad treatment which his characters suffer from. The feuds and betrayals, the fools and madmen. But it is never a

God-like wrath, apocalyptic in its extent, though when he spoke through Moses or Freud, this is what he was aiming for: 'it's nothing but sneerers and smiters, attack after attack, enemies, enemies', wails Freud, about his psychoanalytical disciples, when they start to devise ideas and make refinements of their own. Burgess was petty and pinched. He was 'perpetually angry' as a child, and the temperamental hobgoblinry never abated, according to him. The honeybee quotation from Waugh and the romantic rebel identification from Joyce show his disdainfulness towards affable, moderate, ordinary people. This is not admirable – his belief that he is their superior.

Thomas Atkinson summed up the John Wilson he knew and saw each working day for four years as a man who 'took himself seriously and worked compulsively. I associate him with wit, rather than humour. Not a man for the belly laugh.' To get another viewpoint, I travelled to Banbury to meet Kathleen Winfield, the school's Senior Mistress. She retired in 1964 – so that'll give you an indication of her great Queen Mother-ish age. Miss Winfield (I doubt if anybody has ever had the courage to address her as anything other than that) lived in the most immaculate house I'd seen outside the illustrations in *The Sedate World of Marguerite Patten*. The garden was weedless. She was proud of her huge kitchen, which twinkled and sparkled, though the last thing I could picture being knocked together in such a space would be lavish feasts for lots of people. She wheeled a trolley into her lounge. A polished silver teapot, fresh scones, homemade jam. When I asked for coffee instead of tea – panic stations. A pure white damask cloth was laid out. Later I had a glass of sherry and some nuts left over from Christmas. I'd surely been pitched headlong into the setting of *The Ladykillers*, for Miss Winfield was the double of Katie Johnson (1878–1957), who played Mrs Wilberforce. Any moment I expected to hear strains of the Boccherini minuet waft from upstairs, as Alec Guinness and his gang plot their robbery in the guise of a string quintet. However, 'I like living alone,' said Miss Winfield. 'I like people to drop in. Old pupils, staff. But I could never live with anybody.' So, no colourful lodgers. There was a bookshelf with each volume lined up in undeviating alphabetical order. There was no television set. She is in *The Worm and the Ring* as Miss Withers, who stalks the school in 'a chalky gown over a sensible costume [and] a heavy wooden necklace'. Burgess obviously didn't dare go further than that.

'I was in Egypt for two years, New Zealand for a year. I'd been to Russia in 1936, so John was interested to hear about abroad. I think he wanted to get away. I saw the manuscript of *The Worm and the Ring* well before he went to Malaya. It had been sent back by several publishers. Maurice Draper read it. He taught chemistry, and played the flute in John's plays. The school secretary, Alice – that was Gwen Bustin to the life. I knew her very well – we were at primary school together – so I could see how accurate it was. The novel came out – there was a review in one of the Sunday papers. Kenneth Carrdus told Gwen that he planned to put a copy in the Library. Gwen rushed out and bought it – and she was in a terrible state. Wanted me to give evidence and support her as the plaintiff. Mr Rose showed that he had a sense of the ridiculous and was very amused. "Gwen's terribly upset," he told me, but he didn't mind in the slightest being put in the book as Mr Woolton. It was actually my copy of the novel that Gwen borrowed. She and her solicitor covered it with blue pencil marks. I never had it back. There was a settlement out of court. Gwen made this fuss – and enjoyed it rather. Her family had money. She didn't need it.

'Moyna Morris, who was Moyna Boyle before she married, lived with her mother, Mary, whilst Alec was doing his research degree in aeronautics in Southampton, and then he was all over the place with the RAF. He had something to do with radar and guided missiles.* I never thought she and John were having an affair. He tried too hard to give that impression, though he did used to go round to their house in Chipping Warden. They were often together, the three of them, Alec, John and Moyna. He was lonely – his wife was dead drunk all the time. In his books he always exaggerates his own womanising and drinking. He was not like that to know. Never any scandal. We had an outing to a restaurant in Coventry. John was there, with Moyna. Lynne never wanted to accompany him anywhere.

'He was keen on ghost stories. He used to like to scare the girl pupils – stir them up! And he brought beer into the staffroom at lunchtime, which nobody had done before. He was eccentric. The children quite liked him – though they considered him a bit strange. He liked to shock the complacent girls. They got to be afraid of what he might suddenly say or do. But he never overstepped the line. He was not a dull careeristic teacher. Marking books and the paperwork was not for him. He liked class discussions with the cleverer ones. His senior in his department was Kenneth

* Exactly so. Having performed radar duties with Number 90 (Signals) Group, 1945–50, he was in the Guided Weapons Department of the Royal Aircraft [later Aerospace] Establishment, 1953–56. (Did the prowling Burgess become a little blip on his screen?)

Carrdus, who was a sort of ladies' man. He and John didn't get on, except in their mutual admiration for Joyce. One would quote from *Ulysses* and the other would continue. But Kenneth was a bit of a toff. He wouldn't have gone into the Bell at Adderbury, only to the bars of the best hotels. They were both involved with putting on plays for the Old Banburians. Kenneth liked Gilbert and Sullivan. John put on these strange modern things and the hall was empty. He also produced *Juno and the Paycock* at the village hall in Swalcliffe. He had a walk-on role as a reporter. He'd said he had to go up to London to see an eye specialist. He came back in the middle of the dress rehearsal. "I can't go on. I'm going blind," he announced in this theatrical way. He loved making a dramatic entrance. I think he'd been told he needed to wear glasses, though I never saw him with any.

'Lynne was quickly disapproved of in Adderbury, going into the pubs all the time. She worked – I don't know for how long – in the English Department of the North Oxfordshire Technical College, Broughton Road. John also gave evening classes there for two years running, for the WEA, the Workers' Educational Association. I remember enthusiastic talks on Ford Madox Ford.* It was Lynne's colleague there, Miss Jane Cowen, who had the job of sending John's manuscripts back and forth to publishers when he was in Malaya. But because Lynne was always inclined to make enemies, she offended Miss Cowen somehow, so I don't think much came of that plan. That was another of his exaggerations – saying he wrote five or six novels in one year. He'd been struggling to be a published writer since the war.

'John was always wrapped up in his own doings. You could never judge him by normal standards of common courtesy, like answering letters or staying in touch and maintaining a friendship. It was laughable, the way he tried to live like a bohemian artist in Banbury, bringing wine, onions, cheese and bread into the staffroom – the others often didn't approve of

* 'There are some, and I am one of them,' he announced in *Homage to Qwert Yuiop*, 'who hold that the greatest British novelist of the century (I naturally exclude Ireland) is Ford Madox Ford.' Burgess admired the concept of the unreliable narrator in *The Good Soldier* and the way, in *Parade's End*, that 'time and space become subjective and fluid'. This would be the precedent, in Burgess's own novels, for being cavalier with facts, history, geography – because you must trust neither the teller nor his tale. If this sounds like a recipe for carelessness and obscurity, you'd have an ally in Anthony Powell, who believed that Burgess was insufficiently sensitive to 'a kind of bogusness in Ford' (*Journals*, 18 May 1988). Toomey meets him in Chapter 30 of *Earthly Powers*, and Ford mocks his best-selling works as being full of 'cliché, half truth, compromise, timidity'. Toomey thinks this is just 'envy . . . I had made money out of writing'.

this, because it was pretentious. But he was a charming man, a sensitive man, oversensitive – and he'd try and cover this up. Kenneth Carrdus was from the officer class, so John played the belligerent sergeant major. He kept having to make excuses for himself – he always kept feeling that the past had treated him badly. He was always scathing about the past, even if he was happy at the time. I used to try and say, "John, I had a secure happy childhood!" and so he went round saying, "Kathleen must have a very satisfactory sex life to be so serene" – he generally felt he'd missed out somehow. He was ashamed of his past – and I never could get him to accept that, "John, you can't be held responsible for it." So he put everything into playing this role of "great writer" – he was crazy about language. He'd read every book ever written, I'm convinced. But what gifts he had he dissipated. It's a shame he didn't put all that effort into fewer, better novels. And in Banbury he was happy – lots of friends – marvellous company, especially on his own, when he wasn't this persecuted creature. He'd certainly have been exciting to be taught by . . .'

His enthusiasm for directing plays is one clue; the way he was a marionetteer is another – putting people in his novels and pulling them about; and his pedagogic skill is also part of the same strain: Burgess enjoyed organising and managing people. It's hard to square this with the snarling recluse of his last years when, except if he came to London to launch a book, he saw absolutely nobody except Liana ('It's a pleasure to speak English again,' I once heard him mutter), for at one time he'd been gregarious, even if only in spite of himself. After the war, he'd lingered as long as he could in uniform, playing his piano. He served in Gibraltar in 1946, and then involved himself with vocational and non-vocational training for demobilised servicemen and had next taught teacher-training for the Ministry of Education until 1950, when he went as a junior (not a senior, as he'd said) master to a grammar school where 'I was one of the pioneers of phonetics, elementary linguistics. I was also teaching Spanish and some music,'* though that must have been on the side because Mr

* To keep up the Burgess image of polymathy and omniscience, Alfred Batts, the Music Master, goes deliberately unmentioned in *Little Wilson and Big God*. Burgess liked to leave the impression that he'd been the one who'd mucked in when it came to this area – and in *The Worm and the Ring*, the music master is Ennis, Burgess's fictional double from *A Vision of Battlements*, which he wrote in Adderbury. Alfred Batts was also the organist and choirmaster of the parish church, St Mary's, for which Burgess produced two wedding marches and a toccata and fugue. He was much involved with the Gilbert and Sullivan productions and the oratorios, though Burgess didn't mention this in his reviews in *The Banburian*.

Tryon taught languages and Mr Batts taught music. He was active. 'I was very happy in many ways. I'm a good teacher, I think. I enjoy teaching. I do it well . . .' The Banbury era was Burgess's sole experiment in normal respectable middle-class living. If, between them, he and Lynne sought to undermine such a 'terribly suburban, horribly clean and quiet' sort of society (they tried to make Banbury a High Bohemia), an ambition which left him 'reviled' by 'the borough philistines', his attempted insurrection and the condemnation of the citizenry existed solely in his dreams. If he claimed to have seduced a fellow schoolmistress, that was fantasy, too. The irony is that when *The Worm and the Ring* elicited a writ for libel, the complaint came not from Hilda/Moyna, the girl he pretended he'd seduced and ditched, but from Alice/Gwen, about whom he'd been completely accurate. He was happily married, here, also, walking the dog, the collie bitch Suky, arguing with Lynne about the merits of Jane Austen ('whom I have never been able to read with pleasure'), listening to Elgar symphonies on a second-hand HMV gramophone acquired from Blinkhorn's. And he was, as he believed, a good teacher. That's one thing he remembered correctly.* In this article from *The Banburian* (July 1951), unsigned but unmistakable, you can see the future author and critic

* Interviewed in May 1971 for the *National Elementary Principal*, Burgess described the term's work that he did for a IIIA form at Banbury. The children were thirteen or fourteen years old: 'I'm going back now to 1950. I taught them how to use the International Phonetic Alphabet, how to read sounds, how to interpret symbols of all languages, how to read a foreign language, how to read the various dialects of their own language, how to distinguish between the ghost of authority and the reality of speech. This was done in relation to what we called "speech training". There was also some speech work done. Then there was "composition", which normally centred on contemporary literature. They learned how to do an interior monologue in the style of James Joyce, learned how to write free verse in the style of T. S. Eliot. They learned how to act poetic drama, even write a little of it themselves. In a single year, we did, either in copies that I gave out or that I read in class, first, H. G. Wells's *The Invisible Man*, for pleasure and also for stimulating the imagination, for dealing with the vocabulary, the scientific background, the ethical implications of this kind of situation . . . The next book was what you call here *The Martian Chronicles*, by Ray Bradbury, and what we call *The Silver Locust*. After that came George Orwell's *Nineteen Eighty-Four*, which in 1950 had only recently come out; Evelyn Waugh's *Decline and Fall*; and Jerome K. Jerome's *Three Men in a Boat*. These books were dealt with in two sessions a week. In addition, I used to have excerpts from *The Times*, from *Life*, from *Time* magazine, odd things, for appreciation, comprehension, vocabulary expansion, and I used to have various general knowledge things that usually related to literature, in which the students were taught about the great world.

'This, I thought, was a very adequate English course. At the end of the year, they knew something. They were interested in literature. Books were no longer things like *Black Beauty*. Books were about the real adult world. The students were building up a modern vocabulary. They were learning how to read newspapers. They were learning to be interested in speech as a phenomenon, as a language phenomenon.'

emerging from the classroom:

TRENDS IN CONTEMPORARY FICTION

The members of Form 4A have spent some time of this last term in writing novels. Few of these are as unconsciously funny as Daisy Ashford's 'The Young Visiters' [*sic*] (written when she was 12) or as brilliant as Marjorie Bowen's 'The Viper of Milan' (written when she was 16). But they contain several memorable passages, and deserve serious study because they enable one to see the novelist's tricks in their crudest and most creaking form, and because they give by reflection a survey of contemporary fiction in much the same way as one can study the movement from cubism to surrealism by looking at posters.

The atmosphere of the thriller is established in a few sentences: 'She fetched her aspro and went to bed; as she climbed into bed there was the sound of thunder in the distance and the wind whistled dismally through the trees. It seemed rather a murderous kind of night.' Another descendant of Monk Lewis and Mrs Radcliffe starts her novel thus: 'It is dusk, the last bird's cry has ceased, the mist is slowly descending, leaving the sun a red ball gradually fading away over the hills, and the first signs of night appear. The scene settles down on Mrs Heighton's secluded country club, Bona Vista, in the Cotswolds . . .'

The horrific class derives from Sydney Horler and Bram Stoker: 'Behind them they saw a great grey shape with two blazing yellow-green eyes and bared fangs, ready to spring . . . As they examined the bite by the light of the shaded torch, they both gasped with horror, for instead of the marks of canine teeth, the tooth-marks were – HUMAN – with one tooth missing in the middle . . . As the Count swung round, the candlelight shone full on his face, his pale and drawn face, his blood-red lips, yellow-green blazing eyes, and a devilish leer exposed his long yellow teeth with (you can guess the rest).' Horror follows us to the distant planets, or to the bottom of the ocean. 'I looked at the rocket ship, a little streak of fire high in the sky; then at the remains of Smith . . .' 'The pressure in the submarine was unbearable. Blood poured from Cawse's nose, and Sir John had fainted.'

There was the usual quota of crime and war stories: 'If that kid of yours gets hold of the ring, it could jail us for 20 years!' 'He had been left on the wire as a warning to other prisoners not to try to escape.' 'The two girls, bound and gagged, were thrown on to some sacks in the back of the lorry. They lay there for about two hours, and they could still hear the sound of the burning timbers of their home.'

After so many pools of blood, on the floors of saloons, the snows of Canada and uranium deserts of Pluto, it is almost a relief to hear the gentle and civilised tones of Angela Brazil and Enid Blyton: '"Gosh, we're marooned! What shall we do?" said Elaine. – "We shall have to stop here until the tide goes out," said Betty!'

There was little humour, probably because most children's fiction inhabits an uneasy region below seriousness and above humour. 'Fascinated, he watched more and more of the shoes come through the porthole until he could see the spats clearly. Suddenly he made a grab at them and to his surprise the heels came away in his hands and the room was flooded with pound notes.'

And, as an unclassifiable last word: 'That evening Peter and Steve were standing round Rosemary's bed talking to her, when into the room walked her mother!'

It's a shame that he'd not won any post at a university. 'Jobs were denied me,' he told Martin Amis in 1980, 'because I hadn't been to Oxford. Manchester, you see. "Manchester". They didn't like that.' Whilst Burgess was at Banbury, England's other rumbustious future novelist was teaching at the University College of Wales, Swansea. I wonder if they had unknowingly met at the interview in 1949, when Kingsley Amis was appointed to his lectureship? Also on the shortlist was a Manchester man with a badly shaved face 'who talked with his mouth almost shut', as Amis reported to Larkin. It's too good to be true if that was Burgess – it would be a brief encounter for *The Devil's Mode*. Amis remained at Swansea until 1961, then got elevated to a Fellowship at Peterhouse, and then packed in teaching to write full-time. It is a similar beginning or trajectory to Burgess: pedagogy in the fifties; angry young manliness in the early works presaging curmudgeonliness in the later ones; a consolidation of their comic novelist reputation and success on the cultural scene as a newspaper pundit, wireless talker, and the rest of it. Amis was the Visiting Fellow in Creative Writing at Princeton in 1958 to 1959. Burgess held the same sinecure from 1970 to 1971. Yet they are crucially different at every point. Amis was a Londoner, Protestant (his grandparents were Baptists), First Class degree from St John's, a CBE and a Knight. Burgess was the Mancunian with a IIi who was never even offered the BEM, which they give to lollipop ladies. Burgess was the sergeant major, who only handled a rifle after the shooting match was over (achieving 'a marksman's score' naturally); Amis was a lieutenant in the Royal Signals, seeing real bullets fly and bombs drop in Normandy – where he couldn't decide whether to use his tin helmet to protect his head or to protect his balls. Burgess travelled abroad as if always on the run; Amis locked himself in the Garrick, a badger not keen to stir from his sett. They were both torn between two women, Amis with Hilly and Elizabeth Jane Howard, Burgess with Lynne and Liana, who called him by the foreign version of his pseudonymous Christian name, *Antonio!* The two novelists became Old Devils with cartoonish Rowlandson heads and bodies, dependable, round the clock, for provocative, calumniatory and reactionary opinions. ('The great Jewish vice is glibness, fluency – also possibly just bullshit, as in Marx, Freud, Marcuse. Pity L. Ron Hubbard['s] not,' said Amis. 'There's no doubt that there is a homosexual mafia. Indeed, we had a homosexual Prime Minister, Edward Heath. He's been very clever about it. He's never been found accosting little boys. It may have been hushed up,' confided Burgess.) Both made jokes about Margaret Drabble and Victoria Glendinning.* Neither managed to drive motor vehicles.

Their styles and tones were poles apart, Burgess with his unduly self-conscious use of words, Amis being more interested in the psychological shifts and shadings that words express or evade. Burgess sent his characters all over the place to create his effects ('take *zarf* . . . a word of Arabic origin for the metal enclosure of a glass from which to drink tea . . . you could develop a whole chapter out of *zarf*'); Amis had two Welsh women in the kitchen sharing a litre bottle of supermarket Yugoslavian Soave and an entire culture comes to life ('the two caught each other's eye and as if by pre-arrangement made remarkably similar frowning, blinking, whistling faces. On instinct they drew closer together in their chairs'). But I don't want to get into all this now. The point at issue is that had he become a don, Burgess may have learned the techniques of, or developed a mind that could be bent on, argument, interchange and the need to listen. Instead of which, as very much the dominie (Scottish for school-

* 'This is the book Margaret Drabble would have written – if she'd had it in her,' said Amis, in the press release for his (I think) *Memoirs* (1991). I remember feeling annoyed that he was made to retract this or spell out that it was a joke. As he said to Larkin in 1980, 'Drabble has no sense of humour so she doesn't notice her own outrageous arrogances.' In an interview with Jonathan Coe (in the *Guardian*, 24 February 1989), Burgess was moaning about the supercilious reviews he received from British women critics. His face contorted and 'as if removing a delicate obstruction from between his teeth he mouths the words "Victoria Glendinning".' This landed him in hot water with her (apparently) and he had to send her a card to apologise.

master – vocative of Latin *dominus*, Lord, and a word he was fond of: he called the *OED* man James Murray 'a god-fearing teetotal non-smoking philoprogenitive bizarrely polymath dominie'), he went in for rhetoric and righteousness. As a former pupil of his, Doreen Neville, recalled, 'he was notable for his bulging eyes and the way he entered the classroom with his gown flowing behind him, stopping only to throw a wooden-backed blackboard duster at any pupil whom he considered was paying insufficient attention'. Schoolmastering, to use the phrase of Garnet Bowen's, in Amis's *I Like It Here*, is putting-in, whereas a higher education concerns drawing-out – and Burgess was too absorbed by himself to have coped well with debate on equal terms with bright adults. His performances on radio discussion programmes, for example, were very off-putting. He was fluent and his tone was authoritative, but there was no analysis, no breaking down of propositions to assess them, weigh them, clarify them. All he could do (though very successfully – very profitably) was hold forth. He came across as enormously condescending and not exactly as someone who wore his learning lightly. These were dislikeable characteristics. Though, of course, he went to a university himself, he was like a cranky autodidact. His egotism, as revealed in his intellectual arrogance and snobbery, concealed a large area of personal weakness. And when he became famous, after 1968, if you disagreed with him – it was a conspiracy, the secret police were behind it.

Moyna had left Banbury for Farnborough to be with Alec at the end of the Autumn Term 1953. Lynne was at a loose end in the Bell, the Coach and Horses, the Red Lion, the White Hart, and the Dog and Partridge. Burgess wanted promotion. The two of them were dissatisfied, restless, and yearning for a new climate, in several senses. In the new year, 1954, Burgess was invited to the Colonial Office and offered the job of teaching English at the Malay College, at Kuala Kangsar in the state of Perak. In *The Banburian*, September 1954, readers were told, after the 'sad farewell' to Miss Clegg, who had taught mathematics for eight years and who 'was very interested in life-saving and square-dancing', and before the valediction to Mr Halsey, who had organised dancing classes and was now off 'to take up a position in a boys' school':

> Mr Wilson, that truly remarkable man, will by now be in Malaya, where he has taken a post in a college for the sons of Malayan aristocrats. We hope he will find the climate a little more to his liking. Certainly we shall never forget his original and unconventional contri-

bution to the life of this school.

His letters home over the next few years circled back to a pair of common themes – first, how happy he'd been in Oxfordshire, and would there still be a job for him at the Grammar School when his contract in the East ended? 'I have nostalgic pangs for Banbury'; 'Any chance of a job at BGS? I think I'd be happy to come back'; 'Is there any likelihood of a vacancy in the English Dept. of BGS? I'm serious about this. I look back on that time as a happy one.' The second recurring motif is to ask after Moyna. 'I didn't even know that Moyna's been in Washington so long. Is Alec an air attaché or something?'* 'As far as Moyna's concerned, I believe I owe her a letter but lost her address. Do tell her, when she's back, that I'd love to hear from her'; 'I'd very much like to hear news from Moyna.'

Burgess and Lynne visited Banbury again but once, in October 1957. He was unsuccessful in persuading Mr Rose to give him his old job back. This was the occasion when they dined with the Atkinsons at the White Lion and carried on like Dylan and Caitlin Thomas. 'People were drawing their chairs up to listen,' recalls Elizabeth Atkinson, still appalled decades later. 'Both John and Lynne kept talking about their mistresses and lovers, bragging about their orgiastic existence. What nonsense! Lynne turned to Thomas and asked – trying to needle him, "What about your mistress then?" John jumped in quick to say, "Anyone married to Elizabeth won't need a mistress!"' Which, to be fair, does sound as if he was trying to salvage the evening with a bit of harmless flattery. Lynne didn't see it that way. She glared and glowered, taking her husband's remark as a deeply personal insult – and from where she stood, as a loose-living dipsomaniac who'd lost her looks and her way, it *was* a put-down. The Atkinsons are elderly now, yet still retain elegance and poise. Lynne was dead at forty-seven, worn out by all the effort that went into ensuring that she was never not the centre of attention. Perhaps because he was crapulous after that humiliating spectacle at the dinner party, Burgess projected his humours on to the town itself. He didn't like the café on the High Street serving espresso and cappuccino; he believed that the links with 'a more gracious past are steadily and stealthily being severed'; and he grew furious about the 'horrible new hardness creeping up all over the place' – which is the dark mood of *A Clockwork Orange*. Banbury used to be a place where 'there are still cakes and ale and ginger is still com-

* Alec Morris was on exchange duty at HQ USAF, 1958–60.

Lynne Jones and John Wilson on their wedding day, Bournemouth, 22 January 1942

'It has been a sin to be prolific only since the Bloomsbury Group made it a point of good manners to produce, as it were, costively.'
Burgess in Etchingham, 1968

'Anyway, I'm actually a composer.'
Burgess in Chiswick, 1968

'That stick makes you look venerable. You look *venerable*, Anthony.'
Graham Greene

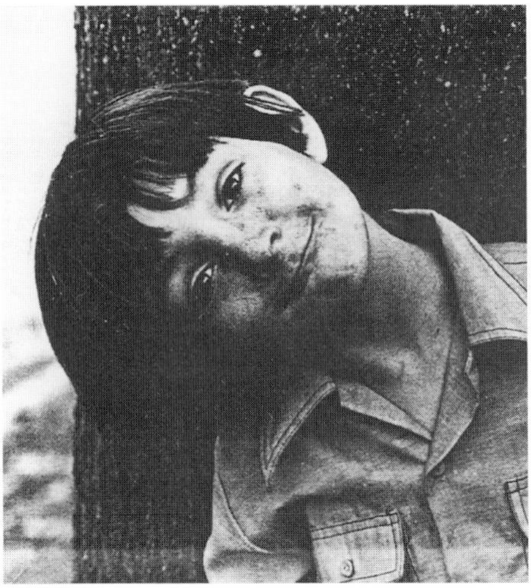

Paolo-Andrea (*aet.* seven), born to Liliana Macellari and Roy Lionel Halliday on 9 August 1964.

Liliana – known as Liana – the daughter of Contessa Maria Lucrezia Pasi della Pergola, arriving at Burgess's Memorial Service, 16 June 1994

Homage to Qwert Yuiop – 'I get angry at the stupidity of critics who wilfully refuse to se what my books are really about. I'm aware of malevolence, especially in England.'

Caesar Burgess – a bust sculpted in Bracciano by Milton Hebald

The Art of Caricature . . .
. . . David Levine (*New York Review of Books*)

. . . William Rushton (*Independent* magazine)

. . . Martin Rowson (*Sunday Telegraph* magazine)

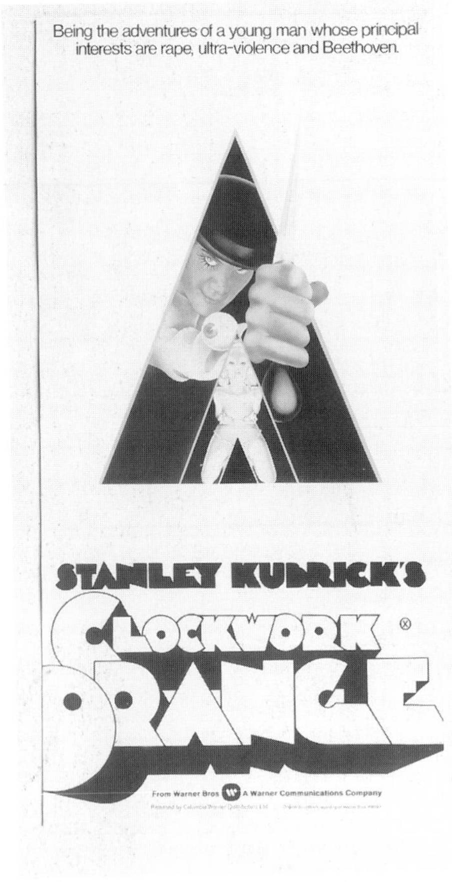

The iconic artwork by Philip Castle for the poster of Stanley Kubrick's *A Clockwork Orange*.

Dust jacket for the first edition of *A Clockwork Orange* (Heinemann, 1962) – '[It] is the book I like least. The over-exposure meant that people could talk about it without having read it.'

Malcolm McDowell as Alex in Kubrick's film of *A Clockwork Orange* – 'Stanley Kubrick produced, directed and wrote the screen version. Have you ever considered that you might also be a creation of Kubrick?' – To which Burgess replied – 'That I'm a creation of Kubrick? Far from it! Kubrick is a creation of mine . . .' (*Transatlantic Review*, May 1976)

The Grand Old Man of Letters – John Wilson, otherwise known as Anthony Burgess, 25 February 1917 – 22 November 1993

paratively hot in the mouth', he said, making a direct reference to the Elizabethan idyll of *Twelfth Night*. It's ironic that a little dozing market town in the English Midlands should have inspired his bleak futuristic vision. The back-projection scenes of roads and villages, when Alex and his droogs steal the car and drive full pelt through the night, were shot by Kubrick in the hinterlands of Oxfordshire and Buckinghamshire.

Moyna, likewise, Burgess only saw the once. 'I had lunch with him in London, in about 1965. I hadn't seen him for twelve years. It wasn't a success. He was not entirely relaxed. Lynne was ill in Sussex – in a psychiatric hospital.' Lady Morris had children by now, twins. The last time she'd seen him, at Christmas 1953, he'd had mumps. Mumps, a swelling of the parotid glands and, in adult males, of the testes, an inflammation called orchitis, can lead to infertility. Mumps, twins, and the problems of paternity form a plot twist in *Earthly Powers*. Domenico, the composer, is married to Hortense, Toomey's sister (for whom Toomey has incestuous thoughts), and as it has been disclosed that Domenico's sperm count is at zero, this means that their twins' biological father is goodness knows whom – and also that Hortense, otherwise believed by everyone to be a saint, has been unfaithful. How many more lessons on the relations of life and Burgess's artistry do you want? Talking to me about it, he was disingenuous. He was now an old man and yet Moyna, to his mind, was still an impressionable girl in her twenties – and he looked back at her with an old man's causticity. 'She's tried to write to me before' – he must have meant the postcard from Greece. 'Not a very clever woman. A diversion at the time. Ancient history now.' This was less than kind. His straightforward forbearance when he told me this was nowhere near being a jest. It was odd how the two of them, young Wilson and momentous Burgess, with his face a stiff and waxy mask, could differ so much and still be the same person.

Before she died of cancer last year, Lady Morris told me that she felt sad she'd never seen him again. 'I should have seen him, especially when he'd fallen ill and was dying in London. We were in the South of France a few times. It would have been easy to get to Monte Carlo, but I was put off by the idea of that frightful woman, Liana. A sad, sad story, old friends, who fail to meet. He loved me – it was a wonderful experience in my life. Yet he did nothing more than put his arms round me – one brief kiss. When I last saw him I said I was having trouble finishing Huxley's *Point Counter Point*, and he said the last page was worth getting to.'* And of the rest of them? Maurice Draper, the Head of

Science, who made the tonic for which nobody could afford the gin, and who painted the scenery for the plays, is ninety-six and still exhibiting his watercolours. His Asian wife who made exotic curries died of Alzheimer's. His daughter, Ann, died of multiple sclerosis. Derrick Rolls ('too handsome to require a degree'), the all-round athlete at whose wedding Burgess played an organ march, moved to Jersey. He slipped and fell on an ice rink and broke his neck. He was six months in intensive care and is now a housebound paraplegic. Mr A. D. Rose (not Dr, as Burgess elevated him) wrote to me on Snoopy notepaper. He retired with his brood of cellists, pianists and violin players to Chichester, and he is now dead. Kenneth Carrdus, flung out by his wealthy wife who'd discovered that he was having an affair with a girl younger than his daughter, was living in Sussex. He bought an expensive sports car, drove to a patch of woodland, doused himself in petrol and lit a match – an agonising suicide by self-immolation. He'd recently discovered he was suffering from cancer. In *The Worm and the Ring* he is 'Turton the exquisite, with his chromatic scale of giggles and his hands, three-ringed, always ready to dismiss the stink of authors he disliked' – and if that makes him sound like Oscar Wilde, he had indeed been a peerless Bunthorne in *Patience*.

How long ago it all was. Pupils in their caps and hats, boating on the river at Windsor, the Mayor and the Aldermen coming to present the borough's coronation gifts (a pencil to the boys, a handkerchief to the girls), Burgess playing cricket (Staff vs. Pupils) in ginger tweeds and bowling underarm, or reading aloud from *Nineteen Eighty-Four*, *Ulysses* and Waugh's *Decline and Fall* and stubbing out his cigarette prior to giving a lesson in one of the portable classrooms, where he'd tell the children about the Russian language, play the piano (improvising a habanera to sing the Tables of Weights and Measures – like Tom Lehrer and the Periodic Table) and reminisce about George Orwell and Dylan Thomas. He took the 'O' Level year to see the film of *The Importance of Being Earnest*, which starred Michael Redgrave and Edith Evans. (Michael Redgrave's querulousness and sense of defiance are very Burgessy qualities.) Afterwards he dictated a model essay for the class to learn by heart and regurgitate in the examination. Wilde's world of hidden lives, topsy-turvy marriages and confused parentage was right up his street.

There is very little music in the name Jack, if any at all, indeed [says

* 'If Don Juans and Don Juanesses only obeyed their desires,' wrote Huxley, 'they'd have very few affairs. They have to tickle themselves up imaginatively before they can start being casually promiscuous.' Burgess, too late, was sending a message through literature.

Gwendolen]. It does not thrill. It produces absolutely no vibrations. I have known several Jacks, and they all, without exception, were more than usually plain. Besides, Jack is a notorious domesticity for John! And I pity any woman who is married to a man called John. She would probably never be allowed the entrancing pleasure of a single moment's solitude.

Following the little tip on household accounting from Moyna, he showed the children his chequebook, with many of the stubs completed in red ink. 'That's when you spend more money than you've got. It's called *overdrawn.*' It was one of his pretences to be clueless about money – that he was the artist figure, or Wildean dandy, way above such mundane matters. An interviewer once suggested that he must earn thousands a week from journalism alone. 'Really? I don't know. We're probably solvent, and I think we must have saved a little money. But I always feel as though I'm going to be poor again. Money goes straight from my agent to Liana and she deals with it and allocates it.' To Martin Amis, ten years before saying this, he'd confided, 'Oh, I've been technically a millionaire for some time now. It doesn't make much difference to anything, after a point . . . I take it you're paying for this lunch?' And in 1983, the script for the ten-hour mini-series *A.D.* completed between 30 January and 1 March, he sat back and announced, 'I am a very rich man, very rich indeed. I'm sorry to say it, but I am.' Asked later about the Booker Prize, he sneered, 'Ten thousand quid, to a millionaire, is not very much.' Kingsley Amis won it in 1986 for *The Old Devils.*

On his last afternoon at the school – the last afternoon of his life when he'd dare risk framing the question, 'Who could not but be happy in such an environment?' – Burgess told his class about how he'd grown up in Manchester, what he'd remembered of looking out from the window, upstairs at the pub. Already he was mythologising Lodge Street and Harpurhey as if it was Joyce's Dublin. He was on his way to a new world of heat and wet, foliage and blooms, diseases and fungi, and John Wilson, a good man determined to be outrageous, was well receding, to be replaced by Anthony Burgess, who was growling for release. Though he was still at that period in his life when (as the protagonist of Greene's *The Comedians* puts it) he 'regarded his future seriously', it was also true that he was already at the stage where we are beginning to put up with falling short. Looking back, and at the changes in oneself, it's a kind of loss.

IV

Jungle Books 1955–59

There is something wrong about Burgess. We all know he was a novelist of some thirty titles; he was a critic with books on James Joyce, Hemingway, Lawrence and Shakespeare (on whom there was also a musical, variously entitled *Will!* or *The Bawdy Bard*); he adapted Rostand's *Cyrano de Bergerac* for Broadway and the Barbican; he rewrote the Old and New Testaments and provided the screenplays for Burt Lancaster's *Moses the Lawgiver*, Franco Zeffirelli's *Jesus of Nazareth* and Ava Gardner's *A.D.*; he invented a stone-age dialect for a film called *Quest for Fire*; he composed symphonies and an operetta (*Blooms of Dublin*, based on *Ulysses*); he translated Bizet's *Carmen* for English National Opera and refurbished the libretto of Weber's *Oberon* for Scottish Opera; he edited *The Coaching Days of England* and *The Age of the Grand Tour*; he digested *Finnegans Wake* into *A Shorter Finnegans Wake*; and he is a man whose talents, acquirements and virtues are so extraordinary, that the more his character is considered, the more he will be regarded by the present age, and by posterity, with admiration and reverence. He was a Doctor Johnson of our *fin de siècle* (and that opening sentence derives from Boswell's closing one); or so he'd have had you believe. But he was berserk. He was obsessive. He tried to grab it all – the musical compositions for concert hall and movies, material which was frequently rejected; the librettos, which were banal in the extreme; painting (actually – that one got away: 'I'm not going back to painting. I was tempted to in Callian but there isn't time'); the unmade films on Edward Lear or Beethoven;* the thousands upon thousands of

* In the eighties, a biopic of Beethoven's last years, *Uncle Ludwig*, was to have been produced by Michael Birkett and Anthony Wilkinson, with a script by Burgess, two drafts of which were completed. Rod Steiger, whose Napoleon in *Waterloo* I alone admire, was to have been Beethoven-as-a-mad-genius. (The perspiring, the Lee Strasberg histrionics, the

literary critical pieces and bouts of cultural commentary, which remain uncollected. It was as if his ambition was to consume the world, to conquer and control it, like Napoleon. Yet his Nappy, in *Napoleon Symphony*, is a glowering goblin, bound by his saucy doubts and fears, rather than a representation of soaring eagle-like freedoms. Bonaparte was always interpreted as the living principle of a romantic dream – to Carlyle, the jumped-up Corsican lieutenant of artillery was 'a piece of silent strength' in the midst of anarchy; to Hazlitt, he was a god of gusto, an irrepressible force of nature and of destiny; to Scott, who also wrote a multi-volume biography, Nappy was a plutocratic landowner or Tory Laird on the grand scale; and to Beethoven, in the 'Eroica' Symphony, for which Burgess (pottily) tried to find verbal analogues, e.g.:

Dumdy DUM
Dee dum dee dumdy
DUM
DUM
DUM diddum diddum
DUM
DUM

– for Beethoven, Napoleon was the composer's idealised self-image as a colonising, charismatic tyrant. Which is how, of course, Brando portrays him in *Desirée*. What all these versions have in common is that Bonaparte's power is an artist's power. Abel Gance's epic film, the six-hour gallimaufry made in 1927, with its tinted and toned celluloid and triptych scenes, again uses Napoleon, this time to show what the cinema is capable of, fadings and dissolvings and apocalyptic visions – you can show the actual twilight of the gods. Kubrick, it goes without saying, had a long-cherished Napoleon project. It's not hard to picture the mechanised marching armies and the megalomania. *Napoleon Symphony* is dedicated 'to Stanley J. Kubrick', our author supplicating for a shot at the script, no doubt. ('The Napoleon project, which began with Kubrick, has now got

embarrassing mannerisms: Steiger's acting is the equivalent of Burgess's prose; it is an artistry that involves being tortured, stupefyingly indulgent, and prone to tantrums.) Steiger read out the script to Wilkinson, who recorded the session on a Philips dictaphone, 'Mr Anthony Burgess, Mr Anthony Wilkinson, I respect you both as artists,' said the actor, who then threw a marble table across the room to demonstrate something-or-other. ('An utterly untamed personality,' said Goethe of Ludwig Van in 1812.) The release of Paul Morrissey's *Beethoven's Nephew* (1985), with Wolfgang Reichmann, Dietmar Prinz and Jane Birkin (and of *Immortal Beloved* [1994] with Gary Oldman) scuppered the project.

beyond Kubrick,' he said in 1972. 'It's a pity about the money and so on, but otherwise I'm glad to feel free' – make of that what you will.)

Napoleon is the spirit of imperialism – of possession and control – and that's Burgess's procedure as a writer, taking over Exodus, Leviticus, Numbers and Deuteronomy, for *Moses the Lawgiver*, or making Leopold Bloom into Enderby and Stephen Dedalus into Mr WS, his Shakespeare, or raiding the anthropological studies of Lévi-Strauss for *MF*, or skirmishing with Orwell for *1985* and Fleming for *Tremor of Intent*, or generally letting John and Lynne Wilson make the mistakes that Burgess could then profit from. Imperialism, or colonialism, is thus straightforward thievery and exploitation, or at least it is when Burgess goes about his business. Lynne was mugged, and this becomes the mob violence of *A Clockwork Orange* and the off-stage attack on the girl in *The Right to an Answer*. An expedition to Russia became *Honey for the Bears*. A spell in a neurological ward became *The Doctor Is Sick*, which itself poaches from Elias Canetti's *Auto da Fé*, where an isolated intellectual, a philologist, like Edwin Spindrift, is threatened and menaced by his environment, as Edwin is by the London underworld fraternity. The notion that syphilis can spark genius, the conceit of *Nothing Like the Sun*, it now occurs to me, is an annexation of Mann's *Doktor Faustus*. 'Very much myself, very much a self-portrait,' said Burgess of the generic anti-hero in his early novels, the disaffected travellers and teachers and writers with women in the background, who are overloaded with words. Yet nothing is enlarged or improved. Even the totemic power of Napoleon, in Burgess's version, becomes fractiousness, bestial aggression, and the Emperor is left to fret about cuckoldry ('The cuckold is always the last to know, isn't he?') and impotence ('my seed will not work in you nor, as I now suspect, in any woman') – with the result that he'll live on only in books, a paper man (like Burgess's characters – like Burgess himself):

> I must seek the way of achievements and monuments and paragraphs in history tomes to secure the continuation of my nature.

The tone of Burgess's work is feverish and cramped and confining. Enderby writes or blasts his poems from the smallest room; *Earthly Powers* presents the world in miniature; and Napoleon is a wormy thing afflicted with dyspepsia. It is a world of crack-ups, annihilations, and of people and their possessions flying apart. His characters exist at a squirming insect level – bed-bugs, crabs, fleas, parasites, leeches. Hence, the titles *The Enemy in the Blanket* or *The Beds in the East*, which star

Victor Crabbe, or the fascination with disease and bacteria and sex as an ungovernable itch. Everything is going wrong and getting worse. It is frenzied material – migrainous, palpitant – and it emanates from a man who seems, by his own admission, mentally ill. If the laws of gravity cross his mind, he has to sit down; standing upright seems so implausible. He panics if he is above the fire-escape level in a hotel. He has nightmares about being shut in a cardboard box. He cannot enter an English cathedral 'without unease and even resentment'. If he meets a deadbeat in a bar at the corner of Broadway and 91st Street, he decides, from the mumbles, that the fellow is 'a specialist in the Northumbrian text of *The Dream of the Rood*'. He seriously believes that Mann's *The Transposed Heads*, the career of Houdini, Virginia Woolf's *Orlando* and Ford's *The Good Soldier* are good subjects for musicals. He is convinced he is being stalked by a seven-foot tall Cherokee who brandishes a tomahawk. When he is corrected for misquoting Eliot (using *voyagers* when the word was *explorers*), he says, with impossible archness, that once, at the Russell Hotel, he overheard Eliot himself misquote the line to a waitress: 'You've been abroad again, Mr Eliot?' 'Ah yes, Mabel. You know what they say? Old men should be voyagers!' And when Richard Cohen, his editor at Hutchinson, tried to suggest that the dead mother-in-law in the boot of the car story, which pads out *The Pianoplayers*, was rather a hoary old chestnut, Burgess said, without a flicker of self-mockery, that it was he, in fact, who had invented the tale back in the thirties, and he was quite aware that it was now well known. It is one thing to be a schoolteacher who'll not be put right or an author who'll not be revised – but these are crazy justifications and of a piece with the Burgess that Kingsley Amis told me about: 'He used to sport a sword-stick, flourishing the fucking thing in the Tube – "If any fucker tries it on with me," he'd say, "he'll fucking get it!" And he meant it, too.' Burgess was more than usually beset by arbitrary and uncontrollable forces. Wherever he went, there were ructions. Marriage bust-ups, suicide attempts, bankruptcies, nervous breakdowns – whilst he, boisterous and indignant, swanned off to the next adventure and locale. His houses would be haunted, ornaments would fall off his mantelpiece, his hotel rooms would mysteriously get trashed, bombs would resound, his cars would get shot at and ex-servicemen would try and beat him up when he went to the Gents – or so he always said.

He also said (or had Toomey say) that 'writers of fiction often have difficulty in deciding between what really happened and what they imagine as having happened'; and though nobody can be meant to believe that it really always rained from a cloudless sky each time Burgess stepped outside on a sunny day, or that he was impelled to start a fist fight with every Italian frontier guard he encountered, the fabrications can supplement his paranormal aura. After he'd been in residence a little while, the cottage in Adderbury started playing up. The rooms were suffused with the aroma of violets. Medieval coins appeared in empty drawers. A telescopic toasting fork clattered out of an empty cupboard. Ghosts and ectoplasm greeted him on empty staircases – and on one occasion he felt himself being throttled. The black magic followed him to Malaya. In Kuala Kangsar, banshees shriek from the trees, kitchen mats rear up and smash the crockery, and the dried blood in the lavatory refuses to be washed away – Burgess decides that the place is haunted by the victims of the Japanese, who'd used his quarters as a torture chamber. Despite the tropical heat, there is always a chill temperature, and outside in the jungle he hears screams. At Kota Bharu, in the sultanate of Kelantan, Lynne is allegedly hypnotised by a Mr Pathan, who casts no shadow and whose servants are zombies. The garden – appropriate for a midnight garden of good and evil – is full of snakes.

Whilst it is fair to say that what went on in John Wilson's life was glamorised, exaggerated, reinvented, generally jazzed up and simplified into the cartoonery of Burgess's books, where an existence or history was never going to be more (or less) than a series of humiliations and disasters, whether the protagonist was called the Man of Nazareth or Cyrano de Bergerac, Enderby or Toomey, the web of deception and lies, the impression Burgess liked to give of writing and living against the odds, suggests a much more interesting mind than that of the minor novelist who dealt with the creation of effects. (He had an Old Testament grandiosity: 'And I contended with them and cursed them and smote certain of them and plucked off their hair, and made them swear by God.' Nehemiah xiii, 25.) Burgess was activated by concealment and corruption, rage and bombast, and Malaya suited his disturbed equilibrium. The sheer culture shock after rainy, grey, ration-ridden post-war Oxfordshire, with its orange street lamps and gloomy dusk, the lone cyclists and worn-out women stooping over pushchairs, cannot be overestimated. I myself spent a summer in the East following in his footsteps, and the smells of sandalwood and open drains, the massive ferns and leaves and carnivorous plants, the swampy jungle and man-eating mosquitoes, the rivers boiling with crocodiles, the violent tropical downpours and the remorseless sun, which sizzles at the dampness, making for phantasmal whorls and whirls of fogs and mist – all this, during the afternoons, he got into his first published books, *Time for a Tiger* ('His characters are splendidly mad,' *Observer*), *The Enemy in the Blanket* ('Mr Burgess really knows this racial melting pot,' *Daily Telegraph*) and *Beds in the East* ('a fascinating chronicle', *Sunday Times*), known now as *A Malayan Trilogy* or *Malesi!* or *The Long Day Wanes*, which is a Tennysonian reference to the fizzling out of the British Empire and the preparation of Malaya for independence. It was a landscape wholly suited to his brightly coloured surface techniques.

How did he get to be there? Burgess would have had you believe that he went on from Banbury to join the Colonial Service, as an educational officer, because he'd posted off the application form as a drunken joke. To me, he laddishly or blokeishly hinted and pretended that he'd been seducing Moyna Morris, and her husband, on the brink of finding out and about to launch an air strike, had suggested he get out of town – just as he'd felt he had to get out of Blackwood when Lynne's old boyfriend reappeared. His script derives from Byron, about whom he wrote in 1988: 'rumours of sexual irregularities, and the growing horror at the tales of his incestuous acts, ended in his ostracism. Annabella [Milbanke], who apparently could not stomach the modes of sexual congress he urged on her, went back to her mother [as Moyna did to Chipping Warden]. Byron cursed England and left it forever.' You can tell that Burgess approves of the sixth baron's pride and heroic stance, his blasphemy and obscenity, high spirits and genuine wit. 'Byron was his own heroes,' too, as Burgess's are his; and the image of the revolutionary artist, mad, bad and dangerous to know, who could leap upon and ravish every woman he met from hotel chamber maids to fancy aristocrats, is one Burgess would like to project for himself. The first thing he did, on arriving in Singapore in 1954, he tells us, was to pick up a Chinese prostitute on Burgis Street. Such a revelation is as likely as going to the West Country to drink cider or to the Wild West to have arrows shot at you by Red Indians. In Düsseldorf, Burgess said he had a friend called Klaus.* Bachelors are unmarried men. All swans are white. These are meaningless statements. Burgis Street used to be nothing but knocking shops. Like his fellow Catholic author and traveller in outlandish parts, Graham Greene, Burgess liked to allege that he was an enthusiastic patron of courtesans. To listen to him, he was soon having it away with waitresses and dance-hall barmaids. 'They were

* Honestly, he did. On his sixty-seventh birthday, in 1984, 'Klaus, my friend from Düsseldorf,' gave him as a present a cassette of Fischer-Dieskau singing Schubert's *Winterreise*.

seductive as few white women are,' he claimed expertly. That he boasted about bedding a twelve-year-old Tamil girl is not something I care to think about – except that it is consistent with his incest fantasies and *Finnegans Wake* exegesis. It is in the East, incidentally, that the last of his memorabilia disappeared. 'I had a photograph of the two of them,' he said of his mother and sister, 'long since eaten up by Malayan humidity and termites, and it showed a firm-featured smiling woman of considerable blonde beauty and a promise of similar beauty in the daughter.' In 1990, returning to this point, he was elegiac. 'No, I have no record of her or of my past at all,' he said, when asked about his mother. 'Such pictures as I once had were destroyed in Malaya and the streets in Manchester where I grew up have quite vanished now. Nothing's left. Only memory.'* That is to say, what was inside his head – and nobody was going to get at *that*.

If this was a film, the next bit, accompanied by the full fruitiness of an Erich Wolfgang Korngold orchestra, would be a close-up of an atlas with one of those red lines moving across the oceans and continents to indicate a journey. 'We dined on half-cooked sausages, and cool chips,' he said of the last night before taking ship. 'We had expected to leave England in a little glow of muted monied glory, but it was not to be.' Burgess and Lynne have booked First Class seats on the train, but owing to a mix-up they are compelled to stand in the corridor. Landladies, hoteliers, ships' stewards and barmen are all obviously belonging to a secret society, the objective of which is to short-change and incense the Burgesses at each and every opportunity. Eventually, having found a vessel which will accept their mean-tempered cat, Lalage, which does little except spit sparks and sink its claws into people (it is Lynne's witch's familiar), they set sail aboard the *Willem Ruys* at Southampton, outward bound for Singapore via Port Said, Colombo and Sumatra. The crew is 'ignorant and brutal' and there are fights with pots of boiling water. Lynne gets paralytic on gin and can't leave her bunk when they dock, eighteen days later. She staggers to Raffles

* Not quite true, as he knew. A clear-out at the house in Malta disclosed a mouldering photograph album, filled with family pictures, including many a snap of the stripling Burgess and the young Lynne (on the beach at Porthcawl), all carefully labelled and inscribed. At the very least Burgess will have known that this material had returned with him from the Far East and had survived no end of moves, address changes and disruptions, particularly after Lynne's death. Perhaps this was part of the problem – Lynne out, Liana in, and a politic obliteration of the past's iconography was in order. In 1986, he told me that the novel he was writing 'is bogging down badly' – this would have been *Any Old Iron*, which was filled with allusions to Lynne and her Welsh world. If he sensed the presence of Liana looking over his shoulder (metaphorically, if not literally), he felt constricted. The manuscript of his memoirs he prudently kept in a safe.

Hotel and, the next morning, they take the Malayan Railways Express to Ipoh and then the branch line to Kuala Kangsar, the royal town of the state of Perak. Lynne was already leafing through *Country Life*, studying house prices and counting off the days until she could return home. It had been a dislocating – unhinging – experience for her, auctioning off their furniture and possessions, as Burgess admitted in 1981: 'It affected my first wife more than it affected me, selling everything, the library, every damn thing, and starting again. And knowing we were going to a country where there was a war on, which was stupid, because we'd had one war for six years . . . But we went straight into a war, straight to the part of Malaya where the war was strongest, and when, if you went to the nearest town, you thought of the danger of being ambushed. It was back into a bloody war . . . Communists infiltrated into the suburbs where I taught. But it did me good, because it enabled me to write.' John Wilson, the man-who-knew-too-much, was metamorphosing into Anthony Burgess, the celebrated polymath. As Lynne swigged down a bottle of gin a day, he slunk off to his typewriter and, in his books, he was detaching himself from all the boring and tragic contingencies of his life. In Malaya, Burgess found himself as a novelist by shutting himself off as a person. His hero Victor Crabbe is, like his creator, a teacher in Malaya and Brunei with a noisy wife. He is placed in the midst of the racial rivalries that were simmering and seething prior to the retreat of British power and protection. Crabbe toils inside the administrative machine because 'duty was duty. Where the British were sent, there they had to go. That was how they built their Empire, an Empire now crashing about their ears.' As the long day of imperialism wanes, dissension is located between the British and the natives, the British amongst themselves, the natives amongst themselves: 'there are no decisive engagements, no real victories. It goes on and on, the sniping, the gutting, the garrotting.' It is a war novel.

Crabbe and his wife, Fenella, are also at odds. To him she is a 'calendar beauty'; to her he is an adulterer – and so Fenella, with much ado, returns to England. Crabbe retires abed, a hollow man: 'there's nothing to get up for'. His salvation is myth. He is a mock-epic hero and Burgess gives him the vestments of Classical allusion. Subsidiary characters aid the process. Che Normah 'was Cassandra, Medea, harpies and furies'. Fenella calls Nabby Adams 'a Minotaur howling piteously in a labyrinth of money worries'. At the beginning of *Time for a Tiger*, 'Victor Crabbe slept soundly, drawn into that dark world where history melts into myth.' By *Beds in the East*, Crabbe is too querulous to sleep soundly and myth unmasks self-pity: 'His state appealed to him – an Education Officer waiting to hand over to the brown man he was training . . . he saw all this as romantic. The last legionary, his aloneness, the lost cause really lost.' Crabbe is regarded as the adrift Ulysses of Tennyson, wallowing in dispossession:

> The lights begin to twinkle from the rocks:
> The long day wanes: the slow moon climbs . . .

We had Virgil for the Gibraltar novel, Wagner's Valhalla for a grammar school; and in Malaya, Burgess is working on a large scale, as always. (Ancient history, the twentieth-century present, a science-fiction future: against it all he raised so great a siege.) The Tennyson references, however, are too droopy, stately and altogether ponderous to evoke the real Malaya, its freshness and freakishness; and whilst we are about it, the Byronic way Burgess kicked the dust of England from his shoes was self-aggrandising to the point of parody. And how much of the way he got there in the first place rings true? He told the story a million times – here it is in 1981: 'I applied for a job on the island of Sark, which is one of the Channel Islands, and this is very ironical, comically so. We had a collie bitch at the time who was a bit restricted in the village where we lived, so we thought it would be nice for her to go and live on an island. Of course, we didn't realise at the time that this was the one island in the world where you couldn't import a bitch. The only person who was allowed to have a bitch on that island is the Dame of Sark. At the same time I must have got drunk on Saturday evening and applied for a job in a Malayan school and forgot about it and posted the letter drunk Then I was summoned for this job in Sark. They sort of looked at me open-mouthed. Since when have the Channel Islands been under the Colonial Office? But then quite accidentally I was given the job in Malaya as an Education Officer . . .' Well, I have no intention of researching the quarantine laws and the movements of livestock regulations for a dependency of Guernsey *c.* 1954; nor am I going to question at this juncture Burgess's alcoholic amnesia ('My God, I had to write *A Clockwork Orange* in a state of near drunkenness, in order to deal with material that upset me so much,' he claimed in 1970; regarding *Finnegans Wake*, 'we must plunge into this dream of history with great tea-or-whiskey-or-Guinness-fortified courage', he advised in 1965; and *Nothing Like the Sun* is presented in the form of a farewell lecture given to Malayan students by a character called Mr Burgess who gets 'progressively drunker and drunker on Chinese rice spirit', according to a Foreword signed 'A. B. Monaco, 1982') – save to suggest it was one of his distancing techniques. There were plenty of Old Banburians (including Burgess's own pupils) who found work in the odd corners of the Empire, e.g. Jack Johnson, who did a tour of duty in Accra, the capital of the Gold Coast, and who then served at the Colonial Office in London; Edna Todd emigrated to Tasmania; Ian Forrest was wounded in a skirmish in Ismailia; Ben Moore was offered the appointment of Education Officer in Nigeria; Malcolm Dalziel was to write to Burgess from Hong Kong, his Christmas card bearing the note 'This should be drunk in Tiger!', a reference to the first of the Malayan books; and when E. E. Oakes got the job of Assistant City Engineer, based at City Hall, Singapore, he, like Burgess and Lynne, left aboard the *Willem Ruys*: 'One snag with this place – they don't speak a civilised language, and I am in the midst of learning Malay,' he complained.

So – Burgess was by no means unique, tramping off abroad; there was expert and first-hand advice to hand, should he have required it. (He wasn't, therefore, the first exile since Lord Byron in 1816 – though look how far away he was willing to transport himself so he could be an outsider.) But this interview at the Colonial Office with 'high functionaries about a post for which I could not remember having applied'? Malaya was an unhandy federation of British colonies in South-East Asia, a conglomeration of Islamic monarchies, sultanates, river states and principalities, specialising in rubber and tin production, which the Crown had governed since 1824. It was always volatile – all those tribes, religions, languages – and the Treaty of Pangkor (1874), which had sought to establish a system of British residential administration, led to revolts in Penang, Selangor, Negri Sembilan and Pahang. The Federated Malay States, so called, came into being in 1876 and it was a further thirty years before Kedah, Perlis, Kelantan and Terengganu accepted British control. And who or what precisely were the British controlling? The trade routes and trunk roads for silks, gold, pearls, cloves and nutmeg; from the Orient to the drooping West tea and opium had to be ferried. The indigenous Malays, interestingly, were almost in a minority. The Indonesians, Ibans, Kadazans, Melanaus, and multifarious islanders and nomadic hunters and gatherers, were not much interested in running the rubber plantations and the tin mines – and these tasks were undertaken by the Chinese, who flooded into the peninsula, escaping the repressions of the Manchu dynasty, bringing with them their dialects, dietary customs, marriage and funeral rites, and superstitious beliefs. Indians, especially Tamils, were encouraged to emigrate to Malaya by the British, who required plentiful manual labourers. (After Independence in 1957, political power devolved upon the Malays, economic power was in the hands of the Chinese – a rift which continues.) The Japanese invaded Kota Bharu in December 1941, and moved remorselessly south, beating, torturing and condemning to starvation thousands of Allied soldiers and civilians of all races. The Chinese received particularly brutal treatment, and many who fled into the jungle became the Communist Freedom Fighters who'd present such post-war problems. Singapore, at the foot of the Malay archipelago, founded in 1819 by an officer of the East India Company, Thomas Stamford Raffles, about whom Toomey writes a novelised biography called *Lion City*,* had the strategic importance of Gibraltar and housed a garrison, which fell to the Japanese in 1942. It had become a Crown Colony in 1867. British rule resumed in Malaya after the defeat of Japan in 1945, but the Malay, Indian and Chinese populations were no longer content with the idea of the Empire and, along with the rise of a Communist influence, armed rebellion began to take place – resulting in the declaration of the Malayan Emergency, as it was termed, which lasted from June 1948 until July 1960. In October 1951, the British High Commissioner, Sir Henry Gurney, was murdered, and his successor, General Sir Gerald Templar, was additionally appointed director of military operations, and a concerted anti-guerrilla offensive was launched in 1952.

This was the world, of bright green light, ferns, orchids and moss, of red ants and white ants, pepper bushes and flying beetles, which Burgess was pitched into, in August 1954. The village of Sungai Siput, near to the Malay College, was reputed to be a headquarters of Chinese Communist terrorists, and the state of Perak was patrolled by troops of the Malay Regiment, which was made up to strength with British conscripts. Planes and helicopters clattered overhead. Raids and ambushes were made by the British upon the rebels, and by the insurgents against European civilians and the military. In the mountainous jungle, both sides were engaged in arduous marches and stealthy combat. Meantime, in the roadside bars, and drinking Tiger beer, Burgess was blithely translating *The Waste Land* into Persian – a lunatic scheme, if you think about it, for what would his pupils, raised in the tropics, know of winter deadness, frost, sleigh rides, dry stones with no sound of water, or commuters crowding over London

* Alternative or rejected titles for this project are *King of the Lion City*, *Man of the Eastern Seas*, *He Built an Island*, and *Flames in the Eastern Sky*. ('My God, what a genius I had then,' says Toomey.)

Bridge? (To the Malays, the cold north is exotic and improbable – a subject Burgess deals with in his story 'Snow', in *The Devil's Mode*: 'It is a kind of frozen water that falls from the sky,' a pupil, who gapes in disbelief, is informed.) Now, the one thing everybody knows about Burgess, once we've made it clear that he wasn't Anthony Blunt *nor* Guy Burgess,* is that he loved word-play and linguistic showing-off. The obsession intensified in Malaya, where he passed the official government languages examination in record time. 'I've had to learn the Arabic alphabet and have developed a beautiful script which makes me feel already half-Oriental,' he explained in February 1955, having sat the test the previous Christmas. Malay words stud his prose like Hemingway tossing in Spanish colloquialisms for cocks and balls. *Dia ta' boleh buat. Dia main-main sahajah* means 'They can't fuck. They can only play about,' which was perhaps the long and the short of it with Burgess.

* For twenty years, people have been assuming I've been writing about a spy. An Australian music-hall artiste, whose father-in-law had corresponded with Guy Burgess in Moscow, tried to give me a cache of letters. A former British Ambassador in Paris offered to describe to me the Top Secret memoranda which had crossed his desk. Everybody gets it wrong. Jan Morris told me she'd, too, met him in Moscow, which got me busy trying to tie up the chronology in the light of Burgess (Anthony)'s remark to Duncan Fallowell: 'Jan Morris lives in Wales – I knew her when she was James – knew *him*, never met *her*. I never suspected he'd change his sex. Seemed quite a masculine type, raised a family and so forth. Bit small-boned, perhaps, but plenty of bristle.' Then I received a follow-up postcard from Llanstumdwy, exclaiming, 'Oh, *that* Burgess!' – as Jan Morris realised her mistake. Roy Jenkins said to me that he met Burgess (Anthony) at the Royal Society of Literature, where he presented him with the Benson Medal, and at a Literary Dinner in Manchester: 'I do not think I handled him very well on either occasion,' confessed The Rt. Hon. Lord Jenkins of Hillhead, O.M. 'I think that this was partly because, by an extraordinary *lapsus linguae*, I inadvertently referred to him as Guy Burgess, and this he greatly disliked.' Burgess claimed that he always sought an apology from a newspaper if they perpetrated the confusion of identities. When the *International Herald Tribune* mentioned 'The spy, Anthony Burgess . . .' in 1983, 'I wrote in, demanding an apology, and also, a sizeable sum of money. I got the apology, but not . . .' he stated to a reporter. He continues to extract regrets and penitence from beyond the grave – or at least it is Liana who polices the press, on the alert for errors or derogatory remarks. On 15 August 1999, Oleg Gordievsky reviewed *The Private Life of Kim Philby: The Moscow Years* by Rufina Philby in the *Sunday Times* and said '[The story] will be familiar not only to Soviet citizens, but also to many western readers acquainted with the vast literature on Philby and the other British defectors, Anthony Burgess, Donald Maclean and George Blake.' You'd have thought Gordievsky would know what he was on about; and doesn't the *Sunday Times* books page possess a sub-editor? Anyway, the following week this appeared:

Correction

Our book review (August 15) of 'The Private Life of Kim Philby: the Moscow Years' wrongly described the late Anthony Burgess as a British defector and spy. The reference should have been to the late Guy Burgess. We fully accept that Anthony Burgess, the

Yet Blunt (Anthony) and Burgess (Guy)? Just as names and words melt and mix together in *Finnegans Wake*, can it be possible that Anthony Blunt and Guy Burgess should have nightmarishly fused to produce Anthony Burgess? He was not, I think, a traitor – for whom could he betray, not being at home in any place? He did say that his fellow Mancunians thought him a traitor for having left town – he was once called 'a stuck-up opinionated bastard!' by a member of a Manchester audience, and when he said he hoped to be buried in Moston Cemetery, a heckler (the same heckler?) said, 'Three graves await you. One for your body. One for your books. One for your ego'; but the trouble with this apocrypha is that when Burgess regaled journalists with it he was full of pride. It was evidence of the littleness he had clambered away from. If it's bigness he'd wanted, however, he found he hated America and Americans, despising the food and linguistic slovenliness, the cheek of acquaintances and colleagues at the many colleges he lurked at who, expecting him to be hospitable, lapped up his whisky. The decadent long hair and casual clothing of the young particularly irked him. 'I resented a lot of the kids who were ragged in appearance, but very rich,' he said of his time at Princeton. 'It's a horrible aspect of the heresy called Americanism.' Psychoanalysis was a Jewish conspiracy or racket – all these neurotic Viennese and hysterical Germans 'coming over to America and having to impose that pattern on America'. The serious attention being given to an emerging

> well-known writer, was never involved in espionage, and apologise to his widow, Mrs Liana Burgess, for our mistake.

Which is a bit grovelling, in my opinion ('the well-known writer'? Was this dictated by a lawyer?). *Anthony Burgess* was a pseudonym, for God's sake, and anyone who has peeped into his work will see that it is all about double lives and deceit. He is one of the great liars – and was haunted by Catholic doctrines of good and evil, the primal struggles between light and dark. His very last novel, *A Dead Man in Deptford*, concerns espionage, treachery, double agents, etc. (*Did* he have personal knowledge of such spookery?) My favourite example of the Burgess touchiness in this regard was his reaction to Jonathan Coe's profile of him in the *Guardian*. Coe had dictated his copy down the phone and *expatriate*, i.e. he who lives abroad for a long period (to avoid British taxes, we might well add), was printed as *ex-patriot*, a pun worthy of Joyce, surely? Coe was to meet up with Burgess later the same week at a literary event in Bristol. 'I've got nothing to discuss with Jonathan,' he told Bridget Sleddon, the publicity girl, shiftily. Turning to Coe, he then said, 'You bastard, you bastard, you bastard.' The misunderstanding struck Coe as funny and he made it the basis for a joke in *What a Carve Up!*, where the hero wants to use the word *brio* in a review and it gets misprinted as *biro*. Finally, in the Harrods' book department in 1989, a chap queued up patiently at a signing session and, when he reached Burgess, handed over *Philby: The Life and Views of the KGB Masterspy* by Phillip Knightley, for an inscription. 'Not mine,' Burgess whimpered, 'No, no. Not my book.'

black culture or to the black voice was incompatible with civilisation, he claimed – for how can we respect 'the quality that made them slaves in the first place'? Successful American artistic icons were as bad – he loathed the way American writers were colonising the world: all those novels by Roth, Ellison and Mailer, which were translated into Italian; and the Malayan books, especially *Beds in the East*, deplore the effects of Coca-Cola and juke boxes on the natives, who presumably should be kept in picturesque isolation, like the bumpkins at Bamber Bridge or the Shakespearean clowns in Adderbury. We can guess, of course, what vulgarians and philistines he thought the British ('an effete race and an effete nation'), who dropped their aitches and had mouthsful of glottal stops. People like Jimmy Savile and Mary Quant are honoured – and 'I *hate* the Queen, because I think she's anti-intellectual, somewhat stupid and somewhat snobbish.' He hated the self-protecting British Establishment, especially over its hypocrisy as revealed in the Profumo scandal. There was a personal animus to this: George Wigg, the Labour Member of Parliament who asked questions in Westminster about sexual morality, bringing the whole Stephen Ward and Christine Keeler business into the open, was the George Wigg who, as the Western Command Deputy Education Officer in the long ago, had vetoed Burgess's speech-therapy classes at the military hospital in Winwick, Warrington. 'Speech therapy is not a specialisation that officially existed in the army,' Wigg told Burgess, who additionally called him facetious. The whirligig of time brings in its revenges, however, and Wigg, created a Life Peer in 1967 by Harold Wilson, was arrested for accosting women at Marble Arch. The beauty part is that three of the black prostitutes he'd approached had turned him down.

England, we are told, in *The Right to an Answer*, 'is the great democratic mess'; and Burgess expanded on this in 1968 – saying that he preferred the precariousness of a Communist state, which makes people aware of 'the existential nature of man's life', and where you can't 'sit back and take for granted the kind of free and moderately well-heeled society we have here'. A little bit of terror does you good, he seems to be saying – and it's the case that the cool and efficient despots in his books always win. There is no reliable counter-check to them. When, in the sixties, he refused to countenance flower-power, student unrest, or the Beatles's first LP, he got to be decried as a crypto-fascist; he also received hate-mail accusing him of being a revolutionary activist and telling him to 'get back to Russia, you limey commie bastard!'. Either way, he was a totalitarian – which can appeal to Catholics, with their need for certainties, or at least rigidity. 'To act evil is better than to have good imposed,' he said – an aphorism which, whilst summing up the theory behind *A Clockwork Orange*, is also a mass of contradictions and a prescription for indulging your own romantic selfishness and libertinism whilst ensuring that others are kept under control; and it also implies that you can provoke trouble if what you want to do is display your own strength. When pressed for his political proclivities, Burgess said he hated capitalism (because 'I've never had any money, therefore I've no sympathy for capitalists') and he hated socialism ('it becomes a totem of terrorism' – eh?); 'I suppose I end up as an anarchist,' he decided. He'd voted Labour only once (in 1945), because it seemed Churchill wanted to keep men in the army to face the Soviet menace; and in Banbury he had served on the local Conservative Committee – but, 'I lean towards anarchy,' he reiterated. He approved of the Catalans and the Basques with their bombs – and in *Any Old Iron*, the Welsh commence a policy of sectarian violence; and when I leaf through Burgess's assessments of other peoples and other places, the only city where his temperament feels at home is Leningrad. Falling apart, brutal, full of suspicion and paranoia, and run by a regime skilled at crushing and mangling people, it is Burgessville or Burgessburg: 'I could see that it was very easy to learn to love Leningrad,' he said of a holiday he'd taken there with Lynne in 1961. 'I had been growing into something of a Leningrader myself.'

It was a curious place to take a vacation, especially forty years ago, before St Petersburg had begun to return to its tsarist glory to attract the tourists. The story he gave was that he'd had this wheeze to earn quick bucks by selling Marks and Spencer's polyester dresses (obtained at the branch in Tunbridge Wells) on the Soviet black market. It seems such a lot of trouble to have gone to. They sailed from Tilbury on a tub of the Baltic Line, the *Alexander Rudishchev*. It was as if the cast and crew of the voyage to Singapore had simply changed costumes and were talking in a different accent. Lynne stayed in her bunk, out of her face on shot glasses of vodka. She'd been unable to totter to the quay in the East; this time, having collapsed in a heap at each port of call during the journey (paralytic in the Tivoli Gardens, Copenhagen, paralytic on the gangplank at Stockholm), she once again couldn't be shifted from her cabin. Burgess kept himself to himself, listing the Russian words he wanted for *A Clockwork Orange*. One way and another, and long after the other passengers had vanished, they made their way in a dishevelled fashion to the Astoria Hotel, then (as now) one of the city's most luxurious billets, overlooking St Isaac's Cathedral. Built in 1910 in the Style-Moderne manner, it was where Hitler had planned to hold his celebration dinner once he'd taken the city. John Reed wrote *Ten Days that Shook the World* in the hotel and Isadora Duncan's husband hanged himself in a bathroom. Burgess found himself short-changed and ripped off by the staff, the receptionist had spots, and the lift was out of order. He stationed himself in the basement lavatories and set out his dress stall. The toilet attendant is easily bribed.

The tale is a familiar one – Burgess getting into scrapes and scraps, Lynne boozing and creating and slapping people. But, here at least, they are indistinguishable from the local citizens, 'an undisciplined lot, given to tears and hard liquor; perhaps they needed communism'. The food is emetic – and Burgess takes perverse pleasure in scowling through meals of over-toasted black bread, cold greasy chunks of beef and mounds of salted sprats. The wine is sugary, the vodka peppery. He tries to play the piano and the lid is forcibly shut on his fingers – though anyone who has heard Burgess's tuneless dirge-filled pianism can only but cheer. (I once heard him plonk out an approximation of 'Here Comes the Bride' that sounded more like a Shostakovich requiem for the 'Death of Stalin'.) Lynne keels over and the KGB, who have been watching, organise a trio of white-coated paramedics to take her in the boot of a Volga saloon car to the hospital. Burgess was happy to see her installed there ('the Soviet hospital system seemed to me highly sensible'), and his wife could be dying yet what preoccupies him are the grammatical niceties of filling in the forms in Cyrillic. Nobody knew how to transliterate 'Llewela', so 'hospital business held up while I gave a lesson on the Cymric hissed lateral'. Lynne is wheeled off on a trolley, and Burgess feels free. Instead of doing what you or I would do – inform the Consulate of the hospital admission, make a few phone calls – he goes to stay in the flat of a chap he met at the Metropol restaurant, Sacha Ivanovich Kornilov. He also has his KGB contact, Oleg Petrovich Potapov, who provides free transportation whenever Burgess dials 03 from a public kiosk. He spends a week, he says, with all his new chums, discussing the character of John F. Kennedy, the merits of jazz, and the shortage of consumer goods. The doctors at the Pavlovskaya Bolnitsa, not having taken long to deduce that Lynne was allergic to vodka (as they diplomatically put it), suggested that she be taken home to England as soon as possible – so Nikita Khrushchev's suite aboard the SS *Baltika* is booked and the Burgesses are finally waved off. ('There were, of course, no hospital fees. This was a socialist country.')

Oleg, of the KGB, makes sure that they are safely aboard – here was one Burgess the Russians *didn't* want defecting. On the voyage back, our man composes a piece for the band, but the passengers can't find any rhythm to it and so sit down, unable to dance. At Tilbury there is a heavy police presence, the customs men are officious, and London is more like Soviet Russia than Soviet Russia.*

How much of any of this is true, I wonder?† Burgess's style when describing the trip (and in *Honey for the Bears*, the fictionalised extrapolation) is pure farce. *Carry On, Ivan*, the sequence ought to be called, directed by Gerald Thomas and produced by Peter Rogers, with Sid James as Burgess, Joan Sims as Lynne, Kenneth Williams and Charles Hawtrey as the comical KGB officers, Hattie Jacques as the matron at the Pavlovskaya Bolnitsa, and Barbara Windsor as a blonde Baltic double agent with whom Sid attempts hanky-panky whilst Joan is prostrate. What, though, was Burgess's actual psychological make-up? His grand quality

* Burgess had been pleased to notice that in the *Dom Knigi*, or House of Books, in Leningrad, the works of Richard Aldington were to be found on sale. Aldington (1892–1962), who married (and divorced) Ezra Pound's old flame Hilda Doolittle (the Imagist poet H. D.), wrote controversial biographies of T. E. Lawrence, whom he thought a fraud, and D. H. Lawrence, whom he considered messianic. 'To read the book(s) at all was an unpatriotic act [in England], and Aldington was pilloried as a traitor,' explained Burgess. He loathed the sham of patriotism and the chivalric hypocrisies which led to the slaughter of a generation in the First World War – an anger he vents in *Death of a Hero* (1929) and *All Men Are Enemies* (1933). Burgess found deep and abiding affinities between Aldington and himself and, by extension, between himself and the Russians, who admired Aldington's 'loud and bitter voice of disaffection'. Burgess compares Aldington with the author of *Sons and Lovers* and when he writes this appraisal the autobiographical code is easy to break: 'Disgust with England drove Lawrence out of it, and made him seek a country which had not yet been defiled . . . Aldington . . . left England to settle in France . . . a gallic allegiance which his British readers must have regarded as unpatriotic. It was enough, anyway, for him to live out of England the better to attack it.' *The Colonel's Daughter* (1931) concerns 'the ghastliness of moral atrophy and total brainlessness' in the English provinces – and in the English mind generally – and Burgess assures us that the satire is no exaggeration: 'The brainless army philistine and his brood outlasted the Great War and the brief peace, and were still going round in the vestigial colonial empire to which I lent my inadequate services in the 1950s.'

† He'd gone to Russia in July 1961, and wrote to Jean Burns of *Woman's Hour* on the 25th of that month to suggest a brief talk on Leningrad life – the price of clothes, the plight of women, how people spend their evenings, what Western books are available, the cuisine, and hospitals: 'my wife was there', he specified. 'I speak some Russian, by the way; it was most necessary,' he added. Jean Burns replied on the 28th to say that Russian women and shopping in the Soviet Union 'have been covered fairly comprehensively', but that if 'you yourself have had sufficient encounters with Russian hospitals one way and another', then that might make a feature. Burgess's script, 'A Rash in Russia', was promptly broadcast on 18 September. They forgot to record it, so Burgess returned to Broadcasting House to read it out again on 27 October (@ 9 gns plus £1.2/- rail fare from Etchingham and 7/6 for taxis).

was a disguise for cowardice, shame, deception and disappointment; and the authoritative citizen of the world act, puffing out cigar smoke, telling us of how he'd put one over on Laura Riding and Robert Graves, or how Duke Ellington had talked to him about Constant Lambert, or that Italian priests possess the evil eye (because they have 'given up sex and are neither men nor women') is of a piece with the charlatanry. He pretends to be this, he pretends to be that. It's all about concealment and illusion. The tales he told about being abandoned as a baby next to the corpses of his mother and sister weren't true – the genealogical documents and facts are at variance with what he wanted us to believe, as if by repeating a story over and over it could become gospel. His mother and sister lying there dead – it's a horror story, all about the origin of his lack of love. His army days he'd misremembered. The Banbury years he'd falsified. His sexual antics are fiction. All the time he is creating this image of action, mystery and suspense. We must trust nothing. This isn't a mere muddle over dates, names, places, events. It's more to do with his taste for secrets, his anxieties and edginess; and the living abroad, as if he's covering his tracks or hoping to vanish, the darting about, the multiple name changes – it would all make him a perfect spy. His misanthropic politics set him apart ('there is no culture coming out of England as far as I can see'; 'American people soar above the purely human, and this probably explains why they make such a mess of the purely human'); and his Catholicism, with its dreams of order, was paradoxically appeased by tumult and revolt; he was aroused by thoughts of evil and damnation. ('Hell from beneath is moved for thee to meet thee at thy coming.' Isaiah xiv, 9.) The drunken bohemianism was a brilliant cover, as it had been for Guy Burgess, who stage-managed his chaos and squalor. Russian misery, to this right-wing radical, was congenial; and as Burgess (Anthony) wrote in 1986, doing his best to confess his own suitability, 'The Intelligence Services were probably founded to accommodate the unloved,' that's to say, with their need for people who'll be permanent outsiders – people who'll often be dealing with paranoid fantasy and idiosyncrasy. If he never did anything else, Burgess was determined to separate himself off from others – and he himself could have been founded to accommodate the Intelligence Services.

Do we ever really know other people? How well? This is the biographer's main question, and one that is infinitely complex when the subject is of an antic disposition (Sellers), replete with theatrical flourishes and subterfuge (Olivier), or a pathological liar (Burgess). Sellers and Olivier expressed themselves through their work – and the paradox with Burgess is that his work is a decoy. In his books you do not find private turmoil, or ambiguity or equivocation. He gives no sense of an introspective mind. He simply presents things, externals. His subjects may be passion, betrayal, deeds of violence, death, yet the tone is supercilious and detached. It is almost as if, in a crazy way, he didn't exist. There is a sort of psychic emptiness or numbness; he was a man who at his centre was a ghost or shadow, such is the dissociation of his sensibility. And look at the reality of the absences in his life. His mother was an essential absence; and Lynne was a volatile presence – until she too became an absence. Women, and their departures from him, and their connection with injuries and pain, ought to be the subject upon which he is an expert. Instead of which we get mother-in-law jokes, shaggy-dog stories, distasteful incest panegyrics, and portraits of Lynne at her most (his word) *couchemaresque*. He was a writer as faker or prankster, who lived by deception, illusion, jokes; and such mavericks have long been of value to the Intelligence community. Somerset Maugham, the main model for Toomey, was recruited as a spy in 1915, and his experience formed the basis of his Ashenden stories. John Betjeman, who was working at the Ministry of Information, was made Press Attaché to Sir John Maffey, the British Ambassador in Dublin, in 1941. Though he had the job of improving Anglo-Irish relations, by organising art exhibitions, writing surveys of local architecture, and helping to arrange for the location shoot of Olivier's *Henry V* at Powerscourt, an adjacent Georgian estate, his secret duty was to send reports and official communications to the Ministry of Information and to Viscount Cranborne, the Secretary of State for the Dominions, about Irish neutrality and attitudes to the war, the Catholics' response to news of Nazi atrocities, and so on. The IRA wanted him killed and despatched an assassin – who aborted his mission when he read some of Betjeman's poems. Such a versifier 'could never have been a spy and so his life was spared', according to Candida Lycett Green. (A back-handed insult, if ever there was one: Betjeman's teddy-bearish encomiums meant he was too wet to be a member of the spy world. Which is also Burgess's dismissive view of him, in *Earthly Powers*.)

Graham Greene, who worked for the Foreign Office during the war, mainly in Sierra Leone, is much more obviously a man of action, slipping off to dangerous countries and perfecting his mask of inscrutability. He once said that his true métier was spying, not writing. 'I'm sure spying is my true spare-time pursuit,' he told Vivien Dayrell-Browning, his future wife, in 1926, when he was still a reporter on the *Nottingham Journal*;

and MI6 would concur with that. A quarter of a century later, according to Cabinet Office files, 'His visits to Indo-China proved of assistance to the local station.' His journeys to Mexico, Liberia, Kenya and Cuba also had intelligence potential – and it is the psychological undercurrent of espionage which is explored in the fiction: commitment, treachery, betrayal, failure. *Devil of a State* is dedicated to Greene, and at one time, I think, when he himself was in a remote spot, it was Burgess's intention to be a Greene-style novelist: an unshaven Englishman abroad, drinking too much Scotch, taking a mistress, missing Mass, and getting shot. Burgess certainly believed he was superior in one respect, being a cradle Catholic and not a convert to the cause; but even this was to rankle: 'It's all right if you're a Catholic convert like Graham Greene or Evelyn Waugh, you can have the best of both worlds. But if you're a cradle Catholic with Irish blood, then you're automatically a renegade.' There's no more cold-blooded an outsider, though, than Greene, and the way he describes the excitement of a moral lapse and living on the edge brings his theological concerns ('I'm a much better Catholic in mortal sin,' he told Catherine Walston) into conjunction with his understanding of the mind of a double agent, which he knew to be filled with pain, lassitude and guilt. His chief at MI6 was Kim Philby, no less, and he was transfixed by the cat's cradle of loyalties and duplicity, virtue and mendacity, attached to Philby's fate. In 1968, he contributed an Introduction to Philby's memoirs, *My Silent War*, where he argued that the defector had been like a Catholic spy working for Philip of Spain in the days of Elizabeth I; the two men kept up a correspondence (monitored by MI6 at one end and the KGB at the other); and they met in Moscow in 1986. 'He is absolutely convinced of his righteousness and absolutely indifferent,' said Greene of Philby. 'Any conviction should leave a chink for doubts, for the possibility of thinking that you're wrong. Otherwise a conviction can turn into a fanatical inquisition,' said Philby of Greene, alluding to the Catholicism. All this went into or was anticipated by *The Human Factor*, a book Burgess praised as being 'ironic, acutely observant of contemporary life, funny, shocking, above all compassionate'. And it is the compassionate that he himself could never bring to his own books. The scenes between the lovers, say, in *The Comedians* ('I suppose it was necessary to say goodbye to her once before I realised that I could not do without her'), or the mysteriousness of adults, as seen from a boy's perspective, in *The Captain and the Enemy*, are quite beyond Burgess's range. Illicit romance in a tropical climate – Burgess had Malaya, but his is a cartoon world, trumped up, full of picturesque exaggerations; and whilst *Little Wilson and Big God* may cover Burgess's boyhood years, he was never a child. He was always preternaturally knowledgeable and disappointed.

Greene wrote favourably of Castro, disapproved of America, visited Russia often and gave talks attended by the KGB; he knew Churchill, the heads of the two branches of the security services and the admiral in charge of Naval Intelligence personally; he had been a member of the Communist Party of Great Britain; he turned down a knighthood, accepted the O.M., and was awarded an honorary degree from Oxford. No wonder Burgess was jealous of him. Their first meeting, in 1957, was not a success. Trevor Wilson, a Malayan Information Officer, had asked Burgess, when they met in Kota Bharu, if he'd take a parcel of silk shirts to Greene's apartment in Albany, off Piccadilly (where Toomey retains a set – E2, previously occupied by Aldous Huxley). Though they proceeded to lunch at the Café Royale, Burgess feels that he is being indulged as an errand boy and, when he inscribes a copy of *Time for a Tiger*, senses that he is patronised as an amateur comic novelist.* His suspicion that he was being silently jeered at marked their final encounter, too, in 1980, when Burgess had caught up with the maestro and they were multimillionaire neighbours on the Côte d'Azur. (I'd give a lot to have witnessed these champion old stagers choreographing their elaborate courtesy and contempt – like a pair of rival mafia dons in a film.) Burgess conducted an interview with Greene for the *Observer*, and when the piece appeared, Greene said, 'He put words into my mouth which I had to look up in the dictionary.' Which is a brilliant boff, and illustrates the difference between them. Burgess's was a galaxy of words and, quite simply, there is this overemphasis on language, which was his hangover from Joyce. His blocks of words don't represent the natural world – nothing is living, evolving, shifting. It's spectacular and majestic – and has a grandiosity – but it is scenic. And the scenes don't flow. They have an element of the tableau. Burgess's work, moreover, is an exercise of the conscious will – he never used a pen, for example (except when composing music), and typed his daily quota straight on to the page, allegedly without any corrections or mistakes. This way, avoiding longhand and using an Olivetti or an Apple Macintosh, 'it separates the words from the body'. The division was the very quality he admired in Napoleon. 'His head was a computer. His body was the body of an ape,' he commented in 1973. Which is all to

* 'We were both published by Heinemann in those days, and I do not doubt that Greene got that copy free,' he sniffed in 1991.

the good if you are a military strategist colonising Europe, but it makes writing as mechanical as a craftsman producing one identical chair after another, or one shoe after another, with nothing of yourself intervening. Though nobody denies that this is hard work, surely it is the equivalent of draughtsmanship, not drawing? (Is it possible to be too efficient?) I am reminded of the remark by Jean-Baptiste-Siméon Chardin, in the eighteenth century, 'One uses colours, but one paints with feeling'; and Greene's novels, by contrast, concern the mysterious inner life and are to do with how we treat each other – how we respect or are careless about each other. Burgess, contrariwise, drags other people into himself. They are judged according to his own whims and habits. Wherever he was, he was driven by an impression of the failings of others – who signally never provide him with sufficient love, respect, money, homage, consideration, acclaim, and so on endlessly. He found human foibles at best exasperating, normally an affront.

Though the treatment of the material is so different, what connects them (as chaps who went to live under palm trees and who had this actorish public persona) is the way they saw life in absolute terms of good and evil – that life was a conflict between good and evil – and that the damned soul, the wrongdoer or hunted creature, is closer to God than the dutifully devout and the dull. Sin, rebellion, imperfection, dissimulation thus become traits worthy of applause – and yet though Greene and Burgess hungered for acclaim, both were uneasy about being understood. (If you met them on the stairs, they are the men who are not there.) If Greene's alter ego was Philby, Burgess was, well, Burgess. Looking at the stock of espionage titles in a bookshop he spotted one on 'my infamous cousin', and seemed rather pleased. In New York, he mentioned 'my distant cousin, Guy Burgess', and evidently he had admitted him into that flexible extended family that included Shakespeare, Lawrence, Joyce and Archbishop Dwyer. Jonathan Meades once asked him if he'd ever met Guy Burgess, and he stated categorically, 'He's a member of the family, a rather remote Scottish branch.' He'd not seen him then? 'Never, never, never. I would have been seduced if I'd met him. He was a powerful and seductive man. That film *An Englishman Abroad* was very good. Coral Browne particularly. "He pissed in our soup and we drank it."'* How far

* *An Englishman Abroad*, written by Alan Bennett and directed by John Schlesinger, was first broadcast by the BBC in 1983. To this viewer, the Englishman didn't look as if he'd gone further afield than Scotland, but you can't blame the production department if I'd managed to spot the locations in Glasgow and Dundee. (That's four years in Fife for you.)

do you regard yourself as being an Englishman? pressed Meades. 'I never was English. It's only the Catholic converts who have the luxury of being genuine Englishmen. Like Graham Greene.' So not only was Burgess (Anthony) politically more in favour of domination and control than anyone else, his sense of exile was more intense than anyone else, and his religion put him patriotically beyond the pale. 'When James II was driven out of England, he was our last monarch,' he said in 1989. Is this why Guy Burgess (or Guy Burgess as portrayed with charismatic dishevelment

---

Coral Browne was given the role of her life – herself. In 1958, the Shakespeare Memorial Company had taken its production of *Hamlet* to Moscow. Michael Redgrave had the main part. Coral Browne, five years his junior, played his mother, Gertrude. During the interval one night, Guy Burgess, at large backstage, ran into her dressing room and puked in her basin. Thus began their friendship, and Burgess showed Miss Browne (who'd later in life become Mrs Vincent Price – you couldn't improve this) around his adopted city. That's the basis of the film (and play – it was adapted for the National Theatre, with Prunella Scales as Coral Browne and Simon Callow as Guy Burgess). Alan Bates's performance is the best that great actor has ever given. Seemingly so cheerful, and his smiles and liveliness so at odds with his physical seediness and distress, his Burgess is grandiloquent – and tough-minded. He's very lonely, and clearly the Communist ideal was a fabrication, but he's defiant and crisp. And, of course, he's more English than the English, with his Reform Club manners, Old Etonian tie, and with his request for suits and shoes from Savile Row. 'I can say I love London. I can say I love England. I can't say I love my country, because I don't know what that means,' Bennett has him say. As, in the end, a pathetic old tosser whose airs and graces fool nobody, Bennett and Bates's Guy Burgess would still make a good dry-run for the elderly Anthony Burgess, sounding off at Durrants Hotel or the Savoy ('Of course, the young know nothing'), dragging on his cigarillo, sneering away like billy-o, and then shooting off back to his tax haven. (A. Bates's hair is as oddly layered and opulent as A. Burgess's was a construction of whitish-yellow strands – so there's another expedient.) Guy Burgess was, as a double agent, a counterfeiter, and Anthony Burgess was like a fake Great Man of Letters. As Coral Browne discovered, beneath the perkiness the spy ached for England. The novelist, in his turn, speaking from Switzerland, where he knew nobody, was equally trying to find or impose a rationale on his predicament: 'I suppose the artist is a lonely man. He cannot integrate into society fully. If he does, can he be an artist and be creative? I don't think so.'

The predicament of the solitary aesthete is the story of Anthony Blunt, whom Bennett dealt with in *A Question of Attribution* (1988). A picture belonging to the Queen is being restored and, when the canvas is X-rayed, other faces, other aspects, are revealed. The analogy is therefore made between the procedures of art history – cleaning and scraping away at the surface to see the truth beneath – and the world of the spy, who conceals, fudges, or reshapes reality to his own ends. As interesting as this is, it wasn't really *dramatic*. Informing us that the mathematical precision of dialectical Marxism excited Blunt's senses in the same way as the formal beauty of a Poussin was a point for the lecture podium, not the stage. *A Question of Attribution* has thus mainly been remembered for Prunella Scales's daunting impression of Her Majesty the Queen – who has seen through Blunt at once. In Miranda Carter's biography, *Anthony Blunt: His Lives* (London, 2001), it is argued that what kept him going was 'the intoxication of playing this wonderfully complex game, like a dazzling piece of choreography' (p. 272). Yet *another* spy-as-artist. Anthony Blunt's face (and I sometimes think I'm going mad noticing such things) was like a leaner, more elongated and desiccated caricature of Anthony Burgess's.

by Alan Bates) would have proved seductive? The mutual interest in sophistry and shocking people? Dadie Rylands called Burgess (Guy) 'a terrific intellectual stimulus', and Noel Annan said he was 'the most brilliant, compelling, promising human being' he had ever met. Tom Driberg, who himself was (or perhaps wasn't) an agent of the Security Service (or a double agent for the Communist Party, at their headquarters in King Street – not even his astute biographer, Francis Wheen, can manage to say more than, 'Tom could never bring himself to regard the spying business as anything more than a game'*), once wrote a discerning book on the subject, *Guy Burgess: A Portrait with Background*. Leaving the politics and ideology to one side, he said that what can motivate a spy is the sheer love of subversion for its own sake; it's an almost aesthetic debate between the devilish and angelic sides of our personalities. And this is precisely Burgess (Anthony)'s position when he suggested that whether one's allegiance is to the East or to the West is an irrelevance: 'As for America, that's just the same as Russia,' it is stated in *Honey for the Bears*. 'You're no different. America and Russia would make a very nice marriage'; and this perception becomes the metaphysical premise, 'All things contain their opposite,' which is adumbrated in the novel during a fancy-dress vicars and tarts party aboard the ship taking Paul and Belinda Hussey to Leningrad. It's the premise of many of the other novels, too: evil and goodness, in *A Clockwork Orange*, miracles and curses, in *Earthly Powers*; also genius and madness, health and disease, pursuit and escape, male and female, impotence and fertility, incest and orphans, madonnas and whores, and all the other fond Burgess pairings and abstractions.

Maugham, with his reptilian watchfulness; Betjeman (so docile – so manipulative); Greene, the anatomist of moral ironies; Philby, named for Kipling's Kim, the scallywag of the Great Game (Britain *vs.* Imperial Russia); Guy Burgess ('I lack what the English call character,' Alan Bennett has him say, 'by which they mean the power to refrain'); Driberg, the High Churchman and member of the Labour Party National Executive, who haunted public lavatories in search of sex and who was admitted to the Upper Chamber as Baron Bradwell of Bradwell-juxta-Mare in the County of Essex, and who felt himself to be persecuted by

* 'The spy is a man of identities and each day he must act many parts,' wrote Leo Abse. 'Driberg could have played the part of the spy with superb skill, and if the officers of MI5 were indeed inept enough to have attempted to recruit him, then, in turn, Tom Driberg would have gained especial pleasure in fooling and betraying them.' Quoted in *Tom Driberg: His Life and Indiscretions* by Francis Wheen (London, 1990), p. 167.

George Wigg ('Harold Wilson's chief snoop'), and who was a colleague and friend of Maurice Edelman, the Labour Member of Parliament for Coventry and a Russian expert, to whom *Honey for the Bears* is dedicated; and then there's the lame and beerishly bloated Roy Campbell, who joined the Army Intelligence Corps in 1941 and who, deemed unfit for active service, was a Talks Producer at the BBC and on their Literary Advisory Committee (another member was Geoffrey Grigson – whom Campbell, brandishing a stick, chased out of Bush House and into a cake shop in the Aldwych), who wrote for Tambimuttu, the Sinhalese editor of *Poetry London*,* and who drank in the pubs off Tottenham Court Road with Dylan Thomas, where Lynne and Burgess (Anthony) knew him:†

* During the war, Burgess sent a copy of *Poetry Gibraltar*, a supplement to *The Rock*, the local magazine, to the editor of *Poetry London*, and 'Tambimuttu had been excited by the title.' The journal contained the verse which had won Burgess the Governor's Poetry Prize ('Useless to hope to hold off/The unavoidable happening . . .' etc. What were the entries which *lost* like, for Christ's sake?).

† Campbell, like a lot of these reprobates, a devout Catholic ('At heart I'm a complete anarchist,' he claimed), fought on Franco's side in the Spanish Civil War and, during the Second World War, his brief was to report news of Spanish proposals for troop movements and military installations to the Consulate in Madrid. Tall, burly, romantic, poetical (drilling with the Intelligence Training Corps in Brecon, Wales, he translated the works of St John of the Cross whilst dossing in a cow-shed), he's like Nabby Adams in *Time for a Tiger*, whom Burgess introduces as '[this] strange spectacle of the huge rambling man with the jaundiced complexion', and as 'a mystery never to be solved'. Burgess stated that the character of Adams, a police lieutenant who befriends Victor and Fenella Crabbe, was based upon a real officer in the Malay Regiment called Donald D. Dunkeley – a man 'of mysterious origin' whose accent was 'hard to place'. He had served in India, 'in what trade was never made clear', and though he is in charge of the Police Transport Section in Kuala Kangsar, he cannot actually drive. There is no reference to the seven-foot tall Lofty Dunkeley in any of Burgess's contemporary letters home, nor have I subsequently traced such a person, in Malaya or anywhere else. (Malcolm Dalziel, Burgess's former pupil, who worked for the British Council and who visited the Malay College in the late fifties, also thought it notable that no Nabby Adams model was to be found – as, in other respects, *Time for a Tiger* and its sequels had translated fact into fiction with little alteration.) Not, of course, that this matters. Why should fictional characters have to have a real-life counterpart? Except that in Burgess they always *do* – and thus my theory that the alcoholic South African colossus Campbell (1902–57) whose sub-Hemingway ne'er-do-well life (bullfighting, octopus fishing) is whipped up in the memoir *Light on a Dark Horse* (1951), contributed to Nabby Adams's appearance and to his personality. The bold statement that 'I believe in comradeship and in standing shoulder to shoulder with my fellow man,' could be a sentiment of Adams's, as could this despondent opinion of the post-war socialist utopia: 'We all become the things we fight/Till differing solely in the palms/And fists that semaphore to Right/or Left their imbecile salaams.' Burgess, in the chapter entitled '1948: An Old Man Interviewed', in *1985*, mentions that he'd had drinks with Campbell at the pub called the George, near Broadcasting House. One of Campbell's best volumes of poetry is suggestively (in this context) entitled *Adamastor* (1930), which contains Burgessy (or Enderbyesque) semi-doggerel such as:

each of these men savoured the art of paradox – of turning things back to front. Their patron saint could be Christopher Marlowe – 'A great man, Marlowe,' as Burgess said in 1983. 'Dead at twenty-nine, stabbed to death in a tavern by double agents. Probably was one himself.' Hence, *A Dead Man in Deptford*, the last novel he was to see published and, if you can look beyond the bad sex sequences ('they . . . rolled and panted and were disengorged of their urgencies'), something of a confession. When Kit (as he is called) signs into Sir Francis Walsingham's service, it is like the sealing of a Faustian pact:

> 'Duty with discretion. Sign your name here' [commands Walsingham]. And he pushed forward abruptly on his paper-loaded table a particular paper, neatly scrivened . . . 'A man who will not put his name to such a testimony of allegiance may well call himself a traitor.'
>
> 'I am no traitor but I am dubious about signing' [replies Kit].
>
> 'Dubiety is in itself a sort of treachery. Sign.'
>
> So Kit dubiously signed with a swan feather and ink black as the gaze of him who was to be his master.

(It is odd how Burgess could write as if his first language was far away from being English – or as if his English is a schoolboy's translation from Latvian or Ibo.) The 'oath of secrecy and livelong fealty and much more of a binding nature' despatched, what is Marlowe's task? 'Watch, watch and learn. Learn what is intended, listen for talk of assassination and rebellion, find out names of traitors who propose treachery.' Such was Burgess's function, likewise. Sir Francis Walsingham (1530?–90), the Member of Parliament for Banbury (1559), travelled widely during Queen Mary's reign, collecting foreign intelligence for Lord Burghley, who had mobilised the secret police to detect plots against Elizabeth. He was made chief of the secret service in London in 1569, and ran the network at his own expense. In *Shakespeare*, Burgess calls him one of 'the great counsellors who had helped guide [Queen Elizabeth I's] hands', and that Gloriana was 'lucky in her chief ministers – men like Sir William Cecil

---

When in dead lands where men like brutish herds
Rush to and fro by aimless frenzies borne,
Firing a golden fusillade of words,
Lashing his laughter like a knotted scourge,
A poet of his own disdain is born
And dares among the rabble to emerge . . .

In the opinion of Peter Thomson, Lecturer in Drama at the University of Manchester, *Adamastor* is a 'boisterously romantic and frankly self-vaunting collection of lyrics'.

[Burghley] and Sir Francis Walsingham'. It was Walsingham who had run the agent Dr Roderigo Lopez, a Portuguese Jew and physician at the court, who forwarded information to and from English spies in Spain. After Walsingham's death, the Earl of Essex accused Lopez of being a double agent and traitor – and it is Lopez's hanging and quartering which is described so avidly in *Nothing Like the Sun* ('The hangman threw the heart and guts into the steaming bowl'); and the politics and duplicity which culminate in the execution is like sixteenth-century le Carré, whose sales always made Burgess emerald with envy. 'The only literature the British can produce on a world-scale is sub-art about spies,' he said in 1986, before coming up with the bizarre rationalisation that, because espionage and defecting involve renewals, a rebirth with new identities, 'It's in and out of the womb all the time . . . [Spies] are literally *motherfuckers*.' He was delighted when William Conrad, the squat, obese homunculus who found fame as Frank Cannon, the television detective, and who had hoped to produce Burgess's Shakespeare movie, the musical *The Bawdy Bard*, worked it out that the title of the novel, *MF*, which up until then had stood for male and female or mezzo-forte, was to be decoded as *m*other*f*ucker – and indeed it had once been Conrad's desire to make an all-black film on Oedipus, entitling it *Mother Fucker*. Not having known his own mother, and despising his stepmother, and then fearing that his stepmother *was* his real mother, or that he'd sleep with somebody and it's his mother (or sister) – this was Burgess's considerable hang-up. He once called America 'our harassed stepmother', and he considered it a grave mistake that the United States had broken with its real mother, England: 'it's a great, great shame that the English-speaking world is divided like this', he claimed, and he hated the way England was being 'absorbed into the Continent of Europe' – even though he personally, of course, only felt at home elsewhere, because (ostensibly) of all the Catholic stuff: 'Our capital was not London but Rome, and our provinces were cities like Dublin and Paris, where you could hear the Angelus at noon and make the sign of the cross in public.' Mother Church took priority over Mother Country; or anyway that was the pretext. The reality was more selfish: 'brought up in the north-west of England and then pulled into the Army and working abroad for England – you know, for the Empire – I always felt that I was supposed to have a responsibility to England and I was disappointed that England felt it had no corresponding responsibility for me'. If Catholicism made him feel 'a sort of traitor', so was his 'patriotism highly qualified'.

How a Walsingham could have exploited Burgess's confusions over what he cared about and his highly charged attitudes to faith and duty – the two very words which make Toomey's eyes prick with tears (there's a line of Whitman's, Toomey confesses to Wignall [the Betjeman character], that always makes him blub: 'all intrepid captains and mates, and those who went down doing their duty'*); and what with his hunger for

* Song for All Seas, All Ships

1
TO-DAY a rude brief recitative,
Of ships sailing the seas, each with its special flag or ship-signal,
Of unnamed heroes in the ships – of waves spreading and spreading far as the eye can reach,
Of dashing spray, and the winds piping and blowing,
And out of these a chant for the sailors of all nations,
Fitful, like a surge.

Of sea-captains young or old, and the mates, and of all intrepid sailors,
Of the few, very choice, taciturn, whom fate can never surprise nor death dismay,
Pick'd sparingly without noise by thee old ocean, chosen by thee,
Thou sea that pickest and cullest the race in time, and unitest nations,
Suckled by thee, old husky nurse, embodying thee,

Indomitable, untamed as thee.
(Ever the heroes on water or on land, by ones or twos appearing,
Ever the stock preserv'd and never lost, though rare, enough for seed preserv'd.)

2
Flaunt out O sea your separate flags of nations!
Flaunt out visible as ever the various ship-signals!
But do you reserve especially for yourself and for the soul of man one flag above all the rest,
A spiritual woven signal for all nations, emblem of man elate above death,

Token, of all brave captains and all intrepid sailors and mates,
And all that went down doing their duty,
Reminiscent of them, twined from all intrepid captains young or old,
A pennant universal, subtly waving all time, o'er all brave sailors,
All seas, all ships.

Toomey (or Burgess) remembers the poem well enough to misquote his favourite line; the words have lodged in his mind and belong there. To make a verification and look the verse up in a book would be a betrayal, like forcing an ageing lover to gaze in a mirror, turning their eyes into their very soul. Burgess misquoted his Anglo-Saxon with Borges in a similar fashion. Margaret Thatcher was the same with Larkin. She told him that she liked his 'wonderful poem about a girl. My face must have expressed incomprehension. "You *know*," she said. "Her mind was full of knives." I took *that* as a great compliment – I thought if it weren't spontaneous she'd have got it right.' (Letter to Julian Barnes, 25 September 1985. The actual line, from 'Deceptions', reads, 'All the unhurried day/Your mind lay open like a drawer of knives.') And what – fuck a duck – a great poem of Whitman's: a song of the sea, like the Anglo-Saxons and their whale-roads, or Melville with Ahab's quest through time and space for Moby Dick. It seems like an improvised piece of oratory – roll on, thou deep and dark blue ocean, roll! Ten thousand fleets sweep over thee in vain! – but the language is biblical, majestic. These are Old Testament

puzzles and codes, his interest in languages, and the fact that he was greedy, grudge-bearing and financially strapped, Burgess was keen to use the Educational Corps as a cover for intelligence work, on the alert for plots and covert operations, initially in Gibraltar. He was assigned to work low-grade tasks like map-reading and the identification of German aircraft. There was a considerable flap when there was an outbreak of smallpox on the Rock. How had that happened? Everybody had to be vaccinated, including the Spanish workmen and all civilian visitors, without the full nature of the threatened epidemic being revealed. On another occasion, a sergeant from the Army Medical Corps went insane and climbed up the face of the Rock, and became stuck, immobilised with fear. He was pinioned to a ledge for over twenty-four hours. Search lights were trained upon him in case he fell asleep and rolled off to the ground. Eventually a Czech doctor from the Military Hospital clambered up with a rope and the chap was lowered to safety. The intelligence people were concerned to know what this was all about – and perhaps they had reason to be agitated. Two saboteurs had been found in the dockyard tunnels and they were condemned to death. A hangman was flown out from England in secret to carry out the execution. The Senior Warrant Officer had to be present, and he was greatly affected by it – as was Burgess? How much of what he saw (or heard about) made its way into the Tyburn scenes with Lopez? We'll never know – though it is worth noting that Shakespeare's (i.e. Burgess's) sympathy is with the victim, 'fading out in humiliation' rather than with the 'intolerable and intolerant' accusers.

Fears about Spain in Shakespeare's and Marlowe's day were replicated by nervousness about Communism in Burgess's. Walsingham was, in effect, the ancestral godfather of the Secret Intelligence Service (SIS or MI6), which is responsible for gathering material overseas; and the founding head of the Secret Service Bureau in 1909, the branch to be

---

cadences. The sea, here, is a nurturing and exacting mother, to whom we must pay homage. The sentiments are echoed in *Ulysses*, where the sea is 'our great sweet mother', and there are plenty of references in the text to the sloshings of amniotic fluid. According to Burgess, in *Here Comes Everybody*, the reference to the sea brings in the theme of 'Stephen's guilt in relation to his mother, recently dead . . . The sea now reminds him of the bowl of sluggish bile "she had torn up from her rotting liver by fits of loud groaning vomiting". Pity for her rests with him and he wears mourning as its outward sign.' Behind Stephen Dedalus and his mother there hover, of course, those Homeric and Shakespearean analogues; and yet when Burgess writes about Joyce, it is his own life that the Dubliner's works parallel and prophesy.

known as MI5, which dealt with defensive counterespionage in Britain, was Major-General Sir Vernon Kell. So that's where the pseudonym for the author of *One Hand Clapping* and *Inside Mr Enderby* comes from. In January 1951, the Joint Intelligence Committee noted that 'Chinese Communist attention to the rest of South East Asia is increasing and must be expected to continue to do so'. If Communism gained ground in Siam and Burma, there was fear of a domino effect and 'our chances of holding Malaya would then become slender'. Secondly, if the Chinese intervened directly in the region, this could escalate into a global thermonuclear war, especially if the Soviets simultaneously supported a coup in the Middle East. It was thus a diplomatic necessity to call the Malayan Emergency an Emergency and not a formally declared war, so as not to incite these superpowers. The French had lost their empire in Indo-China; and it was felt that the best way of limiting the impact of the Communist insurgency in Malaya – the sniping and bombing provoked by the Malayan Communist Party, whose members included the disaffected Chinese who'd particularly suffered from the Japanese occupation – was to grant the place its own independence, but with a pro-British president. Hence, Tunku Abdul Rahman, who took charge of the new republic in September 1957. In order for the Malays to outnumber the Chinese community, the Borneo territories of Sabah (then known as British North Borneo), Sarawak and Brunei (a sultanate under British protection), which were already British Crown Colonies, were to be brought into the Federation. This, though, was opposed by Indonesia, and the Soviets began to send financial and military aid to Jakarta; as did the Americans, who were keen to foster any anti-Chinese sentiment. The Anglo-Malayan Defence Agreement of October 1957 meant that Britain was to remain responsible for the republic's safety (the other side of the deal was that Malaya's currency reserves would be held in London); and I wonder, had Indonesia (with its Russian–American support) confronted the British, whether Britain would have found itself as isolated as Grand Fenwick, in the Peter Sellers film *The Mouse That Roared*? A guerrilla force based in Brunei seized the oil town of Seria in 1962. British troops, including two companies of gurkhas, put down the revolt. The Borneo provinces joined the Federation of Malaysia (now so called) in 1963. Sultan Omar Ali Saifuddin, the construction of whose mosque in Brunei is a subplot in *Devil of a State*, preferred, however, to retain his autonomy. This move was supported by British Petroleum and Shell Oil, who didn't want to see their oil revenues coming under the control of

Kuala Lumpur. Burgess had gone from Brunei for good by then, having fallen to the floor in a fit, foaming at the mouth, and by and by breaking out to savage madness, but he had spied upon his neighbours, Azahari and Che Gu' Salleh, who were to be involved with the failed rebellion, and who ran the Party of Freedom, in opposition to the Islamic monarchy, and his conclusion was that their project to overthrow the Sultan was 'unrealistic'.

On the one hand, with Burgess, there's this love of obfuscation and concealment; and on the other, he's the teacher whose mission is to explain and illuminate – a dichotomy proposed by Miranda Carter for Anthony Blunt, the traitor and Courtauld lecturer: 'You felt he had a radical streak. He was somehow fun to talk to if you were young,' said a former student of Blunt's – a sentiment echoed by Burgess's pupils, too, when I met them. It's Enderby, with his taste for secrets and his travelling and his proliferating names, and Cyrano, defiantly himself, flourishing his rapier wit, relishing an audience and being on parade. The spartan and the frugal, and the epicurean. It was Lynne who'd begun all this for him, after a fashion. During the war, as we know, she'd been organising cargo for the ships involved in the D-day landings. This brought her into contact with the security services. The head of her section, the Assistant Secretary at the Ministry of Supply, from 1939, was Sir William Dale. He had been a legal assistant at the Colonial Office since 1935 and it was to that department he returned after the war, when he formed a commission to ascertain whether Rajah Brooke's offer to cede Sarawak to the British government would be acceptable to the native population. It was Dale's belief that the hasty abandoning of the Empire would be a catastrophe – and as Chinese Communist terrorists were active in Malaya, particularly in Perak and Kelantan, it was essential that an Education Officer, such as Burgess, whilst teaching the sons of the rich Malays who'd be ruling the Federation, also reported to the SIS (Far East) outstation in Singapore, or to the British Resident in Kuching, any news of Communist sympathy among pupils, their parents, or the staff. Thus, Victor Crabbe, in *Time for a Tiger* (and 'one draws on one's personal physical experiences', Burgess told Bernard Levin), pads around the dormitories at night, on patrol, and finds a group of Chinese pupils holding a secret meeting: 'He was also certain that other indoctrination sessions were being held in other houses.' The headmaster, however, will do nothing about this simmering rebellion ('there was the big public school tradition of not sneaking'), which was indeed Burgess's own dispute with Jimmy Howell, the real headmaster of the Malay College – and yet in his memoirs Burgess has to say that 'the deterioration of the relationship between myself and Jimmy Howell' was over the issue of accommodation. Burgess and Lynne didn't like the rooms they were assigned in King's Pavilion, because the water supply is erratic and the children too noisy. Non-ideal flats and billets had never vexed him before – indeed, he has always been remarkably indifferent to his surroundings. What is consistent, however, is the impression he always liked to give that he was surrounded by enemies; this, plus the drunken bohemianism, was part of the strategic appearance of being undisciplined. His guard fell just once. Asked, in 1973, about his views on Vietnam, he said, 'Our war in Malaya was a prelude to your war in Vietnam. The war, incidentally, the Malayan War, was a war which the Americans would not learn from. It's a bit curious.' Burgess had fraternised with the local people in order to get word to their friends and relatives, the insurgents in the jungle, about the offer of amnesties and free passages to China. He was also involved in cutting off food supplies – or providing food (swill from the school canteen), which the rebels would try to collect. 'This is one way of doing it. The best way of doing it, really, is just to flush them out of the jungle. They come to search for food, and then you capture them.' Again, Victor Crabbe is implicated in this adventure; and 'it would be stupid to invent in an area like that. You can take it from me that life was like that in Malaya,' said Burgess.*

It had always been the intention of the Colonial Office to move Burgess to the Malayan Teachers' Training College at Kota Bharu, which had been declared open by His Excellency Sir Donald MacGillivray, High Commissioner of the Federation of Malaya, on 11 October 1954 ('in the eleventh year of the reign of His Highness Tengku Sir Ibrahim Ibui Al-Marhum Sultan Mohamed IV of Kelantan',† as it Grand Fenwickianly

* The weapon of the picaro – and one not available to people outside a novel – is indeed his innocence. Mr Jaganathan flutters before Crabbe undergraduate articles espousing Communism, and threatens, 'You will have only trouble now, Crabbe, nothing but trouble.' When the terrorists emerge from the jungle, however, and stay at Crabbe's house, instead of being arraigned as a traitor he is crowned as a hero – a hero who daringly enticed the enemy into a clever trap. The second novel in the trilogy ends with Crabbe, deserted by Fenella and by his mistress, Anne Talbot, sitting on his veranda, spinning yarns to the Malays, mythologising his autobiography: 'And as he developed wings and an unconquerable fist and the gift of invulnerability he ceased to be a man from a far country, he joined the heroes of the Malay Valhalla . . .' (It is Valhalla's destiny to combust, I seem to recall.)

† A 'dwarf prince', according to Burgess. The prostitutes milling about the parks were allegedly his discarded wives.

says on the plaque outside); for by teaching English as a Second Language (ESL) to the multiracial students, the Asiatics, Tamils, Chinese, Afghans and Arabs, he'd have a wider base for his operations than at Kuala Kangsar. Once more he contrived to quarrel with his colleagues, and the time he spends absorbing the mixed culture of the Chinese and the Hindus is misconstrued, he says, as potential treachery. As he says in *The Enemy in the Blanket* (a title, by the way, which was a term used locally to mean a traitor or, jocularly, one's wife), where Kota Bharu is Kenching (urine) and Kelantan is Dahaga (thirst), Crabbe gets to be 'set upon by hatred of the British, black magic, and fear of being arraigned on the capital charge of aiding the Communist terrorists'. And the precariousness was genuine. Burgess, the low-grade gatherer of rumours and gossip, signs and whispers, was part of the plan, in 1955, though he'd not have been apprised of the bigger picture, for the Chief Ministers of Malaya and of Singapore, Tunku Abdul Rahman and David Marshall, to meet the leader of the outlawed Malayan Communist Party, Chin Peng, for talks in a jungle clearing. Chin Peng, having heard news of the impending self-government of the Federation, wanted to open up negotiations for a political settlement. Rahman and General Sir Geoffrey Bourne, the Director of Operations in Kuala Lumpur, also wanted an end to the sniping and raiding – but meeting the insurgents, and thereby implicitly recognising a terrorist organisation, was as equivocal then as the British government's parleys with the Irish Republican Army are now. The intermediary was to be Lieutenant-Colonel John Davis who, like Chin Peng, had served in a guerrilla force against the Japanese – this was to be how they'd bond. The talks all failed, alas, because Chin Peng's demands that the Malayan Communist Party would operate in the new Federation as a legal political entity were refused. The Emergency continued. A valiant try, however, and one preceded by a vast amount of co-operation between the regional councils, civil groups, the police and the army. How people felt about what? Would Chin Peng turn up? Or be bumped off? Or tipped off? All intelligence was germane.

Summoned to the Colonial Office in early 1954 (return rail fare enclosed) to be offered the job not on the island of Sark, and to meet Dale*

* Dale, who was legal advisor to the Commonwealth Relations Office, 1961–66, and to the Ministry of Education, 1954–61, was also the translator of the Italian author Massimo Bontempelli (1878–1960), a colleague of Joyce's at the *Cahiers d'Italie et d'Europe* (in 1926) and a precursor of magical realism – or what he called the effort to 'discover surreality in reality'.

or his functionaries, Burgess also used his day out in London (Banbury–Bicester–Princes Risborough–High Wycombe–Beaconsfield–Denham–Marylebone) to visit the offices of William Heinemann, at 15 Queen Street, Mayfair, where Roland Gant, the editor-in-chief, informed him that, though he liked neither *A Vision of Battlements* nor *The Worm and the Ring*,* perhaps Burgess did have potential – and to go away and try again. Burgess's personal and professional feel for codes, traps and assignations, his conviction that he was always fighting against the odds and surrounded by enemies, his preference for the hidden life and a clandestine atmosphere, and his aptitude for language and linguistics and spinning a yarn, had come into conjunction, like aspects of the zodiac. As Burgess remembered in 1993, eight months before he died, 'Malaya had to be recorded before the British abandoned it to self-rule. I felt that Somerset Maugham had never done this adequately and not even Joseph Conrad had known the inner working of the Malay mind sufficiently well to delineate it. I got down to the planning and plotting and eventual composition of my *Malayan Trilogy* . . .' He had ticked off Maugham before – in, for example, the Introduction to Maugham's collected *Malaysian Stories*, in 1978, where the old party is disparaged as a visitor, who'd talk and eat with the Colonial Office civil servants and estate managers, but as for the actual Malays and Chinese themselves, they 'would merely bring drinks and serve dinner'. Perhaps he has to be forgiven his era: 'If Maugham had started writing Malayan short stories in, say, 1954, his plots and main characters might have been very different' – if, that is to say, Maugham had been Burgess (or Burgess, Maugham). It is an extraordinary admission. He really did have a very high opinion of himself. How well does he measure up? On his repatriation, in the sixties, he tried to get radio assignments on the basis of Far Eastern experiences; successfully so – on 25 May 1960, he suggested to *Woman's Hour* that he deliver a six-minute talk on the temperaments and modes of behaviour of the ladies he and Lynne had met and befriended in Malaya and Borneo, including an old bat who'd adopted him as an *anak angkat*, or spiritual ward;† on 14 December 1962, he received six guineas for a broadcast entitled 'Rebellion in Brunei'; and in July 1965, for example, he record-

* When Burgess resubmitted the typescript without comment in 1960, Gant thought it was 'masterly'.

† The talk, which Burgess had called 'Some Oriental Wives', was retitled 'The Gentle Sex – Malay Fashion', and was broadcast on 8 July 1960.

ed a discussion with V. S. Naipaul* on the 'Literature of Empire', taking in Kipling in India and Orwell in Burma, as well as his own Malayan experiences and novels. It's this memorandum from the Controller of the Third Programme, P. H. Newby,† to Joseph Hone, on 5 April 1963, however, which I find interesting:

* Burgess and Naipaul, there's a pairing. Both of them are unanchored and strange. Naipaul, after the migrations of his people, wants to be in England, and to settle; Burgess – all he wanted to do was wander. Looking at the Caribbean, Africa and India, in Naipaul's case, and at Malaya, in Burgess's, they wrote about the loss of stability – moral, political, spiritual. The decay of colonialism and the emergence of African and Malayan independence released such bitterness, such expressions of aggression and bigotry. In the end, contemplating the sheer 'instability of our faiths and moral systems' (as Burgess wrote in *Quarto*, October 1979, when reviewing Naipaul's *A Bend in the River*), you have to face the facts of our inability to govern ourselves. We perhaps need the occupation by foreign powers. This is the theme of *A Clockwork Orange*, when order is imposed upon anarchy – and I never quite believe that Burgess genuinely prefers the instabilities of free will.

Though fifteen years Burgess's junior, Naipaul was already, in 1965, with *The Suffrage of Elvira* (1958) and *A House for Mr Biswas* (1961), and with his non-fiction works *The Middle Passage* (1962), about a return to the Caribbean, and *An Area of Darkness* (1964), about the search for his Indian roots, the senior artist – and it was Naipaul who stipulated the time and date of this recording (5.30–7.30 p.m. on Wednesday 14 July at Broadcasting House, out of which a nineteen-minute discussion was prepared and edited and transmitted as *The World of Books*, 10.10–10.45 p.m., on 24 July. Burgess received 20 gns plus £1.19/- for the train and 15/- for taxis).

If their interests in the exotic overlapped, so did their personal manner. Burgess was always trying to be grand – look at the pose he adopts for photographers, or how frequently he'll drop the 'my cousin George Dwyer, the Archbishop' or the 'my wife is Contessa Pasi' stuff into the conversation. This is a quality he got from the Empire, when an invitation or letter from the consulate or embassy would be guaranteed to set the heart fluttering – though no doubt Burgess would have denied all this strenuously. (I can just hear him: 'Boy, tell Missy's amah to take this chit to the Residency chop-chop.') I never mind this – his artifice and falsities are so obviously part of an act. With Naipaul, however, the arrogance is total – and has been well rewarded (a knighthood, the Nobel). His editor, Diana Athill, whilst admiring the work, couldn't help but decide that he was an obnoxious human being, super-sensitive, quick to take offence, self-important, imposing on his publishers, 'the exhausting, and finally tedious, task of listening to his woe'; and Paul Theroux wrote a whole book on the subject of Naipaul's shittiness, the Oedipal narrative called *Sir Vidia's Shadow*. Nobody liked that work much ('I wonder if the author was conscious of how much he was giving away about himself?' asked the *London Magazine*, April/May 1999), but I think that the device of the disenchanted Boswell gives the narrative great animus. Theroux's book is a love story, in its way, and is full of the drama and betrayals of romance. It is so much more rich and fascinating than any conventional biography of Naipaul could have been. Less than chronology, Theroux is interested in the patterns and shapes to be found in a person's life, and as Burgess says in *Ninety-Nine Novels*, Naipaul is 'a sad observer whose will to survive alone defines him'. Burgess found his work 'profoundly depressing. But depression is sometimes a stone on the road to literary exaltation.' Which is a way of saying that Naipaul thinks *important* and *serious* are synonymous; that the comic spirit is a lapse; and that personal rudeness or unkindness are permissible if what you are doing is conjuring away false positions.

† Howard Newby, as he was known to his friends, had joined the BBC in 1949 and was

> Listening to Anthony Burgess last night* it occurred to me that rather than have him talk about Lowry or Joyce it would be more interesting to have him talk directly out of his own experience as a writer. He said that the tone of some of his fiction had been established by the fact that he was giving an account of oriental experiences which seemed not at all unusual at the time but which to an English audience might seem strange indeed. It made me think of the story by Henry James, 'Lesson of the Master', in which a young man had written a novel about foreign parts and the Master had said 'it was very good but next time write a novel about life here in England so that we can measure it against our own experience'. Burgess must be conscious of the difficulty of writing about situations which readers cannot measure against their own experience. There are all sorts of dangers in this situation – charlatanry, the exploitation of local colour and so on. What kind of relationship to his readers does he envisage when he is treating exotic material?

This is perspicacious – for who *did* Burgess think he was addressing? Malaya was as far off for most people as Moses' Egypt or, to leap from the distant past to the future, the spaceship *America*, in *The End of the World News*, is for all of us. His genuine fascination and engagement with Malaya set him at odds with his fellow expatriates, whom he deemed bridge-playing, scandal-mongering Home Counties suburbanites who spoke with Raj-accents and who 'motored into Ipoh to see the new American films', as if that was the height of philistinism. He and Lynne, by contrast, spurned the club and did their drinking in the roadside tin

---

Controller of the Third Programme, later Radio 3, for many years, before being promoted to Director of Programmes. In 1975, he was made Managing Director of BBC Radio. He wrote approximately thirty novels and received the Somerset Maugham Prize, the *Yorkshire Post* Fiction Award and the Booker (in 1969 – for *Something to Answer for*); he was a successful all-round man (CBE, etc.), but how many people have heard of him today? Newby had worked in post-war Egypt, teaching at the University of Cairo, and in his early books, *The Picnic at Sakkara* and *A Guest and His Going*, he discussed what Burgess (who'd read them, of course) called 'the agonizing divisions between races and cultures . . . Newby seems to imply that all a man has in a world without maps is his individuality, his instincts, his capacity to be himself', which to me seems rather a lot to be going on with, but there you are (see *The Novel Now*, p. 69).

* It had been an abstruse programme on Joyce, Malcolm Lowry and Flann O'Brien, which had then led into a discussion of what critics mean by the words *good*, *wonderful* and *bad* – and how should we define *good*? Burgess found his preparation for the broadcast 'useful to oneself, I mean: a chance to sort out what one really thinks'. It's an example of how long ago and far away this was, that radio could be filled with such cerebral matters, such philosophic boffinry. It's as remote as a summer's day in the reign of Queen Anne.

shacks run by the Chinese – Anchor or Tiger beer, 'sometimes warm as tea'. For culture, he went with his Fifth Form to a production of *Macbeth* in Ipoh, where 'a luscious long-haired Chinese teacher played Lady Macbeth and Chinese–Scottish bleeding sergeants ching-chonged away at the immortal lines. The audience loved it and obviously think the Western genius is a comic one entirely.' Back at the house, Burgess's cook had a sex change and had his photograph taken as a woman.* Yusof dyed his hair red and started sprouting breasts. 'He is probably hermaphroditic,' Burgess told Kathleen Winfield sagely. 'He is also too fond of bringing hot water into my bathroom when I'm already bathing.' But he was a good chef, all the same, producing real English Sunday dinners, shark's fin soup and hair-raising curries. 'This was worth going out East for,' Burgess persuaded himself. An amok Tamil chased another with a lead pipe and left him bloody and crying for some mother-goddess or other in the school next to their quarters. At the local cinema, a Hindustani film about Baghdad dubbed in Malay lasted for days. At the fair in the grounds of the Istana Iskandra, there were Chinese operas and dances and everybody drank potent rice spirit . . .

It is such sights and sounds and smells as these that make the *Malayan Trilogy* a success. Yusof, for example, becomes Ibrahim bin Mohamed Salleh, who undulates through the market as, 'in crepitating silk, hair clips holding curls in place, basket swinging, [and] fist clutched tightly round two crumpled dollar notes', he goes to do the morning shopping. 'I teach away, dripping on to the set-books, watching my white shirt become greyish and diaphanous as the morning sweats and blast-furnaces by,' Burgess

* Burgess was fascinated by homosexuality (Toomey, Marlowe, the state-enforced faggotry of *The Wanting Seed*, the way homosexuality is a metaphor for the similitude and interpenetration of East and West in *Honey for the Bears* – a notion foreshadowed in *Time for a Tiger*, where the East is called 'a horrible sweating travesty of Europe'), and yet he denied this vociferously to Duncan Fallowell: 'I wish I could approve of homosexuality, but I'm enough of a Catholic to regard homosexuality as an aberration, as the spending of seed in barren places . . . I don't know why the hell it exists, you see. It must be a genuine aberration, it's not natural. I've just been reading Aldous Huxley's essay about parrots, which imitate human speech, although they don't have the apparatus and there's no earthly biological reason for it . . . This is like homosexuality. What is nature up to here? Only God would be interested in playing such games with nature. In making parrots speak – or homosexuality.' The idea of a sex change really got him going, like the Pope drafting an encyclical. Fallowell was the author of a book about April Ashley, prompting Burgess to say, 'The subject, you know – change of sex – is not a romantic one, it's apocalyptic. Sends theology sky-high. A sex-change is something the Church Fathers never thought of. Male and female created He them and that was that . . . This is the relationship between mind and body, spirit and flesh.'

told a former colleague. 'I shall make a novel out of it, I hope. On the other hand, perhaps not. As Shakespeare says, "Besok dengan besok dengan besok . . ."' The exoticism you can impart on a postcard, however, or in an aerogramme, is less than the half of it. This is the physical life. We have to rely on Burgess that the way his house filled up with monkeys, scorpions, a polecat and a turtle is true – that his intention to translate *The Waste Land*, Pound's *Cantos* and Huxley's *Ape and Essence* into Malay was not a joke – that his partial addiction to opium and his saying it's such a shame that the British working class can't still dose themselves on it is *indeed* a joke. But as regards the puzzle of Burgess's own real nature, you can be sure of nothing save that he has willed himself to be on the dangerous edge of things and wants to shock. 'I knew very well the opium dens of old Penang, before they built the airport. Very sad,' he'd say philosophically. 'To write well,' he said, on another occasion, 'you have to touch pitch and be defiled. Novels are a record of what life's like. The lower depths – squalor – vomit – defecation – drinking.' Yet he can't see that screaming at Egyptians at Port Said, getting into fist fights with shoe-shop salesmen, shouting at waiters and bar managers as if they are natives you can slap and command isn't colourful and daring and wonderful. It is to behave rudely and inconsiderately and to reveal your own disagreeableness and egotism. One of the most embarrassing moments in television history is included in the documentary he made about a return journey to Malaya, 'A Kind of Failure', shown on BBC2 on 17 January 1981 in the *Writers and Places* series. Having boasted about the Malays that, 'I taught their sons. I spoke their language. I knew them better than Conrad'; and mindful of the bragging in his memoirs about 'my growing mastery of the Malay language' and his contempt for other expatriates who 'did not take language-learning seriously enough' – well, here he is in this restaurant, completely failing to make himself understood to the waitresses. The few words he barks gets them giggling. 'Do you understand the language of your own country?' he snapped, in English. He turned to the camera and said, unarguably, 'The country and I have nothing to say to each other.' If only a cook with a cleaver or an Iban with a blowpipe had let him have it at that very moment. Let's be charitable and suggest that he wasn't being a bully, he wasn't a hypocrite – he was merely being Burgess, i.e. overblown and carrying on like a caricature of himself, incapable of admitting, even in the face of all the evidence, that his Malay wasn't up to the scratch needed to order a meal or give basic instructions to the kitchen.

It makes you wonder, though, about the reach of his lies. 'I had better say a little now about love-making in the East,' he announces (and launches into a few pages on prostitutes and dance hall girls), and one really wishes he wouldn't. Why does he consider himself a ladies' man? There's Rahimah, who works in a Chinese coffee shop; Che Isa, a young widow; the nymphomaniac wife of Frank Jones, the State Education Officer; and 'I had sexual encounters with Tamil women blacker than Africans, including a girl who could not have been older than twelve.' Is this delusional? It connects with the incest–paedophile theme he was so keen on teasing out from *Finnegans Wake* and with his fantasies about the pupils at the grammar school. At least when Nabokov rhapsodised about nymphets he could channel it through Humbert Humbert, an insane fictional character. Burgess was always playing to an audience, but what this confession of his reveals is that he had absolutely no sense of what the effects of his outpourings could ever actually be having on an audience – in this case, disgust and revulsion. When he was asked how he'd imagine the ideal reader for his material, he replied that what was required was 'a lapsed Catholic and failed musician, short-sighted, colour-blind, auditorily biased, who had read the books that I have read. He should also be about my age.' His speciality audience was the looking-glass. This would account, I think, for his curious sort of coldness. There's no intimacy in his writing, or in his life. No one else existed, not even Lynne. When he'd written home to say she'd 'narrowly missed ambush on the way to the Siamese border last week', and everybody in Banbury laughed that it was a miracle she'd not been ambushed in the English Midlands, I do find her a thing of pity. She was always a handful (Welsh, see) and her capacity for gin was prodigious, and the breathlessly hot Malayan weather lacerated her temper and drove her to consume more and more booze – the garden outside their quarters glinted with Tanquerary bottles. Her delinquency, which culminated splendidly at an ambassadorial reception, when she managed both to throw a punch at one of the Sultan of Brunei's cousins and to swear at the Duke of Edinburgh ('Welsh, is she?' he was heard to murmur), was an attempt to get her husband's attention. For, if he wasn't writing or dreaming about sleeping with the locals (in *Time for a Tiger*, Perak is called Lanchap, which is Malay for masturbation), he was trying to learn their language (if less competently than he'd later allege). Either way, she was neglected and desperately homesick. When news reached her that her mother had died of throat cancer, she attempted suicide. Burgess got her to vomit up the sleeping pills by forcing mustard down her gullet.

Recovering consciousness, she babbled about wanting a divorce and shook with dengue fever and malaria. In a letter to Kathleen Winfield, no mention is made of this – rather, 'Lynne looks younger' and the circumambient Emergency was vivifying, too. 'The mountains resound with bombs and ornaments are shaken off our wall-ledges . . . There is a heady atmosphere of not knowing how much longer one has to live.'

The prospect of the end of the world always gave him a thrill. 'I fear death,' he said in 1989. 'What'll happen at that moment of dissolution? Perhaps the eschatology of my childhood will come true and there'll be a Hell of spitting serpents and endless privation.' He was far more comfortable with punishment and torment than happiness and eternal rest. In 1927, he watched the total eclipse of the sun through a piece of smoked glass and he was convinced the solar system was collapsing. He believed the planet Mars was on a collision course with Earth, and when a dustbin exploded in a Moss Side back alley he was sure that was the start of the cosmic crack-up. If, during his last few years, interviewers tried to flatter him about a lifetime of achievement, all he could do was worry about time being 'very short, and I worry about dying before I've done what I want to do' (1989); and he was convinced he was unappreciated. 'I've had a long swathe of time in which people have been snide and uncomprehending – this should not happen. After all, one's writing in English. Madness. Total madness. But one pushes on' (1990). He'd always been drawn to the theme of a decline and fall, of Valhalla collapsing in flames, and his heroes, too, are defeated and are superceded. ('He seems, dear dear, to have been somewhat incontinent in his sleep. Gracious, the weaknesses of the great!' we are told of Enderby's end.) Victor Crabbe is drowned, at the conclusion of *Beds in the East*, but nobody is much interested – as the people of the borough aren't, either, in George Crabbe's *Peter Grimes*, when the anti-hero gets into difficulties at sea. His long day has waned into a kind of inconsequential suicide.* What concerns the community is the forthcoming Independence

* As Malaya, to Burgess, comes to be seen through its languages, its babble of tongues – Chinese, Urdu, Bengali, Persian, Hindi, Arabic, Tamil, Sanskrit, Malay itself – the characters in *A Malayan Trilogy* come to be seen through the literature that they themselves have read. The self-reflexive allusiveness is a form of incest: fiction feeds from fiction. *The Enemy in the Blanket* promotes Crabbe to a headmastership in Negeri Dahaga – a province only tenuously yoked 'to the kindly pressure of the British'. Crabbe's prototype is the Duke in *Measure for Measure*, a sublunary god whose power is failing; a god, says Burgess, 'whom all men might touch'. Fenella casts herself as a heroine from Jacobean tragedy, glamorising her plight in terms of 'that play of adultery and jealousy . . . that play with the unironic title of *A Woman Killed with Kindness*'. She still, however, will not think of Malaya as anything other than primitive: 'Things were all too simple.' The society in

Day – which to Burgess meant that Malaya was to be subjugated by yet another power, America. Syed Omar gets given a left-hand drive white van and 'on this van was painted a picture of an eagle shaking claws with a tiger, symbolic of new friendship between peoples'. Burgess had written a *Sinfoni Melayu*, which from what I can gather was Elgar plus bongo-bongo drums and xylophones, and in the novel he fathers it upon Robert Loo ('a young Chinese composer of genius'), who promptly destroys it and instead, when he goes to see the officers at the United States Information Service, claims that what he produces is 'a lot of the better class of film music'.

Empires rise, fall, and strike back. There is a cycle of ruin and change – and Burgess is alert to the mythical dimensions of this. Crabbe – and the British in the East whom he represents – are as otiose as the Wotan of *Götterdämmerung*, who does not even trouble to appear in the opera and who sits in Valhalla waiting to be destroyed: 'The Western sky put on a Bayreuth montage of Valhalla,' we are told. The image has become a step more degraded. No longer are the British even idle Wotans; they are demoted to embodying a theatrical performance of an idle Wotan, their power now a chimerical allusion (and illusion). The Empire is a stage representation of a sinking star. The differing races revert to their tribes. Nationalism means xenophobia – the destruction of former colonial services and residences, the return of jungle and scrub, the rivers choked with weed. There is murder, arson, corruption, inefficiency, despotism and economic collapse. As Burgess wrote in the summer of 1957, 'Work, frankly, has been hell.' At Kota Bharu, they were trying to implement a new teacher-training scheme with hopelessly inadequate material and Burgess's own minimum lecturing programme was running at over twenty man-hours per week. 'This is one of the earlier fruits of Independence. It's a good thing we're leaving,

---

Thomas Heywood's drama, 'reflected a civilization a thousand times more complex'. Fenella departs from the tropics for London, and Crabbe later hears that she becomes a distinguished poet and lecturer – much in demand as an authority about Malaya.

Fenella's moody generalising and simplifying unfortunately affects Burgess's own tone. Crabbe's name was not poked fun at before; now it is mocked frequently. Dining with Talbot, the District Education Officer, we catch: '"I always have a couple of baked crabs." "Yes," said Crabbe.' Talbot confuses Crabbe with Bishop and then unravels the associative reasoning beneath his mistake: 'Let me see. Yes. Bishop was an eighteenth-century drink. Dr Johnson was very fond of it. And you use crab-apples for making lamb's wool. That, you'll remember, was an Elizabethan drink. "When roasted crabs hiss in the bowl." . . . Are you any relation to the poet?' To which Crabbe responds, 'Distant. But my grandmother was a Grimes.'

We find this excessive because it is intrusive. The information does not volley forth from character or context but from the overstocked aviary inside Burgess's head.

because really there's no other work to do which the Malayans are likely to appreciate. The Malays are now cocky, the Herrenvolk, and the other races, having hated the British for being here, and now hating them for leaving. But what to do now, I just don't know.' The heat was intense, the monsoon refused to break, odd diseases abounded, the rivers dried up, the water was undrinkable. 'One is perpetually bathed in sweat, and the night brings no relief.' In Hardy's novels, thunderstorms or meteorological disquiet in the natural world symbolise agitation at the human level, and so it is with Burgess and Lynne, who were covered with heavy grey clouds. At Kuala Kangsar, his interest in the local language and people 'did not make me popular', and when he passes an examination, 'This made me hated.' He loathes his superior, Jimmy Howell, because the headmaster prefers recording popular songs to listening to Japanese language tapes. ('I did not think this funny,' says Burgess, sounding like Augustus Carp, who is always accusing his neighbours of culpable carelessness.) At Kota Bharu, their servant, Mat bin Salleh, fills the house with twenty-five cats, a cockerel and an otter, and, to Burgess's alarm, allows the Tamil magician Mr Pathan across the threshold. ('A magician, I had read, should never receive hospitality: it put you somehow in his power.') There's so much drinking in the evenings and at weekends, no wonder he and Lynne see ghouls and demons in the night and in the forest. What with the triple gins and an affair with a Punjabi police corporal, conducted in full view on the veranda under the revolving ceiling fan, Lynne was going mental. She so looked forward to their leave in 1957. She boxed up their possessions and sent them off to be stored at her widowed father's house at Aylestone, near Leicester (*Beds in the East* is dedicated 'To Edward Jones, Esq., M.Sc.'), whither he'd retired to be near his other daughter, Hazel, whose husband was the headmaster of the local primary school. Hazel played Lynne a tape-recording of her mother's farewell speech, a ghoulish incident that would provide the dénouement for *Beard's Roman Women*. The nearby town of Enderby, where Burgess was to fulminate at the sight of the post-austerity English 'tearing into beef and lapping up cream ices', gave the name to our man's crapulous poet.

Burgess later seemed to forget that he and Lynne had wanted to be done with the East and to come home. ('I revert to ignorant Tennyson's view,' he said. 'Better fifty years of Europe than a cycle of Cathay.') In his memoirs he maintains that when he revisited Britain he hated the place and felt a stranger. 'The mess of post-war England,' he moaned codgerishly in 1987, 'all television, fornication, and a rising generation given to rock music and violence.' Thirty years previously, I think it is fair to say, his howls and execrations suggest somebody who resents being left out, who wanted to be part of the excitement. Espresso and cappuccino, Teddy Boys and layabouts. 'There was a new laxness about. I did not like this hedonistic Britain,' he frowned in *Little Wilson and Big God*. He reminds me of Davidson, the zealous missionary in Maugham's story 'Rain',* who says that the most difficult part of his work is trying 'to instil into the natives the sense of sin', and who dedicated his energies, during a fortnight of enforced idleness in Pago-Pago, to haranguing and berating the cheerful prostitute, Sadie Thompson. ('He'll wear himself out. He doesn't know what it is to spare himself.') The twist in the tale is that when, after his intense praying and Bible-thumping sessions, the wrathful Davidson is found to have cut his own throat, it's because he succumbed to sexual temptation, to passion. This is Burgess, a majestic spoilsport, who craves the very sensations he condemns. The spirit was released only once, and then not in his work (or life) but Kubrick's – in Malcolm McDowell's performance as Alex in *A Clockwork Orange*.† Despite what the liberal intelligentsia argued at the time, that the film is a critique of mindless violence and not a celebration of it – it is a celebration of it. Violence is the only element in the entire one hundred and thirty-six minutes that's handled with style or panache, and it is McDowell, a dandy in his bowler hat and single false eyelash, wielding a gigantic ceramic phallus, or putting the boot in with glee, whose personal energy holds the movie together. He's a sexy little Satan – a sulky piece of rough trade. His body is pale and faintly translucent, like marble – and as with marble, there isn't an inside, there's no emotion. He's a creature of basic drives and conditionings, whether purely cruel, at the start, or completely nauseated, after his treatment. He gives off a chill glow and he's the rebellious and demonic counterforce to Burgess the weak-eyed motherless swot who thought that being a bookworm would get him anywhere. 'You know how placid I

* To be found in *The Complete Short Stories*, Volume One (1951), and filmed as *Sadie Thompson* (1928), with Gloria Swanson and Lionel Barrymore, *Rain* (1932), with Joan Crawford and Walter Huston, and *Miss Sadie Thompson* (1954), with Rita Hayworth and José Ferrer.

† And it is McDowell's performance which is the one that reverberates. Phil Daniels, in the Royal Shakespeare Company's stage adaptation (1990), played Alex as a cockney weasel, a whiplash Bill Sikes, and quite lacked the potent sadomasochistic eroticism – which, in fact, McDowell brought to all his roles, from *If* to *Caligula*, before his pretty-boy looks went and he was condemned to playing villains in straight-to-video television movies that turn up on Channel 5.

normally was,' Burgess exclaimed to Kathleen Winfield, after sending her a note asking if she had such a thing as a Turkish phrasebook lying around. 'I now find myself ready to insult strangers, fight with anybody, or sink into a deeply depressive state corresponding with the preceding manic one.' There being fat chance of anyone in such a volatile mood getting another job at Banbury Grammar School, and as nobody was keen on giving him a reference, and though he'd told people non-prophetically, 'It's satisfying to know that one needn't ever go East again: that duty has been fulfilled,' the only job he could land was as an instructor at the Omar Ali Saifuddin College, Brunei. I myself have been to Brunei. No wonder the Sultan's family spend as much time as possible at the Dorchester or the Beverly Hills Hotel with the houris and the three-star Martell.

Who cared about Brunei until Shell mined for oil in 1929? It was a trading post situated in a swamp. The natives went in for sago production, boat-making, cloth-weaving, slave auctions and piracy. The White Rajah of Sarawak's protection bankrupted the Sultan and in 1888 the enclave came under the control of the British, who already occupied next-door Sabah, or British North Borneo as it was then called. The region as a whole generated timber, tobacco, rubber, camphor and seed pearls. The British North Borneo Co. was chartered in 1881. A governor was appointed by the Company with the approval of the Colonial Secretary, and a Court of Directors met in London. I loved what nineteenth-century vestiges I could find, the mouldering colonial bungalows and municipal buildings of crumbling white stucco, the Edwardian museums with mahogany and glass cabinets filled with fossils, taxidermised fauna, and terrifying native artefacts like scalping knives and rite-of-passage genitalia attachments and adornments. Brunei is an Islamic state (you can't do this, you can't do that), and though we hear so much about the gas and oil revenues and the lavish spendings of the royal family (polo ponies, race horses, fleets of aeroplanes and custom-made motor cars being the least of it), the population live in hovels on stilts above the mud flats and raw pollution. 'Brunei itself,' Burgess was to say, like Hamlet complaining about Denmark, 'was a kind of prison, walled in by sea and jungle.' How apt, therefore, for his antic, increasingly frenzied disposition. He and Lynne were put up in various Public Works Department shacks where the furniture was home to munching termites – he shook his fist at the State Treasurer who, as chairman of the housing committee, had failed to find the Burgesses anything better, but did they deserve anything better? There were endless parties over at their place, with Tamil civil servants, Iban dog-catchers, Dayak headshrinkers and Chinese hitmen making such a racket that complaints were made to the British Resident in Kuching, the ruling official who had authority over the expatriate officers in Brunei. Burgess claimed that he was summoned to see this functionary because he was to be rebuked for calling the country 'an unhappy place at an unhappy time'; in fact the drunkenness and noise was again a cover for snitching, sniffing and snooping and Burgess had been purposefully inciting political comment from his neighbours. The rest of Malaya may have had to fade away to the melancholy strains of Tennyson or Wagner, all sunsets, rainbow bridges and sweet sorrow, and the Empire could no doubt learn to live without the income from rubber (Dunlop tyres, school erasers, contraceptives), but the windfall from oil was in a different league, and Sultan Omar Ali Saifuddin was to remain at the helm, and let's not worry about niceties like democracy. With the assistance of British gurkha troops from Singapore, political dissidents were deported, and though, after the one and only parliamentary election, fifty-four of the fifty-five seats were won by the opposition Brunei People's Party, the upshot was that the constitution was suspended and the country became an autocratic monarchy. The fear, for the British, was that Indonesia, the former Dutch East Indies, which ruled the bulk of the giant island of Borneo, would absorb the territory, with a little help behind the scenes from sundry superpowers; and indeed Britain was responsible for Brunei's foreign and defence policies and played a key role in its affairs up until full independence in 1984.

During his spells in Sarawak, visiting the Residency in Kuching, Burgess claimed he once spent the night in an Iban longhouse impregnating the chief's daughters. 'The Ibans waved me off with smiles of gratitude . . . I sometimes think of the child I may have fathered . . . I hope I have given something to the East.' Now, I have travelled the length and breadth of Borneo, shooting up and down the Skrang River and the Rejang River in wooden canoes, and poking my nose in and out of many an Iban longhouse, where I placated tribal elders with my Hornbill Dance and willingness to buy crates of crappy ethnic carvings, and I have yet to find, hiding in the jungle, any whey-faced Burgess clones interspersing blowpipe lessons and headshrinking class with James Joyce recitals and lectures on how to pronounce *omnifutuant.** Incest is an orphan's mad fantasy; scattering seed and founding dynasties is the megalomaniac's or

* *Adj.* All-fucking: 'He was probably an omnifutuant swine who could do it with anything.' *Earthly Powers* (p. 96).

the impotent cuckold's. *Nothing Like the Sun* concludes with the idea that the Dark Lady of the Sonnets returned to her homeland, pregnant with Shakespeare's child ('A gift from him, was it not?'); and the fantasy is made flesh by Napoleon, whom Burgess called a 'fertility god, a wandering Priapus . . . A great man was expected to scatter bastards abroad.' Is that what Burgess thought he was doing in Borneo – or what, rather, in his dreams he'd like us to believe he'd been doing? Napoleon, whom Burgess otherwise says was (as it were) weaponless, nevertheless needed to surround himself with family. 'He wants to have everything in the family,' a character explains in *Napoleon Symphony*. 'He'll bring in more sisters and cousins and try to have us married to them . . . Family everywhere . . . The clan, so to speak.' The nepotism is a self-protective strategy, a hedge against disloyalty. None of Napoleon's family exists for him as individuals – it's all the fantasy of loneliness; power and control without responsibility. Which appears to be Burgess's own stance. Other people had less and less reality, particularly Lynne. Where Burgess got into fights with broken bottles (easy to find all over the lawn), and was picked up by the police, who'd wait for him outside bars, Lynne, not to be outdone, was bitten by a monkey, caught sand-fly fever, and started to get the shakes. Rabies? No, delirium tremens. If Burgess sounds irresponsible over the Boys from Borneo – the Iban-cross-Mancunian-cross-Irish Catholic-cross-cannibals – he'd wish us to credit he fathered, his off-handedness over Lynne, as she descended, lonely and pitiable, into cirrhosis – well, he deserved to be eaten up with guilt. Except that when he tells us he's 'black with guilt', he's being very self-enclosed or self-pitying; he savours it, actually, because sin and failure tone up his relations with God. As a Catholic, he'd feel he could communicate with God better if things were going badly. Whether this is symptomatic of his solipsism or callousness, I just don't know. If he couldn't see that he was responsible for her, what's to be said? Perhaps, like the way he shouted at the Malay waitresses because they couldn't follow his phrasebook fumblings, he simply wasn't very bright – the view Carlyle uniquely held, incidentally, about Napoleon, whom he judged to be a diminutive dictator, a comic quack.

The mystery really is why Lynne allowed herself to be dragged back East, from Leicester to Brunei. First, where else had she to go? Her mother was dead. She didn't get on with her sister. Her father had remarried 'a local widow of no education but a powerful thirst for stout', which suggests that Maggie Dwyer had been reincarnated. There was nobody left in Wales whom she knew – and, apart from a long weekend in Abergavenny, in 1965, when Burgess refused to sleep with her ('I could take no pleasure in a body that had once been as sweet as cinnamon but was now being wrecked through drink'), she was not to visit the place again. Her erstwhile paramours, along with the confidence she'd shown in London, during the war, had vanished. When she was beaten during the blackout it was her positiveness that had been killed. Now she didn't mind being doomed. Secondly, why would she want to leave Burgess particularly? His sexual infidelities were the inventions of later years – there was no cause for bitter jealousy at the time. He'd done no wrong. For, though he'd portray himself in his memoirs and in interviews as savage and selfish, I think John Wilson was more various than that – much nicer, in fact. Burgess did his utmost to depict himself as prickly, quarrelsome, bellicose, frequently drunk, filled with rancour; he's so masculine and provocative. Yet this is a performance. Who isn't hell to live with? Biographers and critics always take it for granted that their subjects are busy expressing themselves, in every thought and word and deed. But what if that isn't always true? Burgess, I think, spent his career concealing himself, hugging his secrets and being magnificently evasive; and what, in later years, when the great and admired cultural icon, Anthony Burgess, had quite overpowered the historical identity of John Wilson, was the biggest secret he wanted to conceal and the consequences of which evade? That he'd loved Lynne, with all his heart, nobly and ludicrously, and Liana was never to know. This would account, at least in part, for his shut face, his nerviness and tension. It was the face of a man who'd had more disappointment and frustration in his life than excitement and contentment. They were strangely married – but what makes a marriage? In the midst of reviewing Susan Cheever's *Home Before Dark*,* he threw in this long quotation from the book under discussion:

> They [Susan Cheever's parents] married in March of 1941, and they stayed married for more than 40 years . . . Why they chose to remain faithful to the final vows of the marriage ceremony is more or less a mystery. They certainly didn't remain faithful to each other. Sometimes they made each other so miserable . . . that their divorce would have been a relief. Maybe it was habit that kept them together, maybe it was perversity, maybe it was love – a kind of love so different from what we mean by love these days that there should be another word.

* *Observer*, 3 February 1985.

Burgess makes no comment (merely saying of John Cheever that, 'if the marriage held, little else did'); but it is Susan Cheever (b. 1943) whose idea of love is dilute and provisional. Her father's generation, which was Burgess's, didn't expect love to alter when it alteration found; and there is a depth to true love that can embrace hate, or anyway active dislike. Strindberg, 'the great demented Swede', as Burgess called him in *English Literature*, the survey he wrote for students in the tropics, is all about this. His plays 'are terrifying experiences'.

Burgess never attempted psychological depth in his work. Indeed, he's alarmingly physical, or even physiological, and external: the pox, stomach cramps, puking, bad teeth, boils and generalised delirium. It's malarial, feverish prose. Everything is described from a distance. Towards the end of his sojourn in Brunei, he threw a party to launch the central panel in the triptych, *The Enemy in the Blanket* (at his reception there were the usual smashed-bottle fights, drawn knives and polyglot imprecations as a prelude to a hearing before the magistrate – or so he maintained); and, amongst the novel's eccentrics is Rupert Hardman, a disfigured war hero and a failed lawyer. He takes over from Nabby Adams the role of wastrel: 'He owed three months' rent for Club chambers in Kuala Lumpur. He owed for his car. He owed various hotel bills. He had spent too much money on a girl called Enid.' Hardman is willing even to marry a Muslim woman to get her dowry – and Nabby Adams once considered this, but only as very much a last, risible resort. Che Normah is a creature of robust appetite who has already outlived two husbands. She 'was lavish in build, with great thighs but a slim waist, bathycolpous as an Homeric heroine'. The community is a cartoon; but it is an erudite cartoon. The potentate – called the Abang – awaits his cue to flee into exile. He will sweep 'into the opulent suites of Ritzes and Waldorfs': a cowardly, indolent Ulysses baring 'a hairy chest to a milder sun by a snakeless sea'. The Abang is condemned to wander from one salubrious oasis to the next. Hardman interprets crepuscular British rule through Wagner – and it's to him that Burgess gives the smug line: 'The white man's day is coming to an end. *Götterdämmerung* . . .' The idea that twilight is falling on gods is at comic variance from what happens. It transpires that the chef, Ah Wing, has been sending packages of leftover food up into the jungle for Communist terrorists. He knows nothing of politics. His motive is that a family member needs feeding. (How simple it was for Burgess to dissimulate his own secret agent activities.) Rumours spread that it is Crabbe who is a prominent Communist, 'here to help

Communist terrorists in the jungle under the disguise of teaching the little ones of Malaya'.

Though it is the frequent fate of a Burgess hero to be mistrusted – to be considered as other than he is; that the front he presents to the world is a camouflage; and that beneath one layer of clothes is another layer of clothes (Enderby is always accidentally bedecked in other people's apparel; the spy, Hillier, in *Tremor of Intent* is first a typewriter salesman, then he borrows the uniform of a Russian soldier – telling Clara as he garbs himself, 'I hope you'll see me dress again . . . But in future in my own clothes' – and by the end he is costumed in the soutane of a Catholic priest); though, as I say, there is this frantic fancy dress and they are harassed and rendered paranoid, Burgess's heroes and picaros do not yield to the corrupt touch. They are unadjustable. They remain the same person. (They are pre-formed – like the hardness or rigidity of persons in a painting.) Despite the wicked societies they are sent into, neither Enderby, nor Spindrift, nor Denham, nor Lydgate, nor Howarth, nor Tristram, nor Paul, nor WS, nor Hillier, nor Toomey modulate into badness. How could they? They possess no consciousness, no natural psychology; and therefore nothing can be absorbed by them. Picaros: they are innocent and innocuous, changing only sartorially. The exception is that they are allowed to grow old – as in *Beds in the East*: 'Crabbe looked at himself: hair now riding back from his forehead, the beginnings of a jowl. He looked down at his paunch.'

By the same token, if, in his books (or in his life), you are bad, you'll remain bad. There's no sympathy or forgiveness. His stepmother, Major Meldrum, Geoffrey Grigson: they have a cartoon villainy. Occasionally, however, the object of the lampoon would try to fight back. Gwen Bustin thought there was more to her character than sexual hysteria, for example; and where, in *The Enemy in the Blanket*, there is the failed lawyer who callously marries a Malay widow for her money, in Alor Setar, the state capital of Kedah, there'd been a European solicitor, called Gilbert Naughton Christie, who suffered very badly as a result of being identified with Rupert Hardman. Burgess was served with a writ. Christie won his defamation suit in Malaya and the book was withdrawn there – but it continued to be published overseas, as the plaintiff could not afford to run the case in another jurisdiction. So winning the case in Kuala Lumpur had little practical effect on restoring his reputation. He'd been a fighter pilot during the war and had been badly burned. His face had been operated upon and given skin grafts, but it was unnaturally white and shiny. To pillory him seemed – and still seems – small-minded and malicious. Was it simply that Burgess had a desk-bound writer's fear and envy of action heroes? If so, it was a trait he shared with Hemingway, about whom, in 1978, he made a television documentary, *Grace Under Pressure* ('I was sixty-one, Hemingway's own age when he put the gun in his mouth'). Tony Cash, the director, filmed Burgess at large in Chicago, Salt Lake City, Kansas City, Key West and Ketchum, Idaho. The commentary derived from the recently published and beautifully designed (by Thames and Hudson) book, *Ernest Hemingway and His World*, where, as with his jaunty biographies of Joyce, Shakespeare or Lawrence, it is the autobiographical undercurrent which I find myself attending to – thus: 'He had to turn himself into a Homeric myth, which meant posing and lying, treating life as fiction, and while some of his lies are transparent (like the one about sleeping with Mata Hari) it is difficult to sort out the self-made legend from a reality less glamorous, though still glamorous enough.' Burgess on Hemingway is Burgess on Burgess, the roaring fellow in bars, on board ship, or strolling through the markets that are piled high with coconuts, tumps of spice, cones of chopped chillies, rows of freshwater prawns and everything so green, such a gash of vermilion, here's the lushness of Eden before the Fall.

So it went. 'When you were a younger man,' said Anthony Clare, 'you faced the possibility that you had very little time left.' To which Burgess answered, 'Yes, in 1959. I had been working in Brunei, which, as you know, is in North Borneo. When I was there it was evident that Brunei was going to be a very rich state because of the massive oil deposits which were being developed and exploited. But I found the life there very frustrating, chiefly because the Malays were aware that money was coming in from oil, so they didn't have to work, they didn't have to learn. I was trying to teach them and they didn't want to be taught. There were other elements of frustration. My first wife was drinking heavily and making a nuisance of herself. We were always being picked up by the police, and so on. I was drinking in the house itself about a bottle of gin a day and about half a bottle of gin in bars or on the town. I was drinking too much . . .' When he lay down on the classroom floor and refused to go on with the lesson about the Boston Tea Party (an eruption over Britain's attempt to tax its colonies – as pertinent in 1959 as in 1773), here was a nervous breakdown or brain-fever caused by the strain he'd imposed on himself – that is to say, brandy and ginger beer poisoning, a bad diet and severe constipation. He couldn't shit straight for years, as a matter of fact. He was convinced, up to nine years after leaving Brunei, that he had a gastric ulcer and that it would kill him. 'Then one night I came home late, and I was hungry, and I decided I might as well go that way. So I ate cold pork and pickled onions and cold potatoes and cabbage and cold Christmas pudding and a bottle of iced claret. The next morning I felt wonderful, not a rumble. No more complaints now.' The dyspepsia is denoted in the Enderby novels: 'PFFFRRRUMMMP . . . Perrrrrp . . . Querpkprrmp . . .' If we add to these trumpetings Bloom's 'Prrprr . . . Fff. Oo. Rrpr . . . Pprrpffrrppfff', we'd have a wind duet. Is farting oneself to death a possibility known to medical science? It was in Borneo that Enderby had flamed into being, in an appropriately lavatorial fashion. 'One day, in early 1959, delirious with sandfly fever, I opened the door of the bathroom in my bungalow and was not altogether surprised to see a middle-aged man seated on the toilet writing what appeared to be poetry. The febrile vision lasted less than a second, but the impossible personage stayed with me . . .' What a change that makes from the usual pink elephants or six-foot tall white rabbit. Nevertheless, the heat and humidity of the tropics, sexual tension, blocked bowels, grumbling guts, a palpitating liver, enervation, hallucinations, and a recurrent nightmare about a pregnant cobra coming to attack him whilst he was trying to teach: he convinced himself he had an inoperable cerebral tumour.

He was invalided back to London, First Class, and given the best possible treatment at the Sultan of Brunei's expense. Burgess responded with a novel, *Devil of a State*, so damning about Brunei and its people that the publishers delayed bringing it out for two years and made the author relocate the story, all about corruption and the building of a mosque, in East Africa.* It's about another Englishman abroad – or the same Englishman

* Did the relocation ever fool people? (Brunei is Naraka, or 'Hell' in Arabic.) So much of the novel is about the building and ceremonial opening of the mosque, 'a crouched leprous sun-beast, bulbous, pillared, the golden dome the spike-nippled breast of a supine giant Amazon', that anybody with half a mind on the material would have recognised this as the Omar Ali Saifuddin Mosque in Bandar Seri Begawan, or Brunei Town, which is one of the biggest and most lavish edifices in South-East Asia, and which was constructed in 1958. The great golden dome speckled with Venetian mosaics, the walls and floors made from sheets of Italian marble, the stained-glass windows and chandeliers: Burgess describes all of this. He saw it go up. The liveliest characters in the novel are Paolo and Nando Tasca – lively, that is, in the way that Dastardly and Muttley are lively. The Italians have come to cut and lay the marble in the mosque, and they are cartoon Latins prone to violent rages and equally violent reconciliations. The father browbeats the son and Burgess overplays the Joyceanisms (Paolo moans his way 'through the back-streets like Stephen Dedalus' – why? Paolo is mumbling to himself in an incoherent rage; Joyce's character is super-articulate and wanders purposefully, pacing out his arguments); and the primal Oedipal battle is intrusive. ('The crime of parricide was of all crimes punished with the most severity.'

abroad, for Burgess's affectless heroes are all one. Lydgate is frantically trying to find out where he is to be billeted; and when this is known, who has the key to the door? Lydgate is hot, sweaty, seedy, like the country in which he is locked out. (It is Greene-land.) Being one of Burgess's petty colonial officials, he is also an exile within the country of exile; he is set apart from the native society as well as from his native land. He resembles

---

Maybe it was – but Nando is a brute and deserves being stood up to; and in any event there is no murder attempt.)

Paolo, as a symbol of filial disobedience, installs himself in a minaret like a defiant saint. To rub in Burgess's theme, the narrative voice mimics a pastiche sermon and the young signore is indicted for having committed in his heart already the parricidal act: 'anger toward thy father, who gave thee thy being, who maintained and schooled thee, who is now the means to enlighten thy mind further through travel in outlandish parts, this is of all sins perhaps the most reprehensible, being the most unnatural'. The grandiosity of the style sits comically – inappropriately – on the activities it describes. Yet the way the rude mechanicals represent mythical schisms is a common Burgess-cum-Joycean technique. Ill-behaved and quarrelsome as the Italians are – there's some operatic dispute over a stolen or broken watch – even the Caliph gives them special treatment if they work efficiently on the mosque: if they save time. Despite their violence, alleged rapes and whoring, the Tascas are immune from the sharp Dunian law. Paolo is only immune from paternalistic law, however, when he conceives the mad plan of legging it up the tower of the incomplete building. Hiding there – having levitated, again a parodic Stephen Dedalus, now an Icarus – rebels advertise him as an exemplum of 'the fight against tyrannical oppression'. What Nando thinks is 'unfilial treachery', though, is actually self-assertion, the need to grow up and be freed from paternal yokes. Paolo's is a necessary battle; Burgess's engaging thug in *A Clockwork Orange* knows this (at least, in the full-text version). Dreaming about having a son, Alex includes in his dream an expectation of rebellion from the malenky googoogooing malchickiwick, 'and I would not be able to really stop him'. Even Enderby, whose hatred for his stepmother is an open secret, is reminded of sublimated strife between himself and his father. The witch, in *Enderby Outside*, disconcerts him by saying that, 'Your father let you down by marrying your stepmother . . .' She quotes at the worried poet lines he cannot recall as being his own:

> Anciently the man who showed
> Hate to his father with the sword
> Was bundled up in a coarse sack
> With a frantic ape to tear his back.

'That's somebody else,' pleads Enderby. 'Honestly, it's not me.' An appendix to the novel ('Some uncollected early poems by F. X. Enderby,' edited by one A.B.) suggests that this is probably juvenilia – unless it comes from a vanity publication of Rawcliffe's called *Balls and Talk* – of which no copies exist. Has the Muse confused Enderby with his poetasting enemy and rival? The alleged title of this volume gooses the remembrance of Jove castrating Cronos and the subsequent derivations of primeval disaffiliation. When Paolo's sulky, frightened exhibition is elevated into a mythical one, and the elevation is represented by the ascent up the mosque, he is compared with St Simon Stylites and is mentioned throughout the world in political speeches as 'the prisoner in the tower yelling for justice'. Dunia's own rebels see him as exemplifying the search for independence from imperial rule. Theirs, too, is a necessary battle. Fathers have to be usurped for sons to rise, and this is the underlying lesson of Burgess's jungle books.

Oedipus in his growing appreciation of his homelessness and crushing loneliness: Lydgate 'acknowledgeth neither kin nor birthplace'. Dominic de Cruz and David Lloyd-Evans, in a cabaret for the Caliph, perform what can be regarded as a choral commentary about the exile's plight:

I'm not in a state of grace,
It's something far far loonier.
I'm a terrible case; see the lines on my face?
I'm in the State of Dunia.

I'm not in a state of sin.
Indeed, I'd very much soonier.
I'm getting so thin; what a mess I'm in.
I'm in the State of Dunia.

Lydgate's reaction to his dilemmas is to keep moving on, as rootless as the deposed Oedipus; pushed out of doors, he's 'the eternal wanderer', in Burgess's phrase. And that's Burgess himself, too. He was to become an ungrateful, bitter man – notwithstanding which *Devil of a State*, dedicated to Graham Greene, was a Book Society choice for 1961 and set him off on the road to riches. Why has it never been made into a film? It would be at least as rib-tickling as the Boulting Brothers' *Carlton-Browne of the F.O.* (starring Terry-Thomas about the island of Gallardia, a British protectorate forgotten for half a century) or Dick Clement and Ian La Frenais's *Water* (starring Michael Caine – about the island of Cascara,* an overlooked British colony in the Caribbean).

Perhaps the effort it took to conceal his real personality and reinvent himself wore him out? As Burgess took over, and became famous, the old John Wilson friends were dropped. He made out that he'd become a recluse. 'Lynne and I are plodding on in our quiet way, keeping our fingers crossed about our health, and perhaps assuming a pattern of senile behaviour rather prematurely,' he said in December 1960, aged forty-three. Lynne, having become notorious in her own right on the literary party circuit for bashing critics with her handbag or, if she was holding too many drinks, for going at people's earlobes with her bared teeth, had eight more years left before her liver finally exploded. Burgess sat down at his typewriter every day and persevered with his novels and journalism. He stopped going out and drank Spanish wine and cider at home. Once he

* *Cascara* is a generic stimulant laxative drug, no doubt stocked up on by Enderby (and Burgess), along with the canisters of bicarbonate of soda.

was back from the tropics, not much of similar intensity or newness was to happen afterwards. He married an obscure Italian translator, Liana Macellari, who in the manner of Hardy's Florence Dugdale or Eliot's Valerie Fletcher, became the traditional author's dragon who'd guard him. (When he got himself into difficulties with a foreign language at a press conference she'd create a diversion by leaping on top of a chair and shouting, 'Let him speak! Let him speak! Why must there be censorship? Why are you afraid of what he has to say?') He shut himself away in his tax exile (Malta, Monaco, Lugano), cranking out unproduced movie scripts or Zeffirelli's biblical screenplays, pretending to know about everything, turning himself into a highly functional machine, deliberate, industrious, and a little bit dead.

V

Renaissance Man 1960–68

'The clubfoot playing the piano? That's Dudley. André has promised to give us some jazz later.'

'He'll be bringing Mia? Or is she with Frank?'

'He still sees Ava, you know, at Ennismore Gardens.'

'Peter! You kill me with that French detective. Ustinov must be green. Britt! Snowflake! Your English is really coming along.'

'I've been to Berlitz.'

'You can't possibly be in love with Halliwell, Joe.'

'Shame Cyril didn't like your book, Wolf. How is the pottery selling? Is that shop in Piccadilly expensive to rent?'

'I don't know if Raymond Mortimer is still alive, but John Mortimer is going to have to decide if he is a lawyer or a playwright. Penelope's at home with the children – heaps of them. She said there was semen on his wig. He told the judge it was bird shit.'

'No, that's not the blind one. That's Naipaul. You're thinking of Ved Mehta, so don't go pulling funny faces.'

'What do you think of Boxer's gravure magazine for Roy?'

'Bailey's got his Rolleiflex and f/2.5 lens out over there, with Terence Stamp. Lives in Albany.'

'Yes, but what about when his looks go?'

'Sassoon thinks hairdressing is the new art form.'

'The fox-hunting man?'

'Vidal – wrote *Myra Breckenridge*.'

'The most moving moment was when all the docklands' cranes dipped in salute.'

'Is Hancock always so lugubrious? Cheers! He'd be good as Enderby.'

'Greene gets a fortune from Hollywood, it's how he affords all those houses. Paris, Antibes, Capri, Berkhamsted.'

'F-f-f-f-fuck! Larry wants me on the inside pissing out.'

'Take it from me, your genius is to be on the outside pissing in. Well, it's your funeral.'

'I loved seeing Robert and Maggie – are they like Benedick and Beatrice at home?'

'Don't hide that Elephant and Castle accent, Michael, it's your fortune. Lieutenant Gonville Bromhead was Welsh, anyway – from Brecon.'

'The Krays are Establishment now, since Boothby took them up. Never trust a man who wears a bow tie.'

'You won't be seeing much of Driberg. He's got the waiters queuing up for blow jobs in the Gents, that's why they can't find any ice.'

'One of Betjeman's enthusiasms, like the Euston Arch. He met him in Melbourne. Thinks he can make a living as a cabaret artiste – dresses up as an Australian housewife.'

'Peter Cook thinks he's funny, anyway.'

'What I love about Julie Christie is she's slightly unkempt, as if she's only just got out of bed. I don't think she was brought up in Rillington Place, it's quite a common name.'

'Agatha Mallowan's on a dig in Persia.'

'There'll never be a better Miss Marple than Margaret Rutherford.'

'Her uncle split the atom.'

'Prockter's more of an artist than David.'

'Blake does album covers now.'

'That's not a surgical instrument, it's Arne Jacobsen's prototype cutlery for St Catz.'

'Tippett's going to conduct *The Knot Garden* wearing a kaftan.'

'Do Keith and Willis expect us not to have read our Thurber?'

'Germaine's got a job at Warwick. She'd fuck a frog if it stopped hopping, I'm told.'

'Have you heard Ronnie Scott play the tenor sax? Or George Melly talk about Magritte?'

'Lionel's going to do Robin Hood as *Twang!* Or was it the blitz as *Blitz!* Or the New Testament as *Christ!*'

'Oh Christ! Here come the Burgesses! He wants to do Shakespeare as *Will!* He's so venerable. She's so lewd. She bit a chunk out of James Michie's ear last week. Took exception to the way he thinks he's a poet. Her teeth met, he said. He put in an expenses claim to Heinemann for iodine and sticking plaster. Writers' wives, eh?'

You would need a director with the flair of a Fellini, or with the skill to organise ensemble acting and rope up everybody with throat mikes like Robert Altman, if you wanted to capture and convey a party in London's high bohemia during the Age of Aquarius. (I myself transcribed the above dialogue from the ether.) Sandy Shaw . . . Jean Muir . . . Twiggy . . . Mandy Rice Davies . . . Christine Keeler . . . Jean Shrimpton . . . Bridget Riley . . . Mary Quant ('Mary Quant OBE invented the miniskirt, which really consists of showing more leg,' ruminated Burgess. 'It's something we've always wanted; and she, probably through insensitivity, was able to push it through and was surprised at the response because she wasn't sensitive enough to expect a response. I don't know. These are not major achievements. The major achievements of a race are great architecture,* great music, great literature. These are not coming out of England as far as I can see at the moment') . . . Centrepoint . . . The Kinks . . . The Stones . . . The Who . . . The Beatles ('Hogg considered that he had never in his whole life heard anything so, at the same time, obscene, noisy and insipid,' according to *Enderby Outside*) . . . Apple . . . Biba . . . *Blow Up* . . . *The Severed Head* . . . *Zulu* . . . *Oh! Calcutta!* . . . *Darling* . . . *Murder Ahoy!* . . . *A Bigger Splash* . . . *Goodbye Baby and Amen* . . . The dense blue smoke; the fashion-model boys and girls; the hair lacquer and high heels; people flitting one to the other with the buoyancy of humming birds; rivals cutting in; editors at large ('Ah, Tom Maschler! He's a nasty piece of work really – used to be my publisher but I couldn't stand him. My then-agent [Deborah Rogers? Peter Janson-Smith?] was deeply in love with Tom Maschler'); the lavish receptions for Time-Life Inc. at Bruton

* To my knowledge, he never wrote much about buildings. This is because he couldn't see them – though not only because he was so short-sighted. He refused to wear spectacles because the 'diopters of correction', as he called them, made the world 'gross and over-sharp'; but the main cause and effect of his myopia was moral rather than having to do particularly with vanity and eccentricity. The blurring, the mistiness, the haze – it's related to his solipsism. As he said in 1968, when his attention was drawn to his shabby furniture and squalid domestic arrangements, 'I'm very short-sighted. I can't really see things like that except when they occasionally swim into focus. I hate these phony Hampstead people who worry about things like that.' So – an appreciation of beautiful objects, from ashtrays to Chartres Cathedral, was spurious? Ostentatious? Gaudi's unfinished church of the Sagrada Familia in Barcelona, however, he didn't mind, because 'he approached the work rather in the manner of a novelist, letting new notions flower as he proceeded'. And anyway, it didn't look like a building but like confectionery, 'with slender pinnacles of crisp sugar'. As for modern architecture, such as James Stirling's Engineering Building at Leicester University, which had been featured in a *Monitor* documentary he reviewed for the *Listener*, he didn't like it: 'the necessary excitement of the concept is so rarely conveyed in the finished product' – a perfect description, by the way, of *MF* or *Napoleon Symphony*.

Street, where Burgess picked up a commission to write a book on New York ('New York is a displaced persons' camp. I – a writer always in exile, an Englishman whose grandmother was a Finnegan from Tipperary, a sort of mediaevalist in a mechanised world – am a paradigm of displacement'), for Reuters at the Reform Club, where Paul Elek nabbed him to write accompanying texts for the big picture books, *The Coaching Days of England* and *The Age of the Grand Tour*,* or the habitual BBC hospitality at Broadcasting House;† we could even add the launch for *Nothing Like the Sun*, at 15–16 Queen Street, Mayfair, on 20 April 1964 (6–8 p.m.); or Royal Society of Literature functions, such as the one where Enderby receives and rejects the Goodby Gold Medal for poetry and Shem Macnamara 'had breathed on Hogg-Enderby, bafflingly (for no banquet would serve, because of the known redolence of onions, onions) onions';‡ and what about the invitation to meet for a drink in the Café Royal downstairs bar ('on the left as you go on') on Wednesday 22 January 1964 ('about 6 o'clock') to celebrate his and Lynne's twenty-second wedding anniversary? – all of these formed yet another world, to be added to the catalogue that included family, schoolmates, fellow students, the armed

* These are amongst the hardest of Burgess's books to find, only very occasionally surfacing in antiquarian booksellers' catalogues, e.g. '*The Age of the Grand Tour*. Yellow cloth boards, very slightly marked on lower edge; 20" x 13½"; decorated end-papers; four full-page reproductions of engravings; 19 coloured illustrations and many black and white illustrations in text. A fine copy. £50. *The Coaching Days of England*. Original cloth/gilt. Large oblong folio. Superb full-size coloured plates & many other illustrations. Fine in dustwrapper. £70.' The Axbridge Bookshop, Axbridge, Somerset. April 1986.

†

2nd December 1966

Dear Anthony Burgess,

I am planning an hour-long live conversation to be called 'A Bond Dishonoured', which will be broadcast on Wednesday 25th January from 9.5 to 10.5 in the Third Programme, and I am very much hoping that you will be willing to take part. The idea is to discuss the spy cult in literature, television and the cinema with particular reference to the Bond novels. The chairman will be T. G. Rosenthal, and the other speakers I am inviting include Kingsley Amis, Bernard Bergonzi, William Plomer, Eric Rhode and David Sylvester. The whole thing will be intended as something quite different from the usual pre-recorded conversation between 3 or 4 speakers, and we should start the evening with a meal and drinks at Broadcasting House at 7.30 p.m. and then move straight down to the studio and into the conversation with the minimum of preliminaries.

I look forward to hearing from you, and very much hope that you will be interested in taking part.

Yours sincerely,
George MacBeth
Producer, Talks Department

‡ After the opening of *Earthly Powers*, this was Burgess's most renowned sentence, which he'd quote on chat shows and which would be quoted to or at him by ingratiating journalists, e.g. the egregious John Walsh.

forces, teachers, colonial officers, barmen, passport controllers, policemen, publicans, shop assistants, old people, children, cats, dogs and guinea pigs, which Burgess could despise and where he could be on maximum resentment alert. 'I don't like literary people,' he declared in 1968. 'They want to know how much you're earning. Or they're jealous. Or they think *you* ought to be jealous. Or they want to talk about your work.' Five years later, the aversion had become pathological. 'Why should one meet writers?' he asked. 'What does one talk about? They only talk about money. I try to keep out of the way of writers and literary cocktail parties . . . In England, unless a writer is also a friend of the Royal Family, like Sir John Betjeman, or a scientist, like Lord Snow, he is pretty well cut off. If you live in a village as I did [Etchingham – though he and Lynne also bought 'what I laughingly call my London residence', 24 Glebe Street, Chiswick, in January 1964], you have no place in the stratification. You are not a retired admiral. You are not a stockbroker. You are not a farmer. You are not a shopkeeper. What the hell are you? You are not the vicar, the rector. You're just somebody there that is a writer. Consequently, you have no real place in the community.'

But Burgess never wanted to be a pillar of the community. Once he'd stopped producing amateur theatricals in Adderbury, he never again moved in a group; and it suited him to pretend there'd been a conspiracy to exclude him. In 1953, Philip Toynbee, Burgess's predecessor as chief book reviewer at the *Observer*, founded the Wednesday Club, which met regularly for lunch at Bertorelli's restaurant in Charlotte Street. Regular attendees included Francis Haskell, Burgess's collaborator on *The Age of the Grand Tour*, Peter Quennell, V. S. Pritchett, Cecil Day-Lewis, A. Alvarez, George Melly, Colin Haycraft, Terence Kilmartin and A. J. Ayer; the literary editors, publishers and authors of the hour. This society was superseded by or overlapped with what became known (jocularly) as the Fascist Lunches, also held at Bertorelli's, which was where you'd find Kingsley Amis, Robert Conquest, John Braine and Anthony Powell holding forth over the rounds of grappa. They'd tried to welcome Burgess as a coeval – and he did call in once or twice, on his fortnightly trips to Chancery Lane to sell his review copies for half price. 'We like to drink, we can afford cigars,' he said of a Bertorelli's luncheon. It couldn't last. He was convinced it was 'an insider's ring to fix reputations and debase his own', said Peter Vansittart. He was convinced everybody was ganging up against him. How wholly typical of Burgess to decline to participate, and then allege it was, all along, a secret plot to bring about his downfall. He wants us to believe he is always mocked and disbelieved; he is so full of condescension.

Peter Vansittart also recalled Burgess as a muttering, manic figure, carrying on at a *Spectator* party, with a full free drink in each hand, wholly unwilling to mix with his fellow guests: 'The usual crowd, the political, the arty, the fake. Very few of them any good. I seldom expect to find anyone worth meeting and certainly won't do so today. These mobs are simply blatant cabals . . . the Homintern . . . the Arts Council Mafia . . . the so-called elite . . . a whacking great hunk of the third rate . . . Golding is over-rated, Anthony Powell belauded by powerful friends, Angus Wilson is past his best, and Kingsley Amis was only established by careful management by Gollancz. The novel needs a convulsion – *A Clockwork Orange* combines originality of language, theme, invention with an appeal to the more strictly literate and erudite . . . I've never quite believed that Graham Greene much likes me . . . *Finnegans Wake* is actually an easy read once you've grasped the intention and method. Too many are expecting what Joyce had no interest in giving. My book on Joyce – that shop off Gower Street should have it. It's well-stocked on classics – will give you all the necessary clues. It's a delusion to imagine that the straight, however straight, cannot be made straighter . . . I don't advise you to try your hand at a novel. There's very little left in it now for anyone without a tie-up with a studio. Too many old nancies and young ponces still clutter the field, together with alleged wits and smart columnists who think they can create the Creator. I speak as something of a Catholic. Only genius can shatter them and re-establish the Novel proper. You need a vocabulary of at least a hundred thousand words and must understand six major languages and thirty-seven dialects.' Vansittart's last sight of Burgess was of the great man arguing with the cloakroom attendant over the tip expected for retrieving his rain coat – a vignette which rings as horribly true as the rest of the reminiscence.*

He was a character (or comedian) in several senses. Burgess so wanted to achieve recognition, he exaggerated what he thought being a writer entailed (the linguistic fluency, the proud apartness, being the kind of chap who was a wandering outlaw in his own dark mind); everything about him was magniloquent, enhanced, and yet instead of endorsing his own

* Nigel Lawson, the editor of the *Spectator* during these years, recalls Burgess rather differently. The Defence wishes to include the following character-witness statement in the record: 'I inherited Burgess as a book reviewer, and formed such a high opinion of his writing that I took him out to lunch somewhere in Soho and persuaded him to become an occasional essayist in the front half of the paper, where he scintillated. We became regular, if infrequent, lunching companions thereafter. His wit, erudition, and the largest (and always correctly used) vocabulary of anyone I have ever known, expressed in his inimitable fruity voice, were a constant delight. I suppose it helped that he was on much the same wavelength as me in political terms.'

legend, when his words started rolling from their mountain springs, it was boastful vainglorious nonsense. He was thus a target for Auberon Waugh,* who decided to compare and contrast him with Alex Comfort, whose *The Joy of Sex* 'gave us an optimism, a degree of hope, for which we should all be grateful':†

Last Literary Lion

While Dr Comfort was working on his first major treatise, *Sex in Society* (1963), his contemporary Anthony Burgess was completing *A Clockwork Orange* (1962). Burgess definitely has a claim to be considered as one of the last literary lions of the 20th century. The film of *A Clockwork Orange* (1972), which appeared a few months before Dr Comfort's magnum opus, *The Joy of Sex*, has just been revived in London [spring 2000].

When I went on Wednesday, the small theatre in the Odeon, Marble Arch, was less than half full, but I urge anyone with a strong enough stomach to go and see it.

Never can two writers have had a more different message for the world. Where Comfort preached the hope of joy and renewal through sex, Burgess argues that sex is no more than one other outlet for the selfishness, brutality, power mania and often sadism which are the main characteristics of human nature.

They were both wrong, of course. But while we welcome Comfort's wishful agenda, knowing it to be false, we are reluctant to consider

* Like architecture or settees, which he also couldn't see, Burgess was wilfully blind about Auberon Waugh, refusing to credit that such a person existed. Graham Greene, however, 'assures me that Evelyn Waugh does have a son. He *does* exist. [He] is a bloody idiot.' It all started when Waugh *fils* had described Burgess's recipe for Lancashire hotpot as 'disgusting', which was quite enough to trigger off all the cradle Catholic *vs.* converts, North *vs.* South, Manchester University *vs.* Oxford paranoia. It was Waugh, nevertheless, who gave the Address at Burgess's memorial service. This was fitting. Waugh, a brilliant satirist, could see the joke in Burgess – that Burgess was to all intents and purposes a parody of a great writer, rather than a great writer. 'Burgess never became pompous or took himself seriously,' Waugh told the congregation. 'When we thought of the murder of James Bulger, we weren't that surprised. We had been there already in *A Clockwork Orange*.' Waugh disagreed that it was lack of appreciation that had driven Burgess abroad. 'We don't honour writers in Britain and we are better for that,' he concluded.

Did Bron ever give a finer performance – that of a man who is in the wrong church, eulogising the wrong person, and pretending not to notice? It is comparable with Barry Humphries mistaking the stage door and Dame Edna Everage appearing unannounced in Act III of *The Seagull* with Joan Plowright.

† That's what the cavemen in *Quest for Fire* look like, I suddenly realise: the bearded man in *The Joy of Sex* illustrations.

> Burgess's more austere proposals. I feel we should confront both. There may be no ultimate truth about human nature, but it must be part of a writer's job to search for it. Otherwise we are left with Jackie Collins and Anthony Powell.

The austerity, which Waugh is correct to distinguish in him (for a Catholic, Burgess was as puritanical and censorious as the Plymouth Brethren), connects directly with the egotism. Burgess was not a generous man, financially, spiritually or morally. John Tydeman once saw Liana, on her husband's behalf, fill her handbag with leftover cakes from tea at the Savoy. 'Would you like some more of those?' he asked dryly. 'Yes,' she said, so another serving of sandwiches and pastries was scooped into the reticule. A scavenger at parties, and adept at running up other people's tabs, Burgess was the first to complain if he was ever expected to buy a drink. One of his objections against the British Council was that it had 'used me to entertain, at my own expense, visiting Hungarian and Finnish writers who soaked up whisky as parched earth rain'; and the problem with teaching at American campuses was 'standing drinks of the students'. He didn't believe in charitable giving because 'only in this fat society, where nobody is really starving, can people talk about compassion' – which was evidently a quality to be overcome. He'd never (for the sake of argument) hand over food or cash to the poor of Calcutta 'because [you] will be killed' in the ensuing riot. He refused to pay any tax in support of 'the kind of welfare state which makes England's particular prosperity, its niceness, as milk-and-watery as possible'.

So far, so parsimonious. There was no hospitality in his nature – for hospitality presupposes that you are looking out for the well-being of the other fellow, and in Burgess's eyes, if the other fellow couldn't be induced to melt away, then he was a walk-on in the conspiracy to undermine him. Burgess might appear friendly, but this didn't imply trust. As Robert Robinson told me, 'I gave him a lift home from the BBC Television Centre, but he made me drop him some way from his house. "No, no," I said, "no hurry. I can take you to your door." "Has it occurred to you," he said, "that I might not want you to see where I live?"' The same thing happened when Robinson conducted an interview with him in Monaco for *The Book Programme* in 1976 ('I have been abroad in the army, I have been abroad in Malaya, and it was quite natural to go abroad again, permanently', he said during the broadcast) – Burgess wouldn't permit Robinson and his crew anywhere near his flat. Was this a legacy of the intelligence services, to move in an atmosphere of secrecy and caution? Did he fear a jungle ambush? Or perhaps he was afraid Robert Robinson would expect him to put the kettle on?*

Beleaguered, irritable and chippy, his guard was always up. This is the Burgess whom Kingsley Amis has fun with in *Difficulties with Girls*, where he appears as Iain Gowrie Guthrie, a demented poet who lives in Rome and Tuscany ('I'm just over for the launch'), rather than Rome and Bracciano, and whose chief characteristic is his social ineptitude. In a dramatisation of the scene in Amis's *Memoirs* where Burgess, having materialised at his side at the Book Fair in Olympia, and even though they'd not met for nineteen years, instantly launched into the technicalities of a bad review he'd once received, Gowrie, likewise, takes issue with remarks made in 1931 or published in a now defunct magazine back in March 1940: 'I had rather hoped you'd trot out a compliment or two even if it went against the grain, just for old times' sake, as you might say.' Gowrie's way of speaking 'seemingly to everybody within hearing', is Burgess's way of not listening; and 'On hearing Iain Gowrie Guthrie's name and taking in his appearance [the other party guests] had immediately resigned [themselves] to not being able to make out a word he said' – which happens to be a monologue on the meaning of art or some such generalised vapidity. 'He was rather awful,' people agree afterwards. 'Have you read any of his poetry? It must be really terribly bad, isn't it? . . . A man like that couldn't write a word that's any good at all.'

Whilst, needless to say, the social being we glimpse – fleetingly, dartingly – is the writer off-duty, and the real work is done (and the real life is lived) in solitude, with pens and paper, nevertheless, did the phantom tumour or quasi-death from terminal flatulence affect his brain, I wonder? It wasn't simply that John Wilson went to Malaya and came back as Anthony Burgess; or that Malaya had made him; or that Malaya was a test of character; or that there was a Faustian pact and he'd been getting ill and was now well – the point is more that the importance to him of not belonging wasn't jubilant, heroic, Homeric, Byronic. It made him cramped and anxious. Leaving aside his intellectual arrogance, his conviction that he was being snubbed or degraded or mocked,† what his

* 'Thou hast betrayed thy secret, as a bird betrays her nest, by striving to conceal it.' Longfellow – quoted in a CIA training manual.

† How would Burgess have taken the news that it was at the editor, Nigel Lawson's, insistence that he was in the *Spectator* every week throughout the sixties? Hilary Spurling, the Literary Editor (1964–70), aware that Burgess was appearing in every other newspaper and magazine in existence, pleaded for a Burgess-Free Zone. But she was overruled. If there was a conspiracy it was a conspiracy to keep Burgess generously employed.

behaviour illustrates is how out of step he was, how his inability to attach himself to people diminished him as a writer. He just wasn't curious or receptive enough. Sexual relationships, for example: Enderby can't understand them, nor does he want them; and this comes from Burgess. With all that happened to him in his life, you expect to experience more from his work. Yet you don't. Instead of psychology or philosophy, what we get is anatomy. Burgess always reminds me of the sanatorium doctor in *The Magic Mountain* talking about his mistress: 'I know her under the skin – subcutaneously, you see: blood pressure, tissue tension, lymphatic circulation; all that sort of thing.' Some metaphysician or other once said that character is fate. With Burgess, character is disease. He reduces the human person to physical events – to bodily parts and nerve impulses, excitable glands and reflexes – to bruised shins, broken teeth, retchings and vomitings. His interest in language – it's an investigation of our snuffles and grunts, of the noises we make, the roars, snarls and splutters. This can be both exhilarating and nauseating. It gives his work the clarity of feverishness, the warpedness of migraine. The diseases of the nervous system, the palpitations, the defective digestion – which Burgess suffered from; which his characters suffer from: the mental and the corporeal are intertwined, thus promulgating a prose style based upon infection and grief, discomfiture and hysteria. (Discomfiture, certainly, is the chief feeling his work induces in me now.)

'I was told that I had a tumour on the brain, I might not last more than a year,' was how he chose to summarise the events of 1959. During the early years of my researches, I met Sir Roger Bannister, the Master of Pembroke College. Though best-known as the athlete who, in May 1954, first ran the mile in under four minutes, he enters this story as the neurologist assigned by the Hospital for Tropical Diseases, Bloomsbury, who trepanned the Burgess cranium. He appears, by the way, in *The Doctor Is Sick* as Dr Railton (banister = rails), who gives Edwin his brain scans and intelligence tests. ('We'll push on. We'll find out what's wrong. We'll send you out of here a fit man.') With all due concern for medical confidentiality – Burgess still being alive when I made my enquiries – and choosing his words very carefully, what Sir Roger told me was that what a patient chooses to believe about his condition is not necessarily the same thing as what his consultants had told him about his condition – or, indeed, had expected or intended him to believe about his condition. Which seems to me a cautious and polite way of indicating that the inoperable cerebral tumour yarn and the terminal twelve-month tale were figments better evaluated by Bruno Bettelheim, the director of the Sonia Shankman

Orthogenic School at the University of Chicago, who in *The Uses of Enchantment* argues that the way a person transcends 'feeling neglected, rejected, degraded' is by the 'repeated hearing of a fairy story' – and Burgess, motherless and sisterless, was to add the dramatic collapse in Borneo to *his* repertoire of fairy stories, as designed to make him seem vulnerable and impregnable, cursed and blessed, like a hero off the pages of *The Boys' Magazine*, which he had enjoyed as a child for its serial about the end of the world.

Burgess was imprecise about his hospital stay, except when he once said (in 1968), 'I went through all the Ben Casey tests, and there's nothing wrong with me now.' *Ben Casey* was a medical drama, made in America, and produced by Bing Crosby, which starred Vince Edwards as the hirsute neurosurgeon at the County General Hospital, a maverick and a genius who flouted the rules to save his patients. Others in the long-running programme were Franchot Tone, one of Joan Crawford's husbands (as Dr Daniel Niles Freeland), Sam Jaffe, the High Lama in *Lost Horizon* (as the venerable Dr David Zorba), and Stella Stevens (as Jane Hancock, a coma victim). It ran on ITV until 1967 and I wouldn't put it past Burgess to have augmented his experiences from what he picked up in a soap. Whatever – the energy or industriousness he found during that first season back from the East, when he revamped old projects and translated recent events into new ones, was never to flag. After that pseudo-terminal diagnosis of his, you could say that this was the longest death-bed speech in history – thirty-odd years. It certainly explains why illness was a recurrent preoccupation in his work. Burgess's diseases, however, owe nothing to the 'becoming frailty' which Henry James thought tuberculosis, for example, engendered. Rather, there is a more dramatic disablement, caused by violence to the body or mechanised assault upon the brain. The body, indeed, is not an object of beauty: Enderby, for instance, is 'a rheumatic robot in pyjamas'; and Howard Shirley, in *One Hand Clapping*, 'had one of those very unusual brains like a camera', which makes him prone to biliousness and headaches. Commonly, in Burgess, the men are atrophied spectators, lumps or dopes to whom things happen, and his women are the vamps who glide into their field of vision and upset their blood pressure, or worse. Shakespeare's genius is ascribed to the spirochete, in *Nothing Like the Sun*: the clap is his legacy from the Dark Lady. Freud's career, and the rise and fall of psychoanalysis, with its morbid fascination with infant sexuality, parallels the growth of his cancer – the tumour being a malign pregnancy – in *The End of the World News*. Wards like chambers of torture; operating theatres hidden in the cellarage; brutal nurses; evil doctors; plugs and coils which convert the private thoughts inside our heads into computer readings upon a screen: these are frequent props in Burgess's fiction.

Which takes us to beds. Burgess is less interested in beds and sleep as euphemisms for sex or repose than in a bed as the place you're not allowed to get out of in a hospital. Beds find us at our most helpless: we are vulnerable to the prying spatulas and probings of the medics, the gallivanting of illness, and the delirious scenarios of our sleep. It is a prison cell. One of his most self-revealing texts is *On Going to Bed*, where coffins, cots and nocturnal horrors are zestfully compared. We lie flat in bed, we are laid out in our coffins. Not only is our posture the same, but to an infant, being sent to bed is the equivalent of being sentenced to death. 'Every child going to his bedroom knows that the laws of the night are on the side of the irrational, and the irrational is usually malignant.' Burgess says that he awakes more exhausted than when he fell asleep – no doubt because he has dreamt fully orchestrated symphonies and a couple of triple-decker novels. The bed, to him, is an engine to sap our energies. So what is the significance of *Beds in the East* and *The Enemy in the Blanket*? Why, the British Empire is drifting towards sleep, and Victor Crabbe's marriage founders upon a bed. First, he has an affair with a Malay girl, and later he flirts with Anne Talbot, the wife of another Englishman. (Victor is his own worst enemy once in action under the blanket.) Anne Talbot is a further appearance in Burgess's work of Moyna Morris – Talbot = Morris = types of automobile. Was anybody fooled by this crude cipher?

Burgess woke up from Borneo to the plight of Edwin in *The Doctor Is Sick*. Physicians want to uncap the hero's head and poke out the uninvited cancerous guest it contains. As in Malaya, the hospital is populated with orderlies with miscellaneous racial origins. Despite the exile's fond dream of England, and its purity or immaculateness, Burgess writes of London as though it contains more undesirable aliens than abroad. Its stock has been adulterated. Like life in the hospital, all it does is disorientate and depersonalise. Dr Railton gives Edwin tests it is impossible for him to pass. Everything he says will be interpreted in the light of the belief that his brain is malfunctioning. Tranquillised and bemused, Edwin is transported to a spotless dungeon to be prodded and poked as if he is already lifeless tissue. As he is given a lumbar puncture, he thinks away the pain with etymological free association: 'Hysterikos, hysteria, the womb. But Freud had shown that there was no connection.' The night before the operation, his head is shaved and he is then given a mirror. Sitting up in bed he sees 'little Edwin in his pram'. The fear and loathing of hospital is babifying him, making him return, despite Freud, to the infant's condition of helplessness and suspended animation. Awaking later out of a drugged sleep, he decides to escape. He'd rather spend a few months as himself than a prolonged period as an altered personality, 'a mere chunk of morphology'. Edwin finds his clothes in an unlocked locker and strolls out into the night, and the alleged neurophysiological ailment gives Burgess the excuse to present England as a society in which spirits generally are depressed. From spiritual Malay to malaise is the route which has been followed. The world into which Edwin escapes is unkempt, fallen, full of folly.

The Right to an Answer is a further anatomy of the Britain Burgess personally found waiting for him on his return from the East. All Denham can find is an epical mess: 'It's a mess that's made by having too much freedom.' What a diseased organism society has become! 'But the horror is that you can get used to rancid food, used to a mess.' This is an ugly book. When Burgess describes squalor he does not do so with the relish of a Jacobean dramatist but with a mesmerised concentration that is most old-maidish; and once more, characters spend an inordinate amount of time boozing and scoffing like pigs. Instead of reading improving books or learning to sing plainchant, or whatever it might be that meets with Burgess's approval, people watch television – and television sets glow through the curtains of every front parlour. The church spire at least attempts to assert traditional values by interrupting reception – 'Like the transmitter of some enemy country, it jammed and scrambled and confused' – but religion, like everything else, is on the wane; and when Burgess casts himself as a social diagnostician, he comes close to being like a malevolent doctor who upbraids his patients for having the cheek to be ill. If his characters have brought their vapid lives upon themselves, then in that case they deserve them. In Burgess, disease is punitive – your tumours or your rashes are created by neurosis and sin, and in *Devil of a State*, which looks at clashes of culture, at warring organisms, the song for the caliph's birthday contains the verse:

> I'm not in a state of health –
>   My voice gets croakier and croonier.
> But I've picked up some wealth, and I've
>   done it by stealth
> For I'm in the State of Dunia.

The linchpin pun is on *state*. It is a psychophysical condition, a theological position and a geopolitical place. At its wobbling pivot is another of Burgess's menopausal heroes, Lydgate (George Eliot's defeated doctor in *Middlemarch*), for whom the rest of the world is never more than a sequence of irritants which'll impinge upon him. Enderby is the culmination of this weariness – the poet who, like Churchill in the Graham Sutherland portrait, can only compose when straining at stool (the *opera omnia* of Burgess's enemy Geoffrey Grigson are on hand as the toilet paper), and who wants to be an observer of life rather than a participant. Yet the impotence of his personality is a parable of art's – or anyway Burgess's – uselessness. He is nothing, to use Joyce's phrase, but an old artificer. For, at best, a writer is a confidence trickster nobody needs to believe. And even if the public will accept his works, do they take *him* seriously? Does the writer desperately want to be loved, or does he shirk affection? Are Burgess's heroes exiles because they are moody and sulky, or do they want to set themselves apart in Romantic isolation? We know the answer, of course: they are self-deceiving pricks. But Burgess himself evades the issue by condemning Enderby to madness, getting him to take the name Hogg and find employment as a barman. In Burgess's 'new England' (the late fifties and early sixties) the pub and the after-hours drinking club are the same as any Hogarthian gin palace – places to get stupefied, like Lynne.

In *A Clockwork Orange* bars are now curtained cubicles, where glasses of milk spiked with narcotics are to be consumed in private.* Alex is a venomous child – how long weaned? It is not so much that he would not grow up as he does not need to. He is moneyed, articulate and preternaturally experienced. This tiny hoodlum sees Burgess play a variation on his theme of art's powerlessness, when the beauty of Beethoven does not promote joy and peace in its listener, but evil. Off Alex goes for a night of violence. One thing Burgess will never allow art, and that is the strength people had always assumed it possessed – its particular charms that can soothe the savage breast. On the contrary, symphonies and what-not are morally neutral, he seems to say: art's effect on the individual is up to the individual. It is thus no business of the government to compel prisoners to undergo 'reclamation treatment', where their brains are being tinkered with to replace the wickedness with good. This is to be transformed into a machine: a clockwork orange wanting only to please, programmed to puke if ever a

* It's one of the ingenious props in Kubrick's film – the alabaster, fetishistic Allen Jones mannequins which dispense *moloko* from their *groody*.

whisper of unpleasantness crosses one's mind. It is a blessing, therefore, that Burgess was not given a taste of his own medicine, for all he is capable of seeing or responding to are nastiness and misery. When he returned from the East as an ostensible invalid ('I was very fit and active. This made me doubt the truth of the diagnosis,' he said in 1971), all he noticed was society's sickness, 'the modern world with its paltry perversions and cheap mockeries of values'. He didn't like local restaurants or home cooking. He liked neither grand hotels nor modest boarding houses. There's simply no pleasing Burgess. He doesn't like other people – the British, for not knowing about the rest of the world, for their cultural isolation; he doesn't like people who have travelled, because they are jaundiced. He doesn't like the young, because they are disrespectful, nor the old, for their prejudices. No wonder, in *The Wanting Seed*, he gets everybody killed. The books he published in the sixties have a common theme – they are about Burgess's anger and destructiveness and impotence. Their common tone – that of a man who minds everything, who is worn down by everything. The funny yokels or comical cockneys in the pub; the damp and cold (especially after Malaya); the stinking outside lavatories; over-boiled greens; unmade beds; greasy plates; municipal gaslight; sticks of celery in a water jug: it all symbolises the moribund mood, it all intensified his misanthropy.

Such is his degree of self-preoccupation, I'm not sure if Burgess has much human relevance. You'll recall that P. H. Newby mentioned James's story *The Lesson of the Master*. Youngish, on-the-make Paul Overt goes to stay with the distinguished Henry St George, and they have this exchange:

> '. . . I've spent many years out of England, in different places abroad.'
>
> 'Well, please don't do it anymore. You must do England – there's such a lot of it.'
>
> 'Do you mean I must write about it?' – and Paul struck the note of the listening candour of a child.
>
> 'Of course you must. And tremendously well, do you mind? [. . .] Hang "abroad"! Stay at home and do things here – do subjects we can measure.'

Overt fails to heed the advice, and old Henry St George gets his girl, too. He believes himself to be so special and clever, vanishing to remote spots, but it puts people off him. (Did Bruce Chatwin know this story?) Anyway, in relation to Burgess, now that he was writing about England, in *The Right to an Answer*, *The Doctor Is Sick*, *One Hand Clapping* and *Inside*

Mr Enderby, or in the resuscitated (and then withdrawn) *The Worm and the Ring*, at least there is a definite geography (Leicester, London, Hove, Banbury); and there's a social reality, of post-war austerity and fifties food-stuffs, like reheated stew, bits of lard in paper, and 'a neglected chicken carcass . . . which would go well' (in one of 'thrifty Enderby's' disgusting casseroles). Yet something is still out of joint. There's still a sense of estrangement.

Burgess was prematurely old and cranky – it's a shock to learn that Alex is only meant to be fourteen; and Enderby: what is he? Fifty-five? In his sixties? He's in his forties. Burgess was always older than he seemed – and thus must have been born before his time, as an Edwardian. Despite, however, his affinity with Elgar and Chesterton, and the rest of the pack, there's no autumnal nostalgia, regret or resignation in his work. When coal fires, hot-water bottles, linoleum floorings, stewed tea, burnt toast, stinking passageways, wearing vests, and commercial travellers in horrible hotel rooms get mentioned in his books, this isn't part of a vanishing social culture – a culture visualised by Keith Vaughan, Robert Colquhoun and Robert MacBryde; it's more to do with his own inconsolable sense of humiliation and failure. Even the anger of Osborne's Jimmy Porter ('Oh heavens, how I long for a little ordinary human enthusiasm. Just enthusiasm – that's all. I want to hear a warm, thrilling voice cry out Hallelujah! Hallelujah! I'm alive!') is on the side of life. The theatre was moving from the Binkie Beaumont and plummy Shaftesbury Avenue world to regional dialects, northern actors and playwrights; the Royal Court, Woodfall Films; Joan Plowright, Alan Bates, O'Toole, Finney – people who'd previously have played comic peasants. There was a class shift in the late fifties, to put them centre stage. Burgess should have been part of this, and wasn't. He continued to fight his lonely battle against the clubmen, army officers, well-born drifters and civilised eccentrics of Anthony Powell or the high-society gossips and snobs of Betjeman – and he's like one of those Japanese soldiers lost in Burma, unaware that the war is over. Often, in magazine profiles, he'd refer to 'Kingsley Amis, my friend and a superb novelist'; and in July 1957 he had told Kathleen Winfield from Kota Bharu that he'd read *Lucky Jim*, the seminal work of the day. They met a few times in the early sixties, but on each meeting Lynne's drunkenness spoiled the occasion – and in any case, 'It was as though Burgess was so far above the hurly-burly that he habitually occupied some private stratosphere,' Amis said, which was exactly Burgess's problem as a writer. Though they emerged as novelists in the same era, can it be possible to have found such opposed temperaments?* With Amis, you get the impression that he knows what he's talking about when it comes to girls; with Burgess the notes struck seem false. Amis has noticed how women wear their hats, gloves and stockings – how girls, before youth was allowed its moment, quickly grew into their mothers. The rules of courtship are in *Lucky Jim* and the books that followed; he is alert to sexual and social shame, the fear of pregnancy and abortion. None of this is in Burgess – the behaviour of males and females to each other, how they are thinking and reacting from moment to moment, passes him by; yet this is the era when women statutorily weren't paid as much as men, and when all they were doomed to do was clean the house and raise the children. But then none of this involved Lynne, who was busy having slurred arguments in pubs.†

* The writer with whom Burgess could be said to have an affinity (five years his senior, yet he began publishing in the thirties) was Lawrence Durrell. 'For those Britons who had endured a dozen years of sweet-rationing, prose-nougat was the next best thing,' wrote John Sutherland in the *Sunday Times* (12 April 1998), when trying to account for Durrell's success. It seems pretty indigestible and innutritious now, the likes of *Justine* (1957), *Balthazar* (1958), *Mountolive* (1958) and *Clea* (1960), or the alarmingly entitled *Avignon Quincunx*, his final collection of five novels (1974–85). Indeed, it's hard to see what the appeal was – the dud and fuzzy aphorisms ('art, like life, is an open secret'); the sexual curiosity (the *Alexandria Quartet* was 'a sort of spiritual butcher's shop with girls on slabs'); the prose, which was like bad poetry, and all about beaches, olive groves, priapism; and the settings had a Thomas Cook glamour, e.g. Paris, Rhodes, Cyprus, Provence, Corfu, Belgrade. Durrell was idolised on the Continent, hired by Hollywood (to doctor the script of the Elizabeth Taylor *Cleopatra*), in demand at international conferences, and generally considered a genius. I think there was a lot of posturing, myself. He worked for the Foreign Office in Egypt and Greece, in low-grade espionage, and the Antrobus stories, mocking the Diplomatic Corps, have a touch of Enderby or Burgess's Malaya. He was also an obnoxious monkey of a man, an inattentive husband and father, whose life was a round of drunkenness and selfishness (he was always having to organise abortions for his mistresses); and one of his daughters, Sappho, committed suicide after accusing him of incest. 'I feel very threatened by the fact that my father is sleeping with women who are my age or younger. I feel he is committing a kind of mental incest,' the poor thing said. *The Alexandria Quartet* is a selection of *Ninety-Nine Novels*, and Burgess says: 'Anything can happen in Alexandria – pederasty, incest, all the convolutions of lust, all the varieties of betrayal.' Personally, when I want to be transported to a bewitching world of colour and light and exotic sensations, I'm happy with Elizabeth David. A study ought to be made of the influence of her food and drink books on the culture of the fifties. She might be the era's major artist.

† Jonathan Cecil reports that when he was a student at the London Academy of Music and Dramatic Art, he used to see Burgess drinking in the Earls Court Tavern. 'In his seedy raincoat he looked pure Patrick Hamilton, as did the rather blowsy woman with him (his wife?).' Hamilton was the author of *Gaslight*, in which Anton Walbrook systematically drives his wife (Diana Wynyard) insane; *Hangover Square*, in which an Edwardian composer becomes a homicidal maniac; and *Rope*, in which a pair of college students kill a friend and hide the body in a trunk for the hell of it. Hitchcock famously filmed the latter, in 1948. The other two evoke a ramshackle fogbound London, where every sight and sound is imbued with menace and suggestiveness, and Hamilton's work generally was about insidiousness. (He lived at K5, Albany, next to Toomey.)

From the way, as a child, he listened to Debussy on his crystal set, to his old age, learning Japanese, there are no instinctive feelings in Burgess. (He's always the conscious self-improver.) Where is the warmth? His hierarchical view of art – with the Joycean novel, almost too good for this world, at the pinnacle – meant that he denied himself the kick and pleasure of anything popular. (Anything popular is an erosion.) I can't think of any reference he made to sport. 'I sold my golf clubs twenty years ago,' he said in 1987, and as there were no courses in Chiswick in the sixties, did he actually own a set in the first place? He won a cricket bat as a child, which splintered. The pub piano playing, the *Cyrano* musical or the television mini-series on Moses and Christ – the reason they are appalling is that he can't stop reminding us of his exacting standards, his contempt and his affectations, shoving in jarring allusions to Stravinsky, Schoenberg and Hindemith, and though Maugham tells us in *The Moon and Sixpence* that, 'To my mind the most interesting thing in art is the personality of the artist; and if that is singular I am willing to excuse a thousand faults,' I do think it is possible to be such a braggart ('I used to teach my students a little Chinese. This was totally heretical. I also taught them a little about Arabic writing'), such a monstrous egotist ('I spoke up [at the Cannes Film Festival] on behalf of the dignity of the land of Racine and Molière and against the debasement of art'), that the personality replaces the art, and the art tells us nothing.

Burgess went to Malta; Amis purchased Lemmons, Hadley Common, Barnet, Hertfordshire, in November 1968. 'I forget how much it is costing,' said Burgess of this establishment. 'It's a hell of a lot of money. A house toward the end of the Piccadilly Line that has five bathrooms or something like that and twenty-seven acres. He's settling there; he's opting to settle in Britain. Well, he's very welcome to it. His way of writing certainly depends greatly on observation of the British scene, but I think my own novelistic future depends more and more on digging into the mythical roots, the mythical expression of human behaviour, rather than the naturalistic expression of what we see around us.' Not that Burgess was capable of seeing what was around him, or of listening, either. Amis could hear and convey the sounds we make – his letters to Larkin are masterpieces of comic mimicry and misspellings. ('Crzmuz is goan' be hairl, son'); and his book about language, *The King's English*, shows him to have been pin-sharp on matters of grammar and linguistics. The paradox with Burgess, in *Language Made Plain* and its ancillary texts, is how it is that he makes words uncommunicative. What's the point of sentences like: 'Twenty-five drawings of a clavigerous lion guarding a rather imbecilic teenage Britannia,' when *clavigerous* just means *guarding*? Or, 'Well, no, we are all septentrional here,' when *septentrional* means – fuck knows *what* it means? Burgess's theories about music and the novel, for example, show such concern for form, style and bravura treatment, that they suggest a man who has run out of content – who has nothing to say, who has no subject matter left (or at least none he dare address). 'Music will always swallow literature, grateful for it as a note-weaving pretext,' he said in 1988. 'Setting words, it will reduce them to sound without much semantic content.' Though his was a life of almost continuous writing, he lost faith in it. 'Really, writing is structure,' he told Lorna Sage in 1992. 'Meaning is a nuisance. Music is pure structure, and that pleases me.' The perpetrator of *MF* and *Napoleon Symphony*, with their rigid systems, was unrepentant. He believed himself to have evolved above and beyond the need to express any human concerns, such as our incongruities or psychological tensions; and his relentless pedantry kills any attempt at humour, too. His review of Amis's *The Old Devils*, in the *Observer* on 14 September 1986, mostly consisted of a paraphrase of the plot, and it is interesting how a Burgess rewrite of an Amis sentence bleeds away the tone, the irony, the comedy. First, Amis, then Burgess:

> The area had once been called Monmouthshire but because of a decision taken in London was now called Gwent, after an ancient Welsh kingdom or whatever it was that might have formerly existed there or thereabouts [. . .] They went outside and stood where a sign used to say Taxi and now said Taxi / *Tacsi* for the benefit of Welsh people who had never seen a letter X before.

> The appeal to ancient history is as factitious and embarrassing as the TAXI/TACSI sign outside Newport Station [*sic*], the Cymric transliteration is for Welshmen unfamiliar with the letter X.

> The section that really took it out of him was the actual donning of clothes, refined as this had been over the years, and its heaviest item was the opener, putting his socks on. At one time this had come after instead of before putting his underpants on, but he had noticed that that way round he kept tearing them with his toenails. Those toenails had in themselves become a disproportion in his life [. . .] These days cutting them was no joke at all [and] he settled on a garden seat under the rather fine flowering cherry [where] at least he could let the

paring fly free, and fly they bloody well did, especially the ones that came crunching off his big toes, which were massive enough and moved fast enough to have brought down a sparrow on the wing, though so far this had not occurred.

Peter Thomas is grossly fat and can only very rarely cut his toenails. When he does, he conducts the operation in the garden, where hallucal chunks of rock fly like bullets at the sparrows.

Hallucal? 'Hallux' is the anatomical word for big toe, which must have something to do with it; and in the review you may also find *allotrope*, *epigone* and *andromorph*. Despite the big words, though, Burgess's article is like a grammar-school pupil's précis; he's so busy with extrapolating things like the degradation and dilapidation of society as a whole, he's unwilling to admit that ageing and getting through the day, the unobtrusive pathos of life, all that's touching and absurd, are the things (in the Jamesian sense) that we can measure ourselves against – the rest is diffuseness and mannerism and why Burgess's books, when they go all mythological and grandiose, have an air of insubstantiality. It's his big themes, God and the Devil, and so forth, that made him small. But Amis and Burgess – am I comparing like with like? Am I complaining that the problem with a beer mug is that it's not a wine glass? Though they were both to become our senior novelists, both of them theatrically curmudgeonly, like a pair of warring elephant seals on an ice shelf in the Antarctic, they were lugubrious and indignant and cocksure in different ways. Amis at the dinner table was full of jokes, impersonations, paradoxes, anecdotes, expostulations. He didn't mind admitting a fondness for Dick Francis and James Bond – and in addition to *The James Bond Dossier* (1965) he wrote a Fleming pastiche, *Colonel Sun* (1968), under the pseudonym Robert Markham. Burgess also wrote about Bond quite frequently, in 1987 contributing an introduction to the novels ('What Fleming did was to dream of an espionage system far more dangerous and ingenious than reality allowed'); and in 1975, Cubby Broccoli and Guy Hamilton had him work on a script for *The Spy Who Loved Me* ('a horrid fascination drove me on'); and back in 1966, there had been *Tremor of Intent*; yet you don't feel he's enjoying himself very much. What he's doing is dismantling the machinery to see how a bestseller comes off, and realising he doesn't have it in him to be popular. Fleming 'concentrated on a fairly lowly genre and perfected it'; and when Burgess, in *Tremor of Intent*, has Hillier explain that 'all of us who are engaged in this sort of work – international intrigue, espionage, scarlet pimpernellianism, hired assassination – seek something deeper than what most people term life, meaning a pattern of simple gratifications', clearly he has taken this genre and misunderstood it.

Amis was good at repartee and at adjusting; Burgess at the dinner table gave lectures about language and literature, obscure books and out-of-the-way authors. Whilst impressive, how could one chip in?* When he met Benny Hill, he led the saucy comedian through a tutorial on *The Good Soldier Schweik*. The Lancashire accent long got rid of, it was difficult for him not to come across as a sneering know-all, blimpish, impersonal, didactic. This, too, is the effect of his books. They are contraptions. Their components are welded or riveted together and the robots he has for characters, who possess only basic drives and appetites, are incapable of emotional subtlety – there's no genuine love or suffering. Toomey's dewy-eyed love for Dr Shawcross is sentimental, Enderby's pursuit by women farcical, Alex's rampaging facile. The problem I have with *The Right to an Answer* is that there are three deaths at the end of the novel: the old father,

* Though the Oliver Wendell Holmes *The Autocrat of the Breakfast Table* act cut no ice with me, there were (and remain) other people who found it awe-inspiring. Here's Michael Ratcliffe, who, as Literary Editor of the *Observer* from 1990, knew Burgess at the haunted end of the day:

> During this time, he and Liliana lived mostly in Monte Carlo, so we discussed work pretty much every week on the phone. He was one of the few real star book-reviewers left, with an appetite for new subjects, however unexpected, and the great gift of transforming them into a rich, yet accessible, article for non-specialist readers. In this I think he was, above all, a true and great teacher. Copy came in on time; we never altered or cut without consultation because I soon became confident that he knew what he was saying, and why he was saying it the way he was. Coinages, neologisms etc. I would sometimes challenge and they would be patiently explained; on the rare occasions when I still wasn't convinced and thought they held up the flow and intake of a review, there would be regret, but no row, and they would go. If anything went wrong in the subbing or proofing, we were reproached more in sorrow than in anger the following Tuesday. Needless to say, neither he nor Liliana missed a thing. What I loved most about him as a reviewer was that there was almost nothing truly interesting that he wouldn't take on.
>
> We only met twice that I can remember. The first occasion was a birthday dinner organised by (I think) Hutchinson for literary editors and younger British writers, like William Boyd, who were Burgess-fans. Anthony was on stupendous form, and conducted what amounted to a riotous tutorial from the head of the table. The second time was at Dartington, where he gave the opening lecture at the first Ways With Words book festival, which the *Observer* then sponsored. He was clearly dying, and knew it, and racked by the most fearful cough; but what struck me at Dartington was that he had attained some kind of exhausted calm in order to complete all the projects he'd set out to do. I don't think he slept much in these last years. He was also (unlike some writers) exceptionally nice to all the kids acting as volunteers at the festival – as if time was now too pressing to be wasted on scenes. I never knew him in the main part of his career, but the Burgess I saw at the end was a man who was working – and he was always working – with an achieved kind of grace.

stuffed with curries; Winterbottom, who is shot; and Mr Raj, who blows his own brains out – and none of them means anything. They are cartoon deaths; it is all cartoon violence. For such a vaunted egg-head, Burgess's work is full of flippancy and short on human reach. He's solemn – yet shallow. His characters are to be seen 'neighing and barking at each other', in the last scene of *The Right to an Answer* – except that's how they always converse; the mood is frantic, desperate, cursory. Was it his medical experiences which gave his work this air of clinical briskness or detachment – e.g. the impetus of the skit format, the padded-out jokes, the formulaic structures? Given the amount of fear, death and disease in his life, he's never likeably vulnerable; he is meant to be forlorn, and prone to collapse, but nothing impeded the efficient thousand-words-a-day regime. His favourite film was Fritz Lang's *Metropolis*, and at the University of Iowa, in 1975, he accompanied a print of the original seventeen-reel version on the piano – 'the improvising of music to cinematic images,' he said ten years later, 'still seems to me one of the most desirable occupations it is possible to have'. In this German Expressionist masterpiece, set in the year 2000, and made in 1926, the mad scientist, Rotwang, creates an evil robotic double of the saintly Maria, each twin played by the metallic Brigitte Helm. A title pops up to explain his scheme: I HAVE CREATED A MACHINE IN THE IMAGE OF MAN, THAT NEVER TIRES OR MAKES A MISTAKE. Whilst I'm not suggesting that Burgess burst out of Wilson, his eyes wild and staring, in convoy with electrical flashes, dark liquids bubbling in the bottom of glass retorts, and fizzing neon lights, it is the case that Burgess was a physiological cybernaut, a soft grey automaton leaking a barrage of stale smoke. The fluency with language was his circuitry coolant, the typographical page a visual display screen.*

The way he constructs his books, the way his mind works, is like clockwork. Energy goes into the presentation of the set piece. In his essay in *Cities*, his description of the evolution of Rome is an analogy for his fiction: 'things are just added, and added again'. Adventures, in Burgess's

* 'I wish you to consider . . . that all the functions which I attribute to this machine, such as digestion, nutrition, respiration, waking and sleeping; the reception of light, sounds, odours, the impression of ideas in the organ of the common sense and imagination; the retention of these ideas in the memory; the interior movements of the appetites and passions; and finally the movements of all the external members; I desire . . . that you consider that these functions occur naturally in this machine solely by the disposition of its organs, not less than the movements of a clock.' Thus, Descartes – for whom a man is not less than the movements of a clock – and hence he's the originator (in the seventeenth century) of the clockwork orange concept.

novels, like Roman buildings, slot on to one another: hence the lengthening histories of Enderby or Napoleon, with torch held aloft, going 'from bivouac to bivouac to bivouac to bivouac to bivouac . . .' Adventures, in Burgess's novels, like Roman sites, build on top of one another like geological strata: hence the mythical abutments of *MF* or the encyclopaedic layerings of *Earthly Powers*. The legacy comes from the picaresque. The drawback with the inheritance is that in the rush onward and upward there is no leisure to penetrate inwards. Words whoosh and gallop by in a pitter-patter of speech, and what interior monologues can survive the din? When Enderby's biography uncoils, Burgess, the third-person narrator, speaks up on behalf of his fictional self, drowning out those occasions when private reminiscence may – just may – have been eavesdropped upon.* Only what is articulated out loud can count. In Burgess, the language most rubicund and full of fiery shapes subjugates all. '"All finished," Enderby said. "*Finito*." But there must be a better Spanish word than that. *Consommado*? It sounded soupish. "*Consummatum*," he said, pushing down the roots.' He takes society, literally, at its word.

Burgess doesn't watch society – he watches language. In *Les Structures élémentaires de la parenté*, Lévi-Strauss states that, 'like language, the social is an autonomous reality . . . The symbols are more real than what they symbolize.' Language, as an independent thing, untethered from the drab need to represent or convey reality, conveys surreality, and as well as

* In the light of this argument, how can Burgess possibly survive V. S. Pritchett's remark (quoted in Peter Vansittart's *In the Fifties*, London, 1995, p. 147), 'One of the reasons why bad novels are bad is not that the characters do not live, but that they do not live with one another. They read one another's minds through the author'? Burgess was somewhat contemptuous of Sir Victor, saying to Duncan Fallowell, in 1989, when he was seventy-two, 'I'm one of the oldest practising writers. There's V. S. Pritchett of course. He's past decrepitude,' which must have been a clever way of meaning senile. They'd met that same year at a Royal Society of Literature bash. Burgess told Pritchett, who was as old as the century, that Shakespeare had called himself 'A Stratford burgess,' but – self-deprecating pause – 'I'm not yet a Manchester Shakespeare.' Pritchett piped up to say that he'd recently discovered (i.e. round about 1950) that his name derived from *pricket*, the Elizabethan word for buck or deer. Come on, boys, I wish I'd been there to add, don't you remember your *Love's Labour's Lost*? ''Twas not an awd grey doe, 'twas a pricket . . . and I say beside that 'twas a pricket that the Princess killed,' to which Holofernes replies, 'The preyful Princess pierced and pricked a pretty pleasing pricket.' Burgess, by the way, used to like to tell people that *Holofernes*, who in the Book of Judith is a general in Nebuchadnezzar's army and who is decapitated, was Elizabethan slang for *penis*. (Prickets, pricks, whatever next?) The Symphony (No. 3) in C, as performed in Iowa City, concluded with a tenor and baritone singing the owl and cuckoos' song from the end of Shakespeare's play – and naming characters after apples, in *A Malayan Trilogy*, derives from *Love's Labour's Lost*, too (Costard, etc.).

becoming a definer of abstractions, can find its way towards the art of caricature. Language may distort in addition to its capacity for precision. Indeed, it may distort in order to be precise. *The Enemy in the Blanket* demonstrates this. The art of the caricaturist is to catch social behaviour in the act of puffing itself up; the caricaturist unmasks its prey as overblown, and so condemns it to being over-simple (as Fenella, an unwitting caricaturist, does with Malaya). He needs life to be presented at an already voiced and visible level – and this level he proceeds to exaggerate. Privacy tends to be inaccessible. Personalities are built from the outside: their traits are pictured on their bodies, deformity being like a costume. Enderby, therefore, can never transcend his own 'horrible potbellied hairy filthy nakedness', because inner lives, in Burgess's work, are composed only of illnesses or palpitations, and minds contain, in place of thoughts, leaping impulses and images, e.g. of fear, hate or hunger.* Transferred to literature, the millinery or exaggerative line of caricature – of (say) Lancaster, Searle, Scarfe and Steadman – becomes the word. Push back the tradition and we find Dickens. In *Urgent Copy*, Burgess described such mammoth novels as the stunt of 'the music-hall chairman's comic sesquipedalian *tour de force*'. Dickens's narrative voice is discerned 'introducing or dismissing turn after turn'. His novels are a grotesque vaudeville. Beyond him lie picaresque fictions; prior to them, the stage. Even though, with Burgess, we are dealing with a novelist – the form of filigree plot and psychological motivation – the outcome, with Burgess, is graphic and noisy. Toomey in *Earthly Powers* creates similarly: 'I went to my study and, sighing, numbered a new sheet of foolscap . . . recalled some of my characters from their brief sleep and set them talking.' A novelist might be expected to allow his characters a life when they are in abeyance from action: that when they slumber or are off-stage they still exist. Not so Toomey. Not so Burgess. Characters have to be busy clashing and colliding with one another, interacting frantically as though haring around a stage, or wriggling nervously and two-dimensionally from one panel to the next in 'the myths of syndicated cartoon' (which Crabbe's pupils read). Members of Burgess's Repertory Company seldom get left on their own. If they do not exchange words and they are silent, they stop existing: signals in the dark

* What does Enderby do, in *The Clockwork Testament*, when he is persecuted by journalists, television presenters and students, when his poetry is derided, his religious beliefs mocked, and women turn into his stepmother? He returns to his apartment and consumes chocolate ice cream, a tin of pâté, potato pieces, mixed pickles, chutney, two cans of corned beef, onion rings, canned carrots, turkey soup, whisky, Lea and Perrins, pickled cauliflowers, raspberry jam, and a packet of Rich Tea biscuits.

providing empty pages. When we first meet Enderby, Burgess pretends a party of schoolchildren is touring through his squalid suite. Their queries and the teacher's answers inform us as to the nature of the lump prostrate in the bed. When he is asleep, all Enderby gives Burgess to write down are transcriptions of bodily gurgles.

The furnished flat, rented off Mrs Meldrum, is in fact Burgess and Lynne's apartment in Hove, the municipal borough in Sussex, immediately west of Brighton, to which they'd retreated for the ozone after the discharge from the hospital. Dyes had been pumped through his veins, X-ray pictures of his skull taken, 'I was inverted and my brain was pumped full of air'; but gradually, now he was further away from the East, Burgess's cerebrospinal fluid, that gin-like stuff which circulates between the ventricles of the brain, and which consists of dissolved glucose, proteins, salts and white blood cells, had returned to normal, and he felt immortal, with his guarantee of three hundred and sixty-five days of life (which he took as his cue to write three hundred and sixty-five thousand words). 'It was rather exhilarating. A lot of people, after all, don't know they've got a year to live,' he said in 1968, adding, two decades later in his memoirs, 'if the prognosis was valid . . . I would not be run over by a bus tomorrow, nor knifed on the Brighton racetrack. I would not choke on a bone. If I fell in the wintry sea I would not drown. I had a whole year, a long time.' This is a whimsy of Dr Faustus's. In May 1593, Marlowe left London to escape the plague. The theatres were shut down. The plague, writes Keith Thomas, in *Religion and the Decline of Magic*, 'terrified by its suddenness, its virulence and its social effects'; and the fundamental thing Faustus sells his soul to Mephistophilis for is the guarantee that he will live for another twenty-four years. For that space of time, contagion, brain fever and murder attempts cannot prevail – he is unkillable:

> Knew you not, traitors, I was limited
> For four-and-twenty years to breathe on earth?
> And had you cut my body with your swords,
> Or hew'd this flesh and bones as small as sand,
> Yet in a minute had my spirit return'd
> And I had breath'd a man made free from harm.*

* See 'Doctor Faustus and Hell on Earth' by Christopher Ricks, *Essays in Criticism*, Vol. XXXV, No. 2, April 1985. In his introduction to Defoe's *A Journal of the Plague Year*, Burgess says that pestilence and epidemics were 'vicissitudes which threaten to eat through the human core and destroy the sense of human identity and pride'.

At Hove ('I did not care much for it'), Burgess was surrounded by the living dead – all those muffled retirees being pushed in their bath chairs along the seafront; the residential hotels for distressed gentlefolk; the prune-faced old fools in cottage hospitals – and what was his precise address in purgatory? *Kelly's Directory*, for 1960, says that an Anthony Burgess lived at 39A Sloane Street, in a district that has since been demolished. A big new housing estate is there now, though a few shabby Regency terraces survive.* It's an extremely minor point – but Sloane Street is in East Brighton, not Hove. Did he simply forget the location of his street? Or, as with Robert Robinson and the Chiswick place, did Burgess feel a need to be circumspect to the point of furtiveness? He told Jeremy Isaacs, in 1989, that 'I was driven out of the Colonial Service for political reasons that were disguised as clinical reasons,' and whilst Lynne's shouting at Prince Philip may have been the last straw, it was Burgess's friendship with Sheik Azahari, leader of the pro-democratic Brunei People's Party, whose armed coup in 1962 was crushed by the British Army gurkhas, which the SIS no longer wished to encourage. Hence, ever afterwards, did Burgess fear assassination by an Iban blow dart? That his body would be discovered one morning, his face frozen into a rictus like that of Bartholomew Sholto, in *The Sign of Four*, after his visit from the Andaman islander? Something must account for his terror.† He was misleading about his address in Manhattan, too. He wrote an article in the *New York Times*, on 29 October 1972, complaining about his cockroach-ridden kitchen, dilapidated apartment block and generally dire neighbourhood, stating that he lived at Broadway and Ninety-Third

* Also in the Brighton edition of *Kelly's Directory* – Gordon D'Arcy-Conyers (31A Franklin Road) and William G. D'Arcy-Conyers (64 Bentham Road), one of whom was the actor Darcy Conyers (1919–73), featured player in *Ha'penny Breeze* (1952), *The Devil's Pass* (1956), *The Night We Dropped a Clanger* (1960), *Nothing Barred* (1961) and *In the Doghouse* (1962), and the dedicatee (as 'D'Arcy Conyers') of *Inside Mr Enderby*. Conyers, whom Burgess was sure was pseudonymous ('I never discovered what D'Arcy's real name was'), purchased the film rights for *The Doctor Is Sick*, which remain in his widow's possession. It's to be regretted that the picture was never made – for Burgess's novels could easily have lent themselves to British cinema in the fifties; they have that flavour. The little black and white comedies by the Boulting Brothers or the pre-*Carry On* films of Peter Rogers and Gerald Thomas. I can quite see John Gregson as Edwin Spindrift, Diana Dors as Sheila, and with Terry-Thomas, Dennis Price and Shirley Eaton in the supporting roles. Music by Muir Mathieson. Directed by Mario Zampi. Certificate 'A'.

† Le Carré's George Smiley is aware of 'the secret fear that follows every professional to his grave. Namely, that one day, out of a past so complex that he himself could not remember all the enemies he might have made, one of them would find him and demand the reckoning.' *Tinker, Tailor, Soldier, Spy* (London, 1974), p. 29.

Street. In fact, he lived on West End Avenue and Ninety-Third in one of the oldest co-operative middle-class buildings in the city. He claimed he overlooked a deserted cotton mill and that the pavements were strewn with broken glass. Actually, his windows faced West End Avenue between Ninety-Second and Ninety-Third and the prospect was of the gracious Upper West Side. The West Ninety-Third Street Block Association, in addition, had worked hard to ensure clean sidewalks, plenty of trash baskets, adequate lighting after dark, and had planted trees – and basically this is Burgess at his most literally and morally myopic, only knowing as much as he wanted to know. Typically, shittily, unrepentant, he told his next-door neighbours, 'If this were London, the bulldozers would already be at work. But conceivably, too, the blitz bombs would have gotten it earlier.' In *You've Had Your Time*, he shifts the location yet again, to Riverside Drive.

If he fantasised about or fudged so many little things, isn't it possible that he fabricated big things, too? These addresses in Hove or New York; a full-blown affair with a teacher at Banbury Grammar School and womanising generally; being found as a baby next to the corpse of his mother and sister; his famous brain tumour and the twelve-month prognosis: his autobiography is a litany of exaggeration and plain lies. As Toomey says cheerfully to the Archbishop, '. . . in my sad trade, we can never be really devout or pious. We lie for a living.' Burgess would never quite be living where he claimed – indeed, after Lynne's death, a lot of the time was spent aboard the Bedford Dormobile, criss-crossing state frontiers to avoid residence requirements and taxation liabilities. Chaste kisses were fictionalised into bawdy romps. Brushes with death turned out to be all in his mind, or his gaseous alimentary canal. He wasn't even cosmopolitan Anthony Burgess, of course – he was the provincial John Wilson. I can't say I object to any of this. He exerted himself to the colourful, and good luck to him. As Cyrano says:

> With spirits high, twirled like mustachios,
> Among the false and mean I walk about

– waving his sword, proud of his conk (it sets him apart), flourishing or flaunting the plumes of his hat: *c'est le panache*! Feckless, grandiose, apparently incapable of distinguishing between truth and untruth, Burgess nevertheless carved quite a career for himself, signing books for Hatchard's window, being interviewed by Emma Freud ('It's a great honour – a great great honour for me – I idolise the family,' he gushed to her),

Jonathan Ross ('I've heard of you, sir – a great man – a great idol of the young,' he said to him) and Terry Wogan ('When you write an article you tend to lie – I knew you all right. Seen you indeed,' he reassured the talk-show host whose existence he had questioned), attending literary luncheons with Susan Hampshire, Fay Maschler and Bamber Gascoigne; and he'd been a guest on *Desert Island Discs* as early as 1966.*

* Here are the eight gramophone records which Burgess chose to have with him, had he been cast away alone on a desert island:

Purcell, 'Rejoice in the Lord Alway' (Alfred Deller/Deller Consort/Oriana Concert Orchestra/Deller)
Bach, 'Goldberg Variations No. 13' (George Malcolm, harpsichord)
Elgar, 'Symphony No. 1 in A flat major' (Philharmonia Orchestra/Barbirolli)
Wagner, 'Walter's Trial Song' from *Die Meistersinger* (Sandor Konya/Berlin Philharmonic/Kraus)
Debussy, 'Fêtes' (Orchestre de la Suisse Romande/Ansermet)
Lambert, 'The Rio Grande' (Philharmonia Orchestra/Lambert)
Walton, 'Symphony No. 1 in B flat minor' (Philharmonia Orchestra/Walton)
Vaughan Williams, 'On Wenlock Edge' (Alexander Young/Sebastian String Quartet)

His choice of book was *Finnegans Wake* and his luxury was music manuscript paper, pencils and an india rubber. The programme was pre-recorded on 25 October 1966, between 12.45 and 14.00, and Burgess had held a preliminary discussion with Roy Plomley, the presenter, in the Gramophone Library. The fee: 25 gns. inclusive.

What's remarkable about this list is how orthodox, even conventional, it is – no Stravinsky, Bartók, Janáček, Schoenberg, Britten or Tippett. It's a wonder he missed off *The Planets* ('about once a month I listen to Solti's recording on my rollerskate headphones and follow it with Holst's autograph score,' he said in his preview of the Proms in 1981) or the Grimethorpe Colliery Band (which performed pieces by Derek Bourgeois, 'my successful namesake from Kingston-upon-Thames', at the Royal Albert Hall).

Burgess's selection is music you can imagine Geoffrey Grigson listening to of an evening in his lounge, whilst Jane and little Sophie are off in the kitchenette baking scones or perfecting their Soupe de Potiron aux Moules. It is so *English* – Guy Burgess, too, sitting in Moscow, could've conjured up a vision of all that he'd lost: fields and farms, greenness, dominoes in the public bar, hunting prints, wild flowers, full ashtrays, lark's eggs, and 'By brooks too broad for leaping/The lightfoot boys are laid;/The rose-lipt girls are sleeping/In fields where roses fade.' It was whilst he was in exile, in Malaya, that Burgess and Lynne listened to the gramophone and dreamt of home: 'Music we get from long-playing records, and these have been a godsend,' he wrote (from Kota Bharu) in 1957.

His own compositions were decidedly Edwardian and only tentatively admit the influence of jazz or modernism. It belongs to the age of wing-collars and straw boaters. As he said in his 'Preview of the Proms' article in the programme brochure for 1981, he had a 'passion for British choral and orchestral music', for music with 'a kind of British boldness in it', and thus his own tunes are inspired by the poems of Eliot and Dryden, the songs of Shakespeare, the translations of Ezra Pound, and the plays of John Osborne. The 'Biographia Musicalis' included in *This Man and Music* only goes up to 1982, after which came settings of D. H. Lawrence, entitled *Man Who Has Come Through*, Nashe's *In Time of Plague* (a chorus), two dozen Preludes and Fugues, called *The Bad-Tempered Electronic Keyboard* (ho-ho-ho: Perelman had a book called *The Ill-Tempered Clavichord*, which was the original pun on Bach's *The Well-Tempered Clavier*, of 1722), and an orchestral piece called *A Manchester Overture*. There are professors of musicology in America who take all this very seriously.

The foppish, roaring pontificator bit was, of course, an act; and behind the alleged flickering sense of reality was considerable strength and endurance – he'd have to have had a pretty collected and compact nature to produce those hundreds of books and millions of articles. (Though let's have a round of applause, here, please, two centuries on, for Walter Scott, who despite attacks of jaundice, bowel trouble, vomiting, stomach cramps and seizures, wrote twenty-seven novels, a three-volume history of Scotland, a nine-volume life of Napoleon, twelve volumes of correspondence, four volumes of ballads, editions of Dryden and Swift, and twelve books of miscellaneous essays and reviews; and whilst we are on the subject of productivity, let's not forget the whopping output of Agatha Christie, Edgar Wallace, Enid Blyton, Arnold Bennett or Hugh Walpole.) Burgess wrote under pseudonyms – out came all those novels, plays, poems, legends; this we know. Burgessian means the creation of grand, cosmic, sulphuric effects. Fine.

The fibbing and the subterfuge, however, the patterns of intrigue, hint at a deeper concealment. So what was Burgess hiding? From what was he hiding? Why did he feel himself mysteriously frightened? (The generic Catholic guilt trip – 'We are born with something guilty in us, waiting for a subject to justify it' – is an unsatisfactory explanation, and anyway Greene does it better.) My suspicions were rather more than aroused when, a few years ago, I was approached by a retired security official or intelligence officer, who wished to tell me, against all the rules of the Official Secrets Act, no doubt, of a deception operation that had involved my man. I remain sceptical – but who can resist the safe houses, dead letter-boxes, secret inks, safety signals, fall-backs and work names of the Circus? The scalp-hunters, lamplighters, babysitters, nightwatchmen, housekeepers, fieldmen, janitors and customers? I met my source outside Trumper's, the barbers and gentleman's toiletries shop in Curzon Street, a few doors down from the old MI5 headquarters, off Fitzmaurice Place. The story in a nutshell is this: that the title Burgess is best known for, the one upon which his reputation depends, wasn't wholly his, and this was the dark secret haunting him.

Burgess grew to hate *A Clockwork Orange*. In 1976, fourteen years after it had first appeared, he growled at an interviewer, 'no author likes for this one book, always this same book, to be picked out'. It was as if, he claimed, Shakespeare was only ever questioned about *Hamlet* or Rachmaninoff about his Prelude in C Sharp Minor, which he'd composed as a youngster. '*A Clockwork Orange* is the book I like least,' he told

Playboy. 'The over-exposure meant that people could talk about it at cocktail parties without having read it,' he said to *Isis*, adding, 'it sold less well than anything else I'd ever written'. Which may have been the case on its initial publication, but Kubrick's film changed all that. James B. Hemesath,* interrogating Burgess for the *Transatlantic Review* (May 1976), intended to 'force Burgess to abandon his collection of stock answers', and found that his subject grew quickly hostile:

> Q: Stanley Kubrick produced, directed and wrote the screen version of *A Clockwork Orange*. Have you ever considered that you might also be a creation of Kubrick?
> A: That I'm a creation of Kubrick? Far from it!
> Q: [. . .] Essentially, you were a lesser English novelist until Kubrick came along with that film.
> A: Not at all, not at all, not at all, not at all, not at all [. . .] I don't think anybody knows who the big English novelists are [. . .] These things come and go. You don't know, nobody knows, you don't have to think in those terms, you mustn't think in those terms, let's get on with the job of writing.
> Q: Don't get upset. But I'm going to push you a little more.
> A: I'm not getting upset. But I get upset when you suggest that I'm a creation of Kubrick. Kubrick is a creation of mine.
> Q: [. . .] But the book was more or less forgotten until Kubrick made the film.
> A: It wasn't forgotten. It was taught in American universities.
> Q: [. . .] Thanks to the film you have been transformed into a personality.
> A: No, I'm not having that. I refuse to accept that. I am myself.

It's nice to see him flustered and floundering – revealing himself as too vain to have a sense of humour about himself; missing the point because he has such an uncertain sense of his own identity; being so defensive his only weapons are indignation and sanctimoniousness. Here's a man going in fear of other people finding out his weaknesses. He appeared in public only as a teacher – when he could be flamboyant and superior. Catch him

* Hemesath went to find Burgess in Iowa City, where he'd been spending a month on the campus, delivering lectures on pornography, the pros and cons of making a film about Shakespeare, the derivation of the word *turd*, the American obsession with oral sex, and James Joyce. Burgess was habitually attired in a blue suit of indeterminate fabric, a purple shirt and a green tie. (He must've resembled Caesar Romero as The Joker, though the *Des Moines Register* declared that Burgess was 'a Renaissance man'.)

off guard, there's a facetiousness, a ponderous self-importance. He'd puff smoke fiercely from his cigarillo, so that black spittle accumulated at the corners of his mouth. His eyes narrowed and became watery. He'd look feverish, his face a mask of angry shadows. Like his characters when they are cornered, there's an arrogance and a peevishness – and an evasiveness. In 1971, Thomas Churchill from the *Malahat Review* asked him whether *A Clockwork Orange* had begun as a futuristic novel 'or had you other purposes in mind?' And Burgess said, 'It didn't begin as a futuristic novel at all. It began as a novel about the present day. The first third of it – I've lost it somewhere, had it in typescript until recently – was written in teenage slang, British teenage slang of the present day. But while I was writing I began to feel, well, look, this slang is already getting out of date'; and two years later, in *Studies in the Novel*, Burgess claimed, 'I don't think any writer is wise to attempt to predict the future. When I wrote *A Clockwork Orange*, which was back in 1959, 1960, 1961 – I forget, now – I was really writing about the present, but I was mythicising it a little.' (Mythicising? Is there such a word? Mythologising?)

What is consistent is Burgess's imprecision; but one way and another he did his best to distance himself from the novel, additionally saying he wrote it whilst drunk or that it was 'a *jeu de* spleen'. He told Michael Parkinson that the idea for the book had come to him in a dream, and that all he'd done was taken down dictation from his subconscious. He even let the movie rights go for a pittance, and if Lynne was meant to be a financial wizard, would she willingly have missed a chance like that?* Or is that another of his falsehoods? I thought she was a totally helpless and

* Burgess always alleged that he was ripped off over the sale of the film and dramatic rights to *A Clockwork Orange*. As usual, the history is a little more complicated than that. On 26 March 1968, Tony Palmer shot an adaptation for the BBC under the working title of *Pop Film*. Burgess was paid twenty guineas to take part in an interview, around which extracts from the novel would be structured.

Mick Jagger wanted to play Alex in a feature film, with the rest of the Stones as his droogs – and I wonder if that would have been iconic, or disastrous? The lame satire on rock music in *Enderby Outside*, with Yod Crewsy and the Fixers, was based on the Beatles and Rolling Stones, but I'm sure Burgess could have been prevailed upon to set aside his reservations. The screenplay was to have been by Terry Southern, who wrote the script for *Doctor Strangelove*, and the putative director was the photographer Michael Cooper, who'd shot Peter Blake's cover for *Sergeant Pepper*. How Age of Aquarius this is! It wasn't to be – and instead Jagger made *Ned Kelly* (1970 – directed by Tony Richardson), about an outlaw in the outback, and *Performance* (also 1970 – directed by Donald Cammell), where he plays a willowy, vampiral version of himself, harbouring James Fox in a run-down Notting Hill villa. Jagger certainly had the androgynousness for Alex – and that way he can suggest the sensuality of danger would have been ideal, too. But I doubt if he could have actually acted this. As Tony Richardson put it, 'Though fire and energy snake out of Mick

chaotic alcoholic, yet when she died, Burgess had to pay seven thousand pounds in death duties on her estate. How had that accumulated? She'd never had a job. Her father was in the teaching profession, so not much of an inheritance there. By March 1960, however, the Burgesses owned 'Applegarth', Etchingham, East Sussex (telephone Etchingham 262), situated, as he'd point out, two miles from Kipling's manor house at Burwash and three miles from the pub in Robertsbridge where Chesterton and Belloc drank port wine (he'd encircled himself with Edwardian ghosts); and by 1964, there was also 24 Glebe Street, Chiswick, W4 – so he was running two establishments? Then, suddenly, in 1968, he shoots off into tax exile, and moans about Britain from a distance. In the *Hudson Review* (autumn 1966) he ascribed his wherewithal somewhat breezily to 'my wife's skill on the London Stock Exchange', and I find this quite impossible to credit. Lynne was sleeping most of the day from hepatic exhaustion. She was banned from the local pub, the Etchingham Arms, for fighting in the ladies' toilets, and so she stayed at home at night drinking cocktails of cider and gin. She attempted suicide at least twice by taking an over-

---

like electricity in concert, he can't produce them cold as an actor.' He's an inspiration for Alex, but he could never play Alex. As Ned Kelly, that unique head of his – lips not so much bee-stung as attacked by killer hornets – was concealed under an iron mask.

Another rumour is that Ken Russell wanted to direct *A Clockwork Orange*. If only he had. His sheer vulgarity and sacrilegiousness – all that bizarre Catholic imagery, masturbating nuns, burning crucifixes, cardinals in fishnet tights – is infinitely preferable to Kubrick's mortuary chill. Russell (he's like Fellini crossed with a *Carry On* film) may be tasteless, but his work is ecstatic, in an acid sex sort of way. Kubrick is frigid – Latin *frigidus*: to be cold or sexually unresponsive. Burgess needed a director who'd transform him, not one who'd so faithfully share his impersonal enervations. Instead of *A Clockwork Orange*, however, Russell made *The Devils* (1971), its monasteries and cathedrals designed by another child of the sixties, Derek Jarman, and *Tommy* (1975), The Who's rock opera. The only problem – Russell may have wanted to cast the disgusting Oliver Reed.

The purchasers of the rights were Si Litvinoff, Terry Southern's New York lawyer, and Max Raab, a haberdasher from Philadelphia. They paid Burgess five hundred dollars initially and two ex-gratia payments taking the total to three thousand dollars. 'I don't want a lot of money,' said Burgess at the time, 'because that means you have to buy a yacht, and you have to find time to devote to these things. I have no time. I have to write seven days a week.' When he heard that Warner Brothers, on behalf of Kubrick, had paid Litvinoff and Raab two hundred thousand dollars plus five per cent of the gross, however, our *jongleur*, on 9 May 1973, issued a writ in the High Court in London against the executive producers, 'alleging conspiracy to defraud the author over the motion picture rights to his work'. Burgess claimed that Litvinoff and Raab had misrepresented their original deal and had deprived him of royalties. The ruling was that Burgess was to receive a share of the executive producers' percentage once the film was in profit. The budget was two million dollars; it grossed two and a half million dollars in Britain before Kubrick, in 1974, imposed a ban on its distribution. It was re-released on 17 March 2000, and the film was generally felt to have dated badly. Its mystique would have benefited from its continued concealment.

dose of barbiturate tablets. She was rushed to hospital in Hastings to have her stomach pumped. The local doctor wanted to see her committed to the county insane asylum – in his memoirs Burgess says that when this suggestion was made and the requisite forms produced for signature, he, Burgess, flung the medicine man out of the house. In fact, he dedicated a book to him, *Tremor of Intent* ('To J. McMichael M.B., Ch.B., gratefully'); and a few years ago, in a shop off the Charing Cross Road, I found a first edition of *Here Comes Everybody*, inscribed 'To Mac/from John (Anthony Burgess)' with an empty envelope tipped-in, addressed to 'Dr John McMichael' in Burgess's hand. I didn't buy it.*

In Russia, in the summer of 1961, Lynne was continuously drunk; at parties in London she was a liability. 'You,' she said to Gore Vidal ('in a loud clear voice'), 'chung cheers boog sightee Joyce yearsen roscoe conkling.' Admittedly, Vidal found Burgess himself equally incoherent: 'Tchess. Boog Joyce venially blind, too, bolder.' Their vituperation, when translated, had to do with the fact that, though Burgess was eight years older than Vidal, Vidal's *Julian* had been selected as a Book Society choice before Burgess's *Devil of a State*. That's the kind of thing which could make the pair of them seethe for weeks – it's what united them. Authors earn nothing and fledgling authors less than nothing. Burgess himself never achieved spectacular sales. Though he was churning out novels every few hours ('The idea was to do a chapter a day. Ten chapters, ten days; with a couple of days extra to finish it off – twelve days, two weeks with taking off weekends') and capering to Broadcasting House whenever they paid his cab fare ('It might be as well to warn other producers who decide to book him that he can be "Difficult" over expenses,' cautioned the accounts department in a memo), the sums still don't add up. Even in 1979, contributing a Foreword to Jeutonne Brewer's *Anthony Burgess: A Bibliography*, he was maintaining that he didn't have a pot to piss in: 'I write these lines in Monaco, where the blue waters are totally obscured by the yachts that are anchored there. Not one of these yachts belongs to a man or woman who writes or has written. It seems to me wrong that one should have had to do so much writing in order to make a living, and not a very good living at that.' His abiding sin – boundless greed. As he himself admitted, the advances on royalties from his publishers would hardly have been suitable 'for the era of Ford Madox Ford and D. H. Lawrence'.

* Nor did I invest £995 in *One Hand Clapping* by Joseph Kell (Peter Davies, 1961), inscribed 'To Hazel for her birthday 20th Sept., 1961, Joseph Kell', Hazel Jones being Lynne's sister.

Burgess was at such pains to discount Lynne as an incapable inebriate, her sudden facility for figures, her knowledge of bonds, gilts, shares and money markets, is inconceivable; and as busy as he himself was, with journalism and the odd film option being taken up – well, it still wouldn't have got him to Monte Carlo, yacht or no yacht. Where did the money come from? What was afoot? There's a mystifying paragraph in *You've Had Your Time* where he describes thousands of pounds appearing in his bank account, and he doesn't know how or why it turned up there, and then he says he was to be paid a further 'genuine unreturnable £3,000 for writing the history of a great metropolitan real property corporation. There was an organisation which looked after the subliterary concerns of great commercial bodies, and it made these pay far more than the small commercial firms which were publishing houses.' Burgess met a 'patrician gentleman' (his case-handler?) at the Travellers' Club (where else?) and he was taken 'to the offices of the corporation' – and surely what's happening here is that Burgess, the former Colonial Officer, was being put back on the beat. Needless to say, 'the book was never published', because there'd been no book; and how reticent he is about naming names, always a suspicious sign with him, especially as he could recall the number of guinea pigs loose on his back lawn (fifteen) on the morning of 6 June 1963, if pressed.* The mighty corporation, the body, organisation or firm, with whom he was involved, was the British Security Service, in particular that department of MI5 dealing with deception operations.

Burgess had been a low-grade collector of intelligence data (or ground-observer) in the Far East, when the Empire was in retreat, and he was the chronicler of that; then when he returned to England, the Cold War got in to, say, *The Wanting Seed*, with its atmosphere of totalitarian practices, of armies mobilising and annihilating each other; but the immediate worry wasn't the build-up of Soviet tanks or troop manoeuvres behind the Iron Curtain. What concerned Whitehall was the mistrust between the American and British secret worlds as a result of the Guy Burgess and Donald Maclean business. The pair had fled in 1951 and had emerged in Moscow five years later. Guy Burgess had been an Executive Officer of the British Foreign Office and Second Secretary under Philby in Washington. Maclean was head of the American Department of the Foreign Office, where he had access to classified material about the war in Korea. Philby

* He'd been up all night typing an article for the *Listener* about the Profumo scandal, finishing it at dawn, just in time to put it on the train from Etchingham to Charing Cross, where a messenger collected it – and it was published as 'A Grave Matter' on 13 June.

himself, as First Secretary at the British Embassy in Washington, and a liaison officer with the CIA, was to disappear to Russia in 1963. Anthony Blunt confessed to his part in espionage the following year, and he continued as a surveyor of the Queen's pictures until his public unmasking in 1979, though knowledgeable readers of le Carré's *Tinker, Tailor, Soldier, Spy* will have recognised him as the mole, Bill Haydon, the maverick and art connoisseur. With Peter and Helen Kroger it was antiquarian books. They lived in Cranleigh Drive, Ruislip, with Gordon Lonsdale, a Canadian businessman who was really Konon Trofimovich Molody, an officer in the KGB. The Krogers weren't New Zealanders – they were Morris and Lona Cohen, long-established Soviet agents. Their dusty books contained hidden compartments for microdot equipment, radio transmitters, and which-what. Then there was the SIS double agent George Blake, the Admiralty clerk John Vassall . . . Christ, hey, there was enough hostility and pressure for the Americans seriously to wonder which side we were on, and thus (or hence, or therefore), the Circus and the Cousins went through a phase of undermining each other, testing each other, running disinformation campaigns. The CIA have since been exposed as being involved in all manner of mad experiments, getting people to jump out of windows under the influence of LSD or embedding transmitters and aerials in the belly and tail of feral cats. Since 1951, the National Security Agency (NSA) had been toying with 'remote neural monitoring' facilities, mind-control and brainwashing techniques, micro-electronic implants and electronic surveillance. Using pain and pleasure as triggers for promoting responses, people could be 'conditioned to be happy in the social situations imposed upon them. People would be wound up like a clockwork machine and made to be good all the time,' as Burgess explained years later, alluding to the organisational diversion, of which *A Clockwork Orange* formed a part. The idea was that he'd lift the corner of the carpet and put into his novel classified material about the (then) new-fangled conditioning experiments and aversion therapies being devised to reform criminals – experiments which had wider implications for the concept of social engineering.

According to my Curzon Street contact, Burgess's collaborator was a former CIA officer called Howard Roman, a languages expert whose particular field had been the Polish Intelligence Service, the Urzad Bezpieczenstwa (UB) – and it was a senior officer in Polish military intelligence, Michal Goleniewski, who upon defecting had told the CIA about the mole at the Underwater Weapons Establishment, Portland. (The double agent, Harry

Houghton, was arrested outside the Old Vic in the act of handing over a carrier bag of secret documents to Gordon Lonsdale.) Roman studied physics at Harvard and wrote a doctorate on the poetry of Rilke. Over the years, three novels have been published in his name, *Pitfall in August* (1961), *Frog* (1978) and *When Victims Meet* (1980). An analysis of the writing patterns in these works, when joined with samples from *A Clockwork Orange* – using a statistical and graphical technique devised by Professor A. Q. Morton (and admissible at the Court of Appeal when recorded and written confessions are compared and contrasted) – suggests that 'it is difficult to tell if these two samples are by different authors' – which is not the same as concluding that it's all the output of the same author, but one has to wonder.* More evident is the use of diction. Burgess has been praised for the Russian-sounding slang he invented for his novel. What nobody has noticed is that the text is full of Americanisms (liquor store, pretzels, sidewalk, candy) and American spellings, and yet, whether the book was meant to be set in the Mods and Rockers present, or the future, Burgess never said we were anywhere other than in England. Or are we? 'Now, in 1960 . . . Lynne and I saw Mods and Rockers knocking hell out of each other when we made a trip to Hastings,' he stated. 'Then a story began to stir.' Fact: pitched battles at southern holiday resorts between besuited motor-scooter-riding Mods and the leather-clad motorcycle gangs of Rockers, youths whom the magistrate at Margate

* A. Q. Morton was the author of 'The Authorship of Greek Prose', *Journal of the Royal Statistical Society*, Series A, vol. CXXVIII, 1965; *Literary Detection* (London, 1978); and the co-author (with S. Michaelson) of 'The Authorship and Integrity of the Athenaion Politeia', *Proceedings of the Royal Society of Edinburgh*, vol. 71, no. 7, 1971/1972; (with S. Michaelson and N. Hamilton-Smith) of 'To Couple Is the Custom', University of Edinburgh, *CSR*, 1978; and (with S. Michaelson) of 'The Qsum Plot', University of Edinburgh, *CSR*, 1990.

Cusum analysis, as I understand it, involves the computation of cumulative sum charts, whereby the number of words in a sentence, the use of nouns, the pattern of variations in sentence length, word order and arrangement, the use of words beginning (or ending) with vowels, and which-what, are run through the computer in order to test an author's habits of composition for consistency – as 'writers can be identified because they use the same habit at a consistent level in all their works, but differ in the habit, one from another, so enabling their works to be separated'.

The formulae and resultant graphs are beyond me – are all Greek to me – I'm afraid. But I can grasp enough of the principles involved ('The technique is negative. It can only prove that utterance X is not by Y. It is parallel to physical description. A person with brown eyes cannot be the same person as one with blue eyes, but two people with blue eyes need not be one person') to be of the opinion that such a reduction of literature to algebra and statistics is depressing, depressing, depressing. It drains language of its flavour, texture, range; it turns literature into linguistics, all form and no content, if you expect it to submit to logic. Burgess would have approved of this evolution.

memorably described as 'sawdust Caesars', didn't commence until 1964, at Easter, Whitsun, and on Bank Holidays throughout the summer, i.e. two years after the book's publication. Burgess hadn't visited America before the appearance of *A Clockwork Orange*, in May 1962, though he and Lynne had been to Leningrad, in June and July 1961, ostensibly to brush up on the *nadsat* and glower at the 'hordes of *stilyagi*', or boozed-up students; except that 'the novel was nearly finished by the time we were ready to travel to Tilbury and board the *Alexander Radishchev*, a well-found ship of the Baltic Line'. What he wrote on his return was *Honey for the Bears* – *A Clockwork Orange* was already done.

Actually, the book's landscape is a James Bond no-man's-land of white-coated technicians, bug-eyed scientists, cipher stations and communications laboratories. This would be consistent with what I was told the book is about – the mind-control experimentation conducted by Dr Ewen Cameron at the Allen Memorial Institute in Montreal, between 1957 and 1963, and the Remote Neural Monitoring facility that operated out of Fort George Meade, in Maryland.* The CIA were funding controversial research programmes into electronic brain stimulation. They induced exhaustion and nightmares in patients; they put hoods or cones over people's heads to broadcast voices directly into their brains; they irradiated the auditory cortex or inner ear. When patients had their own speech played back to them, incessantly, they went insane. There was a misuse of civilians in these covert operations, and intelligence on these devices remains classified.† It sounds to me like *The Manchurian Candidate*, where Angela Lansbury programmes Laurence Harvey to kill without

* At the NSA's Fort Meade, the world's most advanced computers are developed. Using artificial intelligence, any communication device in existence – personal computers, telephones, radio and video-based gadgetry, car electronics and even the minute electrical fields given off by human beings – can be subject to non-obtrusive surveillance. Communications are tapped for key words that should be brought to the attention of the NSA agents and cryptologists. This is known by the acronym SIGINT (Signals Intelligence), and the electronic surveillance network, its development and implementation, like other electronic warfare programmes, is classified. Signals Intelligence Remote Computer Tampering involves the NSA's stratagems to tune into the emissions from personal computer circuit boards and gain wireless modem-style access to – or even alter – digital information and data. This all seems like the treatment for a *Mission: Impossible* episode with Tom Cruise.

† See Appendix B: *The Cousins*, for my attempts to unearth documentation on Burgess by invoking the Freedom of Information Act (FOIA). It would seem that to divulge his involvements with the intelligence services would compromise national defence or foreign policy. My letters from the CIA are out of the Marx Brothers ('the first part of the party of the first part . . .').

mercy or memory; or *Invasion of the Body Snatchers*, where messy, muddled human beings are replaced by their bland, soulless doubles, who emerge out of pods during the night; or of course Ionesco's *Rhinoceros*, where the population turns into a herd of harrumphing beasts and we are told that '*C'est une chose anormale de vivre*' – it's crazy to be living at all.

Spies; the fraternal love–hate bond between Britain and America, let alone the West and the East; Howard Roman and his Warsaw secret servicemen in the UB; Burgess and his wanderings; Hollywood classics of McCarthyite paranoia; the CIA, FBI, SIS, MI5, GCHQ, JIC, and (why not?) the Komitet Gosuderstvennoy Bezopasnosti – all of them crackbrained fucking fools who misspend their money and muck us about: whether the form is sci-fi, political reality, surrealism, reportage or a scientific paper in a learned journal, whether the tone is macabre, capricious, thrillerish or farcical, the subject is hanging on to your identity (both national and individual), and *A Clockwork Orange* is a distillation of the theme. I don't think Burgess had expected the novel to take off; nor did it, until Kubrick's film a decade later, when it sold fifty thousand copies in a fortnight.* By then he'd become the cigar-puffing megalomaniac on television chat shows, notorious for his Old Testament words and pretending to be outraged that his book may have inspired muggings or deeds of random violence. In 1972 he explained, 'the violence in the book is really more to show what the State can do with it. I'm more scared of the possibility of the individual being cured under the State; of people being made to be good; of evil being rationalised out of existence.' That is exactly the point to pick up in the novel (and film): the denial of freedom of choice, the obliteration of free will – and with or without the encouragement of hidden hands, this was a subject Burgess returned to again and again in his subsequent books. There's me thinking the fallen world and the flowers of evil were legacies from the Catholic childhood. It is difficult at this distance to separate the original novel from the film made a decade later – they are of a piece, and indeed *A Clockwork Orange* is a period piece: the white plastic modernism of the sixties; the cynicism of moneyed louts looking for thrills; the drugs. It's part of the Burgess mythology – the book, the film, its design, its effects on clothes and attitudes. The conno-

* According to the Heinemann archive, it sold 3,872 copies in its first hardback edition. At a Sotheby's sale of Valuable Printed Books and Manuscripts recently (13 December 2001), a lot described as *A Clockwork Orange*, London: Heinemann, 1962. 8vo, FIRST EDITION, FIRST ISSUE, original black cloth, dust jacket (with '16s' on inner flap), slight localised abrasion to dust-jacket, spine creased at head, had an estimate of £2,000.

tations of the book are bigger than the book itself. I can muffle myself up in my overcoat and totter around Mayfair like George Smiley until the cows come home; and it is tempting to connect the 'Ludovico Technique' in the novel with the assassination of JFK and Jack Ruby's shooting of Lee Harvey Oswald whilst under the influence of hypnosis. And why stop there? Conspiracy theorists might like to bring on Freemasonry, Rosicrucianism, the sinking of Atlantis, crop circles, UFOs, Elvis sightings in Merthyr Tydfil, the Loch Ness monster, and that underground installation in New Mexico where boffins are allegedly oscillating the Earth's magnetic field to shift the weight of polar ice caps (why?) – so that the Earth unpeels itself, like an orange.

'You realise,' said the spook, as we sat on a bench in Berkeley Square opposite Maggs Bros. Ltd., by appointment to Her Majesty the Queen, purveyors of rare books and manuscripts, 'that the capitalised lines on page twenty-nine of *A Clockwork Orange* give the HQ location of the psychotronic warfare technology?'

I stared into the middle distance, polishing my glasses with the fat end of my tie and looking simultaneously inscrutable and bewildered. The passage in question refers to the college pennants on Alex's wall, each of these 'being like remembrances of my corrective school life since I was eleven, O my brothers . . .':

SOUTH 4; METRO COR-SKOL BLUE DIVISION; THE BOYS OF ALPHA.

It does sound like an encryption. But of what precisely? It was patiently explained to me that if you look at a map of America, then Utah, Colorado, Arizona and New Mexico are the only states with a right-angled four-corner conjunction ('4 . . . COR') and that there is a military reservation to the 'SOUTH'. It runs north into New Mexico and is based around the *metro*politan area called El Paso. It is a training school ('SKOL' – Russian). The Navy ('BLUE DIVISION') were initially in charge of the technology. Analysing, isolating and interfering with the 'ALPHA' wavelengths of the human collective unconsciousness was part of the set-up. The name of the establishment is Fort Bliss. The word *bliss* appears on page twenty-nine of Burgess's novel no less than six times.

Where are the verifiable facts?* A lot of people told me he was on the

* Fort Bliss, at El Paso, exists, at least. Named after Lieutenant-Colonel William Wallace Smith Bliss, adjutant general during the Mexican War (1846–48), and the headquarters of Brigadier General John J. Pershing, it is situated beside the Rio Grande at the strategic pass

lam with his loot. An associate on *A Blast from the Smallest Room*, the aborted Enderby film, stated that Burgess used to smuggle large denomination Swiss banknotes back to Britain in his shoes. This raised his height by three inches, and Burgess was already not a short man. The trouble was, after walking through customs and getting clear of prying eyes, the paper money had started to disintegrate – so he'd spend hours with Sellotape, trying to piece the serial numbers back together. Burgess, an expert in withholding and exposing, was inexplicably flush, he removed himself to Malta (the retirement ground of intelligence officers), there are similarities between his sentence construction and Howard Roman's, the novel itself contains anomalies, the spook outside Trumper's (where I bought a bottle of cologne: 'Every move must be accountable, Smiley had warned him: assume that the Circus has the dogs on you twenty-four hours a day') was jumpy, handing me a file of material and fretting about telephone intercepts, and my subsequent enquiries made the Cousins jumpy; but the allegations, even though rather exciting, are of a flimsy nature, and I'm on firmer ground revealing that first, as regards the title of *A Clockwork Orange* – 'I had always liked the cockney expression and felt there might be a meaning in it deeper than a bizarre metaphor of, not necessarily sexual, queerness' – nobody had heard it before. Kingsley Amis was adamant: 'Unknown to me, a Londoner (John is a Mancunian), and unrecorded in Eric Partridge's monumental (1065 pp.) *Dictionary of Historical Slang*.' The closest usage I can find is Caryl Brahms's 'it was all Lombard Street to a china orange', a phrase to mean the equivalent of in for a penny, in for a pound; and Jeffrey Bernard said that a man who could outfumble his friends and dodge buying a round of drinks all night was a person, 'as the cockneys say, who could peel an orange in his pocket'. The combination of petty acts of meanness with a certain sort of what-the-hell risk-taking is apt for Burgess.*

---

through the Franklin Mountains and the Sierra Madre. At one time the base for the largest cavalry force in the United States, in 1943 the horses were replaced by mechanised infantry units and Fort Bliss became an anti-aircraft artillery centre – indeed, *the* United States Army Air Defense Artillery Center.

It is a test bed and training installation for joint and combined warfare, employing state-of-the-art technologies and fostering interservice, intergovernmental and civic partnerships. A model installation supporting a variety of missions, with a world-class information technology and communications infrastructure, Fort Bliss was where Training Aids, Devices, Simulators and Simulations (TADSS) were developed. It was a post to 'conduct realistic exercises in a realistic environment [and] maintain all equipment at operation levels capable of executing required tasks' (according to the *Fort Bliss Vision*).

* Burgess was expected to be the expert on oranges (and other strange fruit – there was an

My second revelation is that the concept of Alex the articulate and dandyish anti-hero, the notion of a marauding young troublemaker, derives from *Les Nouveaux Aristocrates* by Michel de Saint-Pierre, first published in France by Calmann-Lévy in 1960. As *The New Aristocrats*, this novel was published in London by Victor Gollancz in 1962 – translated into English 'by Anthony and Llewela Burgess'. Apart from its regular appearance in the bottom right-hand corner of the extensive pre-title page's 'by the same author' list, *viz.*:

TRANSLATION
The New Aristocrats
The Olive Trees of Justice
The Man Who Robbed Poor Boxes
Cyrano de Bergerac
Oedipus the King
Carmen

– and apart from a breathtaking instance of throwaway boasting in his memoirs ('I sometimes improved the style of the Frenchman, so much so that when [the book] appeared in America, a critic acclaimed its elegance and searing imagery and asked why Anglo-Saxon novelists could not write like that'*) nothing more was ever said. The Rostand and the Bizet we know about; *Les Oliviers de la justice* by Jean Pelegri (1962) and *Deo Gratias* by Jean Servin (1965) have vanished without trace (one day I'll find them in a damp and musty West Country second-hand bookshop that smells of drains next to the long unread Storm Jamesons and Warwick Deepings); but the Michel de Grosourdy, Marquis de Saint-Pierre, is quite enough to be going on with. He was born on 12 February 1916, the son

article in the *American Scholar* [autumn 1966] entitled 'An Electric Grape', a reaction to Marshall McLuhan's ideas about popular culture: 'Professor McLuhan's electric grapes can so far only impart some very sour shocks; I await the treading and the vintage,' said Burgess obscurely). There was an encyclopaedic essay, 'About Oranges,' published in *Gourmet* (November 1987), which reads as if he'd upended his reference books to be able to tell us about oranges in poems, oranges in antiquity, oranges as Christmas presents during his 'somewhat deprived childhood', the cities called Orange, the Orange Lodges in Ulster, King William III and the House of Orange, the uses of an orange in the kitchen, and so on and on until his ingenuity ran out. I cherish one wee sidelight: 'I lived in Malta for a few years. Indeed, my house is still there, uninhabited and unsaleable by government decree. The orchard contained not only oranges, limes, and lemons, but also citranges, an ideal compromise of sweet and sour. What could be done with all that fruit, especially at Christmas when it was ready for picking? My answer was marmalade, pots of which made useful and parsimonious presents.'

* *The New Aristocrats* was published in Boston by Houghton-Mifflin in 1963.

of an army officer, and educated at private Catholic schools, the Collège Saint-Jean-de-Béthune and the Institut Catholique et Faculté des Lettres de Paris. After a distinguished war (Chevalier de la Legion d'honneur, Médaille militaire, Croix de guerre, Rosette de la Résistance, Croix du combatant voluntaire, etc.), he settled to fiction writing in 1951. He was a municipal councillor for the sixteenth arrondissement and the Mayor of Saint-Pierre-du-Val, in the Eure. Is he still about? He'd be one year Burgess's senior. His addresses were: 15, rue Dupin, 75006, Paris, and Chateau de Saint-Pierre, 27210, Beuzeville. Give him a call.

From the books of his I've glanced at in the Taylor Institution Library, Oxford,* it looks like here we have the mother and father of Catholic philosophisings: the Church and the state; the devil and the deep blue sea; the individual and how he copes with company; good and evil; right and wrong; war and peace – his subject was what he called '*me compromettre*', his search for a little give and take, for compromises, in the light of Catholicism's dogmatic extremes and hard facts. In each of his books, and in each of his characters, there's '*une division binaire*' – a compelling sense of contradiction or of things in opposition – that he likes to try and resolve. His rebels ultimately respect the values they contest or mock. Parental authority is undermined by the young – and then the young themselves become parents. Burgess talked about *A Clockwork Orange* in exactly this fashion. 'Young people,' he said in his memoirs, 'were expressing the Manichean principle of the universe, opposition as an end in itself, *yin* versus *yang*, X against Y. I foresaw that [life] was going to be greatly disrupted by the aimless energy of these new young, well-fed with money in their pockets.' He didn't foresee the post-war world in these terms at all – Saint-Pierre did, or at least Saint-Pierre did first. In novel after novel he'd been contemplating the disquiet of a younger generation – the effects of bullying and of the strong subjecting the weak. A youngster can be a '*bourreau de soi-même*' – literally, hangman of himself, or his own worst enemy; but there is such energy and vitality, can it not be usefully channelled? The moral problem, or sociological problem, becomes religious – inevitably; father figures and authority figures being as nothing compared with the unconditional obedience required by the Church. Indeed, all the dichotomies and dilemmas of growing up mirror the tussles and skirmishes along the road to faith. A person, during his life, has a wild need to change things and resists all the changes that have already come

* *Contes pour les Sceptiques* (1945), *Les Ecrivains* (1957), *Les Murmures de Satan* (1959), *L'Ecole de la Violence* (1962) and *Les Nouveaux Prêtres* (1964).

about – or that he knows about. This is what being independent means. You are at war with yourself.

The epigraph for *The New Aristocrats* is Matthew, XVIII, 11–15:

> For the Son of Man is come to save that which was lost.
>
> How think ye? If a man have a hundred sheep, and one of them be gone astray, doth he not leave the ninety and nine, and goeth into the mountains, and seeketh that which is gone astray?
>
> And if so be that he find it, verily I say unto you, he rejoiceth more of that sheep, than of the ninety and nine which went not astray.
>
> Even so it is not the will of your Father which is in heaven, that one of these little ones should perish.

Burgess's Alex, like Saint-Pierre's Denis Prullé-Rousseau, is just such a lost sheep – the sinner who is made a fuss of. We are told that the new aristocrats are those who 'are destined to belong to the elite of the future'; they are characterised by 'sensitivity, strong impulses, and restlessness'; and 'on the forehead of him who is destined to lead others . . . there shines a light, and that light is indifference to happiness'. Saint-Pierre says he wants to be clear that such fellows, whilst seemingly impudent or cold, are not tricksters ('*tricheurs*' – better translated as cheats), as uppermost in their minds is an 'honesty with themselves and with others'.

We are in a school, though without difficulty all these themes and appurtenances – people in emotional isolation from each other; the pride of a lonely hero proving in the end to be corrosive – could be decked out as sci-fi, travelogue, spy novel, historical or biblical fiction, all Burgess's modes. Burgess gives the school, in *The New Aristocrats*, the flavour of Stephen Dedalus's Clongowes – Father Philippe de Maubrun, appointed to teach 'our young philosophers', enters the classroom, 'a tall priest, athletic, smiling', and could be from Dublin (or Xaverian College, Manchester); as could Father Spitzwald, the French master, besotted with Racine: 'he taught them much more than literature. He taught them wonder.' The headmaster of Pierre Favre College, however, the Reverend Father Raphael Menuzzi, is an autocrat ('He would have made a first class head of a spy ring'), his office a mission control with maps and coloured pegs. He knows all that is going on. A school, like a city or the army, or a marriage, is a microcosmos, and there can be no disorder. Menuzzi:

> You've a class [de Maubrun is told] of sorcerer's apprentices – undisciplined, critical, insolent; a revolution of a class, a state-within-a-state,

with its own idols, customs, and rituals . . . I get the feeling that I'm looking at an island, and I rely on you to make it part of the continent again.*

. . . I believe we're living in an age when rules have become so relaxed, that an authoritarian education at least retains the merit of being original.

Against this, there's the boys: 'They've learned to doubt everything . . . The parents have given up, abdicated.' Joyce's Jesuits face not cowering striplings, however, but a roomful of Malcolm McDowells, 'these young bloods and braggarts, a new breed that disconcerts the finest educationalists'; '. . . the youth of today is a new breed'. Nevertheless, these coming men are to be cherished: 'In them you'll find a certain refinement – something *aristocratic*. They have taste and quality' – like Alex's knowledge of Mozart and Beethoven, or (much later) the hooligans in *1985* whose idea of playing truant is to bunk off and read Greek and Latin lyric poetry. 'They insist that no one is their master, yet a master is what they are desperately searching for . . .' Did Saint-Pierre want us to think of the *Hitlerjugend*? Was Burgess aware of the latent homoeroticism? (Is there a *comtesse* de Saint-Pierre?)

My problem with Saint-Pierre's work (it's a problem I have with a lot of French literature) happens to be the same as my reservation about Burgess's: the material is too programmatic.† They have a thesis or a

* Burgess was drawn to islands (remember that he wanted to live on Sark?). There's Malta, obviously; and Borneo is technically an island, the third largest on the globe. Perhaps what he really liked was the small self-contained community, such as Brunei or Monte Carlo; small kingdoms or principalities – Ruritanias or devils of a state. Bracciano and Lugano have this quality of lakeside seclusion. Not that there's much nature or alfresco activity in Burgess's work. His characters live an indoor life – pubs, bars, libraries, barracks, classrooms, the lavatory where Enderby stews. There's not much countryside. No hills and rivers. No plants, sun, sky, trees. The jungle of Malaya is there to express the morbidity of the characters – it's part of the claustrophobia. For all his travelling (Malta, Italy, New York, etc.), these were worlds he occupied, but didn't live in. From early on, there was this expatriate mentality, that he'd be moving on, as if island hopping. So where was his personality rooted? Manchester? ('Should I come back to England, to the Moston Cemetery where my family is buried? I don't fancy the idea of being buried in France, Italy, Monaco.') His fantasy of Joyce's Ireland and his ancestry? In all the books he read or ingested? With Lynne and the memory of Lynne? With Liana and the emptiness of his exiles? Anywhere, I suppose, where there's a legion of the lost ones and a cohort of the damned.

† The particular value of Saint-Pierre's novel, for me, is its odd prophecy of Burgess's work. In Denis Prullé-Rousseau's room there is a large portrait of Bonaparte, 'a pouting, potbellied, chubby Napoleon, much like a naughty baby' – exactly the characterisation of the Emperor in *Napoleon Symphony*; the boy's emotions about home are Burgess's: 'He didn't

conundrum and then deck out a story to illustrate it – it's all rather false and unreal. In *A Portrait of an Artist as a Young Man* there's a palpable human drama to Stephen's certain hardness and austerity – as his fear of sentimentality or the clinging nature of love condemns him to taciturnity and solitude. His refusal to surrender is noble – but it is foolish, too. Joyce shows how his young affections run to waste and the ramifications and re-examinations are described with much irony and suggestiveness. Burgess's style and manner cannot admit such qualities. His art is synthetic. As with Saint-Pierre, our responses are being anticipated and directed. We are told what to think. This is the paradox of *A Clockwork Orange* – it is about free will, but there's no freedom in it. His first collection of essays and reviews was called *Urgent Copy* – but where's the urgency? The journalistic deadline is a specious excuse. He always looked desperately tired, struggling on and on, except nobody is required to read Burgess because he could deliver manuscripts and articles on time.* Art needs a deeper impetus than that, if it is not to be a series of tricks. Are there any depths to his work? Is there any build-up? I don't think so. For me, art needs a sort of trembling – like Keats's hare which 'limp'd trembling through the

really know what he felt about his mother; wrapped up in her valiant snobbery, she was something to marvel at. Denis contemplated her face, still beautiful enough . . . the eyes which could express passion and a sort of sad avidity.' This is a vision of the Beautiful Belle Burgess – with a shadow of the vulturine Maggie Dwyer cast across it. Denis's father, like Burgess's, is distant – 'He plays at being a father, a three-minute show in front of others'; and that's also Burgess himself with Liana's son. Finally, the description of the chapel at the school is like the pub on Lodge Street, Manchester, in Burgess's memoirs: 'the dark light of a forest and the hospitality of silence . . . the gold of an eagle-lectern, its old wings outspread'. In an interview in 1981, you'll recall, he said that the sign outside the Golden Eagle was later recycled to decorate a pulpit.

* Though it is this sort of thing that he became famous for – and why editors who believed he was representative of high literary standards were prepared to pay him big bikkies for his guaranteed craftsmanlike eight-hundred word slabs. William Boyd noted that literary journalists were 'sickened with envy by the fact that Burgess always read and reviewed a book the day it arrived in the post'. The secretary at the *Observer* once sent him along the wrong volume of something or other by mistake – and he reviewed that too.

In the sparkling opuscule *On Going to Bed* (creamy Rizzoli paper and over-inky illustrations), we see how his day revolved around serendipitous commissions: 'The world is for the most part so puritanical that it will not accept the conjunction of bed and work. When the postman comes to deliver parcels (always of books to review or unpaid commendation) at eleven in the morning, he say reprovingly: "Ah, well, some of us have to work." This is because he is in uniform and has been up for hours. I myself, though in bed, may well have completed a thousand words of prose by that time.'

It turns out that his bed, or cock-pit, is actually a mattress on the floor, surrounded by his tea-making apparatus, digital clock, record player, tape recorder, radio, a piano-accordion, a medicine chest, and 'even a small refrigerator'. (Is this a bed or a flatlet? He must have spent as much time in his pyjamas as Hugh Hefner, though to different ends.)

frozen grass'; I want this air of alert mystery and self-determination. In Arnold Bennett's *The Old Wives' Tale*, a character has a bundle of banknotes which must be hidden in a cupboard, so: 'She got on a chair, and pushed the fragments out of sight on the topmost shelf, where they may very well be to this day.' David Lodge, the novelist and academic, has commented that it would be a very stupid reader who'd think that those papers are really still there, shoved in a cabinet in a French provincial hotel. Well, that stupid reader is me – for as John Bayley says, censuring Lodge (for it is Lodge who is literal-minded), 'it would be an ungenerous reader of novels who did not take for granted the convention to which Arnold Bennett is archly drawing our attention. Why read novels at all unless we, in some sense, believe what they tell us? The novel which insists that there is no truth in it, and that it is simply an artificial machine devised for our entertainment, is like the film which wants us only to notice how it was shot: both seem to be made only for critics and professional connoisseurs of form.' Thus, the reputation of Burgess – and of Kubrick, who is similarly cold and oppressive. Academics love them. Whilst they are at their seminars and retrospectives, however, I'm more likely to be found carrying on up the jungle in Borneo, or checking the rates books at Albany for the period of Aldous Huxley and Toomey's residence (1936 to 1938), or looking at the lake in Lugano. To me, these are acts of faith – leaps of the imagination. It's a private game, for the most part, and one with a touch of melancholy, like searching for an abandoned path on Puck's Pook Hill – a path so overgrown you would never know there was once a road through the woods. And who, for example, can walk down Baker Street and not think of Sherlock Holmes, a man who because he never lived can never die?

It is the reader's willingness to suspend disbelief – and an author's ways of encouraging us to do this – which John Bayley's own criticism sought to explain. He was my tutor at Oxford, taking over when Ellmann pegged out from motor neurone disease, but I'd actually been attending his classes and seeing him (and Dame Iris) regularly as a friend since 1982. No one has ever had a greater influence on me – counselling that criticism is more a creative process than a reductive or judgemental one; and Bayley hated the idea of an apparatus or any brand of academic orthodoxy. What counted were the reader's (and author's) sensibility and instincts. It was a fallacy, he claimed, to think that poetry (say) has 'no separate realities of its own' – all abstract, or a confection of thought which, as Keats said, 'made the visible a little hard to see'. Ideally, poetry is not a fanciful thing running parallel to one's life, like other people, or outside of one's life, like a billiard ball or sheet music in the piano stool; it is what makes up one's life. Bayley certainly achieved this. He lived the life of art, could penetrate it, and see, in *The Waste Land*, Phlebas the Phoenician, and the small house agent's clerk, with one bold stare, as real individuals.*

* The delightful paradox with John Bayley is that despite knowing him for twenty years I don't think we've ever had a serious conversation. You get the impression quite quickly that such a thing would be disagreeable – a breach of etiquette, like gentlemen of similar rank shaking hands. With the Dame it was a different thing altogether. There was a heaviness to her (intellectually, socially, physically) which Judi Dench, inevitably cast for *Iris*, quite missed. Jim Broadbent's Bayley, by the way, was far too lugubrious and baritonal. The Academy Award notwithstanding, he was as much like John Bayley as if they'd cast Robert Mitchum. You needed Charles Hawtrey or Jonathan Cecil. But the Bayleys were long a feature on the literary landscape – as the Burgesses MK I (John and Lynne) and MK II (Antonio and Liana) must have been.

If I now think that Burgess's work was too mechanical, Murdoch's became too diffuse and elaborate, her novels being like those great wildernesses of flowers and clogged lakes, matted grasses and rat-infested hollow trees that you see surrounding abandoned or gutted stately homes. I never thought to ask her if she'd met Burgess. (She'd met Laurence Olivier, but couldn't remember anything about him.) The pair of them may be compared and contrasted, even so. Burgess began publishing in the years of *The Sandcastle* and *The Bell*, and both he and Murdoch were interested in good and evil as active forces. (Did the writers who emerged in the fifties get this from the war?) Yet where Murdoch could apply her interest in religion and morals and questions of spiritual belief to her characters' personal dramas, in Burgess such abstract deliberations remain as lectures, as chunks of teaching. Murdoch was also interested in goodness and in trying to be good in one's daily life (naturally her biographer, Peter Conradi, has delighted in revealing her string of naughty affairs – as if she were the first girl at Oxford ever to want a bang from every buck); and though she was painfully self-absorbed, she did try to find a way into the 'dramas of the human heart', as Rachel Billington put it (in *The Times*, 25 April 1983), and she was a wonderful listener, like a wise old nun. Burgess, in complete contrast, wasn't ever going to be bothered with the secrets and obsessions of others. Nobody was to expect sympathy or understanding from him. It is intriguing to speculate whether his egotism was similar to an egotism Murdoch sensed in herself, and which she had to accept (as part of an artist's self-protectiveness – who was it who said that a writer has to have a splinter of ice in their heart?) and try to obliterate (for it can foster bad art or anti-art – and it makes you a shit as a human being).

At Xaverian College, Burgess recalled, across half a century, a little rhyme of Brother Cajetan's:

> There once was a metaphysician
> Who proved that he didn't exist.
> When others had learned his position,
> They said that he wouldn't be missed.

Compare that with a remark of Murdoch's (made to Billington in that same piece – an interview conducted in Janet Stone's house in Salisbury, incidentally):

> I believe we live in a fantasy world, a world of illusion, and the great task in life is to find reality.

Which was certainly true in the Dame's case, as those who have met her will attest. She was always the mournful-looking elf-maiden stealthily telling herself stories.

Objects, figures, stories, in art, 'have their own selves which can be like nothing else' – e.g. Achilles' armour, Leopold Bloom's breakfast kidney, or the furniture in those Los Angeles rooms of Raymond Chandler's where 'something nasty has occurred'. What, in Burgess, takes on magical powers? Or is it all words and self-consciousness? Bayley thinks so – he had devastating demurrals. We corresponded about this, and his most cogent critique appears within a piece on Betjeman, in *Selected Essays* (1984):

> Burgess singles ideas out for treatment [and] the way his own prose makes points [is by being] chatty, ingenious, witty, informative. Burgess, one might say, turns art into non-art, fascinating, energetic, even suspenseful non-art, rather as his novel about Shakespeare sought to turn the art into the man. In this, he is not unlike those actual Elizabethan writers – Hall, Nashe, Greene – who created a whole great literary Elizabethan world of non-art, hardly read today . . .

There's grandiosity, but not grandeur; artistry, but not art. Burgess knew his Greene, Nashe and Hall, needless to say.* His account of their work, in *English Literature: A Survey for Students*, displays an infectious enthusiasm for their vulgarities and pace:

> The popular but minor prose writings of Elizabeth's day – prose for entertainment – bubble with life: we have the impression that the author is talking directly to us, words rushing out like a river, non-stop. It is the modulations of a voice that we hear, not the scratchings

* Robert Greene (*c.* 1558–92). *Complete Works*, edited by A. B. Grosart in fifteen volumes (London, 1881–86). Rather a rogue, he died after dining on pickled herring washed down with Rhenish wine. Churned out pastiches of Sidney, Chaucer, Gower, Marlowe – anybody who was popular with the public. His best works are his confessions, *A Notable Discovery of Cosenage*, or *A Groatsworth of Wit Bought with a Million of Repentance*, which, like Burgess's *Little Wilson and Big God* and *You've Had Your Time*, affect the tone of a penitent sinner. (In *Finnegans Wake* there is a pun on 'An ounceworth of onions for a pennywealth of sobs'.)

Thomas Nashe (*c.* 1567–1601) was a pamphleteer, whose *Works* are edited by R. B. McKerrow in five volumes (Oxford, 1904–10). His *The Unfortunate Traveller, or the Life of Jack Wilton*, is an early (1594) example of picaresque fiction – its plague-ridden landscape is Burgess's. Enderby is right there.

Joseph Hall (1574–1656), who became the Bishop of Exeter in 1627 (though he was turned out of his palace in 1647), and whose *Works* were edited by P. Wynter in ten volumes (Oxford, 1863), wrote books with titles like *Characters of Virtues and Vices* (1608), and as is usual with satirists, he was morbidly drawn to that which he wanted to chastise.

There is much on the 'brilliant chatter' of these men in Burgess's *Shakespeare* biography. He argues that their 'odd scraps of learning, strange words invented or out of books [move] towards something we can call Shakespearean language' – not true, of course. They are moving towards a Burgessian language.

of a pen. These minor books seem to be written rapidly, without undue care – sheer cheap journalism churned out to pay the rent – but even the cheapest pamphlet has a vitality that we have long ceased to look for in our modern journalistic prose.

Burgess, a New Elizabethan, can certainly be said to have put a similar bubbliness and scratchy rapidity into his own work. *Nothing Like the Sun*, for example, is entirely composed from sixteenth-century verbiage: *oaklings*, *footsticks*, *cinques*, *moxibustion*, *dittany*, *face-ague* . . . It is the book Shakespeare's contemporaries may have wanted written about him; the conceit is Greene's *Groatsworth of Wit* – 'For there is an upstart crow, beautified with our feathers, that with his tiger's heart wrapped in a player's hide . . . etc.' – tossed in the salad bowl with Joyce's Stephen. With Joyce, however, the prose creates worlds within worlds: Buck Mulligan's appearances are marked by a sarcastic jauntiness; then there's broody Stephen on Sandymount Strand and over-rehearsed Stephen in 'Scylla and Charybdis', actually lecturing us on Shakespeare. Bloom, frying his kidney, talking to his cat, attending a funeral, calling into pubs and walking the streets, has another style again, deferential, dignified, muted, observant. To Joyce, language marks psychological change, even physiological change. *Ulysses*, though it contains the melodrama of fist fights and adultery, finds its real drama in the minuscule fluctuations of daily mood: hunger, tiredness, indigestion, arousal, pity. Joyce draws our attention to the way we inhabit our bodies. Burgess, on the other hand, knows only what it is like to inhabit costumes. There's no depth of feeling. His language, and his stylistic use of it, is a sartorial virtuosity. Joyce tailors a mental language, calibrating very finely the deportments of thought across a twenty-four-hour period. The soul of Burgess's characters is simply in their garments and accoutrements. Remove the layers and you'll be lucky to find blood and bones, nerves and viruses. Their language is a fabrication of fabrics, as he might have put it. In the *TLS*, on 16 June 1972, Bloomsday to the professors, Burgess told how, as a novelist, he made his characters: 'I'll hang draperies on them – see how the contours press through that piece of jazz-patterned calico . . .' And when discussing the plutopolis in his Time-Life book *New York*, it is the rag trade and garment district that Burgess singles out for scrutiny. He is bored by all the museums and galleries – except for the Costume Institute: 'a candid mixture of commerce and aesthetic instruction', and hence a pantheon of Burgess's predicaments about making money and producing high art, about being visibly popular (going on *Wogan* and *Parkinson*), and not remaining an unseen experimenter. (For when did *you* last see Samuel Beckett autographing novels in Harrods under a sign saying TOILETS AND BOOKS?*)

That Stephen grows up from *A Portrait* and into *Ulysses* is self-evident; but Bloom, too, changes during the day in which we see him. Burgess's Enderby, though, is the same at the end of *Enderby's Dark Lady* (1984) as he was at the start of *Inside Mr Enderby* (1963). The voice of the exasperated artist, whose advice nobody will heed, runs through other novels beside his. Ronald Beard, in *Beard's Roman Women*, is an Enderby who lives more opulently after having worked in movies. Toomey is a rich confectioner of lending-library pulps: an Enderby who is far wealthier, and more guilty, than the bowel-obsessed poet from whom he derives. Enderby is Burgess's fictional sibling, a surrogate brother who endures in novels caricatured versions of what Burgess endured – or claimed to endure – in reality. A composite of Enderby and Burgess is the narrative voice that blasts and bellows in book after book, like the garrison sergeant-major. No ruse or stratagem managed to shake this off. The more dexterous Burgess attempted to be, the more he drew attention to himself. *The Clockwork Testament*, for instance, breaks up into film scripts, transcriptions of TV chat shows and scenarios: and yet we leave the book with Burgess uppermost in our minds. Toomey, in *Earthly Powers*, is designed in contradistinction to his designer: a homosexual, an octogenarian, a mixer with every famous name and face the twentieth century possessed. And yet we leave the book with Burgess uppermost in our minds.

If Burgess's tone has a tendency to glare like the varnish on a Victorian canvas; if, whilst fluent, his fluency is stylistically unvariable – this is why Bayley says it is non-art. There is no differentiation. As an author he could never veer away from himself. Enderby, Toomey, Crabbe – and, later, Freud, Moses, Christ and Keats: their opinions and conversational mannerisms could be interchanged. Stephen and Bloom, by contrast, are entirely divergent, as are all Joyce's other Dubliners distinct, because the language that shapes them is newly customised for each character. Burgess's Shakespeare, therefore, is no more than Burgess, which is why, for Bayley, *Nothing Like the Sun* pays diminishing returns.† WS, or Will, the bawdy

* 'Sounds a fair combination,' said Burgess, unscrewing his pen.

† Amongst my papers I found a sixty-thousand-word manuscript, a whole monograph, on Shakespeare, Joyce and Burgess, its epigraph taken from Borges' *Labyrinths*: 'Do not the fervent readers who surrender themselves to Shakespeare become, literally, Shakespeare?' It was all about Joyce's absorption in Victorian Shakespearian scholarship, Burgess's absorption in Joyce, and thus the genesis of *Nothing Like the Sun*, the non-fiction *Shakespeare*, *Enderby's*

bard, could never have written the dramas performed in his name. He is too vain and stingy. There's no spaciousness. He lacks tenderness – a caressingness. He's no more than machinery or a bundle of neurosis and disease. Though about Shakespeare, Shakespeare is missing from it. The book is not Shakespearean in spirit; it's all infirmities, faults and follies. It has a ghastly creepiness – which Burgess derived from his reading of Nashe's *A Litanie in Time of Plague*, which he also set to music, and his plundering of J. B. Harrison's *Elizabethan Journals, 1591–1603* (three volumes, London, 1928–33) and *A Jacobean Journal* (London, 1940), from which he took 'a lot of notes feverishly, making a chronological

---

Dark Lady, and the film that never was, *Will!* or *The Bawdy Bard*. It's a phenomenally erudite piece of work (a relic of my donnish phase), and I recall summers at the Bodleian and in the library at Wolfson reading Sir Sidney Lee's *A Life of William Shakespeare* (1898), James Halliwell-Phillipps's *Outlines of the Life of Shakespeare* (1881, revised 1887), the Professor of English at Trinity College, Dublin, Edward Dowden's *Introduction to Shakespere* [*sic*] (1893), Georg Brandes' *William Shakespeare: A Critical Study* (Copenhagen, 1895), and Frank Harris's *The Man Shakespeare and His Tragic Life-Story* (1909). I looked at the work of the Early English Text Society, founded by F. J. Furnivall, 'a fine old fellow', according to Ezra Pound, who put him in the *Cantos*, and which produced facsimiles of the Quartos in forty-three volumes (1880–89); and of the New Shakespeare Society, founded in 1874 to examine Elizabethan life and literature – it was less about than around Shakespeare. Joyce possessed a copy of its list of *All the Songs and Passages Which Have Been Set to Music* (1884), edited by Furnivall, J. Greenhill and W. A. Harrison.

It was literary archaeology, with C. W. Wallace undertaking research at the Public Record Office, for *Three London Theatres of Shakespeare's Time* (1909), and W. W. Greg making an edition of Henslowe's *Diary* – about which Burgess wrote, 'Thank God for Philip Henslowe. This was not the view of many who knew him personally, for so to know him meant mainly to owe him money' (remember Burgess himself, to the student in *Granta*: 'Do I owe you something?') 'A typical Elizabethan entrepreneur . . . he owned a starch-works, various brothels, a pawnbroker's shop, and a theatre.' His account book tells us that on 3 March 1592 the season's highest dividends were for *Harry the Sixth* by an unknown author from Warwickshire, William Shakespeare. (Henslowe was to have been played in *The Bawdy Bard* by that master of saturnine shrewdness, James Mason.)

Such was the passion to make a mythical figure historical, historical documents were frequently forged. (A similar game was afoot with Christ, e.g. Albert Schweitzer's *The Quest of the Historical Jesus* [1906] – Burgess was there, too, with his biblical novels and television adaptations.) Legal warrants and mortgage deeds, records signed by Shakespeare, registers containing Shakespeare's name – John Jordan's *Original Collections on Shakespeare and Stratford-on-Avon* (1780) and William Henry Ireland's *Miscellaneous Papers and Legal Instruments under the Hand and Seal of Shakespeare Including the Tragedy of 'King Lear' and a Small Fragment of 'Hamlet' from the Original MSS* (1796) – have the quaint antiquarianism of gothic novels, where old vellum documents in locked drawers get the plots going and are connected with haunted houses and headless monks. John Payne Collier's *New Facts* (1835), *Particulars* (1836) and *Further Particulars* (1839) about Shakespeare promulgated forgeries and lies with such ingenuity, e.g. inserting Shakespeare's name in petitions about the Blackfriars Theatre, documenting performances of *Hamlet* and *Richard II* given by the crews of the vessels of the East India Company's fleet off Sierra Leone, that you can see why Coleridge and Wilde wanted to make the fabrications canonical, and why Joyce has fun with

table which related the known facts of Shakespearean biography to the wider events of the time'. Harrison's *Shakespeare Under Elizabeth* (New York, 1933) gave him the idea that the Dark Lady was a Black Lady;* and though Mann's *Docktor Faustus* made the syphilis–genius correlation, even here Joyce was first. The relevant passage is picked out in *A Shorter Finnegans Wake*: 'A baser meaning has been read into these characters the literal sense of which decency can scarcely hint. It has been blurtingly bruited by certain wisecrackers . . . that he suffered from a vile disease.' And to that add Frank Harris's portrait of 'the passionate, melancholy, aesthete-philosopher', with which Burgess was also familiar, and we are a long way off from, say, Gwyneth Paltrow and Joseph Fiennes capering in the motes of fair and natural light.

---

them in the sections on Shem the Penman in *Finnegans Wake*. The grandest efforts of the imagination have been called forth; there is a rejection of all control, all confinement. As Wilde says in 'The Decay of Lying', the temper of the true liar is marked by 'his healthy, natural disdain of proof of any kind. After all, what is a fine lie? Simply that which is its own evidence.'

Related to the counterfeiters are the cryptographers. Ignatius Donnelly's *The Great Cryptogram: Francis Bacon's Cypher in the So-Called Shakespeare Plays* (two volumes, 1887) is again mentioned in *Finnegans Wake*; and between December 1901 and January 1902, the period of Stephen's diary at the end of *A Portrait of the Artist as a Young Man* (with its wordplay on forging in his soul's smithy this, that, and the other thing), there were letters and articles in *The Times* on the Bacon–Shakespeare controversy – and the idea of literature as riddles and crossword puzzles both underpins Joyce's method and anticipates Burgess's: 'Cypher-jugglers going the highroads. Seekers on the great quest. What town good masters? Mummed in names,' as it is stated in *Ulysses*. The cycle is completed in *Enderby's Dark Lady* when the poet, in America to write lyrics for a musical on the bard, is compelled to don the doublet and hose and go on stage, the real leading man having walked out. In costume and make-up he looks exactly like that moon-faced bust in the church at Stratford: 'Shakespeare looked at Enderby from the mirror and coldly nodded' – an echo of the last page of Burgess's biography of Shakespeare, where we are told, 'To see his face we need only look in a mirror.'

* These were texts with which Burgess had become familiar at Manchester, as an undergraduate. In an essay, 'Genesis and Headache', included in *Afterwords: Novelists on Their Novels*, edited by Thomas McCormack (New York, 1968), however, Burgess wanted us to believe that he'd kept up with his studies: 'I had been reading pretty widely, ever since my student days, in books about Shakespeare, in Elizabethan documents, in close scholarly background history.' He was thus surely a match for that other specialist in the period, A. L. Rowse? Both of them imperious; both tending to talk at the tops of their voice; both, in John Kerrigan's phrase, deploying tones 'of Olympian effrontery' (*London Review of Books*, 21 June–4 July 1984): they were all set to meet, like Absalom and Achitophel, at the Brighton Literary Festival. What a clash of the titans this promised to be, in a balloon debate about the identity of Shakespeare's Dark Lady. A few hours before the off, Burgess backed out, claiming he was ill. Gyles Brandreth obligingly understudied for him. Later that evening, Brandreth returned to his hotel, switched on the television – who should be roaring away on a live late-night chat show but Burgess? The illness was a lie. Did he do the TV instead because the fee was bigger, or because Rowse was likely to have wiped the floor with him? It is a shame their bout never did take place, however, for Rowse and Burgess were similarly conceited and absurd – both of them pugnacious and struggling for

When Will visits Madge the cartomancer, he is told, 'You will be pushed and hurried and told to write with speed'; that is, he's a glorified journalist or broadcaster, who'd fit in his five-minute spots on *Woman's Hour*, had it existed then. Like Greene and his crew, Burgess insists on giving Shakespeare a prolixity, a language that's gaudy and obsessed with the body – everything is to do with eating, swilling, excreting and decaying – and the effect is cartoonish and abrading. Shakespeare's motives, too, are graceless. 'Money must still be earned,' is his cry, as it was Burgess's. 'When I buy a house it will be in Stratford. London is for work. There will be time enough for sitting by the fire, telling my children stories.' Parsimonious, he's Shylock. 'WS extended his hands like, he thought, some usurious Jew.' Of the commission for the Sonnets: 'I did it for

---

ascendancy. Where Burgess, regardless of the specific subject, will work in Catholicism and political bondage, remind us of his musical ambitions and insist that writers are despised persons in Britain – had you asked him for directions to the Gents, you feel, you'd get a speech along those lines – Rowse, too, had his crotchets and fixations, which he'd throw in every five minutes, i.e. being working class and from Cornwall, winning his scholarship to Oxford, oh his struggles: 'I have sometimes been tempted to write up the other side of the village life from *A Cornish Childhood*. It would show that one need not go to the Congo or Central America, the Mau-Mau Reserve or Viet-Nam for horrors,' he sniffed, complaining about the insanitary worlds of Graham Greene. He was particularly unforgiving with those who disputed or failed adequately to applaud his theories about the Sonnets: 'When we were young we were mystified, like everybody else, by Mr W. H. and wondered who it could possibly be. When, as a leading authority on the age, I had cleared up all these confusions and at last reduced the career of our greatest writer to common sense, David [Cecil] never troubled to go into the matter; he merely thought that I "might be right".'

Here is the overriding reason for Burgess's avoidance of Rowse: cowardice. Rowse was as abreast of his reviewers and critics' opinions as ever Burgess was; and like Burgess he brooded on negative notices, whilst trying to dismiss them, because 'one has no need to defend oneself against the third-rate'. (Or, as Burgess himself says in *Little Wilson*, 'reviewing does not necessarily entail reading'.) Burgess's notice of Rowse's *Christopher Marlowe: His Life and Work* appeared in the *Nation* on 1 February 1965, as 'Dr Rowse Meets Dr Faustus' (it reappears as 'Dr Rowstus' in *Urgent Copy*), and the article is full of abuse: 'Dr Rowse may be said to be wasting our time'; 'For a scholar, Dr Rowse asks us to take rather too much on trust'; 'Dr Rowse disappoints'; 'Dr Rowse will have to try harder'; 'Dr Rowse gives us the coroner's facts and no more'. In an interview conducted by Charles T. Bunting, for *Studies in the Novel* (1973), the book review seems very sweet-natured by comparison. Seven years on, Burgess's animosity is personal: 'I don't trust Rowse at all. I have never trusted him. I think he's a bigot and pigheaded and, of course, violently Protestant, violently anti-Catholic. I took an instant dislike to his book on Marlowe, which I thought was a bad book, and the work that he did on Shakespeare . . . I thought didn't give us anything new.'

If only they had met at Brighton; there'd have been blood on the sand. Burgess and Rowse: both extraordinarily sour, and both with a deep sense of (provincial) inferiority. By the way, when, after his death, Rowse's library was sold off by G. Heywood Hill Ltd., a copy of *You've Had Your Time*, defaced with angry annotations ('Bloody Fool', 'Feminine Nuisance', 'Irish' and 'Drink BORE' etc.), was priced at £18.

money. I must live.' Though these are Burgess's own excuses, the posturing derives from *Ulysses* and the challenge to 'Prove that he was a Jew,' put by John Eglinton. Shakespeare the Jew is an allusion to Bloom's background, of course; in Joyce's novel we are given a snapshot of the exotic East, of haggling in the bazaar or speculating on the Rialto. Joyce, however, stresses Shakespeare's acumen rather than meanness (and Bloom is nothing but generous); yet Burgess's Shakespeare will only lend money if he can charge punitive rates of interest. *Nothing Like the Sun* would have us believe that in the plays, scenes are shaken together, lines left unblotted, artistic merit unregarded, and all only to make a financial killing. At best, Shakespeare will be craftsmanlike. He stitches plays as his father had stitched gloves. There's to be no distracting absorption in the subject matter, no concentration of thought. Instead of being an artist, he's a cunning popular novelist – and it was Georg Brandes, the Danish literary critic, who gave Burgess this conception of Shakespeare the preincarnation of the grandee on rue Grimaldi (or, as he was in 1964, the squire of Etchingham, the Chiswick swell): 'He longed for land and houses, meadows and gardens, money that yielded sound yearly interest, and, finally,' wrote Brandes, 'a corresponding advancement in rank and position.' In *Nothing Like the Sun*, this becomes: 'Only land is truly gentlemanly, land and property. Well, I shall do my best to buy land'; and 'I am glad we are now acknowledged to be gentlemen,' Will says to his father when the armorial bearings are granted. Shakespeare's eagerness to obtain a coat of arms ('Honour is a mere scutcheon . . . A *mere* scutcheon?') oddly prophesies Burgess's pride over Liana's heraldic devices; like Shakespeare, too, he was to buy a new place in every place – all those houses he acquired and, once title had been established, abandoned.

The plague-pit prose; the worms and skulls; the general grotesquerie of Burgess: his own life was full of death (his mother and sister, his hospitalisation, Lynne's decline); and you don't need to be a biographer of Ellmann's eminence to make connections between fiction and fact – or to see the point of contact between Burgess and the illness or grossness of his characters and their society. But I never personally feel that those real experiences were making their demands on him as an artist – for his art, or non-art, isn't about what people are like; he prefers artifice and burlesque. His work is a species of complex games and lies. What he wants, as he said in his Introduction to *A Journal of the Plague Year*, is a style that's 'all for contrivances and somewhat artificial manipulation'. This is his aesthetic – and you either accept it and relish it or, like Bayley, you go back to Pushkin and writing the recipes for Dame Iris to put in *The Sea, The Sea*. Burgess praises the way Defoe 'amassed a solid little library of reference works' on the plague; he'd gathered coffee-house reminiscence and had interviewed survivors; and when he got down to scribbling the book, Defoe's 'methods were that of the working journalist' – a point that is repeated in praise: Defoe was 'a journalist to the last'. Burgess admires the homework, the legwork, the amalgam of invention and research which results, and he explicitly relates this to Nashe and Greene, whose prose is 'highly contrived and reeking of the lamp'. This is precisely how Burgess himself proceeded. Whether he's recalling Malaya or presenting us with Marlowe, in *A Dead Man in Deptford*, writing about Shakespeare fictionally, in *Nothing Like the Sun*, or non-fictionally, in *Shakespeare*, or, in his memoirs, transfiguring Little Wilson as Big Burgess, he jumbles up verifiable fact with obvious fiction, with the intention of pulling off (as Defoe did) a 'confidence trick of the imagination'.*

The connection, therefore, with Burgess, isn't between art and life; it's between the deceptions and disguises of art and the deceptions and disguises of the artist. His characters are always making quick changes of clothes or identity, so as to move about unobserved. They are always pretending to be other than themselves – and in *Enderby's Dark Lady* it is Ben Jonson who is a spy, plotting with Guido Fawkes to remove the oafish Caledonian who has claimed the throne; except really he is a double agent, handing to Sir Robert Cecil (with Shakespeare as his intermediary) a list of the genuine conspirators. In the meantime, he is happy in the sanctuary of gaol ('I am safe enough here'); and Marlowe makes an appearance, as another spy, so that this song may be sung:

> I sing of a spy, of a spy sing I,
> That under the cloak of tobacco smoke
> And drink and boys and blasphemous noise
> Had sharp enough eyes for other eyes.

– and there is also a (gratuitous) reference to 'Sir Francis Walsingham. Dead these two years, but once head of Her Majesty's Secret Service. He recruited you, Kit.' Burgess's world is full of deception and mendacity. Another of his tales concerns Shakespeare's script-doctoring session on

* 'In five years he turned out book after book – fiction and non-fiction,' said Burgess of Defoe. '*A Journal of the Plague Year* appeared in 1722, twenty-five days after *Religious Courtship* and forty-nine days after *Moll Flanders*. *Colonel Jack*, *Due Preparations for the Plague* and the *Life of Cartouche* completed a year remarkable for industry, but not more remarkable than other years.' Another antecedent, then.

Psalm XLVI, in the King James Bible. The forty-sixth word in from the beginning is 'shake' ('. . . the mountains *shake* with the swelling thereof'); the forty-sixth word from the end is correspondingly 'spear' ('he breaketh the bow and cutteth the *spear* in sunder). In 1611, Shakespeare had his forty-sixth birthday. A brilliant cryptogrammic fancy – quite ingenious. But did Burgess really expect at least somebody not to notice that he'd stolen the story from Kipling, whose 'Proofs of Holy Writ' was published in the *Strand Magazine* in April 1934?* What makes a man do this sort of thing? What is life like when you do it? As an author he's all too alive to his themes, images and meanings (hence his characters are automata – they are imprisoned by the author's calculations); the intentions of his work are all too open to us ('to act evil is better than to have good imposed' – what more need possibly be said about *A Clockwork Orange*?); and yet at his core are fraud and lies. The heroine of *Enderby's Dark Lady* is April Elgar, a negress – Edward Elgar died in the spring of 1934. Is this what Burgess would call an acknowledgement? Her real name, in any event, is May Johnson. Liana, when Burgess met her, was married to a black man called Ben Johnson. There are hidden messages-within-messages here – but do they add up to anything, other than create what Bayley called a mood of 'claustrophobic deliberation'?

The fabrications are pervasive – from his mother and sister not dying in the manner he said they did, to Lynne's famous rape (my bet is that she fell down a manhole in Berkeley Square during the blackout when pickled), to his cerebral ailment, which was actually the migrainous result of malnutrition – and the need to hoodwink was intense. 'And, ah,' sighs Tennyson in *Maud*, 'for a man to arise in me,/That the man I am may cease to be.' Burgess was doing everything he could to make himself intriguing. As he said of Joyce's Stephen, so can we say of Burgess himself: 'What he needs . . . is a spiritual or mystical father, a father who is not "consubstantial". This father will be a mother as well, and we are given a hint as to where he lies.' But whereas Joyce organises the encounter between Stephen and Bloom, Burgess has to be in charge of his own destiny. He has to make allusions to himself. That he does so makes the apocalypse at the end of *Nothing Like the Sun*, where the self-dramatising narrator descends from Shakespeare, and *Abba Abba*, where he comes from Keats, less of a flippant gag. It makes it a vainglorious one.

* First published in book form by the Tragara Press in 1981, with an introduction by Philip Mason. Edition limited to one hundred and twenty-five copies printed in Bembo on Cream Glastonbury paper in red wrappers. Thirty-four pages.

In *Nothing Like the Sun*, Will is sacked from his post as a private tutor (for alleged pederasty) and apprenticed, instead, to the law. He is found in the office at Stratford 'blotting the name WILSON'. Burgess's own real name is embossed by the bard. Later, when the construction of the Globe is celebrated by a drinking bout, the actor called John Wilson baptises the building with a flagon of wine: '*Ego te baptiso . . . in nominee Kyddi et Marlovii et Shakespearii*.' Burgess has given himself a small part in the story, a Hitchcockian walk-on as a mock priest like Buck Mulligan. He was fond of the role. On leaving England, in October 1968, with Liana and her son in the Dormobile – he'd have us believe he was on the run, with garage mechanics, money-changers, waiters, customs officers and the police all tipped-off in advance to give him a hard time – 'It was, of course, raining heavily' (Burgess was a man who'd take a sunset personally); and they get as far as France when, 'I took the opportunity, while Liana was sleeping, to baptise Paolo Andrea in rain-water: *Ego te baptiso Paulum* – did *Andrea* take Latin or a Greek accusative? – *in nominee Patris et Filii et Spiritus, Amen*.' Names are important to Burgess – and likewise name changes have a particular power. It's as if one substance is being transformed into another, as in the mystery of the Mass. All this, and then the local equivalent of Customs and Excise will try and leave him for dead up an alley.

Homer's Ulysses, in returning to Ithaca, the point where he first started, returns to his roots; Oedipus returns to the roots of his own name.* He

* Oedipus's name does not praise him; it condemns him. Oedipus: the *swell-foot*, the feet tied to the ground. Lévi-Strauss has made much of the claudication, an affliction Burgess was proud to share. He insisted that the BBC paid for his private transport within London owing to 'the crippling ailment of thrombo-angiitis obliterans' ('expenses not justified', stated the accounts department bluntly. 'He chose recording date and time to suit himself'); his intermittent claudication, as he called it, a vascular ailment caused by heavy smoking and an arterial fur-up exacerbated by a diet based on lard, 'disappeared one day when I was walking down a street in Brooklyn. Maybe it was a miracle.' The limping, however, was to come and go – perhaps it was psychosomatic. (It went away in Malaya.) Hobbling around with a walking stick, Burgess's *venerability* was mocked by Greene. Several names in the Oedipus myth refer to crippled walking: Labdacos, Laius's father, means *lame*; Laius means *left-sided*. In *The Right to an Answer*, the journey to the heart of darkness which is England is a journey to the heart of darkness which is Denham. 'I can feel damnation being broken in like a pair of shoes,' he boasts, Oedipally registering sin in his feet.

A blinded drifter at the end, a foundling at the beginning, Oedipus is the paradigmatic outcast. What is unique about his name is that it both connects him to his real family and contains the information about his severance from it. Piercing his feet was carried out on the instruction of his parents when they wanted to dispose of him. Killing his father and marrying his mother, Oedipus has been paradoxically involved with his parents whilst they had considered him absent and destroyed.

recognises he has reached the crossroads of his life for the second time. The first occasion was when he killed his father; now it is when he learns that it was his father he killed. Onomastically, he is his own clue in the search to solve the riddle of Laius's death.* The secret of Oedipus's name emerges, for – as Burgess explained in his adaptation for the Guthrie Theater, Minneapolis, in 1972:

He is simultaneously deeply rooted and rootless; his fears about his own conception and birth are our own fears about our conception and birth. Everything prior to an individual's emergence from the womb and his acquisition of self-consciousness is but hearsay evidence. (Burgess's mythical or larger than life heroes, Shakespeare, Napoleon, Keats, Moses, Jesus, even Freud, all mistrust their family trees.) The lesson we learn is to ask how can we be sure that the strangers we grow up with are our genuine parents? Oedipus, his true parentage eventually revealed, blinds himself – he plunges himself in darkness; he does not want to see any more revelations. But he does not kill himself. He wanders the world as a blown husk –

> As blown husk that is finished
>   but the light sings eternal
> a pale flare over marshes
>   where the salt hay whispers to tide's change
> Time, space,
>   neither life nor death is the answer.

Ezra Pound, Canto CXV: unloving, undead – this is the period before we are born – it is the state of history we have to take on trust; equally, it is the limbo in the uterus when we are still subsumed within the greater life of the mother. The unliving, undead state is also the world of myth – and of art. Being a sort of time machine, myths and legends drift into the future and attempt to make sense for us of the past. Despite the best efforts of Lévi-Strauss, Sir James Frazer, Robert Graves and his white goddesses, or modern mystics and mythologists like Iris Murdoch and Angela Carter, however, we can never clutch it: myths slide through our fingers, they speak in riddles, their meanings are ambiguous. This is the value of myriad translation and adaptation. They are all fragments that are greater than any single story.

* Amongst the Lewis Papers (which make the Aspern Papers look like Enoch Soames's lecture notes), I found another monograph, provocatively entitled *Anthony Burgess and Incest*. Using *MF* as the launch pad, the Temporary Lecturer in English Literature at Magdalen College, Oxford (they paid me cleaning-lady rates whilst John Fuller was on sabbatical), shot off into literary critical hyperspace to discuss [i] Joyce's use of mythology, the forensic intelligence of Sherlock Holmes, the figure of Tiresias, versions of the Oedipus legend (Stravinsky, Pasolini, Freud); and [ii] the bearing of such an eclectic heritage on Burgess, with his wanderers, outcasts, and fondness for riddles and puzzles. 'If no God, there must at least be a pattern-making demiurge,' Burgess has a character say in *The Wanting Seed* – and it is deep in the subconscious mind that the shapings and connections are being made. As we are informed in Burgess's *Oedipus the King*:

> It is dangerous to answer riddles,
> But some men are born to answer them.
> It is the gods' doing – they hide themselves in riddles.
> We must not try to understand too much.

According to Freud, in *The End of the World News*, the mainspring is the libido – killing

> . . . the stigma is in your name,
> Oedipus. A man's name always means something
> Though that something be lost in time.

Names advertise our history. 'What's in a name? That is what we ask ourselves in childhood when we write the name that we are told is ours,'

---

rivals (i.e. father figures) to possess perfected womanhood (i.e. mother figures). Mother and son, father and daughter, 'it's one of the oldest things in the world . . . There's no crime, no dirtiness . . . I find it's the wish, the desire, that matters, and the truth means nothing.' Claude Lévi-Strauss, too, believed what counted was 'the living myth' – the story or fiction which a person propounded in front of a psychoanalyst or anthropologist, this being 'an emotional crystallization which is moulded by a pre-existing structure'. What this means is that one's fantasies, no matter how Bosch-like or wayward, can be decoded by the experts and fitted into their tables and graphs – and thus seen to be not so very peculiar and mad after all. This was a consolation to Burgess. He reviewed Lévi-Strauss's *The Scope of Anthropology* in *Book World* on 26 November 1967 (an article reproduced in *Urgent Copy* as 'If Oedipus Had Read His Lévi-Strauss'), and was thrilled to discover the prevalence of an Oedipus legend, from the Greeks to the Viennese, to the Algonquin and Iroquois Indians. The puzzle-solving aspect of the myth is linked, apparently, to the sexual taboo on incest – riddles and incest both being involutions, the one lexical, the other biological. If this seems abstruse, not to say implausible, that's why Burgess wrote *MF*, to give the theory a leg to stand on. Riddle-asking beasts, doubles, inadvertent deaths and seductions that fulfil ancient prophecies: what Lévi-Strauss found amongst the Pueblo nation, Burgess used to confect a plot; and he also found all this jiggery-pokery in *Finnegans Wake*, where 'the dream is expressed in the language of riddles', and he foisted it upon Sophocles, for the Minneapolis adaptation of *Oedipus the King*. And as conclusive proof that 'the riddle–incest nexus is deep in human culture', Burgess put forward *Tremor of Intent*, which he'd written in 1965, allegedly all unawares of Lévi-Strauss. 'My hero, a spy, receives a message he cannot decode; almost immediately he becomes attracted to a girl who is a kind of daughter-substitute . . . "The love he proposed, still marvelling at himself, was the only genuine kind: the incestuous kind." . . .' The Catholic Emancipation (Relief) Act was in 1829 – just the other day, according to Burgess; so imagine how he growled about the prohibition on incest: 'In England, certainly, incest only became a crime in 1908,' so recently, he concludes, that we feel no deep-seated horror about it.

The Scope of Anthropology was Burgess's choice as *Book World* Book of the Year for 1967. He had actually heard of Lévi-Strauss at least as early as January 1965, for he reviewed in the *Listener* a television programme the professor had made about St Nicholas. In the *Spectator* (11 July 1970), Burgess reviewed *The Raw and the Cooked*, Lévi-Strauss's lengthy study of the nature/culture dichotomy, seen in terms of the kitchen. Basically, savages eat raw food, civilised societies make a fuss about preparing and transforming it in some fashion. Table manners separate the civilised from the barbarous. Nearly every conversation and debate in *Earthly Powers* is dramatised over a meal. The plot, also, concerns the Eucharist, cannibalism, the sanctity of eating, and mass poisoning. In 1984, I wrote to Lévi-Strauss himself, at the Laboratoire d'Anthropologie Sociale, Paris, asking him about all the Burgessian inspiration – telling him what he'd initiated. Perhaps they'd met, indeed, these *intellectuels*, these *Commandeurs des Arts et des Lettres*, for didn't Burgess have a high standing in France? His reply is one of my treasures: 'Much to my regret I have not read *MF*, and I do not believe any myth to have a universal meaning. I am due to the airport in a few hours . . .'

meditates Stephen Dedalus, who whether he likes it or not is going to have an existence that'll involve (symbolically) the creation of a labyrinth (i.e. the novel *Ulysses* itself) and the theory of flight (not a literal set of wings from wax and feathers, but exile abroad). *Daidalos* is Greek for 'cunning worker'. How plausible is it as a Dublin family? Leopold Bloom's family were originally Virags; his secret name, when corresponding with Martha Clifford, is Henry Flower. Burgess's *Blooms of Dublin* at least has the wit to do something with the floral imagery, from the rhododendrons on Howth Head, to the bouquet on Rudy's grave, to the scents and roses Molly recalls in Gibraltar. In *Shakespeare*, he pondered the bellicosity of the cognomen and the impressionistic ways it was spelt, e.g. Shogspar, Choxper, etc. Joyce, in *Finnegans Wake*, suggested Shaggspick and Shakhisbeard and, in a compound that involves both Shakespeare and James Hogg, the Ettrick Shepherd, there's Shitric Shilkanbeard ('I am known throughout the world . . . by saints and sinners alike as a cleanliving man'). Burgess quotes the last of these in his sprightly *Joysprick* – and in that Enderby goes to the lavatory, like Bloom, feeds the gulls, like Bloom, and has difficulties with girls, like Bloom, here's another Joycean link: Enderby merges into Hogg as Joyce has Hogg merge into Shakespeare, in a mad plot about doubles and usurped identities.

In *Shakespeare*, Burgess finds the baptismal Will significant – heavy with sexual puns: 'lust, phallus, vagina . . . the name is a small hymn to male thrust, Him that shaketh his spear and breaketh hymens'. Is this a procreative connotation? Does it involve Burgess's ideas about art as a sexual (or masturbatory, in his case) activity? Or is it a puerile notion? ('Was Shakespeare such a prick?' asked John Kerrigan, in his article on *Enderby's Dark Lady* in the *London Review of Books*.) What if the bard had gone by the name of Willy instead (like Somerset Maugham); or if he'd been a Dick, John Thomas or Percy? What if he married a Fanny?* Joyce, we are told in *Joysprick*, 'took seriously the business of the appositeness of a name to its owner', and Burgess, similarly, is cheerfully slavish to both chance and false etymology.

Shakespeare's coat of arms is emblazoned with an eagle shaking a spear

* Willy and Fanny – such a couple must exist. I was always self-conscious about calling Ellmann *Dick*, but it's what he wanted. *John Thomas* was Lawrence's favourite and *Percy* inspired a film about a penis transplant. Playing a comic policeman in the sequel, *Percy's Progress*, is Milo O'Shea, Bloom in the movie version of *Ulysses*. There's plenty on Fanny Brawne, Keats's inamorata, in *Abba Abba*.

in its claw. The name is meant to conjure up a race of heroes and warriors, bloody, bold and resolute ancestors from whom Will derived his zeal. Names are the family's ensign or standard. Shakespeare's crest was a boast about this pedigree – names are sacred; and as Loewe tells Miles in *MF*: 'Your very name implies duty. That's its meaning . . . You were enrolled before birth in the regiment of your family name. Miles in the service of the Fabers.' *Faber* is Latin for maker or manufacturer; the earliest designation was for a metal-worker. Hence, the equivalent of the Greek *daidalos*. The other characters in *MF* are named for animals and birds – like the ones in Saint-Pierre: Menuzzi is obese with talons, Brother Marcel looks like 'a monkey at the end of a chain', and Father Dalival has 'something of the hawk' about him. In Burgess's novel, there is a menagerie of owls, ants, lions, lambs, rabbits and parrots.

John Wilson appears in *Nothing Like the Sun*; and here he is in the epigraph to *MF*:

> *Enter Prine* [sic], *Leonato, Claudio, and Jacke Wilson*
> *Much Ado About Nothing* (First Folio)

The stage direction in the Quarto (1600) for Act II, scene iii, line 35 had 'Enter prince, Leonato, Claudio and Muficke' and the Folio (of 1623) spelt the name as Iacke Wilfon. In the notes to John Dover Wilson's edition (of 1923), the one with which Burgess was familiar, there is a vague reference to a book (?) or article (?) called *Who Was Jack Wilson?*, published in 1846 by Rimbault. (The question is, who was Rimbault? What is the precise source?) Anyway, this Rimbault identified Wilson as Dr John Wilson, who was born in 1595 and became, in 1656, professor of music at Oxford. He was apparently 'Mr Wilson, the singer' who had attended Edward Alleyn's wedding in 1623. He was a 'gentleman of the Chapel Royal' in 1626; and in his book *Cheerful Ayres* (1660) he gave a musical setting for Autolycus's 'Lawn as white as a driven snow.'* Wilson's role in *Much Ado* was Balthazar; his famous line is 'Men were deceivers ever.' Burgess's *This Man and Music*, where the chapter 'Oedipus Wrecks' dismantles *MF*, informs us that 'Jacke Wilson . . . was an actor-singer in the Lord Chamberlain's company of players. Jack Wilson is the real name of Anthony Burgess. There is no true riddle

* It is a line from *The Winter's Tale* that Burgess had intended as an epigraph for *A Clockwork Orange*: '. . . There were no age between ten and three-and-twenty, or that youth would sleep out the rest; for there is nothing in the between but getting wenches with child, wronging the ancientry, stealing, fighting . . .' (III, iii)

here. Either one knows the identification or one does not. The question that ought to be asked is: why did one name change into the other? There is no easy answer.'

Indeed not – and he relied upon the obliquity. 'Few people are any good at piercing disguises,' he taunted, in the midst of discussing Nabokov's *Pale Fire*, that masterpiece about doubles and duplicity and mock scholarship. Hidden names suggest a hidden world, for as Greene says in *Ways of Escape*, there is 'a magical quality in names. To change the name is to change the character'; and by converting his name, Burgess converted himself into a character. Consulting *A Dictionary of British Surnames* we find Burges, Burgis, Burgiss, Burgess and Borges: from the Old French *burgeis*, the inhabitant of a borough, or a freeman. 'I never cease to read Anthony Burgess,' Jorge Luis Borges told Paul Theroux. 'He is good – a very generous man, by the way. We are the same – Borges, Burgess. It's the same name.' By what spell did the old necromancers convince onlookers in Washington that they were two people, when they jointly recited Caedmon's hymn? It is one of Dr Jekyll's observations that 'man is not truly one, but truly two' – he can be born twice, like a butterfly, with its larval and pupal stages. I'd like to imagine that the Burgess–Borges twin thing was an insectile apparition; that the mirror world of their books found expression in their lives – Borges blind, Burgess colour-blind, the shrouded flat with its heavy furniture in Buenos Aires exactly duplicated down to the last cactus flower and silver fork in Monte Carlo; the minor Edwardian authors on the shelf in Argentina matched copy for copy by Burgess's holdings of Chesterton, Stevenson and Wells ('I reviewed *Experiment in Autobiography* when it was first published by Gollancz in 1934 . . . for the school magazine,' claimed Burgess – no, I've not checked). The tilt of the Roman senator's head is the same for both of them, too; pallid, haunted, and with the glaucous eyes dreaming up tales of conspiracy and violence. (Or maybe it's that the rectal suppositories aren't working.) They are authors highly conscious of a book as a bag of tricks – literature as chimerical, conjured by special effects. The style of Borges, said Burgess, is continuously to be 'casting doubt on the reality of what he's saying'. It's true – in *Labyrinths* (1962), *The Book of Imaginary Beings* (1969), and the rest of the parade of paper puzzles, he plays games with the passage of time. He's tireless – and something of a charlatan. Nothing has sprung from feeling, only from feigning. He couldn't be more Burgessian; or Burgess more Borgesian.

(From the *Sunday Correspondent*, 28 October 1990.)

Burgess is an invention. Being an invention, he could fabricate a past from which he might have sprung and a future into which he might head off. What has happened is that he has constructed for himself an entirely new personality. 'This is not unusual,' said Burgess, in the midst of discussing Myra Hindley's realignment of herself in prison. 'Few of us know what we really are: most of us present a persona to the world. We are all, in a sense, actors.'* The name-changing is connected with his travels and his exiles – the theme is that of flight or escape: from his history, from his country, from his grief and guilt. The transubstantiation is like that of Saul into Paul, in *The Kingdom of the Wicked*. The son, his new name bereft of any connotations in so far as the mother is concerned, can be a son no more. Saul she knew; Paul is 'disinherited and disowned'. That's what Burgess felt

* *Daily Mail*, 21 November 1986. He continued, 'Myra Hindley's new personality explains or excuses the lack of remorse. Remorse would only apply to the person who existed in 1965. In effect, she denies knowledge of that person.' Is this, then, how Burgess himself blocked off the feelings and loyalties of John Wilson? How he can manipulate the past, re-rewrite it?

had happened to him, with the Tollitts and the Byrnes and the Dwyers, and he tried to turn isolation (or self-creation) to his advantage. (Let's not blame the stepfamily – let's blame Manchester. It is such an unromantic – anti-romantic – place. It flattens the soul. This can't be helped.*) Unable to convince me that his characters are somebody else entirely, even St Paul, who by his preaching and missionary work did more than anyone to develop Christianity from a Jewish sect into a world religion, is made by Burgess into a Burgess simulacrum. He's Autolycus, 'purveyor of scraps and trifles' (*A Winter's Tale* allusion), and a Joycean Odysseus sniffing the sea: '*Thalassa* . . . Or *thalatta*, according to the dialect you prefer.' Mulligan trills, looking at Dublin bay, 'Thalatta! Thalatta! She is our great sweet mother.' When he leaves Rome, Paul is even sung the Caruso aria from the French romantic opera *Martha*, which Bloom hears: 'Come back again, come back . . .' But the borrowings from other literatures (there are several Shelley and Shakespeare gags), besides making a nonsense of the Burgess-as-great-Biblical-scholar business, don't do any work. They are little authorial games, like an interior decorator who scribbles on the plaster before putting up the wallpaper. Paul is gradually ridiculed. His famous letter to the Corinthians is dictated like a busy tycoon – 'And the greatest of all these is love. Got all that?' he enquires of the stenographer.

Burgess is facetious – but when did he ever tell you anything real about himself?† One of his famous pranks, when Joseph Kell's *Inside Mr Enderby* came out, was to review it personally. As he said in his lecture, 'Confessions of the Hack Trade', delivered at Dartington in 1992, he had the precedent of Walter Scott, who'd reviewed *Waverley* in the *Edinburgh Review* – and: 'There is something to be said for allowing a novelist to notice his own novel. He knows its faults better than any casual reader, and he has at least

* What is there in Manchester to ignite the imagination? Nothing about it is festive, especially when you compare it with a maritime city like Liverpool. Manchester's famous literary progeny are few: Richmal Crompton (born in Bury), Francis Thompson, author of *The Hound of Heaven*, Ian Hay, a friend of Wodehouse's, Paul Dehn, who wrote the screenplays for the James Bond films, the *Planet of the Apes* films and *Murder on the Orient Express*, and, lastly, Ernest Bramah (born in Moss Side in 1868). 'We know nothing about Ernest Bramah, except that his name is not Ernest Bramah,' said Borges.

† In the autobiographical *Little Wilson and Big God* and *You've Had Your Time*, he paradoxically tells us all and gives nothing away. He tried to return to his roots – to the John Wilson realities behind the Anthony Burgess masks. Though seldom the truth (in the police court sense), the representation of self-disgust and resentment smacks of being true (in an emotional sense). They are a fine pair of novels. Burgess, as an autobiographer, living in Lugano, Switzerland, was by then almost totally depersonalised as an artist (and starting to die of cancer as a man). His distant past could be written about with candour because he had no living connection with it. He had no friends left.

read the book.' The Literary Editor of the *Yorkshire Post*, however, hadn't known about the pseudonym – he'd sent the copy to Burgess in all innocence. 'I was attacked by the Editor of the *Yorkshire Post* on Yorkshire Television and promptly, and perhaps justly, dismissed.' Terence Kilmartin was then made to worry about Burgess's pieces for the *Observer* on V. S. Naipaul, Iris Murdoch and Brigid Brophy. 'I was now untrustworthy and might conceivably be all these authors, and more, masquerading under the name Anthony Burgess, a name that was itself a masquerade.' How he loves the truth and cover. An invisible man, said Wells, is a man of power. Here's what Burgess had to say about Joseph Kell:

THE YORKSHIRE POST THURSDAY MAY 16 1963

POETRY FOR A TINY ROOM

JOSEPH KELL'S first novel, 'One Hand Clapping', was a quiet and cunning female monologue that fell from the presses almost unnoticed.

One Australian periodical acclaimed its virtues in a two-page review that, giving a thorough synopsis of the plot, must have made purchase of the book seem supererogatory. For the rest, reviewers had other things to think about. That little book now thinly stalks the bookstalls as a paperback, its bright eyes quietly watching the reception of its successor.

Whatever readers may think of the content of 'Inside Mr. Enderby,' they are hardly likely to ignore the cover. This shows a lavatory seat (wood, not plastic) entwined with ivy. It is Mr. Enderby's lavatory seat, wherefrom he blasts his poetry at the world. (Mr. Eliot said recently – and in The Yorkshire Post, too – that poetry is a lavatorial or purgative art.)

Rejected the world

If the world takes no notice, Mr. Enderby will not worry. He has rejected the world: he has retreated to the smallest room in the house; there, scratching bared knees, he writes the verse that his Muse dictates to him.

But the world will not leave him alone altogether. It drags him out of his lavatory to receive a poetry prize and a proposal of marriage from Vesta Bainbridge, a *chic* vision from a woman's magazine. Soon, Enderby is on his honeymoon in Rome.

This eternal city is the antithesis of the toilet: here is the Church, here is the State, here, in lapidary form well-preserved, is the meanest history known to man. Here, too, is treachery, for Rawcliffe, a jealous fellow-poet, has stolen a poetic plot from Enderby and persuaded Cinecittá to turn it into a bosomy horror-film. Enderby, appalled, flees.

Normal and unpoetic

But his Muse flees also. He can no longer write. He attempts – unhandily, as with everything except his craft – a suicide which the State tut-tuts over. He is turned into a useful citizen, normal and unpoetic. There is a middle way between greatest Rome and smallest room – the way of the decent job and the decent life. Enderby is cured.

This is, in many ways, a dirty book. It is full of bowel-blasts and flatulent borborygms, emetic meals ('thin but over-savoury stews,' Enderby calls them) and halitosis. It may well make some people sick, and those of my readers with tender stomachs are advised to let it alone.

It turns sex, religion, the State into a series of laughing-stocks. The book itself is a laughing-stock.

This is a jaunty précis, perhaps suspiciously confident in its knowledge of the plot, but Burgess can't be accused of recommending himself wholeheartedly. Far from it. Yet there's a glee about these aliases. As he says of his alter ego in *Byrne*, which he wrote whilst undergoing terminal cancer care at Sloane-Kettering, 'He loved mendacity!' The *Dictionary of British Surnames* finds Chelle (1219), Chel (1250) and Kelle (1311), and it comes from the Old Norse *Kel* and the Old Swedish *Kael*, which in English became *Ketill*, or Kettle. Burgess uses 'Kettle' as the slang or code in *The Doctor Is Sick* for a stolen good. As for Enderby himself, there's a remote and uninhabitable chunk of Antarctica called Enderby Land, and in a poem about a shipwreck by Jean Ingelow,* called 'The High Tide on the Coast

* Jean Ingelow (1820–97) wrote twenty-five books of verse and stories for children, such as *Mopsa the Fairy*, *Fated to be Free* and *Sarah de Beranger*. Successful in her day, she's now completely forgotten. Somebody ought to examine how and why authors date and fall from social fashion. Authors people devoured simply vanish – Marie Corelli, Bulwer-Lytton, Mary Webb. Will Alan Bennett, whom the public currently can't get enough of, go the same way as Arnold Bennett? Who decides these things? I was reading about Dame Rebecca West recently. Her novel *The Birds Fall Down* (1966) earned her £53,000 in the first royalty period. Who has heard of that book today – or of Dame Rebecca West herself (1892–1983), come to that? Children's literature is particularly prone to shifts in taste. The illustrations in the Edmund Dulacs and Arthur Rackhams, which were meant to entertain my grandmother, terrified me – all those gnarled tree trunks and gnarled goblins. The literature produced for children by adults ought to be a clue to how or what we think of the tiny swine from one generation or era to the next.

Burgess wrote two children's books, *The Land Where the Ice Cream Grows* (1979) and *A Long Trip to Teatime* (1976), both illustrated in febrile Edward Gorey cross-hatch style by Fulvio Testa. The former must've taken Burgess all of ten minutes – Jack and Tom fly by airship to a frozen land where the snow is ice cream, wafer cones are pointy rocks and the lakes consist of chocolate sauce. *A Long Trip to Teatime*, however, is a much more significant work, and the author clearly conceives of his audience as being dwarf versions of himself. Intended for children, no real child would endure it – for it is a cryptograph.

The tale of Edgar climbing through a hole in his desk (it's Alice's rabbit hole), and wandering amongst the adventures recounted in his history primers, is told with arcane vocabulary and dense neologisms. Burgess is also strenuously allusive, especially to Dickens's *The Mystery of Edwin Drood*. Famously, that novel is unfinished. Its author dropped dead with the pen in his hand. Burgess borrows Dickens's characters from their suspended animation in the incomplete manuscript and gives them walk-on parts: a talking flower mentions Mr Grewgious (the lawyer in *Drood*); Edwin is the forename of many citizens in Edenborough, where Edgar ends up; when he falls into a ditch, he is helped out by Durdles (the grave digger

of Lincolnshire, 1571', church bells clang out 'Play uppe "The Brides of Enderby"': both references, as Burgess said, imply loneliness, a character who is 'cold and removed'. In 1976, he wrote a song cycle for soprano, flute, oboe, cello and keyboard entitled *The Brides of Enderby*. I wonder what that is like? I'd have thought the subject required tubular bells, hand bells, gongs, musical glasses and a Hammond organ. But Enderby's trouble with wives and would-be wives, moon-women, dark ladies and stepmothers is definitely Burgess's theme. When Enderby marries, says Burgess, 'he has to be destroyed'. The jangling church bells have 'shipwreck connotations'.

Robert de Enderbi (d. 1198), Thomas de Enderby (d. 1298) and Robert Enderby (d. 1384) are the Leicestershire Enderbys giving their name to the manor near where Lynne's family had settled. Burgess never chose to tell us that, evidently a conscious decision by the man who can remember (say) the name of a motel he stayed in once in North Carolina where they sold cheap cigarettes (the Carolina Inn, Chapel Hill), or how Shirley Conran spelt 'cunt' ('coynte').* Come to that, Nabokov omitted to inform

in *Drood*). In Dickens's text, there are references which spookily prefigure its non-fulfilment: we are told of an unfinished portrait, an unfinished house, an unfinished tomb. And when we read the fragment we are conscious that each page registers time running out for the author. *The Mystery of Edwin Drood* becomes a piece of clockwork.

A Long Trip to Teatime encourages any amount of enquiry – 'You have to look very deep into it,' says Burgess – and when we do so, we find a manual of the author's fancies. Edgar, like a very great many Burgess heroes, is lost in an alien land and his papers aren't in order. He joins, for example, Crabbe in Malaya, Lydgate in Dunia (*Devil of a State*), Paul in Russia, (*Honey for the Bears*), Hillier in Istanbul (*Tremor of Intent*), Miles on Castita (*MF)*, Enderby everywhere, and Toomey adrift in the twentieth century (*Earthly Powers*). Though it affects to be Scottish, the alien land in *A Long Trip to Teatime* is Hibernicised. Edenborough is less a contortion of Edinburgh than a reference to *Finnegans Wake*: Earwicker 'will be ultimendly respunchable for the hubbub caused in Edenborough'. In Dublin, the two quays on the Liffey are known as the Eden and the Borough. With Burgess, all roads lead to Joyce. Edgar himself is a tiny Ulysses whose ambition is to return home to an Ithaca of 'fish-paste sandwiches and cherry cake'.

The Liliths and Sirens who bedevil the hero are mother figures or mother substitutes ('You watch out, son, for the mother of the Blatant Beast'); the gulls cry out 'Liddell and Scott, Liddell and Scott,' a reference to Carroll's Alice; there's a grisly bit of Freudianism involving an oven, a cat, an old lady's burnt hand ('Oh, oh, the pain's terrible') and a man called Mr Quimby; and lots of nineteenth-century sages seem to be capering about – Matthew Arnold, Carlyle, Trollope, Sir James Stephen.

Frankly, it's a *fucking farrago*, if I may be permitted to use a slightly crude expression.

* Burgess never did quite enough to scotch the rumour that he'd ghosted Shirley Conran's *Lace*, for which Simon and Schuster paid a million dollars. Each evening, she'd come to his apartment in Monaco with a few more pages for correction and improvement, he alleged. Why not? As she says in her indispensable *Superwoman* (1975), 'The most important aspect of cooking is knowing what you can get away with and what you can't.'

us that Quilty is a town in County Clare, and yet what is the purpose of naming Humbert 'Humbert Humbert' unless to reinforce a theme of doubleness? What all this sport with nomenclature signifies are the divisions that go on in people. Was Burgess in reality delicate and effete, and hence busied himself creating a persona as rough and coarse? On the one hand we have Cyrano and his flamboyance – and look at who is drawn to the role: Olivier, Welles (for whom Burgess hoped to write a musical on the life of Houdini), Antony Sher; actors who are showy-offy, hogging the limelight relentlessly and conscious of their high spirits. Cyrano is a man's life as a continuous performance – and then, on the other hand, we have Enderby, who is forever changing his name and trying (without success) to get away from people. Yet, in his own way, he's also always calling attention to himself, proud not to have a permanent job, indifferent to his clothes, hygiene and habitat; like Cyrano he exists best on public occasions, when giving a public performance, improvising a tirade (like Burgess himself) 'against vulgarity and debasement'. He's something you'd want to avoid on a full moon.

Cyrano and Enderby are both Burgess's self-portraits, and whilst they are perpetually exasperated and in turmoil, can they really be said to possess private lives? Inner lives? States of mind can only be made manifest in Burgess if they become part of a wardrobe or something to do with the flesh. Mind is a symptom of the body. In *The Kingdom of the Wicked*, the Roman Empire is a body and revolts and uprisings are contaminations, illnesses. For the Apostles, 'The Body is God's work and very wonderfully made.' The ingestion of wine and bread, at Communion, is a way of exalting it. Saul's collapse on the road to Damascus is interpreted as an epileptic fit. Burgess presents the frothing and the spasms, but is not willing to peer at mental activity: 'I can only guess at Saul's dreams, which must have been manifold and complex.' That's the one area you'd expect a novelist to venture, inside the head. From the cogitations of another character, Ananias, the disciple who was sent to Paul at the period of his blindness, we are again kept away. He casts 'a look of inner torment, perhaps intestinal'.

When Dr Jekyll knocked back his potion, it 'shook the very fortress of identity'; as Hyde, he hasn't only taken a different name, he assumes a different personality, as Paul does when he casts out Saul, who had been a bitter persecutor of the Christians. The dual nature of good and evil is exposed – evil coming from the Old Teutonic *ubiloz*, 'going beyond due measure'; that is, immoderation, or self-assertion, against which must be balanced self-restraint. To carry on with the etymology: the Hebrew word *satan* means 'one who opposes, obstructs or acts as an adversary'; the Greek *diabolos* means 'one who throws something across one's path'. The Christian idea is that evil is simply the absence of good, the actions of sinners, of unclean spirits – their resentments and grudges, malice and negativity. The Manichean belief, to which Burgess subscribed,* sees good and evil as two entities or masses, contrary to one another, active and independent, a cosmic conflict between light and darkness, revelation and falsification. The purpose of art – and certainly the point of a life of moral integrity – is to achieve a balance between chaos and order; to be aware of this paradox, perfectly put by Alfred Brendel (who was in fact discussing his piano-playing): 'You have to be in control and at the same time lose yourself completely. You have to think and feel in advance what you want to do and, simultaneously, to listen to what you are doing and react to that.'† Everything is dualistic – and choices have to be made. *A Clockwork Orange* instructs us that individual freedom means you can choose evil; and in *Tremor of Intent*, Hillier the spy-as-priest says, 'Don't you think we'd all rather see devil-worship than bland neutrality?' This is Milton's Satan, isn't it, 'preferring hard liberty before the easy yoke of servile pomp'? But Burgess himself went beyond moral classifications and into a realm of algebraic banality. 'Life is binary,' he told the *Paris Review*, 'this is a duoverse. What I mean is that the notion of essential opposition – not God/Devil but just x/y – is the fundamental one, and this is a kind of purely structuralist view. We end up with form as more important than content, with speech and art as mere phatic processes ["used to convey general sociability rather than to communicate a specific meaning", *OED*] with the big moral imponderables as mere hot air.'‡

* 'I call myself a Manichee. I believe, if you like, that God and the Devil are possibilities, but it is not foreseeable, it is not inevitable that God should win over the Devil.' Interview with Geoffrey Aggeler, 30 July 1969. Quoted in his *Anthony Burgess: The Artist as Novelist* (Alabama, 1979), p. 28.

† *The New Yorker*, 1 April 1996.

‡ Burgess's most interesting article on all this is 'Two's Company', a review of Karl Miller's *Doubles: Studies in Literary History* (in the *Observer*, 30 June 1985): 'We are binary beings, and everything in our language and culture is based on structures of opposites. Out of certain dualisms – the raw and the cooked; the vowel and the consonant; the stop sign and the go sign – we are able to weave complex cultural networks, but we are so programmed by the formation of our brains that we cannot escape from the duoverse.' Is this Burgess the Lawgiver again? What possible evidence is there that 'language is a mirror of the cerebral cortex'? (What language? Whose cerebral cortex? Burgess's – with its erudite babbling and gabbling?) I thought it was seven that had the cabbalistic good vibrations – seven seas, deadly sins, wonders of the world, pillars of wisdom, dwarves, and brides for

This must be his extrapolation from Lévi-Strauss's boiled/roasted and sun/moon pairings, as found in the four immense volumes of *Mythologiques*; and yet where Lévi-Strauss was celebrating the richness and variety of savage and civilised minds, Burgess's philosophy is empty of all humanity. It's an evaporation, with no roots clutching or branches growing out of the stony rubbish; and this is much as he described his change of name. He never gave a satisfactory answer as to why he'd done this. 'The real reason,' he told Samuel Coale, a professor of English at Wheaton College, Massachusetts, 'was that I started publishing when I was in the Civil Service overseas, and you were not allowed to use your name if you were writing anything of a frivolous nature, like fiction. It was recommended strongly, indeed it was enjoined, that I use another name.' Was there such a prohibition? This sounds like an evasion, especially as Burgess wasn't fully Burgess until well after he'd returned from the Far East; and he was always having to explain to the BBC (particularly the confused accounts department) that 'my work may possibly be known to you under a pseudonym' – and he'd habitually sign letters with a confident fountain-pen flourish:

Anthony/John

– which at the very least is having it both ways, as if Stevenson's doctor were to correspond on potential health scares with the editor of *The Lancet* as Jekyll/Hyde or Wilde's aesthete with the *Yellow Book* as Dorian Gray Jr/Dorian Gray Snr; and don't you love the official structuralist patented forward slash, to denote parity and opposition?

On other occasions, Burgess stated that there were just too many Wilsons on the literary and cultural landscape – Angus (whose *The Old Men at the Zoo* gets into *Ninety-Nine Novels*: 'We are in a world of pri-

---

brothers? Burgess attempted to impute numerological significance to the chapters in *A Clockwork Orange*: 'I had structured the work with some care. It was divided into three sections of seven chapters each, the total figure being, in traditional arithmology, the symbol of human maturity.' Unfortunately, his editors, particularly Eric P. Swenson at W. W. Norton, didn't appreciate the final chapter, where Alex has unconvincingly matured into a family man – and it is indeed more of an epilogue or afterthought – and so until recently (when Penguin added the novel to their Twentieth-Century Classics list in 1996), the book came to a halt at the end of Chapter Twenty.

Swenson, by the way, is the name of the date- and number-obsessed astronaut in 'The Muse', the sci-fi story added to *Enderby's Dark Lady*, who operates the dials and consoles of the spaceship, but who is a philistine: 'I've never had much time for poetry.'

To the cosmological duos, however, may I add the critic and the artist and the biographer and the biographee?

vate nightmare, as Dickens often was, but Wilson has the un-Dickensian courage to let the nightmare take over'); Ethel, the author of *Swamp Angel* and *Mrs Golightly*; Edmund, the learned literary and social critic (who in *Homage to Qwert Yuiop* is deemed 'crotchety and unreasonably vindictive'); August, who wrote a play enticingly entitled *Ma Rainey's Black Bottom*; Colin, whose *The Outsider* defined the angry young men with a smack of Hamlet in them; John Dover, the Shakespearean scholar; Roy, the strip cartoonist, who provided 'Chimpo's Circus' for *Happy Days* in 1938; Teddy, the pianist and bandleader; and William Griffith, the founder of Alcoholics Anonymous. (A. N. Wilson, however, wasn't around half a century ago – it only seems as though he was.) Lecturing at the University of Rochester, in 1972, Burgess noticed that the institution's benefactor was Joseph Chamberlain Wilson, the founder of the company manufacturing Xerox machines, and 'I felt I had to go since, as I told several unbelieving audiences, my father's name was Joseph Wilson . . .' Indeed, this plethora of Wilsons does seem to be photocopied;* they proliferate endlessly. There are fewer Burgesses. There is the espionage cousinage, of course – Guy Francis de Moncy Burgess (1910–63); and the back flap on the jacket for the hardback edition of *The End of the World News* singles out for praise Frank Gelett Burgess ('a very distant relative of your present, or actual, author') who invented the term 'blurb', a 'puffy gobbet of sales talk'. I've heard him say that he was an invention of Roland Gant and James Michie at Heinemann. They tugged at each end of John Wilson and Anthony Burgess popped out, like a paper hat from a Christmas cracker, which simply needed unfolding. In the opening pages of *Little Wilson and Big God* he laments the trouble he's had over the years at the check-in desk of the British Airways terminal at Kennedy airport, at Rome airport and at Luqa in Malta, all

* The *DNB* catalogues heaps of worthy John Wilsons. The Celestial Xerox Machine has brought forth, in addition to the lutenist we know about, the editor of the New Cambridge Shakespeare, and the one who was 'Christopher North', Hogg's coeval in *Noctes Ambrosianae*, these tinkers, tailors, soldiers and sailors: a secretary to the viceroy of Ireland, a botanist, a parish schoolmaster in Lesmahagow, a judge at the Middle Temple, a scene-painter at Astley's Theatre, London, a governor of the province of Minho and General Officer Commanding in Ceylon, the compositor who set Scott up in type, the founder of the *Oriental Christian Spectator* and author of *The Parsi Religion Unfolded*, a principal of the Royal Agricultural College, Cirencester, a Wykeham Professor of Logic at Oxford, the author of *The Practice of the Sheriff Courts of Scotland in Civil Causes*, a Chairman of the Educational Board of the Booksellers Association, a Bishop of Singapore, the editor of the *Berwick Advertiser*, a Whyte's Professor of Moral Philosophy at Oxford, and a major-commandant of the Royal Hospital, Chelsea.

because of his double identity. His passport names him as John Wilson, tickets and hotel bills are habitually made out to Anthony Burgess. His first and last names, he said, 'show the carapace of my nominal shrimp, the head and tail I pull off to disclose the soft edible body'. It's not only Kingsley Amis who found this a baffling metaphor. 'God knows what that last phrase refers to,' he announced. 'Anyway, "John" he was and is to me . . .'

The crustacean imagery is interesting – for here's a writer who'll not be willingly exposed and vulnerable; who lives in fear of giving too much away. Like L. P. Hartley's shrimp, what if he gets sucked inside a sea anemone? His head would be mangled. His ideal was to have no name at all. 'I don't know what we mean by identity,' he confessed in 1968, soon after Lynne's death. 'I don't think it matters ultimately. One is defined by what one does. If one ceases to act, one ceases to have any identity. The whole business about names and so forth is all rather amusing but fundamentally irrelevant. Call me X. Call me K. It doesn't really matter.' Well, X is Enderby's middle initial; K has Kafkaesque reverberations aplenty. The white marble gravestone in Monaco (number forty-seven, on the terrace as you go up the hill) reduces him to the set of carved initials that is:

A B B A
A B B A

– the infinite repetition, a circularity, a world without end, of *A*nthony and *B*urgess. John Wilson has gone for ever. Instead of shrinking him to a pair of capital letters, however, the effect is far from modest – it's the magniloquence of the devil's party: 'Father, father, why hast thou forsaken me?' is Christ's cry on the cross. It's typical of Burgess that his erudite posthumous pun and great cryptogram (the Bible, sonnets, an English romantic buried in a foreign field, an allusion to Joyce's poem 'Ecce Puer') has had to misfire so farcically. Everybody thinks it's the tomb of a seventies Swedish pop group.

Despite his attempt at dismissing the name-changing business, this issue is far from irrelevant, though it is fundamental – for when Burgess changed his name it determined the kind of writer he would become. He didn't just do it for documents and title pages, to appease government officials or indulge editors. It went far deeper than that. Changing his name, shedding an identity – I mean, he didn't belong to the generation, like George Eliot or Jane Austen, where you had to be anonymous. John

Wilson – what's *wrong* with that?* To say there's Harold Wilson or Richard Wilson is no kind of answer. What it means is that he wasn't writing from his centre; he never put his soul into his work. Let's have a war book, a spy novel, something on Beethoven's 'Eroica'; lots of different kinds of projects, like the cobbler, carefully, attentively, producing his boots and shoes.† That one could possess or be permeated by a creative mood, or that there should be such a thing as the breath of emotional life

* I'd be happy to read a book about the psychological or occult significance of pseudonyms. Lynne had recommended 'Anthony Powell' (not knowing there already was one) or 'Anthony Gilwern', after the village near Abergavenny where she had relatives (the Powells). Burgess allowed her to share the credit on the Pelegri ('and Lynn [*sic*] Wilson') and Saint-Pierre ('and Llewela Burgess') translations – and pseudonyms are a form of translation, in the 'Bless thee, Bottom! Thou art translated' sense. You can understand an actor wanting to be more glamorous. Marion Morrison would reach for a hairdryer; John Wayne for a Colt 45. But *authors*? The Clemens/Twain split personality must have to do with the rascality and innocence of the writing and the writer's actual vision of mankind as self-deceiving and hypocritical. Truman Capote plays a character called Lionel Twain in *Murder by Death*. His address is Two-Two Twain. The Eric Blair/George Orwell division (or doubling) has yet to be fathomed by his biographers. 'When George Orwell emerged from Eric Blair, he wore the clothes of common sense,' says Bernard Crick, which hardly explains the Old Etonian's strange desires to live as a down-and-out, dress as a tramp, and go out of his way to spend time in prisons and dosshouses. What middle-class imperialist sins are being atoned for? Other pressing issues: why am I bored by Ruth Rendell yet think Barbara Vine the equal of Dame Iris? Dame Iris, by the way, hated being officially gazetted as Dame Iris Bayley. 'Murdoch is my *name*,' she said to me fiercely. Burgess kept calling le Carré (born John Cornwell) John the Square, as if there was a Masonic association. I don't regard the Martin Amis/John Self games in *Money* as being of any significance – sub-Nabokovian pseudo-conundrums by a writer with nothing to say. There used to be a man, by the way, who went around London pretending to be Stanley Kubrick – i.e. an impostor whose pseudonym was that of a real (but reclusive) person. As Frederic Raphael said, this is 'something like the hero of Nabokov's *Despair* . . . This man has usurped another's identity without, so they say, looking in the least like him.' Spooky.

† Frederic Raphael, in *Eyes Wide Open* (London, 1999), makes a characteristically perceptive remark: Burgess's problem is that he 'confuses innovation with originality. By never doing the same thing twice, yet never reaching a new level of achievement, he displays a kind of monotonous versatility. Like Kubrick, he is a Proteus who ceaselessly, obsessively avoids being himself.' Proteus, a character in the *Odyssey*, doesn't assume different shapes quite for that reason, however, as Raphael ('a major scholar in classics at St John's College, Cambridge', as his blurb informs us proudly) must have known. He changes shape in order to escape being questioned.

The Kubrick/Burgess association is interesting – for both of them were cold, calculating practitioners, the director with his chessboard and computers, Burgess with his typewriter and self-imposed deadlines. As a glorified old hack, however, with delusions of grandeur, a literary style that's purple to the point of puce, and an air of being so pleased with himself he could burst, Burgess's closest disciple is – Frederic Raphael. The Oscar for *Darling* was a long time ago (1965) and *The Glittering Prizes*, for which he remains best known, is also a period piece (1976). The subject of his work, paradoxically, is shallowness – the transitoriness of fame, the emptiness of worldly success. None of this would matter, except that the

inspiring a novel, a musical composition or a painting, were ideas unworthy of serious consideration. Hard work – graft – grit; but never art, which Burgess looks down on. He's this northern puritan, who could never really connect with what art means – as, for example, with the elements of decadence in Modernism: Moreau, Wilde, Lautrec, Pound, and even Joyce, had a sensuousness that was beyond him; ottomans, orientalism, the occult; a prose that's all arabesques, pulse, ardour, and an expression of human sentiment and passion – you'll find none of that in Burgess. Instead of which we got four books a year, much of the stuff a 'silly verbose stew' (Larkin on Auden); and yet the effect wasn't of plenitude and the opening up of magical horizons – because the man who lived in a Dormobile, as he was too mean to pay for a bed-and-breakfast place, was artistically miserly, too. He's cramped and dank. Sometimes I think that, such was his puritanism, for all his output and complaining about being unappreciated, he's actually contemptuous of art and of artists; he has no real understanding of any inwardness or inner consciousness; no patience with what another A. B., Arnold Bennett, called 'the transient gleam of a drop of true human juiciness'. The interviewer from the *Paris Review* was told: 'By extension of vocabulary, by careful distortion of syntax, by exploitation of various prosodic devices traditionally monopolised by poetry, certain indefinite or complex areas of the mind can . . . be rendered. Only through the exploration of language can the personality be coaxed into yielding a few more of its secrets.' This is propounded with such insistence, such rhetoric, it's not instantly obvious that it's nonsense. (Burgess the Lawgiver was as hard to argue with as Moses or Freud.) If sophisticated monkey business with words is what matters, literature has already come to an end, with *Finnegans Wake*. Burgess's law is inhuman. It's like his interest in music as an international language, a generalised flow – and the effect is boring and alienating because it won't admit uncertainty, unruliness, the indirect hints and murmurs that make us more interesting than apes and less predictable than mathematics.

He changed his name, took flight, and became somebody else; he worked out of necessity – but what necessity? Burgess's story is the oppo-

---

persona he projects – the fastidious, sophisticated cosmopolitan with beautiful homes round the Med; the intellectual background and the Hollywood pay cheques – is so arrogant and conceited, glittering prizes and fame evidently matter very much indeed. The shallowness runs deep. (This is a not insignificant observation.) Peter Sellers always used to say to him, 'Haven't they rumbled you yet?' To his credit, Raphael enjoyed the teasing. *Q:* Why did no one ever say to Burgess, 'Haven't they rumbled you yet?'

site of self-exploration. Its theme is self-avoidance. His work is a distraction – from his moral failure; from his relationship with the past. Despite all those losses in his life, his work wasn't a rueful compensatory search; far from it – it's an evasion. He's detached and ambivalent. For what, he felt, was the alternative? Succumb to self-pity and drink? As Lynne did? She'd bang on the floor of the bedroom, and he'd have to take up more drink. 'Thank God – one day the banging stopped,' he said to Joe McGrath. 'Except she was dead.' The strange callous jokiness belies the suffering, pain, anguish, loneliness and insomnia that was closing round them. 'Lynne and I daren't go out very much in case one or other of us suddenly collapses far from home,' he told Kathleen Winfield. 'Still, we went into St Leonards yesterday and didn't collapse, *Gott sei dank*.' This invalidish existence went on for ever – it was like being buried alive. By 1967, Lynne was losing gallons of blood from what Burgess kept telling people was a duodenal ulcer. He visited her in hospital, getting there by train and bus, and he himself was now drinking pints of gin mixed with canned grapefruit juice. 'Llewella slowly improves,' he told a producer at *Woman's Hour*, spelling her baptismal name wrong. At night, he was finishing *Enderby Outside*. He'd begun it in the autumn of 1965 and the yellowing typescript had been hammered piecemeal on a variety of manual typewriters, a testament to his fits and starts. What he most wanted to do was produce a novel about the life and times of a professional musician named Charles Levey Clegg, which would cover the period from Debussy to the advent of the Beatles. 'I envisage half a million words,' he said. It never materialised, unless it was transmuted as *Earthly Powers*, which is the history of a popular novelist from the Edwardians to the era of Burgess himself on Malta and in Italy. 'One settles to the typewriter with a sigh of weariness,' he stated. 'One ends by writing in a void, throwing words into an emptiness. And yet one goes on writing.' And if that's how he felt in the sixties, in Etchingham, matters were never to improve. In 1971, three years after Lynne's death, he was drinking wine in a picturesque Italian town and feeling suicidal. He found Rome intolerable, the food abominable and the people coarse. 'I am a lost soul,' he wails. He ran around Trastevere tearing down what he took to be fascist posters – only to discover that the streets had been roped off for a film location and he was destroying the set. In America, he's all alone in a Holiday Inn surrounded by snow, 'wondering, as the lecture hour approaches, whether anyone will remember I am here at all'. What a vision of desolation – Burgess is like a definition of Hell.

'I was twenty-five when I met him,' a former editor at Heinemann,

David Burnett, told me. 'He was very much in the centre of the literary world. The *Malayan Trilogy* had done very well – fourteen thousand in hardback. *Devil of a State* was a Book Society choice. He was producing potboilers like *Honey for the Bears* and *One Hand Clapping*, published under a different name. But *Tremor of Intent* didn't do very well, so he had this notion that he wasn't highly enough regarded at Heinemann, so he went to Cape for *MF* and *Napoleon Symphony*.

'He was living at 24 Glebe Street, Chiswick, and at Applegarth, a cottage in Etchingham, Sussex. Both were terrible slums.' The former was in an ugly terrace seven miles west of central London. Hogarth is buried in Chiswick in the church of St Nicholas. Applegarth, despite the cottagy name, was a solid redbrick Victorian semi-detached with a large garden. Its rooms were filled with review copies, barrels and kegs, a dog, four cats, a tortoise and a mouse. The Hammer horror-film contingent of glowering villagers, who followed Burgess wherever he went, were well in evidence. They poisoned one of his cats. Michael Ripper, playing a pop-eyed publican in Hastings, made sure there was no ice for Lynne's gin, and Burgess has to biff him. When Lynne is in hospital, more of the Hammer cast are there on hand to be cold-eyed and sinister medical orderlies. Burgess, on a return journey to Gibraltar, throws drinks over retired army officers and 'played hell in broken Andalusian' with a waiter at the Rock Hotel, impersonated no doubt by Sam Kydd.

It was Burgess's habit to go out once a week to Soho with Bill Holden,*

* It was William Holden's task, as Publicity Manager of William Heinemann Ltd, Publishers, London, Melbourne & Toronto (telephone HYDE PARK 4141), to invite radio producers and literary editors out to lunch, to badger them and eulogise the firm's authors and its forthcoming list, as for example in this letter to Miss Joanna Scott Moncrieff, Broadcasting House, Portland Place, on 9 March 1960:

> Proofs of Anthony Burgess's book *The Right to an Answer* will be ready in a few days, and I will send one to you as soon as it comes in.
>
> Just in case you are interested, I am enclosing also a tape recording which Anthony Burgess made for us, which I thought you might like to play through and see what sort of person he is. I would be grateful if you could return it as soon as you have finished with it.

I wonder what sort of home-made concert Burgess had produced? Favourite ballads ('Come into the Garden, Maude', 'Love's Old Sweet Song', 'Bless this House', 'On the Road to Mandalay')? Negro Spirituals ('Swing Low, Sweet Chariot', 'Nobody Knows the Trouble I've Seen', 'He's Got the Whole World in His Hands')? Or an off-air recording of his broadcasts on Radio Malaya and Radio Singapore, which he claimed to have made? Burgess had a splendid ham-actor voice, like Freddie Jones (whom I increasingly believe *is* Anthony Burgess whenever I glimpse him striding through Charlbury or at my London club); and Miss Joanna Scott Moncrieff will not have missed that his voice – emphatic, ostentatious – was the voice of a musician.

the Heinemann publicity manager. 'He'd bring authors he knew, like William Burroughs* or Thomas Hinde,'† continued Burnett. 'They ought to have been wonderful evenings – but for Lynne, a terrible alcoholic.

Burgess released three spoken-word long-playing records commercially: *A Clockwork Orange* (Chapters One, Two and Three), Caedmon TC 1417, with sleeve notes by Burgess and M. Mantell (1973), *Anthony Burgess Reads from The Eve of St Venus and Nothing Like the Sun*, Caedmon TC 1442, with sleeve notes by E. P. Swenson (1974), and *Anthony Burgess Reads from A Clockwork Orange and Enderby*, Spoken Arts SA 1120 (1974).

Parenthetically, what a come-down for William Holden, the corpse in the swimming-pool in *Sunset Boulevard*. It happens. David Lodge, the co-star of Peter Sellers in *Two-Way Stretch* and *The Return of the Pink Panther*, is also an Emeritus Professor of English Literature. ('Burgess set an example to the English literary world, which can become insular, gossipy and bland,' he stated in 1993, perhaps only half-subconsciously referring to his own campus novels.) Tony Curtis was the Literary Editor of the *Financial Times*.

* Burroughs was in London to pick up boys down the Dilly. Burgess went to see Burroughs in Tangier – Enderby's time with the doped Beat poets in North Africa derives from the vacation. It's an odd liaison. Why should Burgess, the huffy puritan, have wanted to seek out the etiolated drawling old gun-crazy woolly-woofterish Southern Regency gent? For a lesson on how to kill your wife? (Burroughs shot his wife 'accidentally' during a game of William Tell; Burgess published a short story called 'I Wish My Wife Was Dead' in the *Transatlantic Review*, no. 34, 1969.) To compare notes on spermatorrhea? Burroughs' books, from *The Naked Lunch* onwards, betray a perverse fascination with the hanging and execution of youths and the splatter of their semen as their necks snap.

If we define Romanticism as a school dedicated to the pursuit of sex and death, then grandees like Burroughs, Ginsberg (who told Burgess to 'Tell Bill Burroughs we'll be back there and up his ass'), Gary Snyder and Kerouac (with his admiration for people who 'burn, burn, burn like fabulous yellow roman candles exploding like spiders across the stars') are the true Last Romantics, far more so than Yeats or Dylan Thomas. In their attempt to make outlaws, drug addicts, hustlers, alcoholics and sexual fantasists glamorous, there's a distinct flowering of evil. The quest for sensation is a search for oblivion – for emptiness and degradation. You can see how the juvenile delinquents of *A Clockwork Orange* would be heroes of such a movement – seen from a distance, Alex and his droogs, cavorting and shooting up in the Korova Milkbar, could be hyper-modern versions of those boys in Chardin paintings, spinning tops and bowling hoops. (They are Burroughs' wild boys from the cities of the red night.)

Though a proud outsider himself, Burgess (or Enderby) was appalled by these gestures of defiance – which he saw as the dangers of idleness. Burroughs' arbitrary arrangements of words, the cut-ups and fold-ins, are of course dead-end literary experiments, but these Beat personages were more thoroughly on the edge than ever Burgess could have been; there was immense vitality, even if it was manic and chemically induced. Burroughs had the dandyism of Dada, and in that *The Naked Lunch* was a hallucinogenic cultural allegory, it has to go in the museum cabinet alongside *A Clockwork Orange*.

Lynne could see this at once and taunted Burgess for his frigidity, in both sexual and moral matters. He made the rather hard to credit claim that she purposefully gave him a knock-out pill to render him unconscious so he couldn't go out and about meeting people in the kasbah.

It was rather false devilry of him to claim (in 1967), 'I myself have smoked marijuana for a long time' – adding carefully, 'although only on annual visits to Tangier'. I believe he went once.

† Thomas Hinde (b. 1926) wrote about Africa, in *A Place Like Home* (1962) and *The Cage* (also 1962). His subject was 'the breakdown of colonial rule and the emergence of

She'd knock back these enormous gin and tonics. You'd keep filling up her glass and try and chat with these other people. But she was appalling. She'd say hurtful, abusive things. She was aggressive and dangerous – there was always a clash.'

'Why did he put up with her?' I asked.

'She was a tormenting fury – his muse to get him going. She was fantastically loyal to him – and ghastly at the same time. She'd say hurtful things, but not as I remember directly to him. I drove them from Etchingham to Rye on one occasion. Frightful scenes from Lynne. She threatened to be sick in the car – so they had to get out and catch a stopping-train back. Took them for ever. She was disruptive. She'd make a scene about anything. He was very English in his reaction – rose right above it. Hardly noticed it. He'd come back from Malaya, and would later return from his homes abroad, as very much the English stiff-upper-lip old buffer. His only interest was literature. Lynne once said to me, in her Welsh sing-song which carried for miles, "You see, John isn't interested in sex anymore. He's gone right off it . . ."'

It had been separate beds for years. Lynne threw a pass at every male she met. She ran around Notting Hill with no clothes on – just a see-through white mac, which she'd soon strip off ('Isn't it hot in here?'), the better to let the cat out of the bag, so to speak. Peter Green, a hectic freelancer, who tipped Burgess off about the lucrative tax-exempt trade in ex-review copies, came to stay one Christmas and Lynne crept into the spare room and leapt on him at three in the morning. 'I left her to it. Eventually she went away.' I'm glad there are no further details to dwell on. When Vivien Leigh carried on like this, who'd mind? She was another nymphomaniacal alcoholic – but she was also Vivien Leigh. A visitation from the witch-faced former Head Girl of Bedwellty Grammar School, middle-aged, sagging and reeking of sour gin, wasn't remotely comparably alluring. Lynne was Lynne.

The drill was that Burgess would spend his evenings in the pub and come home with a fresh bottle of Gordon's for his wife, which he'd hand over as if in propitiation. He did nothing to help her cut down on her drinking. Was this selfish and cold, or (paradoxically) loving and generous? What with her drunkenness and his paranoia, it was as if they were trying to wreak vengeance on each other – and on the cosmos? On the one hand, there he was, as David Burnett testifies, exemplifying old world courtesy, being so

. . . new patterns of life in newly independent territories' (*The Novel Now*, p. 158). Hinde's work is not known to me, though its subject matter would seem to chime with Burgess on Malaya or Paul Scott on India, or V. S. Naipaul on just about everywhere else.

definite and gallant, despite the provocation; and then there's his hyper-sensitivity – and he's fearful and rebellious. He was so self-absorbed, what was touching him? Later on, he'd have all those houses and apartments and yet remain curiously homeless; he was never belonging anywhere, and withdrew from life to write – but to write about what? Part of him relished Lynne's delinquencies; he must have done, for these are what get into his books. Slatternliness, cuckoldry, licentiousness, transgressiveness: in a way he was enjoying himself, cataloguing the sin and guilt. Hence the queasy feelings the Enderby novels or *Beard's Roman Women* leave me with. Burgess was sadomasochistic in his dealings with women. They'd punish him, and he'd come back for more. This was the emotion generated between himself and Lynne. Her excessive displays were his contact with the world. But there's such a marked contrast between his experience and his style. Outward behaviour wholly masks and blocks private thoughts – the books are cartoons or museum frescoes; he can tell us and describe what his characters are up to, as they climb the stairs to 16A Piazza Santa Cecilia (Beard – at Burgess's Roman apartment), mix a drink in the salon of 168 Triq Il-Kbira (Toomey – at Burgess's Maltese villa), or write the last words of a manuscript ('a mania for total liberty is really a mania for prison, and you'll get there by way of incest') on the terrace at 1 and 2 Piazza Padella (Miles Faber – at Burgess's Bracciano house); he can let you know people are being restless and reckless – but this prose is disciplined and stiff. The impression isn't of mobility and slipperiness – it's of fixity and inertia. He never gets beneath the surface.

Had he done so, what was bubbling? 'I'm wrestling with a very difficult theme at the moment,' he said in 1960, 'a piece of fantastic future fiction, in which the great enemy is a growing population and diminishing food supply and social virtues are based on infertility. It means creating a whole new world' – a world where The Man Who Can't Shoot Straight is King. The last thing *The Wanting Seed* could be described as, however, is new – not if you've read *Brave New World*. Burgess has copied Huxley's idea of a hierarchical society in the future controlled by biological engineering and psychochemistry. Happiness is attained and guaranteed by drugs. Work is carried out by the lobotomised masses, who are killed off in contrived wars. Huxley's novel is about the disgust of controlled reproduction; so is Burgess's, which had the effect on me of immersion in a soapy, slimy stream or drain. At the Homosex Institute they are working on divesting intercourse of its procreative ends; fashionable women are being advised to 'leave motherhood to the lower orders, as nature intended'; and metaphysicians have decided that history and mythology form an endless cycle: the Pelphase, where 'the sinful acquisitive urge is lacking, brute desires are kept under rational control'; the Interphase, where people start torturing each other; and the Augustinian or Gusphase, where 'a kind of philosophical pessimism supervenes'. It is a lot of trouble to go to, to celebrate impotence; for if 'a kind of aura of fertility surrounds you', you are for the chop. Beatrice-Joanna, with her twins, is pursued by the Population Police. Elsewhere, when children vanish, it is assumed cannibals have taken them – or is the state behind that, too? 'An army,' we are told, 'being primarily an organisation set up for mass murder, morality could never be its concern.' Though there's a character in a cell at Winwick Hospital, near Warrington, where Burgess himself had worked, who rails that 'There's a curse settling on us, God forgive us all, with our blaspheming against life and love,' as with *A Clockwork Orange*, the author's energy is on the side of the violence and the forces of darkness. The book yearns for annihilation.

In 1968, Burgess said that sex was 'as much a purgative as senna or rhubarb'; and by relegating it in this way, making the whole business no better than a bowel movement, clearly the very idea filled him with shame. It's like Enderby composing his poems in the lavatory – is that what he thought of art, too? Before leaving for Malaya, in 1954, he had to dispose of his possessions, furniture, winter clothes, bric-a-brac – and his books. He gave one of his pupils, Malcolm Dalziel, half a dozen odd volumes, dating from his own time in the Fifth and Sixth Forms – anthologies and selections from Hazlitt and Boswell, all with pencilled annotations.* In the back of a collection of Swift, the young Burgess wrote:

POETRY EXTRACTS A MATERIALLY
UNREAL SIGNIFICANCE FROM THE
SURFACE OF THINGS. IT DEALS WITH
THINGS AS THEY APPEAR RATHER
THAN AS THEY ARE.

* *Selections from Swift*, edited by W. T. Williams and G. H. Vallins (Methuen, Third Edition, 1932); *The Book of Hazlitt*, edited by P. P. Howe (Methuen, Fourth Edition, 1932), with a newspaper cutting of the drawing of James Joyce by Augustus John loosely inserted; *Paradise Lost Books I and II*, edited by A. W. Verity (Cambridge University Press, 1928); *Tennyson* ('The Lady of Shalott', 'The Lotus-Eaters', 'Ulysses', 'Oenone', 'Lancelot and Elaine', 'The Passing of Arthur'), Introduction and Notes by F. J. Rowe and W. T. Webb (Macmillan, 1931); *King Richard II*, edited by Henry Newbolt (Thomas Nelson & Sons, 1925); *A Shorter Boswell*, edited with an Introduction by John Bailey (Thomas Nelson & Sons, 1929), with a pencil cartoon by Burgess of Boswell with a tape measure and saying '5 inches shorter'.

It is as if, in the schoolroom at Xaverian College, twenty years before he began to be published, he was determined only to register the unadorned facts: not love, but lust or lubricious itches; not human warmth and affection, but need and exploitation; not beauty, but stench, decay and going to the toilet; not the miracle of being, but a lot of suffering and loneliness which climaxes with madness and death. The indignation is Swiftian – and Swift's 'meat is sometimes too powerful even for a healthy stomach', wrote Burgess in *English Literature: A Survey for Students*. The author of *A Modest Proposal* ('for preventing the Children of Poor People from being a Burden to Their Parents, or the Country, and for Making Them Beneficial to the Public'), with its satirical suggestion that cannibalism makes sound economic sense, possessed, said Burgess, 'this mad horror of the human body . . . [a] terror of dirt and shame at the body's functions'; and I don't think Burgess himself was ever so very different. In the Foreword to *Urgent Copy*, he tells us that 'Book-writing is hard on the brain and excruciating to the body: it engenders tobacco-addiction, an over-reliance on caffeine and dexedrine, piles, dyspepsia, chronic anxiety, sexual impotence.' Toiling at the studios of Radiotelevisione Italiana on the *Moses the Lawgiver* project, in the summer of 1973, he was heard to complain of 'constipation, impotence, crapula, and the other ailments that Geoffrey Grigson doesn't have'. He turned his morbidity into a rhyme – an epitaph:

> Mr Anthony Impotent Burgess
> Pretends he's controlling his urges.

The theme of impotence was first introduced in *Time for a Tiger*. The various racial groups in Malaya demand breeding stock. 'I was bludgeoned into marriage, I was told I was betraying the clan if I remained single,' laments Alladad Khan. Even the homosexual cook, Ibrahim, is married. He was conjugally united as a child but ran away from his wife as soon as he could. She not infrequently materialises to embarrass him publicly. She calls him a *nusus*: an Arabic word meaning the inability to engage in procreative intercourse. The word is a curse, a brand. In the sci-fi section of *The End of the World News*, it is an administrative convenience. Married couples are not permitted aboard the spaceship, so Vanessa files a petition of divorce from her husband, Valentine. He's shocked by this and wants to know the grounds. 'The Muslims have a useful short word – *nusus*. It means the unwillingness of one of the marital partners to cohabit with the other,' he's informed. 'Val had nothing to say to that . . .' Like his spermatorrhea, which Burgess suffered from, and which his characters suffer from ('It was seed-spilling functioning in a void,' says Hillier in *Tremor of Intent*. 'But the psychiatrist I went to told me that it was an unconscious assertion of the progenitive impulse'), impotence, to which it is surely related (all this meaningless discharge, or no discharge at all), is again the ubiquitous affliction. Burgess had lost his libido, not that it had ever added up to a hill of beans. There's a revealing side-light in *Enderby Outside*. Burgess's alter ego is in Seville, under one of his pseudonyms, and says, 'I was going to write a poetic drama about Don Juan who bribed women to pretend that he'd done it to them because really he couldn't do it, not with anybody.' Moyna Morris told me that Burgess was incapable of cranking his infatuation up a notch to make it physical, 'because, you see, he was impotent'. Impotence, therefore, if pervasive, not to say prevalent, had to become something he could be proud of, like a priest and his celibacy. 'You can't be a eunuch priest,' he told the *Paris Review*, 'and you can't be a eunuch artist. I think art is sublimated libido' – or an alternative to the libido.

Burgess's impotence, which he was paradoxically open about, one way and another, led to some of his more spectacular lies. The half man and half goat of the memoirs is a fiction; and his tale about the attack on Lynne in the blackout, and how she aborted, and how she could never conceive afterwards ('We were to avoid, on doctor's orders, the making of a human family'), was not one he came out with when she was still alive. His army colleagues knew nothing of the assault or of his skirmish with Meldrum over compassionate leave – and these were men who shared all their news from home. In any event, Burgess said he'd heard all about it from Sonia Brownell, who was to marry Orwell in October 1949 (three months before he died), and whose name he misspells as Brownwell; so it wasn't exactly Lynne who'd told him anything.* He additionally said that the correspondence back and forth to Gibraltar was inked over and sliced to ribbons by the military censors. So either the

* Just as I'm suspicious that Burgess derived much of his material in *Little Wilson and Big God* on London in the forties from the memoirs of Julian Maclaren-Ross, fabricating his familiarity with that world, so I'm dubious about the Sonia Brownell connection. It's as if Burgess found the other eccentric, volatile woman from Soho and Fitzrovia in that period and concocted the tale that she and Lynne would have been friends. Maybe they were – but Sonia Orwell (1918–80), as she was always called, despite another marriage in the meantime to Michael Pitt-Rivers, was famous for her literary salon in South Kensington (William Burroughs used to attend), and yet the Burgesses never went, nor were they spoken of there.

incident was an invention, or else the elements of actuality are put together to cover up his own shortcomings. Maybe she was pregnant, but she'd been such a tart, Burgess had insisted, how can he expect us automatically to assume he was the father? Perhaps she'd simply been slapped by a pick-up? Or, as I said earlier, maybe she'd tripped and fallen in a bomb crater when inebriated. It's all a convenient way of explaining why they'd never had children – a lie to cover his impotence; he's like one of those aged lesbians one used to meet who wanted you to believe that their fiancé had been killed in the war.

When his memoirs came out, Lynne's surviving family, up in Leicester, were more than outraged by the calumniations. Her niece, Ceridwen, daughter of Hazel, the dedicatee of *One Hand Clapping*, has said that she well remembered, as a child, this tall imposing figure appearing for tea with her aunt, who at no time seemed to be 'an alcoholic, a nymphomaniac who humiliated him in public, and an hysterical woman bent on suicide'. Perhaps Lynne kept that side of herself away from her sister and other relatives? As Ceri Berry (as she now is) says, however, 'The attack in the autobiography was completely unexpected and shocked us because it was untrue. He exaggerated and invented . . .' Unlike Norman Parker, Burgess's colleague on the Rock, who was mildly admonishing about the falsifications – well, it was a long time ago – Lynne's family, to this day, are unforgiving. The Joneses, after all, in Bedwellty, provided Burgess with affection and acceptance back in the days when he had nothing. 'Our family was very much a solid unit. My grandparents were both teachers, there was lots

---

Hilary Spurling, who is the author of *The Girl from the Fiction Department: A Portrait of Sonia Orwell* (London, 2002), and who was a personal friend of her subject, says that there was never any reference to Burgess (or to Lynne) in any conversation or in any written material – a significant lapse.

Burgess will have known about Sonia from the many volumes on Orwell with which he was familiar (and which he reviewed); and everybody's depiction of Sonia is exactly like his own characterisation of Lynne – a rebellious, perturbed spirit, vehement and provocative; a virago all too easy to mock and deride.

I'm cautious about the Lynne/Sonia association – it is too convenient, for one thing. It's Sonia who was Julia, 'the girl from the fiction department' glimpsed by Winston Smith in *Nineteen Eighty-Four*, yet Burgess thinks that it is Lynne who may have inspired Orwell, when he caught sight of her at the Mandrake Club. During the war, Sonia did work at the Ministry of War Transport, as Lynne did; and she drank heavily and slept around as if in defiance of her strict Catholic upbringing, with its insidious strictures. Sonia, like Lynne, was a creature of boldness – and of sorrow. She wasn't made for happiness. My belief is that Burgess appropriated this – 'that lovely blonde girl, later to be ravaged through drink' – for his presentation of his own wife.

of love, a lovely home, a family car and an income of nine pounds a week, even during the Depression,' fumed Mrs Berry, echoing what was very much Lynne's view. To her dying day, inside her head she was still in her first bloom as the Headmaster's daughter at Bedwellty Grammar School, superior to everybody.

For a time, after Lynne's death, Burgess remained in touch with Hazel, and he sent Ceri a cheque when she married in 1973. Then – complete silence. The family duly looked themselves up in *Little Wilson and Big God*, to find that Lynne was permanently drunk and stripping her clothes off, and that Hazel herself was an oppressive puritan who drove her sister close to suicide. Ceri Berry wanted to bring an injunction, but her mother decided that 'Burgess had suffered a rotten life. Lynne always used to feel sorry for him, too.' It was decided best not to drag it all up in the courts. Ceri, however, wanted to confront her evil old uncle. 'I'd like him to look me in the eye. I have even been to Monte Carlo to find him, but he was not at his home. The lady in the local boulangerie said he was away. Then I thought, well, I'm bound to catch him in London, he's bound to come and do a *Wogan* show. When I saw him on the television, I rushed around to the Sherlock Holmes Hotel, but he'd checked out an hour earlier! But I won't give up. One day, very soon, I will find him and ask why he chose to remember my family this way, why he has left us this legacy.' If Burgess wasn't going to allow Robert Robinson to drop him off near the gaff in Glebe Street, he wasn't going to divulge his whereabouts to the public, and Lynne's relatives had been consigned to this mass of strangers, as had the colleagues in Banbury, or chums from the Army Educational Corps, or the native population of Malaya, whom it had been his proud boast he'd known better than Joseph Conrad and Somerset Maugham put together. He dumped people remorselessly, as if there'd never been any interaction. I'd liked to have hired a photographer, however, to record Burgess being apprehended by Ceri Berry. It would have been like one of Enderby's colourful showdowns. Alas, he died six months after war had been declared, conking out as plain John Wilson in a hospice ward at the Hospital of St John and St Elizabeth, Grove End Road, St John's Wood. He had indeed mentioned from time to time, though, that when in London he'd reside at the Sherlock Holmes Hotel. This was a ruse – and as so often with him, nearly true. He'd take breakfast there – as, for example, with Jonathan Kent, the director of the Almeida Theatre, who was to produce Burgess's adaptation of Griboyedov's *Chatsky*.* ('He talked for two hours about the play and the advisability of smoking or drinking more coffee,' recalls Kent, and he completely beflummoxed the waitress by insisting on trying to speak German.) But there was no need to have stayed the night. He had an apartment in adjacent Chiltern Court, off Baker Street. He signs off *This Man and Music*, 'Baker Street, 1982.' There was also a house in Twickenham. After dining with Lorna Sage at the Savoy, 'He and Liana put their coats on, and scoff gently at the thought that they might be *staying* at the Savoy. They're in Twickenham . . .', which is where Burgess was assembling *A Mouthful of Air*, growling and mumbling as he pottered down to the Pakistani corner shop for the evening paper and a pint of milk and writing blimpish pieces for the press. On the television, the only people who speak correct English are 'evidently not Anglo-Saxon', and 'I have been in exile long enough to preserve my deepest regret for the death of £.s.d. A penny is now a p – how mean, how foreseeable, how vulgar': this in 1989, eighteen years after decimalisation.

He would, of course, stay in rather grand places, but never at his own expense. If a publisher or film company were paying, he'd transfer to 47 Park Street, a service flat in Mayfair (where his personal telephone number was 491 7282), to Durrants, off Marylebone High Street, or the Britannia Inter-Continental, Grosvenor Square, which was like going around the world whilst staying in one place: cocktail bar, piano bar, a business centre, a fitness centre, an English pub, and with English, American, French, Italian and Japanese cuisine. Burgess filed expenses claims for £258.50 per night. He liked its blandness, but went off it when Arabs started using it. Helen Fraser, who edited *You've Had Your Time*, was summoned up to his room and found the extent of the bohemianism rather unexpected: a tape recorder playing one of his own compositions at full blast, discarded clothes on the bed, he and Liana arguing, like characters in a subtitled comedy film. Duncan Fallowell also called in on them: Burgess was slumped in an armchair, smoking his cheroot, frowning deeply and refusing to look you in the eye; Liana was bustling about,

* Aleksander Sergeyevich Griboyedov's *Woe from Wit* (1822), as it's normally known, was translated by G. R. Noyes in 1960. It is 'a satire of self-seeking and complacent Moscow society as viewed by an idealist returned from travel', according to my encyclopaedia, which if you substituted a *jaundiced* man for an *idealist*, makes it sound like a proleptic *The Right to an Answer*.

Jonathan Kent's production starred Colin Firth, Dinsdale Landen, Jemma Redgrave, Sarah Crowe, Minnie Driver and John Fortune. After previewing at the Malvern Festival Theatre, 24–29 May 1993, it had a limited run in Islington.

dressed like a gypsy fortune-teller, hanging up clothes in the wardrobe and taking them out again. What John Tydeman, another visitor, and the producer of *Blooms of Dublin*, who had to deal with the contraltos when they went on strike over the swear words, most remembers is that Burgess's pockets were stuffed with banknotes.

Being clandestine about his whereabouts is part of the pattern – part of his fear of getting caught, or caught out. ('An honest man doesn't conceal his place of business!' expostulates Watson in *The Three Gables*.) The addresses listed in *Who's Who* were printed only when he'd actually moved on – from 44 rue Grimaldi, Monaco, to another studio across the road; from Callian to Lugano (where his telephone number was 41-91-52-67-89). 'I have a house in Malta,' he said in 1973, 'but I've not been in Malta now for three years. I'm going back to the house to see how it is getting on, but I may be put in gaol as soon as I arrive for evasion of taxes. I have a house in Bracciano [actually two*], which is about twenty miles north of Rome, and a flat in Rome. That suits me well enough.' If the scattered real estate is an earnest of his restlessness and dissatisfaction, it also suited his cunning, shifty nature. This was exasperating if an assignment involved collaboration. 'Burgess's libretto was unsingable,' a spokesman of Scottish Opera told me, regarding the *Carmen* adaptation in 1986. 'It was also full of errors of spelling and grammar, and the Greek epigraph he pretentiously put on the front was wrongly transliterated. The board were upset that he was contractually insistent on the production being billed as "Anthony Burgess's *Carmen*"; audiences expected it to be Bizet's. For the translation, he was paid five thousand pounds. Plus whatever deal he had with Hutchinson for its publication as a booklet. We found him and his wife very difficult to negotiate with – Liana was very protective. He was often unavailable and purposefully gave out the wrong telephone number. John Wells, when he adapted *La Vie Parisienne* for us, worked alongside a singer – they made sure the words could be sung. Burgess worked in isolation – and he had a tin ear.'

His lyrics went something like:

* Milton Hebald, the sculptor, tells me that he sold the first house in Bracciano on Piazza Padella ('Frying Pan Square') in 1970 to Burgess for twenty thousand dollars. It is now (2002) worth at least four hundred thousand dollars – as it is situated in the desirable Historic Section of the town. It has not been lived in for years – and Hebald has asked me whether 'Liana is still around?' and where is the bust he made of Burgess? He kindly sent me photographs of it – Caesar Burgess, as I call it.

Under the walls of Sevilla,
Stands Lillas Pastia's tavern,
Where folk dance the gay seguedilla
And drink manzanilla –
Tra la la la la la la la la la
Tra la la la la la la la la LAH!

Carmen came forth for the English National Opera in St Martin's Lane, as well as Scottish Opera in Glasgow. Andalusia was moved to modern America, the gypsies and bullfighters were decked out as used-automobile lot salespersons (car men) – and though he was in London for the première, with gala tickets reserved, Burgess refused to attend, remaining in his room at Durrants Hotel. Despite being absent, however, he was not indifferent. He wrote an angry article in the *Observer*, expounding disapproval of impresarial tinkering and directorial ineptitude. 'Changing One's Tune' is an egregiously self-serving piece, in which he complains, in addition, about the alterations made to his matchless scripts for *A.D.* ('the text so disparaged was not mine: it was what had been made out of mine by producer, director, actors and, for all I know, somebody in the cutting room with a gift for mimicry'), *Moses the Lawgiver* ('It was only my own talent for mimicry that stopped Burt Lancaster from substituting deplorable Americanisms for the staid patriarchal idioms I gave to him') and *Jesus of Nazareth* (written 'with the dangerous assistance of Zeffirelli'). It never seems to have dawned on Burgess, up in the clouds as he was, that it is axiomatic of these biblical epics that they are going to be dead scraps. They are as stagey as Victorian genre paintings and, traditionally, they provide a home for bombastic old actors, like Sir Cedric Hardwicke, Charlton Heston and Anthony Quinn. There can never be any verve. Such implacability is an allegory of the self-righteousness of the talents involved – the actors, directors and writers who think they are God. It's no wonder that Gore Vidal is often involved with such projects (he wrote the screenplay for *Ben-Hur* – and Burgess was the Gore Vidal people could afford); or that Burt Lancaster would gravitate towards them and that Lew Grade, the financier, would impose upon the Pope to bless a copy of the leather-bound script. These granite-thick shows, with guest stars like Ava Gardner, John Houseman and Fernando Rey, or Donald Pleasence, Ernest Borgnine and Christopher Plummer (Burgess's Cyrano), who were reincarnated from the Roman Empire in any event, are about despotism, command, conquest and bad haircuts. It was

Burgess's destiny to become the stalwart of such heavy labour – of these things conceived on a cosmic scale – of the reconstruction of historical events. On the shelf at the Lugano house was a video cassette of *Monty Python's Life of Brian*, which had been filmed on Zeffirelli's left-over sets in Tunisia. Did Burgess know it was a comedy? No one who has seen *Moses the Lawgiver* can forget Burt Lancaster, as the portentous prophet with improbable white teeth, having to say to Anthony Quayle, 'I am uncircumcised of lips' – Burgessian for 'I am slow of speech'; on another occasion, Burgess had Moses tongue-twistingly refer to 'the punctilious observance of the Sabbath, as you so grandiloquently term it'. He thought this periphrastic style was witty. Little wonder that people changed it where they could.

He'd be unreachable in a physical sense (Duncan Fallowell once drove to Callian to discover the house shrouded and shuttered – the Burgesses had nipped back to Monaco); and there's an unreachable aspect to much of his work, because there's nothing there. I sometimes think – Burgess: was he real or imagined? (He's ridiculous.) How helpful was it, for instance, when Michael Langham, who proposed directing *Oedipus the King* at the Guthrie Theater, was told, 'It was written in a kind of hypnotic daze, non-alcoholic, with the Greek to the left and an Italian–Greek lexicon to the right, but it was stimulated and qualified by my reading for the novel on Napoleon I'm writing . . . also by memories of my reading in Lévi-Strauss for my novel *MF*, which is about this relationship between riddle and incest'? Not much guidance there, I'd have thought, were you trying to organise a stage presentation of Burgess's sawdust and tinsel. Yet this is how tricksters operate. There is this triumph of style over substance. Through sheer effort of will he made a reputation for himself (there has to be an audience for the trickster – he's not interested in leaving a masterpiece locked in the safe), and the fame, glory and money did duly accrue. It is interesting, too, that many of his novels are about conspiracy – are about the fear of exposure and humiliation; it is as if, within the texts themselves, in the process of their creation, there was this nervous tension, this anxiety, even a sense of futility, concerning deception, concerning loss (particularly the loss of face). His other, deeper, losses – mother, sister, wife – are submerged beneath a tone that's musty-smelling, airless, heavy going. His attempts at light-heartedness, in *Mozart and the Wolf Gang*, or his retelling of Strauss and Hofmannsthal's *Der Rosenkavalier* (as 'The Cavalier of the Rose'), intend invoking whipped creaminess and friskiness, but that cold mask of his kills the comic spirit.

This is how he killed Lynne, also, at least in his memoirs. She's the dark lady in his books, a symbol of everything that gets snatched away. (What survived of her is unease.) Whereas, I am sure, in reality, the balance of power had alternated between them, Lynne being variously robust, fragile, coarse, a nuisance or essential, and Burgess himself being either impenetrable and aloof or focused yet distracted – 'I remember standing with them in a pub in Adderbury, when John loudly called Lynne "a stupid bitch" for not knowing who wrote the music to "A Shropshire Lad". The locals must have had some strange thoughts,' a retired teacher from Banbury, Maurice Draper, told me – it is the case that Burgess consigned her to hell, that's to say, a place without human warmth. What I feel about her, looking at the Welsh background and beginnings and her horrific finish, is that there was this refined sensibility, but suddenly – with Manchester and meeting Burgess – there was this dislodgement, and her nerves were always on edge. Burgess made the significant comment that Bedwellty remained her anchor or core experience (he realised that much at least); it was where she'd been invincible, and she was tormented by vestigial feelings of invincibility, hence her aggressiveness in literary London, where she felt stranded. It was an adult life of disappointed hope and gnawing misery, and Burgess was a party to her destruction, to the damaging of her, because he could never entirely trust anybody – and without trust, where's love? Burgess had a weak capacity for love and could only look at people from the outside. When asked about Lynne's alcoholism, he said: 'I deliberately shut my mind to it. I didn't want to know what was going on from a clinical angle. Should one feel guilty for the actions of another person? Whether we are responsible for other people, I don't know.' I think Ceri Berry and Lynne's sister, Hazel, could provide him with one or two answers; and only a first-rank egotist would have framed such questions in the first place. Pain and bitterness were only to be seen from his angle.

He was never to be very good at other people's emotional demands. Like an income tax demand, it was confiscatory; he'd be left feeling less. ('Everybody is entitled to dodge paying income tax if he can,' he said in 1970, safe in Malta. 'Authors, I think, have a duty to dodge paying it.') All he wanted, he'd have told you, is freedom. 'Women,' thinks Victor Crabbe, in *Time for a Tiger*, 'they will cling to a man like a liana, like a jungle leech. How he hated women.' One of Crabbe's problems is that Fenella is his second wife; though his first wife is dead, he still feels guilty – and so by some strange logic, 'infidelity to one's second wife was an act of homage to one's first. His dead wife was in all women.' The curious thing is, he wrote this a dozen years before Lynne's actual death, and yet it prophesies exactly how he'd feel and behave. In 1955, beginning to compose the *Malayan Trilogy*, it was Moyna Morris with whom he had an idealised, imagined relationship, wholly inside his head. As a fresh widower, in 1968, he was invited to Hollywood by William Conrad to lay (as it were) Lynne's ghost. Clearly the tom-catting expedition was not a success: 'Conrad's a big fellow, and he had to demonstrate, you see, his potency,' Burgess recalled in 1971. 'It became wearisome, night after night, much as I love the man (love the man dearly), but he had to go to night clubs and he had to pick up a woman, and he had to meet this woman the following night and be told how good he was in bed. And his main aim – I'd just become a widower at that time – was to get me laid, you know. He even paid a woman to do it. Of course nothing's more off-putting than that, to know you've got a lay in the bank waiting for you . . . I found it rather charming, in a way.' It sounds to me like he made his excuses and left; but didn't Burgess claim that at one time he'd been quite the frequenter of brothels? All the time, he's living a lie. Once more, it's all there in *Time for a Tiger*, his first published novel: 'The truth about one's feelings must be masked in a show of indifference or even the lineaments of a very different emotion.' The intelligence services call this tradecraft.

How numinous, too, that the word *liana* should appear in one of Burgess's sentences eight years before he met a person known as that – and when *did* he meet the person known as that? He always wanted it to have the quality of a fairy tale. In December 1963, leaving Lynne coughing blood into her glasses of gin in Etchingham, he travelled up to London to meet an Italian woman who was compiling a report on contemporary English novels for the publishing house Bompiani. Burgess buys her lunch in Chiswick and, 'after our sucking pig, we made love', in the conveniently recently acquired Glebe Street pad. She then vanishes, only to reappear after Lynne's funeral as a genuine temptress in a Mao outfit:

> Her name was Liana Macellari, lately divorced in Boston from the black Ben Johnson, at present working in Cambridge on projects of applied linguistics. She had, all those four years back, entered my life very briefly and then disappeared to Paris, but not before giving birth to a child in a London hospital on 9 August 1964. The child was mine, a boy named, though not baptised, Paolo-Andrea. She announced this fact almost incidentally.

It's hard to credit that any normal person would accept this information without wanting a little more corroboration. Perhaps he was still mad with grief, and didn't understand what he was being told? (Ed Victor, in those days a humble picture researcher at Jonathan Cape, remembers Burgess wandering the streets, baying at the moon, because there was nobody to cook him custard.) Perhaps Liana was forceful? But if somebody reappeared years after a one-night stand, or its equivalent, and said, 'Oh, by the way, this is yours' – who'd not be dubious? Or was Mr Anthony Impotent Burgess only all too eager to go along with the Joycean idea that paternity is a legal fiction? If he was actually impotent, what better than to be able to give the lie to this by 'acknowledging fatherhood'? He told Liana that 'she must . . . bring my son to Chiswick and at once marry his father'.* It was a miracle that she'd been 'willing to give birth to my child' and she 'filled my heart at once and for ever'. Burgess himself may have wanted to believe all this, but he couldn't have expected his readers not to be sceptical – though foundlings and changelings do abound in his books, especially *Earthly Powers*, where nobody is who they think they are, and blood families and stepfamilies, nature and nurture, are in need of constant re-evaluation. The past refuses to sit still. 'Memory as a human faculty is subject to human limitations,' says Toomey. 'We are condemned to invent so much of the past.' Anyway, I have before me a Certified Copy of an Entry of Birth for Paolo-Andrea, born, as Burgess stated, on 9 August 1964 in Bethnal Green Hospital. Unless, which I doubt, the informants were knowingly giving false particulars, in which case they were exposing themselves to prosecution under the Forgery Act 1861 (a felony punishable with penal servitude), then the boy's actual or biological father was Roy Lionel Halliday, a teacher, of 19 Elder Street, Stepney, E1. This was also Liana's address. Both father and mother signed the certificate on 4 September. Burgess married Liana four years later, on 9 September 1968, at the Register Office, Hounslow, in the presence of Sylvia and Michael Rapaport. Bride and groom were both then living at 24 Glebe Street. Lynne had been dead since 20 March (of [a] cardiac failure [b] liver failure – certified by Richard Page M.B.). The white marble Maltese villa in the township of Lija (constructed in 1798)

* We must be extremely glad that Liana arrived with a boy and not a girl. Burgess would have gone to prison. In an article called 'Women in My Life', written in 1985 (from internal evidence for an Irish magazine, though I only have his typescript), he makes the sickening observation that: 'One glorious relationship with a woman I have never had and will now never have – that is the dangerous but fulfilling nexus of father and daughter. I say dangerous because (Freud was right) the incestuous has to be in it.'

was bought for seventeen thousand pounds in August. By the autumn, the Bedford Dormobile had been acquired, and off they went. What a lot had happened in a short space of time. 'The Mediterranean is where the great work will be done, and has been done,' announced Burgess. 'It was done by Joyce. Remember Joyce didn't write *Ulysses* in Dublin; he wrote it in the Mediterranean, much of it, or the Adriatic.'

That's going to be my abiding image of him – aboard the motor caravan, his typewriter on his lap, Liana at the wheel ('We were not robbed until we got to Avignon'), and with Paolo-Andrea about his inquisitive, destructive business. Walt Litz, a Princeton professor, recalls sitting at a café in Ferrara, and suddenly this jalopy wheezed to a halt in a cloud of burnt oil and exhaust fumes. Burgess and Liana hopped out, ran into a bookshop, totted up the number of copies of *Un' Arancia a Orologeria* that were on sale, and sped away again. This is how they filled their days. It is difficult to know exactly what to make of the child, however – or, more accurately, to work out quite what Burgess's attitude and behaviour were like toward him. ('It is the mystery of the relationship,' as he says in *Here Comes Everybody*, 'between non-begetting father and unbegotten son.') The impression from *You've Had Your Time* is of astonishing neglect, and the infant is allowed to clamber everywhere, strip off his clothes, piss where he stood, like a monkey. Paolo-Andrea eats raw bacon, shins up the curtains, spills milk and smashes glasses. He becomes the leader of a gang which systematically wrecks the place when Burgess is away, as he so often is, lecturing in America or touring Australia and glowering at the philistines: 'Marvellous women – terrible men, pot-bellied chauvinists, totally asexual. The men simply don't know what sex is.' During the marriage ceremony in Hounslow, Paolo-Andrea is left outside on his own to play in the road – and that's indicative of the way he's left to his own devices generally. He mixes spectacular messes and leaves dollops of it around the house – salt, cigarette ash and spit, or shampoo, nail-polish remover and butter. He widdles on a near-finished novel ('carbon copy and all'), pours treacle in his own hair, and decides to make his own concrete out of faeces and yoghurt. Burgess had been such a strict schoolteacher, and one for the proprieties generally, this over-liberal attitude is peculiar, to say the least. It amounts to abuse. Keen, on the one hand, to rub in what are either lies or a deliberate misunderstanding – 'I, the father of a son I was still to see'; 'I refused to allow my son, still an abstraction, to grow up illegitimate'; 'a child not quite four with something of my nose' – yet, on the other hand, where is the warmth and the care? You don't have to be Melanie Klein to work out that Burgess, who'd complained endlessly about the uninvolved way he'd been raised by his own stepfamily, was repeating the process. Burgess was the lonely child who'd brought himself up – so was Paolo-Andrea, who had a disrupted formal education and who was thrust into one new language and culture after another. One year he's having to speak Maltese; then it's Italian, at Bracciano; then they are in Princeton, so his English acquires New Jersey idioms; then it's Rome, with its own dialect ('Roman has resisted the dipthongisation of Tuscan,' states Professor Burgess); finally, because the child is on the Mafia's kidnap list, and they decide to flee to Monte Carlo, it's French, and Andrea becomes André. Except he doesn't. He's had enough by now and decides to become a Scot, 'appropriate for the blood he had inherited from his grandmother on the British side', explains Burgess. He takes to wearing a kilt and playing the bagpipes. 'He chose a nation to which he could be devoted. He wore the tartan of the Wilson sept of the Gunn clan, learned Gaelic, read Burns and Hugh MacDiarmid. He was to be called Andrew Burgess Wilson.' This is madness, surely?

Burgess had reinvented himself with such frequency and facility – the Great Man of Letters act took every ounce of his histrionic energy – he couldn't see (or didn't care about) what damage was being done. If Paolo-Andrea sounds like a monster-child, that's only because he was trying to provoke or elicit some love and attention. On Malta he actually moved out, and went to live at the grocery shop down the street. At Princeton (where Burgess says he himself was snubbed by the Faculty – actually they found him graceless and obstreperous), the boy was found asleep in the snow, half dead. He was resuscitated by the police. This was considered scandalous at the time – I've talked to people who were there. Burgess makes nothing of it. Liana had refused to cook or to celebrate Christmas (she slinks off to study Modern Greek), because she did not want to become like any other 'Italo-American, a species not much admired'; Burgess himself blithely watches television . . . In our more scrupulous and vigilant era, with Esther's Childline and educational psychologists on patrol, a lot of this would constitute an offence. Consider Michael Mewshaw's experience. He made a pilgrimage to Piazza Santa Cecilia, a far grander quarter of Rome than Burgess's own descriptions would leave you to believe, only to find that the Great Man was in Minneapolis and Liana was in what can only be described as a devil of a state. Her handbag had been stolen – all her cash, cards, keys gone, again. She insists on rushing off to find a locksmith – and doesn't reappear for twelve hours.

Having been asked if they'd look after her baby, Mewshaw and his girlfriend, Linda, discover that they've been left in sole charge of 'a boy of six or seven', who is just about the last word in obnoxiousness. Overexcited, forward, crude, a pain, Paolo-Andrea proceeds to sit on the draining board and gush water from the taps, slobber over the sandwiches Mewshaw makes, wipes his nose on Linda's pullover, and entertains everybody with karate kicks and yelps. The day limps by. Finally, Liana returns. 'She offered no apology and no explanation . . . "Now, if you don't mind . . . I must rest and you must go."' Not a word about why the assignation with the locksmith should have taken so long; not a word of gratitude for the childminding or any apology for being away longer than she'd expected. What kind of parents dump a kid on complete strangers and then clear off, and without a single phone call back to the flat to see how things were going? Yet had she not brought Paolo-Andrea to come and live in Chiswick with Burgess without discovering how he'd be as a father?

It's immensely imperious, behaving in the expectation that you'll be cosseted and obeyed, presuming upon other people's good nature and good manners. You wouldn't want to be wrapped up in difficulties with a person like that – it's easier to let them have their own way. Liana was a complex creature, warm and Italian, or else she would put on airs, as the contessa. She's all volubility, fizz, flirtatiousness; she crackled with love and animosity, and if he'd closed his eyes, Burgess must have believed that Lynne had been swiftly reincarnated in her prime, a girl dreaming down the vista of years. 'Well,' Kingsley Amis thought to himself, 'people do go *on* about men, some men, marrying the same woman over again.' Martin Amis, who as a child had also met Lynne, was to make a similar point: 'The second Mrs Burgess seems to be a woman of the same voluble genre.' Burgess had found a soulmate – and they were so wrapped up in each other, when he died, Liana refused at first to announce the news to the press. Obituary editors were going frantic trying to verify basic facts and figures. He'd cooled on 22 November 1993, but announcements and tributes* weren't printed until four days later. Liz Sich, the Random House publicity director, was having to field worldwide enquiries, yet Antonio's demise was to be a strictly personal matter. Such was her grief, how could Liana instruct or authorise any firm of funeral directors to collect the corpse? She'd have

* 'If a spirit hovers, as some believe, for an hour or two over the cadaver it has abandoned, what banalities it is doomed to hear, while it waits in a despairing hope that some serious thought will be uttered, some expression which will lend dignity to the life it has left.' Graham Greene, *The Comedians* (1965), p. 54.

been in denial about the realities of her husband's death and its affairs. She fought against it hard. Eventually, the hospital had to point out politely that their fridge was getting a bit full. We need Donizetti to come and make a tragic opera in three acts out of all this; instead, at the memorial service, they had Burgess's own setting of Nashe's 'In Time of Pestilence':

Wit with his wantonness
Tasteth death's bitterness;
Hell's executioner
Hath no ears for to hear
What vain art can reply.
I am sick, I must die.
Lord have mercy on us.

His illness, too, Liana had tried to keep a secret, though everybody *knew* – he went to meet the cast of *Chatsky* in a wheelchair. Richard Cohen had a particularly sticky experience. He'd been Burgess's editor for *The Pianoplayers* and *Any Old Iron*, and he was to introduce Burgess's inaugural 'European Lecture', on the art of translation, at the Cheltenham Festival of Literature, in the autumn of 1992. Burgess arrived early and took Cohen aside to say that he himself was soon about to be translated, that he'd be going from one state to another, for he'd just been told his cancer was terminal. Cohen commiserated – did the best he could in the circumstances; and he said to Liana, a little later, how sorry he was to hear about Anthony, etc. 'What?' she snapped at him. '*What* cancer?' She completely made out that this was the first she'd ever heard of it, putting Cohen in a very awkward spot. Ten minutes later, Burgess told the public audience, 'Good evening, ladies and gentlemen. The term "translation" has taken on a new connotation for me since I have recently been undergoing clinical tests which point to a very dark end . . . a possible transmigration or elevation . . .' At other moments in his life he'd predicted his death would feel like 'a sense of total privation', or listening for eternity to Beethoven's Ninth Symphony 'played on a million-piece orchestra', or 'like a gas bill one can't pay'.

Being the son or daughter or stepchild or ward of a Great Man is never much of a picnic: Richard Cromwell returned after the Restoration and lived under a feigned name in Cheshunt; one of Chaplin's offspring wrote a memoir called *I Couldn't Smoke the Grass on My Father's Lawn*; Kingsley Amis's daughter, Sally, died of alcoholism; Peter Sellers' daughter, Victoria, moved to Los Angeles and believed becoming a hooker was a good career move. Burgess, as much as any driven public figure, had a stony heart. He was proud of his emotional glaciation; that's to say, he never did anything to prompt a thaw. 'I sense a coldness in myself,' he told Russell Davies in 1987, 'a certain fear of commitment, I think it's as simple as that.' Of the thousands of interviews he gave, though he'd be improbably sentimental about Liana ('I have no difficulty in declaring love for my present wife,' he told Anthony Clare. 'Possibly this small civilisation of marriage is enough'), Paolo-Andrea was never mentioned – or if he were ('He trained as a chef but you know what kids are like. He won't stick to one line – works at all sorts of odd jobs'), it is with irritation and exasperation. What were Burgess's expectations, if any? He had said, of the way he was taken in by Maggie Dwyer, 'I was regarded as something of an intruder,' and this is how he's treating Liana's son. The boy is always bullied at school and, later, when he wants to become a cook, he doesn't seem to hold any job down for long. We hear that he drinks heavily and that he has attempted suicide. What we never hear about is Burgess intervening, helping out, or simply being there. Andrea – André – Andrew's existence is happening at a distance. That is not how fathers behave. In 1984, Burgess took him to see *Tristan und Isolde*. Three days later he found the twenty-year-old in a pool of blood with severed wrists. 'The idea of a couple of people dying with a wonderful wave of music made it seem like a good thing to die,' Burgess alleged he was told. And he approved of this. 'Art is dangerous,' he said. 'It is one of the attractions. When it ceases to be dangerous, you don't want it.' So it was Wagner's fault, then, not the parents' – or the step-parent's?

In an article published in the *Spectator*, on 6 September 1968, 'Thoughts of a Belated Father', Burgess rather more plausibly calls himself a stepfather, and says that 'a four year old boy called Paolo-Andrea' is part of his 'Italian bride's dowry'. There's none of the claim to biology and virility we'd get two decades later in the memoirs. It's a revealing – and chilling – article. Burgess is open about his lack of affection. 'To be quite honest, I can do without Paolo-Andrea,' he confesses. 'I sometimes wonder if there is anything in all this that lies beyond duty.' Children, he generalises, 'are bores. They're ineffable, unutterable crashing bores . . . I don't see why I should be charmed by their slow lumbering along the road to rationality. It's the finished state I want; there's no substitute for adulthood.'* Burgess is incapable of interaction; he's fearful of making

* Children appear seldom in Burgess's work. When they do, they are superarticulate hoodlums – midget Anthony Burgesses. Alex, in *A Clockwork Orange*, is a futuristic musketeer ('It was usually like one for all and all for one') whom the state take to a hospital and

emotional attachments, because that exposes you to hurt: all these things which were the result of his own childhood now came into play as he helped to damage somebody else's. 'I must contrive a pretence that this boredom is really interest, concern, and something that may as well be called love,' he told the *Spectator* audience, virtually defining himself as a psycho – all that banality, indifference, dissimulation.* And, fifty years on from his own infancy in Manchester, a note of grief and bitterness had been introduced, too. He had little patience, for example, with his stepson's unrequited love affairs during adolescence. 'We must always expect betrayal,' was the only advice he'd dispense.

In the television documentary on Burgess, *Le Mecanique de L'Orange*, made in 1997, Andrew Wilson popped up on the screen to say, rather wryly and humorously, that everything said about him in *You've Had Your Time* was a lie. Indeed, had one expected the adult Paolo-Andrea to be half hoodlum from *A Clockwork Orange* and half Billy Connolly with

brainwashes until he is meek and docile. When Alex is evil he has a certain charm; when he is good he is mindless. Miles, in *MF*, is another trickster, impressed by shows of violence, 'intrigues, stabs in the back, fraternal treachery, poisoned banquets'; and like Alex, he is fastidious about his dress, a fop. If his precocity comes from Alex – or Burgess, who cannot begin to imagine what it is like to be young; or Saint-Pierre – the original lordling of misrule is Albert Rich, in *The Worm and the Ring*. That is to say, the source is Wagner: Albert Rich is Burgess's Alberich. *Das Rheingold* is alluded to when the repellent tot molests a classmate in the rain and steals her diary. The journal is like gold. It contains salacious secrets about the schoolmasters. Albert becomes 'the only one in the school who could, with a wrist-flick, send packing the man at the top'. Albert's power is based upon fear; he is lucky to have pinched the incriminating book. Like Alberich, he had no idea, at first, of what he had in his possession. When its implications emerge, he is quick to educate himself in being wily – his power corrupts.

Though dwarfish and beastly, Albert Rich is a clue to Burgess's boys: they are stunted grown-ups. Albert is stunted and ugly; Alex and Miles are stunted in that they are clever beyond the years their bodies give them. *Nothing Like the Sun* registers here: Will has a magical facility for words from earliest childhood; Harry Wriothesley, his patron, is a clever, spoilt, petulant brat. The most extreme brain-box, however, is Alan Walters in *Tremor of Intent*. He is thirteen, smokes, boozes, and wears a tailored, miniature dinner jacket. As the novel in which he appears deals with spies, codes, secret messages, disguises – the stuff of fast-paced ripping yarns – he's a munchkin James Bond. Alan becomes Hillier's accomplice. When cornered by Wriste, the foreign agent posing as a ship's steward, the boy makes a timely entrance and, with a silencer strapped on the hand gun, blasts the villain and frees the hero. Like a leprechaun Lévi-Strauss, he is proficient at riddles and conveys encyclopaedic knowledge in epigrammic sallies. Hillier, at first, is not disposed to tolerate him: 'Look. Any more nonsense from you, you bloody young horror, and I'll repeatedly jam a very pointed shoe up your arse.' This reader's sentiments exactly.

* In *Time for a Tiger*, Alladad Khan, chafing at the responsibilities of paternalism, and left alone, 'dandled unhandily his child in unfatherly arms'. In the *Spectator*, Burgess complains about having to carry Paolo-Andrea home from the pub, 'a dead weight in my unhandy arms'.

a false eyelash and a black bowler, then here was this perfectly nondescript bespectacled classroom swot who gave us a few toots on his oboe. Burgess had misdescribed him, in the same way as he'd traduced Lynne, hence outraging Ceri Berry, the only surviving person who might have remembered that there was more to her aunt than the cartoon drunk. I'm sure Lynne was quite aware of her own awfulness – and yet what were the outlets for her curiosity and intelligence? This, however, was his method. In order for Burgess to convey this sense of being badly treated, and that he'd lived in a disturbing world where people, things, fate and the gods were all conspiring to make his life hard, everybody in his estimation becomes misshapen, a little deformed and dark. This happens to Liana, even though we are meant to believe she was his salvation. Perhaps she was. She did the grown-up chores, like handling the money, buying the houses, dealing with the business, and driving the boss about. She's always there on the margins when he gave interviews, like she's his babysitter, who gets sent off to find a tray of drinks, or who pipes up to say that Antonio chops tomatoes the wrong way, or who'll argue with him about the merits of garlic. She was attentive, in ways that Lynne was not, and journalists and publishers always used to smile at how charming the double act was. (Smiles were a little more fixed and frozen, however, when I'd be told of her habit of taking video cameras and recording equipment into business meetings – she wanted to retain evidence in the event of any swindling or reneging.)

I'm afraid I find the total commitment performance rather off-putting – the subjugated wife image. There has to be more to her than that. Left to Burgess, though, what we have is a description of a Gina Lollobrigida glamour girl more accident prone than Inspector Clouseau. In the memoirs, Liana breaks her leg twice, in two places, in as many pages; she trips up carrying a typewriter and cuts her arm; she bruises her big toe. The brake fluid is drained from the Bedford Dormobile and she has to crash-land in some scaffolding. A hire car is knocked into a ditch. She gets out and the vehicle bursts into flames. She's spent more time at a police station reporting the theft of her passport and purse than anyone in history – it is a daily occurrence. Her papers are never in order – there's endless trouble with immigration officials over mislaid or out-of-date visas. Keeping hold of a set of keys is quite impossible – they are always having to be recut and replaced. Burgess, meantime, comes to her aid like the Light Brigade's charge at Balaclava, throwing punches and shouting, and being of about as much material assistance. Dockers smash their possessions at the quayside on Malta, the villagers at Bracciano are cheats, the Mafia are after them in Rome. Everybody is gloomy and suspicious, from the neighbours to men from the electricity board. The typescript of *Joysprick* is stolen, so Burgess simply bangs it out again, with little difficulty, he says, because he has retained it in his photographic memory (a facility which enables Howard Shirley, in *One Hand Clapping*, to memorise the names and dates of authors as disparate as Herrick and Congreve, and win big bucks in a quiz). I don't know why he has a tantrum with the frontier police who suspect him of smuggling cash over the Italian border to Switzerland, however, because that is exactly what he and Liana are up to. He'd made Lynne's and his adventures seem like the scenario of a fifties caper with Dirk Bogarde and Kay Kendall; wasn't he getting too old for this? The disorder is very laboured and contrived – or at least his attempts to make high-minded farce out of it are. I'm sure the mixture of wealth and squalor, e.g. the domestic muddle scattered across real estate worth millions or appearing at the Ritz or the Savoy scruffily dressed and carrying plastic bags, is quite authentic. It's a replay of the slumminess of Etchingham and Chiswick and going with Lynne back to Banbury to shock the wee provincials by being haughty and affected. The idea that he lived in a permanently perilous atmosphere, however, makes it an effort to go on taking him seriously.

With Liana entering his life, perhaps it was like being born again – but did she really restore hope and love? Lynne and Liana: both of them possessing swift feelings; both dusky and, if left to Burgess's powers of description, each capable of being the love interest in *A Vision of Battlements*; both translators; both having (he claimed) financial acumen; both wild, bold and unconventional. So – the same woman? He was so isolated, so self-centred; you never heard of Burgess giving to charity or throwing parties; he didn't, like Amis, have his clubs or, like Iris Murdoch, his college common rooms; he didn't espouse any political or social cause or make any altruistic gesture. What he had was his two women, his constant companions; and was it a fusion, of sorts? When he met Lynne at Manchester, she was jokey and (apparently) fast. I think he mistook her free-and-easy nature for shamelessness; and faced with her psychological deterioration and apparent uncaringness, as she wounded and taunted him, he felt entirely alone – hence he could indulge his self-pity, fume and fluster, and as in his novels he's all his own heroes, he could create these characters who are assailed by external pressures – their lives thrown into disarray or poverty or the general horror of things. Liana, also, is a strong or difficult woman; he was plainly drawn to this sort of temperament – someone capable of embracing and punishing, who'd hug and bully. He liked to be mothered and smothered. Liana's function was to be at his side – to make sure that his critics and interviewers were not inattentive, that we were all being vigilant. In the documentary called *The Burgess Variations*, broadcast in 1999, she paid eloquent testimony to his 'unquenchable human soul – energy and optimism – and this is what you find in his writing and what I always liked so much'. This is like a professional assessment or glowing reference for a job application, not one spouse remembering another. Liana is more in the tradition of an all-in helpmeet like Nabokov's Vera, Eliot's Valerie and F. R. Leavis's Queenie, than Joyce's Nora, yet for me I don't think you can beat Nora's comment on Joyce for affection and perception, when she said, 'Jim knows nothing about women.' For it doesn't do to encourage Burgess's highly conscious feeling for greatness, and yet this is what characterised him in his latter years, and was essentially bogus, as he clattered around doing any old stuff that paid. You go wrong as an artist when you start to believe this – and appear on *Wogan*, pretending to be nice to lesser mortals; doing the omniscient act in public – 'The word *ait* from the Old English *ieg* means a small island in a lake'; 'In Ancient Rome, when you provided a testimony you put your hand on your testicles to show you were telling the truth' – and everything is directed towards projecting a genial persona, but clearly he wasn't genuinely genial. He knew you weren't his equal, and I find this an insult.

The drunker and madder Lynne became, the more she helped to harden his nature, which was industrious, walled-in, and he was always only too willing to avoid having a good time. This is why he didn't seek to save her. He tacitly condoned or encouraged her bad behaviour because he could conceal himself behind it. He was similarly manipulative with Liana – she'd be full of her own anxieties and suspicions, and he'd be camouflaged by the bluster. There was seldom need to notice any defects in himself. In his account, she threw herself at him, and he remarried and realigned himself right away. There'd been loss, and now regeneration. What Lynne was to him had to be suppressed, and the way he hurled himself off into the disruptions of exile was one of the ways he accomplished this. Yet with Lynne's death you'd think he'd have unravelled – a terrifyingly traumatic experience; a turning point. You just don't know what moves him, though, or what's inside him – except that he loved two women, and one of them was a ghost. His novels similarly lack any investigation of the emotional level. Howard Shirley, in *One Hand Clapping*, is gloomy and disaffected and suicidal, but this isn't gone into much. He's upset by television; everybody seems on the take and the make – and that seems to be it. Depths of frustration and alienation aren't probed. Burgess has no interest in his characters as people – this isn't suppression: psychology simply isn't there. The private hell – of Enderby and his brothers – is a vacuum. The best we get (in *One Hand Clapping*) is: 'He was changing inside in a queer sort of way.' This is something of a paradox – that Burgess was a writer who couldn't express himself; or more accurately, wouldn't do so.

Personally, I don't mind it when he's found to be lying to your face – that's the teller of tall stories, like Baron Munchausen. The fact that this knowledge of foreign languages was limited to salutations, valedictions and requests for the time (the extent of Denham's Swedish, Dutch and Indonesian in *The Right to an Answer*) is part of his enjoyable preposterousness. But his emotional dishonesty is another matter. Artificial and improbable constructs like *MF* or *Napoleon Symphony* we can disregard; novels where there is no change or progress in the characters, and where they all sound like Burgess (because there's no differentiation), may also be left on the shelf with the unshiftable stock of Humbert Wolfes and Rod McKuens. *Any Old Iron*, for example: the *Titanic* sinks in that one, the First World War is fought, the Russian Revolution shakes the planet, the Spanish Civil War occurs, the Second World War comes along, the sword Excalibur is found, and it's all rather counterproductive; his energy is dire. Like his Attila endlessly conquering cities (the novella 'Hun', in *The Devil's Mode*, bristles with tribes, languages, religions), or his endless voyager,* criss-crossing the world on aeroplanes (where he meets a Mr Meldrum: 'So some day, I said to myself, I'll bloody show them about their stuff and nonsense about bloody documents'), it is meaningless exertion, which puts me in mind of a soporific long train journey across the steppes, with nothing to see except birch trees. It's as if he didn't have a biography, only a bibliography. The reality of Malaya or Enderby's England, detailed, actual, recognisable, gave way to books about books and literature about language. He wrote about writing. He wrote to keep back pain, betrayal, failing health, hatred and disgust. He wrote about everything *except* what was on his mind, i.e. the intensity of his feelings of loss. That is how I make sense of him. His mother was a missing person, as was his sister. (There's a character in the sci-fi section of *The End of the*

* 'The Endless Voyager', a short story included in *The Devil's Mode*, was first published in the *Independent Magazine*, 28 October 1989.

World News called Muriel who talks 'in a childish little voice'.) He never had or knew anyone who'd be protective until Lynne and Liana – except, of course, he'd fantasised about Lynne and Moyna. In *The Worm of the Ring*, which is less a novel than a dream journal of the Banbury years, Howarth returns from the Paris trip, contemplates Veronica and Hilda, and concludes: 'Perhaps one always had to have two women. Perhaps polygamy was more natural than the laws of the West would allow.' It's interesting, isn't it, the frequency of emotional triangulations in writers' lives? Eliot's Vivienne and Valerie, who variously appear as the hyacinth girls and lynxes, with spotted fur and sharp ears, in his poems; or Pound's Dorothy (a painter) and Olga (a musician); or Betjeman's the Hon. Lady Penelope Chetwode and Lady Elizabeth Cavendish; Larkin's Monica and Maeve; Amis's Hilly and Elizabeth Jane. Coping with two women – it is impossible, whether it's the trouser-dropping farce of having them both around simultaneously (shrewish, suspicious wives and concealed, impatient mistresses); or having them around in memory, like Hardy, or Homer's Helen. 'Some cook, some do not cook/Some things cannot be altered,' said Pound philosophically – orientally – about his dilemma and division, which contributed to his crack up and incarnation in a lunatic asylum for twelve years. Amis tried to become reconciled with Hilly in his novels – in *The Old Devils* and *You Can't Have Both*; and in the poem 'Instead of an Epilogue', dedicated 'To H.', which concludes his *Memoirs*, there's an endnote of harmony and forgiveness which he didn't quite pull off in real life. Knowing this – knowing that, in actuality, Amis was living on his own upstairs whilst Hilly was with her subsequent husband in the basement flat: it's the material of a comedy play about the last days of Casanova; and it does give his novels this underswell of regret, self-dislike and anxiety. What Burgess, also, was unable to do, to his credit, was convince himself that his first marriage had been a disaster. He didn't wish to have those days back again, as Amis did, but he knew that Lynne had been his tragic muse, his muse o' fire; and he can't prevent any mention of her from being steeped in the pathos of her eventual fate, most obviously in *Beard's Roman Women*, which is full of the bereaved person's longing to write a letter or to pick up the telephone.

After Lynne's death in March, he appeared so purposeful in the ensuing weeks, rattling off thirty-one long pieces of journalism, flying hither and thither to discuss the Shakespeare film with William Conrad, Joseph Mankiewicz (the putative director), Jessica Tandy (Queen Elizabeth I – the Judi Dench role) and Hume Cronyn (Burleigh); he oversaw the reissue of

Time for a Tiger, *The Enemy in the Blanket*, *Beds in the East*, *Devil of a State*, *The Eve of Saint Venus* and *The Right to an Answer*; there was the publication in America of an Enderby omnibus, and *Enderby Outside* appeared in London for the first time; 'The Muse' appeared in the *Hudson Review* and there was a German translation of *Here Comes Everybody* to deal with, called *Ein Mann in Dublin Namens Joyce*. The collection of essays and reviews, *Urgent Copy*, was published – no wonder that Geoffrey Grigson's hostile notice (on 7 November, in the *Listener*) caught him at a bad moment. In one of the Guiseppe Gioacchino Belli poems he used to enjoy freely translating, we find a long list of what coarse name a man's balls might go by, which concludes:

> I would prefer to jettison such junk
> And give them Geoffrey Grigson's name,
> If only Grigson had a speck of spunk.

(That's his worst insult, taunting somebody's virility; a very Italianate curse, or *maledizione*.) In addition to this workload, there was Liana's reappearance with Paolo-Andrea, the house-hunting trip to Malta, the remarriage and the Great Escape. Little wonder, therefore, that he felt he may have rushed into things. He sat in a café, in Rome, whilst Liana was in some office arguing with consular staff about missing visas and lost passports, and contemplated swallowing a bottleful of barbiturate tablets that had belonged to Lynne. Why had he retained those? How were they so conveniently to hand? Liana, he says, threw the pills down a drain. The two of them go off romantically to buy the chemicals for the Dormobile's toilet.

He'd been training for exile again since his return from Malaya. Those books published during or soon after the pseudo-terminal year, when he was dancing attendance upon his phantom tumour – each of them is saying farewell to life. Denham, in *The Right to an Answer*, calls himself a 'professional expatriate', and Burgess was mentally prepared for that state himself. 'But you don't really know me,' says Denham. 'It's not as though I'm a close friend you've known all your life. I'm a complete stranger, somebody just passing through. I mean, you've no claim on me.' That's exactly how Burgess, too, wanted to be perceived and treated. There was a withdrawal from England, an uprooting, which matched his psychological detachment. The words he so often uses – *resent*, *distaste*, *revulsion*, *sneer* – are words of scorn and rejection. He went abroad – he transported himself far away, so he could in a very literal sense be an outsider; but his real journey was inwards, where Lynne lurked. Exile, in practice, was agony, because 'being away from home you still sort of imagine home is the same'. His rage against England in the eighties, the requiems he wrote about the New Vulgaria, was really his despair that the clocks hadn't stopped in the spring of 1968, when Lynne was last alive. 'I went into a shop and bought a present for her, when she was dead, you know, that kind of business,' he confessed, years after she'd handed in her martini glass. On a radio programme, *Writers Revealed*, in 1989, he described her as a lively revenant, who still came to him. 'You can't efface the dead – they leave marks on your life when they are gone. Lynne appears in dreams, fit and well, and finds me in bed with another woman. "Now stop that!" she says. "We're married!"' In *You've Had Your Time*, published the following year, the dreams have become nightmares – 'nightmares I still occasionally have'. Born and raised in Manchester under pewter skies filled with cold rain, though professing to be Irish, he believed himself to have been, in the final analysis, 'a kind of orphan' – by which he seems to have meant self-created, though I think pathological liar would be more precise. His mother died when he was an infant, and what with the early death of Lynne later on, Burgess's personality, his combination of pride and courtesy, ferocity and elusiveness, gets to be about shields, shells, the construction of an emotional carapace. I believe what he liked about Liana, whom 'I married a few months after the death of my first wife, and this ménage has been going strong for twenty years' (as he said in 1988), is that, strong-willed and practical, she dealt with property and money matters, and made this buoyancy around him, leaving him free to focus on creative work. She wasn't going to threaten the deep-seated grief and chaos inside him. But what was the effect on his actual work of these layers of protective armour? Aren't they the cause of his falseness? His flatness? Isn't this how he misdirects and evades, and avoids having to be honest with himself?

I am particularly fascinated by the way he was caught between his two women. Lynne was feisty and brilliant – and unfulfilled. She filled him with guilt. Liana, with whom he fled abroad, filled him with passion. ('My first wife was blonde and Welsh. She died young. My second and last wife is dark and Italian.') The novel about all this, *Beard's Roman Women*, is thus one of his most revealing texts – given that Burgess's art was that of concealment. Try to love two people, the novel implies, and stay true to both, and you'll go mad; you'll vaporise. Death doesn't end a relationship and new liaisons are haunted by the old. Beard had had 'a dream last night about his first wife alive again and saying *darling here I am, did you miss me?* In the dream Paola [Liana] was in his life but not in the house, wherever it was, not one he recognised, and he faced the horror of telling Leonora [Lynne] that he'd understood she was dead, he made a new start, loved someone else. There the dream ended.'

As did much else. There was always a grandness to Burgess's work, and a trace of archaism, but after Lynne's death there is very little living emotion that I can detect. He became disinclined to write anything psychologically penetrating or discerning. Talking, in 1990, about his hallucinations that Lynne kept coming back, and that he'd repeatedly have to explain that he has now made other arrangements, he said: 'A great deal of work is done by the unconscious, though actually putting the work together is a very self-conscious process. I wrote a novel called *Beard's Roman Women* based on that dream, in which I resolved the enigma of a wife seeming to come back from the dead. An actress, an impersonation . . . not very convincing.' No, indeed. The resolution is a feeble and evasive cop-out. Here was his opportunity for a Henry James tale of the supernatural, a poignant and vivid investigation of obsession and wretched, ambiguous passion; of the sinister and neurotic aspects of possession – instead of which, he raises his theme and, fancifully and efficiently, he kills it. The dream came back, however, in *Any Old Iron*, where the personal pronouns are reversed. 'L. Jones' is coming to terms with the practicalities of being a widow when she discovers that her husband is not dead after all: 'He's alive. They made a mistake. He's not dead.' In 1976, in conversation with Robert Robinson, *Beard's Roman Women* is given a different genesis altogether: 'The novel was written on commission. I didn't want to write it, but a young Bostonian had some very good photographs of Rome and came to me and said to me, would I write some text to go with his photos? I said yes. I couldn't write a text of the kind he wanted, so I wrote a novel instead, and said: "Let's see if we can combine fiction and photographs." I must have been lacking in inventiveness at the time, so I fell back more than ever I would normally on the facts of my own life.' This is pusillanimous. David Robinson's snaps are of Rome in the rain – Rome reflected in puddles and droplets, everything drenched, blurred, damp and rotting. The marble statues are crying black, sooty tears; the cobblestones and the pavements glisten with oil and slime. There's a great measure of darkness, gloom and shadow – it's Manchester! As for Burgess's contribution, the use of English is so ugly and contorted, it is like a bad translation. His dialogue is so convoluted, when had he last listened to people talk?

Why does he give his characters a vocabulary that nobody would use in conversation? Burgess's books get to be about their own form, intellectual play, arcane diction, and he grew fond of big abstract themes like free will and the triumph or persistence of evil and sin. It was part of his superhuman persona, to deal with cosmic themes, as if he was a god, handing down punishment. He went in for overblown pastiche pseudo-classics about Shakespeare, Jesus, Marlowe, Moses, Freud. (He was determined to bring everybody in.) But he didn't trouble to invent realistic, recognisable people. Burgess's characters are on the same footing as rats and elephants – animals dominating weaker animals, despotically or reasonably, according to the laws of the jungle. That's what the metaphysics of earthly power means: being persecuted – especially by petty officials who want you to fill in forms and give your consent to being pinned down. Burgess saw everything in terms of a battle for possession.

Burgess had a cold, winter-bound genius, for all that he expressed a need for heat: 'I found it easy to write there,' he said of Malaya. 'You sweat so much that it seems to encourage you sweating out words.' He was fascinated by the body and by its fevers, chills, illnesses and addictions – by the complex machines we inhabit; and the great divide between the mind and the body, the way they are always punishing each other and the comic inappropriateness of their conjunction, is his major theme. He was never reckless: there's always an architecture of design in his books – everything is logically constructed, highly conscious. At his best he's flamboyant, epic; at his worst, shallow and ingenious, his productions are static and the intellectual content is empty. Paradoxically, however, that is what he wanted. He disdained a literature that had to do with what Tolstoy called the 'relations of married couples, of parents to children, of children to parents, of men to their fellow-countrymen . . . to the land'; of a literature that was based upon the subtlety, irony, honour, loyalties, understanding – and love, in human conduct. All he'll record is his own flailing fists and rancour; and instead of convincing me he's a put-upon man of action, a giant surrounded by fools, who are trying to destroy him, he simply seems as foolish and mad as a player in an empty theatre. His acting is covering up all sorts of odd and extreme emotions. Any (retrospective) show of affection to Lynne was a kind of betrayal of Liana – and this was very unsatisfying, because he needed both, and one of them was dead. 'Loving two women at the same time had damned him,' wrote Burgess of Scobie in Greene's *The Heart of the Matter*; and in respect of Burgess himself, his rhetoric or graphomania concealed his refusal to engage with that growing drama inside him. He compelled himself to be deeply superficial. He refused to supply his books with real problems drawn from any experience of life – only with artifice, deliberate riddles, and illusion.

He was avid for money and fame, but he could enjoy neither. He accumulated heaps of houses; the dwellings would fill up with books and papers; he'd lock the door and on he'd go, never to return. He was like Timon of Athens:

> Put armour on thine ears and on thine eyes;
> Whose proof nor yells of mothers, maids, nor babes,
> Nor sight of priests in holy vestments bleeding,
> Shall pierce a jot.*

It was as if, like Rimbaud, he was travelling to ward off the horrors

* Act IV, scene iii. Further on in his misanthropic rant, Timon says: 'I'll example you with thievery:/The sun's a thief, and with his great attraction/Robs the vast sea: the moon's an arrant thief,/And her pale fire she snatches from the sun': so that is where Nabokov derived his title for a book about the thieving magpie aspects of poetry and scholarship, *Pale Fire*. In his review of Pushkin's *Eugene Onegin*, translated with a commentary by Nabokov, published in *Encounter* (May 1965), Burgess makes the brilliant point that this labour of love, upon which Nabokov lavished at least fourteen years' work (the translation takes up 228 pages, the commentary 1,172 pages), is itself like Kinbote's mad edition of John Shade. With his verbal eccentricities and temperamental crankiness, his pedantry and braggadocio, the imperious Nabokov is an extreme (and extremely successful) version of the Burgessian artiste, i.e. one who'd prefer to be beheaded rather than reveal or address any personal crisis in their work, and whose books are full of puzzles, chess games, smoke, mirrors and general quirkiness – all of which, though highly polished, somehow suggest darkness and the macabre. 'Nabokov,' Burgess says in *Urgent Copy*, 'is one of the few living writers I honestly admire and would, had I the equipment, like to emulate.' There's Nabokov in his splendid fur-trimmed brocade robes, a Tartar prince; and there's Burgess in his cheap check shirts and ginger jackets looking like a Thai sex tourist. The cerebral or stylistic tricks aside, one way he did echo the maestro (quite happily – and possibly all unawares) was to ape Nabokov's magisterial or snooty personal manner, quick to put down competition or opposition. It tickled Burgess no end to see all those unsaleable paperbacks of *Pale Fire*, 'the ultimate in rarefaction, on Tunbridge Wells Station's bookstall'; and he was jealous of the fluke commercial prowess of *Lolita* – just as he was mightily covetous of the allusive post-structuralist raving, *The Name of the Rose* by Umberto Eco. He said it did for the monastery what Arthur Hailey had done for airports.

In the *Paris Review*, envy got the better of him. 'Nabokov won't go down in history as one of the greatest names. He's unworthy to unlatch Joyce's shoe.'

You should have heard Burgess pronounce Nabokov's name. When he threw it into a sentence it was like an industrial accident in a firework factory – mumbling and droning and then full lung-power for Vla-DEEM-ear Nah-BOAK-off . . . He did do wonders with foreign words and phrases.

The lesson (or moral) of *Timon of Athens* isn't the protagonist's hatred of mankind; it's that his cantankerousness is a vehicle for (or an expression of) intense self-admiration.

accumulating in his mind. He produced much science fiction and historical fiction – he worked so hard it was as if he was trying to keep back or bypass his memories, rather than confront them. Once he'd gone abroad with Liana – an exile which he made sound like an elopement – and had begun a wanderer's life in southern Europe, he cut himself off from society; there was literally no one that spoke his own language. There he is, in Bracciano, 'writing in English, surrounded by Italian speakers', an island unto himself – but at least this brings him closer to Joyce, 'to whom Italian became a first domestic language'. He justified this by claiming (in a postlude to *Moses: A Narrative Poem*, of all out-of-the-way places): 'It is a British writer's duty . . . to get out of Britain if he can and examine the English language against the foil of other tongues, occasionally going back as a tourist and staying at Claridge's.' Marginally less pompously, he made the same declaration on *Parkinson* in 1982: 'One of the reasons I live abroad is because, as a writer, I can see England better when removed from it.'* I suddenly realise the virtue of Philip Larkin staying put in Hull or Julian of Norwich remaining in her cell. The result of Burgess's long-distance perspective was that Britain came to exist in a different, feebler dimension. Which is what he really wanted, of course.

Though he was being vainglorious, his remarks were true in their way. Burgess's high dedication was indeed to language; language held the only reality for him. In *MF*, the Maltese novel, language seems to play at its games all on its own. There is no feeling in the writing. To shut out his private griefs, Burgess's work grew egotistical and as cold as if he'd swallowed snowballs instead of pills. In *MF*, for example, Miles Faber wants to 'get beyond structure and cohesion and find that it's not quite silent and empty. Words and colours totally free because totally meaningless.' However, the point of his adventures is to prove the impossibility of

* Point to ponder: 'Travelling broadens the mind? No, it narrows it. Jesus never travelled; not more than a hundred miles. Michelangelo, Rembrandt, Milton: they are people who made a journey of scarcely any consequence at all and subsequently never travelled further. Travel is for people without imagination: dullards, clods; those who need to animate the landscape otherwise they see nothing there at all.' Sir Ralph Richardson, quoted in *An Actor's Life* by Garry O'Connor (Limelight Edition, New York, 1985, p. 102). Burgess, some time in the sixties, wrote an essay on Coleridge which was included in an edition of 'The Ancient Mariner', with Doré's illustrations, and tucked into the back flap was 'a nice little record of Ralph Richardson reading the poem . . . That seemed to work easily enough. You could do that with the novel, too . . . This is what the people sound like, this is how it was conceived . . . You're hearing a novel. Could be done.' Yes, Anthony – they are called *plays*. The Coleridge project was published by Time-Life Inc. I've never found it and Garry O'Connor had never heard of it, when I asked.

independent and spontaneous action. Where accident is attempted, there is design. Hoping, on the island of Castita (Malta), to 'be wholly free', Miles is revealed as everywhere in chains. He tries to locate a surrealist painter called Sib Legeru ('I hungered for Sib Legeru as for the only sanity in the world'), and it helps to know that *siblegeru* is Anglo-Saxon for incest.* Oedipus flutters, or limps, through the book. ('Keeping sex in the family . . . Oedipus, Electra, all that.') If, in his other novels, Burgess always delighted in making his heroes come to terms with confusion, here the difference is that Miles wants confusion – so Burgess makes him come to terms with the confusing notion of the preordained.

We can see what he is up to: Burgess was denying the concept of free will. By extension, he was trying to convince himself that Lynne's fate was not his fault. She'd have predeceased him in any event. The Catholic side of him searched for certainties, unities, patterns. (In *Earthly Powers* a miracle, hundreds of pages later, turns itself inside out to be an evil deed: a baby saved from meningitis in an orphanage grows up to become a murderous fanatic.) He affected to be fatalistic, to believe that he was innocent of his own guilt, but in fact he was in flight. *MF* is all scaffolding and no building; as is *Napoleon Symphony*, his next novel, where language is made to ape the noises and movements of Beethoven's 'Eroica'. Burgess, who had nothing really to write about except his own past, to avoid his recent past, was left producing abstract, cerebral games. Mothers, dispossession, traps, power: these themes nonetheless criss-cross the texts like cryptic crossword-puzzle clues. (Decoded, what do they mean? That he was still contemplating his origins? Trying to get to the bottom of who he was?) He became his own endless voyager, shuttling between Rome and Lake Bracciano, spending much time in America, as Visiting Professor at City College, New York, and as a Visiting Fellow of Creative Writing at Princeton. He was at Iowa, Chapel Hill, Buffalo, Kenyon College, Ohio (to deliver the John Crowe Ransom Memorial Lectures), and every campus in between, giving lectures for ready tin, to use Kipling's phrase. When I made enquiries, I received letters from places I'd never heard of, e.g. the Choate School in Wallingford, Connecticut. Keith S. Orenstein, who is now Senior Partner at Orenstein

* *Siblegeru* (neuter plural, from *sibleger*, or the law of kinship: see Bosworth-Toller, *An Anglo-Saxon Dictionary*, for the etymology, where you should look at the two elements of the compound) occurs in Bishop Wulfstan's *Sermo Lupi ad Anglos*, a homily on the evils of the times (*c.* 1014) and the imminence of Judgement Day. Burgess had studied this text at Manchester in the edition published by Dorothy Whitelock (Methuen Old English Library, 1939). Incest, like divorce, was one of the 'violations of holy orders' [*hadbrycas*], and Wulfstan was concerned at the disregard in his diocese of the Church's laws on marriage.

and Orenstein, attorneys at law, Madison Avenue, took a course, in 1974, on Burgess's works, and the English professor, William Maillet, invited the Great Man to join in a roundtable discussion in the library. Burgess puffed away about Joyce.* He went from coast to coast like Humbert Humbert traipsing from motel to motel. In the early eighties he went north, to McMaster, in Ontario, where whom should he meet but the erstwhile piano-playing nymphet, Valerie Tryon. Her father, Kenneth Tryon, who had taught German and French at Banbury, also attended the two days' worth of lectures. 'He really had not changed,' they told me – or more accurately, what he'd done was to change back into John Wilson, well fitted in the arts, glorious in arms: nothing became him ill that he would well.

Burgess worked at the Guthrie Theater in Minneapolis – the *Oedipus* translation; the *Cyrano* adaptation – and in Iowa City he had one of his symphonies performed. As if acknowledging the emptiness that had entered his life, he said: 'I rather despise the [novelistic] craft I practise because it is not the craft of the musician. Most musicians know about literature, but few litterateurs know about music . . . I thank America, or rather part of the cornbelt of America, for granting me the only true artistic exaltation I have ever experienced. In Iowa . . . there was a performance of my Third Symphony. My father would have been proud.' (When, later, he accompanied *Metropolis* on the piano, there was 'this . . . mystical identification of paternity and filiality'.) The Iowa campus, I can tell you in passing, was awash with glassy-eyed Vietnam war veterans killing time pretending to be graduate students. The place was lost under a rolling thunder cloud of marijuana fumes. Music, charting, trance-like, the ebb and flow of our internal states, is the supreme mode of expression; it makes us feel we are divining the root cause of a mystery because it is itself mysterious. It is composed to fit mathematical and technical laws, but the laws are infinitely accommodating (as the Debussy tale in *The Devil's Mode* explains). Language, too, is an unpredictable creature which, even as we try to command it, eludes our grasp. New meanings, new words and expressions; the processes of semantics and morphological change – all this obsessed Burgess ('It could be regarded as a kind of masturbation . . . to cosset the words themselves, like so many budgerigars . . .'); and he was more aroused by language than by any of its users.

In his book, *Language Made Plain*, he attempted to argue that language is the wielding of an arbitrary fiction. Beyond all the learned stuff ('what

* A recording was made of the discussion. 'They are usually pretty good at preserving these things at Choate,' said Judge Orenstein. You may telephone the college on 203-697-2000.

I liked was the word *weald* and how, through such processes as I-mutation, vowel rounding, and the vocalisation of the dark L, it tied up with *wold*, *wood* and the German *Wald*'*), Burgess was evidently claiming that language, as a fickle instrument, was coquettish – womanly. Language was his girl and etymology, the cross-breeding of words ('*maudlin* goes back to the weeping of Mary *Magdalene*'), was a family tree – a pedigree. Burgess, who loved language, makes the concept of love, in *Cyrano*, actually equal (=) language. It is not Christian whom Roxanne fancies; she is aroused by his 'game of words', his eloquence – which, as it happens, Cyrano stage-manages and articulates:

> My heart is open wide – your words can't miss
> So large a target. Or, heavy with the honey of
> Desire, it zigzags to the orifice
> Of your tiny ear, and buzzes blunderingly,
> Seeking its way in, its wings a haze of love.
> Or, should these not suffice, then, finally,
> Since your words fall, they yield to gravity:
> Mine have to rise and fight it.

Words, as arrows of desire, are a courtship stratagem here. You'd never have known Edmond Rostand was a Frenchman, though: this has the metrical clink-clank of *Beowulf*. In *A Clockwork Orange*, Burgess had devised harsh, yelping Russian neologisms for a fable of violence. For *Quest For Fire* he crafted that primordial speech of grunts out of Greek, or was it *The Flintstones*? As ever, the buzzes, hisses and bangs are elements of warfare.

He was always hitting out, like the troubled child in the corner, worked up and panic-stricken. This is the mentality of Alex, especially as characterised by Malcolm McDowell, and the release of Kubrick's film made Burgess unfailingly famous, at least whilst he was alive. To the end of his days he was the media's pundit on good and evil, e.g. the piece he always wrote for the *Daily Mail*† each time Myra Hindley came up for parole.

* He was fond of giving impromptu tutorials along these lines. On a train outward bound from Paddington to Cardiff, he suddenly asked Bridget Sleddon, the Hutchinson publicity handmaiden, 'What county is Swindon in? Wiltshire? It means Swine Town. Wiltshire is a bacon-producing district . . . *Shit* and *schizoid* have the same root. Old English via Greek and Old Scots: it means "split", the sensation of the body rent in two by the onset of diarrhoea. This to me is fascinating.' 'Yes,' said Bridget, vaguely.

† Burgess would insist on a few thousand pounds in cash for his why-oh-why pieces. The money had to be left in an envelope at the reception of a hotel. Only then would he dictate his copy down the phone, speaking off the cuff. A most lucrative ten minutes' work.

('What we want from her is a full admission of the enormity in which she was involved and, with her new piety and apparent intelligence, a soul-racking repentance'); and his last article, dictated from his deathbed, was a review of *Art and the Beauty of God: A Christian Understanding* by Richard Harries, Bishop of Oxford. Burgess said that His Grace's waffling on about divine creativity rather overlooked the existence of pain and evil, and God's 'undeniable responsibility' for such things. Art is not 'kittens and daisies', wrote – or spoke – Burgess;* this is all the more poignant and personal if you visualise him lying there, the cancer transforming him into a Francis Bacon portrait. 'The Devil was quite as powerful as God, perhaps more so,' said Jean Rhys. 'I was passionately on the side of God, but it was very difficult to see what I could do about it.' This is rather as I interpret *A Clockwork Orange* (the film), for all the Wulfstan-esque homilies that really it condemns violence, which Burgess was prone to come out with, in *The Clockwork Testament* and elsewhere (e.g. 'The important thing is moral choice . . . life is sustained by the grinding opposition of moral entities,' blah blah blah: *vide* 'A Clockwork Orange Resucked', in *One Man's Chorus*). It's the devilishness of McDowell that we want – his horniness. His Alex is a perfect piece of chicken, like Orton's Mr Sloane – or, to be more true to the period (1972), Robin Askwith in the *Confessions* films. Like Askwith, whose attempt to be a driving instructor or a window cleaner is merely a pretext for frantic fornication, McDowell's Alex seeks sensation. 'Enjoying that are you, my darling?' he says leeringly to a girl sucking a lollipop. In the next scene, she and her friend are stripping off in fast motion for a bout of high-speed rumpy-pumpy with Alex at his flat. It is exactly a Robin Askwith scene – McDowell's hairless, trim body is the same ('a swimmer's build' as they say in the gay contact mags); the cartoonery is the same. Adrienne Corri, in her leotard, is exactly like one of the dolls in *Confessions of a Pop Performer*. Why do critics think Kubrick is such an exalted artist? *A Clockwork Orange* could have been directed by Val Guest – and may have been the better for it. What are Michael Bates's comical prison warder and Patrick Magee's boiling-with-rage rape victim's husband, other than Peter Sellers-type caricatures? Sellers worked with Guest long before Kubrick came along, with *Lolita* and *Doctor Strangelove*; and ever afterwards there'd be a Sellers role in Kubrick's films, usually cast with Leonard Rossiter or Hardy Kruger.

* The dictation was taken down and later typed up by Leslie Gardner, his London agent, who distributed the article on 3 December 1993 – the first of Burgess's posthumous works.

My problem with Kubrick is that he had no sense of humour; it is utterly, totally lacking. He is one of those death's heads who deem the comic spirit of lesser magnitude than tragedy, with its alleged catharsis (which I personally have never experienced. All those bodies at the end of *Hamlet* or *King Lear*? So what? I'm not purged – though the professors continue to preach that one should be); and what this means is that he brought out the portentousness in Burgess, his intellectual snobbery, when actually his novels are full of randy wives and cuckolded husbands, bungled hanky-panky and music-hall puns. 'When a man cannot choose, he ceases to be a man,' we are told in the film, and it's like one of those moralistic Sunday School captions in an old silent picture beloved of Hollywood tyrants. It is sentimental – and sentimentality is cruel because it is indulgent. Nobody has a decent impulsion or motive in Kubrick's *A Clockwork Orange*: the clergyman is creepy, Alex's parents turf him out so as to earn rent on his room, and the social worker is a pederast. Was it pure chance, or did Kubrick intentionally fill the film with grotesque men who look like doubles or hall-of-mirror deformations of Burgess himself? Apart from Alex, with his exaggerated codpiece – he's literally cocky, and he brains Miriam Karlin with a gigantic porcelain penis – every other male person on display, rheumy-eyed, veiny-nosed, dewlapped, is leering and ugly: not only Bates and Magee, but Warren Clarke (one of the droogs), Paul Farrell (the tramp), Aubrey Morris (Deltoid), Godfrey Quigley (the prison chaplain), John Savident (a conspirator), Anthony Sharp (the minister), Philip Stone (Alex's father) and David Prowse (Magee's assistant – a giant in green underpants). Each of them is shot in looming close-up with a distorting wide-angle lens. This only accentuates the homoeroticism in the presentation of McDowell, who lolls next to a reproduction of Michelangelo's statue of David, wanders his house nearly nude, has a long scene lying in the bath, and who is strip-searched at the prison. He didn't have to vary his performance much to play Gore Vidal's Caligula.

Progressively humiliated and broken, betrayed and abandoned: in this sense Alex in the film is a typical Burgess hero, a suffering Lost Boy. 'Where was I to go who had no home and no money?' he asks. His parents have northern accents – Manchester accents; and the image of the lonely child, thrown to the mercy of the elements, unwanted, unloved, is one that Burgess had always claimed as his own. One doesn't quite believe in it, however, in the film. Alex is too sparky and savage to be oppressed for long. Simply by his performance, McDowell undermines the premise that behaviour can be programmed and engineered. He is a consummate rebel – as he was in *If*. (When he's bleeding it looks like war paint.) The rest of the film, however, has no depth; it is nerveless. Is that why it was hidden from view for decades, to generate an air of mystery and myth when actually it was rather piss-poor? Those claims that it inspired violent deeds and copycat killings, from the rape of a nun in Berwick-upon-Tweed to a mugging in Poughkeepsie: specious? To whip up publicity? Burgess was certainly put to work by Warner Brothers to market the movie, doing the round of chat shows, giving endless interviews to the press, churning out his articles. Why didn't anybody say that, despite the rapes and fights, *A Clockwork Orange* is inert, like Alex in his straitjacket, his eyes clamped wide shut? Yet what survives from it, viewed today, are the very features Burgess would have liked least, its magentas and raspberry reds, its late sixties/early seventies psychedelia (against which Enderby railed so ineffectually). Kubrick had seen the future, and it was Uxbridge (Brunel University), Radlett, South Norwood and Thamesmead.

Roaring boys – the droogs – were not only in *A Clockwork Orange*: there are American teenage hoodlums in *The Right to an Answer*; and in *The Kingdom of the Wicked*, Nero and Domitian join street gangs and run wild because, causing havoc, they create a depraved sort of performance art. The Imperial droogs spill blood as artists splash ink and paint. (There'd been artistry, too, in the way Alex warbled Gene Kelly's number 'Singin' in the Rain' in counterpoint to putting the boot in. Burgess claimed that it was he who gave Kubrick that idea, thumping on the piano one day at the director's house during pre-production.) Human life is 'fissile and susceptible of new shapes', and as Emperors, Nero and Domitian are raised above the law – 'and it follows that only the individual whom rank has raised above the law is free to pursue beauty to the limit'. This is virtually Dorian Gray's metaphysics; Nero's own Lord Henry Wotton is Petronius, a tutor in temptation, and the outcome of debauchery is a paradox and a contradiction: 'true wisdom,' says Nero, sexually spent, 'lies in the nerves and in the arousing of the imagination' – which is exactly the lesson *Flame into Being** blesses Lawrence for having pointed out. For Lawrence, 'the centre of his response to the external world was the solar plexus, not the cerebral cortex . . . Well, there are plenty of scientific truths which reason has to accept, but there is no reason why our guts

* This is the book Burgess had recently completed when I first met him. I saw him in London, too, when *The Kingdom of the Wicked* was published. I was amazed at the number of eminent Fleet Street hacks who flocked around him, pretending to have read the thing. I was very young, still at Oxford, and shocked by the hypocrisy and bluff.

and instincts should have to bow to them.' The apparent antagonism in Burgess between castigating Roman emperors for what a Nottingham wordsmith rediscovered is no real antagonism. Burgess has filled many books with the glandular and the occult, the magical and the invisible. His Shakespeare is superintended by Venus; *The Eve of Saint Venus* brings the goddess to an English village; voodoo is in the Malayan novels and *Earthly Powers*. The paganism *Flame into Being* enjoys – Burgess entranced by Lawrence's quest for strange gods – *The Kingdom of the Wicked*, despite itself, is enthralled by as well. (What else are boys and girls to do with their natural energies?)

Consider incest, again. Evidently the characters in this late work have proleptically studied the Belgian anthropologist, Lévi-Strauss – who said that incest is a taboo initiated to proscribe endogamy and insist upon exogamy. Thus a tribe will make alliances and flourish; there will be no turning-in, no inbreeding. Claudius, to marry Agrippina, barks that 'The Emperor is above taboos like incest.' Censure comes from Seneca, who anachronistically propounds *The Scope of Anthropology* and *The Elementary Structures of Kinship*. Incest taboos are not invented; somehow they are immanent: 'There is an instinctive abhorrence of these acts which is based on an instinctive knowledge of what makes for stability of society.' Seneca, played in the mini-series with appropriate gravitas by Fernando Rey, tells his pupil to read his play on Oedipus or 'your aversion to my style being so great, the play by Sophocles on which it is based'. And as Oedipus and incest cannot get far without Freud, Tiberius refers to his mother as 'you unkillable bitch' and Philip cures a cripple's hand by coaxing the patient to confess he'd 'struck his mother in a rage' and had found 'as he had thought, that God struck that hand and rendered it paralysed'. Psychoanalytically, the apostle heals. Psychoanalytically, Nero rebels. 'No boy,' he says, striking Agrippina, 'likes hitting his mother. Except, that is, in those bouts of love play one particular mother taught her son.' He thrusts his hand into her dress and fondles her nipple. (In *A.D. Anno Domini*, that's exactly what Anthony Andrews does to Ava Gardner.) With Petronius he postulates a production of a real *Oedipus Rex*, with real incest and real mutilations on the stage. His rage against his mother is explicitly Freudian: 'To put it bluntly, liberation from the womb' is what he desires by her demise.

In the Lawrence book, Burgess makes the fascinating suggestion that he'll never fathom *Sons and Lovers* because, having lost his own mother when young, he never knew the luxury of the Oedipus Complex. Burgess's mother was a pretty music-hall singer, of whom spectral photos survived, only to be destroyed by the humidity in Malaya. It is my contention that the fiery muse and Venusian goddess who stalks so many of his pages, guarding, flirting, is in fact an incarnation of the lost maternal force. He has created the luxury in art – or non-art, where he had an outlet for his fantasies and lechery. Why the interest in incest? It is the secret dream of the dispossessed and lost. Oedipus thought himself an exile, a wanderer; suddenly, madly, he learns he'd been in the embrace of his family all along. Incest is a way of coming home.

Orgiastic Romans, with their themes of lust and death, Burgess counterpoints with the chaste Nazarenes. *The Kingdom of the Wicked* does not succeed in making the religious life appealing, or interesting. Moral debate palls. The love of God, so much touted, is little evidenced by the omnipresent cruelty and surliness. To try and prevent the apostles from coming over as weak and wimpish, Burgess makes them comic. They are comic in the sense that Mel Brooks is comic. Baptising is hard work; thousands to get through every day, like a novelist's wordcount. Thomas is given a Scottish accent. Peter winces when roosters crow (like the crone in *Young Frankenstein*, mention of whose name causes horses to neigh). When they are flagellated the disciples sing a shanty (like the tortured Jews in *History of the World*):

Beat us and bash us
Lick us and lash us.

Death is jolly. Christians go to the lions as to a bank-holiday spree. A cured cripple complains he's now made redundant from his profitable job as a beggar. Dining on leeks and onions, the holy twelve fart like the *Blazing Saddles* cowboys (or is the allusion Joycean: 'Gone with the wind. Hosts at Mullaghmast and Tara of the Kings'?). I am convinced that those people who wrote his obituaries and delivered their eulogies and who allowed Burgess to retain this reputation as the great twentieth-century truly international master had never read his works.

Leaving the divine dozen aside, Paul does furnish a few opportunities for intelligence and wit, chiefly in his private battles with the pricklings of the flesh. He has bodily cravings for an anonymous woman – 'faceless as Eve and with Eve's body to comfort him, our first mother . . .' The primal parent is the premier mistress, the source of all fantasies of lechery. Burgess, not quite able to excite us with bland and flatulent Christians, certainly cannot make Christianity compete with 'Aphrodite and Astarte or Ashtaroth who was Hellenized to Artemis and Romanized to Diana'. Diana, the huntress, and Venus are in cahoots. (They pursue Enderby through *Enderby Outside*.) Though Luke has to treat a temple prostitute for the clap, the goddess of love is dangerously real. Her paganism and voluptuousness easily puts Nazarene restraint to rout. 'The goddess . . . is no wraith or fiction – she is real enough,' says Paul. 'The goddess is a great nuisance.' Paul joins many other Burgess heroes in being rewarded, at long last, with 'a nocturnal emission', a wet dream. 'He wished, of course, to be back in bed with his mother, comforted to sleep.' The book concludes with *una nox dormienda* when the Earth Mother sinks Pompeii: 'our mother our killer' intones the text.

It's curious that Burgess had to go to ancient Rome to bring up his obsessions; and then he only mentions them rather than explores them. Having decided that Lucky Luciano and his henchmen were after him, he left modern-day Rome for Monaco and set up his headquarters at 44 rue Grimaldi. Here he wrote *Earthly Powers*, which is all his other books in one. In it he recapitulates his career and sings a song of himself; he also fills the text with lots of real people (Betjeman, Wells, Henry James, etc.*) and gooses them in the manner of scurrilous Beerbohm cartoons: graphic satire that is also literary and personal criticism. Kenneth Toomey, in addition, is a plurality of paper men: the saga of the Campanatis is like Galsworthy's Forsytes; the oriental short stories make Toomey into Maugham; as a popular wartime playwright he is Noel Coward. But basically the book – a history of the last century – is about Burgess. It deals with the dilemma which beset him towards the end of his career: was he a true artist? What was posterity going to think? Toomey (i.e. Burgess) wants to know whether it is possible to be a great writer *and* produce a bestseller. There is a tension between wanting to be experimental and wanting to be popular. (*Is he demotically beerbarrelish or classically pocular?* as Burgess asked of Ogden Nash.) He was tormented by trying to be innovative and wanting to be read. *Beard's Roman Women* splits the author into warring selves: the script-writing hack and the posh novelist-cum-professor. Writers whom Burgess admired managed to straddle the extremes: Defoe, Hemingway, Fitzgerald, and ultimately Shakespeare.

* Wells is 'a satyromaniac', Norman Douglas is 'boy-shagging', James Agate is 'a well-known sodomite', T. S. Eliot is a 'dilettante' . . . Burgess humiliates the elder statesmen in the guise of paying homage to them. At one point Toomey is asked about the concept of humiliation and replies, 'I practically invented it'; this echoes the line in *Cyrano de Bergerac* where the protagonist is asked if he knows *Don Quixote*: 'Know it? I've practically lived it,' he responds.

These combine the extremes, and marry the extremes; a miraculous match. Dickens, we read in *Urgent Copy*, won the creation of 'serious literary art out of pop material . . . Language and morality add dimensions to his cartoons and turn them into literature.'

Did Burgess's own alchemy succeed? He enjoyed being topsy-turvy – one minute assuring us that 'One of my few endowments is an ability to read Persian' and the next admitting that he couldn't dress himself. You think I'm joking? On his way to the publication party at Calder and Boyar's office in Walker's Court, Soho, for Robert Nye's first novel, *Doubtfire*, in 1967, Burgess, standing to attention on the tube, was mystified to see his underpants beginning to appear from the bottom of his trouser leg. He was too embarrassed to pull them out and put them in his pocket and couldn't understand how or why they'd begun such a descent. Eventually he understood that the day before he had removed his knickers along with his breeches, put on a fresh pair in the morning and the others had been working their way down . . . But the prosaic explanation isn't any good – with Burgess we want sartorial pixies to be afflicting him and laughing at his harm; from Burgess we expect it to snow on him in New Orleans, or that he'll go in a pub, miles from anywhere, and there, framed on the wall, are certificates from the Ancient Order of Buffaloes bearing his father's name,* or that, invited to a literary dinner in his honour in Bristol, he'll throw a tantrum: 'The image of Chatterton swam into my mind – so I gave these complacent Bristolians hell. "If Chatterton reappeared, you'd do it again, kill him at eighteen." They didn't like that.' ('Please be nice to them today,' pleaded Bridget Sleddon, his emissary from Hutchinson.) It seems a bit tough on the good people who'd turned out to support him to accuse them over the death of a poet two hundred years previously. It's like when he was invited to deliver the commencement address at Fordham University, at the Robert Moses Plaza, Lincoln Center. He hated the pop song which had preceded him, which had exhorted people to reach out and touch each other – 'I could not and would not.' He then scowled at the black students

* During his childhood (which Burgess would have us believe was more deprived than Smike's – indeed, Smike's was like the Princesses Lilibet and Margaret Rose's by comparison), when he was banished to his bed in the attic, Burgess found a complete set of the *Manual of Freemasonry*. 'A secret society apparently, with passwords and obscure rites. Was my father a member? . . . I fancy he was a quiet low-degree apron-wearer.' He was not. I have checked the indexes for Lancashire prior to 1938, at the Library and Museum of Freemasonry, in the United Grand Lodge, and the only Joseph Wilsons on the books are a wool comber from Bradford and a waterworks manager from Blackburn.

There is much on freemasonry in *Ulysses*, but it is one of those subjects which deranges people. You'd end up arguing that Burgess's father was Jack the Ripper.

and told the hooded and gowned graduates: 'There are some who can benefit from a university education and some who cannot.' He then wonders why he had to creep from the podium to scant applause. Did he really not know when his behaviour was inappropriate and his irritable self-advertising offensive?

His belief in a hierarchy of taste and decorum, and the way he continually runs into trouble, is comic, bashful, buffoonish. He is fond of noble folly undercut by base wisdom. It's a version of his battle between high art and low art. *Earthly Powers* is a comedy which pretends to be a tragedy. History is a trickster allowing saints to be devils and fat greedy pigs elected as Pope. It's all as unlikely as a generation of Oxford undergraduates drowning themselves for the love of Zuleika Dobson: 'One is taught to refrain from irony, because mankind does tend to take it literally. In the hearing of the gods, who hear all, it is conversely unsafe to make a simple and direct statement,' counsels Beerbohm. The problem with Burgess is to know how much we are to take him at his word; what is the precise degree of irony in his descriptions and reports? Did he really lack humility, or is that another layer of pretence? Wilde once said that 'One's real life is the one we do not lead'; thus the primacy of the imagination or the world inside the head, or of books where you may find what Jean Rhys calls 'sharp flashing things'; or it is the way Wilson readjusted himself as Burgess – Burgess being a hotch-potch of duplicities, disguises, condescension and extravagant silliness. In *Seven Men and Two Others*, Enoch Soames makes a Faustian pact to time travel to the British Museum Reading Room, where he'll look himself up in the works of reference. He is startled to discover that he is but 'an immajnari karrakter' invented by 'a riter ov the time, naimd Max Beerbohm'. All he's learnt is that he is a figment of somebody else's fancy, 'a ghostly visitation'. Such is the fate of literature. It can do little in the end but haunt itself, which is the conceit of *Enderby's Dark Lady*, where Shakespeare's plays are beamed from the future into the past. Burgess, whose works have shimmered in from who knows what grove or green, by fountain clear or spangled starlight sheen, showed 'much power . . . great ability there is assuredly – long and careful study – considerable humour – untiring industry – all of them qualities entitled to high praise'. This is from Ruskin's report about the Royal Academy Exhibition of 1858, and concerns Frith's *Derby Day*. He continues, however, to remark that the painting is compromised by its appeals to popularity, and thus 'is necessarily, because popular, stooping and restricted'. Burgess's work likewise droops under its own weight. But this is perhaps to judge him on issues that don't affect him. His concern is language, not character; he wants to teach and give orders, not bother with the nuances of psychological realism; he is interested in the phenomenon of style and technique rather than in any semblance of nature. Hence the self-conscious caricatures which result. Burgess's novels – *crossmess parzels*, to use his favourite Joyceanism: crossword puzzles and Christmas parcels – are (as Auden said of Oxford colleges) 'utterly satisfied with their own weight'. They are about nothing except themselves. Or, more accurately, when they come off they are about themselves, but when they don't they are about Burgess and his efforts to keep control over his waking mind.

When I got to know him, making an appearance in his story as a Recording Angel,* it was when he was beginning to dwell on matters of life and death – though when had such matters ever been far off? *Enderby's Dark Lady* was composed 'to placate kind readers . . . who objected to my casually killing my hero', and in *Tremor of Intent*, Hillier, a spy meant to be liquidated and who is disguised as a priest in Dublin, remarks that 'Only after death . . . was regeneration possible.' Burgess's favourite bit of the Gospels was the raising of Lazarus: 'Of course, you never know why God singles people out for special treatment. Take Lazarus – pissed every night, screwing everyone, slain in a tavern . . .'

Christopher Marlowe was slain in a tavern. 'A great man, Marlowe – died at twenty-nine, stabbed to death in a tavern by double agents. Probably was one himself . . . Writers in the old days brawled for their work.' Marlowe, the dead man in Deptford, and the subject of the final novel, is symbolic of talent attenuated; Burgess is representative of talent protracted. His career was a phantasmal, enigmatic enterprise: everything beyond that cerebral-tumour terminal year was miraculously accomplished during a stay of execution. Hence perhaps the paper trail of aliases and the acting: hospitalised Wilson fled into the world, as Spindrift does in *The Doctor Is Sick*, bedecked in a wardrobe of different identities. Language itself was a component in the disguise. Yet, slippery and amorphous as he was, Burgess hated not to be grasped: 'I like understanding from those who read my books,' he once bellowed. 'I don't get much from

* I appear, a Welshman at Oxford, transmuted into 'a Canadian academic' who'd approached him 'a week before in London with a view to writing my biography', in the opening chapter of *Little Wilson and Big God*. I'm also in Jonathan Meades' *The Fowler Family Business* (London, 2002) as Fancy Lewis, an incest-ridden Herefordshire yokel with a yen for women whose 'nipples are like the starter-buttons on a Massey-Fergusson'. Where will it all end?

the people in England.' Well, he's had plenty of understanding from me, fair play. I can see for example that (a) he was a great writer who never wrote a great book: his talent was too widely dispersed; (b) his life was circumscribed by deaths: his mother, his sister, his first wife, his own first death sentence – and his real death sentence. In 1993 he returned to England to die – 'I'll want to come back, and find a place to be buried in, an honourable grave' – and if it is true that he wrote to live (and to make a living), he also worked to forget, to block out, rather than to remember. He did his best to disengage himself from his feelings; this is why there is no sensuality in his writing. There is wordplay, but no actual skylarking or any spirit of intimacy. There is a lack of positive, warm emotion. (He was hopeless, by the way, at sex scenes; he may as well have had bicycles coupling.) He was stiff and withdrawn. What does come through, in his best work, is a sense of doom. Empires collapsing; the end of the world. His vanity, too, could be curiously innocent and winning; he was not continuously megalomaniacal. He dared to become a genius, and this book has shown you how and why; and in the distance there will always be that one sound which haunted him and terrified him equally, which he tried to shut out, but from which his inspiration had sprung: the cry of a mother weeping. Fade to black, printer.

Epilogue

Telemessage

OXF0702 LMX9896 P800001 P12 40480XF

08 DEC 1985/1515

08 December 1985

TELEMESSAGE
ROGER LEWIS
7 THE MANOR HOUSE
STRATTON AUDLEY
OXFORD

SEATS BOOKED FOR YOU AND YOUR WIFE APOLLO THEATRE OXFORD TUESDAY EVENING. SEE YOU 18.45 IN VESTIBULE.

ANTHONY BURGESS

'So great a man he seems to me,' wrote Thackeray of Swift, 'that thinking of him is like thinking of an empire falling.' Burgess, too, in any summing up, would seem to require cataclysmic imagery. He's a prince of the powers of the air; a mountain range full of ravines and waterfalls, torrents, crags and snowfields, casting a shadow for leagues over the plains. He demands hyperbole. Yet, as Henry James said of Tennyson's funeral, 'something – I don't know what – of real impressiveness – was wanting.' Burgess's house of fiction, for all its flights of stairs, antechambers, labyrinthine libraries, annexes, sliding panels, trapdoors, secret rooms, chambers of horrors and ornate carvings, is a bit gimcrack. As I have already concluded, he was a great writer who, paradoxically, never wrote a great book. But he perfected, instead, a great writer act – only ever emerging fully in character for the journalism, films, radio and television pontifications; and he was famous for never turning away a commission. He was the toiling artisan, extravagant, gassy, pedantic and pompous; and this is the Burgess that John Sessions imitates, which rather doubles (or cubes) the theatrical effect.

For all the panoramic range – the vastness – there is, however, a narrowness to his vision. He was easily slighted, quick to take offence, and his resentments did him no credit. He would always complain he was a victim of metropolitan snobbery – that he was looked down upon as being from Manchester, with all that the north–south division entailed. 'John, I did not realise you were so well connected,' Olivia Manning had said to him, having heard about George Patrick Dwyer, Archbishop of Birmingham. When he told her that this was a Catholic diocese, she reputedly replied, 'Oh, that explains it then.' Yet his attitudes *were* provincial, for all his exotic voyaging and inhabiting the farthest distances.

It's he who was ashamed of his origins, who goes on about it in interviews: 'Mancunians don't take kindly to people who leave their own city,' he said in 1989. 'They think I'm a stuck-up opinionated bastard.' He also claimed that, in Waterstone's, he was shouted at 'to stop writing books and get a proper job for a change' – which is either apocryphal, or it might have been a comment tossed at him as a joke. But he took it (real or imagined) as an insult, and as the reason for his banishment.

If 'I'm still very much a Mancunian', and one who'd wanted to be buried in Moston Cemetery at that, why is he in a pot behind a marble slab in Monte Carlo, which everybody thinks houses the remains of Benny Andersson and Bjorn Ulvaeus? Why, in any event, did he go out of his way to try to become Celtic, claiming Irish and Scottish allegiance? He was determined never to fit in. 'Manchester, when I was a boy in the thirties, was much more cosmopolitan than it is today. It had a booming cotton industry, German chophouses, a lot of foreign technologists and Jews,' he once said, recreating the place, in his mind, as a turn-of-the-century Budapest or Vienna, filled with parades, brass bands, nights at the opera and Sundays in the park. Retrospectively, he was making himself a European – and he was always to vilify the writers who remained behind in England, paring their nails in Hampstead or Mayfair; and as for the rest of Britain – that's where 'you revert to feudalism, folksongs, that sort of thing. I'm not quite English enough to be at home in the English countryside.' It's a fascinating delusion, thinking that Lancashire has fallen off the landmass of the British Isles and is floating far away, like the orchestra in *The Marx Brothers at the Circus*.

When he returned from his self-imposed exile, however, which he did more than periodically, he was the first to complain about the coinage, the beer in the pubs, the trains, the clothes people were wearing, the television; he was like a peppery, gouty retired Major Bloodrok tut-tutting over the Rees-Mogg leaders in the lounge of his Angmering-on-Sea nursing home. (He'd become Major Meldrum.) He was a parody of the very personality he'd always ridiculed. 'I felt towards the officers who gave me orders a great deal of contempt,' he'd said of his experience in the ranks during the war – yet look how he was to behave. 'Two young negresses (or female blacks) were sitting by, loudly playing a transistor radio. I politely asked them to turn the thing off and was told obscenely to turn myself off. What is the right response?' March them back to the jungle is what he wants to do, but instead, 'I did nothing.' He'd like Britain still to be 1954, when he went to Malaya, or at least 1968, when he went to Malta. How dare his country have carried on and changed in his absence. It was another sign of betrayal.

Burgess did all that travelling and yet he didn't inhabit anywhere fully. It was a life of wandering, as if he was plunging himself into abroad as if into an abyss. Britain was wrong; he had a brainstorm and returned from Borneo in a dramatic fashion. Malta was evacuated under cover of darkness ('We had to get out quickly'). In Italy, the Mafia were on his tail ('We had better get out of Bracciano'). Coming to the end of his year as Visiting Fellow, 'Liana, Andrea and I crept out of Princeton.' It's a life of misadventure and humiliation. He was on the jury at the Cannes Film Festival and the police had to be called. He gave a lecture in Venice at a conference organised by the European Parliament on the problem of a common language, suggested that we revert to speaking in Latin, and was surprised when 'I was cold-shouldered and ate my buffet lunch in an enclosure of human backs.' Perhaps nobody felt they had the necessary or adequate Ciceronian skills to dare broach him? He was so determined to present himself as embattled; he was so keen to think of himself as a romantic individualist; and the effect of all this is so farcical – it is easy to forget that the laceration and disruption were deliberate. He was covering up for his childhood (and I still can't imagine him as a child) and for the fact that mothers meant death to him: his actual mother's death; the hateful deadly stepmother; Lynne's miscarriage; and his obsession with the Oedipus myth, with its deaths and entrances. He was concealing the fact that though he wanted us to believe his sexual energies were unstoppable (maids, girls in the Malay bazaar, students), actually he was impotent ('. . . his heart began to sink rapidly as the flaccid cold of failure crept towards him . . . "It doesn't matter. You can't help it I suppose,"' we read in *A Vision of Battlements*); he immersed himself in any number of fancy languages, but couldn't communicate ('Mr Burgess,' said an interviewer, interrupting him at a foreign press conference, 'I can't understand a word you're saying. Could you please answer in English?'); he shut himself off with big words, which he savoured morphologically and etymologically, not as aids to being sociable or making friends. ('We spend a lot of our time keeping away from people,' he told Duncan Fallowell in 1989. 'It sounds cold-blooded to say it but time is so short. Too short for the kind of social life which friends demand.') Bamber Bridge, for example, was remembered as a Never-Neverland of old dialects and genial customs. 'The Malay language, and later the Chinese, changed not just my attitude to communication in general but the whole shape of my mind,' he was to say – of a mind that would be closed off, secretive, extremely defensive. There was all that energy, yet the work gets to be inert: e.g. in *Any Old Iron*, where he grabs at anything, from the *Titanic* going down to Arthurian legends; there's nothing living or impulsive. There are plenty of big themes, but no characters for whom it is possible to feel affection. Everybody has always noted how generous Burgess was, how prodigal, but was he really? The extravagance of the prose, the exoticism of his locales, the curlicues of his vocabulary, were underpinned with a very Mancunian parsimoniousness. It was always a very important consideration: who's paying for lunch? He and Liana once met Richard Cohen and made a big fuss that it was their wedding anniversary. A bottle of champagne was ordered. Cohen was left to pick up the bill.

The Malaya books, *Nothing Like the Sun*, *MF*: each closes with a grandiose cosmic coming together, of East and West, black and white; there's a marriage of Russia and America in *Honey for the Bears*, even in the neologisms of *A Clockwork Orange*. Yet, as his least sentimental novel, *The Right to an Answer*, demonstrates, different cultures and peoples are incompatible; and in his own life there were plenty of mutual misunderstandings, between himself and America, or himself and the young, whom he despised. 'I blame the young for the impoverishment of language,' he said once, standing on a jetty in Venice in the rain. 'I blame the young for this – the tremendous lexicon becoming a slim little volume.' In defence of those of us the right side of seventy, may I just say it can take much of a lifetime to build up to *zeugma*, *zim* and *zinzulation*. But his own preferences were for disgruntlement and disillusion; his books are full of loveless, homeless, isolated figures. What's remarkable about his documentary on Rome, where he is to be seen in crimpolene flares and a yellow shirt (what colour did he think that was? Beige?) shouting above the traffic, is that he in effect empties the city of human beings. There he is, like an antique Roman in modern dress – a bronze cast of the Burgess hair with its adrift horns and crescents ought to have been placed in the British Museum; and he pops up in long shot, in the Colosseum arena or on a bridge, or down a side street, to point out that the Borghese Gardens are 'my gardens', for example, or he assures us that the place is like 'what most men seek in a woman: a whore and a mother, corrupt and vicious but never ungenerous'. Yet there's no family feeling here – no parents and children going on outings; no bustling restaurants and cafés; he doesn't think to direct the camera at people enjoying themselves. Burgess doesn't talk to or mix with the locals. There's no fun or entertainment in Burgess's Rome – he turns it into Manchester.

You should see his look of disapproval at a papal mass, in the basilica of St Peter's. Rome, he maintains, is a city of worldly pomp and grandeur, closer to 'dung and copulation' than to any spiritual or eternal truths. Which leads to my next paradox: for all his Catholic anxiety, Burgess was a puritan. He's very austere – against relaxation, against frivolity. How about this rant, from 1973:*

> They're all impotent. They're a rather impotent, flaccid lot – which is a pity [he said of his students at City College, New York]. They shouldn't be like that. They should be vigorous; they're not vigorous. They are not vigorous even in their demeanours. They sit in the classroom, not with the intention of learning, not with that rather uptight, tense posture. They relax. You cannot learn relaxed. You cannot play music relaxed, but, you know, the virtues of relaxation have been promoted so much in this country that it is about time people began to think seriously about what the virtue is. Why should we?
>
> You know, I always associate America with: you pull off your tie as soon as you get into a room; you slouch; you take off your jacket. The British view has always been different. You regard dress or deportment as an aspect to action. When the Americans laugh at the British for having dressed for dinner in the jungle, the British were perfectly right to dress for dinner. If they did not dress for dinner in the jungle, they would just wear the same clothes they were wearing all day long: sweaty, dirty clothes that they would probably put on again in the morning. They would relax. Everything would relax. Law would relax. Discipline would relax. The jungle would creep back again. So they deliberately did this. It was not foolishness. It was a deliberate technique for maintaining self-discipline. There is not enough self-discipline. This may be a very English thing to say, I don't know.

It's a mad and fearful thing to say, I know that. Burgess reminds me of one of those terrified passengers who think that if they stop concentrating or meditating the plane will crash and burn. Despite his endless articles and polemics about free will; although he took up the libertarian position in an extreme form with Lynne, standing back and allowing her the latitude to drink herself to death – actually he mistrusted the progress of

* From 'An Interview in New York with Anthony Burgess' by Charles T. Bunting, *Studies in the Novel* (Winter 1973).

human liberty. He's proscriptive and rigid. His view of freedom is more like cynicism – he's like Patrick Magee, in the Kubrick film, who gives a gibbering apoplectic impersonation of Burgessian wrathfulness. 'I live in a state of almost perpetual rage,' he told Anthony Clare. This is true: staying in Kent, he wanted to blow up Canterbury Cathedral; at the Franco–Italian border at Ventimiglia, 'I hit out and guns were drawn.' When Clare, no doubt hoping that the tranquilliser gun was loaded and in his briefcase, asked why was it he'd agreed to appear on *In the Psychiatrist's Chair*, Burgess said, 'I wondered how far I could voluntarily submit to the kind of probing you do, how deep the probing was, and what I could learn about myself.' This was disingenuous. Despite the host's best efforts ('Contemporary psychiatrists would be interested in the fact that you didn't have much experience as a child in relating to your peers'), the pseudo-patient sped easily away, protecting himself with his familiar, robust crotchets: 'I feel rejected by the English'; 'I was writing continually – two thousand words a day'; etc. Such is his manner, he's not a man you'd like to contradict. Fourteen years prior to that encounter,* he'd been asked by an American interviewer if he'd ever consent to a psychoanalytic enquiry and his reply was unequivocal. 'No. Nor ever will I. *Never* . . . It's my job *not* to be fully aware of the unconscious process . . .' It's not A B B A/A B B A that should be on his tombstone – 'Trespassers will be prosecuted' would be more apt.

He didn't want his guilt dispelled, or dispersed. All his characters are beset by a sense of sin and guilt; they are in a state of mortification because of a God who is fierce, who loves destruction. And if the early novels (*The Doctor Is Sick*, *The Right to an Answer*, *The Wanting Seed*) are about adulterous and squabbling youngish couples – men and women who are paradoxically sustained by the strain and tension and animal magnetism that exist between them – the later work, the post-Lynne work, is about the search for forgiveness and the impulse to make confession. ('I have spent much of my life apologising, asking for pardon first and then deciding what I should be pardoned for afterwards,' he slyly said.) With *Beard's Roman Women*, *Man of Nazareth*, *Earthly Powers* and *The Kingdom of the Wicked*, Burgess became a religious writer, or at least a moralising one. Guilt, he knew, was the 'source of [my] writing strength; once you cease to be guilty, then you won't write so well'; and so is this that altar upon which Lynne was sacrificed? 'I should have stopped her

* The *In the Psychiatrist's Chair* episode was usefully if selectively transcribed in the *Listener* on 28 July 1988.

drinking,' he said, twenty years after her death. 'But being Welsh and self-willed she wouldn't be told. Guilt attached to me for her situation – but I deliberately shut my mind to the clinical condition. But it was evident that here was a woman not fit for normal life.' All this puffing and blowing about guilt (when what he means is shame: ashamed to be from Manchester; ashamed not to be posh; ashamed to be a novelist because 'I am a musician really'); yet he needed guilt. He nurtured it. He was in a permanent mood of moral transgression and he luxuriated in it; all these feelings of disobedience and embarrassment – he wallowed in his own weaknesses, as Greene did (except he lacks the irony and compassion of Greene). But surely it is such a useless and arrogant feeling, guilt? Especially if you feel guilty about things you are not responsible for; or if you think everything in the universe is down to you? He may or may not have been able to help Lynne more, but it's not guilt we want from him – it's penitence.

Fat chance. By pouring out books and articles, Burgess could make his fortune by being wrapped up in himself. Writing is a solitary pursuit – it is the consolation of the essentially lonely – and as Burgess grew more busy (as Burgess became Burgess), Lynne was further and further excluded. She'd seen it as her function to try and single out and biff those critics who'd been less than adulatory about her husband's productions (Kingsley Amis and Gore Vidal were amongst the many victims; Christopher Ricks was assaulted with a handbag); and such displays were rather pathetic attempts to reach the man she was married to – and so at least we can say of Liana that she'll have known what was expected from her. Here they all are in Bracciano – in an account kindly sent to me by Milton Hebald, the sculptor whose Roman emperor bust of Burgess appears in the soft-focus photograph on the jacket of *Little Wilson and Big God* and *You've Had Your Time*:

> I was having a one-man show of sculpture and graphics at the Galleria La Margherita in Rome, during June of 1970, and I made a point to be in attendance each day. It was an important exhibition for me, posters were spread around town, and I had a good crowd coming and going all the time. At the opening, I saw Liana Johnson, who had been away from Rome since my days at the academy in the 1950s. Liana was a north Italian countess who, together with her husband, Ben Johnson, had been part of the convivial literary group of American and Italian writers which included Ralph Ellison, Giuseppe

Berto and Stanley Kauffmann.* They would meet at open-air bars and have supper together with Cecille and me outdoors at Ristaurante Sabatini on Piazza Santa Maria, in Trastevere.

I felt warmly toward both of the Johnsons, although Ben, gentle and conversational, had an unquenchable thirst, and one hesitated to bring out a bottle at home when they came to visit, as Ben would make short work of it! He was lithe with delicate features. He came from Boston where his father was the first Negro doctor in the city. Both of them were translators, working principally on contemporary Italian writing. Liana had the dark eyes and delicate frame of a typical Mediterranean type, as well as an excellent English vocabulary delivered with great speed. It was difficult to latch on to the content, as she inevitably made such a confusion by joining syllables together in the wrong places.

Liana quickly informed me that she had divorced Ben years back, had been living in Cambridge, and had remarried and had a son, and introduced me to her present husband, Anthony Burgess. The name at that time meant little – but taking me aside, she told me that he was a well-known author, and that they were at that time living in Malta. She was interested in finding a home in Rome, as her six-year-old son, the product of an English father and Italian mother, could only speak Maltese. Liana got really excited when I told her that we lived in Bracciano and had a house that we were interested in selling.

After the exhibition, we had supper together, with some Roman lawyers, at a nearby Abruzzese restaurant, where I discovered the fascinating man she had married. Anthony Burgess kept the conversation going over clouds of cigar smoke and glasses of Spumante. He too was interested in living in Italy, and above all in getting down to writing.

* Ralph Ellison (1914–94): black American novelist and short-story writer, born in Oklahoma City. He studied music at university and sculpture in New York. *Invisible Man* (1952) was his autobiographical account of rejection and isolation – and it remains a classic of its kind, like *Uncle Tom's Cabin*; Giuseppe Berto – I'm afraid I can't find anything on him, unless he's Enrico Bertoia (1915–78), who became Harry Bertoia, a sculptor and designer from San Lorenzo, Italy, who taught painting and metal-craft in America. You'd recognise his slender metal chairs with their wire-mesh seats if you saw them; Stanley Kauffmann (1916–) was a leading New York film and theatre critic (*New Republic*, *Commentary*, *New York Times*). He was to review *Nothing Like the Sun*, (in *Book Week*, 20 September 1964), *The Long Day Wanes* (in *New Leader*, 10 May 1965); he mentions Burgess in 'Literature of the Early Sixties' in the *Wilson Library Bulletin*, no. 9 (May 1965); and he reviewed the Kubrick film in the *New Republic* on 1 January 1972.

He had such a diversity of projects to do: a novel, a musical comedy on *Ulysses*, words *and* music; a translation of Rostand's *Cyrano*.

The Burgesses collected exotically placed houses as others collected works of art, adding to their list our little Seicento house, completely furnished in the period with Cecille's taste in Porta Portese bargains. They adapted themselves to the environment in no time, not at all disturbed by the noise and vermin that infested the area. My one-eyed assistant, Luigino, was in demand with his keen vision to locate and destroy the lice that occupied Liana's abundant mop of hair.

Their six-year-old precocious son, upon being introduced to me formally by Anthony – 'And this is Mr Hebald' – acted by extending his hand and, to everyone's astonishment, gave my genitalia a hearty squeeze. When I recovered from the shock, Anthony explained that it was envy. His growing up in Arabic Malta had produced a product new to provincial Bracciano. He quickly assumed the leadership of the beragged band of boys in the neighbourhood. He was a veritable terror.

Burgess plunged himself into uninterrupted writing, as we witnessed on an unexpected visit to Piazza Padella one afternoon. If ever there was an ambience less suited to concentration, we were right in the heart of the maelstrom itself: Liana and a group of women were holding an animated discussion in that small room, while the television was delivering its meaningless drone and fluttery images; little Paolo-Andrea was sailing paper airplanes back and forth; and in the midst of this pandemonium was Anthony Burgess, in front of his portable typewriter, with the typed pages emerging to the unbroken pounding of the keys.

During that summer, Liana was a constant visitor to my studio alone, as Anthony was hard to get out of the house. The arched window of the room where he typed had a view equal to any of the lake and no amount of urging could get him to the beach. I imagine the years in East Asia, where he worked as an education officer, had put him off exposure to the ultraviolet rays of the sun. He described the house and his neighbour, the garbage collector, on the last pages of his novel, *MF*.*

* 'The *tramontana* is raging like Antichrist . . . Lake Bracciano breaks on its shores like the North Sea, and from the cleared dining table on which I write I can watch the heads of foam racing in . . . This morning Lupo Sassone, the garbage collector and oddjobman who lives next door [secured the window-shutter] . . . I gave him a five-thousand lire note . . . I get a good rate of exchange for my dollars.'

Even if we couldn't get him to the beach, we saw a good deal of Burgess, as he was fascinated with sculpture and would drop in at the studio frequently. I encouraged him to see if he could wrestle something tangible out of a mass of clay. He soon tired of keeping the floppy result on its feet. My literary friends all do, as the materials of sculpture and writing are exact opposites.

Yet, he did learn a good deal about clay manipulation, watching me do his head in terra cotta, and this portrait must have been in his imagination when he described an elegant apartment in New York in his futuristic novel, *The End of the World News*: 'On a teak plinth was a bronze bust of Vanessa by Hebald, queenly neck exaggerated as to length, breasts brazenly or bronzely offered.'

Until he bought an unwieldy camper, and departed for somewhere north, we would take trips out into the surrounding Etruscan countryside . . .

There is a similar scene of Burgess managing to keep his head whilst all about him people are losing theirs, another example of his facility to insulate or isolate himself, in the Introduction to *One Man's Chorus*. In the midst of the chaos of a busy hotel lobby, thronged by groups of tourists, bellhops, busboys and harassed reception-desk staff, there's Burgess, at a table with his portable typewriter, the plume rising from his panatella. 'The keys clanged, the roller turned, the carriage slammed to the right, the bell rang, the smoke puffed upward,' remembered Ben Forkner. 'The Burgess engine was at work.' Though his professionalism was admirable, there's something inhuman about it; and though there used to be lots of jokes about his productivity ('Burgess went home, did the kitchen, spring-cleaned the flat, wrote two book reviews, a flute concerto and a film treatment, knocked off his gardening column for *Pravda*, phoned in his surfing page to the *Sydney Morning Herald*, and then test-drove a kidney-machine for *El Pais* – before settling down to some serious work,' jested Martin Amis), his discipline and purpose and the critics' compliments and amazement are really nothing. It gives us no reason to read him. What counts is the quality of the result. But then again, there is indeed something classical and heroic about his endeavours. He had such persistence.

He'd bang on about the need to work ('One pushes on because one has to pay bills,' he told Russell Davies, in 1987 – and indeed the maintenance charges and local rates on all those properties must have added up); critics would praise his will to work. He could write with authority about the art of the novel, but could he do it himself? It is a further paradox. He was passionate and spontaneous as a critic, swirling back and forth from the blackboard; as a creator, however, he's too self-conscious. The results are faintly ludicrous. (Not that this prevented him from advancing and prospering – unless the hopper was being topped up by the Cousins.) *Ninety-Nine Novels*, which he'd boasted about writing in a few days, is nevertheless a painfully revealing text – and he was the first to admit that 'the personality of the novelist is important to us – the personality as revealed in his work and not in his private life' (though he did add, 'the private lives of many artists do not bear looking at'); because it is in this book that it's clear there was no *art* of the novel, only a series of contrivances. He had no idea how to make that leap from talent to inspiration. He's like one of those actors who reads his Stanislavsky and his Lee Strasberg, but just can't put the theories and discriminations into practice. He studies the techniques and mechanisms, he watches the masters at work, he can pass any stiff examination on technical considerations – but Salieri is Salieri. He does everything right, yet he's not Mozart. Thus, the distinctive mood of Burgess: he's that most perfect paradox, a genuine fake.

I reported my deliberations to Ellmann, and he was unusually forthright. He wheezed and shook at *genuine fake*[*] – dons laugh at the slightest provocation, as if there are unaccountable layers of irony and epigram in attendance upon the most banal of remarks – and then, chewing the ear-pieces of his National Health horn-rims (Geoffrey Rhodes One Price Specs, Cornmarket), he said, 'You sometimes seem to have this need to compete in allusion and allusiveness with Burgess. I worry a little about your tone – outsmarting its subject. I feel sure that you regard Burgess as an extraordinary phenomenon, without whom literature would be poorer. If he writes a lot, that's because writing comes so naturally to him, even though he loves artifice. I can't think of anyone in the history of literature who provides us with so many books,[†] none of them simple-minded, all

[*] See Appendix C: *Burgess's Keats, Keats's Burgess*.

[†] His archive, sold by Liana to the Harry Ransom Humanities Research Center, Texas, for a quarter of a million dollars, comprises in excess of three thousand items. Though the Burgess bibliography is vast – get this: it could have been vaster. Heard melodies are sweet, we are told, and those unheard are sweeter. Here are some proposed new departures and unrealised or unsung projects mentioned over the years: a novel in the style of Jane Austen based upon the structure of a Mozart symphony; a novel about the Marquis de Sade; a biographical novel in the style of a broadsheet newspaper, complete with a crossword puzzle and personal columns; a contribution on *Neologism* for a Methuen series called The Critical Idiom, the General Editor for which was John D. Jump, Burgess's old tutor at Manchester (whom he'd described as 'unsure of himself'); *Rag Week*, a novel about

vastly ambitious, much more ambitious than necessary (or advisable) for a popular success. Of course you know all this and to some extent say it, but I'd like to feel that you were not above patting him on the back. I realise that you have somewhat striated feelings about your subject. Still, in the hierarchy of virtues, kindness ranks above unkindness . . .'

Manchester's students; an epic about a dynasty of actors, from the Corpus Christi plays to the present day, entitled *All the Men and Women*; the lyrics for a musical based upon *Les Enfants du Paradis*, in collaboration with Michel Legrand; a novel about Jason and the Golden Fleece (he presumably knew William Morris's *The Life and Death of Jason* [1867]); a novel based on the fourth book of the *Aeneid*, called *I Trust and Love You* (i.e. ITALY); an anthology of Victorian humour (in Italian); a musical for Diana Rigg adapted from Virginia Woolf's *Orlando*; a rewrite of Verdi's *Rigoletto* set amongst the world of *The Godfather*; *A Princeton Romance*, in which the Burgess figure, Cyrano-fashion, writes poems for a Mafia don; a stage show about Houdini for Orson Welles; the life story of an Elgar-esque composer called Charles Levey Clegg; 'I would like to translate Wagner from the German'; an assemblage of Shakespeare's Falstaff scenes (translated into Italian) for Mario Maranzana, who'd dubbed the Michael Bates part in *Arancia Meccanica*; a script for a film about Cyrus the Great, the founder of the Persian Empire, for the late Shah of Iran; film treatments and tie-in novels on George III (*The Man Who Lost America*), Patton (*The True Patton Papers*), and George Gershwin (*The Rhapsody Man*); original screenplays about Edward Lear and Beethoven; a screenplay adapted from Mary Stewart's *The Crystal Cave*; television scripts about the career of General 'Vinegar Joe' Stilwell, commander of the American forces in the Pacific, and the life of Aristotle Onassis; 'I shall write a book some day about the appropriateness of names'; and a novel derived from Ford's *'Tis Pity She's a Whore*.

There'll have been many others, certainly. A production of *Peer Gynt* with Paul Newman ('I began to work on my Norwegian'); 'Whistle a Tune from Thomas Mann': 'Anthony Burgess and Stephen Schwartz to collaborate on a musical film version of *The Transposed Heads*. . .', *New York Times*, 3 June 1973. Not a day goes by (still) when I don't expect a Burgess project to pop up – an operetta called *General Pinochet in Weybridge*; the text for a book of paparazzi pictures of Di and Dodi; another more oleaginous homage, that he'll have called *Death of a Princess*; articles in the press about the total eclipse of the sun, the new millennium, the evils of terrorism, the upsurge of French fascism, the abomination of the single European currency and Mick Jagger's knighthood.

It's quite easy to predict his range and his responses – which though wide were derivative, prone to latch on to any historical, epic figure (with an anniversary coming up), and desperately in search of that popular success. How he'd have entered into a Faustian pact to be involved with a *Les Misérables* musical or a novel like Umberto Eco's *The Name of the Rose*, of which he was madly jealous. He was never to recapture the success or appeal of *A Clockwork Orange*. According to an article, 'Taking Best Sellers Seriously: Where Sex Meets Self-Improvement' (*New York Times* Book Review section, 1 June 1986), he once spent more than a month immersed in James A. Michener, Arthur Hailey and Eco, pulling apart their books, desperate to find their formula, and I can just picture him in rue Grimaldi, in a wizard's pointy hat, analysing these lumps of prose, as if he were an alchemist aiming to discover the philosopher's stone, a universal solvent, and the elixir of life.

There's something panic-stricken about the profusion of his projects – Burgess lacked the laid-back salamander manner of Gore Vidal, another (or *the* other) great exponent of *rodomontade*.

That was on 7 September 1985. Have my feelings towards Burgess changed over the years? He was a whole world to me once, when I was young and what I published was academic in inspiration. He himself knew how one's mind is chopped and changed. *Inside Mr Enderby* was composed in dribs and drabs, and 'the author changes between periods of resumed activity on it: he undergoes new influences, makes new resolutions'. It's Wordsworth revisiting Tintern Abbey ('Though changed, no doubt, from what I was when first I came among these hills . . .'); and my awestruck admiration was later replaced by a hung-over replay. How sickly his books seem to me now – they are crammed with the themes of illness – we've had our time; and the *Malayan Trilogy*, for example: its dwelling is the light of setting suns. There's an end-of-empire atmosphere about Burgess; of high Victorian imperialism fading away in a remote outpost. Even when he returned from Monte Carlo, there was this touch of anachronism; he was dapper, gentlemanly, and very uncomfortable with the twentieth century. (Guy Burgess, in permanent exile in Moscow, listening to his Jack Buchanan record and hankering for Jermyn Street, likewise pined for a way of life that had all gone into the past.) If you spoke to him on the phone, invariably, in the background, there'd be Elgar or Holst (or one of his own Edwardian compositions?) blaring away, as the mood-setting soundtrack of another era. You'd have to listen to a litany of domestic woes, as if he and Liana had just suffered a mass walk-out by their servants, and how in God's name did one boil water? What was a tea bag? 'The house in Callian hasn't been visited in ages. I paid the electricity bill, but the electricity was still cut off. You have to speak very good French to negotiate the re-instatement. We don't know where the key is, either. It's difficult to cut another, because it is an old-fashioned kind, of mediaeval dimensions . . . Here in rue Grimaldi, the apartment is three floors up and no elevator. The neighbours are nasty. They hate writers . . . My heart is bad. I thought it was bronchitis, but it is a faulty mitral valve. Liana had blood-pressure of two hundred and ten. She does yoga to relax . . .'

Occasionally, she'd come on the line. She was never easy to follow – a mixture of Italian, French and English, delivered very fast and idiosyncratically, like Salvador Dali. 'I'm translating *Kingdom of the Wicked* into Italian. A translator has a very close relationship with a text, and can appreciate its small details and excellence. Such a powerful book – life then like life now . . . You must get this detail right. What's this about my jalopy? I always anticipate trends, and I was interested in vintage cars long before anyone else. My father had many beautiful cars. My first was an

Alvis Fiat, 1956; then a 1924 Sunbeam; thirdly, a Morgan. Then, a Bedford Dormobile, in 1968. All vandalised and broken into at one time or another. I actually cry when I think of it. Now I have an ordinary Mercedes. In America, I refused to have a car, which was considered unpatriotic. Oh – and we don't have houses in all those places, only *pieds-à-terres*.'

Or did she say *pommes-de-terre*? It was such a *Finnegans Wake* gabble, no wonder he cherished her. Once asked, 'Which talent would you most like to have?' Burgess answered, 'Ability to drive a car.' (And whilst we are on the topic, *jalopy* – 'dilapidated old motor vehicle' [20th c.; orig. unkn.], *OED* – may surely be used affectionately?*) For a change, therefore, he was planning a route to England (from Lugano) by train – except 'Liana refuses to travel in Germany'; and whether she overcame this restraint I don't know, but when I met him next he was alone. I was bidden to the Apollo Theatre, Oxford, on a Tuesday evening in December. The Scottish Opera was in town with Weber's *Oberon*, in 'A New Version by Anthony Burgess'. The text had been published a month previously, so by the looks of *Oberon Old and New* we were in for a fine old farrago. The original production, in 1826, was a spectacular event. The stage machinery at Covent Garden brought forth storms and sunsets, desert islands and Arabian palaces. This was theatre anticipating the special effects of cinema – and in Graham Vick's interpretation of Burgess's libretto, the opera unfolded inside one of those gigantic picture houses of the thirties, all art deco trapezoids and arabesques.

Carl Maria von Weber was mortally ill when he composed the score; he wanted to be able to leave behind a work that would earn royalties for his widow. (So is *that* what inspired Burgess to a similar end in 1959?) James Robinson Planché's text, which Burgess overhauled, was itself a translation of an old legend about Huon of Bordeaux, one of Charlemagne's knights, whose virtue and fidelity are to be tested by Oberon and Titania

* I'd discussed the Bedford Dormobile thus in my review article on *But Do Blondes Prefer Gentlemen? Homage to Qwert Yuiop and Other Writings*, which appeared in *The World and I* (no. 7, July 1986), an out-of-the-way magazine in Washington. Burgess was quick to notice mentions of himself – exactly like Kubrick who, from local newspapers, would monitor the times and dates of screenings in, say, Ciudad Rodrigo or Clermont-Ferrand, calculate his percentage of the gross, and if box-office receipts didn't tally with his estimates, go berserk. I'd also said that Liana was the one at the wheel of the jalopy, and I'd imagined an Italian Mr Toad – Anna Magnani in a flying-helmet and goggles. The Burgesses, however, were far too suspicious to take being teased. Or praised. When, in her novel, *Serenissima*, Erica Jong mentioned Anthony and Liana in Lugano, meaning this as an indication of success and salubriousness, Burgess was uneasy. 'We rest in comparative humility,' he countered.

– so Shakespeare is thrown into the brew as well; or if we want to be scholarly about it, Shakespeare's own sources – Chaucer's *The Knight's Tale* and Reginald Scot's *Discoverie of Witchcraft* (1584) – are what Planché was drawing upon. The effect, however, is rather more reminiscent of *Die Zauberflöte* – that is to say, Emmanuel Schikaneder's words, not Mozart's music. Instead of a magic flute, there's a magic horn – surrealistically depicted, in Burgess's production (or was this a fancy of Vick's?), by a dwarf dressed up as a silver tuba, like an ambling Hoffnung cartoon. Frank Jones, whose role as The Horn was his first opera appearance, was born in Oldham, worked as a clown in circuses, had performed in charity shows for children's homes and mental hospitals, and was an Ewok in *The Return of the Jedi*.

The horn is to protect Huon (or Hugh MacLaren, as Burgess makes him – and he's updated from being a knight to an American test pilot) against adversity. It was plainly difficult to modernise the plot. What with Puck and the fairy king and queen, tempests that come and go at one's command, and the prevalence of protective talismans, the supernatural elements are integral – so why attempt deconsecration? Burgess made Baghdad into Teheran; he got rid of the fanciful oriental excrescences; and people are apparently singing because this is now an opera-within-an-opera and what we see is a show by the Embassy's amateur dramatic society in the Sultanate of Naraka. Burgess places the new *Oberon*, therefore, in his old world of *Devil of a State* or even of the Old Banburians, rehearsing in the village hall, as the evenings were drawing in and the lamps were being lit, back in the fifties. *Naraka* is Arabic for hell. In place of goblins and Saracens in brocade robes, Burgess demanded khaki-clad guards with dark glasses and sub-machine guns.

Planché's dialogue is sub-Shakespearean ('Tardy Spirit, is it thou?/ Where hast thou been since cock-crow?'); Burgess's, as fans of *Moses the Lawgiver* will readily attest, is unmistakable. 'The stability of the universe,' says Oberon, 'depends on the harmony of the yin and the yang, or the Oberonic and the Titanian'; and the jokes would have made Form III groan. 'My gentle Puck, come hither' – 'That, sir, is the wrong play.' Which is a pity, for where, in the wood near Athens and in Weber's original opera, the theme is that of constancy, here the dilemma is racial or tribal. Rezia and Selina (another Burgess lunatrix) have been taken hostage because they are American, not because they are fickle and a danger to clean-thinking grail knights. With the girls, we switch from the plot of *Die Zauberflöte* to that of *Die Entführung aus dem Serail*, and there is much haring around the harem, as Hugh and his chum Geoffrey Cabot, in disguise, fool the ayatollahs, Haroun and Lot ibn Abdul Rahab, and escape aboard the SS *Mohammed Ali*. The enchanted horn induces paralysis in the troops giving chase – 'the higher harmonics working on the centres of muscular control' do the trick; there's a shipwreck scene; some business with a nuclear bomb; and it all concludes with Oberon, 'the god from the machine', praising people for their 'powers of tough endurance', and deciding to restore harmony to the planet. 'Yeah – *deus ex machina*.'

Bing and Bob could have made it work when, like *Webster's Dictionary*, they were Morocco bound. ('The dictionary I like best is old and American, the 1926 Webster. It's pre-electronic but it's enormous and full of obscure dialect,' Burgess told Jonathan Meades.) But the trouble with opera singers is that few of them can act – and *Oberon* required the agility of vaudevillian hoofers, who'd bring a light-hearted, frolicsome manner to the work's essential nonsensicality. Dennis Bailey and Geoffrey Dolton, the Hugh and Geoffrey in Oxford, whilst they could warble, simply lumbered around the stage. Robin Leggate was a camp Oberon, shaven-headed and clad as Erich von Stroheim. Basically, what I liked best was The Horn. Maybe the Italian cast, for this was a co-production with Gran Teatro La Fenice, Venice,* better captured the crackerjack rhythms? Or were the Italians, perforce singing and speaking in English, even more wooden? ('A seraglio must learn that it is only an expendable parcel of nugatory sweets': Pavarotti himself would have had a job getting his larynx around that.) I have seen productions of Jánaček by British performers given in Czech and it's plain nobody has a clue what they are saying – and this only enhanced the alienating, startling modernity of the material (all those Jenůfas and Kátas determined to lead an independent existence); but Burgess's *Oberon*? It was damaged by one of his own fatal divisions – his intellectual pretensions and his desire to be popular, and the one always undermining the other. In interviews he gave at the time, he discussed his adaptation as being 'post-Brechtian . . . It is an apology for the panache before you get it'; and he also said he wanted to be Lorenz Hart.† 'His lyrics are brilliant. But, of course, it's regarded as a low form of art.

* The theatre burned down soon afterwards. Burgess had attended the opening, on a wet day in February 1987. A ticket tout, on the steps of La Fenice, offered him a good pair of seats for the afternoon's performance. 'No, thank you,' he said. 'I wrote it. I know it quite well.'

† He also wanted to be Auden, who (with Chester Kallman) wrote the text for Stravinsky's *The Rake's Progress* (which had its first performance in Venice in 1951), and who also adapted *Die Zauberflöte*, turning Tamino, Pamina and the rest of the cast into Americans. Auden got rid of the romantic quest theme and turned the opera into a debate (chaired by

I don't see why it should be. To be able to take a tune given to him by Richard Rodgers and put very nearly deathless words to it is great art. I have always had this hankering after doing the same sort of thing.' To a lonely man like Burgess, involvement with the popularity of a musical was his idea of company. Unfortunately, is 'New Mexico, New Mexico,/The state where I was born' superior to Planché's 'O Araby, dear Araby,/My own, my native land'? And does not the substitution of President Reagan for the Emperor Charlemagne, and the general effort to be topical by introducing political hostages, kidnaps and oil-cartel ransom demands, induce what the Scarlet Pimpernel used to call the fatigues?*

Was he aware that *Oberon* was doing the equivalent of sailing full pelt into an iceberg? Burgess had a masochistic side which welcomed pain and disaster; it allowed him to put on his hurt-quality look, as if Little Wilson was being roughly picked on by the cruel world. He was already waiting in the foyer of the Apollo when I arrived.† He was in rather a fluster about

---

Sarastro) on Reason *vs.* Instinct. It was produced (and broadcast) by the NBC Opera Theatre in January 1956. *The Magic Flute* was published by Faber in 1957. Other Auden–Kallman translations and adaptations include *Don Giovanni* ('the defiant counter-image of the ascetic saint'; for NBC in April 1960) and *Elegy for Young Lovers*, with music by Hans Werner Henze (first performed in 1961). In *Oberon*, we find this exchange:

GEOFFREY: It's called *Oberon*. That means he has to come in at the end.
HUGH: To recite an elegy for dead lovers.
GEOFFREY : No. I'm pretty sure this isn't a tragedy.

They also adapted *Love's Labour's Lost*, with music composed by Nicolas Nabokov (the première took place in 1973; the vocal score was published in 1972); it is this Shakespeare play which underpins Burgess's Symphony No. 3 in C; and in 1963, Auden and Kallman had worked on lyrics for *Man of La Mancha*.

'Auden, of course, wrote several librettos,' said Burgess in October 1985, 'including Stravinsky's *Rake's Progress*, but I don't recall them being performed terribly frequently. There are very few writers now who can write and read music and writing opera librettos is the most difficult thing in the world.'

* The reviews were uniformly abysmal. 'A total mess' (*The Times*); 'cheap, trite and unfunny' (*Glasgow Herald*); 'It goes beyond entertainment and alienation to distraction, and from there to send-up (*Guardian*); 'His text is dogged by a heavy-handed facetiousness' (*Observer*).

† Of all the writers I have known personally over the years, the one Burgess most resembled in temperament was Wolf Mankowitz. A swaggerer who was also commanding and precise, pernickety, and with a sense of drama, Mankowitz was a difficult man. He went on about his Jewishness like Burgess complained about Catholicism; he was convinced he wasn't appreciated enough, paid enough (money and attention), respected enough. Like Burgess, he was fond of attaching himself to American colleges as a Distinguished Visiting Professor so that he'd be guaranteed acclaim. He was morose, self-pitying and, when I met him, a spent force. After some trouble with the Inland Revenue (he nearly went to gaol), he lived as a tax-exempt artist in County Cork, producing childishly bad collages as a pretext for his residence status in the Irish Republic. Most of the time, however, he was in a flat

tickets, whether to smoke or not, whether to have another drink or not; but I steered him to the bar and he calmed down by listing the deprivations of exile: HP Sauce, pickles and chutneys, decent cheese, sausages. 'I sometimes fly to England for a sausage.' He told me he'd read Ellmann's biography of Joyce 'about twenty times' (why?), and what did I think of all these new works by Shakespeare which Oxford University Press kept publishing? 'I've written about the controversy for the Italian press. The *New York Times* will be running the piece.* I recently saw *Pericles* in Rome. It was set in a brothel.'

Burgess wanted to know if I'd met Gary Taylor (I'd not – still haven't), an Oxford academic who'd turned up, in the Bodleian, a poem included in a volume dated 1630, and which may or may not be canonical: 'Shall I die? Shall I fly/Lover's baits and deceits,/Sorrow breeding?' etc. Burgess was evidently absorbed by the mystery – and mystifications – of authorship. What's authentic? What's fake? What is the difference? If the lines were Shakespeare's own, are they imbued with more magic and meaning than if they were the work of an Elizabethan songwriter, his name now lost? This was one of those knotty scholarly squabbles the Victorians enjoyed, as they pottered amongst their collections of dusty parchment; we are back in the gothick libraries with the forgers and the fantasists.

which he called 'the shit-hole' in Upper Montagu Street, London. He took me to an Afghan restaurant in Paddington Street, I remember, and though I was an indigent Clerke at Oxenforde, and he'd been a millionaire, he was very slow on the uptake when the bill came. (I paid.)

Like Burgess, he had success in the fifties and sixties, with *A Kid for Two Farthings* and *The Bespoke Overcoat* (adapted from Gogol – though this wasn't acknowledged); he then moved off into musicals (*Expresso Bongo*) and film scripts, transferring Shaw's *The Millionairess* and Fleming's *Casino Royale* to the screen for Peter Sellers. Much journalism was tossed off; novels came and went; there were histories of Wedgwood pottery, biographies of Dickens, guides to antiques. Everything was done at top speed – the effect was of a 'gigantic brain' (like Pickwick's) behind it all. You were to gain the impression that, should he ever feel like it, or could be bothered, one day he might deign to give us that masterpiece he had within him; but in the meantime, here's a novella about Casanova, a spoof biography of a lost surrealist painter, a version of *Don Quixote* set in the East End. Being versatile disguised an unsettled talent and personality.

I stood amazed – abashed – before Wolf Mankowitz, when I was younger. He (and Burgess) had the effect on me that the toy theatre had on that little boy in *Fanny and Alexander*. I was transfixed by something so brightly lit up. A musical about Crippen; an appointment as Honorary Consul to the Republic of Panama in Dublin; a study of Edgar Allen Poe: these sound like Burgessian conjurings, but they were Mankowitz's projects. 'Tricksterism is an essential element of the artist,' he vouchsafed. He died of liver cancer in May 1998, his sole income deriving from the royalties of Harry Secombe's touring production of *Pickwick!* A cautionary tale.

* And duly did so: 'Is It Really Shakespeare?' was in the Book Review section, on 22 December 1985.

Despite modern computer technology and literary scrupulousness, Burgess still thought you couldn't beat instinct, 'the subtle testimony of the ear. The same kind of instinct informs us we are listening to Mozart, not Salieri; to Beethoven, not to Weber.' It was his belief that the poem wasn't actually Shakespeare's – it was too ingenious; too many internal rhymes. 'Shakespeare was too impatient to carve and cut and polish his lyrics'; he wasn't enough of a 'careful craftsman' to scribble lute lyrics or madrigals. Therefore, 'In a dream it did seem/But alas dreams do pass/As do shadows' etc. was the verse 'attributed to a writer called Anonymous. Anonymous wrote much . . . songwriters were modest enough not to wish to disclose their names' – like Jacke Wilson, or the John Wilson concealed behind Joseph Kell and Anthony Burgess.

'I used to recite Shakespeare with a northern accent,' he was now telling me. 'His rhymes and puns would make more sense – *reasons* and *raisins*. Much ado about *noting*, taking *note* of *nothing*. The apocryphal lost play, *Love's Labour's Won*, that's the one with Beatrice and Benedick in it. Wonderful opera by Berlioz. Very little of *Henry VIII* is by Shakespeare. He wanted to be a land-owning gentleman in Stratford, and handed over chunks of new plays to assistants or collaborators, like Francis Beaumont and John Fletcher. Shakespeare is not always present in his own works.'

We took our seats in the auditorium. A few patrons recognised the maestro, or at least some dignified and discreet nodding went on. The set for *Oberon*, by Russell Craig, was spectacular. There was a cinema screen flanked by a Grauman's Chinese Theater-calibre gilt and gold palm court, with heavily ornate curtains, minarets and models of eagles; it had a Fellini-esque opulence. The silver costumes were out of *Things to Come* or *Flash Gordon*, and throughout the evening people dressed as an old-style film crew, with a hand-cranked camera on a wooden tripod, followed the action. An opera-within-an-opera, therefore, depicted as a film-within-a-film – and a silent film at that. Bizarre. At the back, on the screen, were sepia projections of a storm, the San Francisco earthquake, Busby Berkeley dance routines, and what looked to me like out-takes from *Tarzan's New York Adventure*. Dressed as Biggles, Hugh and Geoffrey, in their plane, suddenly crashed through the screen, the propeller whirring. 'Andrew saw the production in Glasgow and said the plane was the best thing,' Burgess whispered.

The oriental design of the cinema became the actual orient. Windows opened in the fretwork to disclose blue skies and a beach. A drop curtain, indicating the Interval, was of a blue art deco cinema with the silhouettes of limousines pulling up outside. The name 'Anthony Burgess' was picked out on the marquee in flashing light bulbs. We went back to the bar. 'Have you read *Edmund Ironside*?' he asked. 'The canon goes on thickening.' He described to me the plot about Ironside's quarrel with the Danes, and told me that there was plenty of Shakespearean violence in the play, hand-loppings and comic confusion; but if it was Shakespeare it was minor Shakespeare and what he'd like to find were texts of vanished works, like *A Knack to Know a Knave* and *If You Know Not Me You Know Nobody*.

He was drinking brown ale by the bottle, like Martha Longhurst in the snug at the Rovers' Return. I asked how *The Sovereignty of the Sword* was progressing, the novel that was to become *Any Old Iron*. He said that before leaving for the theatre he had torn up the typescript. 'I was on completely the wrong tack. It was to be about Wales. I'm learning Welsh for it. I've found it hard to find a decent grammar or textbook. My copy of *Living Welsh* is all about rugby and beer. I spoke Welsh in the house with Lynne. Her father lived in Blackwood, taught at Bedwellty. You know all that.' He pronounced *Bedwellty* in an extraordinarily Cymric way, with much sloshing and swishing going on amongst his dentures. At such moments Welsh can sound like somebody doing an impersonation of tempests and hurricanes very close to a microphone. Thank God Lynne hadn't been raised in Llanfairfechan, at the foot of the Penmaenmawr mountain, or Machynlleth, in Powys, for Burgess's teeth might have shot clean out of his mouth and bitten somebody fifty yards away, in the stalls. As with his go at 'Vladimir Nabokov', which could knock you flat, I'm sure he believed he was saying these proper nouns in the way they should be said. But still.

'I've also been thinking about my autobiography, but writing it is slow, so slow. I want the second volume to be finished by next June – get that life out of the way so that I can live this one, or another one. *The Pianoplayers*'ll be published next year. The blurb on the jacket is all wrong. It says the girl was born before the First World War. She was born in 1917, the same as me. I've had to correct the proofs of *Homage to Qwert Yuiop* two times' – and he held up two fingers, in Churchill's V-for-Victory fashion. In fact, he did a lot of gesticulating, like an Englishman abroad signalling for the bill or for a waiter. He actually slapped all his trouser and jacket pockets when he mentioned he'd forgotten something – in this case the scripts of the unmade Shakespeare film, *The Bawdy Bard*, which I'd asked to see. As he had the theatrical manner of a stage magician, I did expect a few hundred pages of typescript to appear out of the air, along with a bouquet of paper flowers.

Back we went to the dress circle. A few old duffers, Burgess's contemporaries, shuffled towards us for his autograph, which he had no hesitation in giving. Some of my own undergraduates smirked in the middle distance. I didn't invite them over. We'd only have been given another impromptu lecture on *Two Noble Kinsman* by the Merton Professor *manqué*. The safety curtain was down, obscuring the 'Anthony Burgess' name-in-lights, which I'd looked forward to seeing him stare at. On the safety curtain were stencilled the words:

'What, has this thing appear'd again to-night?'

Hamlet, Act I, scene i

'For thine especial safety'

Hamlet, Act IV, scene iii

'That *thine* is wrong, surely,' he said. 'Shouldn't the possessive pronoun by *thy*?'

'Not necessarily before a vowel,' I answered, feeling a bit of a prat as I continued: 'Also, Claudius is talking to the prince, his stepson, hence the second-person singular. The Folio has "this deed of thine, especial safety . . . must send thee hence . . ."'

And so on. Who else in the world would you converse with like that except Burgess – or, in the previous century, James Murray, of the *Oxford English Dictionary*? Burgess was caught in a web of words. That's what Shakespeare, and literature, meant to him; not the characters or the emotions or the themes and sentiments; just the language.

'They should emend it to *thy*, though, because the reference is to all of us, out here in the auditorium . . .' He was like this when Kubrick took him to Trader Vic's, the Polynesian restaurant in Park Lane. The grammar in the match-book wasn't up to scratch ('a finite verb is camouflaging itself as an infinitive'), and he spent hours puzzling over such 'linguistic trivialities', except they were not quite trivial to him. They are what bolted, strapped down and lashed the cosmos together; words were his ligatures.

I complimented him on his Brancusi tie. He was pleased I'd recognised the design – the parallel lines and spiral representing the 'Scylla and Charybdis' episode in *Ulysses*, a narrow channel and a whirlpool. The drawing was originally meant to depict Joyce himself, and the abstract sketch served as the frontispiece of *Tales Told of Shem and Shaun*, published by the Black Sun Press, in 1929. More helpful for my immediate purpose was the fact that the Brancusi appeared on the jacket of Vincent

John Cheng's *Shakespeare and Joyce: A Study of Finnegans Wake* (Colin Smythe Press, Gerrards Cross), which I had recently been sent for favour of review by the charmingly named *Notes and Queries*.

'This book you'll be writing about me,' he said eventually, 'now I offer you this – and you mustn't make anything of it. But Joyce told Herbert Gorman, who was working on his biography, that it didn't matter what he wrote, but he, Joyce, had to come over as a saint whose life was one long martyrdom.'* That was certainly how Burgess was to present himself, in *Little Wilson and Big God*, a title which grows in sacrilegiousness, as obviously he means it to be taken as *Little Wilson and Big Burgess*. The stoning of Stephen, the 'protomartyr', is described at length in *The Kingdom of the Wicked*; and in *Joysprick* we are told that Stephen Dedalus's name 'has evidently been well thought out. Stephen was the protomartyr; his namesake will become a martyr for art'; and the surname Dedalus turns himself into Icarus, 'a winged being falling from heaven'. Enderby and Toomey are presented as martyrs – to poetry, to the twentieth century; and the word, as Burgess explained, comes from the Greek for *witness*: somebody who'll undergo suffering in order to establish their belief in some great cause. And Burgess's particular great cause? Why, the creation of Burgess. When Carlo is elected Pope, he appears on the balcony of St Peter's to decree that he is to be known henceforward as Gregory XVII. 'Today I am reborn, with a new name.' Saul, in *The Kingdom of the Wicked*, transmogrifying into Paul, announces, 'What I was I was. What I am you see – a man reborn, refashioned, even renamed.'

On the stage, in another filmed insertion, and in quite another dimension, Oberon was chasing Titania, a platinum blonde like Jean Harlow, back to her dressing room. They clinched, they squeezed, and Oberon turned to the camera – to us – and winked. The curtain fell. 'Was that a boo?' Burgess yelped, as the polite applause died away and a discreet solitary jeer echoed from the balcony (or gods) above us. 'A good sign,' he said, turning to me with a look of relish on his face. 'Rossini was booed. *Brava*!' he yelled, when Janice Cairns took her last bow.

The theatre quickly emptied – it was a sparse house. 'This is not how I pictured it at all,' Burgess announced to the deserted orchestra pit. 'None of this is mine. *None of this is mine*. I've had nothing to do with any of this.' The last few patrons scurried off in embarrassment. The cleaners

* Herbert Gorman's *James Joyce* was published by Farrar and Rinehart in New York in 1939. Gorman told his editors, 'I will never write another biography of a living man. It is too difficult and thankless a task.'

made their way along the stalls with black bin liners. All that visual trickery of Graham Vick's, and suddenly nothing, except the coming dark.

We waited in the rain for a taxi to take him to the last train for Paddington. Back he had to go to his own little world. For I think it was little. Despite the world-circumnavigating publicity tours and transcontinental lecturing; the books about ancient history and the distant future; his epic scope: how *little* he was,* scratching around on afternoon television shows with Sue Lawley, doing late-night call-in radio spots with Emma Freud; always on the move – literally shifty. 'I once did a show on American radio – an all-night radio station. All they were interested in, the callers, it was a phone-in show, was how much I earned. Commerce, finance, obsesses people.'

For something to say, I said, 'It's a hard life, isn't it, being a writer?' I had in mind flensing whales, or mining for emeralds with your bare hands in Colombia, but he overlooked my irony, clutched at the door frame like Henry Irving at the corner of the velvet tabs at the Lyceum, closed his eyes, took a cigarillo out of a big flat tin and lit it in dumbshow and muttered, 'It's the hardest work there is!', and he hit his balled fist into his palm for emphasis. It is now nearly twenty years later – and I thought: facing the blank sheet every morning and having to cover it with meaningful hieroglyphics; collecting and marshalling the facts; finding the traceries, shapes and patterns in a life which will form a biography; living inside the mind too much; all those battles with oneself to get the complexity, the multiformity, of a person across; then there's the grotesquerie of the literary world, the false friendships, the cold-shouldering, the spite, the slyness, the incompetence, the indifference; the having to deal with agents and publishers, the unending betrayals, discourtesies, letters not answered, phone calls not returned; the cabbalistic reviewers, who are wilfully obtuse or genuinely stupid; and the racing ahead of less talented rivals

* I don't only mean in the way Picasso called Henry Moore a *petit-maître*; for the way Burgess is smaller and less over-inflated improves him, makes him more human. Do you know those jokey squibs Thorne Smith was writing in the thirties, which became the *Topper* movies? That's Burgess's imagination, I think, once you scrape the barnacles off and allow him to be prankish. Cosmo Topper is a henpecked little man who is haunted by the ghosts of his friends, played by Cary Grant and Constance Bennett: *Topper* (1937) was followed by *Topper Takes a Trip* (1939), where they are on the Riviera, and *Topper Returns* (1941), set in a spooky old house. Not only is this the half astral, half earthbound world of *The Eve of Saint Venus*, but Topper is Enderby and Burgess's other freaked heroes, too. Though played by Roland Young, the role was intended for W. C. Fields. The supporting cast had wonderful names: Verree Teasdale, Eugene Pallette and Theodore von Eltz. What happened to ensemble acting like that?

because they are more photogenic or better connected; and the money and space given to anything on cookery or gardening or interior design by soap-opera starlets who were in the SAS and are dying of cancer; and the lunches where you drink too much Soave and believe that the people on the other side of the table who'll be picking up the tab actually like and/or are interested in you; the hollow praise from editorial directors who only want to talk about their geraniums and take early retirement so as to spend more time at their Dordogne house; and these flotillas of twenty-four-year-old publicity handmaidens who flirt and laugh at your jokes but whom you'll never *in a million years* get to fuck because they have fiancés in marine reinsurance or coffee futures in the City who all look like Jeremy Northam; and the literary parties with the same puffy faces and the diarists prowling like the hyenas in *The Lion King* for gossip; and the wireless shows you do where the host says, 'I'm sorry but I haven't had time to read the press release'; and the former school friends who won't come to your own book launches because 'Some of us have to work for a living and get up in the morning'; the indexers who compile their lists from the wrong set of proofs; the picture captions which end up in the wrong order; the fan letters which turn out to be from elderly lesbians, creeps who do voices from *The Goon Show*, and a man from Grimsby with a metal plate in his head; the low turn-out for a signing session at the Royal Festival Hall; the bitch of an assistant in Waterstone's (Hereford) who wouldn't permit you to sign copies of your own titles 'because then we can't return them to the warehouse'; the disdain of academics (time-servers, wankers); the contempt of journalists (hacks, illiterates); the loneliness and suicide attempts; the arrogance that's bred by low self-esteem; the depression, grind and anxiety; other people's niceness that's on a short lease; the dust and ashes: and I'd respond again today as I did then, though my heart would be going like mad and I'd be in fuller agreement and shorn of all satire –

'Yes, John,' I said. 'Yes!'

APPENDIX A
AB's BA, Manchester 1937–40

As it is important to appreciate Burgess's thorough knowledge of language and his grounding in literature, here are the precise syllabus regulations for his BA degree at Manchester, 1937–40:

Honours School of English Language and Literature

All candidates are required to complete a specified number of courses in both literature and language. The examination in these constitutes Part I of the Honours examination, and will be held at the end of the second year, or one year before Part II of the Honours examination. Candidates who satisfy the Examiners in Part I may proceed to a course affording opportunities either mainly for linguistic study (Part IIA) or mainly for literary study (Part IIB).

Candidates who intend to take courses mainly linguistic in Part IIA may also take special linguistic courses in their second session. They will be examined in such additional courses only in Part II of the Honours Examination.

A. SUBJECTS OF STUDY

The subjects of study for Part I are:

1. The History of the English Language.
2. Translation from specified and unspecified Old and Middle English Texts (to 1300), with literary, historical and linguistic questions arising out of them.
3. Chaucer and the literature of the fourteenth and fifteenth centuries, with specified texts.
4. Shakespeare.
5. The History of English Literature (1550–1760), with specified books.

The examination will consist of six papers, one on each of the subjects enumerated above except No. 5, on which there will be two papers.

The names of candidates who have satisfied the Examiners in this Part will be published in alphabetical order, and the Examiners may test candidates orally and take into account the work done previously in the candidates' academic course. Such candidates as are not admitted to continue their Honours course may be excused from completing such courses in English for the ordinary degree as the Board of the Faculty may on the recommendation of the Examiners, determine.

The subjects of study for Part IIA (mainly linguistic) are:
1. The History of the English Language.
2. Old English Texts and translation.
3. Middle English Texts and translation.
4. English Literature, comprising (*a*) Medieval Literature, and (*b*) Literary History, 1760–1830 *or*, Literary History, 1830–1880.
5. Old and Middle English Philology.
6. Gothic.
7. Old Icelandic *or* a subject chosen from the following:-
(*a*) Germanic Philology.
(*b*) Anglo-Norman French, with reference to specified texts.
(*c*) Old Saxon, with a study of the *Heliand*.
(*d*) Modern Icelandic, with reference to specified texts.
(*e*) A period of Anglo-Saxon or Medieval English History, with a study of specified historical documents.
(*f*) Any other linguistic subject approved by the Board of the Faculty.
8. Essay.

The examination will consist of nine papers, one on each of the subjects numbered 1 to 3 and 5 to 8, and two papers on the subject numbered 4. Candidates whose special study of English language is limited to one year may substitute for subject 7, subject 2 or subject 3 under Part IIB.

The subjects of study for Part IIB (mainly literary) are:
1. Old and Middle English. Translation from specified and unspecified books, with questions relating to Literature, History, and Institutions.
2. History of Criticism and Literary Theory.
3. History of Literature, 1760–1830.
4. History of Literature, 1830–1880.
5. Essay.
6. A special subject, chosen from the following:-
(a) Old French Literature, with reference to specified texts.

(*b*) Old Norse Literature, with reference to specified texts.

(*c*) A subject from English Literature treated in connection with *either* (i) Political and Social History *or* (ii) one or more continental literatures.

(*d*) The Middle English lyric.

(*e*) The English language 1575–1675, with special reference to Shakespeare and Milton.

(*f*) Any other subject in English Literature approved by the Board of the Faculty.

7. Thesis.

The examination will consist of seven papers, two on the subject numbered 1, and one on each of the subjects numbered 2 to 6.

Every candidate for Part II is required to submit *two* copies of the thesis, one of which shall be filed in the English Seminar Library. The Examiners in each section of Part II have the power to take into account the work done throughout the candidate's academic course, and to test candidates orally.

B. ATTENDANCE

Candidates are required to attend during three academic years courses of instruction in the subjects of the school, of not less than six hours a week during each year. Provided that such students as may be allowed by the Board of the Faculty may, in lieu of attendance at the University during the Summer term immediately preceding their last academic year, attend approved courses during that term at the University of Iceland, and may take there their Part I examination and the written papers in any General or Special subject required by them under the Regulations for the Honours School of English.

C. SPECIAL REQUIREMENTS.

1. Candidates are required to complete courses of at least Intermediate grade in the following subjects:

(*a*) Greek *or* Latin.

(*b*) French *or* German *or* Italian, *or* Spanish.

(*c*)Modern History, *or* Medieval History, *or* Philosophy and Psychology, *or* any other non-linguistic subject approved by the Board of the Faculty.

2. Candidates are required to complete a course of at least General grade in Greek, Latin, French, German, Italian, *or* Spanish.

In the case of Second or Third Year Students who have received the special permission of the Board of the Faculty specified in B above, they may present as evidence of having completed their General or Special course certificates of satisfactory attendance at the end of the Lent term. Such candidates, however, may, if they so desire, satisfy this requirement by passing either the General or Special Examination in the subject chosen, and in this case, any oral part of the General or Special Examination may be taken at the end of the Lent term instead of in June.

Candidates who at the end of their first year have decided to specialise for two years in English Language and who in their first year were not qualified to pursue a course of General grade in any of the preceding subjects may substitute a prescribed course in Old Icelandic as a General subject.

3. Candidates who offer Part IIB are required in their third year to attend a course of instruction of not more than two hours a week in the department of History. The subject studied shall in general be the one most closely bearing on the Special Subject or Thesis; but, if no course suitable for that purpose is provided, the appropriate instruction will be determined by the Board of the Faculty.

4. In determining the class lists the Examiners have the power to take into account the work of each candidate during his academic course.

APPENDIX B

The Cousins

If, in Elysium, Laurence Sterne, James Joyce and Vladimir Nabokov pooled their resources, they'd not devise anything more beautiful and opaque than this correspondence, which has a shimmering, serpentine unintelligibility.

Washington D.C.
Dec. 17 1999

Reference: F-1999-02499

Dear Mr. Lewis:

This is in response to your 9 November 1999 Freedom of Information Act (FOIA) request for

"any files [CIA] might hold on Burgess/Wilson [British novelist John Anthony Burgess Wilson, 1917–1993]."

We have assigned your request the reference number above for identification purposes. Please refer to it in any future correspondence.

The CIA can neither confirm nor deny the existence or nonexistence of any CIA records responsive to your request. The fact of the existence or nonexistence of records containing such information—unless it has been officially acknowledged–would be classified for reasons of national security under Sections 1.5(c) [intelligence sources and methods] and 1.5(d) [foreign relations] of Executive Order 12958. Further, the Director of Central Intelligence has the responsibility and authority to protect such information from unauthorized disclosure in accordance with Subsection 103(c)(6) of the National Security Act of 1947 and Section 6 of the CIA Act of 1949.

Accordingly, your request is denied on the basis of FOIA exemptions (b)(1) and (b)(3). By this action, we are neither confirming nor denying the existence or nonexistence of such records. An explanation of cited FOIA exemptions is enclosed. The CIA official responsible for this denial is Kathryn I. Dyer, Acting Information and Privacy Coordinator. You may appeal this decision by addressing your appeal to the Agency Release Panel within 45 days from the date of this letter, in my care. Should you choose to do this, please explain the basis of your appeal.

I regret that we cannot be more helpful on this matter.

Sincerely,

Kathryn I. Dyer
Acting Information and Privacy Coordinator

Enclosure:

Explanation of Exemptions

Freedom of Information Act:

(b)(1) applies to material which is properly classified pursuant to an Executive order in the interest of national defense or foreign policy;

(b)(2) applies to information which pertains solely to the internal rules and practices of the Agency;

(b)(3) applies to the Director's statutory obligations to protect from disclosure intelligence sources and methods, as well as the organization, functions, names, official titles, salaries or numbers of personnel employed by the Agency, in accord with the National Security Act of 1947 and the CIA Act of 1949, respectively;

(b)(4) applies to information such as trade secrets and commercial or financial information obtained from a person on a privileged or confidential basis;

(b)(5) applies to inter- and intra-agency memoranda which are predecisional and deliberative in nature;

(b)(6) applies to information, release of which would constitute an unwarranted invasion of the personal privacy of other individuals; and

(b)(7) applies to investigatory records, release of which could (C) constitute an unwarranted invasion of the personal privacy of others, (D) disclose the identity of a confidential source, (E) disclose investigative techniques and procedures, or (F) endanger the life or physical safety of law enforcement personnel.

Privacy Act:

(b) applies to information concerning other individuals which may not be released without their written consent;

(j)(1) applies to polygraph records; documents or segregable portions of documents, release of which would disclose intelligence sources and methods, including names of certain Agency employees and organizational components; and, documents or information provided by foreign governments;

(k)(1) applies to information and material properly classified pursuant to an Executive order in the interest of national defense or foreign policy;

(k)(5) applies to investigatory material compiled solely for the purpose of determining suitability, eligibility, or qualifications for Federal civilian employment, or access to classified information, release of which would disclose a confidential source; and

(k)(6) testing or examination material used to determine individual qualifications for appointment or promotion in Federal Government service, the release of which would compromise the testing or examination process.

Washington D.C.
Feb. 14 2000

Reference: F-1999-02499

Dear Mr. Lewis:

This is in response to your letter dated 18 January 2000 and received in this office on 8 February 2000. You are appealing our 17 December 1999 response to your 9 November 1999 Freedom of Information Act request for:

"any files [CIA] might hold on Burgess/Wilson [British novelist John Anthony Burgess Wilson, 1917–1993]."

Specifically, you appealed our determination that we can neither confirm nor deny the existence or nonexistence of records responsive to your request on the basis of Freedom of Information Act exemptions (b)(1) and (b)(3).

Your appeal has been accepted and arrangements will be made for its consideration by the appropriate members of the Agency Release Panel. You will be advised of the determinations made.

In order to afford requesters the most equitable treatment possible, we have adopted the policy of handling appeals on a first-received, first-out basis. At the present time, our workload consists of approximately 320 appeals awaiting completion. In view of this, some delay in our reply must be expected, but I can assure you that every reasonable effort will be made to complete a response as soon as possible.

Sincerely,

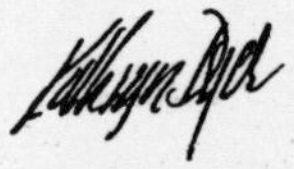

Kathryn I. Dyer
Acting Information and Privacy Coordinator

Washington D.C.
April 14 2000

Reference: F-1999-02499

Dear Mr. Lewis:

This is in response to your 18 January 2000 letter in which you appealed the 17 December 1999 determination of this Agency in response to your 9 November 1999 Freedom of Information Act request for:

"any files [CIA] might hold on Burgess/Wilson [British novelist John Anthony Burgess Wilson, 1917–1993]."

Specifically, you appealed our determination to neither confirm nor deny the existence or nonexistence of records responsive to your request on the basis of Freedom of Information Act exemptions (b)(1) and (b)(3).

Your appeal has been presented to the appropriate member of the Agency Release Panel, the Information Review Officer for the Directorate of Intelligence. Pursuant to the authority delegated under paragraph 1900.43 of Chapter XIX, Title 32 of the Code of Federal Regulations (C.F.R.), the Information Review Officer has determined that we must neither confirm nor deny the existence or nonexistence of any records. It has been determined that such information, that is, whether or not any responsive records exist, would be classified for reasons of national security under Sections 1.5(c) [intelligence sources and methods] and 1.5(d) [foreign relations] of Executive Order 12958. Further, the fact of the existence or nonexistence of such documents would relate directly to information concerning intelligence sources and methods which the Director of Central Intelligence has the responsibility to protect from unauthorized disclosure in accordance with Subsection 103(c)(6) of the National Security Act of 1947, as amended, and Section 6 of the Central Intelligence Agency Act of 1949, as amended. Accordingly, pursuant to Freedom of Information Act exemptions (b)(1) and (b)(3), your appeal is denied. By this statement, we are neither confirming nor denying that any such documents exist. Further, in regard to your appeal and in accordance with CIA regulations appearing at 32 C.F.R. paragraph 1900.41 (c)(2), the Agency Release Panel has affirmed this determination.

In accordance with the provisions of the Freedom of Information Act, you have the right to seek judicial review of this determination in a United States district court.

We appreciate your patience while your appeal was being considered.

Sincerely,

Gregory L. Moulton
Executive Secretary
Agency Release Panel

APPENDIX C

Burgess's Keats, Keats's Burgess

If I've accused somebody of being a *genuine fake*, the claim needs a little substantiation. Here's a detailed account of one particular book, *Abba Abba*, which is representative of his illusions, deceptions, homages, copies, brilliance, ingenuity and manipulation. His miracles, I think, are explicable.*

It was Anthony Burgess's practice to pit himself against other gods and monsters. Freud, Shakespeare, Moses, Jesus, Marlowe, Orwell – and Keats. On each of these he extrapolated grandiose novels, verse epics or motion pictures directed by Zeffirelli. *Nothing Like the Sun* is a dazzling evocation of Elizabethan Stratford-upon-Avon; *Man of Nazareth*, the book of the television series, is a lusty, rollicking reinterpretation of the Gospels; *1985* is a brisk riposte to *Nineteen Eighty-Four*, which, Burgess argued, was actually set in Orwell's own 1948, a post-war era of deprivation, paranoia and bakelite radios. *Napoleon Symphony*, which is dedicated to Stanley Kubrick, takes on Beethoven, Prometheus and conquering the world, its themes so egotistically sublime, I wonder if the author wore a tricorn hat whilst composing it?

And so it goes – Burgess's highly coloured vision of life was to be imposed

* Mine is by no means the prevailing view. A. S. Byatt, in her Introduction to the recent reprint (Vintage, 2000), believes Burgess's over-literary manner to be quite the thing. Burgess has a walk-on part, incidentally, in her novel *Babel Tower* (1996), where Byatt gets him to appear for the defence in the prosecution of an allegedly obscene book. Byatt captures Burgess's over-ready fluency and public self-assurance very well – such that he inadvertently gets the book successfully banned. Her sequence would seem to be based upon a trial he actually was involved with – the attempt to ban Hubert Selby Jr's *Last Exit to Brooklyn* (Calder and Boyars, 1968). 'It is the frivolous mind that responds with pious horror to distasteful subject matter and ignores the genuinely moral purpose for which the subject-matter is deployed,' he stated in a preface to a paperback edition of Selby's grisly fable.

upon any cultural icon which came his way. Viennese witchdoctors are the subject of *The End of the World News*; Claude Lévi-Strauss's structural anthropology underpins *MF*; the twentieth century, no less, from the sinking of the *Titanic* to the rise of the Nazis, is the subject of *Earthly Powers*. All these books are acts of generous attention, of great learning. They are prodigal. But if Burgess was trying to exalt great men – and there is something anachronistic and Victorian about Burgess; he's like Carlyle or Ruskin – it is the case that he is measuring himself against their achievements too. Burgess can never quite suppress his envy or vanity – and other people are always rivals in terms of reputation, sales, popularity, acclaim and general wherewithal. He adopts their language, their ways. He tries to turn himself into them – or find himself in them; but the effect is like seeing Orson Welles or Laurence Olivier in heavy make-up. The last thing they can do is disguise themselves and disappear. Hence, Burgess is always in character as Burgess, under his pounds of verbiage.

As a writer, therefore, his gift was theatrical, expansive; and his genius was for mannerism and pastiche. Keats would not, at first sight, seem an obvious bit of Burgess casting. You'd expect him to go for Byronic swaggerings or violent Turneresque thunderstorms. What's the appeal of 'a poet of nature, romance, fairyland, heartache, the classical worlds as seen in a rainy English Garden', as Keats's themes are listed in *Abba Abba*? Isn't Keats too modest for Burgess? Possibly – but Joyce wasn't. If there's one artist Burgess wished he was it's Joyce. I can never get over how saturated he was in Joyce, his prose rhythms and allusions. The young Shakespeare in *Nothing Like the Sun* is Stephen Dedalus, with his pride, his loneliness, his cunning; and the biographical background is derived from Stephen's pontifications in the National Library, from *Ulysses*. Burgess wrote two critical books on Joyce, *Here Comes Everybody* and *Joysprick*, and in his very first opus, *A Vision of Battlements*, written in the forties though not published until 1965, Molly Bloom's injunction is heard on the very first page: 'Aw, come on, tell us in plain words.' (Note: my copy of the Ballantine paperback ['A high-spirited cadenza among the brassy cacophony of war,' *Time*] once belonged to Richard Ellmann. Molly's line is underlined in thick green felt pen.)

Plain words were not Burgess's predilection. Think of Burgess and you'll think of the buffalo stampede of eccentric vocabulary – in *Abba Abba* there's 'engulesced', 'chthonian' and 'wax-sigillaed' to furrow one's brows; and though he tries to convey frivolity, Burgess can never stop being pedantic, heavy, formal. Highly self-conscious in his use of language, this is the lesson he learned from Joyce. 'His mountain looms at the end of the street where so many of us work with the blinds down, fearful of looking out.' Joyce was the mighty artificer, filling his texts with scraps of Greek mythology, the plot of *Hamlet*, references to popular songs, the Dublin dialect, foreign phrases; the whole flotsam and jetsam of the streams of consciousness. 'A sculptor rejoices in stone, a painter in pigment, Joyce in words,' claimed Burgess; and as he gave this Joycean facility to Shakespeare (and to Moses, Jesus and Napoleon), so his conception of Keats is as a wordsworth. Keats, in *Abba Abba*, has a greed for words and for language; he feeds on words, from the 'damnable chiming bells' of Italian to the definitions in Florio's dictionary, *Queen Anne's New World of Words*, which he is reading the day he dies.

The narrative of *Abba Abba* derives, unattributed, from Robert Gittings' Standard Life of *John Keats*, published in 1968. (Did the busy Burgess review it? He reviewed most things.) The novel concerns a dying man, begging for laudanum to free him from the agonies of tuberculosis. He hallucinates; he rants. Reading Gittings, I was surprised at how little Burgess had to invent: Joseph Severn's tender ministrations; the disposition of the Roman lodging house; the fountain in the piazza; the meetings with Lieutenant Elton of the Royal Engineers, a fellow consumptive; the encounter with Pauline Buonaparte; the Scottish doctor, Clark, and his blood-letting treatments; the piano-playing and critique of Haydn; the facts of the post-mortem examination – all this, so to speak, is true. Gittings describes the dome of St Peters as 'a dark grape colour in the lemon-tinted dusk', and Burgess's Keats, looking at the same view, comments on the building 'grape-hued in the citron twilight'. Is that how people imagine Romantic writing to be like – all fruit and sunsets?

Where the biographer records events, however, the novelist is free to transcribe conversation and eavesdrop upon thoughts. The Keats of *Abba Abba* is an irresistible punster, his talk a torrent of quips and quiddities. He can't introduce himself without saying, 'Junkets? Oh yes. Jun Kets.' Hearing of the sculptor Ewing, he says, 'Ewing in Italy, hewing so prettily.' Mister Kettis or Kattis ('Keats, *signore* . . . You have the combination of sounds already in your language. As in *cazzo*, as in *cazzica*') at one point even burbles stuff from *Finnegans Wake*: 'By the waters of babble on there we shat down and flung our arses on the pillows.' Whatever that might conceivably mean.

If, on the one hand, there is a great deal of bawdy, which Burgess could have argued he'd lifted from the cocksure tones of Keats's letters, on the other the book is stiff with theological and aesthetical debates – the nature of identity, the purposes of God, the immortality of the soul. High-mindedness and basic bodily functions, the civil war going on between our brains and carcasses, is a major Burgess preoccupation, best known through his idea (or ideal) of the clockwork orange – juicy, fleshy pulp married to the efficiency of a machine. We are, in this book, after all in Rome, the *Urbs Lucis*, which is also crammed with 'the dirt and madness of the body', i.e. with the real people who live and work there. It would seem to be a particularly Catholic vexation, the carnal needs and drives versus the clear abstractions of faith and duty; and, as ordinary people can't hope to measure up, they'll be disabled with guilt and sin. All this palaver Burgess gives to Keats, who says, 'I am all disease, and disease is to be burnt out. I am a living tumour, a kind of devil.' His poetry, meantime, like music, is sublime and rises above the ego, shedding 'the shameful rotting stuff' of the physical being who created it.

The problem, though, in *Abba Abba*, is that Keats wasn't, like Joyce and Burgess (and Graham Greene), a guilt-ridden Catholic, lovingly picking his sores. He was quite bracingly agnostical, it seems to me. To get over this, Burgess introduces us to the Roman poet and Vatican censor Giuseppe Gioacchino Belli, the author of several thousand sonnets in the local dialect – which by 'presenting realistically the demotic life of a great capital city, may be regarded as a kind of proto-*Ulysses*,' says Burgess (off-puttingly) in an Afterword. Belli gave, we are assured, 'full scope to the employment of the blasphemy of the Roman gutters' – so poem after poem is wearingly about pricks, tools, shit, turds, balls. The conceit is that Keats met Belli and much enjoyed the liberalities of such verse; Belli, in his turn, was impressed by Keats's knowledge of formal structures and properties such as rhymes, odes, sonnets; and these, it is argued, represent or symbolise unchanging truths. That's to say they mirror God's perfection; that's to say Keats is a Catholic after all. The octet of a sonnet is inviolably A / B / B / A / A / B / B / A. 'Abba Abba' is also (pure Burgess, this) Aramaic for 'Father! Father!', the words Christ cried out on the cross. (Keats on his deathbed becomes a kind of Christ.)

Poetry, it is implied, is a magical codex; it is about more than we know. The trouble with *Abba Abba*, however, is the presentation of the poet Belli. Though he was real enough (d. 1861), Burgess doesn't bring him alive. He growls, he snarls, he laughs harshly. His guilt, about wanting to be intellectual but speaking coarsely – the way he is 'torn between his soul and his lower instincts' is very schematic. And does it in any event make sense? I think it is a false division. You might as well divide people up as tragic and jovial, or categorise their feelings as having to do with death or desire, or their temperaments as gauche or confident. Burgess, the novelist who owes most to Joyce, yet completely misunderstood Joyce's appreciation of overpowering details, blissful commonplaces, unimportant things. (Burgess always has to be titanic.) On his deathbed, Burgess's Keats goes into a delirious meltdown and becomes a clockwork orange – viewing himself as 'a clever machine, with the tongue and the teeth and the lips clacking and cooing'; and these noises are 'attached to things and thoughts and [are] eager to be juggled in pretty poesy'. For if there's one thing Burgess couldn't abide it was disunity, the slippings and slidings of our natures; he's always the schoolmaster (as he actually was in Banbury) afraid of loss of control. He couldn't see that the opposite of chaos and decay needn't be mechanical disengagement, it could be the freedom of consciousness – and if he's a Joycean who missed the point of Joyce, his Keats fails to be Keatsian. As a writer Burgess could never convey illusions of immediacy or appearances of effortlessness. Part of his theatricality is that he's contrived, intractable. He can't cope with real people that don't stay still. And despite all those rude sonnets – the form immaculate; the content blasphemous – I don't believe in Burgess's enjoyment of the scatology. He's disdainful, fastidious. Indeed, he's disgusted, filled with revulsion: snot, piss, shit, seed; there's no sensuality. It's Enderby on the lavatory.

How far away he is from Keats. Though both writers fill up their work with bright lights and dark shadows, though both are fascinated with death and decay – autumnal ripeness that's about to become rot; the flow of life immobilised on an ancient urn – Keats is warm, erotic, embracing, yielding; Burgess cold, rusting, metallic, aloof. Keats is youthful, sexually aware, puzzled about mortality. The lambs gambol; Porphyro is a 'puzzled urchin'; Madeline is the rose that can become a bud again. I can absolutely picture that castle, snowy, dusty, cobwebby in 'The Eve of St. Agnes' – I can smell the perfumes; imagine I can touch the underclothes and beads of perspiration. Burgess's world, by contrast, isn't about to die: it is already dead. The epic debates of his Keats and Belli are moribund – as are their replays in the conflict between Carlo, the Pope, and Toomey, the novelist, in *Earthly Powers*. And other than their being enraptured with language itself, they are books generally without love and about loneliness and isolation. Moses, Shakespeare, Jesus, Freud and the rest of them – plus Enderby and Toomey – are embattled loners, excluded, alienated, weird. Though Burgess copied Gittings so closely, the main item on Keats's mind, his greatest obsession, Burgess quite omits: Fanny Brawne. Whilst he may have travelled to the sun for a cure, Keats had also gone to Italy resolved not to see or speak again to his merciless lady. This is a glaring gap in *Abba Abba*: Keats's love which agonised him to the last. It is like playing Othello white. Her last letters, which he couldn't bear to open and read, were placed in his coffin. The sight of her handwriting on the envelope was enough to send him into a spasm of coughing up blood.

Did Burgess find the demands of love too embarrassing, too demeaning? Yet look at his own life. His mother, sister and first wife, all the key women, all died dramatically of disease – his mother and sister in the influenza epidemic of 1918, Lynne Wilson of cirrhosis in 1968. What could have been his chief subject – loss, oblivion – is paradoxically absent from his work. He never addresses the needs and importunities of love; it's the main theme he hardened himself against and avoided. He replaced or laid aside his emotions in favour of learning and knowledge: books, philosophy, music, 'impressive spiritual essences, God and country and the roaring giants of history'. ABBA ABBA, God and the Petrachan sonnet, are the letters inscribed on his tombstone, high above the tax haven of Monte Carlo. How impersonal – and how lordly, biblical and (unpitiably) omnipotent; how stern and cerebral a monument. For what Burgess did have or gain, you feel, was literature, or anyway language, or anyway writing. He couldn't stop writing. There's something manic about him, aggressive; yet something in him is seized up, too, arrested. He made his art out of art, which I think he took too solemnly. Keats, by contrast, made his art out of observing life – the gingerbread and sweetmeat world, of foxgloves and fragile dewdrops, going dark.

Sources and Acknowledgements

[i] Interviews and Profiles

Amis, Martin, 'Burgeoning Burgess', *Observer*, 12 October 1980.

Anon., 'Playboy Interview: Anthony Burgess', *Playboy*, September 1974.

Anon., 'Anthony Burgess: The Author of *A Clockwork Orange* Now Switches His Attention to Napoleon's Stomach', *Publishers Weekly*, 31 January 1972.

Barber, Michael, 'Getting Up English Noses: Burgess at Seventy', *Books*, April 1987.

Bunting, Charles T., 'An Interview in New York with Anthony Burgess', *Studies in the Novel*, Winter 1973.

Burkham, Chris, 'Lust for Language', *The Face*, April 1984.

Burn, Gordon, 'The Droogs Are Back', *Telegraph Weekend Magazine*, 3 February 1990.

Churchill, Thomas, 'An Interview with Anthony Burgess', *Malahat Review*, January 1971.

Clare, Anthony, 'Unearthly Powers', *Listener*, 28 July 1988.

Clemons, Walter, 'Anthony Burgess: Pushing on', *New York Times Book Review*, 29 November 1970.

Coale, Samuel, 'An Interview with Anthony Burgess', *Modern Fiction Studies*, Autumn 1981.

Coe, Jonathan, 'Any Old Burgess', *Guardian*, 24 February 1989.

Christopher, James, 'Stage Blood', *Time Out*, 6–13 December 1989.

Cullinan, John, 'Anthony Burgess', in *Writers At Work: The Paris Review Interviews*, Fourth Series, edited by George Plimpton (London, 1977).

Davies, Russell, 'A Happy Birthday for a Friendless Man', *Listener*, 26 February 1987.

Dempsey, Judy, 'An Interview with Anthony Burgess', *Literary Review*, 28 November–11 December 1980.
Dix, Carol, 'The Mugging Machine', *Guardian*, 1 January 1972.
Dix, Carol, 'Anthony Burgess', *Transatlantic Review*, May 1972.
Edelhart, Mike, 'More Fiction Writing Tips', *Writer's Digest*, August 1975.
Ellis, Alice Thomas, 'Beer, Brandy and Burgess', *Sunday Telegraph Magazine*, 22 February 1987.
Fallowell, Duncan, 'Anthony Burgess in Monaco and London', unpublished typescript.
Greenstreet, Rosanna, 'The *Correspondent* Questionnaire', *Sunday Correspondent*, 10 December 1989.
Grove, Valerie, 'This Old Man Comes Ranting Home', *The Times*, 6 March 1992.
Heller, Richard, 'Burgess the betrayer', *Mail on Sunday*, 11 April 1993.
Hemesath, James B., 'Anthony Burgess', *Transatlantic Review*, May 1976.
Horder, John, 'Art that Pays', *Guardian*, 10 October 1964.
Hicks, Jim, 'Eclectic Author of His Own Five-Foot Shelf', *Life*, 25 October 1968.
Jackson, Paul, 'The Cynical Confessions of Big Burgess', *Western Mail*, 25 February 1987.
Jones, Bruce, 'Anthony Burgess', *Isis*, 4 March 1983.
Lambert, Angela, 'The True Confessions of Anthony Burgess', *Independent*, 1 November 1990.
Lewis, Anthony, 'I Love England, But I Will No Longer Live There', *New York Times Magazine*, 3 November 1968.
Mandrake [column], 'This Guy Burgess Is a Bit Blunt', *Sunday Telegraph*, 22 January 1984.
Maxwell, Olivia, 'Unearthly Powers', *Time Out*, 10–17 December 1986.
May, Derwent, 'The Wily Colonial Boy', *Radio Times*, 10–16 January 1981.
Meades, Jonathan and Rayner, Richard, 'In Conversation with Anthony Burgess', *Fiction Magazine*, Summer 1984.
Mitgang, Herbert, 'On the Trapeze with Anthony Burgess', *International Herald Tribune*, 13–14 August 1983.
Murphy, Michael, 'English Literature Belongs to the Irish', *Sunday Tribune*, 20 May 1985.
Pagano, Margareta, 'The Selling of Anthony Burgess', *The Times*, n.d., *c.* 1981.

Parker, Ian, 'Clockwork Wind-Up', *Time Out*, 15–22 March 1989.
Parkinson, Michael, *The Best of Parkinson* (London, 1982).
Pearce, Edward, 'Let Us Now Honour a Wordsmith of Unearthly Powers', *Sunday Times*, 31 July 1988.
Riemer, George, 'An Interview with Anthony Burgess', *National Elementary Principal*, May 1971.
Robinson, Robert, 'Anthony Burgess – On Being a Lancashire Catholic', *Listener*, 30 September 1976.
Sage, Lorna, 'Still Angry After All These Years', *Observer*, 23 February 1992.
Walsh, John, 'Myth and Maverick', *Evening Standard*, 19 May 1988.
Wansell, Geoffrey, 'Man of the Week', *Sunday Telegraph Magazine*, 8 September 1985.

[ii] Books
Aggeler, Geoffrey, *Anthony Burgess: The Artist as Novelist* (Alabama, 1979).
Amis, Kingsley, *The Amis Collection: Selected Non-Fiction 1954–1990* (London, 1990).
Amis, Kingsley, *Memoirs* (London, 1991).
Amis, Martin, *The War Against Cliché: Essays and Reviews 1971–2000* (London, 2001).
Barclay, William, *Jesus of Nazareth* (London, 1977).
Bartholomew, James, *The Richest Man in the World: The Sultan of Brunei* (London, 1989).
Boytinck, Paul, *Anthony Burgess: An Enumerative Bibliography with Selected Annotations* (Norwood Editions, 1977).
Brewer, Jeutonne, *Anthony Burgess: A Bibliography* (Metuchen, New Jersey, 1980).
Byatt, A. S., *Babel Tower* (London, 1996).
Coale, Samuel, *Anthony Burgess* (New York, 1981).
Cradock, Percy, *Know Your Enemy: How the Joint Intelligence Committee Saw the World* (London, 2002).
Devitis, A. A., *Anthony Burgess* (New York, 1972).
Dick, Susan, *et al.*, *Omnium Gatherum: Essays for Richard Ellmann* (Gerrards Cross, 1989).
Dix, Carol M., *Anthony Burgess* (British Council, 1971).
Ellmann, Richard, *James Joyce* (Oxford, revised edition, 1982).
Enright, D. J., *Man Is an Onion* (London, 1972).

Enright, D. J., *A Mania for Sentences* (London, 1983).
James, Clive, *From the Land of Shadows* (London, 1982).
Leach, Edmund, *Lévi-Strauss* (London, 1970).
Lévi-Strauss, Claude, *Myth and Meaning* (Toronto, 1978).
Lévi-Strauss, Claude, *Les Structures elementaires de la parenté* (Paris, 1949; revised edition 1967).
Lévi-Strauss, Claude, *Structural Anthropology* (London, 1968).
Lévi-Strauss, Claude, *The Raw and the Cooked* (London, 1970).
Lobrutto, Vincent, *Stanley Kubrick* (London, 1997).
Mewshaw, Michael, 'Do I Owe You Something?' in *Granta* no. 75 (London, 2001).
Morris, Robert K., *The Consolations of Ambiguity: An Essay on the Novels of Anthony Burgess* (Missouri, 1971).
Raphael, Frederic, *Eyes Wide Open* (London, 1999).
Rhodes, Neil, *Elizabethan Grotesque* (London, 1980).
Rosny-Aîné, J. H., *Quest for Fire* (1911; new edition, New York, 1967).
Spurling, Hilary, *The Girl from the Fiction Department: A Portrait of Sonia Orwell* (London, 2002).
Theroux, Paul, *My Other Life: A Novel* (London, 1996).
Vansittart, Peter, *In the Fifties* (London, 1995).
Vansittart, Peter, *Survival Tactics* (London, 1999).
Vidal, Gore, *United States: Essays 1952–1992* (London, 1993).
West, W. J., *The Quest for Graham Greene* (London, 1997).
Zeffirelli, Franco, *Jesus: A Spiritual Diary* (San Francisco, 1984).
Zeffirelli, Franco, *The Autobiography* (London, 1986).

[iii] Institutions

I wish to thank the curators, administrators and librarians of the following places for their assistance with the research for this book: Anthony Burgess Center, Université d'Angers, (e-mail: *Valerie.Neveu@univ-angers.fr;* web site: *http://buweb.univ-angers.fr/EXTRANET/AnthonyBURGESS*); BBC Written Archives Centre; Birmingham Archdiocesan Archives, Cathedral House, St Chad's; Bodleian Library, Oxford; Durrants Hotel, London; English Faculty Library, University of Oxford; Harry Ransom Humanities Research Center, the University of Texas at Austin (the direct web address for the Burgess holdings is: *http://www.hrc.utexas.edu/research/fa/burgess.hp.html*); Helen Day Center, Stowe, Vermont; University of Manchester, Department of English Language and Literature; Wolfson College, Oxford; Yorkshire Post Newspapers Ltd.

[iv] Individuals

I am grateful to the following people for their correspondence, recollections, enlightenment, or for granting me interviews: first and foremost, the late Anthony Burgess – John Wilson – himself ('I look forward to your completion of the task'); and then the late Sir Kingsley Amis; Mark Amory; Suzanne Anderson; Shelagh Aston (University of Manchester, Department of English Language and Literature); Thomas and Elizabeth Atkinson; Eric Bailey; Michael Ball (National Army Museum); Sir Roger Bannister; Lynn Barber; Philippa Bassett (University of Birmingham); John Bayley; Monica Beckett; Brigid Bell (Methuen); Sarah Bell (Pan Books); Bernard Bergonzi; Martin and Sonia Blinkhorn; Susan and William Boyd; Tony Bonnici (Malta High Commission); Lee Brackstone (Faber); the late Sir Malcolm Bradbury; Lord Bragg; Betty Brimble; Robert Burchfield; David Burnett; Simon Burt (English Centre of PEN); Christopher Butler; A. S. Byatt; the late Kenneth Carrdus; Peter Carson (Penguin); Jonathan Cecil; Valerie M. Chamberlain (A. & C. Black Ltd); Jonathan Coe; Richard Cohen; the late William Cooper; Alan Coren; Michael Cosby; Valentine Cunningham; Malcolm Dalziel; Jenny Dent (University of Manchester); Roger Dobson (The Lost Club); Morris Dodderidge (British Council Representative, Rome); Maurice Draper; the late Richard Ellmann; D. J. Enright; Peter Evans; Duncan Fallowell; Ariane and Jean-Claude Fasquelle; James Fergusson; Judith Flanders; Ben Forkner; the late Roy Fuller; Karen Game; John Gammons (John Murray); Leslie Gardner; Michael W. Gardner; Professor R. E. Z. Gillon; the late Lord Grade of Elstree; Peter Green; Paul Griffiths; Maria Guarnaschelli (W. W. Norton); Doreen M. Hall (née Neville); Marion Harding (Department of Archives, National Army Museum); David Huw Harries; Caroline Hart; Michael Hastings; A. T. Heagren (Board of the Inland Revenue); Milton Hebald; Michael Herbert; Bevis Hillier; Jennifer Hodge (University of St Andrews); the late George Jack; Eric Jacobs; the Right Honourable Lord Jenkins of Hillhead O. M.; Nicholas John (English National Opera); Jay Jones (*Transatlantic Review*); K. A. Jowett (Library and Museum of Freemasonry); the late Pauline Kael; Philip Kemp; Sir Frank Kermode; John Kerrigan; the late Terry Kilmartin; Simon King (Random House); Eric de Kuyper (Netherlands Filmmuseum); the Right Honourable Lord Lawson P. C.; Claude Lévi-Strauss; Jeremy Lewis; Professor A. Walton Litz (Princeton); Harriette Lloyd (Victor Gollancz); Dame Moura Lympany; Alison Macdonald; Joanna Mackle (Faber); Corinne Mallet-Russo (Consulat Général de Monaco); the late Wolf

Mankowitz; Carole Mansur; Terry McCarthy (Bedwellty School); Joe McGrath; Don Mead (International Technical Co-Ordination Services); Jonathan Meades; John Mills (Royal Army Educational Corps Museum); Sir Alec and the late Lady Moyna Morris (née Boyle); David Morris (Arts Club); Desmond Morris; Jan Morris; the late Dame Iris Murdoch; Paul Napier (*Banbury Guardian*); Rodney Needham (All Souls College, Oxford); C. Nicholson (Ministry of Defence); Garry O'Connor; Ulick O'Connor; Keith S. Orenstein; Gabriele Pantucci; Norman Parker; Sarah Paterson (Imperial War Museum); Kate Perry (Channel Four); the late Michael Powell; Janice Price (Methuen); the late Sir Victor Pritchett; Denis Quilley; Lord Quirk; Jonathan Raban; Lyssa Randolph; Michael Ratcliffe; the late Cyril Ray; Richard Rayner; Stanley Reynolds; Bernard Richards; Christopher Ricks; Jon Riley (Faber); Robert Robinson; Deborah Rogers; the late A. D. Rose; Ann Rosenberg (BBC Publicity Officer); Martin Rowson; Celia Sisam (St Hilda's College, Oxford); Hilary Spurling; Thomas Staley (Harry Ransom Humanities Research Center); George Steiner; Margot Strickland; Bo Svenson (Svenska Akademien); Peter Sykes (*Oxford Times*); Janet Thompsett (Heinemann); David Thompson; Ian Todd (Pace University); Angela Tollitt; Claire Tomalin; Valerie Tryon; John Tydeman; Sir Peter Ustinov; Peter Vansittart; the late John Wain; Philip Waller; Kate Ward (Faber); Julia Wassell (Sidgwick and Jackson); Keith Waterhouse; Tony Watson (*Yorkshire Post*); the late Auberon Waugh; Professor D. S. R. Welland (University of Manchester); Francis Wheen; Simon Whittaker; Anthony Whittombe (Hutchinson); Nigel Williams; Kathleen Winfield; Roger Witts (Scottish Opera); Dai Woosnam; John Wyatt; Alan Yentob; plus various officers from the Security Service (MI5), the Secret Intelligence Service (MI6, SIS) and the Joint Intelligence Committee (JIC) who must remain anonymous.

R. L.
Gozo, 1982 – *Herefordshire*, 2002

Index